GMAT™

GMAT™ Official Guide Quantitative Review 2025-2026

From the makers of the GMAT™ exam

- Only study guide that features **real exam questions**
- **230+ practice questions** with detailed answer explanations
- Digital flashcards, games, a **customizable question bank**, and more
- Exclusive **tips and tricks** for exam success from the exam creators

GMAT™ Official Guide Quantitative Review 2025–2026

Published by John Wiley & Sons, Inc., Hoboken, New Jersey.

For general information on our other products and services or to obtain technical support please contact our Customer Care Department within the U.S. at (877) 762-2974, outside the U.S. at (317) 572-3993 or fax (317) 572-4002.

Wiley also publishes its books in a variety of electronic formats. Some content that appears in print may not be available in electronic books. For more information about Wiley products, please visit our Web site at www.wiley.com.

ISBN 978-1-394-33387-5 (pbk); ISBN 978-1-394-33504-6 (ePub)

Printed and bound in the United Kingdom by CPI Group (UK) Ltd, Croydon, CR0 4YY

10 9 8 7 6 5 4 3 2 1

Table of Contents

Dear GMAT™ Test Taker,

Thank you for taking this important step toward your graduate management education. The GMAT exam stands as the global standard in business school admissions, used by more than 7,700 graduate programs worldwide to identify excellence in candidates for MBA, business master's, and other graduate-level management degrees. Seven out of ten business school applicants choose to differentiate themselves with a GMAT exam score.*

By choosing the GMAT™ Official Guide, you're preparing with the most authoritative resource available—the only guide featuring real GMAT questions published by the Graduate Management Admission Council (GMAC™), the makers of the GMAT exam. Combined with our prep tools at **www.mba.com**, this guide will build your confidence and help you achieve your personal best on exam day.

For more than 70 years, the GMAT exam has empowered candidates like you to demonstrate their readiness for academic success and signal their commitment to business education. Schools use and trust the GMAT because it consistently predicts classroom performance and indicates your potential to excel in your chosen program.

At GMAC, our purpose is to ensure no talent goes undiscovered. We're committed to providing the tools and insights you need throughout your business school journey, continuously enhancing the GMAT exam, and helping you connect with programs that match your aspirations. We applaud your commitment to advancing your education and wish you every success in your future educational and professional endeavors.

Sincerely,

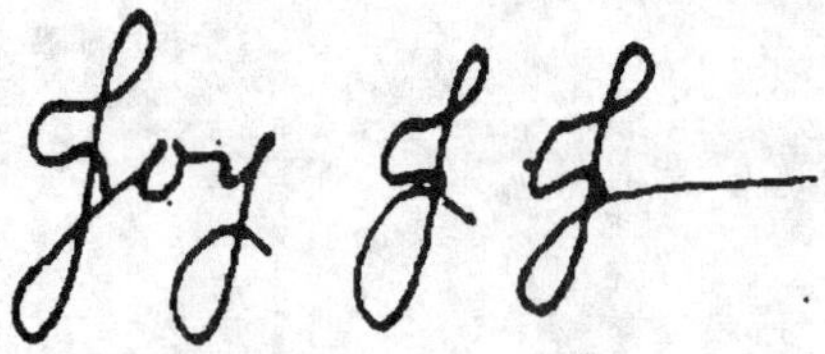

Joy J. Jones

CEO, Graduate Management Admission Council

* Top 100 *Financial Times* full-time MBA programs

GMAT™ Official Guide
Quantitative Review 2025–2026

1.0 What Is the GMAT™ Exam?

1.1 What Is the GMAT™ Exam?

The Graduate Management Admission Test™ (GMAT™) is used in admissions decisions by more than 7,700 graduate management programs at over 2,400 business schools worldwide. Unlike undergraduate grades and courses, whose meanings vary across regions and institutions, your GMAT scores are a standardized, statistically valid, and reliable measure for both you and these schools to predict your future performance and success in core courses of graduate-level management programs.

Hundreds of studies across hundreds of schools have demonstrated the validity of GMAT scores as being an accurate indicator of business school success. Together, these studies have shown that performance on the GMAT predicts success in business school even better than undergraduate grades.

The exam tests you on skills expected by management faculty and admission professionals for incoming graduate students. These skills include problem-solving, data analysis, and critical thinking, which all require complex judgments and are tested in the three sections of the GMAT exam: Quantitative Reasoning, Data Insights, and Verbal Reasoning. These three sections feature content relevant to today's business challenges and opportunities, ensuring you are prepared for graduate business school and beyond.

Your GMAT Official Score is meant to be an objective, numeric measure of your ability and potential for success. Business schools will use it as part of their holistic admissions processes, which may also consider recommendation letters, essays, interviews, work experiences, and other signs of social and emotional intelligence, as well as leadership. Even if your program does not require a GMAT score, you can stand out from the crowd by doing well on the exam to show you are serious about business school and have the skills to succeed.

The exam is always delivered in English on a computer, either online (such as at home) or at a test center. The exam tests your ability to apply foundational knowledge in the following areas: algebra and arithmetic, analyzing and interpreting data, reading and comprehending written material, and reasoning and evaluating arguments.

Myth -vs- **FACT**

M **– My GMAT score does not predict my success in business school.**

F – The GMAT exam measures your critical thinking skills, which you will need in business school and your career.

1.2 Why Take the GMAT™ Exam?

Taking the exam helps you stand out as an applicant and shows you're ready for and committed to a graduate management education. Schools use GMAT scores in choosing the most qualified applicants. They know an applicant who has taken the exam is serious about earning a graduate business degree, and they know the exam scores reliably predict how well applicants can do in graduate business programs.

No matter how you do on the exam, you should contact schools that interest you to learn more about them, and to ask how they use GMAT scores and other criteria in admissions decisions. School

admissions offices, websites, and publications are key sources of information when you are researching business schools. Note that schools' published GMAT scores are *averages* of the scores of their admitted students, not minimum scores needed for admission.

While you might aim to get a high or perfect score, such a score is not required to get into top business school programs around the world. You should try your best to achieve a competitive score that aligns with the ranges provided by the schools of your choice. Admissions officers will use GMAT scores as one factor in admissions decisions along with undergraduate records, application essays, interviews, letters of recommendation, and other information.

To learn more about the exam, test preparation materials, registration, and how to use your GMAT Official Score in applying to business schools, please visit **www.mba.com/gmat**.

Myth -vs- **FACT**

M **– If I don't get a high GMAT score, I won't get into my top-choice schools.**

F – Schools use your GMAT score as a part of their holistic evaluation process.

1.3 GMAT™ Exam Format

The GMAT exam has three separately timed sections (see the table on the following page). The Quantitative Reasoning section and the Verbal Reasoning section consist of only multiple-choice questions. The Data Insights section includes multiple-choice questions along with other kinds of graphical and data analysis questions. Before you start the exam, you can choose any order in which you will take the three sections. For example, you can choose to start with Verbal Reasoning, then do Quantitative Reasoning, and end with Data Insights. Or you can choose to do Data Insights first, followed by Verbal Reasoning, and then Quantitative Reasoning. You can take one optional ten-minute break after either the first or second section.

All three GMAT sections are computer adaptive. This means the test chooses from a large bank of questions to adjust itself to your ability level, so you will not get many questions that are too hard or too easy for you. The first question will be of medium difficulty. As you answer each question, the computer uses your answer, along with your responses to earlier questions, to choose the next question with the right level of difficulty. Because the computer uses your answers to choose your next question, you cannot skip questions.

Computer adaptive tests get harder as you answer more questions correctly. But getting a question that seems easier than the last one doesn't always mean your last answer was wrong. At the end of each section, you can review any question(s) and edit up to three answers within the allotted section time.

Though each test taker gets different questions, the mix of question types is always consistent. Your score depends on the difficulty and statistical traits of the questions you answer, as well as on which of your answers are correct. If you don't know how to answer a question, try to rule out as many wrong answer choices as possible. Then pick the answer choice you think is best. By adapting to each test taker, the exam can accurately and efficiently gauge a full range of skill levels, from very high to very low. Many factors may make the questions easier or harder, so don't waste time worrying if some questions seem easy.

To make sure every test taker gets equivalent content, the test gives specific numbers of questions of each type. While the test covers the same kinds of questions for everyone, some questions may seem harder or easier for you because you may be stronger in some questions than in others.

At the end of the exam, you will see your unofficial score displayed on the screen. A few days after your exam, you will receive your Official Score Report, which includes detailed performance insights. Once you receive your report, you can select to send your Official Score to schools of your choice.

Format of the GMAT™ Exam

	Questions	Timing
Quantitative Reasoning Problem-Solving	21	45 min.
Data Insights Data Sufficiency Multi-Source Reasoning Table Analysis Graphics Interpretation Two-Part Analysis	20	45 min.
Verbal Reasoning Reading Comprehension Critical Reasoning	23	45 min.
	Total Time	135 min.

A ten-minute optional break can be taken after the first or the second section.

Each section of the GMAT exam contains the following features:

- **Bookmarking:** Mark any questions you are unsure about so you can easily get back to them after you complete the section. Bookmarking can make the Question Review & Edit process more efficient.
- **Question Review & Edit:** Review as many questions as you would like (whether or not they're bookmarked) and change or edit up to three answers per section, within the section's allotted time.

Myth -vs- **FACT**

M **– Getting an easier question means I answered the previous one wrong.**

F – Many factors may make the questions easier or harder, so don't waste time worrying if some questions seem easy.

1.4 What Is the Testing Experience Like?

You can take the exam either online (such as at home) or at a test center—whichever you prefer. You may feel more comfortable at home with the online delivery format. Or you may prefer the uninterrupted, structured environment of a test center. It is your choice. Both options have the same content, structure, features, optional ten-minute break, scores, and score scales.

At the Test Center: Over 700 test centers worldwide administer the GMAT exam under standardized conditions. Each test center has proctored testing rooms with individual computer workstations that allow you to take the exam in a peaceful, quiet setting, with some privacy. To learn more about exam day, visit **www.mba.com/gmat**.

Online: In available regions, the GMAT exam is delivered online and is proctored remotely, so you can take it in the comfort of your home or office. You will need a quiet workspace with a desktop or laptop computer that meets minimum system requirements, a webcam, microphone, and a reliable internet connection. For more information about taking the exam online, visit **www.mba.com/gmat**.

Whether you're taking the GMAT exam online or at a test center, there are several accommodations available. To learn more about available accommodations for the exam, visit **www.mba.com/accommodations**.

1.5 What Is the Exam Content Like?

The GMAT exam measures several types of analytical reasoning skills. The Quantitative Reasoning section gives you basic arithmetic and algebra problems. The questions present you with a mix of word or pure math problems. The Data Insights section asks you to use diverse reasoning skills to solve real-world problems involving data. It also asks you to interpret and combine data from different sources and in different formats to reach conclusions. The Verbal Reasoning section tests your ability to read and comprehend written material and to reason through and evaluate arguments.

The test questions are contextualized in various subject areas, but each question provides you everything you need to know to answer it correctly. In other words, you do not need detailed outside knowledge of the subject areas.

1.6 Quantitative Reasoning Section

The GMAT Quantitative Reasoning section measures how well you solve math problems and interpret graphs. All questions in this section require solving problems using basic arithmetic, algebra, or both. Some are practical word problems, while others are pure math. Answering these questions correctly relies on logic, analytical skills, and basic knowledge of algebra and arithmetic skills. You **cannot** use a calculator while working on this section.

Chapter 3 of this book, "Math Review," reviews the basic math you need to know to answer questions in the Quantitative Reasoning section. Chapter 4, "Quantitative Reasoning," includes test-taking tips, as well as practice questions and answer explanations both in this book and in the Online Question Bank.

1.7 How Are Scores Calculated?

The Quantitative Reasoning, Data Insights, and Verbal Reasoning sections are each scored on a scale from 60 to 90, in 1-point increments. You will get four scores: a Section Score each for Quantitative Reasoning, Data Insights, and Verbal Reasoning, along with a Total Score based on your three section scores. The Total Score ranges from 205 to 805. Your scores depend on:

- Which questions you answered correctly.
- How many questions you answered.
- Each question's difficulty and other statistical characteristics.

There is a penalty for not completing each section of the exam. If you do not finish in the allotted time, your score will be penalized, reflecting the number of unanswered questions. Your GMAT exam score will be the best reflection of your performance when all questions are answered within the time limit.

Immediately after completing the exam, your unofficial scores and percentile for the Quantitative Reasoning, Data Insights, and Verbal Reasoning, as well as your Total Score, are displayed on-screen. You are **not** allowed to record, save, screenshot, or print your unofficial score. You will receive an email notification when your Official Score Report is available in your **www.mba.com** account.

The following table summarizes the different types of scores and their scale properties.

Score Type	Scale	Increment
Quantitative Reasoning	60–90	1
Data Insights	60–90	1
Verbal Reasoning	60–90	1
Total	205–805	10

Your GMAT Official Scores are valid for five years from your exam date. Your Total GMAT Score includes a percentile ranking, which shows the percentage of tests taken with scores lower than your score.

In addition to reviewing your Total and Section Scores, it's important to pay attention to your percentile ranking. Percentile rankings indicate what percentage of test takers you performed better than. For example, a percentile ranking of 75% means that you performed better than 75% of other test takers, and 25% of test takers performed better than you. Percentile ranks are calculated using scores from the most recent five years. Visit **www.mba.com/scores** to view the most recent predicted percentile rankings tables.

To better understand the exam experience and view score reports before exam day, we recommend taking at least one GMAT official practice exam to simulate the test-taking experience and gauge your potential score. The more practice exams you take, the better prepared you will be on your actual testing day. Visit **www.mba.com/examprep** to learn more about the practice exams offered by GMAC.

2.0 How to Prepare

2.1 How Should I Prepare for the GMAT™ Exam?

The GMAT™ exam has several unique question formats. We recommend that you familiarize yourself with the test format and the different question types before you take the test. The key to prepping for any exam is setting a pace that works for you and your lifestyle. That might be easier said than done, but the ***GMAT™ Official 6-Week Study Planner*** does the planning for you! Our step-by-step planner will help you stick to a schedule, inform your activities, and track your progress. Go to **www.mba.com/examprep** to download the planner.

Here are our recommended steps to starting your prep journey with your best foot forward.

1. **Study the structure.** Use the study plan in our **free GMAT™ Official Starter Kit** to become familiar with the exam format and structure. The study plan will guide you through each question type and give you sample questions. This will boost your confidence come test day when you know what to expect.
2. **Understand the question types.** Beyond knowing how to answer questions correctly, learn what each type of question is asking of you. GMAT questions rely on logic and analytical skills, not underlying subject matter mastery, as detailed in the ***GMAT™ Official Guide 2025–2026* and Online Question Bank**.
3. **Establish your baseline.** Take the **GMAT™ Official Practice Exam 1 (FREE)** to establish your baseline. It uses the same format and scoring algorithm as the real test, so you can use the Official Score Report to accurately assess your strengths and growth areas.
4. **Study the answer explanations.** Take advantage of each question you get wrong by studying the correct answers, so you know how to get it right the next time. **GMAT™ Official Practice Questions** provide detailed answer explanations for hundreds of real GMAT questions. This will help you understand why you got a question right or wrong.
5. **Simulate the test-taking experience.** Take the **GMAT™ Official Practice Exams.** All GMAT™ Official Practice Exams use the same algorithm, scoring, and timing as the real exam, so take them with test-day-like conditions (e.g., quiet space, use the tools allowed on test day) for the truest prep experience.

Remember, the exam is timed, so learning to pace yourself and understanding the question formats and the skills you need can be a stepping stone to achieving your desired score. The timed practice in the **Online Question Bank** can help you prepare for this. The time management performance chart provided in practice exam score reports can also help you practice your pacing.

Because the exam assesses reasoning rather than knowledge, memorizing facts probably won't help you. You don't need to study advanced math, but you should know basic arithmetic and algebra. Likewise, you don't need to study advanced vocabulary words, but you should know English well enough to understand writing at an undergraduate level.

> **"The GMAT is not a math test. 'Textbook' math will work—but you'll take longer than you need to. Approach the GMAT from a business mindset: What's the least-effort path to a legitimate answer? Estimate, logic it out, test real numbers—whatever works for each problem."**
>
> **—A test instructor from Manhattan Prep Powered By Kaplan**

2.2 Getting Ready for Exam Day

Whether you take the exam online or in a test center, knowing what to expect will help you feel confident and succeed. To understand which exam delivery is right for you, visit **www.mba.com/plan-for-exam-day**.

Our Top Exam Day Strategies:

1. Get a good night's sleep the night before.
2. Pacing is key. Consult your on-screen timer periodically to avoid having to rush through sections.
3. Read each question carefully to fully understand what is being asked.
4. Don't waste time trying to solve a problem you recognize as too difficult or time-consuming. Instead, eliminate answers you know are wrong and select the best from the remaining choices.
5. Leverage the bookmarking tool to make your question review and edit process more efficient.

"Don't take a 'brute force' approach to GMAT questions—think strategically instead."
— A test instructor from GMAT Genius

"Compile summarized notes that can be reviewed on the morning of the test. Awareness of the key points and types of mistakes will boost your scores."
— A test instructor from LEADERSMBA

Myth -vs- **FACT**

M **– You need advanced math skills to get a high GMAT score.**

F – The exam measures your reasoning ability rather than your advanced math skills.

2.3 How to Use the *GMAT™ Official Guide Quantitative Review 2025–2026*

The GMAT™ Official Guide series is the largest official source of actual GMAT questions. You can use this series of books and the included Online Question Bank to practice answering the different types of questions. The *GMAT™ Official Guide Quantitative Review* is designed for those who have completed the Quantitative Reasoning questions in the *GMAT™ Official Guide 2025–2026* and are looking for additional practice questions, as well as those who are interested in practicing only Quantitative Reasoning questions. Questions of each type are organized by difficulty level of easy, medium, and hard. Your rate of accuracy in each category might differ from what you expect. You might be able to answer the "hard" questions easily, while the "easy" ones are challenging. This is common and is not an indicator of exam performance. The questions in this book are not adaptive based on your performance but are meant to serve as exposure to the range of question types and formats you might encounter on the exam. Also, the proportions of questions about different content areas in this book don't reflect the proportions in the actual exam. To find questions of a specific type and difficulty level (for example, easy arithmetic questions), use the index of questions in Chapter 5.

We recommend the steps below for how to best use this book:

1. Start with the review chapters to gain an overview of the required concepts.

> **"Building a strong foundation is crucial to achieve a high score. If you struggle with fundamental questions, your progress on more advanced questions will be hindered."**
>
> **—A test instructor from XY Education**

2. Go through the practice questions in this book. Once you've familiarized yourself with the concepts and question types, use the Online Question Bank to further customize your practice by choosing your preferred level of difficulty, category of concepts, or question types.

> **"The Official Guide offers in-depth answer explanations. After completing a question, reviewing it alongside the explanation helps you gain a deeper understanding of the question's key concepts and solution strategies. On the result interface of the online question bank, it serves a dual purpose: on one hand, it encourages us to review incorrect answers; on the other hand, it provides detailed insights into the time spent on each question, aiding in optimizing our pace during exercises."**
>
> **—A test instructor from JiangjiangGMAT**

3. Use the **Online Question Bank** to continue practicing based on your progress. To better customize and enhance your practice, use the Online Question Bank to:

    a. Review and retry practice questions to improve performance by using the untimed or timed features along with a study mode or an exam mode.

    b. Analyze key performance metrics to help assess focus area and track improvement.

    c. Use flashcards to master key concepts.

> **"The biggest mistake students make is completing too many new problems. Completing problems doesn't move your score! Learning from problems does. Keep a list of questions you want to go back to and redo. Redo at least three of these questions every time you study. This book is one of the most important resources you can use to create the future you want. Make sure you understand every question you complete extremely well. You should be able to explain every problem you complete to someone who is new to the exam. Don't focus on simply 'getting through' the book. That mindset will work against you and your dreams."**
>
> **—A test instructor from The GMAT Strategy**

TIP

Since the exam is given on a computer, we suggest you practice the questions in this book using the **Online Question Bank** accessed via **www.mba.com/my-account.** It includes all the questions in this book, and it lets you create practice sets—both timed and untimed—and track your progress more easily. The Online Question Bank is also available on your mobile device through the GMAT™ Official Practice mobile app. To access the Online Question Bank on your mobile device, first create an account at **www.mba.com,** and then sign into your account on the mobile app.

2.4 How to Use Other GMAT™ Official Prep Products

We recommend using our other GMAT™ Official Prep products along with this guidebook.

- **For a realistic simulation of the exam:** GMAT™ Official Practice Exams 1–6 are the only practice exams that use real exam questions along with the scoring algorithm and user interface from the actual exam. The first two practice exams are free to all test takers at **www.mba.com/gmatprep**.
- **For more practice questions:** *GMAT™ Official Guide Data Insights Review 2025–2026* and *GMAT™ Official Guide Verbal Review 2025–2026* offer over 225 additional practice questions not included in this book.
- **For focused practice:** GMAT™ Official Practice Questions for Quantitative, Data Insights, and Verbal products offer 100+ questions that are not included in the Official Guide series.

> **"Build teaching-level depth; don't just finish content mindlessly. Even if you solve thousands of questions on a shaky foundation, you will remain stuck on a really low accuracy."**
>
> **—A test instructor from Top One Percent**

2.5 Tips for Taking the Exam

Tips for answering questions of the different types are given later in this book. Here are some general tips to help you do your best on the test.

1. **Before the actual exam, decide in what order to take the sections.**
The exam lets you choose in which order you'll take the sections. Use the GMAT™ Official Practice Exams to practice and find your preferred order. No order is "wrong." Some test takers prefer to complete the section that challenges them the most first, while others prefer to ease into the exam by starting with a section that they're stronger in. Practice each order and see which one works best for you.

2. **Try the practice questions and practice exams.**
Timing yourself as you answer the practice questions and taking the practice exams can give you a sense of how long you will have for each question on the actual test, and whether you are answering them fast enough to finish in time.

> **TIP**
>
> After you've learned about all the question types, use the practice questions in this book and practice them online at **www.mba.com/my-account** to prepare for the actual test.

3. **Review all test directions ahead of time.**
The directions explain exactly what you need to do to answer questions of each type. You can review the directions in the GMAT™ Official Practice Exams ahead of time so that you don't miss anything you need to know to answer properly. To review directions during the test, you can click on the Help icon. But note that your time spent reviewing directions counts against your available time for that section of the test.

4. **Study each question carefully.**
Before you answer a question, understand exactly what it is asking, then pick the best answer choice. Never skim a question. Skimming may make you miss important details or nuances.

5. **Use your time wisely.**
Although the exam stresses accuracy over speed, you should use your time wisely. On average, you have just about 2 minutes and 9 seconds per Quantitative Reasoning question; 2 minutes and 15 seconds per Data Insights question; and under 2 minutes per Verbal Reasoning question. Once you start the test, an on-screen clock shows how much time you have left. You can hide this display if you want, but by checking the clock periodically, you can make sure to finish in time.

6. **Do not spend too much time on any one question.**
If finding the right answer is taking too long, try to rule out answer choices you know are wrong. Then pick the best of the remaining choices and move on to the next question.

Not finishing sections or randomly guessing answers can lower your score significantly. As long as you've worked on each section, you will get a score even if you didn't finish one or more sections in time. You don't earn points for questions you never get to see.

Pacing is important. If a question stumps you, pick the answer choice that seems best and move on. If you guess wrong, the computer will likely give you an easier question, which you're more likely to answer correctly. Soon the computer will return to giving you questions matched to your ability. You can bookmark questions you get stuck on, then return to change up to three of your answers if you still have time left at the end of the section. But if you don't finish the section, your score will be reduced.

7. **Confirm your answers ONLY when you are ready to move on.**
In the GMAT Quantitative Reasoning, Data Insights, and Verbal Reasoning sections, once you choose your answer to a question, you are asked to confirm it. As soon as you confirm your response, the next question appears. You can't skip questions. In the Data Insights and Verbal Reasoning sections, several questions based on the same prompt may appear at once. When more than one question is on a single screen, you can change your answers to any questions on that screen before moving on to the next screen. But until you've reached the end of the section, you can't navigate back to a previous screen to change any answers.

Myth -vs- FACT

M **– Avoiding wrong answers is more important than finishing the test.**

F – Not finishing can lower your score a lot.

Myth -vs- FACT

M **– The first ten questions are critical, so you should spend the most time on them.**

F – All questions impact your score.

2.6 Quantitative Reasoning Section Strategies

Utilize the strategies below to better prepare for the exam. Creating a solid study plan and selecting the right prep materials are two key elements of getting accepted into your top business schools. But knowing how to strategically approach the exam is another crucial factor that can increase your confidence going into test day and help you perform your best.

> **"Don't just read explanations. Review your notes and learn from your mistakes."**
> **—A test instructor from Admit Master**

Problem-Solving Questions

- Familiarize yourself with the rules and concepts of arithmetic and algebra.
- For questions that require approximations, skim answer choices first. If you are unable to get some idea of how close the approximation should be, you may waste time on long computations when a short mental process would serve you better.
- Take advantage of your whiteboard or note board. Solving problems in writing may help you avoid errors. Make sure you understand how the whiteboard will work on test day. If you are taking the exam online, you also have the option to use an online whiteboard tool—make sure you understand how the online whiteboard works and practice using it before test day.

To register for the GMAT™ exam, go to www.mba.com/register

3.0 Math Review

3.0 Math Review

This chapter reviews the math you need to answer GMAT™ Quantitative Reasoning questions. This is only a brief overview. If you find unfamiliar terms, consult other resources to learn more.

Unlike some math problems you may have solved in school, GMAT math questions ask you to **apply** your math knowledge. For example, rather than asking you to list a number's prime factors to show you understand prime factorization, a GMAT question may ask you to **use** prime factorization and exponents to simplify an algebraic expression with a radical.

To prepare for the GMAT Quantitative Reasoning section, first review basic math to make sure you know enough to answer the questions. Then practice with GMAT questions from past exams.

Section 3.1, "Value, Order, and Factors," includes:

1. Numbers and the Number Line
2. Factors, Multiples, and Remainders
3. Exponents
4. Decimals and Place Value
5. Arithmetic Shortcuts and Properties of Operations

Section 3.2, "Algebra, Equalities, and Inequalities," includes:

1. Algebraic Expressions and Equations
2. Linear Equations
3. Factoring and Quadratic Equations
4. Inequalities
5. Functions
6. Graphing
7. Formulas and Measurement Conversion

Section 3.3, "Rates, Ratios, and Percents," includes:

1. Ratio and Proportion
2. Fractions
3. Percents
4. Converting Decimals, Fractions, and Percents
5. Working with Decimals, Fractions, and Percents
6. Rate, Work, and Mixture Problems

Section 3.4, "Statistics, Sets, Counting, Probability, Estimation, and Series," includes:

1. Statistics
2. Sets
3. Counting Methods
4. Probability
5. Estimation
6. Sequences and Series

Section 3.5, "Reference Sheets"

3.1 Value, Order, and Factors

1. Numbers and the Number Line

A. All ***real numbers*** match points on ***the number line***, and all points on the number line represent real numbers.

The figure below shows the number line with labeled points standing for the real numbers $-\frac{3}{2}$, 0.2, and $\sqrt{2}$.

The Number Line

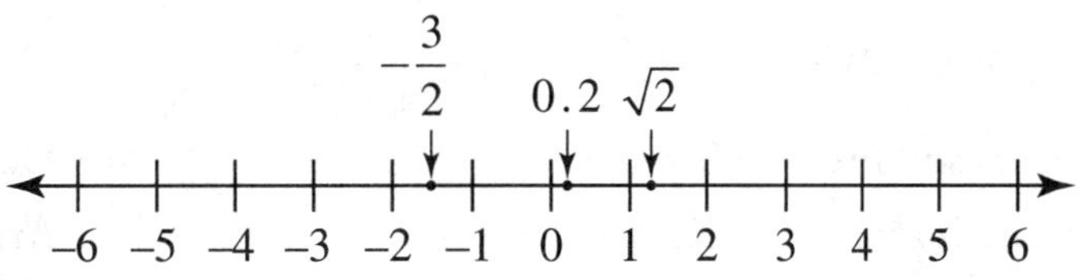

B. On the number line, points to the left of zero stand for ***negative*** numbers, and points to the right of zero stand for ***positive*** numbers. Every real number except zero is either positive or negative.

C. On the number line, each number is less than any number to its right. So, as the figure above shows, $-4 < -3 < -\frac{3}{2} < -1$, and $1 < \sqrt{2} < 2$.

D. If a number n is between 1 and 4 on the number line, then $n > 1$ and $n < 4$; that is, $1 < n < 4$. If n is "between 1 and 4, inclusive," then $1 \le n \le 4$.

E. The ***absolute value*** of a real number x, written as $|x|$, is x if $x \ge 0$ and $-x$ if $x < 0$. A number's absolute value is the distance between that number and zero on the number line. Thus, –3 and 3 have the same absolute value since each is three units from zero on the number line. The absolute value of any nonzero number is positive.

Examples:

$|-5| = |5| = 5$, $|0| = 0$, and

$\left|-\frac{7}{2}\right| = \frac{7}{2}$.

For any real numbers x and y, $|x + y| \le |x| + |y|$, and $|xy| = |x||y|$.

Examples:

If $x = 10$ and $y = 2$, then $|x + y| = |12| = 12 = |x| + |y|$.

And $|xy| = |20| = 20 = |x||y|$.

If $x = 10$ and $y = -2$, then $|x + y| = |8| = 8 < 12 = |x| + |y|$.

And $|xy| = |-20| = 20 = |x||y|$.

2. Factors, Multiples, and Remainders

A. An ***integer*** is any number in the set $\{\ldots -3, -2, -1, 0, 1, 2, 3, \ldots\}$. For any integer n, the numbers in the set $\{n, n + 1, n + 2, n + 3, \ldots\}$ are ***consecutive integers***.

B. For integers x and y, if $x \neq 0$, x is a ***divisor*** or ***factor*** of y if $y = xn$ for some integer n. Then y is ***divisible*** by x and is a ***multiple*** of x.

> *Example:*
>
> Since $28 = (7)(4)$, both 4 and 7 are divisors or factors of 28.
>
> But 8 isn't a divisor or factor of 28 since n isn't an integer if $28 = 8n$.

C. Dividing a positive integer y by a positive integer x and then rounding down to the nearest nonnegative integer gives the ***quotient*** of the division.

To find the ***remainder*** of the division, multiply x by the quotient, then subtract the result from y. The quotient and the remainder are the unique positive integers q and r, respectively, such that $y = xq + r$ and $0 \leq r < x$.

> *Example:*
>
> When 28 is divided by 8, the quotient is 3 and the remainder is 4 because $28 = (8)(3) + 4$.

The remainder r is 0 if and only if y is ***divisible*** by x. Then x is a divisor or factor of y, and y is a multiple of x.

> *Example:*
>
> Since 32 divided by 8 has a remainder of 0, 32 is divisible by 8. So, 8 is a divisor of 32, and 32 is a multiple of 8.

When a smaller integer is divided by a larger integer, the quotient is 0 and the remainder is the smaller integer.

> *Example:*
>
> When 5 is divided by 7, the quotient is 0 and the remainder is 5 since $5 = (7)(0) + 5$.

D. For any positive integers x, y, and z, suppose that r is the remainder when x is divided by z, and that s is the remainder when y is divided by z. Then the remainder when $x + y$ is divided by z equals the remainder when $r + s$ is divided by z. Similarly, the remainder when xy is divided by z equals the remainder when rs is divided by z.

Examples:

When 142 is divided by 13, the remainder is 12 because 132 = (13 × 10) + 12. And when 29 is divided by 13, the remainder is 3 because 29 = (13 × 2) + 3.

So, the remainder when 142 + 29 is divided by 13 equals the remainder when 12 + 3 = 15 is divided by 13; that is, it's 2.

And the remainder when 142 × 29 is divided by 13 equals the remainder when 12 × 3 = 36 is divided by 13; that is, it's 10.

E. Any integer divisible by 2 is ***even***. The set of even integers is {… −4, −2, 0, 2, 4, 6, 8, …}. Integers not divisible by 2 are ***odd***, so {… −3, −1, 1, 3, 5, …} is the set of odd integers. For any integer n, the numbers in the set $\{2n, 2n + 2, 2n + 4, \ldots\}$ are ***consecutive even integers***, and the numbers in $\{2n + 1, 2n + 3, 2n + 5, \ldots\}$ are ***consecutive odd integers***.

If a product of integers has at least one even factor, the product is even; otherwise, it's odd. If two integers are both even or both odd, their sum and their difference are even. Otherwise, their sum and their difference are odd.

F. A ***prime*** number is a positive integer with exactly two positive divisors: 1 and itself. That is, a prime number is divisible by no integer but itself and 1.

Examples:

The first six prime numbers are 2, 3, 5, 7, 11, and 13.

But 15 is not a prime number because it has four positive divisors: 1, 3, 5, and 15.

Nor is 1 a prime number because it has only one positive divisor: itself.

3. Exponents

A. An expression of the form k^n means the nth ***power*** of k, or k raised to the nth power, where n is the ***exponent*** and k is the ***base***.

B. A positive integer exponent shows how many instances of the base are multiplied together. That is, when n is a positive integer, k^n is the product of n instances of k.

Examples:

x^5 is $(x)(x)(x)(x)(x)$; that is, the product in which x is a factor 5 times with no other factors. We can also say x^5 is the 5th power of x, or x raised to the 5th power.

The second power of 2, also called 2 ***squared***, is $2^2 = 2 \times 2 = 4$. The third power of 2, also called 2 ***cubed***, is $2^3 = 2 \times 2 \times 2 = 8$.

Squaring a number greater than 1, or raising it to any power greater than 1, gives a larger number.

Squaring a number between 0 and 1 gives a smaller number.

Examples:

$3^2 = 9$, and $9 > 3$.

$(0.1)^2 = 0.01$, and $0.01 < 0.1$.

C. A ***composite number*** is an integer greater than 1 that's not prime. Any composite number is a product of a unique set of prime factors, each raised to some positive integer power. The ***prime factorization*** of a composite number shows it as such a product.

Examples:

Some prime factorizations of composite numbers are $14 = (2)(7)$, $81 = 3^4$, and $484 = (2^2)(11^2)$.

D. For any two positive integers x and y, y is divisible by x if and only if the prime factorization of y includes each prime number in the prime factorization of x, raised to at least as great a power as it is in the prime factorization of x.

Examples:

$1080 = (2^3)(3^3)(5)$ is divisible by $24 = (2^3)(3)$, because the prime factorization of 1080 includes both 2 and 3, which are the only prime factors in the prime factorization of 24, and each is raised to at least as great a power as it is in the prime factorization of 24.

But 1080 is not divisible by $16 = 2^4$, because the prime factor 2 in the prime factorization of 16 is raised to a higher power than it is in the prime factorization of 1080.

Nor is 1080 divisible by $21 = (3)(7)$, because its prime factor 7 isn't in the prime factorization of 1080.

E. A ***square root*** of a number n is a number x such that $x^2 = n$. Every positive number has two real square roots, one positive and the other negative. The positive square root of n is written as $\sqrt{n}$ or $n^{\frac{1}{2}}$.

Example:

The two square roots of 9 are $\sqrt{9} = 3$ and $-\sqrt{9} = -3$.

For any x, the nonnegative square root of x^2 equals the absolute value of x; that is, $\sqrt{x^2} = |x|$.

The square root of a negative number is not a real number. Only real numbers appear on the GMAT

F. Every real number r has exactly one real ***cube root***, the number s such that $s^3 = r$. The real cube root of r is written as $\sqrt[3]{r}$ or $r^{\frac{1}{3}}$.

Examples:

Since $2^3 = 8$, $\sqrt[3]{8} = 2$.

Likewise, $\sqrt[3]{-8} = -2$ because $(-2)^3 = -8$.

4. Decimals and Place Value

A. A ***decimal*** is a real number written as a series of digits, often with a period called a ***decimal point***. The decimal point's position sets the ***place values*** of the digits.

> *Example:*
>
> The digits in the decimal 7,654.321 have these place values:

Thousands		Hundreds	Tens	Ones or units		Tenths	Hundredths	Thousandths
7	,	6	5	4	.	3	2	1

B. Some decimal numbers extend rightward by infinitely many digits. In a ***repeating decimal***, a finite sequence of digits that are not all 0s repeats forever. A repeating decimal may be written showing the finite sequence of digits to the right of the decimal point only once, with a bar over them. There are never digits to the right of the repeating sequence.

> *Example:*
>
> The repeating decimal $12.34\overline{56}$ has the digits 12.3456565656..., with the digit sequence 56 repeating forever.

C. In ***scientific notation***, a decimal is written with only one nonzero digit to the decimal point's left, multiplied by an integer power of 10. To convert a number from scientific notation to regular decimal notation, move the decimal point by the number of places equal to the absolute value of the exponent on the 10. Move the decimal point to the right if the exponent is positive or to the left if the exponent is negative.

> *Examples:*
>
> In scientific notation, 231 is written as 2.31×10^2, and 0.0231 is written as 2.31×10^{-2}.
>
> To convert 2.013×10^4 to regular decimal notation, move the decimal point 4 places to the right, giving 20,130.
>
> Likewise, to convert 1.91×10^{-4} to regular decimal notation, move the decimal point 4 places to the left, giving 0.000191.

D. To add or subtract decimals with many finite digits, line up their decimal points. If one decimal has fewer digits to the right of its decimal point than another, insert zeros to the right of its last digit.

Examples:

To add 17.6512 and 653.27, insert zeros to the right of the last digit in 653.27 to line up the decimal points when the numbers are in a column:

$$\begin{array}{r} 17.6512 \\ +\,653.2700 \\ \hline 670.9212 \end{array}$$

Likewise for 653.27 minus 17.6512:

$$\begin{array}{r} 653.2700 \\ -17.6512 \\ \hline 635.6188 \end{array}$$

E. Multiply decimals with many finite digits as if they were integers. Then insert the decimal point in the product so that the number of digits to the right of the decimal point is the sum of the numbers of digits to the right of the decimal points in the numbers being multiplied.

Example:

To multiply 2.09 by 1.3, first multiply the integers 209 and 13 to get 2,717. Since 2 + 1 = 3 digits are to the right of the decimal points in 2.09 and 1.3, put 3 digits in 2,717 to the right of the decimal point to find the product:

$$\begin{array}{rl} 2.09 & \text{(2 digits to the right)} \\ \times 1.3 & \text{(1 digit to the right)} \\ \hline 627 & \\ 2090 & \\ \hline 2.717 & (2+1=3 \text{ digits to the right}) \end{array}$$

F. To divide a number (the ***dividend***) by a decimal (the ***divisor***), when both have many finite digits, move the decimal points of the dividend and the divisor the same number of digits to the right until the divisor is an integer. Then divide as you would integers. The decimal point in the quotient goes directly above the decimal point in the new dividend.

Example:

To divide 698.12 by 12.4, first move the decimal points in both the divisor 12.4 and the dividend 698.12 one place to the right to make the divisor an integer. That is, replace 698.12/12.4 with 6981.2/124. Then do the long division normally:

$$
\begin{array}{r}
56.3 \\
124\overline{)6981.2} \\
\underline{620} \\
781 \\
\underline{744} \\
372 \\
\underline{372} \\
0
\end{array}
$$

5. Arithmetic Shortcuts and Properties of Operations

A. For any two nonnegative integers x and y, the final digit of $x + y$ is the final digit of the sum of x's final digit and y's final digit. And for any two integers x and y, the final digit of xy is the final digit of the product of x's final digit and y's final digit.

Examples:

The final digit of 345 + 789 is the final digit of 5 + 9 = 14, which is 4.

The final digit of 345 × 789 is the final digit of 5 × 9 = 45, which is 5.

B. Here are some shortcuts to help tell whether one integer is divisible by another:

An integer is divisible by 2 if and only if its final digit is even.

An integer is divisible by 3 if and only if the sum of its digits is divisible by 3.

An integer with 3 or more digits is divisible by 4 if and only if its final 2 digits make a number divisible by 4.

An integer is divisible by 5 if and only if its final digit is 5 or 0.

An integer is divisible by 9 if and only if the sum of its digits is divisible by 9.

An integer is divisible by 10 if and only if its final digit is 0.

Examples:

The integer 180 is divisible by 2, 5, and 10, because its final digit is 0. It's also divisible by 3 and 9, because its digits sum to 1 + 8 + 0 = 9, which is divisible by both 3 and 9. And it's divisible by 4, because its final 2 digits, 80, make a number divisible by 4.

But the integer 121 is not divisible by 2, because its final digit is odd. Nor is it divisible by 3 or 9, because its digits sum to 1 + 2 + 1 = 4, which is divisible by neither 3 nor 9. And it's not divisible by 4, because its final two digits, 21, make a number not divisible by 4. Finally, because its final digit is neither 5 nor 0, it's not divisible by 5 or 10.

C. Here are some basic properties of arithmetical operations for any real numbers x, y, and z:

- Addition and Subtraction

  $x + 0 = x = x - 0$

  $x - x = 0$

  $x + y = y + x$

  $x - y = -(y - x) = x + (-y)$

  $(x + y) + z = x + (y + z)$

  If x and y are both positive, then $x + y$ is positive.

  If x and y are both negative, then $x + y$ is negative.

- Multiplication and Division

  $x \times 1 = x = \frac{x}{1}$

  $x \times 0 = 0$

  If $x \neq 0$, then $\frac{x}{x} = 1$.

  $\frac{x}{0}$ is undefined.

  $xy = yx$

  If $x \neq 0$ and $y \neq 0$, then $\frac{x}{y} = \frac{1}{\left(\frac{y}{x}\right)}$.

  $(xy)z = x(yz)$

  $xy + xz = x(y + z)$

  If $y \neq 0$, then $\left(\frac{x}{y}\right) + \left(\frac{z}{y}\right) = \frac{(x + z)}{y}$.

  If x and y are both positive, then xy is positive.

  If x and y are both negative, then xy is positive.

  If x is positive and y is negative, then xy is negative.

  If $xy = 0$, then $x = 0$ or $y = 0$, or both.

- Exponentiation

  $x^1 = x$

  If $x \neq 0$, then $x^0 = 1$.

  If $x \neq 0$, then $x^{-1} = \frac{1}{x}$.

  $(x^y)^z = x^{yz} = (x^z)^y$

  $x^{y+z} = x^y x^z$

  If $x \neq 0$, then $x^{y-z} = \frac{x^y}{x^z}$.

  $(xz)^y = x^y z^y$

  If $z \neq 0$, then $\left(\frac{x}{z}\right)^y = \frac{x^y}{z^y}$.

  If $z \neq 0$, then $x^{\frac{y}{z}} = (x^y)^{\frac{1}{z}} = \left(x^{\frac{1}{z}}\right)^y$.

3.2 Algebra, Equalities, and Inequalities

1. Algebraic Expressions and Equations

A. Algebra is based on arithmetic and on the concept of an ***unknown quantity***. Letters like ***x*** or ***n*** are ***variables*** that stand for unknown quantities. Other numerical expressions called ***constants*** stand for known quantities. A combination of variables, constants, and arithmetical operations is an ***algebraic expression***.

Solving word problems often requires translating words into algebraic expressions. The table below shows how some words and phrases can be translated as math operations in algebraic expressions:

<table>
<tr><th colspan="5">3.2 Translating Words into Math Operations</th></tr>
<tr><th>$x + y$</th><th>$x - y$</th><th>xy</th><th>$\frac{x}{y}$</th><th>x^y</th></tr>
<tr><td rowspan="3">x added to y
x increased by y
x more than y
x plus y
the sum of x and y
the total of x and y</td><td rowspan="3">x decreased by y
difference of x and y
y fewer than x
y less than x
x minus y
x reduced by y
y subtracted from x</td><td>x multiplied by y
the product of x and y
x times y</td><td>x divided by y
x over y
the quotient of x and y
the ratio of x to y</td><td>x to the power of y
x to the yth power</td></tr>
<tr><td>If $y = 2$:
double x
twice x</td><td rowspan="2">If $y = 2$:
half of x
x halved</td><td>If $y = 2$:
x squared</td></tr>
<tr><td>If $y = 3$:
triple x</td><td>If $y = 3$:
x cubed</td></tr>
</table>

B. In an algebraic expression, a ***term*** is a constant, a variable, or a product of terms that are each a constant or a variable. A variable in a term may be raised to an exponent. A term with no variables is a ***constant term***. A constant in a term with one or more variables is a ***coefficient***.

Example:

Suppose Pam has 5 more pencils than Fred. If F is the number of pencils Fred has, then Pam has $F + 5$ pencils. The algebraic expression $F + 5$ has two terms: the variable F and the constant 5.

C. A ***polynomial*** is an algebraic expression that's a sum of terms and has exactly one variable. Each term in a polynomial is a variable raised to some power and multiplied by some coefficient. If the highest power a variable is raised to is 1, the expression is a ***first degree*** (or ***linear***) ***polynomial*** in that variable. If the highest power a variable is raised to is 2, the expression is a ***second degree*** (or ***quadratic***) ***polynomial*** in that variable.

Examples:

$F + 5$ is a linear polynomial in F, since the highest power of F is 1.

$19x^2 - 6x + 3$ is a quadratic polynomial in x, since the highest power of x is 2.

$\frac{3x^2}{(2x-5)}$ is not a polynomial because it's not a sum of powers of x multiplied by coefficients.

D. You can simplify many algebraic expressions by factoring or combining ***like*** terms.

Examples:

In the expression $6x + 5x$, x is a factor common to both terms. So, $6x + 5x$ is equivalent to $(6 + 5)x$, or $11x$.

In the expression $9x - 3y$, 3 is a factor common to both terms: $9x - 3y = 3(3x - y)$.

The expression $5x^2 + 6y$ has no like terms and no common factors.

E. In a fraction $\frac{n}{d}$, n is the ***numerator*** and d is the ***denominator.*** In a numerator and denominator, you can divide out any common factors not equal to zero.

Example:

If $x \neq 3$, then $\frac{(x-3)}{(x-3)} = 1$.

So, $\frac{(3xy-9y)}{(x-3)} = \frac{3y(x-3)}{(x-3)} = 3y(1) = 3y$.

F. To multiply two algebraic expressions, multiply each term of one expression by each term of the other.

Example:

$$(3x - 4)(9y + x) = 3x(9y + x) - 4(9y + x)$$
$$= 3x(9y) + 3x(x) - 4(9y) - 4(x)$$
$$= 27xy + 3x^2 - 36y - 4x$$

G. To ***evaluate*** an algebraic expression, replace its variables with constants.

Example:

If $x = 3$ and $y = -2$, we can evaluate $3xy - x^2 + y$ as

$3(3)(-2) - (3)^2 + (-2) = -18 - 9 - 2 = -29$.

H. An ***algebraic equation*** is an equation with only algebraic expression. An algebraic equation's ***solutions*** are the sets of assignments of constant values to its variables that make it true, or "satisfy the equation." An equation may have no solution, one solution, or more than one solution. For equations solved together, the solutions must satisfy all the equations at once. An equation's solutions are also called its ***roots***. To confirm the roots are correct, you can substitute them into the equation.

I. Two equations with the same solution or solutions are ***equivalent***.

Examples:

The equations $2 + x = 3$ and $4 + 2x = 6$ are equivalent, because each has the unique solution $x = 1$. Notice the second equation is the first equation multiplied by 2.

Likewise, the equations $3x - y = 6$ and $6x - 2y = 12$ are equivalent, although each has infinitely many solutions. For any value of x, giving the value $3x - 6$ to y satisfies both these equations. For example, $x = 2$ with $y = 0$ is a solution to both equations, and so is $x = 5$ with $y = 9$.

2. Linear Equations

A. A ***linear equation*** has a linear polynomial on one side of the equals sign and either a linear polynomial or a constant on the other side—or can be converted to that form. A linear equation with only one variable is a ***linear equation with one unknown***. A linear equation with two variables is ***a linear equation with two unknowns***.

Examples:

$5x - 2 = 9 - x$ is a linear equation with one unknown.

$3x + 1 = y - 2$ is a linear equation with two unknowns.

B. To solve a linear equation with one unknown (that is, to find what value of the unknown satisfies the equation), isolate the unknown on one side of the equation by doing the same operations on both sides. Adding or subtracting the same number on both sides of the equation doesn't change the equality. Likewise, multiplying or dividing both sides by the same nonzero number doesn't change the equality.

Example:

To solve the equation $\frac{5x-6}{3} = 4$, isolate the variable x like this:

$$5x - 6 = 12 \quad \text{multiply both sides by 3}$$

$$5x = 18 \quad \text{add 6 to both sides}$$

$$x = \frac{18}{5} \quad \text{divide both sides by 5}$$

To check the answer $\frac{18}{5}$, substitute it for x in the original equation to confirm it satisfies that equation:

$$\frac{\left(5\left(\frac{18}{5}\right) - 6\right)}{3} = \frac{(18-6)}{3} = \frac{12}{3} = 4$$

So, $x = \frac{18}{5}$ is the solution.

C. Two equivalent linear equations with the same two unknowns have infinitely many solutions, as in the example of the equivalent equations $3x - y = 6$ and $6x - 2y = 12$ in Section 3.2.1.I above. But if two linear equations with the same two unknowns aren't equivalent, they have at most one solution.

When solving two linear equations with two unknowns, if you reach a trivial equation like $0 = 0$, the equations are equivalent and have infinitely many solutions. But if you reach a contradiction, the equations have no solution.

Example:

Consider the two equations $3x + 4y = 17$ and $6x + 8y = 35$. Note that $3x + 4y = 17$ implies $6x + 8y = 34$, contradicting the second equation. So, no values of x and y can satisfy both equations at once. The two equations have no solution.

If neither a trivial equation nor a contradiction is reached, a unique solution can be found.

D. To solve two linear equations with two unknowns, you can use one of the equations to express one unknown in terms of the other unknown. Then substitute this result into the second equation to make a new equation with only one unknown. Next, solve this new equation. Substitute the value of its unknown into either original equation to solve for the remaining unknown.

Example:

Let's solve these two equations for x and y:

$$(1)\quad 3x + 2y = 11$$
$$(2)\quad x - y = 2$$

In equation (2), $x = 2 + y$. So, in equation (1), substitute $2 + y$ for x:

$$\begin{aligned} 3(2 + y) + 2y &= 11 \\ 6 + 3y + 2y &= 11 \\ 6 + 5y &= 11 \\ 5y &= 5 \\ y &= 1 \end{aligned}$$

Since $y = 1$, we find $x - 1 = 2$, so $x = 2 + 1 = 3$.

E. Another way to remove one unknown and solve for x and y is to make the coefficients of one unknown the same in both equations (ignoring the sign). Then either add the equations or subtract one from the other.

Example:

Let's solve the equations:

$$(1)\quad 6x + 5y = 29 \text{ and}$$
$$(2)\quad 4x - 3y = -6$$

Multiply equation (1) by 3 and equation (2) by 5 to get

$$18x + 15y = 87 \text{ and}$$
$$20x - 15y = -30$$

Add the two equations to remove y. This gives us $38x = 57$, or $x = \frac{3}{2}$.

Substituting $\frac{3}{2}$ for x in either original equation gives $y = 4$. To check these answers, substitute both values into both the original equations.

3. Factoring and Quadratic Equations

A. Some equations can be solved by ***factoring***. To do this, first add or subtract to bring all the expressions to one side of the equation, with 0 on the other side. Then try to express the nonzero side as a product of factors that are algebraic expressions. When that's possible, setting any of these factors equal to 0 makes a simpler equation. The solutions of the simpler equations made this way are also solutions of the factored equation.

Example:

Factor to find the solutions of the equation $x^3 - 2x^2 + x = -5(x - 1)^2$:

$$x^3 - 2x^2 + x + 5(x - 1)^2 = 0$$
$$x(x^2 - 2x + 1) + 5(x - 1)^2 = 0$$
$$x(x - 1)^2 + 5(x - 1)^2 = 0$$
$$(x + 5)(x - 1)^2 = 0$$
$$x + 5 = 0 \text{ or } x - 1 = 0$$
$$x = -5 \text{ or } x = 1$$

So, $x = -5$ or $x = 1$.

B. When factoring to solve equations with algebraic fractions, note that a fraction equals 0 if and only if its numerator equals 0 and its denominator doesn't.

Example:

Find the solutions of the equation $\frac{x(x - 3)(x^2 + 5)}{x - 4} = 0$.

The denominator must not equal 0, so $x - 4 \neq 0$. Thus, $x \neq 4$.

But the numerator must equal 0: $x(x - 3)(x^2 + 5) = 0$.

Thus, $x = 0$, or $x - 3 = 0$, or $x^2 + 5 = 0$. So, $x = 0$, or $x = 3$, or $x^2 + 5 = 0$.

But $x^2 + 5 = 0$ has no real solution because $x^2 + 5 \geq 0$ for every real number x. So, the original equation's solutions are 0 and 3.

C. Here are some common algebraic equations used for factoring. They hold for any real numbers x, y, and z:

Examples:

$(x + \frac{1}{x})^2 = x^2 + \frac{1}{x^2} + 2$

$(x + y)^2 = x^2 + 2xy + y^2$

$(x - y)^2 = x^2 - 2xy + y^2$

$(x + y)(x - y) = x^2 - y^2$

$x^2 + y^2 = (x + y)^2 - 2xy = (x - y)^2 + 2xy$

$(x + y + z)^2 = x^2 + y^2 + z^2 + 2xy + 2xz + 2yz$

$(x + y)^3 = x^3 + 3x^2y + 3xy^2 + y^3$

$(x - y)^3 = x^3 - 3x^2y + 3xy^2 - y^3$

D. A ***quadratic equation*** has the standard form $ax^2 + bx + c = 0$, where a, b, and c are real numbers and $a \neq 0$.

Examples:

$$x^2 + 6x + 5 = 0,$$
$$3x^2 - 2x = 0, \text{ and}$$
$$x^2 + 4 = 0.$$

E. Some quadratic equations are easily solved by factoring.

Example (1):

$$x^2 + 6x + 5 = 0$$
$$(x + 5)(x + 1) = 0$$
$$x + 5 = 0 \text{ or } x + 1 = 0$$
$$x = -5 \text{ or } x = -1$$

Example (2):

$$3x^2 - 3 = 8x$$
$$3x^2 - 8x - 3 = 0$$
$$(3x + 1)(x - 3) = 0$$
$$3x + 1 = 0 \text{ or } x - 3 = 0$$
$$x = -\frac{1}{3} \text{ or } x = 3$$

F. A quadratic equation has at most two real roots but may have just one or even no real root.

Examples:

The equation $x^2 - 6x + 9 = 0$ can be written as $(x - 3)^2 = 0$ or $(x - 3)(x - 3) = 0$. So, its only root is 3.

The equation $x^2 + 4 = 0$ has no real root. Since any real number squared is greater than or equal to zero, $x^2 + 4$ must be greater than or equal to 4 if x is a real number.

G. An expression of the form $a^2 - b^2$ can be factored as $(a - b)(a + b)$.

Example:

We can solve the quadratic equation $9x^2 - 25 = 0$ like this:

$$(3x - 5)(3x + 5) = 0$$
$$3x - 5 = 0 \text{ or } x + 5 = 0$$
$$x = \frac{5}{3} \text{ or } x = -\frac{5}{3}$$

H. If a quadratic expression isn't easily factored, we can still find its roots with the ***quadratic formula***: If $ax^2 + bx + c = 0$ and $a \neq 0$, the roots are

$$x = \frac{-b + \sqrt{b^2 - 4ac}}{2a} \text{ and } x = \frac{-b - \sqrt{b^2 - 4ac}}{2a}$$

These roots are two distinct real numbers unless $b^2 - 4ac \leq 0$.

If $b^2 - 4ac = 0$, the two root expressions both equal $-\frac{b}{2a}$, so the equation has only one root.

If $b^2 - 4ac < 0$, then $\sqrt{b^2 - 4ac}$ is not a real number, so the equation has no real root.

4. Inequalities

A. An ***inequality*** is a statement with one of these symbols:

$\neq$ is not equal to

$>$ is greater than

$\geq$ is greater than or equal to

$<$ is less than

$\leq$ is less than or equal to

Examples:

$5x - 3 < 9$ and $6x \geq y$

B. Solve a linear inequality with one unknown the same way you solve a linear equation: isolate the unknown on one side. As in an equation, the same number can be added to or subtracted from both sides of the inequality. And you can multiply or divide both sides by a positive number without changing the order of the inequality. However, multiplying or dividing an inequality by a negative number reverses the order of the inequality. Thus, $6 > 2$, but $(-1)(6) < (-1)(2)$.

Example (*1*):

To solve the inequality $3x - 2 > 5$ for x, isolate x:

$3x - 2 > 5$

$3x > 7$ (add 2 to both sides)

$x > \frac{7}{3}$ (divide both sides by 3)

Example (*2*):

To solve the inequality $\frac{5x - 1}{-2} < 3$ for x, isolate x:

$\frac{5x - 1}{-2} < 3$

$5x - 1 > -6$ (multiply both sides by -2)

$5x > -5$ (add 1 to both sides)

$x > -1$ (divide both sides by 5)

5. Functions

A. An algebraic expression in one variable can define a ***function*** of that variable. A function is written as a letter like f or g along with the variable in the expression. Function notation is a short way to express that a value is being substituted for a variable.

Examples:

(i) The expression $x^3 - 5x^2 + 2$ can define a function f written as $f(x) = x^3 - 5x^2 + 2$.

(ii) The expression $\frac{2z+7}{\sqrt{z+1}}$ can define a function g written as $g(z) = \frac{2z+7}{\sqrt{z+1}}$.

In these examples, the symbols "$f(x)$" and "$g(z)$" don't stand for products. Each is just a symbol for a function. Pronounce "$f(x)$" as "f of x" and "$g(z)$" as "g of z."

The substitution of 1 for x in the first expression can be written as $f(1) = -2$. Then $f(1)$ is called the "value of f at $x = 1$."

Likewise, in the second expression the value of g at $z = 0$ is $g(0) = 7$.

B. Once a function $f(x)$ is defined, think of x as an input and $f(x)$ as the output. In any function, any one input gives at most one output. But different inputs can give the same output.

Example:

If $h(x) = |x + 3|$, then $h(-4) = 1 = h(-2)$.

C. The set of all allowed inputs for a function is the function's ***domain***. In the examples in Section 3.2.5.A above, the domain of f is the set of all real numbers, and the domain of g is the set of all numbers greater than -1.

Any function's definition can restrict the function's domain. For example, the definition "$a(x) = 9x - 5$ for $0 \le x \le 10$" restricts the domain of a to real numbers greater than or equal to 0 but less than or equal to 10. If the definition has no restrictions, the domain is the set of all values of x that each give a real output when input into the function.

D. The set of a function's outputs is the function's ***range***.

Examples:

(i) For the function $h(x) = |x + 3|$ in the example in Section 3.2.5.B above, the range is the set of all numbers greater than or equal to 0.

(ii) For the function $a(x) = 9x - 5$ for $0 \le x \le 10$ defined in Section 3.2.5.C above, the range is the set of all real numbers y such that $-5 \le y \le 85$.

E. A ***quadratic function*** has the form $f(x) = ax^2 + bx + c$ where a, b, and c are constants and $a \ne 0$. If $a > 0$, then $f(x)$ has a unique minimum value but no maximum value. Otherwise, it has a unique maximum value but no minimum value. In either case, the unique minimum or maximum value of $f(x)$ is $c - \frac{b^2}{4a}$. This value occurs only when $x = -\frac{b}{2a}$.

Examples:

(i) The quadratic function $f(x) = 2x^2 - 3x + 4$ has a unique minimum value of $4 - \frac{(-3)^2}{4 \times 2} = 4 - \frac{9}{8} = \frac{25}{8}$. This minimum value occurs only when $x = -\left(\frac{-3}{2 \times 2}\right) = \frac{3}{4}$.

(ii) The quadratic function $g(x) = -3x^2 + 2x + 1$ has a unique maximum value of $1 - \frac{2^2}{4 \times -3} = 1 - \frac{-1}{3} = \frac{4}{3}$. This maximum value occurs only when $x = -\left(\frac{2}{2 \times -3}\right) = \frac{1}{3}$.

6. Graphing

A. The figure below shows the rectangular ***coordinate plane.*** The horizontal line is the ***x-axis*** and the vertical line is the ***y-axis.*** These two axes intersect at the ***origin***, called *O*. The axes divide the plane into four quadrants: I, II, III, and IV, as shown.

The Coordinate Plane

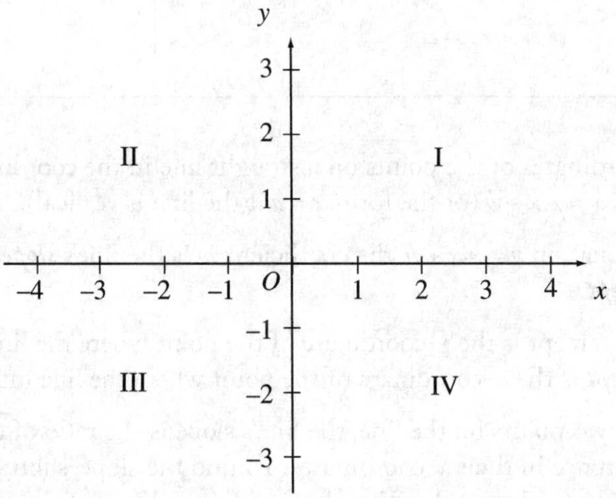

B. Any ordered pair (x, y) of real numbers defines a point in the coordinate plane. The point's ***x-coordinate*** is the first number in this pair. It shows how far the point is to the right or left of the *y*-axis. If the *x*-coordinate is positive, the point is to the right of the *y*-axis. If it's negative, the point is to the left of the *y*-axis. If it's 0, the point is on the *y*-axis. The point's ***y-coordinate*** is the second number in the ordered pair. It shows how far the point is above or below the *x*-axis. If the *y*-coordinate is positive, the point is above the *x*-axis. If it's negative, the point is below the *x*-axis. If it's 0, the point is on the *x*-axis.

Example:

In the graph below, the (x, y) coordinates of point P are $(2, 3)$. P is 2 units to the right of the y-axis, so $x = 2$. Since P is 3 units above the x-axis, $y = 3$.

Likewise, the (x, y) coordinates of point Q are $(-4, -3)$. The origin O has coordinates $(0, 0)$.

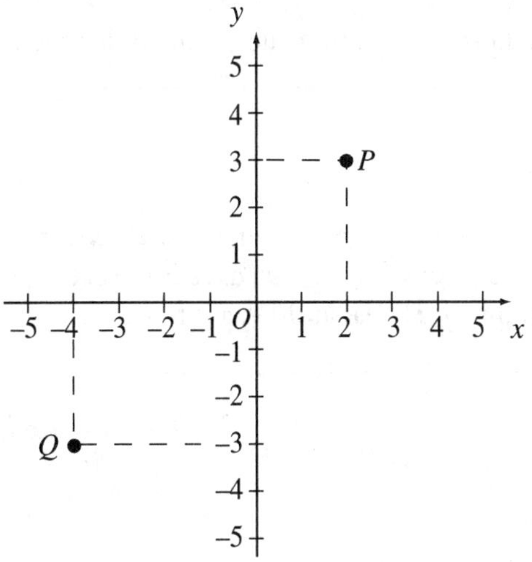

C. The coordinates of the points on a straight line in the coordinate plane satisfy a linear equation of the form $y = mx + b$ (or the form $x = a$ if the line is vertical).

In the equation $y = mx + b$, the coefficient m is the line's ***slope,*** and the constant b is the line's ***y-intercept.***

The y-intercept is the y-coordinate of the point where the line intersects the y-axis. Likewise, the ***x-intercept*** is the x-coordinate of the point where the line intersects the x-axis.

For any two points on the line, the line's slope is the ratio of the difference in their y-coordinates to the difference in their x-coordinates. To find the slope, subtract one point's y-coordinate from the other's. Then subtract the former point's x-coordinate from the latter's—not the other way around! Then divide the first difference by the second.

If a line's slope is negative, the line slants down from left to right.

If the slope is positive, the line slants up.

If the slope is 0, the line is horizontal. A horizontal line's equation has the form $y = b$, since $m = 0$.

A vertical line's slope is undefined.

Example:

In the graph below, each point on the line satisfies the equation $y = -\frac{1}{2}x + 1$. To check this for the points $(-2, 2)$, $(2, 0)$, and $(0, 1)$, substitute each point's coordinates for x and y in the equation.

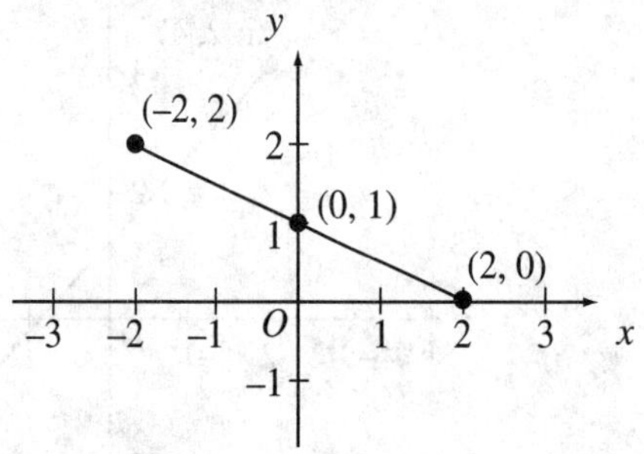

You can use the points $(-2, 2)$ and $(2, 0)$ to find the line's slope:

$$\frac{\text{the difference in the } y\text{-coordinates}}{\text{the difference in the } x\text{-coordinates}} = \frac{0-2}{2-(-2)} = \frac{-2}{4} = -\frac{1}{2}.$$

The y-intercept is 1. That's y's value when x is 0 in $y = -\frac{1}{2}x + 1$.

To find the x-intercept, set y to 0 in the same equation:

$$-\frac{1}{2}x + 1 = 0$$

$$-\frac{1}{2}x = -1$$

$$x = 2$$

Thus, the x-intercept is 2.

D. You can use the definition of slope to find an equation of the line through two points (x_1, y_1) and (x_2, y_2) with $x_1 \neq x_2$. The slope is $m = \frac{y_2 - y_1}{x_2 - x_1}$. Given the known point (x_1, y_1) and the slope m, any other point (x, y) on the line satisfies the equation $m = \frac{(y - y_1)}{(x - x_1)}$, or equivalently $(y - y_1) = m(x - x_1)$. Using (x_2, y_2) instead of (x_1, y_1) as the known point gives an equivalent equation.

Example:

The graph below shows points (–2, 4) and (3, –3).

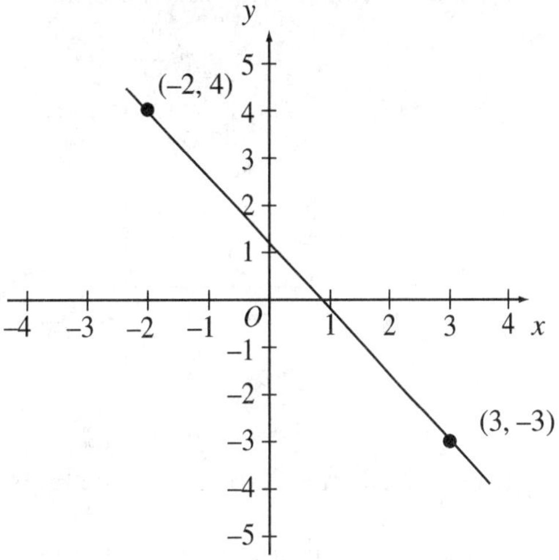

The line's slope is $\frac{(-3-4)}{(3-(-2))} = -\frac{7}{5}$. To find an equation of this line, let's use the point (3, –3):

$$y-(-3) = \left(-\frac{7}{5}\right)(x-3)$$
$$y+3 = \left(-\frac{7}{5}\right)x + \frac{21}{5}$$
$$y = \left(-\frac{7}{5}\right)x + \frac{6}{5}$$

So, the y-intercept is $\frac{6}{5}$.

Find the x-intercept like this:

$$0 = -\frac{7}{5}x + \frac{6}{5}$$
$$\frac{7}{5}x = \frac{6}{5}$$
$$x = \frac{6}{7}$$

The graph shows both these intercepts.

E. If two linear equations with unknowns x and y have a unique shared solution, their graphs are two lines intersecting at the shared point that is the solution.

If two linear equations are equivalent, they both stand for the same line and have infinitely many shared solutions.

Two linear equations with no shared solution stand for two parallel lines.

F. Graph any function $f(x)$ in the coordinate plane by equating y with the function's value: $y = f(x)$. For any x in the function's domain, the point $(x, f(x))$ is on the function's graph. For every point on the graph, the y-coordinate is the function's value at the x-coordinate.

Example:

Consider the function $f(x) = -\frac{7}{5}x + \frac{6}{5}$.

If $f(x)$ is equated with the variable y, the function's graph is the graph of $y = -\frac{7}{5}x + \frac{6}{5}$ in the example above.

G. For any function f, the x-intercepts are the solutions of the equation $f(x) = 0$. The y-intercept is the value $f(0)$.

Example:

To see how the quadratic function $f(x) = x^2 - 1$ relates to its graph, let's plot some points $(x, f(x))$ in the coordinate plane:

x	$f(x)$
–2	3
–1	0
0	–1
1	0
2	3

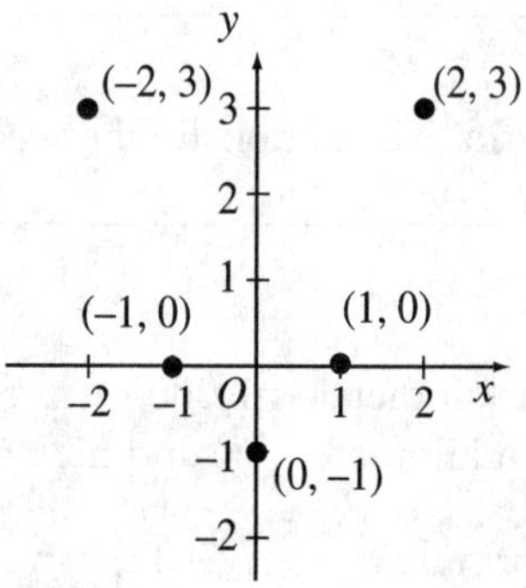

The graph below shows all the points for $-2 \le x \le 2$:

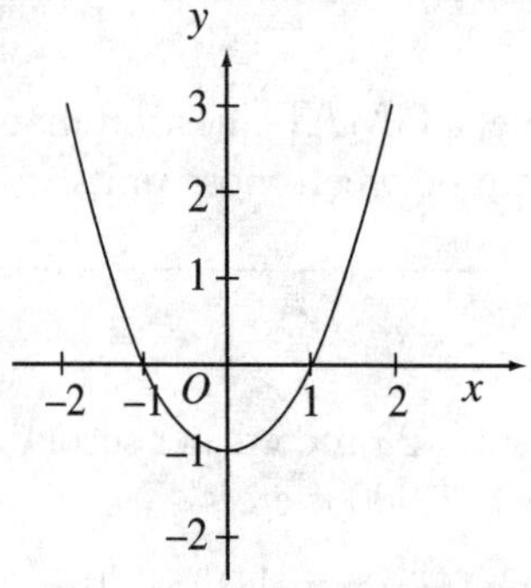

The roots of this equation $f(x) = x^2 - 1 = 0$ are $x = 1$ and $x = -1$. They match the x-intercepts since x-intercepts are found by setting $y = 0$ and solving for x.

The y-intercept is $f(0) = -1$ because that's the value of y for $x = 0$.

7. Formulas and Measurement Conversion

A. A ***formula*** is an algebraic equation with variables that have specific meanings. To use a formula, assign quantities to its variables to match these meanings.

Example:

In the physics formula $F = ma$, the variable F stands for force, the variable m stands for mass, and the variable a stands for acceleration. The standard metric unit of force, the newton, is just enough force to accelerate a mass of 1 kilogram by 1 meter/second^2.

If we know a rock with a mass of 2 kilograms is accelerating at 5 meters/second^2, we can use the formula $F = ma$ by setting the variable m to 2 kilograms, and the variable a to 5 meters/second^2. Then we find that 10 newtons of force F are pushing the rock.

Note: You don't need to learn physics formulas or terms like this for the GMAT, but some specific GMAT questions may give you the formulas and terms you need to solve them.

B. Any quantitative relationship between units of measure can be written as a formula.

Examples:

(i) Since 1 kilometer is 1,000 meters, the formula $m = 1000k$ can stand for the relationship between kilometers (k) and meters (m).

(ii) The formula $C = \frac{5}{9}(F - 32)$ can stand for the relationship between temperature measurements in degrees Celsius (C) and degrees Fahrenheit (F).

C. Except for units of time, a GMAT question that requires converting one unit of measure to another will give the relationship between those units.

Example:

A train travels at a constant 25 meters per second. How many kilometers does it travel in 5 minutes? (1 kilometer = 1,000 meters)

Solution: In 1 minute the train travels (25)(60) = 1,500 meters, so in 5 minutes it travels 7,500 meters. Since 1 kilometer = 1,000 meters, we find 7,500 meters = 7.5 kilometers.

3.3 Rates, Ratios, and Percents

1. Ratio and Proportion

A. The ***ratio*** of a number x to a nonzero number y may be written as $x{:}y$, or $\frac{x}{y}$, or x to y. In each of these expressions, x is the numerator and y is the denominator.The order of a ratio's terms is important. Unless the absolute values of x and y are equal, $\frac{x}{y} \neq \frac{y}{x}$.

Examples:

The ratio of 2 to 3 may be written as 2:3, or $\frac{2}{3}$, or 2 to 3.

The ratio of the number of months with exactly 30 days to the number of months with exactly 31 days is 4:7, not 7:4.

B. A ***proportion*** is an equation between two ratios. Remember, the denominator on either side of the proportion must not equal zero.

Example:

2:3 = 8:12 is a proportion.

C. One way to solve for an unknown in a proportion is to cross multiply, then solve the resulting equation.

Example:

To solve for n in the proportion $\frac{2}{3} = \frac{n}{12}$, cross multiply to get $3n = 24$, then divide both sides by 3 to find $n = 8$.

D. Some word problems can be solved using ratios.

Example:

If 5 shirts cost a total of $44, then what is the total cost of 8 shirts at the same cost per shirt?

Solution: If c is the cost of the 8 shirts, then $\frac{5}{44} = \frac{8}{c}$. Cross multiplying gives $5c = 8 \times 44 = 352$, so $c = \frac{352}{5} = 70.4$. Thus, the 8 shirts cost a total of $70.40.

2. Fractions

A. In a fraction $\frac{n}{d}$, n is the ***numerator*** and d is the ***denominator***. A fraction's denominator can never be 0 because division by 0 is undefined.

B. ***Equivalent*** fractions stand for the same number. To check whether two fractions with numerators and denominators that are integers are equivalent, divide each fraction's numerator and denominator by the largest factor common to that numerator and that denominator, their ***greatest common divisor*** (GCD). This is called ***reducing each fraction to its lowest terms***. Two fractions are equivalent if and only if reducing each to its lowest terms makes them identical.

Example:

To check whether $\frac{8}{36}$ and $\frac{14}{63}$ are equivalent, first reduce each to its lowest terms. In the first fraction, 4 is the GCD of the numerator 8 and the denominator 36. Dividing both the numerator and the denominator of $\frac{8}{36}$ by 4 gives $\frac{2}{9}$. In the second fraction, 7 is the GCD of the numerator 14 and the denominator 63. Dividing both the numerator and the denominator of $\frac{14}{63}$ by 7 also gives $\frac{2}{9}$. Since reducing $\frac{8}{36}$ and $\frac{14}{63}$ to their lowest terms makes them identical, they're equivalent.

C. To add or subtract two fractions with the same denominator, just add or subtract the numerators, leaving the denominators the same.

Examples:

$\frac{3}{5}+\frac{4}{5}=\frac{3+4}{5}=\frac{7}{5}$ and

$\frac{5}{7}-\frac{2}{7}=\frac{5-2}{7}=\frac{3}{7}$

D. To add or subtract two fractions with different denominators, first express them as fractions with the same denominator.

Example:

To add $\frac{3}{5}$ and $\frac{4}{7}$, multiply the numerator and denominator of $\frac{3}{5}$ by 7 to get $\frac{21}{35}$. Then multiply the numerator and denominator of $\frac{4}{7}$ by 5 to get $\frac{20}{35}$. Since both fractions now have the same denominator 35, you can easily add them: $\frac{3}{5}+\frac{4}{7}=\frac{21}{35}+\frac{20}{35}=\frac{41}{35}$

E. To multiply two fractions, multiply their numerators, and also multiply their denominators.

Example:

$\frac{2}{3}\times\frac{4}{7}=\frac{2\times4}{3\times7}=\frac{8}{21}$

F. The ***reciprocal*** of a fraction $\frac{n}{d}$ is $\frac{d}{n}$ if neither n nor d is 0.

Example:

The reciprocal of $\frac{4}{7}$ is $\frac{7}{4}$.

G. To divide by a fraction, multiply by its reciprocal.

Example:

$$\frac{2}{3} \div \frac{4}{7} = \frac{2}{3} \times \frac{7}{4} = \frac{14}{12} = \frac{7}{6}$$

H. A ***mixed number*** is written as an integer next to a fraction. It equals the integer plus the fraction.

Example:

The mixed number $7\frac{2}{3} = 7 + \frac{2}{3}$

I. To write a mixed number as a fraction, multiply the integer part of the mixed number by the denominator of the fractional part. Add this product to the numerator. Then put this sum over the denominator.

Example:

$$7\frac{2}{3} = \frac{(7 \times 3) + 2}{3} = \frac{23}{3}$$

3. Percents

A. The word ***percent*** means ***per hundred*** or ***number out of 100.***

Example:

Saying that 37 percent, or 37%, of the houses in a city are painted blue means that 37 houses per 100 in the city are painted blue.

B. A percent may be greater than 100.

Example:

Saying that the number of blue houses in a city is 150% of the number of red houses means the city has 150 blue houses for every 100 red houses. Since 150:100 = 3:2, this means the city has 3 blue houses for every 2 red houses.

C. A percent need not be an integer.

Example:

Saying that the number of pink houses in a city is 0.5% of the number of blue houses means the city has 0.5 of a pink house for every 100 blue houses. Since 0.5:100 = 1:200, this means the city has 1 pink house for every 200 blue houses.

Likewise, saying that the number of orange houses is 12.5% of the number of blue houses means the ratio of orange houses to blue houses is 12.5:100 = 1:8. Therefore, there is 1 orange house for every 8 blue houses.

4. Converting Decimals, Fractions, and Percents

A. Decimals with many finite digits can be rewritten as fractions or sums of fractions.

Examples:

$$0.321 = \frac{3}{10} + \frac{2}{100} + \frac{1}{1{,}000} = \frac{321}{1{,}000}$$

$$0.0321 = \frac{0}{10} + \frac{3}{100} + \frac{2}{1{,}000} + \frac{1}{10{,}000} = \frac{321}{10{,}000}$$

$$1.56 = 1 + \frac{5}{10} + \frac{6}{100} = \frac{156}{100}$$

B. Repeating decimals can also be rewritten as fractions. To do this, set a variable x equal to the repeating decimal. Next multiply both sides by a power of 10 just large enough to make the repeating digits start right after the decimal if they don't already. Call this Equation A. Then make another equation by multiplying both sides of Equation A by a power of 10 just large enough to move one copy of the repeating digits from the right to the left of the decimal point. From this, subtract Equation A, and solve for x.

Examples:

(i) To rewrite the repeating decimal $3.\overline{6}$ as a fraction, first let $x = 3.\overline{6}$. This equation already has the repeating digit 6 starting right after the decimal, so it's our Equation A. Next we multiply both sides by 10 to move one repeating 6 from the right to the left of the decimal point: $10x = 36.\overline{6}$. From this, subtract Equation A to get $9x = 36.\overline{6} - 3.\overline{6} = 33$. Finally divide both sides by 9 to solve for x: $x = \frac{33}{9} = 3\frac{2}{3}$.

(ii) To rewrite the repeating decimal $1.2\overline{79}$ as a fraction, first let $x = 1.2\overline{79}$. Next multiply both sides by 10 to make the repeating digits start right after the decimal: $10x = 12.\overline{79}$. This is our Equation A. Then multiply both sides by 100 to move one copy of the repeating digits 79 from the right to the left of the decimal point: $1000x = 1279.\overline{79}$. From this, subtract Equation A to get $990x = 1279.\overline{79} - 12.\overline{79} = 1267$. Finally divide both sides by 990 to solve for x: $x = \frac{1267}{990} = 1\frac{277}{990}$.

C. To rewrite a percent as a fraction, write the percent number as the numerator over a denominator of 100. To rewrite a percent as a decimal, move the decimal point in the percent two places to the left and drop the percent sign. To rewrite a decimal as a percent, move the decimal point two places to the right, then add a percent sign.

Examples:

$37\% = \frac{37}{100} = 0.37$

$300\% = \frac{300}{100} = 3$

$0.5\% = \frac{0.5}{100} = 0.005$

D. To find a percent of a number, multiply the number by the percent written as a fraction or decimal.

Examples:

$20\% \text{ of } 90 = 90\left(\frac{20}{100}\right) = 90\left(\frac{1}{5}\right) = \frac{90}{5} = 18$

$20\% \text{ of } 90 = 90(0.2) = 18$

$250\% \text{ of } 80 = 80\left(\frac{250}{100}\right) = 80(2.5) = 200$

$0.5\% \text{ of } 12 = 12\left(\frac{0.5}{100}\right) = 12(0.005) = 0.06$

5. Working with Decimals, Fractions, and Percents

A. To find the percent increase or decrease from one positive quantity to another, first find the amount of increase or decrease. Then divide this amount by the original quantity. Write this quotient as a percent.

Examples:

Suppose a price increases from \$24 to \$30. To find the percent increase, first find the amount of increase: \$30 – \$24 = \$6. Divide this \$6 by the original price of \$24 to find the percent increase: $\frac{6}{24} = 0.25 = 25\%$.

Now suppose a price falls from \$30 to \$24. The amount of decrease is \$30 – \$24 = \$6. So, the percent decrease is $\frac{6}{30} = 0.20 = 20\%$.

Notice the percent **increase** from 24 to 30 (25%) doesn't equal the percent **decrease** from 30 to 24 (20%).

A percent increase may be greater than 100%, but a percent decrease cannot be.

Example:

Suppose a house's price in 2018 was 300% of its price in 2003, which was above 0. By what percent did the price increase?

Solution: If n is the price in 2003, the percent increase is $\left|\frac{(3n-n)}{n}\right| = \left|\frac{2n}{n}\right| = 2, \frac{3n-n}{n} = \frac{2n}{n} = 2,$ or 200%.

B. A price discounted by n percent is $(100 - n)$ percent of the original price.

Example:

A customer paid $24 for a dress. If the customer got a 25% discount off the original price of the dress, what was the original price before the discount?

Solution: The discounted price is 100% – 25% = 75% of the original price. So, if p is the original price, $0.75p = \$24$ is the discounted price. Thus, $p = (\$24/0.75) = \$32$, the original price before the discount.

Two discounts can be combined to make a larger discount.

Example:

A price is discounted 20%. Then this reduced price is discounted another 30%. These two discounts together make an overall discount of what percent?

Solution: If p is the original price, then $0.8p$ is the price after the first discount. The price after the second discount is $(0.7)(0.8)p = 0.56p$. The overall discount is 100% – 56% = 44%.

C. ***Profit*** equals revenues minus expenses, or selling price minus total costs.

Example:

A certain appliance costs a merchant a total of $30 to acquire and sell. At what price should the merchant sell the appliance to make a profit of 50% of the appliance's total cost to the merchant?

Solution: The merchant should sell the appliance for a price $\$s$ such that $s - 30 = (0.5)(30)$. So, $\$s = \$30 + \$15 = \$45$.

D. ***Simple annual interest*** on a loan or investment is based only on the original loan or investment amount (the ***principal***). It equals (principal) × (interest rate) × (time).

Example:

If $8,000 is invested at 6% simple annual interest, how much interest is earned in 3 months?

Solution: Since the annual interest rate is 6%, the interest for 1 year is $(0.06)(\$8{,}000) = \$480$.

A year has 12 months, so the interest earned in 3 months is $\left(\frac{3}{12}\right)(\$480) = \$120$.

E. ***Compound interest*** is based on the principal plus any interest already earned.

Compound interest over n periods = (principal) × (1 + interest per period)^n – principal.

Example:

If \$10,000 is invested at 10% annual interest, compounded every 6 months, what is the investment's value after 1 year?

Solution: Since the interest is compounded every 6 months, or twice a year, the interest rate for each 6-month period is 5%, half the 10% annual rate. So, the investment's value after the first 6 months is 10,000 + (10,000)(0.05) = \$10,500.

For the second 6 months, the interest is based on the \$10,500 balance after the first 6 months. So, the investment's value after 1 year is 10,500 + (10,500)(0.05) = \$11,025.

The investment's value after 1 year can also be written as $10{,}000 \times \left(1 + \frac{0.10}{2}\right)^2$ dollars.

F. To solve some word problems with percents and fractions, you can organize the information in a table.

Example:

In a production lot, 40% of the toys are red, and the rest are green. Half of the toys are small, and half are large. If 10% of the toys are red and small, and 40 toys are green and large, how many of the toys are red and large?

Solution: First make a table to organize the information:

	Red	Green	Total
Small	10%		50%
Large			50%
Total	40%	60%	100%

Then fill in the missing percents so that the "Red" and "Green" percents in each row add up to that row's total, and the "Small" and "Large" percents in each column add up to that column's total:

	Red	Green	Total
Small	10%	40%	50%
Large	30%	20%	50%
Total	40%	60%	100%

The number of large green toys, 40, is 20% of the total number of toys (n), so $0.20n = 40$. Thus, the total number of toys $n = 200$. So, 30% of the 200 toys are red and large. Since (0.3)(200) = 60, we find that 60 of the toys are red and large.

6. Rate, Work, and Mixture Problems

A. The distance an object travels is its average speed multiplied by the time it takes to travel that distance. That is, ***distance = rate × time.***

Example:

How many kilometers did a car travel in 4 hours at an average speed of 70 kilometers per hour?

Solution: Since distance = rate × time, multiply 70 kilometers/hour × 4 hours to find that the car went 280 kilometers.

B. To find an object's average travel speed, divide the total travel distance by the total travel time.

Example:

On a 600-kilometer trip, a car went half the distance at an average speed of 60 kilometers per hour (kph), and the other half at an average speed of 100 kph. The car didn't stop between the two halves of the trip. What was the car's average speed over the whole trip?

Solution: First find the total travel time. For the first 300 kilometers, the car went at 60 kph, taking $\frac{300 \text{ kilometers}}{60 \text{ kph}} = 5$ hours. For the second 300 kilometers, the car went at 100 kph, taking $\frac{300 \text{ kilometers}}{100 \text{ kph}} = 3$ hours. So, the total travel time was 5 + 3 = 8 hours. The car's average speed was $\frac{600 \text{ kilometers}}{8 \text{ hours}} = 75$ kph. Notice the average speed was not $\frac{(60 + 100) \text{ kilometers}}{2 \text{ hours}} = 80$ kph.

C. A ***work problem*** usually says how fast certain individuals work alone, then asks you to find how fast they work together, or vice versa.

The basic formula for work problems is $\frac{1}{r} + \frac{1}{s} = \frac{1}{h}$, where r is how long an amount of work takes a certain individual, s is how long that much work takes a different individual, and h is how long that much work takes both individuals working at the same time.

Example:

Suppose one machine takes 4 hours to make 1,000 bolts, and a second machine takes 5 hours to make 1,000 bolts. How many hours do both machines working at the same time take to make 1,000 bolts?

Solution:

$$\frac{1}{4} + \frac{1}{5} = \frac{1}{h}$$

$$\frac{5}{20} + \frac{4}{20} = \frac{1}{h}$$

$$\frac{9}{20} = \frac{1}{h}$$

$$9h = 20$$

$$h = \frac{20}{9} = 2\frac{2}{9}$$

Working together, the two machines can make 1,000 bolts in $2\frac{2}{9}$ hours.

If a work problem says how long it takes two individuals to do an amount of work together, and how long it takes one of them to do that much work alone, you can use the same formula to find how long it takes the other individual to do that much work alone.

Example:

Suppose Art and Rita both working at the same time take 4 hours to do an amount of work, and Art alone takes 6 hours to do that much work. Then how many hours does Rita alone take to do that much work?

Solution:

$$\frac{1}{6} + \frac{1}{R} = \frac{1}{4}$$

$$\frac{1}{R} = \frac{1}{4} - \frac{1}{6} = \frac{1}{12}$$

$$R = 12$$

Rita alone takes 12 hours to do that much work.

D. In ***mixture problems***, substances with different properties are mixed, and you must find the mixture's properties.

Example:

If 6 kilograms of nuts that cost \$1.20 per kilogram are mixed with 2 kilograms of nuts that cost \$1.60 per kilogram, how much does the mixture cost per kilogram?

Solution: The 8 kilograms of nuts cost a total of 6(\$1.20) + 2(\$1.60) = \$10.40. So, the cost per kilogram of the mixture is $\frac{\$10.40}{8} = \$1.30$.

Some mixture problems use percents.

Example:

How many liters of a solution that is 15% salt must be added to 5 liters of a solution that is 8% salt to make a solution that is 10% salt?

Solution: Let n be the needed number of liters of the 15% solution. The amount of salt in n liters of 15% solution is $0.15n$. The amount of salt in the 5 liters of 8% solution is $(0.08)(5)$. These amounts add up to the amount of salt in the 10% mixture, which is $0.10(n + 5)$. So,

$$0.15n + 0.08(5) = 0.10(n + 5)$$

$$15n + 40 = 10n + 50$$

$$5n = 10$$

$$n = 2 \text{ liters}$$

So, 2 liters of the 15% salt solution must be added to the 8% solution to make the 10% solution.

3.4 Statistics, Sets, Counting, Probability, Estimation, and Series

1. Statistics

A. A common statistical measure is the ***average*** or ***(arithmetic) mean***, a type of center for the numerical values in a data set. The average or mean of n values is the sum of the n values divided by n. If a number appears more than once in the data set, each instance of that number is a separate value and is added separately to find the sum. To learn more about values in data sets, see Chapter 5, "Data Insights Review."

Example:

The average of the 5 values 6, 4, 7, 10, and 4 is $\frac{(6 + 4 + 7 + 10 + 4)}{5} = \frac{31}{5} = 6.2$. Notice that 4 appears twice in the list of 5 values, so it is added twice when finding the sum.

B. The ***median*** is another type of center for ordered values in a data set. As above, if a number appears more than once in the data set, each instance of that number is a separate value. To find the median, arrange the values from least to greatest. If the number of entries in the list is odd, the median is the middle entry in the list. But if the number of entries in the list is even, the median is the average of the two middle entries. The median may be less than, equal to, or greater than the mean.

Example:

To find the median of the 5 values 6, 4, 7, 10, and 4, arrange them from least to greatest: 4, 4, 6, 7, 10. The median is 6, the middle entry in this list.

The median of the 6 values 4, 6, 6, 8, 9, and 12 is $\frac{(6 + 8)}{2} = 7$. But the mean of these 6 values is $\frac{(4 + 6 + 6 + 8 + 9 + 12)}{6} = \frac{45}{6} = 7.5$.

Often about half the values in a data set are less than the median, and about half are greater than the median. But not always.

Example:

For the 15 values 3, 5, 7, 7, 7, 7, 7, 7, 8, 9, 9, 9, 9, 10, and 10, the median is 7. Only $\frac{2}{15}$ of the values are less than the median.

C. The ***mode*** of a data set is the value appearing most often in the list.

Example:

The mode of the list of values 1, 3, 6, 4, 3, and 5 is 3, since 3 is the only value appearing more than once in the list.

A list may have more than one mode.

Example:

The list 1, 2, 3, 3, 3, 5, 7, 10, 10, 10, and 20 has two modes, 3 and 10.

D. The ***dispersion*** of numerical data is how spread out the data is. The simplest measure of dispersion is the ***range,*** which is the greatest value in the data minus the least value.

Example:

The range of the values 11, 10, 5, 13, and 21 is 21 – 5 = 16. Notice the range depends on only 2 of the values.

E. Another common measure of dispersion is the ***standard deviation***. Generally, the farther the values are from the mean, the greater the standard deviation. To find the standard deviation of n values:

(1) Find their mean

(2) Find the differences between the mean and each of the n values

(3) Square each difference

(4) Find the average of the squared differences, and

(5) Take the nonnegative square root of this average

Examples:

Let's use the table below to find the standard deviation of the 5 values 0, 7, 8, 10, and 10, which have the mean 7.

x	$x - 7$	$(x - 7)^2$
0	–7	49
7	0	0
8	1	1
10	3	9
10	3	9
	Total	68

The standard deviation is $\sqrt{\frac{68}{5}} \approx 3.7$

The standard deviation depends on every value in the data set, but more on those farther from the mean. This is why the standard deviation is smaller for a data set grouped closer around its mean.

As a second example, consider the values 6, 6, 6.5, 7.5, and 9, which also have the mean 7. These values are grouped closer around the mean 7 than are those in the first example. That makes the standard deviation in this second example only about 1.1, far below the standard deviation of 3.7 in the first example.

F. How many times a value occurs in a data set is its ***frequency*** in the set. When different values have different frequencies, a ***frequency distribution*** can help show how the values are distributed.

Example:

Consider this data set of 20 numbers:

−4	0	0	−3	−2	−1	−1	0	−1	−4
−1	−5	0	−2	0	−5	−2	0	0	−1

We can show its frequency distribution in a table showing each value x and x's frequency f:

Value x	Frequency f
−5	2
−4	2
−3	1
−2	3
−1	5
0	7
Total	20

This frequency distribution table makes finding statistical measures easier:

Mean: $= \dfrac{(-5)(2) + (-4)(2) + (-3)(1) + (-2)(3) + (-1)(5) + (0)(7)}{20} = -1.6$

Median: −1 (the average of the 10th and 11th numbers)

Mode: 0 (the number that occurs most often)

Range: $0 - (-5) = 5$

Standard deviation: $\sqrt{\dfrac{(-5+1.6)^2(2) + (-4+1.6)^2(2) + \ldots + (0+1.6)^2(7)}{20}} \approx 1.7$

2. Sets

A. In math, a ***set*** is a collection of numbers or other things. The things in the set are its ***elements***. A list of a set's elements between braces stands for the set. The list's order doesn't matter.

Example:

$\{-5, 0, 1\}$ is the same set as $\{0, 1, -5\}$. That is, $\{-5, 0, 1\} = \{0, 1, -5\}$.

B. The number of elements in a finite set S is written as $|S|$.

> *Example:*
>
> $S = \{-5, 0, 1\}$ is a set with $|S| = 3$.

C. If all the elements in a set S are also in a set T, then S is a ***subset*** of T. This is written as $S \subseteq T$ or $T \supseteq S$.

> *Example:*
>
> $\{-5, 0, 1\}$ is a subset of $\{-5, 0, 1, 4, 10\}$. That is, $\{-5, 0, 1\} \subseteq \{-5, 0, 1, 4, 10\}$.

D. The ***union*** of two sets A and B is the set of all elements that are each in A or in B or both. The union is written as $A \cup B$.

> *Example:*
>
> $\{3, 4\} \cup \{4, 5, 6\} = \{3, 4, 5, 6\}$

E. The ***intersection*** of two sets A and B is the set of all elements that are each in **both** A and B. The intersection is written as $A \cap B$.

> *Example:*
>
> $\{3, 4\} \cap \{4, 5, 6\} = \{4\}$

F. Two sets sharing no elements are ***disjoint*** or ***mutually exclusive***.

> *Example:*
>
> $\{-5, 0, 1\}$ and $\{4, 10\}$ are disjoint.

G. The ***empty set*** is the set with no elements. It's written as $\emptyset$ or $\{\}$.

H. A ***Venn diagram*** shows the unions and intersections of two or more sets. Suppose sets S and T aren't disjoint, and neither is a subset of the other. The Venn diagram below shows their intersection $S \cap T$ as a shaded area.

A Venn Diagram of Two Intersecting Sets

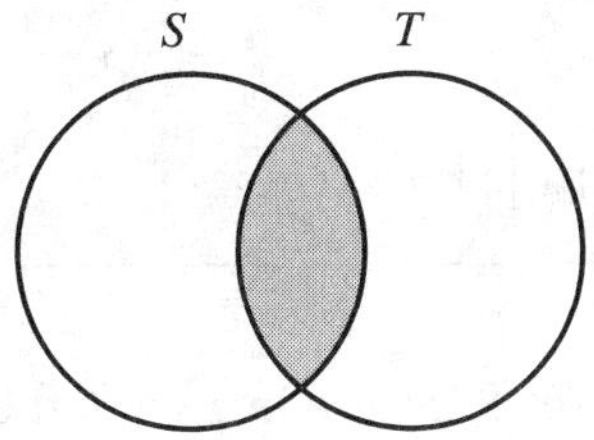

A Venn diagram of sets S and T, with their intersection $S \cap T$ shaded.

I. The number of elements in the union of two finite sets S and T is the number of elements in S, plus the number of elements in T, minus the number of elements in the intersection of S and T. That is, $|S \cup T| = |S| + |T| - |S \cap T|$. This is the ***general addition rule for two sets***.

Example:

$$|\{3, 4\} \cup \{4, 5, 6\}| = |\{3, 4\}| + |\{4, 5, 6\}| - |\{3, 4\} \cap \{4, 5, 6\}| =$$

$$|\{3, 4\}| + |\{4, 5, 6\}| - 1\{4\}| = 2 + 3 - 1 = 4.$$

If S and T are disjoint, then $|S \cup T| = |S| + |T|$, since $|S \cap T| = 0$.

J. You can often solve word problems involving sets by using Venn diagrams and the general addition rule.

Example:

Each of 25 students is taking history, mathematics, or both. If 20 of them are taking history and 18 of them are taking mathematics, how many of them are taking both history and mathematics?

Solution: Separate the 25 students into three disjoint sets: the students taking history only, those taking mathematics only, and those taking both history and mathematics. This gives us the Venn diagram below, where n is the number of students taking both courses, $20 - n$ is the number taking history only, and $18 - n$ is the number taking mathematics only.

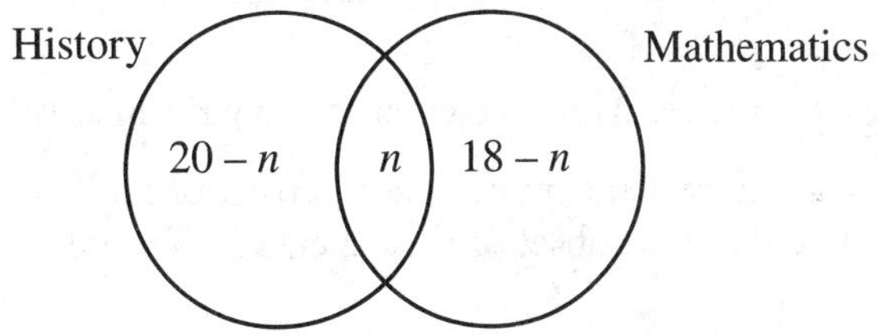

Since there are 25 students total, $(20 - n) + n + (18 - n) = 25$, so $n = 13$. So, 13 students are taking both history and mathematics. Notice that $20 + 18 - 13 = 25$ uses the general addition rule for two sets.

3. Counting Methods

A. To count elements in sets without listing them, you can sometimes use this ***multiplication principle***:

If an object will be chosen from a set of m different objects, and another object will be chosen from a disjoint set of n different objects, then mn different choices are possible.

> *Example:*
>
> Suppose a meal at a restaurant must include exactly 1 entree and 1 dessert. The entree can be any 1 of 5 options, and the dessert can be any 1 of 3 options. Then $5 \times 3 = 15$ different meals are available.

B. Here's a more general version of the multiplication principle: The number of possible choices of 1 object apiece out of any number of sets is the product of the numbers of objects in those sets. For example, when choosing 1 object apiece out of 3 sets with x, y, and z elements, respectively, xyz different choices are possible. The general multiplication principle also means that when choosing 1 object apiece out of n sets of exactly m objects apiece, m^n different choices are possible.

> *Example:*
>
> Each time a coin is flipped, the 2 possible results are heads and tails. In a sequence of 8 consecutive coin flips, think of each flip as a set of those 2 possible results. The 8 flips give us a sequence of 8 of these 2-element sets. So, the sequence of 8 flips has 2^8 possible results.

C. A concept often used with the multiplication principle is the ***factorial***. For any integer $n > 1$, n factorial is written as $n!$ and is the product of all the integers from 1 through n. Also, by definition, $0! = 1! = 1$.

> *Examples:*
>
> $2! = 2 \times 1 = 2$
>
> $3! = 3 \times 2 \times 1 = 6$
>
> $4! = 4 \times 3 \times 2 \times 1 = 24$, etc.

A useful equation with factorials is $n! = (n - 1)!(n)$.

D. Any sequential ordering of a set's elements is a ***permutation*** of the set. A permutation is a way to choose elements one by one in a certain order.

The factorial is useful for finding how many permutations a set has. If a set of n objects is being ordered from 1st to nth, there are n choices for the 1st object, $n - 1$ choices left for the 2nd object, $n - 2$ choices left for the 3rd object, and so on, until only 1 choice is left for the nth object. So, by the multiplication principle, a set of n objects has $n(n-1)(n-2)\ldots(3)(2)(1) = n!$ permutations.

> *Example:*
>
> The set of letters A, B, and C has $3! = 6$ permutations: ABC, ACB, BAC, BCA, CAB, and CBA.

E. When $0 \le k \le n$, each possible choice of k objects out of n objects is a ***combination*** of n objects taken k at a time. The number of these combinations is written as $\binom{n}{k}$. This is also the number of k-element subsets of a set with n elements, since the combinations simply are these subsets. It can be calculated as $\binom{n}{k} = \frac{n!}{k!(n-k)!}$. Note that $\binom{n}{k} = \binom{n}{n-k}$.

> *Example:*
>
> The 2-element subsets of $S = \{A, B, C, D, E\}$ are the combinations of the 5 letters in S taken 2 at a time. There are $\binom{5}{2} = \frac{5!}{2!3!} = \frac{120}{(2)(6)} = 10$ of these subsets: {A, B}, {A, C}, {A, D}, {A, E}, {B, C}, {B, D}, {B, E}, {C, D}, {C, E}, and {D, E}.
>
> For each of its 2-element subsets, a 5-element set also has exactly one 3-element subset containing the elements not in that 2-element subset. For example, in S the 3-element subset {C, D, E} contains the elements not in the 2-element subset {A, B}, the 3-element subset {B, D, E} contains the elements not in the 2-element subset {A, C}, and so on. This shows that a 5-element set like S has exactly as many 2-element subsets as 3-element subsets, so $\binom{5}{2} = 10 = \binom{5}{3}$.

4. Probability

A. Sets and counting methods are also important to ***discrete probability***. Discrete probability involves ***experiments*** with finitely many possible ***outcomes***. An ***event*** is a set of an experiment's possible outcomes.

> *Example:*
>
> Rolling a 6-sided die with faces numbered 1 to 6 is an experiment with 6 possible outcomes. Let's call these outcomes 1, 2, 3, 4, 5, and 6, each number being the one facing up after the roll. Notice that no two outcomes can occur together.
>
> One event in this experiment is that the outcome is 4. This event is written as {4}.
>
> Another event in the experiment is that the outcome is an odd number. This event has the three outcomes 1, 3, and 5. It is written as {1, 3, 5}.

B. The probability of an event E is written as $P(E)$ and is a number between 0 and 1, inclusive. If E is the empty set of no possible outcomes, then E is ***impossible***, and $P(E) = 0$. If E is the set of all possible outcomes of the experiment, then E is ***certain***, and $P(E) = 1$. Otherwise, E is possible but not certain, and $0 < P(E) < 1$. If F is a subset of E, then $P(F) \le P(E)$.

C. If the probabilities of two or more outcomes are equal, those outcomes are ***equally likely***. For an experiment with outcomes that are all equally likely, the probability of an event E is

$$P(E) = \frac{\text{the number of outcomes in } E}{\text{the total number of possible outcomes}}.$$

> *Example:*
>
> In the earlier example of a 6-sided die rolled once, suppose all 6 outcomes are equally likely. Then each outcome's probability is $\frac{1}{6}$. The probability that the outcome is an odd number is
>
> $P(\{1, 3, 5\}) = \frac{|\{1, 3, 5\}|}{6} = \frac{3}{6} = \frac{1}{2}$.

D. Given two events E and F, these further events are defined:

(i) "not E" is the set of outcomes not in E;

(ii) "E or F" is the set of outcomes in E or F or both, that is, $E \cup F$;

(iii) "E and F" is the set of outcomes in both E and F, that is, $E \cap F$.

The probability that E doesn't occur is $P(\text{not } E) = 1 - P(E)$.

The probability that "E or F" occurs is $P(E \text{ or } F) = P(E) + P(F) - P(E \text{ and } F)$. This is based on the general addition rule for two sets, given above in Section 3.4.2.G.

Example:

In the example above of a 6-sided die rolled once, let E be the event $\{1, 3, 5\}$ that the outcome is an odd number. Let F be the event $\{2, 3, 5\}$ that the outcome is a prime number. Then $P(E \text{ and } F) = P(E \cap F) = P(\{3, 5\}) = \frac{|\{3, 5\}|}{6} = \frac{2}{6} = \frac{1}{3}$. So, $P(E \text{ or } F) = P(E) + P(F) - P(E \text{ and } F) = \frac{3}{6} + \frac{3}{6} - \frac{2}{6} = \frac{4}{6} = \frac{2}{3}$.

We get the same result by noticing that the event "E or F" is $E \cup F = \{1, 2, 3, 5\}$, so $P(E \text{ or } F) = \frac{|\{1, 2, 3, 5\}|}{6} = \frac{4}{6} = \frac{2}{3}$.

Events E and F are ***mutually exclusive*** if no outcomes are in $E \cap F$. Then the event "E and F" is impossible: $P(E \text{ and } F) = 0$. The special addition rule for the probability of two mutually exclusive events is $P(E \text{ or } F) = P(E) + P(F)$.

E. Two events A and B are ***independent*** if neither changes the other's probability. The multiplication rule for independent events E and F is $P(E \text{ and } F) = P(E)P(F)$.

Example:

In the example above of the 6-sided die rolled once, let A be the event $\{2, 4, 6\}$ and B be the event $\{5, 6\}$. Then A's probability is $P(A) = \frac{|A|}{6} = \frac{3}{6} = \frac{1}{2}$. The probability of A occurring **if B occurs** is $\frac{|A \cap B|}{|B|} = \frac{|\{6\}|}{|\{5, 6\}|} = \frac{1}{2}$, the same as $P(A)$.

Likewise, B's probability is $P(B) = \frac{|B|}{6} = \frac{2}{6} = \frac{1}{3}$. The probability of B occurring **if A occurs** is $\frac{|B \cap A|}{|A|} = \frac{\{6\}}{|\{2, 4, 6\}|} = \frac{1}{3}$, the same as $P(B)$.

So, neither event changes the other's probability. Thus, A and B are independent. Therefore, by the multiplication rule for independent events, $P(A \text{ and } B) = P(A)P(B) = \left(\frac{1}{2}\right)\left(\frac{1}{3}\right) = \frac{1}{6}$.

Notice the event "A and B" is $A \cap B = \{6\}$, so $P(A \text{ and } B) = P(\{6\}) = \frac{1}{6}$.

The general addition rule and the multiplication rule discussed above imply that if E and F are independent, $P(E \text{ or } F) = P(E) + P(F) - P(E)P(F)$.

F. An event A is ***dependent*** on a nonempty event B if B changes the probability of A.

The probability of A occurring if B occurs is written as $P(A|B)$. So, the statement that A is dependent on B can be written as $P(A|B) \neq P(A)$.

A general multiplication rule for any dependent or independent events A and B is $P(A \text{ and } B) = P(A|B)P(B)$.

Example:

In the example of the 6-sided die rolled once, let A be the event $\{4, 6\}$ and B be the event $\{4, 5, 6\}$. Then the probability of A is $P(A) = \frac{|A|}{6} = \frac{2}{6} = \frac{1}{3}$. But the probability that A occurs **if B occurs** is $P(A|B) = \frac{|A \cap B|}{|B|} = \frac{|\{4, 6\}|}{|\{4, 5, 6\}|} = \frac{2}{3}$. Thus, $P(A|B) \neq P(A)$, so A is dependent on B.

Likewise, the probability that B occurs is $P(B) = \frac{|B|}{6} = \frac{3}{6} = \frac{1}{2}$. But the probability that B occurs **if A occurs** is $P(B|A) = \frac{|B \cap A|}{|A|} = \frac{|\{4, 6\}|}{|\{4, 6\}|} = 1$. Thus, $P(B|A) \neq P(B)$, so B is dependent on A.

In this example, by the general multiplication rule for events,

$P(A \text{ and } B) = P(A|B)P(B) = \left(\frac{2}{3}\right)\left(\frac{1}{2}\right) = \frac{1}{3}$. Likewise, $P(A \text{ and } B) = P(B|A)P(A) = (1)\left(\frac{1}{3}\right) = \frac{1}{3}$.

Notice the event "A and B" is $A \cap B = \{4, 6\} = A$, so $P(A \text{ and } B) = P(\{4, 6\}) = \frac{1}{3} = P(A)$.

G. The rules above can be combined for more complex probability calculations.

Example:

In an experiment with events A, B, and C, suppose $P(A) = 0.23$, $P(B) = 0.40$, and $P(C) = 0.85$. Also suppose events A and B are mutually exclusive, and events B and C are independent. Since A and B are mutually exclusive, $P(A \text{ or } B) = P(A) + P(B) = 0.23 + 0.40 = 0.63$.

Since B and C are independent, $P(B \text{ or } C) = P(B) + P(C) - P(B)P(C) = 0.40 + 0.85 - (0.40)(0.85) = 0.91$.

$P(A \text{ or } C)$ and $P(A \text{ and } C)$ can't be found from the information given. But we can find that $P(A) + P(C) = 1.08 > 1$. So, $P(A) + P(C)$ can't equal $P(A \text{ or } C)$, which like any probability cannot be greater than 1. This means that A and C can't be mutually exclusive, and that $P(A \text{ and } C) \geq 0.08$.

Since $A \cap B$ is a subset of A, we can also find that $P(A \text{ and } C) \leq P(A) = 0.23$.

And C is a subset of $A \cup C$, so $P(A \text{ or } C) \geq P(C) = 0.85$.

Thus, we've found that $0.85 \leq P(A \text{ or } C) \leq 1$ and that $0.08 \leq P(A \text{ and } C) < 0.23$.

5. Estimation

A. Calculating exact answers to complex math questions is often too hard or slow. Estimating the answers by simplifying the questions may be easier and faster.

One way to estimate is to ***round*** the numbers in the original question: replace each number with a nearby number that has fewer digits.

For any integer n and real number m, you can ***round m down*** to a multiple of 10^n by deleting all of m's digits to the right of the digit that stands for multiples of 10^n.

To ***round m up*** to a multiple of 10^n, first add 10^n to m, then round the result down.

To ***round m to the nearest*** 10^n, first find the digit in m that stands for a multiple of 10^{n-1}. If this digit is 5 or higher, round m up to a multiple of 10^n. Otherwise, round m down to a multiple of 10^n.

Examples:

(i) To round 7651.4 to the nearest hundred (multiple of 10^2), first notice the digit standing for tens (multiples of 10^1) is 5.

Since this digit is 5 or higher, round up:

First add 100 to the original number: 7651.4 + 100 = 7751.4.

Then drop all the digits to the right of the one standing for multiples of 100 to get 7700.

Notice that 7700 is closer to 7651.4 than 7600 is, so 7700 is the nearest 100.

(ii) To round 0.43248 to the nearest thousandth (multiple of 10^{-3}), first notice the digit standing for ten-thousandths (multiples of 10^{-4}) is 4. Since 4 < 5, round down: just drop all the digits to the right of the digit standing for thousandths to get 0.432.

B. Rounding can simplify complex calculations and give rough answers. If you keep more digits of the original numbers, the answers are usually more exact, but the calculations take longer.

Example:

You can estimate the value of $\frac{(298.534+58.296)}{1.4822+0.937+0.014679}$ by rounding the numbers in the dividend to the nearest 10 and the numbers in the divisor to the nearest 0.1:

$$\frac{(298.534+58.296)}{1.4822+0.937+0.014679} \approx \frac{300+60}{1.5+0.9+0} = \frac{360}{2.4} = 150$$

C. Sometimes it's easier to estimate by rounding to a multiple of a number other than 10, like the nearest square or cube of an integer.

Examples:

(i) You can estimate the value of $\frac{2447.13}{11.9}$ by noting first that both the dividend and the divisor are near multiples of 12: 2448 and 12. So, $\frac{2447.13}{11.9} \approx \frac{2448}{12} = 204$.

(ii) You can estimate the value of $\sqrt{\frac{8.96}{24.82 \times 4.057}}$ by noting first that each decimal number in the expression is near the square of an integer: $8.96 \approx 9 = 3^2$, $24.82 \approx 25 = 5^2$, and $4.057 \approx 4 = 2^2$. So, $\sqrt{\frac{8.96}{24.82 \times 4.057}} \approx \sqrt{\frac{3^2}{5^2 \times 2^2}} = \sqrt{\frac{3^2}{10^2}} = \frac{3}{10}$.

D. Sometimes finding a ***range*** of possible values for an expression is more useful than finding a single estimated value. The range's ***upper bound*** is the smallest number found to be greater than (or no less than) the expression's value. The range's ***lower bound*** is the largest number found to be less than (or no greater than) the expression's value.

Example:

In the equation $x = \frac{2.32^2 - 2.536}{2.68^2 + 2.79}$, each decimal is greater than 2 and less than 3. So, $\frac{2^2 - 3}{3^2 + 3} < x < \frac{3^2 - 2}{2^2 + 2}$. Simplifying these fractions, we find that x is in the range $\frac{1}{12} < x < \frac{7}{6}$. The range's lower bound is $\frac{1}{12}$, and the upper bound is $\frac{7}{6}$.

6. Sequences and Series

A. A ***sequence*** is an ordered list of elements, starting with a first element. Any sequence may be defined as the range of a function $a(n)$ with a domain that is the positive integers. Its value a_i for a specific positive integer i is its ***i*th term**.

An ***arithmetic sequence*** has the form $a_n = b + cn$, where b and c are constants. The first term of an arithmetic sequence is $a_1 = b + c$. For each term a_i, the next term $a_{i+1} = a_i + c$.

A ***geometric sequence*** has the form $a_n = bc^n$, where b and c are constants. The first term of an arithmetic sequence is $a_1 = bc$. For each term a_i, the next term $a_{i+1} = a_i c$.

Sometimes a sequence is defined only by giving the value of the first term or terms, then giving an equation for finding each subsequent term's value based on the value of one or more earlier terms.

Examples:

(i) The function $a(n) = n^2 + \left(\frac{n}{5}\right)$ with a domain that is the positive integers is an infinite sequence $a_1, a_2, a_3, \ldots$. Its third term is its value at $n = 3$, which is $a_3 = 3^2 + \frac{3}{5} = 9.6$.

(ii) $a(n) = n^2 + \left(\frac{n}{5}\right) b_n = (-1)^n(n!)$ The function $a(n) = 2 + 3n$ with a domain that is the positive integers is an arithmetic sequence. Its first term $a_1 = 5$. For any positive integer i, $a_{i+1} = ai + 3$. Thus, $a_2 = a_1 + 3 = 8$.

(iii) The function $b(n) = 2(3^n)$ with a domain that is the positive integers is a geometric sequence. Its first term $b_1 = 6$. For any positive integer i, $b_{i+1} = 3b_i$. Thus, $b_2 = 3 \times 6 = 18$.

(iv) We can define a sequence $c(n)$ just by stating that its first term $c_1 = 1$, its second term $c_2 = 1$, and each subsequent term $c_{n+2} = c_n + c_{n+1}$. Thus, $c_3 = c_1 + c_2 = 1 + 1 = 2$.

B. A ***series*** is the sum of a sequence's terms.

For an infinite sequence $a(n)$, the ***infinite series*** $\sum_{n=1}^{\infty} a(n)$ adds up the sequence's infinitely many terms, $a_1 + a_2 + a_3 + \cdots$. Some infinite series add up to finite sums, but others don't.

Example:

The infinite series based on the function $a(n) = n^2 + \left(\frac{n}{5}\right)$ is $\sum_{i=1}^{\infty} n^2 + \left(\frac{n}{5}\right)$. It adds up the infinitely many terms $\left(1^2 + \frac{1}{5}\right) + \left(2^2 + \frac{2}{5}\right) + \left(3^2 + \frac{3}{5}\right) + \cdots$. This series has no finite sum.

The partial sum of the first three terms $a(n) = n^2 + \left(\frac{n}{5}\right)$ is

$$\sum_{i=1}^{3} a_i = \left(1^2 + \frac{1}{5}\right) + \left(2^2 + \frac{2}{5}\right) + \left(3^2 + \frac{3}{5}\right) = 1.2 + 4.4 + 9.6 = 15.2.$$

3.5 Reference Sheets

Arithmetic and Decimals

ABSOLUTE VALUE:

$|x|$ is x if $x \geq 0$ and $-x$ if $x < 0$.

For any x and y, $|x + y| < |x| + |y|$, and $|xy| = |x||y|$.

$\sqrt{x^2} = |x|$.

EVEN AND ODD NUMBERS:

Even × Even = Even	Even × Odd = Even
Odd × Odd = Odd	Even + Even = Even
Even + Odd = Odd	Odd + Odd = Even

ADDITION AND SUBTRACTION:

$x + 0 = x = x - 0$

$x - x = 0$

$x + y = y + x$

$x - y = -(y - x) = -y + x$

$(x + y) + z = x + (y + z)$

If x and y are both positive, then $x + y$ is positive.

If x and y are both negative, then $x + y$ is negative.

DECIMALS WITH MANY FINITE DIGITS:

Add or subtract decimals by lining up their decimal points:

17.6512	653.2700
+ 653.2700	−17.6512
670.9212	635.6188

To multiply decimal A by decimal B:

First, ignore the decimal points and multiply A and B as if they were integers.

Next, if decimal A has n digits to the right of its decimal point and decimal B has m digits to the right of its decimal point, place the decimal point in $A \times B$ so it has $m + n$ digits to its right.

To divide decimal A by decimal B, first move the decimal points of A and B equally many digits to the right until B is an integer. Then divide as you would integers.

QUOTIENTS AND REMAINDERS:

The quotient q and the remainder r of dividing positive integer x by positive integer y are unique positive integers such that

$y = xq + r$ and $0 < r < x$.

The remainder r is 0 if and only if y is divisible by x. Then x is a factor of y.

MULTIPLICATION AND DIVISION:

$x \times 1 = x = \frac{x}{1}$

$x \times 0 = 0$

If $x \neq 0$, then $\frac{x}{x} = 1$.

$\frac{x}{0}$ is undefined.

$xy = yx$

If $x \neq 0$ and $y \neq 0$, then $\frac{x}{y} = \frac{1}{\left(\frac{y}{x}\right)}$.

$(xy)z = x(yz)$

$xy + xz = x(y + z)$

If $y \neq 0$, then $\left(\frac{x}{y}\right) + \left(\frac{z}{y}\right) = \frac{(x + z)}{y}$.

If x and y are both positive, then xy is positive.

If x and y are both negative, then xy is positive.

If x is positive and y is negative, then xy is negative.

If $xy = 0$, then $x = 0$ or $y = 0$, or both.

SCIENTIFIC NOTATION:

To convert a number in scientific notation $A \times 10^n$ into regular decimal notation, move A's decimal point n places to the right if n is positive, or $|n|$ places to the left if n is negative.

To convert a decimal to scientific notation, move the decimal point n spaces so that exactly one nonzero digit is to its left. Multiply the result by 10^n if you moved the decimal point to the left or by 10^{-n} if you moved it to the right.

ARITHMETIC SHORTCUTS:

For any two nonnegative integers x and y, the final digit of $x + y$ is the final digit of the sum of x's final digit and y's final digit. And for any two integers x and y, the final digit of xy is the final digit of the product of x's final digit and y's final digit.

An integer is divisible by	if and only if
2	its final digit is 0, 2, 4, 6, or 8.
3	the sum of its digits is divisible by 3.
4	its final two digits make a number divisible by 4.
5	its final digit is 5 or 0.
9	the sum of its digits is divisible by 9.
10	its final digit is 0.

Exponents

SQUARES, CUBES, AND SQUARE ROOTS:

Every positive number has two real square roots, one positive and the other negative. The table below shows the positive square roots rounded to the nearest hundredth.

n	n^2	n^3	$\sqrt{n}$
1	1	1	1
2	4	8	1.41
3	9	27	1.73
4	16	64	2
5	25	125	2.24
6	36	216	2.45
7	49	343	2.65
8	64	512	2.83
9	81	729	3
10	100	1,000	3.16

EXPONENTIATION:

Formula	Example
$x^1 = x$	$2^1 = 2$
If $x \neq 0$, then $x^0 = 1$.	$2^0 = 1$
If $x \neq 0$, then $x^{-1} = \frac{1}{x}$.	$2^{-1} = \frac{1}{2}$
If $x > 1$ and $y > 1$, then $x^y > x$.	$2^3 = 8 > 2$
If $0 < x < 1$ and $y > 1$, then $x^y < x$.	$0.2^3 = 0.008 < 0.2$
$(x^y)^z = x^{yz} = (x^z)^y$	$(2^3)^4 = 2^{12} = (2^4)^3$
$x^{y+z} = x^y x^z$	$2^7 = 2^3 2^4$
If $x \neq 0$, then $x^{y-z} = \frac{x^y}{x^z}$.	$2^{5-3} = \frac{2^5}{2^3}$
$(xz)^y = x^y z^y$	$6^4 = 2^4 3^4$
If $z \neq 0$, then $\left(\frac{x}{z}\right)^y = \frac{x^y}{z^y}$.	$\left(\frac{3}{4}\right)^2 = \frac{3^2}{4^2} = \frac{9}{16}$
If $z \neq 0$, then $x^{\frac{y}{z}} = (x^y)^{\frac{1}{z}} = (x^{\frac{1}{z}})^y$.	$4^{\frac{2}{3}} = (4^2)^{\frac{1}{3}} = (4^{\frac{1}{3}})^2$

Algebraic Expressions and Linear Equations

TRANSLATING WORDS INTO MATH OPERATIONS:

$x + y$	$x - y$	xy	$\frac{x}{y}$	x^y
x added to y x increased by y x more than y x plus y the sum of x and y the total of x and y	x decreased by y difference of x and y y fewer than x y less than x x minus y x reduced by y y subtracted from x	x multiplied by y the product of x and y x times y	x divided by y x over y the quotient of x and y the ratio of x to y	x to the power of y x to the yth power
		If $y = 2$: double x twice x	If $y = 2$: half of x x halved	If $y = 2$: x squared
		If $y = 3$: triple x		If $y = 3$: x cubed

MANIPULATING ALGEBRAIC EXPRESSIONS:

Technique	**Example**
Factor to combine like terms	$3xy - 9y = 3y(x - 3)$
Divide out common factors	$\frac{(3xy - 9y)}{(x - 3)} = \frac{3y(x - 3)}{(x - 3)} = 3y(1) = 3y$
Multiply two expressions by multiplying each term of one expression by each term of the other	$(3x - 4)(9y + x) = 3x(9y + x) - 4(9y + x)$ $= 3x(9y) + 3x(x) - 4(9y) - 4(x)$ $= 27xy + 3x^2 - 36y - 4x$
Substitute constants for variables	If $x = 3$ and $y = -2$, then $3xy - x^2 + y =$ $3(3)(-2) - (3)^2 + (-2) = -18 - 9 - 2 = -29$.

SOLVING LINEAR EQUATIONS:

Technique	Example
Isolate a variable on one side of an equation by doing the same operations on both sides of the equation.	Solve the equation $\frac{(5x-6)}{3} = 4$ like this: (1) Multiply both sides by 3 to get $5x - 6 = 12$. (2) Add 6 to both sides to get $5x = 18$. (3) Divide both sides by 5 to get $x = \frac{18}{5}$.
To solve two equations with two variables x and y: (1) Express x in terms of y using one of the equations. (2) Substitute that expression for x to make the second equation have only the variable y. (3) Solve the second equation for y. (4) Substitute the solution for y into the first equation to solve for x.	Solve the equations A: $x - y = 2$ and B: $3x + 2y = 11$: (1) From A, $x = 2 + y$. (2) In B, substitute $2 + y$ for x to get $3(2 + y) + 2y = 11$. (3) Solve B for y: $6 + 3y + 2y = 11$ $6 + 5y = 11$ $5y = 5$ $y = 1$ (4) Since $y = 1$, from A we find $x = 2 + 1 = 3$.
Alternative technique: (1) Multiply both sides of one equation or both equations so that the coefficients on y have the same absolute value in both equations. (2) Add or subtract the two equations to remove y and solve for x. (3) Substitute the solution for x into the first equation to find the value of y.	Solve the equations A: $x - y = 2$ and B: $3x + 2y = 11$: (1) Multiply both sides of A by 2 to get $2x - 2y = 4$. (2) Add the equation in (1) to equation B: $2x - 2y + 3x + 2y = 4 + 11$ $5x = 15$ $x = 3$ (3) Since $x = 3$, from A we find $3 - y = 2$, so $y = 1$.

Factoring, Quadratic Equations, and Inequalities

SOLVING EQUATIONS BY FACTORING:

Techniques	Example
(1) Start with a polynomial equation. (2) Add or subtract from both sides until 0 is on one side of the equation. (3) Write the nonzero side as a product of factors. (4) Set each factor to 0 to find simple equations giving the solutions to the original equation.	$x^3 - 2x^2 + x = -5(x-1)^2$ $x^3 - 2x^2 + x + 5(x-1)^2 = 0$ (i) $x(x^2 - 2x + 1) + 5(x-1)^2 = 0$ (ii) $x(x-1)^2 + 5(x-1)^2 = 0$ (iii) $(x+5)(x-1)^2 = 0$ $x + 5 = 0$ or $x - 1 = 0$. So, $x = -5$ or $x = 1$.

FORMULAS FOR FACTORING:

$(a + \frac{1}{a})^2 = a^2 + \frac{1}{a^2} + 2$

$a^2 - b^2 = (a - b)(a + b)$

$a^2 + 2ab + b^2 = (a + b)^2$

$a^2 - 2ab + b^2 = (a - b)^2$

$a^2 + b^2 = (a + b)^2 - 2ab = (a - b)^2 + 2ab$

$(a + b + c)^2 = a^2 + b^2 + c^2 + 2ab + 2ac + 2bc$

$(a + b)^3 = a^3 + 3a^2b + 3ab^2 + b^3$

THE QUADRATIC FORMULA:

For any quadratic equation $ax^2 + bx + c = 0$ with $a \neq 0$, the roots are

$$x = \frac{-b + \sqrt{b^2 - 4ac}}{2a} \text{ and } x = \frac{-b - \sqrt{b^2 - 4ac}}{2a}$$

These roots are two distinct real numbers if $b^2 - 4ac \geq 0$.

If $b^2 - 4ac = 0$, the equation has only one root: $-\frac{b}{2a}$.

If $b^2 - 4ac < 0$, the equation has no real roots.

SOLVING INEQUALITIES:

Explanation	Example
As in solving an equation, the same number can be added to or subtracted from both sides of the inequality, or both sides can be multiplied or divided by a positive number, without changing the order of the inequality. But multiplying or dividing an inequality by a negative number reverses the order of the inequality. Thus, $6 > 2$, but $(-1)(6) < (-1)(2)$.	To solve the inequality $\frac{(5x-1)}{-2} < 3$ for x, isolate x: (1) $5x - 1 > -6$ (multiplying both sides by -2, reversing the order of the inequality) (2) $5x > -5$ (add 1 to both sides) (3) $x > -1$ (divide both sides by 5)

LINES IN THE COORDINATE PLANE:

An equation $y = mx + b$ defines a line with slope m which has a y-intercept that is b.

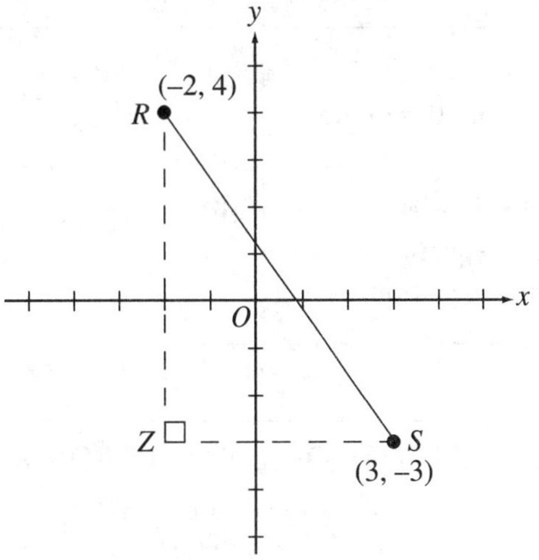

For a line through two points (x_1, y_1) and (x_2, y_2) with $x_1 \neq x_2$, the slope is $m = \frac{(y_2 - y_1)}{(x_2 - x_1)}$. Given the known point (x_1, y_1) and the slope m, any other point (x, y) on the line satisfies the equation $m = \frac{(y - y_1)}{(x - x_1)}$.

Above, the line's slope is $\frac{(-3 - 4)}{(3 - (-2))} = -\frac{7}{5}$. To find an equation of the line, we can use the point (3, –3):

$$y - (-3) = \left(-\frac{7}{5}\right)(x - 3)$$
$$y + 3 = \left(-\frac{7}{5}\right)x + \frac{21}{5}$$
$$y = \left(-\frac{7}{5}\right)x + \frac{6}{5}$$

So, the y-intercept is $\frac{6}{5}$.

Find the x-intercept like this:

$$0 = \left(-\frac{7}{5}\right)x + \frac{6}{5}$$
$$\left(\frac{7}{5}\right)x = \frac{6}{5}$$
$$x = \frac{6}{7}$$

The graph shows both these intercepts.

Rates, Ratios, and Percents

FRACTIONS:

Equivalent or Equal Fractions:
Two fractions stand for the same number if dividing each fraction's numerator and denominator by their greatest common divisor makes the fractions identical.

Adding, Subtracting, Multiplying, and Dividing Fractions:

$\frac{a}{b} + \frac{c}{d} = \frac{ad}{bd} + \frac{bc}{bd}$; $\frac{a}{b} - \frac{c}{d} = \frac{ad}{bd} - \frac{bc}{bd}$

$\frac{a}{b} \times \frac{c}{d} = \frac{ac}{bd}$; $\frac{a}{b} \div \frac{c}{d} = \frac{ad}{bc}$

MIXED NUMBERS:

A mixed number of the form $a\frac{b}{c}$ equals the fraction $\frac{ac + b}{c}$.

RATE:

distance = rate × time

PROFIT:

Profit = Revenues – Expenses, or

Profit = Selling price – Cost.

INTEREST:

Simple annual interest =
(principal) × (interest rate) × (time)

Compound interest over n periods =
(principal) × (1 + interest per period)^n – principal

PERCENTS:

$x\% = \frac{x}{100}$.

$x\%$ of y equals $\frac{xy}{100}$.

To convert a percent to a decimal, drop the percent sign, then move the decimal point two digits left.

To convert a decimal to a percent, add a percent sign, then move the decimal point two digits right.

PERCENT INCREASE OR DECREASE:

The percent increase from x to y is $100\left(\frac{y - x}{x}\right)\%$.

The percent decrease from x to y is $100\left(\frac{x - y}{x}\right)\%$.

DISCOUNTS:

A price discounted by n percent becomes $(100 - n)$ percent of the original price.

A price discounted by n percent and then by m percent becomes $(100 - n)(100 - m)$ percent of the original price.

WORK:

$\frac{1}{r} + \frac{1}{s} = \frac{1}{h}$, where r is how long one individual takes to do an amount of work, s is how long a second individual takes to do that much work, and h is how long they take to do that much work when both are working at the same time.

MIXTURES:

	Number of units of a substance or mixture	Amount of an ingredient per unit of the substance or mixture	Total amount of that ingredient in the substance or mixture
Substance A	X	M	X × M
Substance B	Y	N	Y × N
Mixture of A and B	X + Y	$\frac{(X \times M) + (Y \times N)}{X + Y}$	(X × M) + (Y × N)

Statistics, Sets, and Counting Methods

STATISTICS:

Concept	Definition for a data set of n values ordered from least to greatest	Example with data set {4, 4, 5, 7, 10}
Mean	The sum of the n values, divided by n	$\frac{(4+4+5+7+10)}{5} = \frac{30}{5} = 6$
Median	The middle value if n is odd; The mean of the two middle values if n is even.	5 is the middle value in {4, 4, 5, 7, 10}.
Mode	The value that appears most often in the data set.	4 is the only value that appears more than once in {4, 4, 5, 7, 10}.
Range	The largest value in the data set minus the smallest	$10 - 4 = 6$
Standard Deviation	Calculate like this: (1) Find the arithmetic mean (2) Find the differences between each of the n values and the mean (3) Square each of the differences (4) Find the average of the squared differences, and (5) Take the nonnegative square root of this average	(1) The mean is 6. (2) −2, −2, −1, 1, 4 (3) 4, 4, 1, 1, 16 (4) $\frac{26}{5} = 5.2$ (5) $\sqrt{5.2}$

SETS:

Concept	Notation for finite sets S and T	Example
Number of elements	$\lvert S \rvert$	$S = \{-5, 0, 1\}$ is a set with $\lvert S \rvert = 3$.
Subset	$S \subseteq T$ (S is a subset of T); $S \supseteq T$ (T is a subset of S)	{−5, 0, 1} is a subset of {−5, 0, 1, 4, 10}.
Union	$S \cup T$	$\{3, 4\} \cup \{4, 5, 6\} = \{3, 4, 5, 6\}$
Intersection	$S \cap T$	$\{3, 4\} \cap \{4, 5, 6\} = \{4\}$
The general addition rule for two sets	$\lvert S \cup T \rvert = \lvert S \rvert + \lvert T \rvert - \lvert S \cap T \rvert$	$\lvert\{3, 4\} \cup \{4, 5, 6\}\rvert =$ $\lvert\{3, 4\}\rvert + \lvert\{4, 5, 6\}\rvert - \lvert\{3, 4\} \cap \{4, 5, 6\}\rvert =$ $\lvert\{3, 4\}\rvert + \lvert\{4, 5, 6\}\rvert - \lvert\{4\}\rvert = 2 + 3 - 1 = 4.$

COUNTING METHODS:

Concept and Equations	Examples
Multiplication Principle: The number of possible choices of 1 element apiece from the data sets $A_1, A_2, \ldots, A_n$ is $\lvert A_1 \rvert \times \lvert A_2 \rvert \times \ldots \times \lvert A_n \rvert$.	The number of possible choices of 1 element apiece from the data sets $S = \{-5, 0, 1\}$, $T = \{3, 4\}$, and $U = \{3, 4, 5, 6\}$ is $\lvert S \rvert \times \lvert T \rvert \times \lvert U \rvert = 3 \times 2 \times 4 = 24$.
Factorial: $n! = n \times (n-1) \times \ldots \times 1$ $0! = 1! = 1$ $n! = (n-1)!(n)$	$4! = 4 \times 3 \times 2 \times 1 = 24$ $4! = 3! \times 4$
Permutations: A data set of n objects has $n!$ permutations	The data set of letters A, B, and C has $3! = 6$ permutations: ABC, ACB, BAC, BCA, CAB, and CBA.
Combinations: The number of possible choices of k objects from a data set of n objects is $\binom{n}{k} = \frac{n!}{k!(n-k)!}$.	The number of 2-element subsets of data set {A, B, C, D, E} is $\binom{5}{2} = \frac{5!}{2!3!} = \frac{120}{(2)(6)} = 10$. The 10 subsets are: {A, B}, {A, C}, {A, D}, {A, E}, {B, C}, {B, D}, {B, E}, {C, D}, {C, E}, and {D, E}.

Probability and Sequences

PROBABILITY:

Concept	**Definition, Notation, and Equations**	**Example: Rolling a die with 6 numbered sides once**
Event	A set of outcomes of an experiment	The event of the outcome being an odd number is the set $\{1, 3, 5\}$.
Probability	The probability $P(E)$ of an event E is a number between 0 and 1, inclusive. If each outcome is equally likely, $P(E) = \frac{\text{(the number of possible outcomes in E)}}{\text{(the total number of possible outcomes)}}$.	If the 6 outcomes are equally likely, the probability of each outcome is $\frac{1}{6}$. The probability that the outcome is an odd number is $P(\{1, 3, 5\}) = \frac{\lvert\{1, 3, 5\}\rvert}{6} = \frac{3}{6} = \frac{1}{2}$.
Conditional Probability	The probability that E occurs if F occurs is $P(E \mid F) = \frac{\lvert E \cap F\rvert}{\lvert F\rvert}$.	$P(\{1, 3, 5\} \mid \{1, 2\}) = \frac{\lvert\{1\}\rvert}{\lvert\{1, 2\}\rvert} = \frac{1}{2}$
Not *E*	The set of outcomes not in event E: $P(\text{not } E) = 1 - P(E)$.	$P(\text{not}\{3\}) = \frac{6-1}{6} = \frac{5}{6}$
E* and *F	The set of outcomes in both E and F, that is, $E \cap F$; $P(E \text{ and } F) = P(E \cap F) = P(E \mid F)P(F)$.	For $E = \{1, 3, 5\}$ and $F = \{2, 3, 5\}$: $P(E \text{ and } F) = P(E \cap F) = P(\{3, 5\}) = \frac{\lvert\{3, 5\}\rvert}{6} = \frac{2}{6} = \frac{1}{3}$
E* or *F	The set of outcomes in E or F or both, that is, $E \cup F$; $P(E \text{ or } F) = P(E) + P(F) - P(E \text{ and } F)$.	For $E = \{1, 3, 5\}$ and $F = \{2, 3, 5\}$: $P(E \text{ or } F) = P(E) + P(F) - P(E \text{ and } F) = \frac{3}{6} + \frac{3}{6} - \frac{2}{6} = \frac{4}{6} = \frac{2}{3}$.
Dependent and Independent Events	E is dependent on F if $P(E \mid F) \neq P(E)$. E and F are independent if neither is dependent on the other. If E and F are independent, $P(E \text{ and } F) = P(E)P(F)$.	For $E = \{2, 4, 6\}$ and $F = \{5, 6\}$: $P(E \mid F) = P(E) = \frac{1}{2}$, and $P(F \mid E) = P(F) = \frac{1}{3}$, so E and F are independent. Thus $P(E \text{ and } F) = P(E)P(F) = \left(\frac{1}{2}\right)\left(\frac{1}{3}\right) = \frac{1}{6}$.

SEQUENCE:

An ordered list of elements, starting with a first element.

Example: The function $a(n) = n^2 + \left(\frac{n}{5}\right)$ with the domain of all positive integers $n = 1, 2, 3, \ldots$ is an infinite sequence a_n.

4.0 Quantitative Reasoning

4.0 Quantitative Reasoning

The GMAT™ exam's Quantitative Reasoning section tests your math skills in the areas reviewed in Chapter 3, "Math Review": Value, Order, Factors, Algebra, Equalities, Inequalities, Rates, Ratios, Percents, Statistics, Sets, Counting, Probability, Estimation, and Series. Quantitative Reasoning questions also test how well you reason mathematically, solve math problems, and interpret graphic data. All the math needed to answer the questions is generally taught in secondary school (or high school) math classes.

To answer a Quantitative Reasoning question, you pick one of five answer choices. First study the question to see what information it gives and what it's asking you to do with that information. Then scan the answer choices. If the problem seems simple, try to find the answer quickly. Then check your answer against the choices. If your answer isn't among the choices, or if the problem is complicated, think again about what the problem is asking you to do. Try to rule out some of the choices. If you still can't narrow down the answer to one choice, reread the question. It gives all the information you need to find the right answer. If you already know about the topic, don't use that knowledge to answer. Use only the information given.

You have 45 minutes to answer the 21 questions in the section. That's an average of about two minutes and nine seconds per question. You may run out of time if you spend too long on any one question. If you find yourself stuck on a question, just pick the answer that seems best, even if you're not sure. Guessing is not usually the best way to score high on the GMAT, but making an educated guess is better than not answering.

Below are question-solving tips, directions for the section, and sample questions with an answer key and answer explanations. These explanations also show strategies that may help you solve other Quantitative Reasoning questions.

4.1 Tips for Answering Quantitative Reasoning Questions

1. **Pace yourself.**

   Check the on-screen timer to see how much time you have left. Work carefully, but don't take too long double-checking an answer or struggling with a problem.

2. **Use the erasable notepad provided.**

   Solving a problem step by step on the notepad may help you avoid mistakes. If the problem doesn't show a diagram, drawing your own may help.

3. **Study each question to understand what it's asking.**

   Approach word problems one step at a time. Read each sentence. When useful, translate the problem into math expressions.

4. **Scan all the answer choices before working on the problem.**

   By scanning the answer choices, you can avoid finding the answer in the wrong form. For example, if the choices are all fractions like $\frac{1}{4}$, work out the answer as a fraction, not as a decimal like 0.25. Similarly, if the choices are all estimates, you can often take shortcuts. For example, you may be able to estimate by rounding 48% to 50% if every answer choice is an estimate.

5. **Don't waste time on a problem that's too hard for you.**

   Make your best guess. Then move on to the next question.

To register for the GMAT™ exam, go to www.mba.com/register

4.2 Practice Questions

Solve the problem and pick the best answer choice given.
Numbers: All numbers used are real numbers.
Figures: A figure in a Quantitative Reasoning question gives information useful in solving the problem. Figures are drawn as accurately as possible, except as noted. Lines shown as straight are straight. Lines that look jagged may also be straight. Points, angles, regions, etc., are positioned as shown. All figures are flat unless otherwise noted.

Questions 1 to 82 — Difficulty: Easy

1. Working at a constant rate, a copy machine makes 20 copies of a one-page document per minute. If the machine works at this constant rate, how many hours does it take to make 4,800 copies of a one-page document?

(A) 4
(B) 5
(C) 6
(D) 7
(E) 8

2. If $x + y = 2$ and $x^2 + y^2 = 2$, what is the value of xy?

(A) –2
(B) –1
(C) 0
(D) 1
(E) 2

3. The sum S of the first n consecutive positive even integers is given by $S = n(n + 1)$. For what value of n is this sum equal to 110?

(A) 10
(B) 11
(C) 12
(D) 13
(E) 14

4. $6(87.30 + 0.65) - 5(87.30) =$

(A) 3.90
(B) 39.00
(C) 90.90
(D) 91.20
(E) 91.85

5. What is the value of $x^2yz - xyz^2$, if $x = -2$, $y = 1$, and $z = 3$?

(A) 20
(B) 24
(C) 30
(D) 32
(E) 48

6. If T is a set of 35 consecutive integers, of which 17 are negative, what is the sum of all the integers in T?

(A) –2
(B) –1
(C) 0
(D) 1
(E) 2

7. If $x > y$ and $y > z$, which of the following represents the greatest number?

(A) $x - z$
(B) $x - y$
(C) $y - x$
(D) $z - y$
(E) $z - x$

8. 38, 69, 22, 73, 31, 47, 13, 82

Which of the following numbers is greater than three-fourths of the numbers but less than one-fourth of the numbers in the list above?

(A) 56
(B) 68
(C) 69
(D) 71
(E) 73

9. A rug manufacturer produces rugs at a cost of $75 per rug. What is the manufacturer's gross profit from the sale of 150 rugs if $\frac{2}{3}$ of the rugs are sold for $150 per rug and the rest are sold for $200 per rug?

(A) $10,350
(B) $11,250
(C) $13,750
(D) $16,250
(E) $17,800

10. The value of Maureen's investment portfolio has decreased by 5.8 percent since her initial investment in the portfolio. If her initial investment was $16,800, what is the current value of the portfolio?

(A) $7,056.00
(B) $14,280.00
(C) $15,825.60
(D) $16,702.56
(E) $17,774.40

11. Company C produces toy trucks at a cost of $5.00 each for the first 100 trucks and $3.50 for each additional truck. If 500 toy trucks were produced by Company C and sold for $10.00 each, what was Company C's gross profit?

(A) $2,250
(B) $2,500
(C) $3,100
(D) $3,250
(E) $3,500

	Profit or Loss (in millions of dollars)				
Division	1991	1992	1993	1994	1995
A	1.1	(3.4)	1.9	2.0	0.6
B	(2.3)	5.5	(4.5)	3.9	(2.9)
C	10.0	(6.6)	5.3	1.1	(3.0)

12. The annual profit or loss for the three divisions of Company T for the years 1991 through 1995 are summarized in the table shown, where losses are enclosed in parentheses. For which division and which three consecutive years shown was the division's profit or loss for the three-year period closest to $0?

(A) Division *A* for 1991–1993
(B) Division *A* for 1992–1994
(C) Division *B* for 1991–1993
(D) Division *B* for 1993–1995
(E) Division *C* for 1992–1994

13. A computer appliance dealer bought a computer at a wholesale price of $500 and then sold it at a 20 percent discount off the suggested retail price. If the dealer made a 12 percent profit on the wholesale price, what was the suggested retail price of the computer?

(A) $560
(B) $580
(C) $660
(D) $700
(E) $730

14. Pat invested x dollars in a fund that paid 8 percent annual interest, compounded annually. Which of the following represents the value, in dollars, of Pat's investment plus interest at the end of 5 years?

(A) $5(0.08x)$
(B) $5(1.08x)$
(C) $[1 + 5(0.08)]x$
(D) $(1.08)^5x$
(E) $(1.08x)^5$

15. There are five sales agents in a certain real estate office. One month Andy sold twice as many properties as Ellen, Bob sold 3 more than Ellen, Cary sold twice as many as Bob, and Dora sold as many as Bob and Ellen together. Who sold the most properties that month?

(A) Andy
(B) Bob
(C) Cary
(D) Dora
(E) Ellen

16. In a field day at a school, each child who competed in n events and scored a total of p points was given an overall score of $\frac{p}{n} + n$. Andrew competed in 1 event and scored 9 points. Jason competed in 3 events and scored 5, 6, and 7 points, respectively. What was the ratio of Andrew's overall score to Jason's overall score?

(A) $\frac{10}{23}$
(B) $\frac{7}{10}$
(C) $\frac{4}{5}$
(D) $\frac{10}{9}$
(E) $\frac{12}{7}$

17. A certain work plan for September requires that a work team, working every day, produce an average of 200 items per day. For the first half of the month, the team produced an average of 150 items per day. How many items per day must the team average during the second half of the month if it is to attain the average daily production rate required by the work plan?

(A) 225
(B) 250
(C) 275
(D) 300
(E) 350

18. A company sells radios for $15.00 each. It costs the company $14.00 per radio to produce 1,000 radios and $13.50 per radio to produce 2,000 radios. How much greater will the company's gross profit be from the production and sale of 2,000 radios than from the production and sale of 1,000 radios?

(A) $500
(B) $1,000
(C) $1,500
(D) $2,000
(E) $2,500

19. Working at their respective constant rates, machine A makes 100 copies in 12 minutes and machine B makes 150 copies in 10 minutes. If these machines work simultaneously at their respective rates for 30 minutes, what is the total number of copies that they will produce?

(A) 250
(B) 425
(C) 675
(D) 700
(E) 750

20. Company X mailed out a questionnaire. Sixty percent of those who received the questionnaire by mail responded. Company X needed 300 responses. What is the minimum number of questionnaires that Company X should have mailed in order to get the necessary responses?

(A) 400
(B) 420
(C) 480
(D) 500
(E) 600

21. The toll T, in dollars, for a truck using a certain bridge is given by the formula $T = 1.50 + 0.50(x - 2)$, where x is the number of axles on the truck. What is the toll for an 18-wheel truck that has 2 wheels on its front axle and 4 wheels on each of its other axles?

(A) \$2.50
(B) \$3.00
(C) \$3.50
(D) \$4.00
(E) \$5.00

22. For what value of x between –4 and 4, inclusive, is the value of $x^2 - 10x + 16$ the greatest?

(A) –4
(B) –2
(C) 0
(D) 2
(E) 4

23. If $x = -\frac{5}{8}$ and $y = -\frac{1}{2}$, what is the value of the expression $-2x - y^2$?

(A) $-\frac{3}{2}$
(B) –1
(C) 1
(D) $\frac{3}{2}$
(E) $\frac{7}{4}$

24. At the opening of a trading day, stock X had a value of \$40.00 per share and stock Y had a value of \$25.00 per share. At the closing of the trading day, stock X had a value of \$41.00 per share and stock Y had a value of \$28.50 per share. For this trading day, the percent increase in the value of stock Y was how many percentage points greater than the percent increase in the value of stock X?

(A) 2.5
(B) 6.25
(C) 10
(D) 11.5
(E) 12.5

25. For positive integers a and b, the remainder when a is divided by b is equal to the remainder when b is divided by a. Which of the following could be a value of ab?

I. 24
II. 30
III. 36

(A) II only
(B) III only
(C) I and II only
(D) II and III only
(E) I, II, and III

26. List S consists of the positive integers that are multiples of 9 and are less than 100. What is the median of the integers in S?

(A) 36
(B) 45
(C) 49
(D) 54
(E) 63

27. A rope 20.6 meters long is cut into two pieces. If the length of one piece of rope is 2.8 meters shorter than the length of the other, what is the length, in meters, of the longer piece of rope?

(A) 7.5
(B) 8.9
(C) 9.9
(D) 10.3
(E) 11.7

28. If x and y are integers and $x - y$ is odd, which of the following must be true?

I. xy is even.
II. $x^2 + y^2$ is odd.
III. $(x + y)^2$ is even.

(A) I only
(B) II only
(C) III only
(D) I and II only
(D) I, II, and III

29. On Monday, the opening price of a certain stock was \$100 per share and its closing price was \$110 per share. On Tuesday the closing price of the stock was 10 percent less than its closing price on Monday, and on Wednesday the closing price of the stock was 4 percent greater than its closing price on Tuesday. What was the approximate percent change in the price of the stock from its opening price on Monday to its closing price on Wednesday?

(A) A decrease of 6%
(B) A decrease of 4%
(C) A decrease of 1%
(D) An increase of 3%
(E) An increase of 4%

30. $1 - 0.000001 =$

(A) (1.01)(0.99)
(B) (1.11)(0.99)
(C) (1.001)(0.999)
(D) (1.111)(0.999)
(E) (1.0101)(0.0909)

31. In a certain history class of 17 juniors and seniors, each junior has written 2 book reports and each senior has written 3 book reports. If the 17 students have written a total of 44 book reports, how many juniors are in the class?

(A) 7
(B) 8
(C) 9
(D) 10
(E) 11

32. $|-4|(|-20|-|5|) =$

(A) −100
(B) −60
(C) 60
(D) 75
(E) 100

33. What is the greatest integer k for which 32.45×10^k is less than 1?

(A) −2
(B) 1
(C) 0
(D) 1
(E) 2

34. How many integers x satisfy both $2 < x \le 4$ and $0 \le x \le 3$?

(A) 5
(B) 4
(C) 3
(D) 2
(E) 1

35. At the opening of a trading day at a certain stock exchange, the price per share of stock K was \$8. If the price per share of stock K was \$9 at the closing of the day, what was the percent increase in the price per share of stock K for that day?

(A) 1.4%
(B) 5.9%
(C) 11.1%
(D) 12.5%
(E) 23.6%

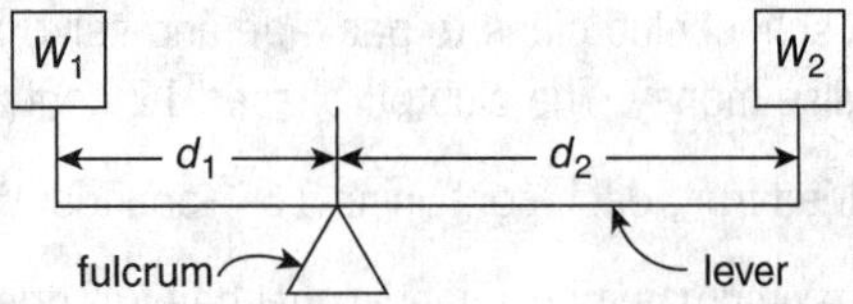

36. As shown in the diagram above, a lever resting on a fulcrum has weights of w_1 pounds and w_2 pounds, located d_1 feet and d_2 feet from the fulcrum. The lever is balanced and $w_1d_1 = w_2d_2$. Suppose w_1 is 50 pounds and w_2 is 30 pounds. If d_1 is 4 feet less than d_2, what is d_2, in feet?

(A) 1.5
(B) 2.5
(C) 6
(D) 10
(E) 20

Day	Change in Dollars
Monday	$+1\frac{1}{2}$
Tuesday	$-\frac{3}{4}$
Wednesday	0
Thursday	$-\frac{1}{8}$
Friday	$+2\frac{1}{4}$

37. The table above shows the daily change in the price of a certain stock last week. What was the net change in dollars in the price of the stock for the week?

(A) $-4\frac{5}{8}$
(B) $-2\frac{7}{8}$
(C) $+2\frac{7}{8}$
(D) $+3\frac{3}{4}$
(E) $-4\frac{5}{8}$

38. Of 120 hotel rooms rented one night, some were suites rented for \$115 each and the rest were double rooms rented for \$85 each. If the total revenue from the room rentals for this night was \$10,890, how many suites were rented?

(A) 23
(B) 35
(C) 54
(D) 94
(E) 99

39. Last week Jack worked 70 hours and earned \$1,260. If he earned his regular hourly wage for the first 40 hours worked, $1\frac{1}{2}$ times his regular hourly wage for the next 20 hours worked, and 2 times his regular hourly wage for the remaining 10 hours worked, what was his regular hourly wage?

(A) \$7.00
(B) \$14.00
(C) \$18.00
(D) \$22.00
(E) \$31.50

40. If $\frac{x}{4}$ is 2 more than $\frac{x}{8}$, then $x =$

(A) 4
(B) 8
(C) 16
(D) 32
(E) 64

41. If $(2^x)(2^y) = 8$ and $(9^x)(3^y) = 81$, then $(x, y) =$

(A) (1, 2)
(B) (2, 1)
(C) (1, 1)
(D) (2, 2)
(E) (1, 3)

42. A certain toll station on a highway has 7 tollbooths, and each tollbooth collects $0.75 from each vehicle that passes it. From 6 o'clock yesterday morning to 12 o'clock midnight, vehicles passed each of the tollbooths at the average rate of 4 vehicles per minute. Approximately how much money did the toll station collect during that time period?

(A) $1,500
(B) $3,000
(C) $11,500
(D) $23,000
(E) $30,000

43. If $y = 2 + 2k$ and $y \neq 0$, then $\frac{1}{y} + \frac{1}{y} + \frac{1}{y} + \frac{1}{y} =$

(A) $\frac{1}{8+8k}$
(B) $\frac{2}{1+k}$
(C) $\frac{1}{8+k}$
(D) $\frac{4}{8+k}$
(E) $\frac{4}{1+k}$

44. If $3^x - 3^{x-1} = 162$, then $x(x - 1) =$

(A) 12
(B) 16
(C) 20
(D) 30
(E) 81

45. The expression $n!$ is defined as the product of the integers from 1 through n. If p is the product of the integers from 100 through 299 and q is the product of the integers from 200 through 299, which of the following is equal to $\frac{p}{q}$?

(A) 99!
(B) 199!
(C) $\frac{199!}{99!}$
(D) $\frac{299!}{99!}$
(E) $\frac{299!}{199!}$

46. A school club plans to package and sell dried fruit to raise money. The club purchased 12 containers of dried fruit, each containing $16\frac{3}{4}$ pounds. What is the maximum number of individual bags of dried fruit, each containing $\frac{1}{4}$ pounds, that can be sold from the dried fruit the club purchased?

(A) 50
(B) 64
(C) 67
(D) 768
(E) 804

Height	Price
Less than 5 ft	$14.95
5 ft to 6 ft	$17.95
Over 6 ft	$21.95

47. A nursery sells fruit trees priced as shown in the chart above. In its inventory 54 trees are less than 5 feet in height. If the expected revenue from the sale of its entire stock is estimated at $2,450, approximately how much of this will come from the sale of trees that are at least 5 feet tall?

(A) $1,730
(B) $1,640
(C) $1,410
(D) $1,080
(E) $810

48. A certain bridge is 4,024 feet long. Approximately how many minutes does it take to cross this bridge at a constant speed of 20 miles per hour? (1 mile = 5,280 feet)

(A) 1
(B) 2
(C) 4
(D) 6
(E) 7

49. A purse contains 57 coins, all of which are nickels, dimes, or quarters. If the purse contains x dimes and 8 more nickels than dimes, which of the following gives the number of quarters the purse contains in terms of x?

(A) $2x - 49$

(B) $2x + 49$

(C) $2x - 65$

(D) $49 - 2x$

(E) $65 - 2x$

50. The annual interest rate earned by an investment increased by 10 percent from last year to this year. If the annual interest rate earned by the investment this year was 11 percent, what was the annual interest rate last year?

(A) 1%

(B) 1.1%

(C) 9.1%

(D) 10%

(E) 10.8%

51. A total of 5 liters of gasoline is to be poured into two empty containers with capacities of 2 liters and 6 liters, respectively, such that both containers will be filled to the same percent of their respective capacities. What amount of gasoline, in liters, must be poured into the 6-liter container?

(A) $4\frac{1}{2}$

(B) 4

(C) $3\frac{3}{4}$

(D) 3

(E) $1\frac{1}{4}$

52. What is the larger of the 2 solutions of the equation $x^2 - 4x = 96$?

(A) 8

(B) 12

(C) 16

(D) 32

(E) 100

$$x = \frac{1}{6}gt^2$$

53. In the formula shown, if g is a constant and $x = -6$ when $t = 2$, what is the value of x when $t = 4$?

(A) −24

(B) −20

(C) −15

(D) 20

(E) 24

54. $\frac{(39{,}897)(0.0096)}{198.76}$ is approximately

(A) 0.02

(B) 0.2

(C) 2

(D) 20

(E) 200

55. The "prime sum" of an integer n greater than 1 is the sum of all the prime factors of n, including repetitions. For example, the prime sum of 12 is 7, since $12 = 2 \times 2 \times 3$ and $2 + 2 + 3 = 7$. For which of the following integers is the prime sum greater than 35?

(A) 440

(B) 512

(C) 620

(D) 700

(E) 750

56. Each machine at a toy factory assembles a certain kind of toy at a constant rate of one toy every 3 minutes. If 40 percent of the machines at the factory are to be replaced by new machines that assemble this kind of toy at a constant rate of one toy every 2 minutes, what will be the percent increase in the number of toys assembled in one hour by all the machines at the factory, working at their constant rates?

(A) 20%

(B) 25%

(C) 30%

(D) 40%

(E) 50%

57. When a subscription to a new magazine was purchased for m months, the publisher offered a discount of 75 percent off the regular monthly price of the magazine. If the total value of the discount was equivalent to buying the magazine at its regular monthly price for 27 months, what was the value of m?

(A) 18
(B) 24
(C) 30
(D) 36
(E) 48

58. At a garage sale, all of the prices of the items sold were different. If the price of a radio sold at the garage sale was both the 15th highest price and the 20th lowest price among the prices of the items sold, how many items were sold at the garage sale?

(A) 33
(B) 34
(C) 35
(D) 36
(E) 37

59. Half of a large pizza is cut into 4 equal-sized pieces, and the other half is cut into 6 equal-sized pieces. If a person were to eat 1 of the larger pieces and 2 of the smaller pieces, what fraction of the pizza would remain <u>uneaten</u>?

(A) $\frac{5}{12}$
(B) $\frac{13}{24}$
(C) $\frac{7}{12}$
(D) $\frac{2}{3}$
(E) $\frac{17}{24}$

60. If $a = 1 + \frac{1}{4} + \frac{1}{16} + \frac{1}{64}$ and $b = 1 + \frac{1}{4}a$, then what is the value of $a - b$?

(A) $-\frac{85}{256}$
(B) $-\frac{1}{256}$
(C) $-\frac{1}{4}$
(D) $\frac{125}{256}$
(E) $\frac{169}{256}$

61. In a certain learning experiment, each participant had three trials and was assigned, for each trial, a score of either –2, –1, 0, 1, or 2. The participant's final score consisted of the sum of the first trial score, 2 times the second trial score, and 3 times the third trial score. If Anne received scores of 1 and –1 for her first two trials, not necessarily in that order, which of the following could NOT be her final score?

(A) –4
(B) –2
(C) 1
(D) 5
(E) 6

62. For all positive integers m and v, the expression $m \Theta v$ represents the remainder when m is divided by v. What is the value of $((98 \Theta 33) \Theta 17) - (98 \Theta (33 \Theta 17))$?

(A) –10
(B) –2
(C) 8
(D) 13
(E) 17

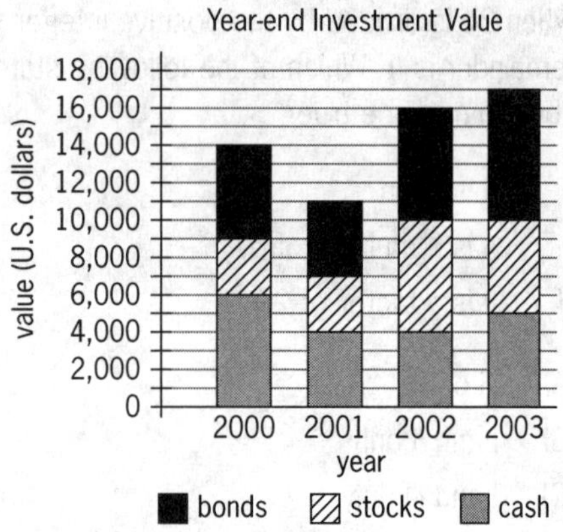

63. The chart above shows year-end values for Darnella's investments. For just the stocks, what was the increase in value from year-end 2000 to year-end 2003?

    (A) $1,000
    (B) $2,000
    (C) $3,000
    (D) $4,000
    (E) $5,000

64. If the sum of the reciprocals of two consecutive odd integers is $\frac{12}{35}$, then the greater of the two integers is

    (A) 3
    (B) 5
    (C) 7
    (D) 9
    (E) 11

65. What is the sum of the odd integers from 35 to 85, inclusive?

    (A) 1,560
    (B) 1,500
    (C) 1,240
    (D) 1,120
    (E) 1,100

66. For all numbers *a*, *b*, *c*, and *d*, $\begin{vmatrix} a & b \\ c & d \end{vmatrix}$ is defined by the equation $\begin{vmatrix} a & b \\ c & d \end{vmatrix} = ad - cb$. Which of the following is equal to $\begin{vmatrix} s & t \\ 1 & 3 \end{vmatrix} - \begin{vmatrix} -t & 2 \\ s & 4 \end{vmatrix} + \begin{vmatrix} 2 & 2 \\ t & s \end{vmatrix}$?

    (A) $\begin{vmatrix} s & t \\ 1 & 5 \end{vmatrix}$
    (B) $\begin{vmatrix} s & t \\ 7 & 1 \end{vmatrix}$
    (C) $\begin{vmatrix} s & t \\ 5 & 7 \end{vmatrix}$
    (D) $\begin{vmatrix} s & -t \\ 1 & 5 \end{vmatrix}$
    (E) $\begin{vmatrix} s & -t \\ 1 & 7 \end{vmatrix}$

67. In a certain sequence, each term after the first term is one-half the previous term. If the tenth term of the sequence is between 0.0001 and 0.001, then the twelfth term of the sequence is between

    (A) 0.0025 and 0.025
    (B) 0.00025 and 0.0025
    (C) 0.000025 and 0.00025
    (D) 0.0000025 and 0.000025
    (E) 0.00000025 and 0.0000025

68. A certain drive-in movie theater has a total of 17 rows of parking spaces. There are 20 parking spaces in the first row and 21 parking spaces in the second row. In each subsequent row there are 2 more parking spaces than in the previous row. What is the total number of parking spaces in the movie theater?

    (A) 412
    (B) 544
    (C) 596
    (D) 632
    (E) 692

69. Ada and Paul received their scores on three tests. On the first test, Ada's score was 10 points higher than Paul's score. On the second test, Ada's score was 4 points higher than Paul's score. If Paul's average (arithmetic mean) score on the three tests was 3 points higher than Ada's average score on the three tests, then Paul's score on the third test was how many points higher than Ada's score?

(A) 9
(B) 14
(C) 17
(D) 23
(E) 25

70. The price of a certain stock increased by 0.25 of 1 percent on a certain day. By what fraction did the price of the stock increase that day?

(A) $\frac{1}{2,500}$
(B) $\frac{1}{400}$
(C) $\frac{1}{40}$
(D) $\frac{1}{25}$
(E) $\frac{1}{4}$

71. For each trip, a taxicab company charges \$4.25 for the first mile and \$2.65 for each additional mile or fraction thereof. If the total charge for a certain trip was \$62.55, how many miles at most was the trip?

(A) 21
(B) 22
(C) 23
(D) 24
(E) 25

72. When 24 is divided by the positive integer *n*, the remainder is 4. Which of the following statements about *n* must be true?

I. *n* is even.
II. *n* is a multiple of 5.
III. *n* is a factor of 20.

(A) III only
(B) I and II only
(C) I and III only
(D) II and III only
(E) I, II, and III

73. Terry needs to purchase some pipe for a plumbing job that requires pipes with lengths of 1 ft 4 in, 2 ft 8 in, 3 ft 4 in, 3 ft 8 in, 4 ft 8 in, 5 ft 8 in, and 9 ft 4 in. The store from which Terry will purchase the pipe sells pipe only in 10-ft lengths. If each 10-ft length can be cut into shorter pieces, what is the minimum number of 10-ft pipe lengths that Terry needs to purchase for the plumbing job?

(Note: 1 ft = 12 in)

(A) 3
(B) 4
(C) 5
(D) 6
(E) 7

74. What is the thousandths digit in the decimal equivalent of $\frac{53}{5,000}$?

(A) 0
(B) 1
(C) 3
(D) 5
(E) 6

75. If a equals the sum of the even integers from 2 to 20, inclusive, and b equals the sum of the odd integers from 1 to 19, inclusive, what is the value of $a - b$?

(A) 1
(B) 10
(C) 19
(D) 20
(E) 21

76. If a, b, c, and d are consecutive even integers and $a < b < c < d$, then $a + b$ is how much less than $c + d$?

(A) 2
(B) 4
(C) 6
(D) 8
(E) 10

77. A retailer sold an appliance for \$80. If the retailer's gross profit on the appliance was 25 percent of the retailer's cost for the appliance, how many dollars was the retailer's gross profit?

(A) \$10
(B) \$16
(C) \$20
(D) \$24
(E) \$25

78. Beth has a collection of 8 boxes of clothing for a charity, and the average (arithmetic mean) number of pieces of clothing per box is c. If she replaces a box in the collection that contains 12 pieces of clothing with a box that contains 22 pieces of clothing, what is the average number of pieces of clothing per box for the new collection, in terms of c?

(A) $c - \frac{5}{4}$
(B) $c + \frac{5}{4}$
(C) $8 - \frac{10}{c}$
(D) $8 + \frac{10}{c}$
(E) $8c - 10$

$$\frac{1 + 0.0001}{0.04 + 10}$$

79. The value of the expression above is closest to which of the following?

(A) 0.0001
(B) 0.001
(C) 0.01
(D) 1
(E) 10

80. If $x + 1 = t$ and $t = 3 - x$, then $x =$

(A) −2
(B) −1
(C) 0
(D) 1
(E) 2

81. If $x = kc$ and $y = kt$, then $y - x =$

(A) $k(t - c)$
(B) $k(c - t)$
(C) $c(k - t)$
(D) $t(k - c)$
(E) $k(1 - t)$

82. If k is a positive even integer, which of the following must be an odd integer?

I. $k^2 - 3k + 4$
II. $k^5 + 3$
III. $7k - 7$

(A) II only
(B) III only
(C) I and III only
(D) II and III only
(E) I, II, and III

Questions 83 to 151 — Difficulty: Medium

83. If $\frac{1}{2}$ the result obtained when 2 is subtracted from 5*x* is equal to the sum of 10 and 3*x*, what is the value of *x*?

(A) −22
(B) −4
(C) 4
(D) 18
(E) 22

84. If Car A took *n* hours to travel 2 miles and Car B took *m* hours to travel 3 miles, which of the following expresses the time it would take Car C, traveling at the average (arithmetic mean) of those rates, to travel 5 miles?

(A) $\frac{10nm}{3n+2m}$

(B) $\frac{3n+2m}{10(n+m)}$

(C) $\frac{2n+3m}{5nm}$

(D) $\frac{10(n+m)}{2n+3m}$

(E) $\frac{5(n+m)}{2n+3m}$

85. If *x*, *y*, and *k* are positive and *x* is less than *y*, then $\frac{x+k}{y+k}$ is

(A) 1
(B) greater than $\frac{x}{y}$
(C) equal to $\frac{x}{y}$
(D) less than $\frac{x}{y}$
(E) less than $\frac{x}{y}$ or greater than $\frac{x}{y}$, depending on the value of k

86. Consider the following set of inequalities: $p > q$, $s > r$, $q > t$, $s > p$, and $r > q$. Between which two quantities is no relationship established?

(A) *p* and *r*
(B) *s* and *t*
(C) *s* and *q*
(D) *p* and *t*
(E) *r* and *t*

87. Carl averaged 2*m* miles per hour on a trip that took him *h* hours. If Ruth made the same trip in $\frac{2}{3}h$ hours, what was her average speed in miles per hour?

(A) $\frac{1}{3}mh$
(B) $\frac{2}{3}mh$
(C) m
(D) $\frac{3}{2}m$
(E) $3m$

88. Of three persons, two take relish, two take pepper, and two take salt. The one who takes no salt takes no pepper, and the one who takes no pepper takes no relish. Which of the following statements must be true?

I. The person who takes no salt also takes no relish.
II. Any of the three persons who takes pepper also takes relish and salt.
III. The person who takes no relish is not one of those who takes salt.

(A) I only
(B) II only
(C) III only
(D) I and II only
(E) I, II, and III

89. If the smaller of 2 consecutive odd integers is a multiple of 5, which of the following could NOT be the sum of these 2 integers?

(A) -8
(B) 12
(C) 22
(D) 52
(E) 252

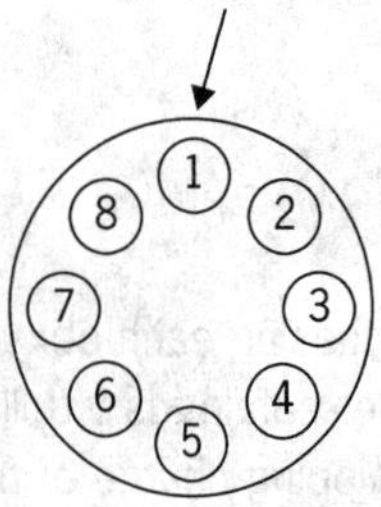

90. Eight light bulbs numbered 1 through 8 are arranged in a circle as shown above. The bulbs are wired so that every third bulb, counting in a clockwise direction, flashes until all bulbs have flashed once. If the bulb numbered 1 flashes first, which numbered bulb will flash last?

(A) 2
(B) 3
(C) 4
(D) 6
(E) 7

Closing Prices of Stock X
During a Certain Week
(in dollars)

Monday	Tuesday	Wednesday	Thursday	Friday
21	19	22	$24\frac{1}{2}$	23

91. A certain financial analyst defines the "volatility" of a stock during a given week to be the result of the following procedure: find the absolute value of the difference in the stock's closing price for each pair of consecutive days in the week and then find the average (arithmetic mean) of these 4 values. What is the volatility of Stock X during the week shown in the table?

(A) 0.50
(B) 1.80
(C) 2.00
(D) 2.25
(E) 2.50

92. If $y = \frac{|3x-5|}{-x^2-3}$, for what value of x will the value of y be greatest?

(A) -5
(B) $-\frac{3}{5}$
(C) 0
(D) $\frac{3}{5}$
(E) $\frac{5}{3}$

93. What values of x have a corresponding value of y that satisfies both $xy > 0$ and $xy = x + y$?

(A) $x \le -1$
(B) $-1 < x \le 0$
(C) $0 < x \le 1$
(D) $x > 1$
(E) All real numbers

94. Employee X's annual salary is \$12,000 more than half of Employee Y's annual salary. Employee Z's annual salary is \$15,000 more than half of Employee X's annual salary. If Employee X's annual salary is \$27,500, which of the following lists these three people in order of increasing annual salary?

(A) Y, Z, X
(B) Y, X, Z
(C) Z, X, Y
(D) X, Y, Z
(E) X, Z, Y

$$C = \begin{cases} 0.10s, \text{ if } s \le 60{,}000 \\ 0.10s + 0.04(s - 60{,}000), \text{ if } s > 60{,}000 \end{cases}$$

95. The formula above gives the contribution C, in dollars, to a certain profit-sharing plan for a participant with a salary of s dollars. How many more dollars is the contribution for a participant with a salary of \$70,000 than for a participant with a salary of \$50,000?

(A) \$800
(B) \$1,400
(C) \$2,000
(D) \$2,400
(E) \$2,800

96. Next month, Ron and Cathy will each begin working part-time at $\frac{3}{5}$ of their respective current salaries. If the sum of their reduced salaries will be equal to Cathy's current salary, then Ron's current salary is what fraction of Cathy's current salary?

(A) $\frac{1}{3}$
(B) $\frac{2}{5}$
(C) $\frac{1}{2}$
(D) $\frac{3}{5}$
(E) $\frac{2}{3}$

97. David and Ron are ordering food for a business lunch. David thinks that there should be twice as many sandwiches as there are pastries, but Ron thinks the number of pastries should be 12 more than one-fourth of the number of sandwiches. How many sandwiches should be ordered so that David and Ron can agree on the number of pastries to order?

(A) 12
(B) 16
(C) 20
(D) 24
(E) 48

98. The cost of purchasing each box of candy from a certain mail order catalog is v dollars per pound of candy, plus a shipping charge of h dollars. How many dollars does it cost to purchase 2 boxes of candy, one containing s pounds of candy and the other containing t pounds of candy, from this catalog?

(A) $h + stv$
(B) $2h + stv$
(C) $2hstv$
(D) $2h + s + t + v$
(E) $2h + v(s + t)$

99. If $x \neq -\frac{1}{2}$, then $\frac{6x^3 + 3x^2 - 8x - 4}{2x + 1} =$

(A) $3x^2 + \frac{3}{2}x - 8$
(B) $3x^2 + \frac{3}{2}x - 4$
(C) $3x^2 - 4$
(D) $3x - 4$
(E) $3x + 4$

100. If $x^2 + bx + 5 = (x + c)^2$ for all numbers x, where b and c are positive constants, what is the value of b?

(A) $\sqrt{5}$
(B) $\sqrt{10}$
(C) $2\sqrt{5}$
(D) $2\sqrt{10}$
(E) 10

101. Last year Shannon listened to a certain public radio station 10 hours per week and contributed \$35 to the station. Of the following, which is closest to Shannon's contribution per minute of listening time last year?

(A) \$0.001
(B) \$0.010
(C) \$0.025
(D) \$0.058
(E) \$0.067

102. Each of the 20 employees at Company J is to receive an end-of-year bonus this year. Agnes will receive a larger bonus than any other employee, but only \$500 more than Cheryl will receive. None of the employees will receive a smaller bonus than Cheryl. If the amount of money to be distributed in bonuses at Company J this year totals \$60,000, what is the largest bonus Agnes can receive?

(A) \$3,250
(B) \$3,325
(C) \$3,400
(D) \$3,475
(E) \$3,500

103. Beth, Naomi, and Juan raised a total of \$55 for charity. Naomi raised \$5 less than Juan, and Juan raised twice as much as Beth. How much did Beth raise?

(A) \$9
(B) \$10
(C) \$12
(D) \$13
(E) \$15

104. The set of solutions for the equation $(x^2 - 25)^2 = x^2 - 10x + 25$ contains how many real numbers?

(A) 0
(B) 1
(C) 2
(D) 3
(E) 4

105. An aerosol can is designed so that its bursting pressure, *B*, in pounds per square inch, is 120% of the pressure, *F*, in pounds per square inch, to which it is initially filled. Which of the following formulas expresses the relationship between *B* and *F*?

(A) $B = 1.2F$
(B) $B = 120F$
(C) $B = 1 + 0.2F$
(D) $B = \frac{F}{1.2}$
(E) $B = \frac{1.2}{F}$

106. The average (arithmetic mean) of the positive integers *x*, *y*, and *z* is 3. If $x < y < z$, what is the greatest possible value of *z*?

(A) 5
(B) 6
(C) 7
(D) 8
(E) 9

107. The product of 3,305 and the 1-digit integer *x* is a 5-digit integer. The units (ones) digit of the product is 5 and the hundreds digit is *y*. If *A* is the set of all possible values of *x* and *B* is the set of all possible values of *y*, then which of the following gives the members of *A* and *B*?

	A	*B*
(A)	{1, 3, 5, 7, 9}	{0, 1, 2, 3, 4, 5, 6, 7, 8, 9}
(B)	{1, 3, 5, 7, 9}	{1, 3, 5, 7, 9}
(C)	{3, 5, 7, 9}	{1, 5, 7, 9}
(D)	{5, 7, 9}	{1, 5, 7}
(E)	{5, 7, 9}	{1, 5, 9}

108. If *x* and *y* are integers such that $2 < x \le 8$ and $2 < y \le 9$, what is the maximum value of $\frac{1}{x} - \frac{x}{y}$?

(A) $-3\frac{1}{8}$
(B) 0
(C) $\frac{1}{4}$
(D) $\frac{5}{18}$
(E) 2

109. Items that are purchased together at a certain discount store are priced at \$3 for the first item purchased and \$1 for each additional item purchased. What is the maximum number of items that could be purchased together for a total price that is less than \$30?

(A) 25
(B) 26
(C) 27
(D) 28
(E) 29

110. What is the least integer z for which $(0.000125)(0.0025)(0.00000125) \times 10^z$ is an integer?

(A) 18
(B) 10
(C) 0
(D) −10
(E) −18

111. The average (arithmetic mean) length per film for a group of 21 films is t minutes. If a film that runs for 66 minutes is removed from the group and replaced by one that runs for 52 minutes, what is the average length per film, in minutes, for the new group of films, in terms of t?

(A) $t+\frac{2}{3}$
(B) $t-\frac{2}{3}$
(C) $21t+14$
(D) $t+\frac{3}{2}$
(E) $t-\frac{3}{2}$

112. A garden center sells a certain grass seed in 5-pound bags at \$13.85 per bag, 10-pound bags at \$20.43 per bag, and 25-pound bags at \$32.25 per bag. If a customer is to buy at least 65 pounds of the grass seed, but no more than 80 pounds, what is the least possible cost of the grass seed that the customer will buy?

(A) \$94.03
(B) \$96.75
(C) \$98.78
(D) \$102.07
(E) \$105.36

113. If $x = -|w|$, which of the following must be true?

(A) $x = -w$
(B) $x = w$
(C) $x^2 = w$
(D) $x^2 = w^2$
(E) $x^3 = w^3$

114. A certain financial institution reported that its assets totaled \$2,377,366.30 on a certain day. Of this amount, \$31,724.54 was held in cash. Approximately what percent of the reported assets was held in cash on that day?

(A) 0.00013%
(B) 0.0013%
(C) 0.013%
(D) 0.13%
(E) 1.3%

$$\begin{array}{r} AB \\ +\ BA \\ \hline AAC \end{array}$$

115. In the correctly worked addition problem shown, where the sum of the two-digit positive integers *AB* and *BA* is the three-digit integer *AAC*, and *A*, *B*, and *C* are different digits, what is the units digit of the integer *AAC*?

(A) 9
(B) 6
(C) 3
(D) 2
(E) 0

116. The hard drive, monitor, and printer for a certain desktop computer system cost a total of \$2,500. The cost of the printer and monitor together is equal to $\frac{2}{3}$ of the cost of the hard drive. If the cost of the printer is \$100 more than the cost of the monitor, what is the cost of the printer?

(A) \$800
(B) \$600
(C) \$550
(D) \$500
(E) \$350

$$3r \leq 4s + 5$$
$$|s| \leq 5$$

117. Given the inequalities above, which of the following CANNOT be the value of *r*?

(A) −20
(B) −5
(C) 0
(D) 5
(E) 20

118. If *m* is an even integer, *v* is an odd integer, and $m > v > 0$, which of the following represents the number of even integers less than *m* and greater than *v*?

(A) $\frac{m-v}{2} - 1$
(B) $\frac{m-v-1}{2}$
(C) $\frac{m-v}{2}$
(D) $m - v - 1$
(E) $m - v$

119. A positive integer is divisible by 9 if and only if the sum of its digits is divisible by 9. If *n* is a positive integer, for which of the following values of *k* is $25 \times 10^n + k \times 10^{2n}$ divisible by 9?

(A) 9
(B) 16
(C) 23
(D) 35
(E) 47

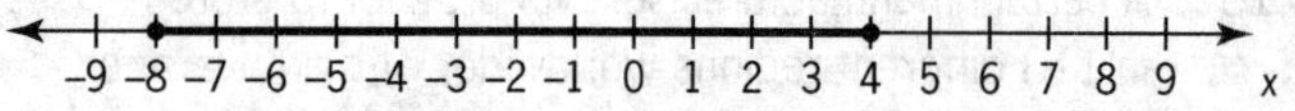

120. On the number line, the shaded interval is the graph of which of the following inequalities?

(A) $|x| \leq 4$
(B) $|x| \leq 8$
(C) $|x - 2| \leq 4$
(D) $|x - 2| \leq 6$
(E) $|x + 2| \leq 6$

121. Last year members of a certain professional organization for teachers consisted of teachers from 49 different school districts, with an average (arithmetic mean) of 9.8 schools per district. Last year the average number of teachers at these schools who were members of the organization was 22. Which of the following is closest to the total number of members of the organization last year?

(A) 10^7
(B) 10^6
(C) 10^5
(D) 10^4
(E) 10^3

122. Of all the students in a certain dormitory, $\frac{1}{2}$ are first-year students and the rest are second-year students. If $\frac{4}{5}$ of the first-year students have not declared a major and if the fraction of second-year students who have declared a major is 3 times the fraction of first-year students who have declared a major, what fraction of all the students in the dormitory are second-year students who have not declared a major?

(A) $\frac{1}{15}$
(B) $\frac{1}{5}$
(C) $\frac{4}{15}$
(D) $\frac{1}{3}$
(E) $\frac{2}{5}$

123. If the average (arithmetic mean) of *x*, *y*, and *z* is 7*x* and $x \neq 0$, what is the ratio of *x* to the sum of *y* and *z*?

(A) 1:21
(B) 1:20
(C) 1:6
(D) 6:1
(E) 20:1

124. Jonah drove the first half of a 100-mile trip in x hours and the second half in y hours. Which of the following is equal to Jonah's average speed, in miles per hour, for the entire trip?

(A) $\frac{50}{x+y}$

(B) $\frac{100}{x+y}$

(C) $\frac{25}{x}+\frac{25}{y}$

(D) $\frac{50}{x}+\frac{50}{y}$

(E) $\frac{100}{x}+\frac{100}{y}$

125. If the amount of federal estate tax due on an estate valued at $1.35 million is $437,000 plus 43 percent of the value of the estate in excess of $1.25 million, then the federal tax due is approximately what percent of the value of the estate?

A. 30%

B. 35%

C. 40%

D. 45%

E. 50%

$$7x + 6y \le 38,000$$
$$4x + 5y \le 28,000$$

126. A manufacturer wants to produce x balls and y boxes. Resource constraints require that x and y satisfy the inequalities shown. What is the maximum number of balls and boxes combined that can be produced given the resource constraints?

(A) 5,000

(B) 6,000

(C) 7,000

(D) 8,000

(E) 10,000

127. If $\frac{3}{10^4} = x\%$, then $x =$

(A) 0.3

(B) 0.03

(C) 0.003

(D) 0.0003

(E) 0.00003

128. What is the remainder when 3^{24} is divided by 5?

(A) 0

(B) 1

(C) 2

(D) 3

(E) 4

129. José has a collection of 100 coins, consisting of nickels, dimes, quarters, and half-dollars. If he has a total of 35 nickels and dimes, a total of 45 dimes and quarters, and a total of 50 nickels and quarters, how many half-dollars does he have?

(A) 15

(B) 20

(C) 25

(D) 30

(E) 35

130. David used part of $100,000 to purchase a house. Of the remaining portion, he invested $\frac{1}{3}$ of it at 4 percent simple annual interest and $\frac{2}{3}$ of it at 6 percent simple annual interest. If after a year the income from the two investments totaled $320, what was the purchase price of the house?

(A) $96,000

(B) $94,000

(C) $88,000

(D) $75,000

(E) $40,000

131. A certain manufacturer sells its product to stores in 113 different regions worldwide, with an average (arithmetic mean) of 181 stores per region. If last year these stores sold an average of 51,752 units of the manufacturer's product per store, which of the following is closest to the total number of units of the manufacturer's product sold worldwide last year?

(A) 10^6

(B) 10^7

(C) 10^8

(D) 10^9

(E) 10^{10}

132. Andrew started saving at the beginning of the year and had saved \$240 by the end of the year. He continued to save and by the end of 2 years had saved a total of \$540. Which of the following is closest to the percent increase in the amount Andrew saved during the second year compared to the amount he saved during the first year?

(A) 11%
(B) 25%
(C) 44%
(D) 56%
(E) 125%

133. If x is a positive integer, r is the remainder when x is divided by 4, and R is the remainder when x is divided by 9, what is the greatest possible value of $r^2 + R$?

(A) 25
(B) 21
(C) 17
(D) 13
(E) 11

134. Each of the nine digits 0, 1, 1, 4, 5, 6, 8, 8, and 9 is used once to form 3 three-digit integers. What is the greatest possible sum of the 3 integers?

(A) 1,752
(B) 2,616
(C) 2,652
(D) 2,775
(E) 2,958

135. Given that $1^2 + 2^2 + 3^2 + \ldots + 10^2 = 385$, what is the value of $3^2 + 6^2 + 9^2 + \ldots + 30^2$?

(A) 1,155
(B) 1,540
(C) 1,925
(D) 2,310
(E) 3,465

136. If water is leaking from a certain tank at a constant rate of 1,200 milliliters per hour, how many <u>seconds</u> does it take for 1 milliliter of water to leak from the tank?

(A) $\frac{1}{3}$
(B) $\frac{1}{2}$
(C) 2
(D) 3
(E) 20

137. When the positive integer k is divided by the positive integer n, the remainder is 11. If $\frac{k}{n} = 81.2$, what is the value of n?

(A) 9
(B) 20
(C) 55
(D) 70
(E) 81

138. The total area of a certain continent is approximately 3.8×10^{16} square inches. Which of the following is closest to the area of the continent, in square miles? (1 square mile is approximately 4.0×10^9 square inches.)

(A) 6.7×10^5
(B) 2.0×10^6
(C) 9.5×10^6
(D) 1.1×10^7
(E) 9.5×10^8

139. If $xy = 1$, what is the value of $\frac{2(x+y)^2}{2(x-y)^2}$?

(A) 2
(B) 4
(C) 8
(D) 16
(E) 32

140. Of the 20 members of a kitchen crew, 17 can use the meat-cutting machine, 18 can use the bread-slicing machine, and 15 can use both machines. If one member of the crew is to be chosen at random, what is the probability that the member chosen will be someone who cannot use either machine?

(A) 0
(B) $\frac{1}{10}$
(C) $\frac{1}{7}$
(D) $\frac{1}{4}$
(E) $\frac{1}{3}$

141. Which of the following is an integer?

I. $\frac{12!}{6!}$
II. $\frac{12!}{8!}$
III. $\frac{12!}{7!5!}$

(A) I only
(B) II only
(C) III only
(D) I and II only
(E) I, II, and III

142. The function f is defined for all nonzero x by the equation $f(x) = x - \frac{1}{x}$. If $x \neq 0$, which of the following equals $f\left(\frac{1}{x}\right)$?

(A) $f(x)$
(B) $f(-x)$
(C) $f\left(-\frac{1}{x}\right)$
(D) $\frac{1}{f(x)}$
(E) $-\frac{1}{f(x)}$

143. In the arithmetic sequence $t_1, t_2, t_3, \ldots, t_n, \ldots$, $t_1 = 23$ and $t_n = t_{n-1} - 3$ for each $n > 1$. What is the value of n when $t_n = -4$?

(A) −1
(B) 7
(C) 10
(D) 14
(E) 20

144. How many seconds will it take for a car that is traveling at a constant rate of 45 miles per hour to travel a distance of 220 yards? (1 mile = 1,760 yards)

(A) 8
(B) 9
(C) 10
(D) 11
(E) 12

145. A store's selling price of $2,240 for a certain computer would yield a profit of 40 percent of the store's cost for the computer. What selling price would yield a profit of 50 percent of the computer's cost?

(A) $2,400
(B) $2,464
(C) $2,650
(D) $2,732
(E) $2,800

146. If a certain coin is flipped, the probability that the coin will land heads up is $\frac{1}{2}$. If the coin is flipped 5 times, what is the probability that it will land heads up on the first 3 flips and not on the last 2 flips?

(A) $\frac{3}{5}$
(B) $\frac{1}{2}$
(C) $\frac{1}{5}$
(D) $\frac{1}{8}$
(E) $\frac{1}{32}$

147. The operation ⊗ is defined for all nonzero numbers a and b by $a \otimes b = \frac{a}{b} - \frac{b}{a}$. If x and y are nonzero numbers, which of the following statements must be true?

I. $x \otimes xy = x(1 \otimes y)$
II. $x \otimes y = -(y \otimes x)$
III. $\frac{1}{x} \otimes \frac{1}{y} = y \otimes x$

(A) I only
(B) II only
(C) III only
(D) I and II
(E) II and III

148. If each term in the sum $a_1 + a_2 + \ldots + a_n$ is either 7 or 77 and the sum equals 350, which of the following could be equal to n?

(A) 38
(B) 39
(C) 40
(D) 41
(E) 42

149. $(1.00001)(0.99999) - (1.00002)(0.99998) =$

(A) 0
(B) 10^{-10}
(C) $3(10^{-10})$
(D) 10^{-5}
(E) $3(10^{-5})$

150. A certain rectangular photograph has an area of $6\frac{1}{2}$ square feet. What is the area of the photograph in square inches? (1 foot = 12 inches)

(A) 36
(B) 78
(C) 432
(D) 864
(E) 936

151. The toll for crossing a certain bridge is \$0.75 each crossing. Drivers who frequently use the bridge may instead purchase a sticker each month for \$13.00 and then pay only \$0.30 each crossing during that month. If a particular driver will cross the bridge twice on each of x days next month and will not cross the bridge on any other day, what is the least value of x for which this driver can save money by using the sticker?

(A) 14
(B) 15
(C) 16
(D) 28
(E) 29

Questions 152 to 207 — Difficulty: Hard

152. Two numbers differ by 2 and sum to S. Which of the following is the greater of the numbers in terms of S?

(A) $\frac{S}{2} - 1$
(B) $\frac{S}{2}$
(C) $\frac{S}{2} + \frac{1}{2}$
(D) $\frac{S}{2} + 1$
(E) $\frac{S}{2} + 2$

153. If m is an integer and $m = 10^{32} - 32$, what is the sum of the digits of m?

(A) 257
(B) 264
(C) 275
(D) 284
(E) 292

154. In a numerical table with 10 rows and 10 columns, each entry is either a 9 or a 10. If the number of 9s in the nth row is $n - 1$ for each n from 1 to 10, what is the average (arithmetic mean) of all the numbers in the table?

(A) 9.45
(B) 9.50
(C) 9.55
(D) 9.65
(E) 9.70

155. In 2004, the cost of 1 year-long print subscription to a certain newspaper was \$4 per week. In 2005, the newspaper introduced a new rate plan for 1 year-long print subscription: \$3 per week for the first 40 weeks of 2005 and \$2 per week for the remaining weeks of 2005. How much less did 1 year-long print subscription to this newspaper cost in 2005 than in 2004?

(A) \$64
(B) \$78
(C) \$112
(D) \$144
(E) \$304

156. A positive integer n is a perfect number provided that the sum of all the positive factors of n, including 1 and n, is equal to $2n$. What is the sum of the reciprocals of all the positive factors of the perfect number 28?

(A) $\frac{1}{4}$
(B) $\frac{56}{27}$
(C) 2
(D) 3
(E) 4

157. The infinite sequence $a_1, a_2, \dots, a_n, \dots$ is such that $a_1 = 2$, $a_2 = -3$, $a_3 = 5$, $a_4 = -1$, and $a_n = a_{n-4}$ for $n > 4$. What is the sum of the first 97 terms of the sequence?

(A) 72
(B) 74
(C) 75
(D) 78
(E) 80

158. The sequence $a_1, a_2, \dots a_n, \dots$ is such that $a_n = 2a_{n-1} - x$ for all positive integers $n \geq 2$ and for a certain number x. If $a_5 = 99$ and $a_3 = 27$, what is the value of x?

(A) 3
(B) 9
(C) 18
(D) 36
(E) 45

159. In a certain medical survey, 45 percent of the people surveyed had the type A antigen in their blood and 3 percent had both the type A antigen and the type B antigen. Which of the following is closest to the percent of those with the type A antigen who also had the type B antigen?

(A) 1.35%
(B) 6.67%
(C) 13.50%
(D) 15.00%
(E) 42.00%

160. On a certain transatlantic crossing, 20 percent of a ship's passengers held round-trip tickets and also took their cars aboard the ship. If 60 percent of the passengers with round-trip tickets did not take their cars aboard the ship, what percent of the ship's passengers held round-trip tickets?

(A) $33\frac{1}{3}\%$
(B) 40%
(C) 50%
(D) 60%
(E) $66\frac{2}{3}\%$

161. If x and k are integers and $(12^x)(4^{2x+1}) = (2^k)(3^2)$, what is the value of k?

(A) 5
(B) 7
(C) 10
(D) 12
(E) 14

162. If S is the sum of the reciprocals of the 10 consecutive integers from 21 to 30, then S is between which of the following two fractions?

(A) $\frac{1}{3}$ and $\frac{1}{2}$
(B) $\frac{1}{4}$ and $\frac{1}{3}$
(C) $\frac{1}{5}$ and $\frac{1}{4}$
(D) $\frac{1}{6}$ and $\frac{1}{5}$
(E) $\frac{1}{7}$ and $\frac{1}{6}$

163. For every even positive integer m, $f(m)$ represents the product of all even integers from 2 to m, inclusive. For example, $f(12) = 2 \times 4 \times 6 \times 8 \times 10 \times 12$. What is the greatest prime factor of $f(24)$?

(A) 23
(B) 19
(C) 17
(D) 13
(E) 11

$$3,\ k,\ 2,\ 8,\ m,\ 3$$

164. The arithmetic mean of the list of numbers above is 4. If k and m are integers and $k \neq m$, what is the median of the list?

(A) 2
(B) 2.5
(C) 3
(D) 3.5
(E) 4

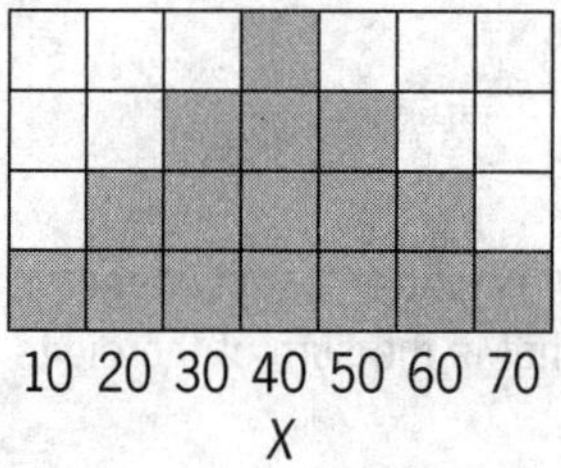

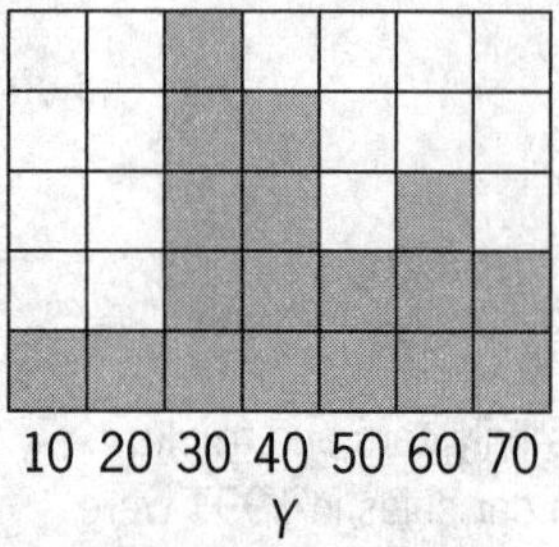

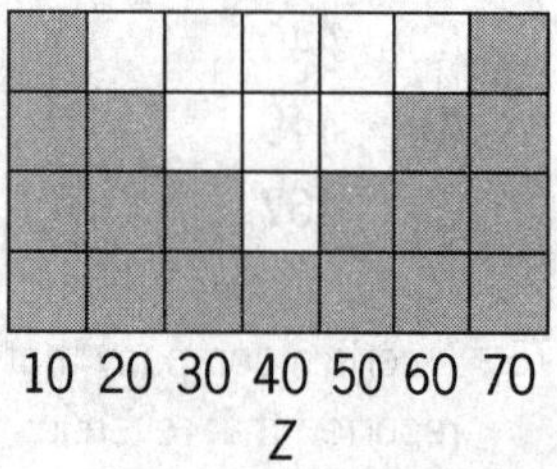

165. If the variables X, Y, and Z take on only the values 10, 20, 30, 40, 50, 60, or 70 with frequencies indicated by the shaded regions above, for which of the frequency distributions is the mean equal to the median?

(A) X only
(B) Y only
(C) Z only
(D) X and Y
(E) X and Z

$$2x + y = 12$$
$$|y| \leq 12$$

166. For how many ordered pairs (x, y) that are solutions of the system above are x and y both integers?

(A) 7
(B) 10
(C) 12
(D) 13
(E) 14

167. The United States Mint produces coins in 1-cent, 5-cent, 10-cent, 25-cent, and 50-cent denominations. If a jar contains exactly 100 cents worth of these coins, which of the following could be the total number of coins in the jar?

I. 91
II. 81
III. 76

(A) I only
(B) II only
(C) III only
(D) I and III only
(E) I, II, and III

168. A certain university will select 1 of 7 candidates eligible to fill a position in the mathematics department and 2 of 10 candidates eligible to fill 2 identical positions in the computer science department. If none of the candidates is eligible for a position in both departments, how many different sets of 3 candidates are there to fill the 3 positions?

(A) 42
(B) 70
(C) 140
(D) 165
(E) 315

169. A survey of employers found that during 1993 employment costs rose 3.5 percent, where employment costs consist of salary costs and fringe-benefit costs. If salary costs rose 3 percent and fringe-benefit costs rose 5.5 percent during 1993, then fringe-benefit costs represented what percent of employment costs at the beginning of 1993?

(A) 16.5%
(B) 20%
(C) 35%
(D) 55%
(E) 65%

170. The subsets of the set {*w*, *x*, *y*} are {*w*}, {*x*}, {*y*}, {*w*, *x*}, {*w*, *y*}, {*x*, *y*}, {*w*, *x*, *y*}, and { } (the empty subset). How many subsets of the set {*w*, *x*, *y*, *z*} contain *w*?

(A) Four
(B) Five
(C) Seven
(D) Eight
(E) Sixteen

171. The number $\sqrt{63-36\sqrt{3}}$ can be expressed as $x+y\sqrt{3}$ for some integers *x* and *y*. What is the value of *xy*?

(A) −18
(B) −6
(C) 6
(D) 18
(E) 27

172. There are 10 books on a shelf, of which 4 are paperbacks and 6 are hardbacks. How many possible selections of 5 books from the shelf contain at least one paperback and at least one hardback?

(A) 75
(B) 120
(C) 210
(D) 246
(E) 252

173. If *x* is to be chosen at random from the set {1, 2, 3, 4} and *y* is to be chosen at random from the set {5, 6, 7}, what is the probability that *xy* will be even?

(A) $\frac{1}{6}$
(B) $\frac{1}{3}$
(C) $\frac{1}{2}$
(D) $\frac{2}{3}$
(E) $\frac{5}{6}$

174. The function *f* is defined for each positive three-digit integer *n* by $f(n) = 2^x 3^y 5^z$, where *x*, *y*, and *z* are the hundreds, tens, and units digits of *n*, respectively. If *m* and *v* are three-digit positive integers such that $f(m) = 9f(v)$, then $m - v =$

(A) 8
(B) 9
(C) 18
(C) 20
(E) 80

175. If $10^{50} - 74$ is written as an integer in base 10 notation, what is the sum of the digits in that integer?

(A) 424
(B) 433
(C) 440
(D) 449
(E) 467

176. A certain company that sells only cars and trucks reported that revenues from car sales in 1997 were down 11 percent from 1996 and revenues from truck sales in 1997 were up 7 percent from 1996. If total revenues from car sales and truck sales in 1997 were up 1 percent from 1996, what is the ratio of revenue from car sales in 1996 to revenue from truck sales in 1996?

(A) 1:2
(B) 4:5
(C) 1:1
(D) 3:2
(E) 5:3

177. Becky rented a power tool from a rental shop. The rent for the tool was \$12 for the first hour and \$3 for each additional hour. If Becky paid a total of \$27, excluding sales tax, to rent the tool, for how many hours did she rent it?

(A) 5
(B) 6
(C) 9
(D) 10
(E) 12

178. If $4 < \frac{7-x}{3}$, which of the following must be true?

I. $5 < x$
II. $|x+3| > 2$
III. $-(x+5)$ is positive.

(A) II only
(B) III only
(C) I and II only
(D) II and III only
(E) I, II, and III

179. On a certain day, a bakery produced a batch of rolls at a total production cost of \$300. On that day, $\frac{4}{5}$ of the rolls in the batch were sold, each at a price that was 50 percent greater than the average (arithmetic mean) production cost per roll. The remaining rolls in the batch were sold the next day, each at a price that was 20 percent less than the price of the day before. What was the bakery's profit on this batch of rolls?

(A) \$150
(B) \$144
(C) \$132
(D) \$108
(E) \$90

180. A set of numbers has the property that for any number t in the set, $t + 2$ is in the set. If –1 is in the set, which of the following must also be in the set?

I. –3
II. 1
III. 5

(A) I only
(B) II only
(C) I and II only
(D) II and III only
(E) I, II, and III

181. A couple decides to have 4 children. If they succeed in having 4 children and each child is equally likely to be a boy or a girl, what is the probability that they will have exactly 2 girls and 2 boys?

(A) $\frac{3}{8}$
(B) $\frac{1}{4}$
(C) $\frac{3}{16}$
(D) $\frac{1}{8}$
(E) $\frac{1}{16}$

182. The closing price of Stock X changed on each trading day last month. The percent change in the closing price of Stock X from the first trading day last month to each of the other trading days last month was less than 50 percent. If the closing price on the second trading day last month was \$10.00, which of the following CANNOT be the closing price on the last trading day last month?

(A) \$3.00
(B) \$9.00
(C) \$19.00
(D) \$24.00
(E) \$29.00

183. How many different positive integers are factors of 441?

(A) 4
(B) 6
(C) 7
(D) 9
(E) 11

184. If n is a positive integer and n^2 is divisible by 72, then the largest positive integer that must divide n is

(A) 6
(B) 12
(C) 24
(D) 36
(E) 48

185. A certain grocery purchased x pounds of produce for p dollars per pound. If y pounds of the produce had to be discarded due to spoilage and the grocery sold the rest for s dollars per pound, which of the following represents the gross profit on the sale of the produce?

(A) $(x - y)s - xp$
(B) $(x - y)p - ys$
(C) $(s - p)y - xp$
(D) $xp - ys$
(E) $(x - y)(s - p)$

186. If x, y, and z are positive integers such that x is a factor of y, and x is a multiple of z, which of the following is NOT necessarily an integer?

(A) $\frac{x+z}{z}$
(B) $\frac{y+z}{x}$
(C) $\frac{x+y}{z}$
(D) $\frac{xy}{z}$
(E) $\frac{yz}{x}$

187. Running at their respective constant rates, Machine X takes 2 days longer to produce w widgets than Machine Y. At these rates, if the two machines together produce $\frac{5}{4}w$ widgets in 3 days, how many days would it take Machine X alone to produce $2w$ widgets?

(A) 4
(B) 6
(C) 8
(D) 10
(E) 12

188. What is the greatest positive integer n such that 5^n divides $10! - (2)(5!)^2$?

(A) 2
(B) 3
(C) 4
(D) 5
(E) 6

189. Yesterday, Candice and Sabrina trained for a bicycle race by riding around an oval track. They both began riding at the same time from the track's starting point. However, Candice rode at a faster pace than Sabrina, completing each lap around the track in 42 seconds, while Sabrina completed each lap around the track in 46 seconds. How many laps around the track had Candice completed the next time that Candice and Sabrina were together at the starting point?

(A) 21
(B) 23
(C) 42
(D) 46
(E) 483

190. If $n = 9! - 6^4$, which of the following is the greatest integer k such that 3^k is a factor of n?

(A) 1
(B) 3
(C) 4
(D) 6
(E) 8

191. The integer 120 has many factorizations. For example, $120 = (2)(60)$, $120 = (3)(4)(10)$, and $120 = (-1)(-3)(4)(10)$. In how many of the factorizations of 120 are the factors consecutive integers in ascending order?

(A) 2
(B) 3
(C) 4
(D) 5
(E) 6

192. Jorge's bank statement showed a balance that was \$0.54 greater than what his records showed. He discovered that he had written a check for \$*x.yz* and had recorded it as \$*x.zy*, where each of *x*, *y*, and *z* represents a digit from 0 though 9. Which of the following could be the value of *z*?

(A) 2
(B) 3
(C) 4
(D) 5
(E) 6

193. One side of a parking stall is defined by a straight stripe that consists of *n* painted sections of equal length with an unpainted section $\frac{1}{2}$ as long between each pair of consecutive painted sections. The total length of the stripe from the beginning of the first painted section to the end of the last painted section is 203 inches. If *n* is an integer and the length, in inches, of each unpainted section is an integer greater than 2, what is the value of *n*?

(A) 5
(B) 9
(C) 10
(D) 14
(E) 29

194. This year, Henry will save a certain amount of his income, and he will spend the rest. Next year, Henry will have no income, but for each dollar that he saves this year, he will have $1 + r$ dollars available to spend. In terms of *r*, what fraction of his income should Henry save this year so that next year the amount he has available to spend will be equal to half the amount that he spends this year?

(A) $\frac{1}{r} + 2$
(B) $\frac{1}{2r} + 2$
(C) $\frac{1}{3r} + 2$
(D) $\frac{1}{r} + 3$
(E) $\frac{1}{2r} + 3$

Machine	Consecutive Minutes Machine Is Off	Units of Power When On
A	17	15
B	14	18
C	11	12

195. At a certain factory, each of Machines A, B, and C is periodically on for exactly 1 minute and periodically off for a fixed number of consecutive minutes. The table above shows that Machine A is on and uses 15 units of power every 18th minute, Machine B is on and uses 18 units of power every 15th minute, and Machine C is on and uses 12 units of power every 12th minute. The factory has a backup generator that operates only when the total power usage of the 3 machines exceeds 30 units of power. What is the time interval, in minutes, between consecutive times the backup generator begins to operate?

(A) 36
(B) 63
(C) 90
(D) 180
(E) 270

196. In a certain region, the number of children who have been vaccinated against rubella is twice the number who have been vaccinated against mumps. The number who have been vaccinated against both is twice the number who have been vaccinated only against mumps. If 5,000 have been vaccinated against both, how many have been vaccinated only against rubella?

(A) 2,500
(B) 7,500
(C) 10,000
(D) 15,000
(E) 17,500

197. Three boxes of supplies have an average (arithmetic mean) weight of 7 kilograms and a median weight of 9 kilograms. What is the maximum possible weight, in kilograms, of the lightest box?

(A) 1
(B) 2
(C) 3
(D) 4
(E) 5

Stock	Number of Shares
V	68
W	112
X	56
Y	94
Z	45

198. The table shows the number of shares of each of the 5 stocks owned by Mr. Sami. If Mr. Sami were to sell 20 shares of Stock *X* and buy 24 shares of Stock *Y*, what would be the increase in the range of the numbers of shares of the 5 stocks owned by Mr. Sami?

(A) 4
(B) 6
(C) 9
(D) 15
(E) 20

199. Last year, sales at Company *X* were 10% greater in February than in January, 15% less in March than in February, 20% greater in April than in March, 10% less in May than in April, and 5% greater in June than in May. In which month were sales closest to the sales in January?

(A) February
(B) March
(C) April
(D) May
(E) June

200. If s and t are integers greater than 1 and each is a factor of the integer n, which of the following must be a factor of n^{st}?

I. s^t
II. $(st)^2$
III. $s + t$

(A) None
(B) I only
(C) II only
(D) III only
(E) I and II

201. How many 4-digit positive integers are there in which all 4 digits are even?

(A) 625
(B) 600
(C) 500
(D) 400
(E) 256

202. If $0 < r < 1 < s < 2$, which of the following must be less than 1?

I. $\frac{r}{s}$
II. rs
III. $s - r$

(A) I only
(B) II only
(C) III only
(D) I and II
(E) I and III

203. Last month, 15 homes were sold in Town X. The average (arithmetic mean) sale price of the homes was \$150,000 and the median sale price was \$130,000. Which of the following statements must be true?

I. At least one of the homes was sold for more than \$165,000.

II. At least one of the homes was sold for more than \$130,000 and less than \$150,000.

III. At least one of the homes was sold for less than \$130,000.

(A) I only
(B) II only
(C) III only
(D) I and II
(E) I and III

204. Pumps A, B, and C operate at their respective constant rates. Pumps A and B, operating simultaneously, can fill a certain tank in $\frac{6}{5}$ hours; Pumps A and C, operating simultaneously, can fill the tank in $\frac{3}{2}$ hours; and Pumps B and C, operating simultaneously, can fill the tank in 2 hours. How many hours does it take Pumps A, B, and C, operating simultaneously, to fill the tank?

(A) $\frac{1}{3}$
(B) $\frac{1}{2}$
(C) $\frac{2}{3}$
(D) $\frac{5}{6}$
(E) 1

205. If n is a positive integer, then $(-2^n)^{-2} + (2^{-n})^2 =$

(A) 0
(B) 2^{-2n}
(C) 2^{2n}
(D) 2^{-2n+1}
(E) 2^{2n+1}

206. Which of the following is equal to $\left(\frac{2\sqrt[3]{3}}{\sqrt{2}}\right)^3$?

(A) $\frac{3\sqrt{2}}{2}$
(B) $3\sqrt{2}$
(C) $6\sqrt{2}$
(D) 12
(E) $12\sqrt{2}$

207. Dara ran on a treadmill that had a readout indicating the time remaining in her exercise session. When the readout indicated 24 min 18 sec, she had completed 10% of her exercise session. The readout indicated which of the following when she had completed 40% of her exercise session?

(A) 10 min 48 sec
(B) 14 min 52 sec
(C) 14 min 58 sec
(D) 16 min 6 sec
(E) 16 min 12 sec

4.3 Answer Key

1. A	32. C	63. B	94. E	125. B
2. D	33. A	64. C	95. D	126. B
3. A	34. E	65. A	96. E	127. B
4. D	35. D	66. E	97. E	128. B
5. C	36. D	67. C	98. E	129. E
6. C	37. C	68. C	99. C	130. B
7. A	38. A	69. D	100. C	131. D
8. D	39. B	70. B	101. A	132. B
9. C	40. C	71. C	102. D	133. C
10. C	41. A	72. D	103. C	134. C
11. C	42. D	73. B	104. D	135. E
12. E	43. B	74. A	105. A	136. D
13. D	44. C	75. B	106. B	137. C
14. D	45. C	76. D	107. D	138. C
15. C	46. E	77. B	108. B	139. D
16. D	47. B	78. B	109. C	140. A
17. B	48. B	79. C	110. A	141. E
18. D	49. D	80. D	111. B	142. B
19. D	50. D	81. A	112. B	143. C
20. D	51. C	82. D	113. D	144. C
21. B	52. B	83. A	114. E	145. A
22. A	53. A	84. A	115. E	146. E
23. C	54. C	85. B	116. C	147. E
24. D	55. C	86. A	117. E	148. C
25. B	56. A	87. E	118. B	149. C
26. D	57. D	88. E	119. E	150. E
27. E	58. B	89. C	120. E	151. B
28. D	59. E	90. D	121. D	152. D
29. D	60. B	91. D	122. B	153. D
30. C	61. E	92. E	123. B	154. C
31. A	62. D	93. D	124. B	155. A

156. C	167. D	178. D	189. B	200. E
157. B	168. E	179. C	190. D	201. C
158. A	169. B	180. D	191. C	202. A
159. B	170. D	181. A	192. E	203. A
160. C	171. A	182. A	193. C	204. E
161. E	172. D	183. D	194. E	205. D
162. A	173. D	184. B	195. C	206. C
163. E	174. D	185. A	196. C	207. E
164. C	175. C	186. B	197. C	
165. E	176. A	187. E	198. D	
166. D	177. B	188. D	199. D	

4.4 Answer Explanations

The following discussion is intended to familiarize you with the most efficient and effective approaches to the kinds of problems common to Problem-Solving questions. The particular questions in this chapter are generally representative of the kinds of problem-solving questions you will encounter on the GMAT exam. Remember that it is the problem-solving strategy that is important, not the specific details of a particular question.

Questions 1 to 82 — Difficulty: Easy

1. Working at a constant rate, a copy machine makes 20 copies of a one-page document per minute. If the machine works at this constant rate, how many hours does it take to make 4,800 copies of a one-page document?

(A) 4
(B) 5
(C) 6
(D) 7
(E) 8

Arithmetic Rate

The copy machine produces 20 copies of the one-page document each minute. Because there are 60 minutes in an hour, the constant rate of 20 copies per minute is equal to $60 \times 20 = 1{,}200$ copies per hour. With the machine working at this rate, the amount of time that it takes to produce 4,800 copies of the document is

$$\frac{4800\ \textit{copies}}{1200\ \frac{\textit{copies}}{\textit{hour}}} = 4\text{ hours.}$$

The correct answer is A.

2. If $x + y = 2$ and $x^2 + y^2 = 2$, what is the value of xy?

(A) –2
(B) –1
(C) 0
(D) 1
(E) 2

Algebra Second-Degree Equations

$x + y = 2$	given
$y = 2 - x$	subtract x from both sides
$x^2 + (2 - x)^2 = 2$	substitute $y = 2 - x$ into $x^2 + y^2 = 2$
$2x^2 - 4x + 4 = 2$	expand and combine like terms
$2x^2 - 4x + 2 = 0$	subtract 2 from both sides
$x^2 - 2x + 1 = 0$	divide both sides by 2
$(x - 1)(x - 1) = 0$	factor
$x = 1$	set each factor equal to 0
$y = 1$	use $x = 1$ and $y = 2 - x$
$xy = 1$	multiply 1 and 1

Alternatively, the value of xy can be found by first squaring both sides of the equation $x + y = 2$.

$x + y = 2$	given
$(x + y)^2 = 4$	square both sides
$x^2 + 2xy + y^2 = 4$	expand and combine like terms
$2 + 2xy = 4$	replace $x^2 + y^2$ with 2
$2xy = 2$	subtract 2 from both sides
$xy = 1$	divide both sides by 2

The correct answer is D.

3. The sum S of the first n consecutive positive even integers is given by $S = n(n + 1)$. For what value of n is this sum equal to 110?

(A) 10
(B) 11
(C) 12
(D) 13
(E) 14

Algebra Factoring

Given that the sum of the first n even numbers is $n(n + 1)$, the sum is equal to 110 when $110 = n(n + 1)$. To find the value of n in this case, we need to find the two consecutive integers whose product is 110. These integers are 10 and 11; $10 \times 11 = 110$. The smaller of these numbers is n.

The correct answer is A.

4. $6(87.30 + 0.65) - 5(87.30) =$

(A) 3.90
(B) 39.00
(C) 90.90
(D) 91.20
(E) 91.85

Arithmetic Factors, Multiples, and Divisibility

This question is most efficiently answered by distributing the 6 over 87.30 and 0.65, and then combining the terms that contain a factor of 87.30, as follows:

$6(87.30 + 0.65) - 5(87.30) = 6(87.30) + 6(0.65) - 5\,(87.30) = (6 - 5)\,87.30 + 6(0.65) = 87.30 + 3.90 = 91.20$

The correct answer is D.

5. What is the value of $x^2yz - xyz^2$, if $x = -2$, $y = 1$, and $z = 3$?

(A) 20
(B) 24
(C) 30
(D) 32
(E) 48

Algebra Operations on Integers

Given that $x = -2$, $y = 1$, and $z = 3$, it follows by substitution that

$$\begin{aligned} x^2yz - xyz^2 &= (-2)^2(1)(3) - (-2)(1)(3^2) \\ &= (4)(1)(3) - (-2)(1)(9) \\ &= 12 - (-18) \\ &= 12 + 18 \\ &= 30 \end{aligned}$$

The correct answer is C.

6. If T is a set of 35 consecutive integers, of which 17 are negative, what is the sum of all the integers in T?

(A) −2
(B) −1
(C) 0
(D) 1
(E) 2

Arithmetic Properties of Numbers

The only set of 35 consecutive integers of which exactly 17 are negative is $\{-17, -16, -15, \ldots, 0, \ldots, 15, 16, 17\}$. The sum of these integers is $(-17 + 17) + (-16 + 16) + (-15 + 15) + \ldots + 0 = 0 + 0 + 0 + \ldots + 0 = 0$.

The correct answer is C.

7. If $x > y$ and $y > z$, which of the following represents the greatest number?

(A) $x - z$
(B) $x - y$
(C) $y - x$
(D) $z - y$
(E) $z - x$

Algebra Inequalities

From $x > y$ and $y > z$, it follows that $x > z$. These inequalities imply the following about the differences that are given in the answer choices:

Answer choice	Difference	Algebraic sign	Reason
A	$x - z$	positive	$x > z$ implies $x - z > 0$
B	$x - y$	positive	$x > y$ implies $x - y > 0$
C	$y - x$	negative	$x - y > 0$ implies $y - x < 0$
D	$z - y$	negative	$y > z$ implies $0 > z - y$
E	$z - x$	negative	$x - z > 0$ implies $z - x < 0$

Since the expressions in A and B represent positive numbers and the expressions in C, D, and E represent negative numbers, the latter can be eliminated because every negative number is less than every positive number. To determine which of $x - z$ and $x - y$ is greater, consider the placement of points with coordinates x, y, and z on the number line.

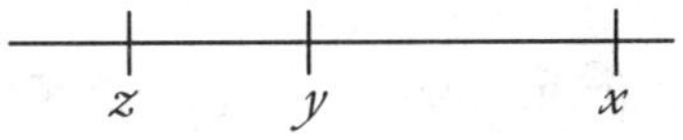

The distance between x and z (that is, $x - z$) is the sum of the distance between x and y (that is, $x - y$) and the distance between y and z (that is, $y - z$). Therefore, $(x - z) > (x - y)$, which means that $x - z$ represents the greater of the numbers represented by $(x - z)$ and $(x - y)$. Thus, $x - z$ represents the greatest of the numbers represented by the answer choices.

Alternatively,

$y > z$	given
$-y < -z$	multiply both sides by -1
$x - y < x - z$	add x to both sides

Thus, $x - z$ represents the greater of the numbers represented by $(x - z)$ and $(x - y)$. Therefore, $x - z$ represents the greatest of the numbers represented by the answer choices.

The correct answer is A.

8. 38, 69, 22, 73, 31, 47, 13, 82

Which of the following numbers is greater than three-fourths of the numbers but less than one-fourth of the numbers in the list above?

(A) 56
(B) 68
(C) 69
(D) 71
(E) 73

Arithmetic Order

Let's rearrange the eight numbers in the list from least to greatest: 13, 22, 31, 38, 47, 69, 73, 82. A number greater than three-fourths of them will be greater than each of the first six but less than either of the last two. Thus, this number must be greater than 69 but less than 73. Among the answer options, only the number 71 meets this condition.

The correct answer is D.

9. A rug manufacturer produces rugs at a cost of \$75 per rug. What is the manufacturer's gross profit from the sale of 150 rugs if $\frac{2}{3}$ of the rugs are sold for \$150 per rug and the rest are sold for \$200 per rug?

(A) \$10,350
(B) \$11,250
(C) \$13,750
(D) \$16,250
(E) \$17,800

Arithmetic Applied Problems; Proportions

The gross profit from the sale of 150 rugs is equal to the revenue from the sale of the rugs minus the cost of producing them. For $\frac{2}{3}$ of the 150 rugs—100 of them—the gross profit per rug is $\$150 - \$75 = \$75$. For the remaining 50 rugs, the gross profit per rug is $\$200 - \$75 = \$125$. The gross profit from the sale of the 150 rugs is therefore $100 \times \$75 + 50 \times \$125 = \$13{,}750$.

The correct answer is C.

10. The value of Maureen's investment portfolio has decreased by 5.8 percent since her initial investment in the portfolio. If her initial investment was \$16,800, what is the current value of the portfolio?

(A) \$7,056.00
(B) \$14,280.00
(C) \$15,825.60
(D) \$16,702.56
(E) \$17,774.40

Arithmetic Percents

Maureen's initial investment was \$16,800, and it has decreased by 5.8%. Its current value is therefore (100% – 5.8%) = 94.2% of \$16,800, which is equal to $0.942 \times \$16{,}800$. To make the multiplication simpler, this can be expressed as $\$(942 \times 16.8)$. Thus multiplying, we obtain the result of \$15,825.60.

The correct answer is C.

11. Company C produces toy trucks at a cost of \$5.00 each for the first 100 trucks and \$3.50 for each additional truck. If 500 toy trucks were produced by Company C and sold for \$10.00 each, what was Company C's gross profit?

(A) \$2,250
(B) \$2,500
(C) \$3,100
(D) \$3,250
(E) \$3,500

Arithmetic Applied Problems

The company's gross profit on the 500 toy trucks is the company's revenue from selling the trucks minus the company's cost of producing the trucks. The revenue is (500)(\$10.00) = \$5,000. The cost for the first 100 trucks is (100)(\$5.00) = \$500, and the cost for the other 400 trucks is (400)(\$3.50) = \$1,400 for a total cost of \$500 + \$1,400 = \$1,900. Thus, the company's gross profit is \$5,000 – \$1,900 = \$3,100.

The correct answer is C.

	Profit or Loss (in millions of dollars)				
Division	1991	1992	1993	1994	1995
A	1.1	(3.4)	1.9	2.0	0.6
B	(2.3)	5.5	(4.5)	3.9	(2.9)
C	10.0	(6.6)	5.3	1.1	(3.0)

12. The annual profit or loss for the three divisions of Company T for the years 1991 through 1995 are summarized in the table shown, where losses are enclosed in parentheses. For which division and which three consecutive years shown was the division's profit or loss for the three-year period closest to \$0?

(A) Division *A* for 1991–1993
(B) Division *A* for 1992–1994
(C) Division *B* for 1991–1993
(D) Division *B* for 1993–1995
(E) Division *C* for 1992–1994

Arithmetic Applied Problems

For completeness, the table shows all 9 of the profit or loss amounts, in millions of dollars, for each of the 3 divisions and the 3 three-year periods.

	1991–1993	1992–1994	1993–1995
A	–0.4	0.5	4.5
B	–1.3	4.9	–3.5
C	8.7	**–0.2**	3.4

The correct answer is E.

13. A computer appliance dealer bought a computer at a wholesale price of \$500 and then sold it at a 20 percent discount off the suggested retail price. If the dealer made a 12 percent profit on the wholesale price, what was the suggested retail price of the computer?

(A) \$560
(B) \$580
(C) \$660
(D) \$700
(E) \$730

Arithmetic Applied Problems

The dealer's profit of 12 percent of the \$500 wholesale price was $0.12 \times \$500 = \$60$. Thus, the dealer sold the computer for \$500 + \$60 = \$560. Since this sale was at a 20 percent discount off the suggested retail price, \$560 was 80 percent $\left(\frac{4}{5}\right)$ of the suggested retail price. Therefore, the suggested retail price was $\frac{\$560}{0.8} = \$700$.

The correct answer is D.

14. Pat invested x dollars in a fund that paid 8 percent annual interest, compounded annually. Which of the following represents the value, in dollars, of Pat's investment plus interest at the end of 5 years?

(A) 5(0.08x)
(B) 5(1.08x)
(C) [1 + 5(0.08)]x
(D) $(1.08)^5x$
(E) $(1.08x)^5$

Arithmetic Applied Problems

The formula for the compound interest earned on a principal x over n periods at percent rate r is $\left(1+\frac{r}{100}\right)^n x - x$. For Pat's investment, that means the compound interest in dollars over 5 years is $(1.08)^5x - x$. The total dollar value of Pat's investment includes the principal x plus the compound interest, so the total dollar value after 5 years is $((1.08)^5x - x) + x = (1.08)^5x$.

The correct answer is D.

15. There are five sales agents in a certain real estate office. One month Andy sold twice as many properties as Ellen, Bob sold 3 more than Ellen, Cary sold twice as many as Bob, and Dora sold as many as Bob and Ellen together. Who sold the most properties that month?

(A) Andy
(B) Bob
(C) Cary
(D) Dora
(E) Ellen

Algebra Order

Let x represent the number of properties that Ellen sold, where $x \geq 0$. Then, since Andy sold twice as many properties as Ellen, $2x$ represents the number of properties that Andy sold. Bob sold 3 more properties than Ellen, so $(x + 3)$ represents the number of properties that Bob sold. Cary sold twice as many properties as Bob, so $2(x + 3) = (2x + 6)$ represents the number of properties that Cary sold. Finally, Dora sold as many properties as Bob and Ellen combined, so $[(x + 3) + x] = (2x + 3)$ represents the number of properties that Dora sold. The following table summarizes these results.

Agent	Properties Sold
Andy	$2x$
Bob	$x + 3$
Cary	$2x + 6$
Dora	$2x + 3$
Ellen	x

Since $x \geq 0$, clearly $2x + 6$ exceeds x, $x + 3$, $2x$, and $2x + 3$. Therefore, Cary sold the most properties.

The correct answer is C.

16. In a field day at a school, each child who competed in n events and scored a total of p points was given an overall score of $\frac{p}{n} + n$. Andrew competed in 1 event and scored 9 points. Jason competed in 3 events and scored 5, 6, and 7 points, respectively. What was the ratio of Andrew's overall score to Jason's overall score?

(A) $\frac{10}{23}$
(B) $\frac{7}{10}$
(C) $\frac{4}{5}$
(D) $\frac{10}{9}$
(E) $\frac{12}{7}$

Algebra Applied Problems; Substitution

Andrew participated in 1 event and scored 9 points, so his overall score was $\frac{9}{1} + 1 = 10$. Jason participated in 3 events and scored $5 + 6 + 7 = 18$ points, so his overall score was $\frac{18}{3} + 3 = 9$. The ratio of Andrew's overall score to Jason's overall score was $\frac{10}{9}$.

The correct answer is D.

17. A certain work plan for September requires that a work team, working every day, produce an average of 200 items per day. For the first half of the month, the team produced an average of 150 items per day. How many items per day must the team average during the second half of the month if it is to attain the average daily production rate required by the work plan?

(A) 225
(B) 250
(C) 275
(D) 300
(E) 350

Arithmetic Rate Problem

The work plan requires that the team produce an average of 200 items per day in September. Because the team has only produced an average of 150 items per day in the first half of September, it has a shortfall of $200 - 150 = 50$ items per day for the first half of the month. The team must make up for this shortfall in the second half of the month, which has an equal number of days as the first half of the month. The team must therefore produce in the second half of the month an average amount per day that is 50 items greater than the required average of 200 items per day for the entire month. This amount for the second half of September is 250 items per day.

The correct answer is B.

18. A company sells radios for \$15.00 each. It costs the company \$14.00 per radio to produce 1,000 radios and \$13.50 per radio to produce 2,000 radios. How much greater will the company's gross profit be from the production and sale of 2,000 radios than from the production and sale of 1,000 radios?

(A) \$500
(B) \$1,000
(C) \$1,500
(D) \$2,000
(E) \$2,500

Arithmetic Applied Problems

If the company produces and sells 1,000 radios, its gross profit from the sale of these radios is equal to the total revenue from the sale of these radios minus the total cost. The total cost is equal to the number of radios produced multiplied by the production cost per radio: $1{,}000 \times \$15.00$. The total revenue is equal to the number of radios sold multiplied by the selling price: $1{,}000 \times \$14.00$. The gross profit in this case is therefore $1{,}000 \times \$15.00 - 1{,}000 \times \$14.00 = 1{,}000 \times (\$15.00 - \$14.00) = 1{,}000\ (\$1.00) = \$1{,}000$. If 2,000 radios are produced and sold, the total cost is equal to $2{,}000 \times \$13.50$ and the total revenue is equal to $2{,}000 \times \$15.00$. The gross profit in this case is therefore $2{,}000 \times \$15.00 - 2{,}000 \times \$13.50 = 2{,}000 \times (\$15.00 - \$13.50) = 2{,}000 \times (\$1.50) = \$3{,}000$. This profit of \$3,000 is \$2,000 greater than the gross profit of \$1,000 from producing and selling 1,000 radios.

The correct answer is D.

19. Working at their respective constant rates, machine A makes 100 copies in 12 minutes and machine B makes 150 copies in 10 minutes. If these machines work simultaneously at their respective rates for 30 minutes, what is the total number of copies that they will produce?

(A) 250
(B) 425
(C) 675
(D) 700
(E) 750

Arithmetic Applied Problems

Over 30 minutes, machine A makes 100 copies $\times \left(\frac{30 \text{ minutes}}{12 \text{ minutes}}\right) = 250$ copies, while machine B makes 150 copies $\times \left(\frac{30 \text{ minutes}}{10 \text{ minutes}}\right) = 450$ copies.

So together, the machines will make $250 + 450 = 700$ copies in 30 minutes.

The correct answer is D.

20. Company X mailed out a questionnaire. Sixty percent of those who received the questionnaire by mail responded. Company X needed 300 responses. What is the minimum number of questionnaires that Company X should have mailed in order to get the necessary responses?

(A) 400
(B) 420
(C) 480
(D) 500
(E) 600

Arithmetic Percents

Since 300, the number of responses received, was 60 percent of the number of copies of the questionnaire that were mailed, the number of copies mailed was $\frac{300}{0.6} = 500$.

The correct answer is D.

21. The toll T, in dollars, for a truck using a certain bridge is given by the formula $T = 1.50 + 0.50(x - 2)$, where x is the number of axles on the truck. What is the toll for an 18-wheel truck that has 2 wheels on its front axle and 4 wheels on each of its other axles?

(A) \$2.50
(B) \$3.00
(C) \$3.50
(D) \$4.00
(E) \$5.00

Algebra Operations on Rational Numbers

The 18-wheel truck has 2 wheels on its front axle and 4 wheels on each of its other axles, and so if A represents the number of axles on the truck in addition to the front axle, then $2 + 4A = 18$, from which it follows that $4A = 16$ and $A = 4$. Therefore, the total number of axles on the truck is $1 + A = 1 + 4 = 5$. Then, using $T = 1.50 + 0.50(x - 2)$, where x is the number of axles on the truck and $x = 5$, it follows that $T = 1.50 + 0.50(5 - 2) = 1.50 + 1.50 = 3.00$. Therefore, the toll for the truck is \$3.00.

The correct answer is B.

22. For what value of x between –4 and 4, inclusive, is the value of $x^2 - 10x + 16$ the greatest?

(A) –4
(B) –2
(C) 0
(D) 2
(E) 4

Algebra Second-Degree Equations

Given the expression $x^2 - 10x + 16$, a table of values can be created for the corresponding function $f(x) = x^2 - 10x + 16$ and the graph in the standard (x,y) coordinate plane can be sketched by plotting selected points:

x	$f(x)$
–4	72
–3	55
–2	40
–1	27
0	16
1	7
2	0
3	–5
4	–8
5	–9
6	–8
7	–5
8	0
9	7

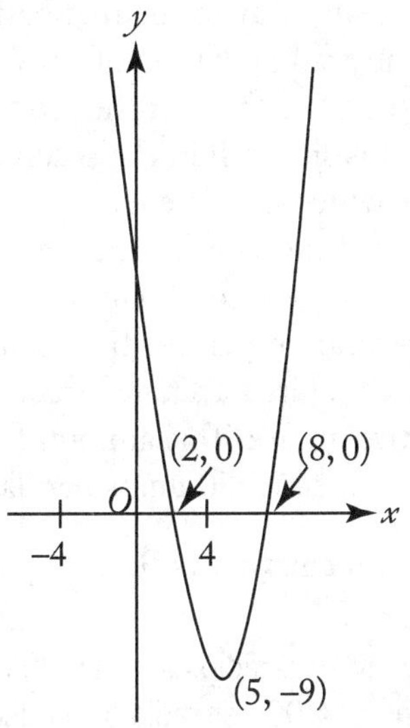

It is clear from both the table of values and the sketch of the graph that as the value of x increases from –4 to 4, the values of $x^2 - 10x + 16$ decrease. Therefore, the value of $x^2 - 10x + 16$ is greatest when $x = -4$.

Alternatively, the given expression, $x^2 - 10x + 16$, has the form $ax^2 + bx + c$, where $a = 1$, $b = -10$, and $c = 16$. The graph in the standard (x,y) coordinate plane of the corresponding function $f(x) = ax^2 + bx + c$ is a parabola with vertex at $x = -\frac{b}{2a}$, and so the vertex of the graph of $f(x) = x^2 - 10x + 16$ is at

$$x = -\left(\frac{-10}{2(1)}\right) = 5.$$

Because $a = 1$ and 1 is positive, this parabola opens upward and values of $x^2 - 10x + 16$ decrease as x increases from –4 to 4. Therefore, the greatest value of $x^2 - 10x + 16$ for all values of x between –4 and 4, inclusive, is at $x = -4$.

The correct answer is A.

23. If $x = -\frac{5}{8}$ and $y = -\frac{1}{2}$, what is the value of the expression $-2x - y^2$?

(A) $-\frac{3}{2}$

(B) –1

(C) 1

(D) $\frac{3}{2}$

(E) $\frac{7}{4}$

Algebra Fractions

If $x = -\frac{5}{8}$ and $y = -\frac{1}{2}$, then

$$-2x - y^2 = -2\left(-\frac{5}{8}\right) - \left(-\frac{1}{2}\right)^2 = \frac{5}{4} - \frac{1}{4} = \frac{4}{4} = 1.$$

The correct answer is C.

24. At the opening of a trading day, stock X had a value of \$40.00 per share and stock Y had a value of \$25.00 per share. At the closing of the trading day, stock X had a value of \$41.00 per share and stock Y had a value of \$28.50 per share. For this trading day, the percent increase in the value of stock Y was how many percentage points greater than the percent increase in the value of stock X?

(A) 2.5

(B) 6.25

(C) 10

(D) 11.5

(D) 12.5

Arithmetic Percents

Stock X's percentage increase in value was $(41 - 40) \times \frac{100\%}{40} = \frac{100\%}{40} = 2.5\%$. Stock Y's was $(28.5 - 25) \times \frac{100\%}{25} = \frac{350\%}{25} = 14\%$. Thus, the percentage increase in stock Y's value was $(14 - 2.5)\% = 11.5$ percentage points greater than that in stock X's value.

The correct answer is D.

25. For positive integers *a* and *b*, the remainder when *a* is divided by *b* is equal to the remainder when *b* is divided by *a*. Which of the following could be a value of *ab*?

I. 24

II. 30

III. 36

(A) II only

(B) III only

(C) I and II only

(D) II and III only

(E) I, II, and III

Arithmetic Properties of Integers

We are given that the remainder when *a* is divided by *b* is equal to the remainder when *b* is divided by *a*, and asked about possible values of *ab*. We thus need to find what our given condition implies about *a* and *b*.

We consider two cases: $a = b$ and $a \neq b$.

If $a = b$, then our given condition is trivially satisfied: the remainder when *a* is divided by *a* is equal to the remainder when *a* is divided by *b*. The condition thus allows that *a* be equal to *b*.

Now consider the case of $a \neq b$. Either a < b or $b < a$. Supposing that $a < b$, the remainder when *a* is divided by *b* is simply *a*. (For example, if 7 is divided by 10, then the remainder is 7.) However, according to our given condition, this remainder, *a*, is also the remainder when *b* is divided by *a*, which is impossible. If *b* is divided by *a*, then the remainder must be less than *a*. (For example, for any number that is divided by 10, the remainder cannot be 10 or greater.) Similar reasoning applies if we suppose that $b < a$. This is also impossible.

We thus see that a must be equal to b, and consider the statements I, II, and III.

I. Factored in terms of prime numbers, $24 = 3 \times 2 \times 2 \times 2$. Because "3" occurs only once in the factorization, we see that there is no integer a such that $a \times a = 24$. Based on the reasoning above, we see that 24 cannot be a value of ab.

II. Factored in terms of prime numbers, $30 = 5 \times 3 \times 2$. Because there is no integer a such that $a \times a = 30$, we see that 30 cannot be a value of ab.

III. Because $36 = 6 \times 6$, we see that 36 is a possible value of ab (with $a = b$).

The correct answer is B.

26. List S consists of the positive integers that are multiples of 9 and are less than 100. What is the median of the integers in S?

(A) 36
(B) 45
(C) 49
(D) 54
(E) 63

Arithmetic Series and Sequences

In the set of positive integers less than 100, the greatest multiple of 9 is 99 (9×11) and the least multiple of 9 is 9 (9×1). The sequence of positive multiples of 9 that are less than 100 is therefore the sequence of numbers $9 \times k$, where k ranges from 1 through 11. The median of the numbers k from 1 through 11 is 6. Therefore, the median of the numbers $9 \times k$, where k ranges from 1 through 11, is $9 \times 6 = 54$.

The correct answer is D.

27. A rope 20.6 meters long is cut into two pieces. If the length of one piece of rope is 2.8 meters shorter than the length of the other, what is the length, in meters, of the longer piece of rope?

(A) 7.5
(B) 8.9
(C) 9.9
(D) 10.3
(E) 11.7

Algebra First-Degree Equations

If x represents the length of the longer piece of rope, then $x - 2.8$ represents the length of the shorter piece, where both lengths are in meters. The total length of the two pieces of rope is 20.6 meters so,

$x + (x - 2.8) = 20.6$	given
$2x - 2.8 = 20.6$	add like terms
$2x = 23.4$	add 2.8 to both sides
$x = 11.7$	divide both sides by 2

Thus, the length of the longer piece of rope is 11.7 meters.

The correct answer is E.

28. If x and y are integers and $x - y$ is odd, which of the following must be true?

I. xy is even.
II. $x^2 + y^2$ is odd.
III. $(x + y)^2$ is even.

(A) I only
(B) II only
(C) III only
(D) I and II only
(E) I, II, and III

Arithmetic Properties of Numbers

We are given that x and y are integers and that $x - y$ is odd, and then asked, for various operations on x and y, whether the results of the operations are odd or even. It is therefore useful to determine, given that $x - y$ is odd, whether x and y are odd or even. If both x and y are even—that is, divisible by 2—then $x - y = 2m - 2n = 2(m - n)$ for integers m and n. We thus see if both x and y are even then $x - y$ cannot be odd. And because $x - y$ *is* odd, we see that x and y cannot both be even. Similarly, if both x and y are odd, then, for integers j and k, $x = 2j + 1$ and $y = 2k + 1$. Therefore, $x - y = (2j + 1) - (2k + 1)$. The ones cancel, and we are left with $x - y = 2j - 2k = 2(j - k)$. Because $2(j - k)$ would be even, x and y cannot both be odd if $x - y$ is odd. It follows from all of this that one of x or y must be even and the other odd.

Now consider the statements I through III.

I. If one of x or y is even, then one of x or y is divisible by 2. It follows that xy is divisible by 2 and that xy is even.

II. Given that a number x or y is odd—not divisible by 2—we know that its product with itself is not divisible by 2 and is therefore odd. On the other hand, given that a number x or y is even, we know that its product with itself *is* divisible by 2 and is therefore even. The sum $x^2 + y^2$ is therefore the sum of an even number and an odd number. In such a case, the sum can be written as $(2m) + (2n + 1) = 2(m + n) + 1$, with m and n integers. It follows that $x^2 + y^2$ is not divisible by 2 and is therefore odd.

III. We know that one of x or y is even and the other is odd. We can therefore see from the discussion of statement II that $x + y$ is odd, and then also see, from the discussion of statement II, that the product of $x + y$ with itself, $(x + y)^2$, is odd.

The correct answer is D.

29. On Monday, the opening price of a certain stock was \$100 per share and its closing price was \$110 per share. On Tuesday the closing price of the stock was 10 percent less than its closing price on Monday, and on Wednesday the closing price of the stock was 4 percent greater than its closing price on Tuesday. What was the approximate percent change in the price of the stock from its opening price on Monday to its closing price on Wednesday?

(A) A decrease of 6%
(B) A decrease of 4%
(C) A decrease of 1%
(D) An increase of 3%
(E) An increase of 4%

Arithmetic Percents

The closing share price on Tuesday was 10% less than the closing price on Monday, \$110. 10% of \$110 is equal to $0.1 \times \$110 = \$11$, so the closing price on Tuesday was $\$110 - \$11 = \$99$. The closing price on Wednesday was 4% greater than this: $\$99 + (0.04 \times \$99) = \$99 + \$3.96 = \$102.96$. This value, \$102.96, is 2.96% greater than \$100, the opening price on Monday. The percentage change from the opening share price on Monday is therefore an increase of approximately 3%, which is the closest of the available answers to an increase of 2.96%.

The correct answer is D.

30. $1 - 0.000001 =$

(A) (1.01)(0.99)
(B) (1.11)(0.99)
(C) (1.001)(0.999)
(D) (1.111)(0.999)
(E) (1.0101)(0.0909)

Arithmetic Place Value

The task in this question is to find among the available answers the expression that is equal to $1 - 0.000001 = 0.999999$. In the case of answer choice C, the first of the two factors, (1.001), is equal to $1 + 0.001$. One may therefore observe that $(1.001)(0.999) = (1 + 0.001)(0.999) = 0.999 + 0.000999 = 0.999999$. Answer choice C is therefore a correct answer.

For answer choice A, $(1.01)(0.99) = (1 + 0.01)(0.99) = 0.9999$. This answer choice is therefore incorrect. For answer choice B, $(1.11)(0.99) = (1 + 0.1 + 0.01)(0.99) = 0.99 + 0.099 + 0.0099 = 1.0989$. This answer choice is therefore incorrect. For answer choice D, $(1.111)(0.999) = 0.999 + 0.0999 + 0.00999 + 0.000999 = 1.109889$. This answer choice is therefore incorrect. For answer choice E, $(1.0101)(0.909) = 0.909 + 0.00909 + 0.0000909 = 0.9181809$. This answer choice is therefore incorrect.

The correct answer is C.

31. In a certain history class of 17 juniors and seniors, each junior has written 2 book reports and each senior has written 3 book reports. If the 17 students have written a total of 44 book reports, how many juniors are in the class?

(A) 7
(B) 8
(C) 9
(D) 10
(E) 11

Algebra Simultaneous Equations

Letting j and s, respectively, represent the juniors and seniors in the class, it is given that $j + s = 17$ or $s = 17 - j$. Also, since it is given that each junior has written 2 book reports and each senior has written 3 book reports for a total of 44 book reports, it follows that $2j + 3s = 44$ or $2j + 3(17 - j) = 44$. Therefore, $j = 3(17) - 44 = 7$.

The correct answer is A.

32. $|-4|(|-20|-|5|) =$

(A) –100
(B) –60
(C) 60
(D) 75
(E) 100

Arithmetic Absolute Value

$|-4|(|-20|-|5|) = 4(20 - 5) = 4 \times 15 = 60$

The correct answer is C.

33. What is the greatest integer k for which 32.45×10^k is less than 1?

(A) –2
(B) 1
(C) 0
(D) 1
(E) 2

Arithmetic Operations with Integers

$32.45 \times 10^{-2} = 0.3245 < 1$, but $32.45 \times 10^{-1} = 3.245 > 1$. Thus, –2 is the greatest integer k for which $32.45 \times 10^k < 1$.

The correct answer is A.

34. How many integers x satisfy both $2 < x \leq 4$ and $0 \leq x \leq 3$?

(A) 5
(B) 4
(C) 3
(D) 2
(E) 1

Arithmetic Inequalities

The integers that satisfy $2 < x \leq 4$ are 3 and 4. The integers that satisfy $0 \leq x \leq 3$ are 0, 1, 2, and 3. The only integer that satisfies both $2 < x \leq 4$ and $0 \leq x \leq 3$ is 3, and so there is only one integer that satisfies both $2 < x \leq 4$ and $0 \leq x \leq 3$.

The correct answer is E.

35. At the opening of a trading day at a certain stock exchange, the price per share of stock K was \$8. If the price per share of stock K was \$9 at the closing of the day, what was the percent increase in the price per share of stock K for that day?

(A) 1.4%
(B) 5.9%
(C) 11.1%
(D) 12.5%
(E) 23.6%

Arithmetic Percents

An increase from \$8 to \$9 represents an increase of $\left(\frac{9-8}{8} \times 100\right)\% = \frac{100}{8}\% = 12.5\%$.

The correct answer is D.

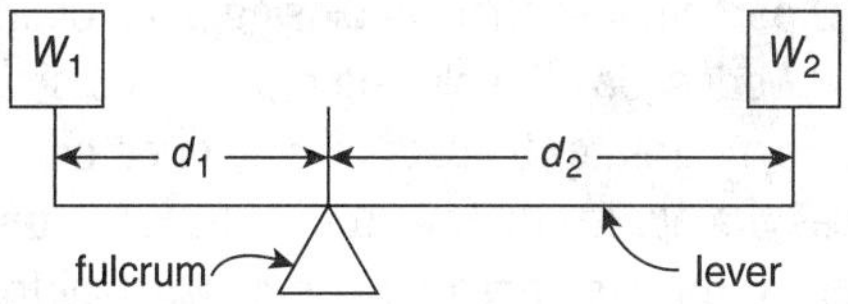

36. As shown in the diagram above, a lever resting on a fulcrum has weights of w_1 pounds and w_2 pounds, located d_1 feet and d_2 feet from the fulcrum. The lever is balanced and $w_1d_1 = w_2d_2$. Suppose w_1 is 50 pounds and w_2 is 30 pounds. If d_1 is 4 feet less than d_2, what is d_2, in feet?

(A) 1.5
(B) 2.5
(C) 6
(D) 10
(E) 20

Algebra First-Degree Equations; Substitution

Given $w_1 d_1 = w_2 d_2$, $w_1 = 50$, $w_2 = 30$, and $d_1 = d_2 - 4$, it follows that $50(d_2 - 4) = 30d_2$, and so

$50(d_2 - 4) = 30d_2$ given

$50d_2 - 200 = 30d_2$ distributive principle

$20d_2 = 200$ add $200 - 30d_2$ to both sides

$d_2 = 10$ divide both sides by 20

The correct answer is D.

Day	Change in Dollars
Monday	$+1\frac{1}{2}$
Tuesday	$-\frac{3}{4}$
Wednesday	0
Thursday	$-\frac{1}{8}$
Friday	$+2\frac{1}{4}$

37. The table above shows the daily change in the price of a certain stock last week. What was the net change in dollars in the price of the stock for the week?

(A) $-4\frac{5}{8}$

(B) $-2\frac{7}{8}$

(C) $+2\frac{7}{8}$

(D) $+3\frac{3}{4}$

(E) $-4\frac{5}{8}$

Arithmetic Interpretation of Tables

The net change in dollars is $\frac{3}{2} - \frac{3}{4} - \frac{1}{8} + \frac{9}{4} = \frac{12 - 6 - 1 + 18}{8} = \frac{23}{8} = 2\frac{7}{8}$. So, that's an increase of $2\frac{7}{8}$ dollars.

The correct answer is C.

38. Of 120 hotel rooms rented one night, some were suites rented for \$115 each and the rest were double rooms rented for \$85 each. If the total revenue from the room rentals for this night was \$10,890, how many suites were rented?

(A) 23

(B) 35

(C) 54

(D) 94

(E) 99

Algebra Simultaneous Equations

Let x be the number of suites rented. Then $\$10,890 = \$115x + \$85(120 - x) = \$115x + \$10,200 - \$85x$, so $\$690 = \$30x$. Thus, $x = 23$.

The correct answer is A.

39. Last week Jack worked 70 hours and earned \$1,260. If he earned his regular hourly wage for the first 40 hours worked, $1\frac{1}{2}$ times his regular hourly wage for the next 20 hours worked, and 2 times his regular hourly wage for the remaining 10 hours worked, what was his regular hourly wage?

(A) \$7.00

(B) \$14.00

(C) \$18.00

(D) \$22.00

(E) \$31.50

Algebra First-Degree Equations

If w represents Jack's regular hourly wage, then Jack's earnings for the week can be represented by the sum of the following amounts, in dollars: $40w$ (his earnings for the first 40 hours he worked), $(20)(1.5w)$ (his earnings for the next 20 hours he worked), and $(10)(2w)$ (his earnings for the last 10 hours he worked). Therefore,

$40w + (20)(1.5w) + (10)(2w) = 1,260$ given

$90w = 1,260$ add like terms

$w = 14$ divide both sides by 90

Jack's regular hourly wage was \$14.00.

The correct answer is B.

40. If $\frac{x}{4}$ is 2 more than $\frac{x}{8}$, then x =

(A) 4
(B) 8
(C) 16
(D) 32
(E) 64

Algebra First-Degree Equations

If $\frac{x}{4} = 2 + \frac{x}{8}$, then we can multiply both sides of the equation by 8 to find that $2x = 16 + x$, so $x = 16$.

The correct answer is C.

41. If $(2^x)(2^y) = 8$ and $(9^x)(3^y) = 81$, then $(x, y) =$

(A) (1, 2)
(B) (2, 1)
(C) (1, 1)
(D) (2, 2)
(E) (1, 3)

Algebra Exponents

If $(2^x)(2^y) = 8 = 2^3$, then $x + y = 3$. Of the five answer options, the only ones satisfying this equation are option A, in which $(x, y) = (1, 2)$, and option B, in which $(x, y) = (2, 1)$. Since $(9^x)(3^y) = 81 = (9^1)(3^2) \neq (9^2)(3^1)$, we find that $x = 1$ and $y = 2$, so $(x, y) = (1, 2)$.

The correct answer is A.

42. A certain toll station on a highway has 7 tollbooths, and each tollbooth collects \$0.75 from each vehicle that passes it. From 6 o'clock yesterday morning to 12 o'clock midnight, vehicles passed each of the tollbooths at the average rate of 4 vehicles per minute. Approximately how much money did the toll station collect during that time period?

(A) \$1,500
(B) \$3,000
(C) \$11,500
(D) \$23,000
(E) \$30,000

Arithmetic Rate Problem

On average, 4 vehicles pass each tollbooth every minute. There are 7 tollbooths at the station, and each passing vehicle pays \$0.75. Therefore, the average rate, per minute, at which money is collected by the toll station is $\$\,(7 \times 4 \times 0.75) = \$\,(7 \times 4 \times \frac{3}{4}) = \$\,(7 \times 3) = \$21$. From 6:00 a.m. through midnight there are 18 hours. And because 18 hours is equal to 18×60 minutes, from 6:00 a.m. through midnight there are 1,080 minutes. The total amount of money collected by the toll station during this period is therefore $1{,}080 \times \$21 = \$22{,}680$, which is approximately \$23,000.

The correct answer is D.

43. If $y = 2 + 2k$ and $y \neq 0$, then $\frac{1}{y} + \frac{1}{y} + \frac{1}{y} + \frac{1}{y} =$

(A) $\frac{1}{8 + 8k}$
(B) $\frac{2}{1 + k}$
(C) $\frac{1}{8 + k}$
(D) $\frac{4}{8 + k}$
(E) $\frac{4}{1 + k}$

Algebra Equations

If $y = 2 + 2k \neq 0$, then $\frac{1}{y} + \frac{1}{y} + \frac{1}{y} + \frac{1}{y} = \frac{4}{y} = \frac{4}{2 + 2k} = \frac{2}{1 + k}$.

The correct answer is B.

44. If $3^x - 3^{x-1} = 162$, then $x(x - 1) =$

(A) 12
(B) 16
(C) 20
(D) 30
(E) 81

Algebra Exponents

If $3^x - 3^{x-1} = 162 = 2(81) = 2(3^4) = 3(3^4) - 1(3^4) = 3^5 - 3^4$, then $x = 5$. Thus, $x(x - 1) = 5(4) = 20$.

The correct answer is C.

45. The expression $n!$ is defined as the product of the integers from 1 through n. If p is the product of the integers from 100 through 299 and q is the product of the integers from 200 through 299, which of the following is equal to $\frac{p}{q}$?

(A) 99!
(B) 199!
(C) $\frac{199!}{99!}$
(D) $\frac{299!}{99!}$
(E) $\frac{299!}{199!}$

Arithmetic Series and Sequences

The number p is equal to $100 \times 101 \times 102 \times \ldots \times 299$ and the number q is equal to $200 \times 201 \times 202 \times \ldots \times 299$. The number $\frac{p}{q}$ is thus equal to $\frac{100 \times 101 \times 102 \times \ldots \times 299}{200 \times 201 \times 202 \times \ldots \times 299} = \frac{100 \times 101 \times 102 \times \ldots \times 199 \times 200 \times 201 \times 202 \times \ldots \times 299}{200 \times 201 \times 202 \times \ldots \times 299}$.

Canceling $200 \times 201 \times 202 \times \ldots \times 299$ from the numerator and the denominator, we see that $\frac{p}{q} = 100 \times 101 \times 102 \times \ldots \times 199$. Note that the multiplication in this expression for $\frac{p}{q}$ begins with 100 (the smallest of the numbers being multiplied), whereas the multiplication in $n! = 1 \times 2 \times 3 \times \ldots \times n$ begins with 1. Starting with 199! as our numerator, we thus need to find a denominator that will cancel the undesired elements of the multiplication (in 199!). This number is $1 \times 2 \times 3 \times \ldots \times 99 = 99!$ That is, $\frac{p}{q} = 100 \times 101 \times 102 \times \ldots \times 199 = \frac{1 \times 2 \times 3 \times \ldots \times 99 \times 100 \times 101 \times 102 \times \ldots \times 199}{1 \times 2 \times 3 \times \ldots \times 99} = \frac{199!}{99!}$.

The correct answer is C.

46. A school club plans to package and sell dried fruit to raise money. The club purchased 12 containers of dried fruit, each containing $16\frac{3}{4}$ pounds. What is the maximum number of individual bags of dried fruit, each containing $\frac{1}{4}$ pounds, that can be sold from the dried fruit the club purchased?

(A) 50
(B) 64
(C) 67
(D) 768
(E) 804

Arithmetic Applied Problems; Operations with Fractions

The 12 containers, each containing $16\frac{3}{4}$ pounds of dried fruit, contain a total of $(12)\left(16\frac{3}{4}\right) = (12)\left(\frac{67}{4}\right) = (3)(67) = 201$ pounds of dried fruit, which will make $\frac{201}{\frac{1}{4}} = (201)(4) = 804$ individual bags that can be sold.

The correct answer is E.

Height	Price
Less than 5 ft	\$14.95
5 ft to 6 ft	\$17.95
Over 6 ft	\$21.95

47. A nursery sells fruit trees priced as shown in the chart above. In its inventory 54 trees are less than 5 feet in height. If the expected revenue from the sale of its entire stock is estimated at \$2,450, approximately how much of this will come from the sale of trees that are at least 5 feet tall?

(A) \$1,730
(B) \$1,640
(C) \$1,410
(D) \$1,080
(E) \$810

Arithmetic Applied Problems

If the nursery sells its entire stock of trees, it will sell the 54 trees that are less than 5 feet in height at the price per tree of \$14.95 shown in the chart. The expected revenue from the sale of the trees that are less than 5 feet tall is therefore $54 \times \$14.95 = \$807.30$. The revenue from the sale of the trees that are at least 5 feet tall is thus equal to the total revenue from the sale of the entire stock of trees minus \$807.30. The revenue from the sale of the entire stock of trees is estimated at \$2,450. Based on this estimate, the revenue from the sale of the trees that are at least 5 feet tall will be $\$2,450 - \$807.30 = \$1,642.70$, which is approximately \$1,640.

The correct answer is B.

48. A certain bridge is 4,024 feet long. Approximately how many minutes does it take to cross this bridge at a constant speed of 20 miles per hour? (1 mile = 5,280 feet)

(A) 1
(B) 2
(C) 4
(D) 6
(E) 7

Arithmetic Applied Problems

First, convert 4,024 feet to miles since the speed is given in miles per hour:

$$4{,}024\ \cancel{\text{ft}} \times \frac{1\ \text{mi}}{5{,}280\ \cancel{\text{ft}}} = \frac{4{,}024}{5{,}280}\ \text{mi.}$$

Now, divide by 20 mph: $\frac{4{,}024}{5{,}280}\ \text{mi} \div \frac{20\ \text{mi}}{1\ \text{hr}}$

$$= \frac{4{,}024\ \cancel{\text{mi}}}{5{,}280} \times \frac{1\ \text{hr}}{20\ \cancel{\text{mi}}} = \frac{4{,}024\ \text{hr}}{(5{,}280)(20)}.$$

Last, convert $\frac{4{,}024\ \text{hr}}{(5{,}280)(20)}$ to minutes:

$$\frac{4{,}024\ \cancel{\text{hr}}}{(5{,}280)(20)} \times \frac{60\ \text{min}}{1\ \cancel{\text{hr}}} = \frac{(4{,}024)(60)\ \text{min}}{(5{,}280)(20)} \approx$$

$\frac{4{,}000}{5{,}000} \times \frac{60}{20}$ min. Then, $\frac{4{,}000}{5{,}000} \times \frac{60}{20}$ min $= 0.8 \times 3$ min ≈ 2 min. Thus, at a constant speed of 20 miles per hour, it takes approximately 2 minutes to cross the bridge.

The correct answer is B.

49. A purse contains 57 coins, all of which are nickels, dimes, or quarters. If the purse contains x dimes and 8 more nickels than dimes, which of the following gives the number of quarters the purse contains in terms of x?

(A) 2x – 49
(B) 2x + 49
(C) 2x – 65
(D) 49 – 2x
(E) 65 – 2x

Algebra First-Degree Equations

Letting Q be the number of quarters, there are $(x + 8)$ nickels, x dimes, and Q quarters for a total of 57 coins.

$(x+8)+x+Q = 57$	given
$2x+8+Q = 57$	combine like terms
$Q = 49-2x$	subtract $2x+8$ from both sides

The correct answer is D.

50. The annual interest rate earned by an investment increased by 10 percent from last year to this year. If the annual interest rate earned by the investment this year was 11 percent, what was the annual interest rate last year?

(A) 1%
(B) 1.1%
(C) 9.1%
(D) 10%
(E) 10.8%

Arithmetic Percents

If L is the annual interest rate last year, then the annual interest rate this year is 10% greater than L, or $1.1L$. It is given that $1.1L = 11\%$. Therefore, $L = \frac{11\%}{1.1} = 10\%$. (Note that if the given information had been that the investment increased by *10 percentage points*, then the equation would have been $L + 10\% = 11\%$.)

The correct answer is D.

51. A total of 5 liters of gasoline is to be poured into two empty containers with capacities of 2 liters and 6 liters, respectively, such that both containers will be filled to the same percent of their respective capacities. What amount of gasoline, in liters, must be poured into the 6-liter container?

(A) $4\frac{1}{2}$

(B) 4

(C) $3\frac{3}{4}$

(D) 3

(E) $1\frac{1}{4}$

Algebra Ratio and Proportion

If x represents the amount, in liters, of gasoline poured into the 6-liter container, then $5 - x$ represents the amount, in liters, of gasoline poured into the 2-liter container. After the gasoline is poured into the containers, the 6-liter container will be filled to $\left(\frac{x}{6} \times 100\right)$% of its capacity and the 2-liter container will be filled to $\left(\frac{5-x}{2} \times 100\right)$% of its capacity. Because these two percents are equal,

$\frac{x}{6} = \frac{5-x}{2}$	given
$2x = 6(5 - x)$	multiply both sides by 12
$2x = 30 - 6x$	use distributive property
$8x = 30$	add $6x$ to both sides
$x = 3\frac{3}{4}$	divide both sides by 8

Therefore, $3\frac{3}{4}$ liters of gasoline must be poured into the 6-liter container.

The correct answer is C.

52. What is the larger of the 2 solutions of the equation $x^2 - 4x = 96$?

(A) 8

(B) 12

(C) 16

(D) 32

(E) 100

Algebra Second-Degree Equations

It is given that $x^2 - 4x = 96$, or $x^2 - 4x - 96 = 0$, or $(x - 12)(x + 8) = 0$. Therefore, $x = 12$ or $x = -8$, and the larger of these two numbers is 12.

Alternatively, from $x^2 - 4x = 96$ it follows that $x(x - 4) = 96$. By inspection, the left side is either the product of 12 and 8, where the value of x is 12, or the product of -8 and -12, where the value of x is -8, and the larger of these two values of x is 12.

The correct answer is B.

$$x = \frac{1}{6}gt^2$$

53. In the formula shown, if g is a constant and $x = -6$ when $t = 2$, what is the value of x when $t = 4$?

(A) −24

(B) −20

(C) −15

(D) 20

(E) 24

Algebra Formulas

Since $x = -6$ when $t = 2$, it follows that $-6 = \left(\frac{1}{6}\right)(g)(4)$ so $g = \frac{3}{2}(-6) = -9$. Then, when $t = 4$, $x = \frac{1}{6}(-9)(16) = -24$.

The correct answer is A.

54. $\frac{(39{,}897)(0.0096)}{198.76}$ is approximately

(A) 0.02

(B) 0.2

(C) 2

(D) 20

(E) 200

Arithmetic Estimation

$$\frac{(39{,}897)(0.0096)}{198.76} \approx \frac{(40{,}000)(0.01)}{200} = (200)(0.01) = 2$$

The correct answer is C.

55. The "prime sum" of an integer n greater than 1 is the sum of all the prime factors of n, including repetitions. For example, the prime sum of 12 is 7, since $12 = 2 \times 2 \times 3$ and $2 + 2 + 3 = 7$. For which of the following integers is the prime sum greater than 35?

(A) 440
(B) 512
(C) 620
(D) 700
(E) 750

Arithmetic Properties of Numbers

A Since $440 = 2 \times 2 \times 2 \times 5 \times 11$, the prime sum of 440 is $2 + 2 + 2 + 5 + 11 = 22$, which is not greater than 35.

B Since $512 = 2^9$, the prime sum of 512 is $9(2) = 18$, which is not greater than 35.

C Since $620 = 2 \times 2 \times 5 \times 31$, the prime sum of 620 is $2 + 2 + 5 + 31 = 40$, which is greater than 35.

Because there can be only one correct answer, D and E need not be checked. However, for completeness,

D Since $700 = 2 \times 2 \times 5 \times 5 \times 7$, the prime sum of 700 is $2 + 2 + 5 + 5 + 7 = 21$, which is not greater than 35.

E Since $750 = 2 \times 3 \times 5 \times 5 \times 5$, the prime sum of 750 is $2 + 3 + 5 + 5 + 5 = 20$, which is not greater than 35.

The correct answer is C.

56. Each machine at a toy factory assembles a certain kind of toy at a constant rate of one toy every 3 minutes. If 40 percent of the machines at the factory are to be replaced by new machines that assemble this kind of toy at a constant rate of one toy every 2 minutes, what will be the percent increase in the number of toys assembled in one hour by all the machines at the factory, working at their constant rates?

(A) 20%
(B) 25%
(C) 30%
(D) 40%
(E) 50%

Arithmetic Applied Problems; Percents

Let n be the total number of machines working. Currently, it takes each machine 3 minutes to assemble 1 toy, so each machine assembles 20 toys in 1 hour and the total number of toys assembled in 1 hour by all the current machines is $20n$. It takes each new machine 2 minutes to assemble 1 toy, so each new machine assembles 30 toys in 1 hour. If 60% of the machines assemble 20 toys each hour and 40% assemble 30 toys each hour, then the total number of toys produced by the machines each hour is $(0.60n)(20) + (0.40n)(30) = 24n$. The percent increase in hourly production is $\frac{24n - 20n}{20n} = \frac{1}{5}$ or 20%.

The correct answer is A.

57. When a subscription to a new magazine was purchased for m months, the publisher offered a discount of 75 percent off the regular monthly price of the magazine. If the total value of the discount was equivalent to buying the magazine at its regular monthly price for 27 months, what was the value of m?

(A) 18
(B) 24
(C) 30
(D) 36
(E) 48

Algebra Percents

Let P represent the regular monthly price of the magazine. The discounted monthly price is then $0.75P$. Paying this price for m months is equivalent to paying the regular price for 27 months. Therefore, $0.75mP = 27P$, and so $0.75m = 27$. It follows that $m = \frac{27}{0.75} = 36$.

The correct answer is D.

58. At a garage sale, all of the prices of the items sold were different. If the price of a radio sold at the garage sale was both the 15th highest price and the 20th lowest price among the prices of the items sold, how many items were sold at the garage sale?

(A) 33
(B) 34
(C) 35
(D) 36
(E) 37

Arithmetic Operations with Integers

If the price of the radio was the 15th highest price, there were 14 items that sold for prices higher than the price of the radio. If the price of the radio was the 20th lowest price, there were 19 items that sold for prices lower than the price of the radio. Therefore, the total number of items sold is $14 + 1 + 19 = 34$.

The correct answer is B.

59. Half of a large pizza is cut into 4 equal-sized pieces, and the other half is cut into 6 equal-sized pieces. If a person were to eat 1 of the larger pieces and 2 of the smaller pieces, what fraction of the pizza would remain <u>uneaten</u>?

(A) $\frac{5}{12}$

(B) $\frac{13}{24}$

(C) $\frac{7}{12}$

(D) $\frac{2}{3}$

(E) $\frac{17}{24}$

Arithmetic Operations with Fractions

Each of the 4 equal-sized pieces represents $\frac{1}{8}$ of the whole pizza since each slice is $\frac{1}{4}$ of $\frac{1}{2}$ of the pizza. Each of the 6 equal-sized pieces represents $\frac{1}{12}$ of the whole pizza since each slice is $\frac{1}{6}$ of $\frac{1}{2}$ of the pizza. The fraction of the pizza remaining after a person eats one of the larger pieces and 2 of the smaller pieces is $1 - \left[\frac{1}{8} + 2\left(\frac{1}{12}\right)\right] = 1 - \left(\frac{1}{8} + \frac{1}{6}\right) = 1 - \frac{6+8}{48} = 1 - \frac{7}{24} = \frac{17}{24}$.

The correct answer is E.

60. If $a = 1 + \frac{1}{4} + \frac{1}{16} + \frac{1}{64}$ and $b = 1 + \frac{1}{4}a$, then what is the value of $a - b$?

(A) $-\frac{85}{256}$

(B) $-\frac{1}{256}$

(C) $-\frac{1}{4}$

(D) $\frac{125}{256}$

(E) $\frac{169}{256}$

Arithmetic Operations with Fractions

Given that $a = 1 + \frac{1}{4} + \frac{1}{16} + \frac{1}{64}$, it follows that $\frac{1}{4}a = \frac{1}{4} + \frac{1}{16} + \frac{1}{64} + \frac{1}{256}$ and so $b = 1 + \frac{1}{4} + \frac{1}{16} + \frac{1}{64} + \frac{1}{256}$. Then $a - b = \left(1 + \frac{1}{4} + \frac{1}{16} + \frac{1}{64}\right) - \left(1 + \frac{1}{4} + \frac{1}{16} + \frac{1}{64} + \frac{1}{256}\right) = -\frac{1}{256}$.

The correct answer is B.

61. In a certain learning experiment, each participant had three trials and was assigned, for each trial, a score of either −2, −1, 0, 1, or 2. The participant's final score consisted of the sum of the first trial score, 2 times the second trial score, and 3 times the third trial score. If Anne received scores of 1 and −1 for her first two trials, not necessarily in that order, which of the following could NOT be her final score?

(A) −4

(B) −2

(C) 1

(D) 5

(E) 6

Arithmetic Applied Problems

If x represents Anne's score on the third trial, then Anne's final score is either $1 + 2(-1) + 3x = 3x - 1$ or $-1 + 2(1) + 3x = 3x + 1$, where x can have the value −2, −1, 0, 1, or 2. The following table shows Anne's final score for each possible value of x.

x	$3x-1$	$3x+1$
−2	−7	−5
−1	−4	−2
0	−1	1
1	2	4
2	5	7

Among the answer choices, the only one not found in the table is 6.

The correct answer is E.

62. For all positive integers m and v, the expression $m \ominus v$ represents the remainder when m is divided by v. What is the value of $((98 \ominus 33) \ominus 17) - (98 \ominus (33 \ominus 17))$?

(A) −10
(B) −2
(C) 8
(D) 13
(E) 17

Arithmetic Operations with Integers

First, for $((98 \ominus 33) \ominus 17)$, determine $98 \ominus 33$, which equals 32, since 32 is the remainder when 98 is divided by 33 $(98 = 2(33) + 32)$. Then, determine $32 \ominus 17$, which equals 15, since 15 is the remainder when 32 is divided by 17 $(32 = 1(17) + 15)$. Thus, $((98 \ominus 33) \ominus 17) = 15$.

Next, for $(98 \ominus (33 \ominus 17))$, determine $33 \ominus 17$, which equals 16, since 16 is the remainder when 33 is divided by 17 $(33 = 1(17) + 16)$. Then, determine $98 \ominus 16$, which equals 2, since 2 is the remainder when 98 is divided by 16 $(98 = 6(16) + 2)$. Thus, $(98 \ominus (33 \ominus 17)) = 2$.

Finally, $((98 \ominus 33) \ominus 17 - (98 \ominus (33 \ominus 17)) = 15 - 2 = 13$.

The correct answer is D.

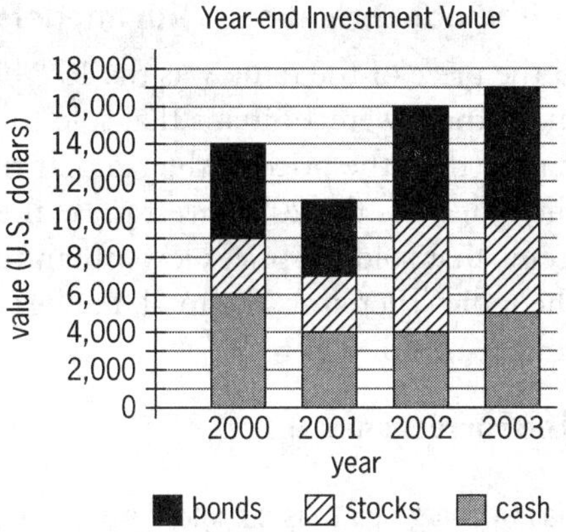

63. The chart above shows year-end values for Darnella's investments. For just the stocks, what was the increase in value from year-end 2000 to year-end 2003?

(A) \$1,000
(B) \$2,000
(C) \$3,000
(D) \$4,000
(E) \$5,000

Arithmetic Interpretation of Graphs

From the graph, the year-end 2000 value for stocks is $9{,}000 - 6{,}000 = 3{,}000$ and the year-end 2003 value for stocks is $10{,}000 - 5{,}000 = 5{,}000$. Therefore, for just the stocks, the increase in value from year-end 2000 to year-end 2003 is $5{,}000 - 3{,}000 = 2{,}000$.

The correct answer is B.

64. If the sum of the reciprocals of two consecutive odd integers is $\frac{12}{35}$, then the greater of the two integers is

(A) 3
(B) 5
(C) 7
(D) 9
(E) 11

Arithmetic Operations with Fractions

The sum of the reciprocals of 2 integers, a and b, is $\frac{1}{a} + \frac{1}{b} = \frac{a+b}{ab}$. Therefore, since $\frac{12}{35}$ is the sum of the reciprocals of 2 consecutive odd integers, the integers must be such that their sum is a multiple of 12 and their product is the same multiple of 35 so that the fraction reduces to $\frac{12}{35}$. Considering

the simplest case where $a + b = 12$ and $ab = 35$, it is easy to see that the integers are 5 and 7 since 5 and 7 are the only factors of 35 that are consecutive odd integers. The larger of these is 7.

Algebraically, if a is the greater of the two integers, then $b = a - 2$ and

$$\begin{aligned} \frac{a+(a-2)}{a(a-2)} &= \frac{12}{35} \\ \frac{2a-2}{a(a-2)} &= \frac{12}{35} \\ 35(2a-2) &= 12a(a-2) \\ 70a-70 &= 12a^2-24a \\ 0 &= 12a^2-94a+70 \\ 0 &= 2(6a-5)(a-7) \end{aligned}$$

Thus, $6a - 5 = 0$, so $a = \frac{5}{6}$, or $a - 7 = 0$, so $a = 7$.

Since a must be an integer, it follows that $a = 7$.

The correct answer is C.

65. What is the sum of the odd integers from 35 to 85, inclusive?

(A) 1,560
(B) 1,500
(C) 1,240
(D) 1,120
(E) 1,100

Arithmetic Operations on Integers

The odd integers from 35 through 85 form an arithmetic sequence with first term 35 and each subsequent term 2 more than the preceding term. Thus the sum $35 + 37 + 39 + \ldots + 85$ can be found as follows:

1st term	35	= 35	
2nd term	37	= 35	+ 1(2)
3rd term	39	= 35	+ 2(2)
4th term	41	= 35	+ 3(2)
…	…	… …	… …
26th term	85	= 35	+ 25(2)

$$\begin{aligned} \text{Sum} &= 35(26) + (1+2+3+\ldots+25)(2) \\ &= 35(26) + \frac{(25)(26)}{2}(2) \quad \text{see note below} \\ &= 910 + 650 \\ &= 1{,}560 \end{aligned}$$

Note that if $s = 1 + 2 + 3 + \ldots + 25$, then $2s = (1 + 2 + 3 + \ldots + 25) + (25 + 24 + 23 + \ldots + 1)$, and so $2s = (1 + 25) + (2 + 24) + (3 + 23) + \ldots + (25 + 1) = (25)(26)$. Therefore, $s = \frac{(25)(26)}{2}$.

Alternatively, to determine the number of odd integers from 35 to 85, inclusive, consider that 3 of them (35, 37, and 39) have tens digit 3. Half of the integers with tens digit 4 are odd, so 5 of the odd integers between 35 and 85, inclusive, have tens digit 4. Similarly, 5 of the odd integers between 35 and 85, inclusive, have tens digit 5; 5 have tens digit 6; and 5 have tens digit 7. Finally, 3 have tens digit 8 (81, 83, and 85), and so the number of odd integers between 35 and 85, inclusive, is $3 + 5 + 5 + 5 + 5 + 3 = 26$. Now, let $S = 35 + 37 + 39 + \ldots + 85$. Then, $S = 85 + 83 + 81 + \ldots + 35$, and it follows that $2S = (35 + 85) + (37 + 83) + (39 + 81) + \ldots + (85 + 35) = (120)(26)$. Thus,

$$S = 35 + 37 + 39 + \ldots + 85 = \frac{(120)(26)}{2} = 1{,}560.$$

The correct answer is A.

66. For all numbers a, b, c, and d, $\begin{vmatrix} a & b \\ c & d \end{vmatrix}$ is defined by the equation $\begin{vmatrix} a & b \\ c & d \end{vmatrix} = ad - cb$. Which of the following is equal to $\begin{vmatrix} s & t \\ 1 & 3 \end{vmatrix} - \begin{vmatrix} -t & 2 \\ s & 4 \end{vmatrix} + \begin{vmatrix} 2 & 2 \\ t & s \end{vmatrix}$?

(A) $\begin{vmatrix} s & t \\ 1 & 5 \end{vmatrix}$

(B) $\begin{vmatrix} s & t \\ 7 & 1 \end{vmatrix}$

(C) $\begin{vmatrix} s & t \\ 5 & 7 \end{vmatrix}$

(D) $\begin{vmatrix} s & -t \\ 1 & 5 \end{vmatrix}$

(E) $\begin{vmatrix} s & -t \\ 1 & 7 \end{vmatrix}$

Algebra Formulas

First, expand the given expression using the given definition.

$$\begin{vmatrix} s & t \\ 1 & 3 \end{vmatrix} - \begin{vmatrix} -t & 2 \\ s & 4 \end{vmatrix} + \begin{vmatrix} 2 & 2 \\ t & s \end{vmatrix}$$

$$= (3s - t) - (-4t - 2s) + (2s - 2t) = 3s - t + 4t + 2s + 2s - 2t = 7s + t$$

Next, compare the result, $7s + t$, with the expanded versions of the answer choices.

A $\begin{vmatrix} s & t \\ 1 & 5 \end{vmatrix} = 5s - t$ (not correct)

B $\begin{vmatrix} s & t \\ 7 & 1 \end{vmatrix} = s - 7t$ (not correct)

C $\begin{vmatrix} s & t \\ 5 & 7 \end{vmatrix} = 7s - 5t$ (not correct)

D $\begin{vmatrix} s & -t \\ 1 & 5 \end{vmatrix} = 5s + t$ (not correct)

E $\begin{vmatrix} s & -t \\ 1 & 7 \end{vmatrix} = 7s + t$ (correct)

The correct answer is E.

67. In a certain sequence, each term after the first term is one-half the previous term. If the tenth term of the sequence is between 0.0001 and 0.001, then the twelfth term of the sequence is between

(A) 0.0025 and 0.025
(B) 0.00025 and 0.0025
(C) 0.000025 and 0.00025
(D) 0.0000025 and 0.000025
(E) 0.00000025 and 0.0000025

Arithmetic Sequences

Let a_n represent the nth term of the sequence. It is given that each term after the first term is $\frac{1}{2}$ the previous term and that $0.0001 < a_{10} < 0.001$. Then for a_{11}, $\frac{0.0001}{2} < a_{11} < \frac{0.001}{2}$, or $0.00005 < a_{11} < 0.0005$. For a_{12}, $\frac{0.00005}{2} < a_{12} < \frac{0.0005}{2}$, or $0.000025 < a_{12} < 0.00025$. Thus, the twelfth term of the sequence is between 0.000025 and 0.00025.

The correct answer is C.

68. A certain drive-in movie theater has a total of 17 rows of parking spaces. There are 20 parking spaces in the first row and 21 parking spaces in the second row. In each subsequent row there are 2 more parking spaces than in the previous row. What is the total number of parking spaces in the movie theater?

(A) 412
(B) 544
(C) 596
(D) 632
(E) 692

Arithmetic Operations on Integers

Row	Number of parking spaces
1st row	20
2nd row	21
3rd row	21 + 1(2)
4th row	21 + 2(2)
…	… … …
17th row	21 + 15(2)

Then, letting S represent the total number of parking spaces in the theater,

$$S = 20 + (16)(21) + (1 + 2 + 3 + \ldots + 15)(2)$$
$$= 20 + 336 + \frac{(15)(16)}{2}(2) \text{ see note below}$$
$$= 356 + 240$$
$$= 596$$

Note that if $s = 1 + 2 + 3 + \ldots + 15$, then $2s = (1 + 2 + 3 + \ldots + 15) + (15 + 14 + 13 + \ldots + 1)$, and so $2s = (1 + 15) + (2 + 14) + (3 + 13) + \ldots + (15 + 1) = (15)(16)$. Therefore, $s = \frac{(15)(16)}{2}$.

The correct answer is C.

69. Ada and Paul received their scores on three tests. On the first test, Ada's score was 10 points higher than Paul's score. On the second test, Ada's score was 4 points higher than Paul's score. If Paul's average (arithmetic mean) score on the three tests was 3 points higher than Ada's average score on the three tests, then Paul's score on the third test was how many points higher than Ada's score?

(A) 9
(B) 14
(C) 17
(D) 23
(E) 25

Algebra Statistics

Let a_1, a_2, and a_3 be Ada's scores on the first, second, and third tests, respectively, and let p_1, p_2, and p_3 be Paul's scores on the first, second, and third tests, respectively. Then, Ada's average score is $\frac{a_1+a_2+a_3}{3}$ and Paul's average score is $\frac{p_1+p_2+p_3}{3}$. But Paul's average score is 3 points higher than Ada's average score, so $\frac{p_1+p_2+p_3}{3}=\frac{a_1+a_2+a_3}{3}+3$. Also, it is given that $a_1=p_1+10$ and $a_2=p_2+4$, so by substitution, $\frac{p_1+p_2+p_3}{3}=\frac{(p_1+10)+(p_2+4)+a_3}{3}+3$. Then $p_1+p_2+p_3=(p_1+10)+(p_2+4)+a_3+9$ and so $p_3=a_3+23$. On the third test, Paul's score was 23 points higher than Ada's score.

The correct answer is D.

70. The price of a certain stock increased by 0.25 of 1 percent on a certain day. By what fraction did the price of the stock increase that day?

(A) $\frac{1}{2{,}500}$
(B) $\frac{1}{400}$
(C) $\frac{1}{40}$
(D) $\frac{1}{25}$
(E) $\frac{1}{4}$

Arithmetic Percents

It is given that the price of a certain stock increased by 0.25 of 1 percent on a certain day. This is equivalent to an increase of $\frac{1}{4}$ of $\frac{1}{100}$, which is $\left(\frac{1}{4}\right)\left(\frac{1}{100}\right)$, and $\left(\frac{1}{4}\right)\left(\frac{1}{100}\right)=\frac{1}{400}$.

The correct answer is B.

71. For each trip, a taxicab company charges $4.25 for the first mile and $2.65 for each additional mile or fraction thereof. If the total charge for a certain trip was $62.55, how many miles at most was the trip?

(A) 21
(B) 22
(C) 23
(D) 24
(E) 25

Arithmetic Applied Problems

Subtracting the charge for the first mile leaves a charge of $62.55 – $4.25 = $58.30 for the miles after the first mile. Divide this amount by $2.65 to find the number of miles to which $58.30 corresponds: $\frac{58.30}{2.65}=22$ miles. Therefore, the total number of miles is at most 1 (the first mile) added to 22 (the number of miles after the first mile), which equals 23.

The correct answer is C.

72. When 24 is divided by the positive integer *n*, the remainder is 4. Which of the following statements about *n* must be true?

I. *n* is even.
II. *n* is a multiple of 5.
III. *n* is a factor of 20.

(A) III only
(B) I and II only
(C) I and III only
(D) II and III only
(E) I, II, and III

Arithmetic **Properties of Numbers**

Since the remainder is 4 when 24 is divided by the positive integer n and the remainder must be less than the divisor, it follows that $24 = qn + 4$ for some positive integer q and $4 < n$, or $qn = 20$ and $n > 4$. It follows that $n = 5$, or $n = 10$, or $n = 20$ since these are the only factors of 20 that exceed 4.

I. n is not necessarily even. For example, n could be 5.
II. n is necessarily a multiple of 5 since the value of n is either 5, 10, or 20.
III. n is a factor of 20 since $20 = qn$ for some positive integer q.

The correct answer is D.

73. Terry needs to purchase some pipe for a plumbing job that requires pipes with lengths of 1 ft 4 in, 2 ft 8 in, 3 ft 4 in, 3 ft 8 in, 4 ft 8 in, 5 ft 8 in, and 9 ft 4 in. The store from which Terry will purchase the pipe sells pipe only in 10-ft lengths. If each 10-ft length can be cut into shorter pieces, what is the minimum number of 10-ft pipe lengths that Terry needs to purchase for the plumbing job?

(Note: 1 ft = 12 in)

(A) 3
(B) 4
(C) 5
(D) 6
(E) 7

Arithmetic **Operations with Integers; Measurement Conversion**

The 7 lengths of pipe Terry needs total 30 feet plus 8 inches, which means Terry will need to buy at least 4 pipes, each 10 feet long. Four pipes will suffice if Terry cuts pieces of the following lengths:

1st pipe: 9 feet 4 inches (with 8 inches left)

2nd pipe: 5 feet 8 inches and 3 feet 8 inches (with 8 inches left)

3rd pipe: 4 feet 8 inches, 3 feet 4 inches, and 1 foot 4 inches (with 8 inches left)

4th pipe: 2 feet 8 inches (with 7 feet 4 inches left)

The correct answer is B.

74. What is the thousandths digit in the decimal equivalent of $\frac{53}{5{,}000}$?

(A) 0
(B) 1
(C) 3
(D) 5
(E) 6

Arithmetic **Place Value**

$\frac{53}{5{,}000} = \frac{106}{10{,}000} = 0.0106$ and the thousandths digit is 0.

The correct answer is A.

75. If a equals the sum of the even integers from 2 to 20, inclusive, and b equals the sum of the odd integers from 1 to 19, inclusive, what is the value of $a - b$?

(A) 1
(B) 10
(C) 19
(D) 20
(E) 21

Arithmetic **Series and Sequences**

$$a = 2 + 4 + 6 + \ldots + 20$$
$$b = 1 + 3 + 5 + \ldots + 19$$
$$a - b = (2 - 1) + (4 - 3) + (6 - 5) + \ldots + (20 - 19)$$
$$= 1 + 1 + 1 + \ldots + 1$$

Since there are 10 even numbers in the expression for a above—note that the expression for a can be written as $2(1 + 2 + 3 + \ldots + 10)$—it follows that there are 10 occurrences of 1 in the expression for $a - b$, and hence $a - b = 10 \times 1 = 10$.

The correct answer is B.

76. If a, b, c, and d are consecutive even integers and $a < b < c < d$, then $a + b$ is how much less than $c + d$?

(A) 2
(B) 4
(C) 6
(D) 8
(E) 10

Algebra Series and Sequences; Simplifying Algebraic Expressions

Since a, b, c, and d are consecutive even integers in this order, we have $b = a + 2$, $c = b + 2 = a + 4$, and $d = c + 2 = a + 6$. Therefore, the amount by which $a + b$ is less than $c + d$ is $(c + d) - (a + b) = (a + 4 + a + 6) - (a + a + 2) = 8$.

The correct answer is D.

77. A retailer sold an appliance for \$80. If the retailer's gross profit on the appliance was 25 percent of the retailer's cost for the appliance, how many dollars was the retailer's gross profit?

(A) \$10
(B) \$16
(C) \$20
(D) \$24
(E) \$25

Algebra Applied Problems; First-Degree Equations

Let $\$C$ be the cost of the appliance. The appliance sold for \$80 and the profit was 25% of the cost. Since selling price equals cost plus profit, it follows that $80 = C + 0.25C = 1.25C$. Dividing both sides by 1.25 (equivalently, dividing both sides by $\frac{5}{4}$), we have $C = 64$. Therefore, the profit is $0.25(\$C) = \frac{1}{4} \times \$64 = \$16$.

The correct answer is B.

78. Beth has a collection of 8 boxes of clothing for a charity, and the average (arithmetic mean) number of pieces of clothing per box is c. If she replaces a box in the collection that contains 12 pieces of clothing with a box that contains 22 pieces of clothing, what is the average number of pieces of clothing per box for the new collection, in terms of c?

(A) $c - \frac{5}{4}$
(B) $c + \frac{5}{4}$
(C) $8 - \frac{10}{c}$
(D) $8 + \frac{10}{c}$
(E) $8c - 10$

Algebra Average

Before the replacement, the total number of pieces of clothing in the 8 boxes was $8c$. After the replacement, the total number of pieces of clothing in the 8 boxes was $8c - 12 + 22 = 8c + 10$. Therefore, the average number of pieces of clothing per box for the new collection is

$$\frac{8c + 10}{8} = \frac{8c}{8} + \frac{10}{8} = c + \frac{5}{4}.$$

The correct answer is B.

$$\frac{1 + 0.0001}{0.04 + 10}$$

79. The value of the expression above is closest to which of the following?

(A) 0.0001
(B) 0.001
(C) 0.01
(D) 1
(E) 10

Arithmetic Estimation

$$\frac{1 + 0.0001}{0.04 + 10} = \frac{1.0001}{10.04} \approx \frac{1}{10} = 0.1$$

Alternatively (and less heuristically), because a small relative change (i.e., a small percentage change) in the value of the numerator of a fraction produces a small relative change in the value of the fraction, and similarly for the denominator, it follows that

$$\frac{1 + 0.0001}{0.04 + 10} \approx \frac{1}{0.04 + 10} \approx \frac{1}{10} = 0.1$$

The correct answer is C.

80. If $x + 1 = t$ and $t = 3 - x$, then $x =$

(A) −2
(B) −1
(C) 0
(D) 1
(E) 2

Algebra First-Degree Equations

$x + 1 = 3 - x$	substitution
$x + x = 3 - 1$	add $x - 1$ to both sides
$2x = 2$	combine like terms
$x = 1$	divide both sides by 2

The correct answer is D.

81. If $x = kc$ and $y = kt$, then $y - x =$

(A) $k(t - c)$
(B) $k(c - t)$
(C) $c(k - t)$
(D) $t(k - c)$
(E) $k(1 - t)$

Algebra Simplifying Algebraic Expressions

$y - x = kt - kc$	given
$y - x = k(t - c)$	distributive property

The correct answer is A.

82. If k is a positive even integer, which of the following must be an odd integer?

I. $k^2 - 3k + 4$
II. $k^5 + 3$
III. $7k - 7$

(A) II only
(B) III only
(C) I and III only
(D) II and III only
(E) I, II, and III

Arithmetic Properties of Integers

The table below shows some results for adding, subtracting, and multiplying even and odd integers. For example, an even integer plus an even integer is an even integer (for example, 4 + 8 equals 12, which is even) and an odd integer times an odd integer is an odd integer (for example, 3 × 7 equals 21, which is odd).

even	±	even	is	even
even	±	odd	is	odd
odd	±	odd	is	even
even	×	even	is	even
even	×	odd	is	even
odd	×	odd	is	odd

Now apply these results to the expressions in I, II, and III when k is an even integer.

I. $k^2 - 3k + 4$ is even − even + even, which is **EVEN.**

II. $k^5 + 3$ is even + odd, which is **ODD.**

III. 7k − 7 is even − odd, which is **ODD.**

The correct answer is D.

Questions 83 to 151 — Difficulty: Medium

83. If $\frac{1}{2}$ the result obtained when 2 is subtracted from $5x$ is equal to the sum of 10 and $3x$, what is the value of x?

(A) −22
(B) −4
(C) 4
(D) 18
(E) 22

Algebra First-Degree Equations

The result obtained when 2 is subtracted from $5x$ is $5x - 2$, and the sum of 10 and $3x$ is $10 + 3x$.

Therefore, it is given that $\frac{1}{2}$ of $5x - 2$ is equal to $10 + 3x$, or $\frac{1}{2}(5x - 2) = 10 + 3x$.

$\frac{1}{2}(5x - 2) = 10 + 3x$	given
$5x - 2 = 20 + 6x$	multiply both sides by 2
$-22 = x$	subtract both $5x$ and 20 from both sides

The correct answer is A.

84. If Car A took n hours to travel 2 miles and Car B took m hours to travel 3 miles, which of the following expresses the time it would take Car C, traveling at the average (arithmetic mean) of those rates, to travel 5 miles?

(A) $\dfrac{10nm}{3n+2m}$

(B) $\dfrac{3n+2m}{10(n+m)}$

(C) $\dfrac{2n+3m}{5nm}$

(D) $\dfrac{10(n+m)}{2n+3m}$

(E) $\dfrac{5(n+m)}{2n+3m}$

Algebra Applied Problems

This is a rate problem that can be solved by several applications of the formula

rate × time = distance.

Let r_A and r_B be the rates, respectively and in miles per hour, of Car A and Car B. Then omitting units for simplicity, for Car A this formula becomes $r_A \times n = 2$, or $r_A = \frac{2}{n}$, and for Car B this formula becomes $r_B \times m = 3$, or $r_B = \frac{3}{m}$. Thus, the average of the two rates is $\frac{1}{2}(r_A + r_B) = \frac{1}{2}\left(\frac{2}{n}+\frac{3}{m}\right) = \frac{1}{2}\left(\frac{2m+3n}{mn}\right) = \frac{3n+2m}{2mn}$.

Therefore, if t is the desired time, in hours, that Car C traveled, then the above formula for Car C becomes $\frac{3n+2m}{2mn} \times t = 5$, or $t = 5 \times \frac{2mn}{3n+2m} = \frac{10mn}{3n+2m}$.

The correct answer is A.

85. If x, y, and k are positive and x is less than y, then $\dfrac{x+k}{y+k}$ is

(A) 1

(B) greater than $\dfrac{x}{y}$

(C) equal to $\dfrac{x}{y}$

(D) less than $\dfrac{x}{y}$

(E) less than $\dfrac{x}{y}$ or greater than $\dfrac{x}{y}$, depending on the value of k

Algebra Ratios

x	$<$	y	given
kx	$<$	ky	multiply by positive k
$xy + kx$	$<$	$xy + ky$	add xy
$x(y+k)$	$<$	$y(x+k)$	factor
x	$<$	$\dfrac{y(x+k)}{y+k}$	divide by positive $y + k$
$\dfrac{x}{y}$	$<$	$\dfrac{x+k}{y+k}$	divide by positive y

Thus, $\dfrac{x+k}{y+k} > \dfrac{x}{y}$.

The correct answer is B.

86. Consider the following set of inequalities: $p > q$, $s > r$, $q > t$, $s > p$, and $r > q$. Between which two quantities is no relationship established?

(A) p and r

(B) s and t

(C) s and q

(D) p and t

(E) r and t

Algebra Order

Using $r > q$ and $q > t$ gives $r > t$, so a relationship is established between r and t. The correct answer is NOT E.

Using $p > q$ and $q > t$ gives $p > t$, so a relationship is established between p and t. The correct answer is NOT D.

Using $s > r$ and $r > q$ gives $s > q$, so a relationship is established between s and q. The correct answer is NOT C.

Using $s > r$, $r > q$, and $q > t$ gives $s > t$, so a relationship is established between s and t. The correct answer is NOT B.

Alternately, the diagram below shows the given relationships and does not establish a relationship between p and r.

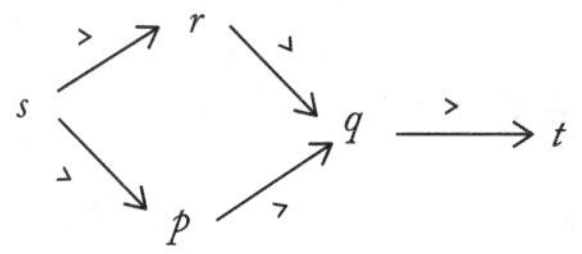

The correct answer is A.

87. Carl averaged $2m$ miles per hour on a trip that took him h hours. If Ruth made the same trip in $\frac{2}{3}h$ hours, what was her average speed in miles per hour?

(A) $\frac{1}{3}mh$

(B) $\frac{2}{3}mh$

(C) m

(D) $\frac{3}{2}m$

(E) $3m$

Algebra Applied Problems

Using distance = rate × time, the distance Carl traveled on the trip was $2mh$ miles. Using rate $= \frac{\text{distance}}{\text{time}}$, Ruth's rate was $\frac{2mh}{\frac{2}{3}h} = \frac{3}{2}(2m) = 3m$.

The correct answer is E.

88. Of three persons, two take relish, two take pepper, and two take salt. The one who takes no salt takes no pepper, and the one who takes no pepper takes no relish. Which of the following statements must be true?

I. The person who takes no salt also takes no relish.

II. Any of the three persons who takes pepper also takes relish and salt.

III. The person who takes no relish is not one of those who takes salt.

(A) I only

(B) II only

(C) III only

(D) I and II only

(E) I, II, and III

Arithmetic Sets (Venn Diagrams)

Although this problem can be solved by the use of a Venn diagram, it is probably simpler to use ordinary reasoning. The single person who takes no salt takes no pepper, and the single person who takes no pepper takes no relish, so exactly one person does not take any of the three. Thus, each of the other two people take all three. The table below shows these results where Person 1 does not take any of the three and Persons 2 and 3 each take all three.

Person	Relish	Pepper	Salt
1	no	no	no
2	yes	yes	yes
3	yes	yes	yes

The only person who takes no salt is Person 1, who also takes no relish, so I must be true.

The only people who take pepper are Persons 2 and 3, and each of them also takes relish and salt, so II must be true.

The only person who takes no relish is Person 1, who is not a person who takes salt, so III must be true.

The correct answer is E.

89. If the smaller of 2 consecutive odd integers is a multiple of 5, which of the following could NOT be the sum of these 2 integers?

(A) −8
(B) 12
(C) 22
(D) 52
(E) 252

Algebra Operations with Integers

Since the smaller of the 2 consecutive odd integers is a multiple of 5, let it be represented by $5n$ for some integer n. Then the other odd integer can be represented by $5n + 2$. The sum of these two integers is $10n + 2$. The sum is −8 when $n = -1$ and $5n = (5)(-1)$ is odd. The sum is 12 when $n = 1$ and $5n = (5)(1)$ is odd. The sum is 22 when $n = 2$, but $5n = (5)(2)$ is not odd. There is no need to check the D and E because it has been determined that 22 cannot be the sum of the 2 consecutive odd integers. For completeness, the sum is 52 when $n = 5$ and $5n = (5)(5)$ is odd. The sum is 252 when $n = 25$ and $5n = (5)(25)$ is odd.

The correct answer is C.

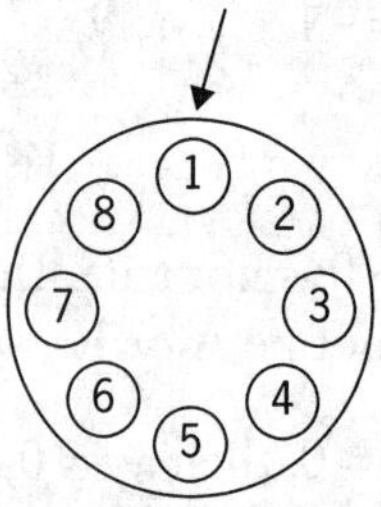

90. Eight light bulbs numbered 1 through 8 are arranged in a circle as shown above. The bulbs are wired so that every third bulb, counting in a clockwise direction, flashes until all bulbs have flashed once. If the bulb numbered 1 flashes first, which numbered bulb will flash last?

(A) 2
(B) 3
(C) 4
(D) 6
(E) 7

Arithmetic Properties of Integers

The easiest way to do this problem might be by just counting every third bulb going clockwise around the circle starting at Bulb 1, which flashes, skipping 2 bulbs and getting to Bulb 4, which flashes, skipping 2 bulbs and getting to Bulb 7, which flashes, skipping 2 bulbs and getting to Bulb 2, which flashes, skipping 2 bulbs and getting to Bulb 5, which flashes, skipping 2 bulbs and getting to Bulb 8, which flashes, skipping 2 bulbs and getting to Bulb 3, which flashes, and finally skipping 2 bulbs and getting to Bulb 6, which flashes. Now, all 8 bulbs have flashed once and the last one to flash was Bulb 6.

The correct answer is D.

Closing Prices of Stock X
During a Certain Week
(in dollars)

Monday	Tuesday	Wednesday	Thursday	Friday
21	19	22	$24\frac{1}{2}$	23

91. A certain financial analyst defines the "volatility" of a stock during a given week to be the result of the following procedure: find the absolute value of the difference in the stock's closing price for each pair of consecutive days in the week and then find the average (arithmetic mean) of these 4 values. What is the volatility of Stock X during the week shown in the table?

(A) 0.50
(B) 1.80
(C) 2.00
(D) 2.25
(E) 2.50

Arithmetic Statistics

The volatility of Stock X during the week is the average of the 4 values associated with the 4 pairs of consecutive days during the week.

$$\frac{(\text{Mon \& Tue})+(\text{Tue \& Wed})+(\text{Wed \& Thu})+(\text{Thu \& Fri})}{4}$$

$$=\frac{|19-21|+|22-19|+|24.5-22|+|23-24.5|}{4}$$

$$=\frac{|-2|+|3|+|2.5|+|-1.5|}{4}=\frac{2+3+2.5+1.5}{4}=\frac{9}{4}=2.25$$

The correct answer is D.

92. If $y=\frac{|3x-5|}{-x^2-3}$, for what value of x will the value of y be greatest?

(A) −5

(B) $-\frac{3}{5}$

(C) 0

(D) $\frac{3}{5}$

(E) $\frac{5}{3}$

Algebra Functions; Absolute Value

Since the absolute value of any real number is greater than or equal to zero, it follows that $|3x-5| \geq 0$. Also, for any real number x we have $x^2 \geq 0$, and hence $-x^2 \leq 0$. Subtracting 3 from both sides of the last inequality gives $-x^2-3 \leq -3$. Therefore, the numerator of the expression for y is greater than or equal to zero and the denominator of the expression for y is negative. It follows that the value of y cannot be greater than 0. However, the value of y is equal to 0 when $|3x-5|=0$, or $3x-5=0$, or $x=\frac{5}{3}$. Therefore, the value of x for which the value of y is greatest (i.e., when $y=0$) is $x=\frac{5}{3}$.

The correct answer is E.

93. What values of x have a corresponding value of y that satisfies both $xy > 0$ and $xy = x + y$?

(A) $x \leq -1$

(B) $-1 < x \leq 0$

(C) $0 < x \leq 1$

(D) $x > 1$

(E) All real numbers

Algebra Equations; Inequalities

First, use $xy = x + y$ to solve for y in terms of x.

xy	=	$x+y$	given
$xy-y$	=	x	subtract y from both sides
$y(x-1)$	=	x	factor
y	=	$\frac{x}{x-1}$	divide both sides by $x-1$

Note that the division by $x-1$ requires $x \neq 1$, and thus $x = 1$ needs to be considered separately. However, if $x = 1$, then $xy = x + y$ becomes $y = 1 + y$, which is not true for any value of y. Using $y=\frac{x}{x-1}$, it follows that the inequality $xy > 0$ is equivalent to $\frac{x^2}{x-1} > 0$. Since $x^2 \geq 0$ for each value of x, the quotient $\frac{x^2}{x-1}$ can only be positive when $x \neq 0$ and $x-1$ is positive, or when $x > 1$.

Alternatively, the correct answer can be found by eliminating the incorrect answers, which can be accomplished by considering the endpoints of the intervals given in the answer choices.

Case 1: If $x = -1$, then $xy = x + y$ becomes $-y = -1 + y$, or $y=\frac{1}{2}$. However, in this case $xy=(-1)\left(\frac{1}{2}\right)$ is negative, and thus $xy > 0$ is not true. Therefore, the answer cannot be A or E.

Case 2: If $x = 0$, then $xy = 0$, and thus $xy > 0$ is not true. Therefore, the answer cannot be B or E.

Case 3: If $x = 1$, then $xy = x + y$ becomes $y = 1 + y$, which is not true for any value of y. Therefore, the answer cannot be C or E.

Since the answer cannot be A, B, C, or E, it follows that the answer is D.

The correct answer is D.

94. Employee X's annual salary is $12,000 more than half of Employee Y's annual salary. Employee Z's annual salary is $15,000 more than half of Employee X's annual salary. If Employee X's annual salary is $27,500, which of the following lists these three people in order of increasing annual salary?

(A) Y, Z, X
(B) Y, X, Z
(C) Z, X, Y
(D) X, Y, Z
(E) X, Z, Y

Algebra First-Degree Equations

Letting x, y, and z represent the annual salary, in dollars, of Employee X, Employee Y, and Employee Z, respectively, the following information is given:

(1) $x = 12{,}000 + \frac{y}{2}$

(2) $x = 15{,}000 + \frac{x}{2}$

(3) $x = 27{,}500$

From (1) and (3), it follows that $27{,}500 = 12{,}000 + \frac{y}{2}$ or $y = 2(27{,}500 - 12{,}000) = 31{,}000$. From (2) and (3), it follows that $z = 15{,}000 + \frac{27{,}500}{2} = 28{,}750$. Therefore, $x < z < y$.

The correct answer is E.

95. $$C = \begin{cases} 0.10s, \text{ if } s \le 60{,}000 \\ 0.10s + 0.04(s - 60{,}000), \text{ if } s > 60{,}000 \end{cases}$$

The formula above gives the contribution C, in dollars, to a certain profit-sharing plan for a participant with a salary of s dollars. How many more dollars is the contribution for a participant with a salary of $70,000 than for a participant with a salary of $50,000?

(A) $800
(B) $1,400
(C) $2,000
(D) $2,400
(E) $2,800

Algebra Applied Problems; Formulas

For a participant with a salary of $70,000, $C = 0.1(\$70{,}000) + 0.04(\$70{,}000 - \$60{,}000) = \$7{,}000 + \$400 = \$7{,}400$. For a participant with a salary of $50,000, $C = 0.1(\$50{,}000) = \$5{,}000$. The difference is $\$7{,}400 - \$5{,}000 = \$2{,}400$.

The correct answer is D.

96. Next month, Ron and Cathy will each begin working part-time at $\frac{3}{5}$ of their respective current salaries. If the sum of their reduced salaries will be equal to Cathy's current salary, then Ron's current salary is what fraction of Cathy's current salary?

(A) $\frac{1}{3}$
(B) $\frac{2}{5}$
(C) $\frac{1}{2}$
(D) $\frac{3}{5}$
(E) $\frac{2}{3}$

Algebra First-Degree Equations

Letting R and C, respectively, represent Ron's and Cathy's current salaries, it is given that $\frac{3}{5}R + \frac{3}{5}C = C$. It follows that $\frac{3}{5}R = \frac{2}{5}C$ and $R = \frac{5}{3}\left(\frac{2}{5}C\right) = \frac{2}{3}C$.

The correct answer is E.

97. David and Ron are ordering food for a business lunch. David thinks that there should be twice as many sandwiches as there are pastries, but Ron thinks the number of pastries should be 12 more than one-fourth of the number of sandwiches. How many sandwiches should be ordered so that David and Ron can agree on the number of pastries to order?

(A) 12
(B) 16
(C) 20
(D) 24
(E) 48

Algebra Simultaneous Equations

Let S be the number of sandwiches that should be ordered and let P be the number of pastries that should be ordered. Then David desires $S = 2P$ and Ron desires $P = 12 + \frac{1}{4}S$.

$S = 2P$	given
$S = 2(12 + \frac{1}{4}S)$	$P = 12 + \frac{1}{4}S$
$S = 24 + \frac{1}{2}S$	distributive law
$\frac{1}{2}S = 24$	subtract $\frac{1}{2}S$ from both sides
$S = 48$	multiply both sides by 2

The correct answer is E.

98. The cost of purchasing each box of candy from a certain mail order catalog is v dollars per pound of candy, plus a shipping charge of h dollars. How many dollars does it cost to purchase 2 boxes of candy, one containing s pounds of candy and the other containing t pounds of candy, from this catalog?

(A) $h + stv$
(B) $2h + stv$
(C) $2hstv$
(D) $2h + s + t + v$
(E) $2h + v(s + t)$

Algebra Formulas

The cost, in dollars, to purchase the 2 boxes of candy is the sum of 2 shipping charges and the cost of $s + t$ pounds of candy.

$$\text{cost} = (2 \text{ shipping charges}) + (v)(s + t)$$
$$\text{cost} = 2(h) + (v)(s + t)$$
$$\text{cost} = 2h + v(s + t)$$

The correct answer is E.

99. If $x \neq -\frac{1}{2}$, then $\frac{6x^3 + 3x^2 - 8x - 4}{2x + 1} =$

(A) $3x^2 + \frac{3}{2}x - 8$
(B) $3x^2 + \frac{3}{2}x - 4$
(C) $3x^2 - 4$
(D) $3x - 4$
(E) $3x + 4$

Algebra Factoring

$\frac{6x^3 + 3x^2 - 8x - 4}{2x + 1} = \frac{(6x^3 + 3x^2) - (8x + 4)}{2x + 1}$	group
$= \frac{3x^2(2x + 1) - 4(2x + 1)}{2x + 1}$	factor
$= \frac{(3x^2 - 4)(2x + 1)}{2x + 1}$	factor
$= 3x^2 - 4$	cancel since $x \neq \frac{1}{2}$

Alternatively, sometimes it is easier or quicker to test one-variable expressions for equality by substituting a convenient value for the variable and eliminating answer choices for which the value of the expression in that answer choice does not equal the value of the given expression. For example, choose $x = 0$, since calculations for $x = 0$ are minimal. Then, as shown in the table below, $\frac{6x^3 + 3x^2 - 8x - 4}{2x + 1} = \frac{-4}{1} = -4$, but $3x^2 + \frac{3}{2}x - 8 = -8$ and $3x + 4 = 4$, neither of which equals -4, so answer choices A and E can be eliminated. Another convenient value to choose for x is 1. There is no need to evaluate answer choices A and E at 1 since they have already been eliminated. As shown, when $x = 1$, $\frac{6x^3 + 3x^2 - 8x - 4}{2x + 1} = -1$, but $3x^2 + \frac{3}{2}x - 4 = \frac{1}{2} \neq -1$, so answer choice B can be eliminated. A third convenient value for x is -1. There is no need to evaluate answer choices A, B, and E at -1 since they have already been eliminated. As shown, when $x = -1$, $\frac{6x^3 + 3x^2 - 8x - 4}{2x + 1} = -1$, but $3x - 4 = -7 \neq -1$, so answer choice D can be

eliminated. Note that, if $x = -1$ had been chosen initially, A, B, D, and E would have been eliminated immediately since $3x^2 + \frac{3}{2}x - 8 = -6\frac{1}{2} \neq -1$, $3x^2 + \frac{3}{2}x - 4 = -2\frac{1}{2} \neq -1$, $3x - 4 = -7 \neq -1$, and $3x + 4 = 1 \neq -1$.

		$x = 0$	$x = 1$	$x = -1$
	$\frac{6x^3 + 3x^2 - 8x - 4}{2x + 1}$	-4	-1	-1
A	$3x^2 + \frac{3}{2}x - 8$	-8		
B	$3x^2 + \frac{3}{2}x - 4$	-4	$\frac{1}{2}$	
C	$3x^2 - 4$	-4	-1	-1
D	$3x - 4$	-4	-1	-7
E	$3x + 4$	4		

The correct answer is C.

100. If $x^2 + bx + 5 = (x + c)^2$ for all numbers x, where b and c are positive constants, what is the value of b?

(A) $\sqrt{5}$
(B) $\sqrt{10}$
(C) $2\sqrt{5}$
(D) $2\sqrt{10}$
(E) 10

Algebra Second-Degree Equations

Given that $x^2 + bx + 5 = (x + c)^2$, since $(x + c)^2 = x^2 + 2cx + c^2$, it follows that $5 = c^2$ and $b = 2c$. The possible values of c are $-\sqrt{5}$ and $\sqrt{5}$, but since c is positive, $c = \sqrt{5}$ and $b = 2c = 2\sqrt{5}$.

The correct answer is C.

101. Last year Shannon listened to a certain public radio station 10 hours per week and contributed \$35 to the station. Of the following, which is closest to Shannon's contribution per minute of listening time last year?

(A) \$0.001
(B) \$0.010
(C) \$0.025
(D) \$0.058
(E) \$0.067

Arithmetic Measurement Conversion

Since there are 52 weeks in 1 year and 60 minutes in 1 hour, 10 hours per week is equivalent to (10)(52)(60) = 31,200 minutes per year. Shannon's \$35 contribution is then $\frac{35}{31,200}$ dollars per minute, which is closest to \$0.001 per minute.

The correct answer is A.

102. Each of the 20 employees at Company J is to receive an end-of-year bonus this year. Agnes will receive a larger bonus than any other employee, but only \$500 more than Cheryl will receive. None of the employees will receive a smaller bonus than Cheryl. If the amount of money to be distributed in bonuses at Company J this year totals \$60,000, what is the largest bonus Agnes can receive?

(A) \$3,250
(B) \$3,325
(C) \$3,400
(D) \$3,475
(E) \$3,500

Algebra Applied Problems

Since the total amount of the bonuses is fixed, the largest possible bonus that Agnes can receive will occur when the total amount received by the 19 employees other than Agnes is the smallest possible. Let A be the bonus, in dollars, that Agnes receives. Then, in dollars, Cheryl will receive $(A - 500)$, and each of the remaining 18 employees will receive between $(A - 500)$ and A. Therefore, the total amount received by the 19 employees other than Agnes is smallest when each of these 19 employees receives $(A - 500)$ dollars.

$19(A - 500) + A$	=	60,000	total of 20 bonuses is \$60,000
$19A - 9{,}500 + A$	=	60,000	distributive law
$20A - 9{,}500$	=	60,000	combine like terms
$20A$	=	69,500	add 9,500 to both sides
A	=	3,475	divide both sides by 20

The correct answer is D.

103. Beth, Naomi, and Juan raised a total of \$55 for charity. Naomi raised \$5 less than Juan, and Juan raised twice as much as Beth. How much did Beth raise?

(A) \$9
(B) \$10
(C) \$12
(D) \$13
(E) \$15

Algebra Simultaneous Equations

Let B, N, and J be the amounts raised, respectively and in dollars, by Beth, Naomi, and Juan.

$B+N+J$	=	55	given
N	=	$J-5$	given
J	=	$2B$	given
J	=	$55-B-N$	subtract $B+N$ from both sides of first equation
J	=	$55-B-(J-5)$	$N=J-5$
$2B$	=	$55-B-(2B-5)$	$J=2B$
B	=	12	solve for B

The correct answer is C.

104. The set of solutions for the equation $(x^2-25)^2 = x^2-10x+25$ contains how many real numbers?

(A) 0
(B) 1
(C) 2
(D) 3
(E) 4

Algebra Second-Degree Equations

$(x^2-25)^2=x^2-10x+25$	given
$(x+5)^2(x-5)^2=(x-5)^2$	factor
$(x+5)^2(x-5)^2-(x-5)^2=0$	subtract $(x-5)^2$
$(x-5)^2[(x+5)^2-1]=0$	factor
$(x-5)^2[(x+5)-1][(x+5)+1]=0$	factor
$(x-5)^2(x+4)(x+6)=0$	subtraction, addition

Thus, the solution set of $(x^2-25)^2=x^2-10x+25$ contains 3 real numbers: 5, –4, and –6.

The correct answer is D.

105. An aerosol can is designed so that its bursting pressure, B, in pounds per square inch, is 120% of the pressure, F, in pounds per square inch, to which it is initially filled. Which of the following formulas expresses the relationship between B and F?

(A) $B=1.2F$
(B) $B=120F$
(C) $B=1+0.2F$
(D) $B=\frac{F}{1.2}$
(E) $B=\frac{1.2}{F}$

Algebra Formulas; Percents

We are given that B is 120% of F, so $B=(120\%)F$, or $B=1.2F$. Note that both B and F are given in pounds per square inch, so there are no unit conversions involved.

The correct answer is A.

106. The average (arithmetic mean) of the positive integers x, y, and z is 3. If $x<y<z$, what is the greatest possible value of z?

(A) 5
(B) 6
(C) 7
(D) 8
(E) 9

Algebra Inequalities

It is given that $\frac{x+y+z}{3}=3$, or $x+y+z=9$, or $z=9+(-x-y)$. It follows that the greatest possible value of z occurs when $-x-y=-(x+y)$ has the greatest possible value, which occurs when $x+y$ has the least possible value. Because x and y are different positive integers, the least possible value of $x+y$ occurs when $x=1$ and $y=2$. Therefore, the greatest possible value of z is $9-1-2=6$.

The correct answer is B.

107. The product of 3,305 and the 1-digit integer x is a 5-digit integer. The units (ones) digit of the product is 5 and the hundreds digit is y. If A is the set of all possible values of x and B is the set of all possible values of y, then which of the following gives the members of A and B?

	A	B
(A)	{1, 3, 5, 7, 9}	{0, 1, 2, 3, 4, 5, 6, 7, 8, 9}
(B)	{1, 3, 5, 7, 9}	{1, 3, 5, 7, 9}
(C)	{3, 5, 7, 9}	{1, 5, 7, 9}
(D)	{5, 7, 9}	{1, 5, 7}
(E)	{5, 7, 9}	{1, 5, 9}

Arithmetic Properties of Numbers

Since the products of 3,305 and 1, 3,305 and 2, and 3,305 and 3 are the 4-digit integers 3,305, 6,610, and 9,915, respectively, it follows that x must be among the 1-digit integers 4, 5, 6, 7, 8, and 9. Also, since the units digit of the product of 3,305 and x is 5, it follows that x cannot be 4 (product has units digit 0), 6 (product has units digit 0), or 8 (product has units digit 0). Therefore, $A = \{5, 7, 9\}$. The possibilities for y will be the hundreds digits of the products $(3{,}305)(5) = 16{,}525$, $(3{,}305)(7) = 23{,}135$, and $(3{,}305)(9) = 29{,}745$. Thus, y can be 5, 1, or 7, and so $B = \{1, 5, 7\}$.

The correct answer is D.

108. If x and y are integers such that $2 < x \le 8$ and $2 < y \le 9$, what is the maximum value of $\frac{1}{x} - \frac{x}{y}$?

(A) $-3\frac{1}{8}$

(B) 0

(C) $\frac{1}{4}$

(D) $\frac{5}{18}$

(E) 2

Algebra Inequalities

Because x and y are both positive, the maximum value of $\frac{1}{x} - \frac{x}{y}$ will occur when the value of $\frac{1}{x}$ is maximum and the value of $\frac{x}{y}$ is minimum. The value of $\frac{1}{x}$ is maximum when the value of x is minimum or when $x = 3$. The value of $\frac{x}{y}$ is minimum when the value of x is minimum (or when $x = 3$) and the value of y is maximum (or when $y = 9$). Thus, the maximum value of $\frac{1}{x} - \frac{x}{y}$ is $\frac{1}{3} - \frac{3}{9} = 0$.

The correct answer is B.

109. Items that are purchased together at a certain discount store are priced at \$3 for the first item purchased and \$1 for each additional item purchased. What is the maximum number of items that could be purchased together for a total price that is less than \$30 ?

(A) 25

(B) 26

(C) 27

(D) 28

(E) 29

Arithmetic Applied Problems

After the first item is purchased, \$29.99 – \$3.00 = \$26.99 remains to purchase the additional items. Since the price for each of the additional items is \$1.00, a maximum of 26 additional items could be purchased. Therefore, a maximum of 1 + 26 = 27 items could be purchased for less than \$30.00.

The correct answer is C.

110. What is the least integer z for which $(0.000125)(0.0025)(0.00000125) \times 10^z$ is an integer?

(A) 18

(B) 10

(C) 0

(D) –10

(E) –18

Arithmetic Decimals

Considering each of the three decimal numbers in parentheses separately, we know that 0.000125×10^6 is the integer 125, 0.0025×10^4 is the integer 25, and 0.00000125×10^8 is the integer 125. We thus know that $(0.000125) \times 10^6 \times (0.0025) \times 10^4 \times (0.00000125) \times 10^8 = (0.000125)(0.0025)(0.00000125) \times 10^6 \times 10^4 \times 10^8 = (0.000125)(0.0025)(0.00000125) \times$

$10^{6+4+8} = (0.000125)(0.0025)(0.00000125) \times 10^{18}$ is the integer $125 \times 25 \times 125$. We therefore know that if $z = 18$, then $(0.000125)(0.0025)(0.00000125) \times 10^z$ is an integer.

Now, if the product $125 \times 25 \times 125$ were divisible by 10, then for at least one integer z less than 18, $(0.000125)(0.0025)(0.00000125) \times 10^z$ would be an integer. However, each of the three numbers being multiplied in the product $125 \times 25 \times 125$ is odd (not divisible by 2). We thus know that $125 \times 25 \times 125$ is not divisible by 2 and is therefore odd. Because only even numbers are divisible by 10, we know that $125 \times 25 \times 125$ is not divisible by 10. We thus know that 18 is the *least* integer z such that $(0.000125)(0.0025)(0.00000125) \times 10^z$ is an integer.

Note that it is not necessary to perform the multiplication $125 \times 25 \times 125$.

The correct answer is A.

111. The average (arithmetic mean) length per film for a group of 21 films is t minutes. If a film that runs for 66 minutes is removed from the group and replaced by one that runs for 52 minutes, what is the average length per film, in minutes, for the new group of films, in terms of t?

(A) $t+\frac{2}{3}$

(B) $t-\frac{2}{3}$

(C) $21t+14$

(D) $t+\frac{3}{2}$

(E) $t-\frac{3}{2}$

Arithmetic Statistics

Let S denote the sum of the lengths, in minutes, of the 21 films in the original group. Since the average length is t minutes, it follows that $\frac{S}{21} = t$.

If a 66-minute film is replaced by a 52-minute film, then the sum of the lengths of the 21 films in the resulting group is $S - 66 + 52 = S - 14$. Therefore, the average length of the resulting 21 films is $\frac{S-14}{21} = \frac{S}{21} - \frac{14}{21} = t - \frac{2}{3}$.

The correct answer is B.

112. A garden center sells a certain grass seed in 5-pound bags at \$13.85 per bag, 10-pound bags at \$20.43 per bag, and 25-pound bags at \$32.25 per bag. If a customer is to buy at least 65 pounds of the grass seed, but no more than 80 pounds, what is the least possible cost of the grass seed that the customer will buy?

(A) \$94.03

(B) \$96.75

(C) \$98.78

(D) \$102.07

(E) \$105.36

Arithmetic Applied Problems

Let x represent the amount of grass seed, in pounds, the customer is to buy. It follows that $65 \le x \le 80$. Since the grass seed is available in only 5-pound, 10-pound, and 25-pound bags, then the customer must buy either 65, 70, 75, or 80 pounds of grass seed. Because the seed is more expensive per pound for smaller bags, the customer should minimize the number of the smaller bags and maximize the number of 25-pound bags to incur the least possible cost for the grass seed. The possible purchases are given in the table below.

x	Number of 25-pound bags	Number of 10-pound bags	Number of 5-pound bags	Total cost
65	2	1	1	\$98.78
70	2	2	0	\$105.36
75	3	0	0	\$96.75
80	3	0	1	\$110.60

The least possible cost is then 3(\$32.25) = \$96.75.

The correct answer is B.

113. If $x = -|w|$, which of the following must be true?

(A) $x = -w$

(B) $x = w$

(C) $x^2 = w$

(D) $x^2 = w^2$

(E) $x^3 = w^3$

Algebra Absolute Value

Squaring both sides of $x = -|w|$ gives $x^2 = (-|w|)^2$, or $x^2 = |w|^2 = w^2$.

Alternatively, if (x, w) is equal to either of the pairs $(-1, 1)$ or $(-1, -1)$, then $x = -|w|$ is true. However, each of the answer choices except $x^2 = w^2$ is false for at least one of these two pairs.

The correct answer is D.

114. A certain financial institution reported that its assets totaled \$2,377,366.30 on a certain day. Of this amount, \$31,724.54 was held in cash. Approximately what percent of the reported assets was held in cash on that day?

(A) 0.00013%
(B) 0.0013%
(C) 0.013%
(D) 0.13%
(E) 1.3%

Arithmetic Percents; Estimation

The requested percent can be estimated by converting the values into scientific notation.

$\dfrac{31{,}724.54}{2{,}377{,}366.30}$	value as fraction
$= \dfrac{3.172454\times10^4}{2.37736630\times10^6}$	convert to scientific notation
$= \dfrac{3.172454}{2.37736630}\times\dfrac{10^4}{10^6}$	arithmetic property of fractions
$= \dfrac{3.172454}{2.37736630}\times10^{-2}$	subtract exponents
$\approx \dfrac{3}{2}\times10^{-2}$	approximate
$= 1.5\times10^{-2}$	convert to decimal fraction
$= 0.015$	multiply
$= 1.5\%$	convert to percent

A more detailed computation would show that 1.3% is a better approximation. However, in order to select the best value from the values given as answer choices, the above computation is sufficient.

The correct answer is E.

$$\begin{array}{r} AB \\ +\ BA \\ \hline AAC \end{array}$$

115. In the correctly worked addition problem shown, where the sum of the two-digit positive integers *AB* and *BA* is the three-digit integer *AAC*, and *A*, *B*, and *C* are different digits, what is the units digit of the integer *AAC*?

(A) 9
(B) 6
(C) 3
(D) 2
(E) 0

Arithmetic Place Value

Determine the value of *C*.

It is given that $(10A + B) + (10B + A) = 100A + 10A + C$ or $11A + 11B = 110A + C$. Thus, $11B - 99A = C$, or $11(B - 9A) = C$. Therefore, *C* is divisible by 11, and 0 is the only digit that is divisible by 11.

The correct answer is E.

116. The hard drive, monitor, and printer for a certain desktop computer system cost a total of \$2,500. The cost of the printer and monitor together is equal to $\frac{2}{3}$ of the cost of the hard drive. If the cost of the printer is \$100 more than the cost of the monitor, what is the cost of the printer?

(A) \$800
(B) \$600
(C) \$550
(D) \$500
(E) \$350

Algebra Simultaneous Equations

Letting *d*, *m*, and *p*, respectively, represent the cost of the hard drive, monitor, and printer, the following equations are given:

(1) $d + m + p = 2{,}500$

(2) $p + m = \frac{2}{3}d$

(3) $p = m + 100$

Using (2) and substituting $\frac{2}{3}d$ for $m + p$ in (1) gives $\frac{5}{3}d = 2{,}500$, from which $d = 1{,}500$. Then from (1), $p + m = 1{,}000$, but $m = p - 100$ from (2), so $2p - 100 = 1{,}000$, $2p = 1{,}100$, and $p = 550$.

The correct answer is C.

$$3r \le 4s + 5$$
$$|s| \le 5$$

117. Given the inequalities above, which of the following CANNOT be the value of *r*?

(A) –20
(B) –5
(C) 0
(D) 5
(E) 20

Algebra Inequalities

Since $|s| \le 5$, it follows that $-5 \le s \le 5$. Therefore, $-20 \le 4s \le 20$, and hence $-15 \le 4s + 5 \le 25$. Since $3r \le 4s + 5$ (given) and $4s + 5 \le 25$ (end of previous sentence), it follows that $3r \le 25$. Among the answer choices, $3r \le 25$ is false only for $r = 20$.

The correct answer is E.

118. If *m* is an even integer, *v* is an odd integer, and $m > v > 0$, which of the following represents the number of even integers less than *m* and greater than *v*?

(A) $\frac{m-v}{2} - 1$
(B) $\frac{m-v-1}{2}$
(C) $\frac{m-v}{2}$
(D) $m - v - 1$
(E) $m - v$

Arithmetic Properties of Numbers

Since there is only one correct answer, one method of solving the problem is to choose values for m and v and determine which of the expressions gives the correct number for these values. For example, if $m = 6$ and $v = 1$, then there are 2 even integers less than 6 and greater than 1, namely the even integers 2 and 4. As the table below shows, $\frac{m-v-1}{2}$ is the only expression given that equals 2.

$$\frac{m-v}{2} - 1 = 1.5$$
$$\frac{m-v-1}{2} = 2$$
$$\frac{m-v}{2} = 2.5$$
$$m - v - 1 = 4$$
$$m - v = 5$$

To solve this problem it is not necessary to show that $\frac{m-v-1}{2}$ always gives the correct number of even integers. However, one way this can be done is by the following method, first shown for a specific example and then shown in general. For the specific example, suppose $v = 15$ and $m = 144$. Then a list—call it the first list—of the even integers greater than v and less than m is 16, 18, 20, …, 140, 142. Now subtract 14 (chosen so that the second list will begin with 2) from each of the integers in the first list to form a second list, which has the same number of integers as the first list: 2, 4, 6, …, 128. Finally, divide each of the integers in the second list (all of which are even) by 2 to form a third list, which also has the same number of integers as the first list: 1, 2, 3, …, 64. Since the number of integers in the third list is 64, it follows that the number of integers in the first list is 64. For the general situation, the first list is the following list of even integers: $v + 1$, $v + 3$, $v + 5$, …, $m - 4$, $m - 2$. Now subtract the even integer $v - 1$ from (i.e., add $-v + 1$ to) each of the integers in the first list to obtain the second list: 2, 4, 6, …, $m - v - 3$, $m - v - 1$. (Note, for example, that $m - 4 - (v - 1) = m - v - 3$.) Finally, divide each of the integers (all of which are even) in the second list by 2 to obtain the third list: 1, 2, 3, …, $\frac{m-v-3}{2}$, $\frac{m-v-1}{2}$. Since the number of integers in the third list is $\frac{m-v-1}{2}$, it follows that the number of integers in the first list is $\frac{m-v-1}{2}$.

The correct answer is B.

119. A positive integer is divisible by 9 if and only if the sum of its digits is divisible by 9. If n is a positive integer, for which of the following values of k is $25 \times 10^n + k \times 10^{2n}$ divisible by 9?

(A) 9
(B) 16
(C) 23
(D) 35
(E) 47

Arithmetic Properties of Numbers

Since n can be any positive integer, let $n = 2$. Then $25 \times 10^n = 2{,}500$, so its digits consist of the digits 2 and 5 followed by two digits of 0. Also, $k \times 10^{2n} = k \times 10{,}000$, so its digits consist of the digits of k followed by four digits of 0. Therefore, the digits of $(25 \times 10^n) + (k \times 10^{2n})$ consist of the digits of k followed by the digits 2 and 5, followed by two digits of 0. The table below shows this for $n = 2$ and $k = 35$:

$$25 \times 10^n = \quad 2{,}500$$
$$35 \times 10^{2n} = 350{,}000$$
$$(25 \times 10^n) + (35 \times 10^{2n}) = 352{,}500$$

Thus, when $n = 2$, the sum of the digits of $(25 \times 10^n) + (k \times 10^{2n})$ will be $2 + 5 = 7$ plus the sum of the digits of k. Of the answer choices, this sum of digits is divisible by 9 only for $k = 47$, which gives $2 + 5 + 4 + 7 = 18$. It can also be verified that, for each positive integer n, the only such answer choice is $k = 47$, although this additional verification is not necessary to obtain the correct answer.

The correct answer is E.

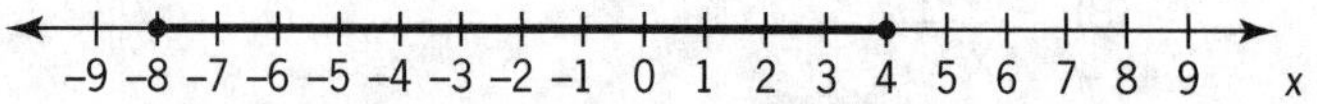

120. On the number line, the shaded interval is the graph of which of the following inequalities?

(A) $|x| \le 4$
(B) $|x| \le 8$
(C) $|x - 2| \le 4$
(D) $|x - 2| \le 6$
(E) $|x + 2| \le 6$

Algebra Inequalities; Absolute Value

The midpoint of the interval from −8 to 4, inclusive, is $\frac{-8+4}{2} = -2$ and the length of the interval from −8 to 4, inclusive, is $4 - (-8) = 12$, so the interval consists of all numbers within a distance of $\frac{12}{2} = 6$ from −2. Using an inequality involving absolute values, this can be described by $|x - (-2)| \le 6$, or $|x + 2| \le 6$.

Alternatively, the inequality $-8 \le x \le 4$ can be written as the conjunction $-8 \le x$ and $x \le 4$. Rewrite this conjunction so that the lower value, −8, and the upper value, 4, are shifted to values that have the same magnitude. This can be done by adding 2 to each side of each inequality, which gives $-6 \le x + 2$ and $x + 2 \le 6$. Thus, $x + 2$ lies between −6 and 6, inclusive, and it follows that $|x + 2| \le 6$.

The correct answer is E.

121. Last year members of a certain professional organization for teachers consisted of teachers from 49 different school districts, with an average (arithmetic mean) of 9.8 schools per district. Last year the average number of teachers at these schools who were members of the organization was 22. Which of the following is closest to the total number of members of the organization last year?

(A) 10^7
(B) 10^6
(C) 10^5
(D) 10^4
(E) 10^3

Arithmetic Statistics

There are 49 school districts and an average of 9.8 schools per district, so the number of schools is $(49)(9.8) \approx (50)(10) = 500$. There are approximately 500 schools and an average of 22 teachers at each school, so the number of teachers is approximately $(500)(22) \approx (500)(20) = 10{,}000 = 10^4$.

The correct answer is D.

122. Of all the students in a certain dormitory, $\frac{1}{2}$ are first-year students and the rest are second-year students. If $\frac{4}{5}$ of the first-year students have not declared a major and if the fraction of second-year students who have declared a major is 3 times the fraction of first-year students who have declared a major, what fraction of all the students in the dormitory are second-year students who have not declared a major?

(A) $\frac{1}{15}$

(B) $\frac{1}{5}$

(C) $\frac{4}{15}$

(D) $\frac{1}{3}$

(E) $\frac{2}{5}$

Arithmetic Applied Problems

Consider the table below in which T represents the total number of students in the dormitory. Since $\frac{1}{2}$ of the students are first-year students and the rest are second-year students, it follows that $\frac{1}{2}$ of the students are second-year students, and so the totals for the first-year and second-year columns are both $0.5T$. Since $\frac{4}{5}$ of the first-year students have not declared a major, it follows that the middle entry in the first-year column is $\frac{4}{5}(0.5T) = 0.4T$ and the first entry in the first-year column is $0.5T - 0.4T = 0.1T$. Since the fraction of second-year students who have declared a major is 3 times the fraction of first-year students who have declared a major, it follows that the first entry in the second-year column is $3(0.1T) = 0.3T$ and the second entry in the second-year column is $0.5T - 0.3T = 0.2T$. Thus, the fraction of students that are second-year students who have not declared a major is $\frac{0.2T}{T} = 0.2 = \frac{1}{5}$.

	First-year	Second-year	Total
Declared major	$0.1T$	$0.3T$	$0.4T$
Not declared major	$0.4T$	$0.2T$	$0.6T$
Total	$0.5T$	$0.5T$	T

The correct answer is B.

123. If the average (arithmetic mean) of x, y, and z is $7x$ and $x \neq 0$, what is the ratio of x to the sum of y and z?

(A) 1:21

(B) 1:20

(C) 1:6

(D) 6:1

(E) 20:1

Algebra Ratio and Proportion

Given that the average of x, y, and z is $7x$, it follows that $\frac{x+y+z}{3} = 7x$, or $x + y + z = 21x$, or $y + z = 20x$. Dividing both sides of the last equation by $20(y + z)$ gives $\frac{1}{20} = \frac{x}{y+z}$, so the ratio of x to the sum of y and z is 1:20.

The correct answer is B.

124. Jonah drove the first half of a 100-mile trip in x hours and the second half in y hours. Which of the following is equal to Jonah's average speed, in miles per hour, for the entire trip?

(A) $\frac{50}{x+y}$

(B) $\frac{100}{x+y}$

(C) $\frac{25}{x}+\frac{25}{y}$

(D) $\frac{50}{x}+\frac{50}{y}$

(E) $\frac{100}{x}+\frac{100}{y}$

Algebra Applied Problems

Using average speed $= \frac{\text{total distance}}{\text{total time}}$, it follows that Jonah's average speed for his entire 100-mile trip is $\frac{100}{x+y}$.

The correct answer is B.

125. If the amount of federal estate tax due on an estate valued at \$1.35 million is \$437,000 plus 43 percent of the value of the estate in excess of \$1.25 million, then the federal tax due is approximately what percent of the value of the estate?

(A) 30%
(B) 35%
(C) 40%
(D) 45%
(E) 50%

Arithmetic Percents; Estimation

The amount of tax divided by the value of the estate is

$$\frac{[0.437 + (0.43)(1.35 - 1.25)]\ \cancel{\text{million}}}{1.35\ \cancel{\text{million}}} \quad \text{value as fraction}$$

$$= \frac{0.437 + (0.43)(0.1)}{1.35} \quad \text{arithmetic}$$

$$= \frac{0.48}{1.35} = \frac{48}{135} \quad \text{arithmetic}$$

By long division, $\frac{48}{135}$ is approximately 35.6, so the closest answer choice is 35%.

Alternatively, $\frac{48}{135}$ can be estimated by $\frac{48}{136} = \frac{6}{17} \approx \frac{6}{18} = \frac{1}{3} \approx 33\%$, so the closest answer choice is 35%. Note that $\frac{48}{135}$ is greater than $\frac{48}{136}$, and $\frac{6}{17}$ is greater than $\frac{6}{18}$, so the correct value is greater than 33%, which rules out 30% being the closest.

The correct answer is B.

$$7x + 6y \le 38{,}000$$
$$4x + 5y \le 28{,}000$$

126. A manufacturer wants to produce x balls and y boxes. Resource constraints require that x and y satisfy the inequalities shown. What is the maximum number of balls and boxes combined that can be produced given the resource constraints?

(A) 5,000
(B) 6,000
(C) 7,000
(D) 8,000
(E) 10,000

Algebra Inequalities

We are to determine the maximum value of $x + y$ given the inequalities above. Note that if $A \le B$ and $C \le D$, then we can "add inequalities" to obtain $A + C \le B + D$, since (roughly speaking) the sum of two smaller numbers is less than the sum of two larger numbers. Adding the inequalities shown above gives $(7x + 6y) + (4x + 5y) \le 38{,}000 + 28{,}000$, or $11x + 11y \le 66{,}000$. Dividing both sides of this last inequality by 11 gives $x + y \le 6{,}000$. Therefore, the values of $x + y$ are at most 6,000, and hence the maximum value of $x + y$ is *at most* 6,000.

The fact that the maximum value of $x + y$ is *equal* to 6,000 follows from the fact that the system of simultaneous equations $7x + 6y = 38{,}000$ and $4x + 5y = 28{,}000$ has a solution, which in turn follows from the fact that these two equations correspond to a pair of nonparallel lines in the standard (x,y) coordinate plane. In particular, the pair $x = 2{,}000$ and $y = 4{,}000$ satisfy both the two inequalities and the equation $x + y = 6{,}000$.

The correct answer is B.

127. If $\frac{3}{10^4} = x\%$, then $x =$

(A) 0.3
(B) 0.03
(C) 0.003
(D) 0.0003
(E) 0.00003

Arithmetic Percents

Given that $\frac{3}{10^4} = x\%$, and writing $x\%$ as $\frac{x}{100}$, it follows that $\frac{3}{10^4} = \frac{x}{100}$. Multiplying both sides by 100 gives $x = \frac{300}{10^4} = \frac{300}{10{,}000} = \frac{3}{100} = 0.03$.

The correct answer is B.

128. What is the remainder when 3^{24} is divided by 5?

(A) 0
(B) 1
(C) 2
(D) 3
(E) 4

Arithmetic Properties of Numbers

A pattern in the units digits of the numbers $3, 3^2 = 9, 3^3 = 27, 3^4 = 81, 3^5 = 243$, etc., can be found by observing that the units digit of a product of two integers is the same as the units digit of the product of the units digit of the two integers. For example, the units digit of $3^5 = 3 \times 3^4 = 3 \times 81$ is 3 since the units digit of 3×1 is 3, and the units digit of $3^6 = 3 \times 3^5 = 3 \times 243$ is 9 since the units digit of 3×3 is 9. From this it follows that the units digit of the powers of 3 follow the pattern 3, 9, 7, 1, 3, 9, 7, 1, etc., with a units digit of 1 for $3^4, 3^8, 3^{12}, \ldots, 3^{24}, \ldots$. Therefore, the units digit of 3^{24} is 1. Thus, 3^{24} is 1 more than a multiple of 10, and hence 3^{24} is 1 more than a multiple of 5, and so the remainder when 3^{24} is divided by 5 is 1.

The correct answer is B.

129. José has a collection of 100 coins, consisting of nickels, dimes, quarters, and half-dollars. If he has a total of 35 nickels and dimes, a total of 45 dimes and quarters, and a total of 50 nickels and quarters, how many half-dollars does he have?

(A) 15
(B) 20
(C) 25
(D) 30
(E) 35

Algebra Simultaneous Equations

Letting n, d, q, and h, respectively, represent the numbers of nickels, dimes, quarters, and half-dollars José has, determine the value of h.

The following are given:

(1) $n + d + q + h = 100$
(2) $n + d = 35$
(3) $d + q = 45$
(4) $n + q = 50$

Adding (2), (3), and (4) gives $2n + 2d + 2q = 130$ or $n + d + q = 65$. Subtracting this equation from (1) gives $h = 100 - 65 = 35$.

The correct answer is E.

130. David used part of \$100,000 to purchase a house. Of the remaining portion, he invested $\frac{1}{3}$ of it at 4 percent simple annual interest and $\frac{2}{3}$ of it at 6 percent simple annual interest. If after a year the income from the two investments totaled \$320, what was the purchase price of the house?

(A) \$96,000
(B) \$94,000
(C) \$88,000
(D) \$75,000
(E) \$40,000

Algebra Applied Problems; Percents

Let x be the amount, in dollars, that David used to purchase the house. Then David invested $(100{,}000 - x)$ dollars, $\frac{1}{3}$ at 4% simple annual interest and $\frac{2}{3}$ at 6% simple annual interest. After one year the total interest, in dollars, on this investment was $\frac{1}{3}(100{,}000 - x)(0.04) + \frac{2}{3}(100{,}000 - x)(0.06) = 320$. Solve this equation to find the value of x.

$\frac{1}{3}(100{,}000-x)(0.04)+$ $\frac{2}{3}(100{,}000-x)(0.06)$	$=320$	given
$(100{,}000-x)(0.04)+$ $2(100{,}000-x)(0.06)$	$=960$	multiply both sides by 3
$4{,}000-0.04x+$ $12{,}000-0.12x$	$=960$	distributive property
$16{,}000-0.16x$	$=960$	combine like terms
$16{,}000-960$	$=0.16x$	add $0.16x-960$ to both sides
$100{,}000-6{,}000$	$=x$	divide both sides by 0.16
$94{,}000$	$=x$	

Therefore, the purchase price of the house was \$94,000.

The correct answer is B.

131. A certain manufacturer sells its product to stores in 113 different regions worldwide, with an average (arithmetic mean) of 181 stores per region. If last year these stores sold an average of 51,752 units of the manufacturer's product per store, which of the following is closest to the total number of units of the manufacturer's product sold worldwide last year?

(A) 10^6
(B) 10^7
(C) 10^8
(D) 10^9
(E) 10^{10}

Arithmetic Estimation

$$\begin{aligned}(113)(181)(51{,}752) &\approx (100)(200)(50{,}000)\\ &= 10^2\times(2\times10^2)\times(5\times10^4)\\ &= (2\times5)\times10^{2+2+4}\\ &= 10^1\times10^8 = 10^9\end{aligned}$$

The correct answer is D.

132. Andrew started saving at the beginning of the year and had saved \$240 by the end of the year. He continued to save and by the end of 2 years had saved a total of \$540. Which of the following is closest to the percent increase in the amount Andrew saved during the second year compared to the amount he saved during the first year?

(A) 11%
(B) 25%
(C) 44%
(D) 56%
(E) 125%

Arithmetic Percents

Andrew saved \$240 in the first year and \$540 – \$240 = \$300 in the second year. The percent increase in the amount Andrew saved in the second year compared to the amount he saved in the first year is $\left(\frac{300-240}{240}\times100\right)\% = \left(\frac{60}{240}\times100\right)\% = \left(\frac{1}{4}\times100\right)\% = 25\%$.

The correct answer is B.

133. If x is a positive integer, r is the remainder when x is divided by 4, and R is the remainder when x is divided by 9, what is the greatest possible value of $r^2 + R$?

(A) 25
(B) 21
(C) 17
(D) 13
(E) 11

Arithmetic Properties of Integers

If r is the remainder when the positive integer x is divided by 4, then $0 \le r < 4$, so the maximum value of r is 3. If R is the remainder when the positive integer x is divided by 9, then $0 \le R < 9$, so the maximum value of R is 8. Thus, the maximum value of $r^2 + R$ is $3^2 + 8 = 17$.

The correct answer is C.

134. Each of the nine digits 0, 1, 1, 4, 5, 6, 8, 8, and 9 is used once to form 3 three-digit integers. What is the greatest possible sum of the 3 integers?

(A) 1,752
(B) 2,616
(C) 2,652
(D) 2,775
(E) 2,958

Arithmetic Place Value

To create 3 three-digit numbers using each of the digits 0, 1, 1, 4, 5, 6, 8, 8, and 9 and having the maximum possible sum, the greatest three digits must be in hundreds place, the next greatest three in tens place, and the three smallest digits in units place. The sum will then be $(9 + 8 + 8)(100) + (4 + 5 + 6)(10) + (0 + 1 + 1) = 25(100) + 15(10) + 2 = 2{,}500 + 150 + 2 = 2{,}652$.

The correct answer is C.

135. Given that $1^2 + 2^2 + 3^2 + \ldots + 10^2 = 385$, what is the value of $3^2 + 6^2 + 9^2 + \ldots + 30^2$?

(A) 1,155
(B) 1,540
(C) 1,925
(D) 2,310
(E) 3,465

Arithmetic Series and Sequences

We can use the fact that each term of the second series is $3^2 = 9$ times greater than the corresponding term of the first series to find the sum of the second series.

$$\begin{aligned}&3^2 + 6^2 + 9^2 + \ldots + 30^2\\&= (3 \cdot 1)^2 + (3 \cdot 2)^2 + (3 \cdot 3)^2 + \ldots + (3 \cdot 10)^2\\&= (3^2 \cdot 1^2) + (3^2 \cdot 2^2) + (3^2 \cdot 3^2) + \ldots + (3^2 \cdot 10^2)\\&= 3^2(1^2 + 2^2 + 3^2 + \ldots + 10^2) = 9(385) = 3{,}465\end{aligned}$$

The correct answer is E.

136. If water is leaking from a certain tank at a constant rate of 1,200 milliliters per hour, how many <u>seconds</u> does it take for 1 milliliter of water to leak from the tank?

(A) $\frac{1}{3}$
(B) $\frac{1}{2}$
(C) 2
(D) 3
(E) 20

Arithmetic Measurement Conversion; Rate Problem

We are given that 1,200 milliliters leak in 1 hour, or 3,600 seconds. Because the leaking is at a constant rate, it takes $\frac{1}{1{,}200}$ as long for 1 milliliter to leak, and so 1 milliliter leaks in $\frac{3{,}600}{1{,}200} = 3$ seconds.

The correct answer is D.

137. When the positive integer k is divided by the positive integer n, the remainder is 11. If $\frac{k}{n} = 81.2$, what is the value of n?

(A) 9
(B) 20
(C) 55
(D) 70
(E) 81

Arithmetic Properties of Integers

When the positive integer k is divided by the positive integer n, there exist unique positive integers q (the quotient) and r (the remainder) such that $k = qn + r$, where $0 \le r < n$. For example, when 43 is divided by 5, we have $43 = (8)(5) + 3$ and $0 \le 3 < 5$. Dividing both sides of $k = qn + r$ by n and using $r = 11$ gives $\frac{k}{n} = q + \frac{r}{n}\ q + \frac{11}{n}$. We are given that $\frac{k}{n} = 81.2 = 81 + \frac{2}{10}$, so $q + \frac{11}{n} = 81 + \frac{2}{10}$. Therefore, $q = 81$ and $\frac{11}{n} = \frac{2}{10}$, or $n = 55$.

The correct answer is C.

138. The total area of a certain continent is approximately 3.8×10^{16} square inches. Which of the following is closest to the area of the continent, in square miles? (1 square mile is approximately 4.0×10^{9} square inches.)

(A) 6.7×10^{5}
(B) 2.0×10^{6}
(C) 9.5×10^{6}
(D) 1.1×10^{7}
(E) 9.5×10^{8}

Arithmetic Measurement Conversion

The following calculations make use of the given approximations.

$$4.0 \times 10^{9} \text{ in}^2 \approx 1 \text{ mi}^2 \quad \text{given}$$

$$1 \text{ in}^2 \approx \frac{1}{4.0 \times 10^{9}} \text{mi}^2 \quad \text{divide both sides by } 4.0 \times 10^{9}$$

$$3.8 \times 10^{16} \text{ in}^2 \approx \frac{3.8 \times 10^{16}}{4.0 \times 10^{9}} \text{mi}^2 \quad \text{multiply both sides by } 3.8 \times 10^{16}$$

$$3.8 \times 10^{16} \text{ in}^2 \approx \frac{3.8}{4.0} \times \frac{10^{16}}{10^{9}} \text{mi}^2 \quad \text{use } \frac{a}{b} \times \frac{c}{d} = \frac{ac}{bd}$$

$$3.8 \times 10^{16} \text{ in}^2 \approx \frac{19}{20} \times 10^{16-9} \text{ mi}^2 \quad \text{use } \frac{a^b}{a^c} = a^{b-c}$$

$$3.8 \times 10^{16} \text{ in}^2 \approx 0.95 \times 10^{7} \text{ mi}^2$$

$$3.8 \times 10^{16} \text{ in}^2 \approx 9.5 \times 10^{6} \text{ mi}^2$$

The correct answer is C.

139. If $xy = 1$, what is the value of $\frac{2^{(x+y)^2}}{2^{(x-y)^2}}$?

(A) 2
(B) 4
(C) 8
(D) 16
(E) 32

Algebra Exponents; Simplifying Algebraic Expressions

Using the property $\frac{2^a}{2^b} = 2^{a-b}$,

$\frac{2^{(x+y)^2}}{2^{(x-y)^2}} = 2^{(x+y)^2 - (x-y)^2}$. Also, since

$$(x+y)^2 - (x-y)^2 = (x^2 + 2xy + y^2) - (x^2 - 2xy + y^2) = 4xy$$

and $xy = 1$, it follows that $\frac{2^{(x+y)^2}}{2^{(x-y)^2}} = 2^{4xy} = 2^{4\times1} = 16$.

The correct answer is D.

140. Of the 20 members of a kitchen crew, 17 can use the meat-cutting machine, 18 can use the bread-slicing machine, and 15 can use both machines. If one member of the crew is to be chosen at random, what is the probability that the member chosen will be someone who cannot use either machine?

(A) 0
(B) $\frac{1}{10}$
(C) $\frac{1}{7}$
(D) $\frac{1}{4}$
(E) $\frac{1}{3}$

Arithmetic Probability; Sets (Venn diagrams)

Since 17 members can use the meat-cutting machine and 15 members can use both machines, $17 - 15 = 2$ members can use only the meat-cutting machine. Similarly, since 18 members can use the bread-slicing machine and 15 members can use both machines, $18 - 15 = 3$ members can use only the bread-slicing machine. The Venn diagram below shows these values, where x is the number of members who cannot use either machine.

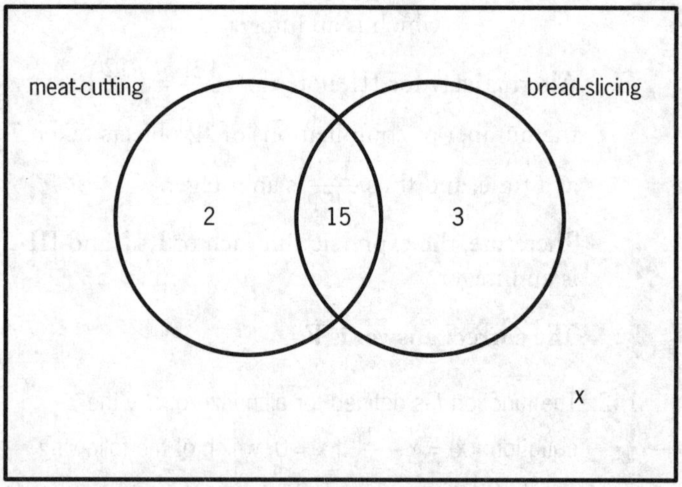

Since there is a total of 20 members, it follows that $2 + 15 + 3 + x = 20$, or $x = 0$. Therefore, the probability that the member chosen cannot use either machine is $\frac{0}{20} = 0$.

The correct answer is A.

141. Which of the following is an integer?

I. $\frac{12!}{6!}$

II. $\frac{12!}{8!}$

III. $\frac{12!}{7!5!}$

(A) I only
(B) II only
(C) III only
(D) I and II only
(E) I, II, and III

Arithmetic Arithmetic Operations

I. $\frac{12!}{6!} = \frac{\cancel{6!} \times 7 \times 8 \times 9 \times 10 \times 11 \times 12}{\cancel{6!}}$
$= 7 \times 8 \times 9 \times 10 \times 11 \times 12$, which is an integer.

II. $\frac{12!}{8!} = \frac{\cancel{8!} \times 9 \times 10 \times 11 \times 12}{\cancel{8!}}$
$= 9 \times 10 \times 11 \times 12$, which is an integer.

III. $\frac{12!}{7!5!} = \frac{\cancel{7!} \times 8 \times 9 \times 10 \times 11 \times \cancel{12}}{\cancel{7!} \times 1 \times 2 \times \cancel{3 \times 4} \times 5}$
$= \frac{8 \times 9 \times \cancel{10} \times 11}{\cancel{2 \times 5}} = 8 \times 9 \times 11$, which is an integer.

Alternatively for III, note that $\frac{12!}{7!5!} = \binom{12}{7}$ is the number of combinations of 12 objects taken 7 at a time, and thus $\frac{12!}{7!5!}$ is an integer.

Therefore, the expression in each of I, II, and III is an integer.

The correct answer is E.

142. The function f is defined for all nonzero x by the equation $f(x) = x - \frac{1}{x}$. If $x \neq 0$, which of the following equals $f\left(\frac{1}{x}\right)$?

(A) $f(x)$
(B) $f(-x)$
(C) $f\left(-\frac{1}{x}\right)$
(D) $\frac{1}{f(x)}$
(E) $-\frac{1}{f(x)}$

Algebra Functions

$$f\left(\frac{1}{x}\right) = \frac{1}{x} - \frac{1}{\frac{1}{x}} = \frac{1}{x} - x$$

$$f(-x) = -x - \frac{1}{-x} = -x + \frac{1}{x} = \frac{1}{x} - x$$

Therefore, $f\left(\frac{1}{x}\right) = f(-x)$.

Alternatively, evaluate all of the expressions for an appropriate value of x, such as $x = 2$.

$$f\left(\frac{1}{x}\right) = f\left(\frac{1}{2}\right) = \frac{1}{2} - 2 = -\frac{3}{2}$$
$$f(x) = f(2) = 2 - \frac{1}{2} = \frac{3}{2}$$
$$f(-x) = f(-2) = -2 + \frac{1}{2} = -\frac{3}{2}$$
$$f\left(-\frac{1}{x}\right) = f\left(-\frac{1}{2}\right) = -\frac{1}{2} + 2 = \frac{3}{2}$$
$$\frac{1}{f(x)} = \frac{1}{f(2)} = \frac{1}{2 - \frac{1}{2}} = \frac{2}{3}$$
$$-\frac{1}{f(x)} = -\frac{1}{f(2)} = -\frac{1}{2 - \frac{1}{2}} = -\frac{2}{3}$$

The correct answer is B.

143. In the arithmetic sequence $t_1, t_2, t_3, \ldots, t_n, \ldots$, $t_1 = 23$ and $t_n = t_{n-1} - 3$ for each $n > 1$. What is the value of n when $t_n = -4$?

(A) –1
(B) 7
(C) 10
(D) 14
(E) 20

Algebra Series and Sequences

From the given information, it follows that if we subtract 3 a total of $n - 1$ times from $t_1 = 23$, then we will obtain $t_n = -4$. Therefore, n satisfies the equation $23 - (n - 1)(3) = -4$. Now solve for n.

$23 - (n - 1)(3)$	=	–4	from above
$23 - 3n + 3$	=	–4	distributive property
$-3n$	=	–30	combine like terms
n	=	10	divide both sides by –3

Alternatively, subtract 3 from 23 until –4 is obtained and count the number of subtractions. One more than this number is the value of n such that $t_n = -4$.

The correct answer is C.

144. How many seconds will it take for a car that is traveling at a constant rate of 45 miles per hour to travel a distance of 220 yards? (1 mile = 1,760 yards)

(A) 8
(B) 9
(C) 10
(D) 11
(E) 12

Arithmetic Rate Problem; Measurement Conversion

First, convert 45 miles per hour to yards per second. We know that 1 hour is equal to 3,600 seconds giving us the fraction $\frac{45}{3{,}600}$. Divide both sides of the fraction by 3,600 to get the miles per second which equals $\frac{1}{80}$ miles in one second. We know that 1 mile is equal to 1,760 yards so the nest step is $1{,}760 \times \frac{1}{80}$. Therefore, it will take the car 1 second to travel 22 yards; hence it will take 10 seconds for the car to travel 220 yards.

Alternatively, let t be the number of seconds it will take for the car to travel 220 yards.

$220 \text{ yd} = \left(45 \frac{\text{mi}}{\text{hr}}\right)(t \text{ sec})$	distance = rate × time
$(220 \cancel{\text{yd}})\left(\frac{1 \text{ mi}}{1{,}760 \cancel{\text{yd}}}\right) = \left(45 \frac{\text{mi}}{\cancel{\text{hr}}}\right)\left(\frac{1 \cancel{\text{hr}}}{3{,}600 \cancel{\text{sec}}}\right)(t \cancel{\text{sec}})$	1 mi = 1,760 yd 1 hr = 3,600 sec
$\frac{220}{1{,}760} \text{ mi} = \left(\frac{45}{3{,}600}t\right)\text{mi}$	cancel units
$\frac{2 \times 11 \times 10}{11 \times 16 \times 10} = \left(\frac{45}{45 \times 80}\right)t$	factor
$\frac{1}{8} = \frac{t}{80}$	cancel common factors
$t = 10$	multiply both sides by 80

The correct answer is C.

145. A store's selling price of $2,240 for a certain computer would yield a profit of 40 percent of the store's cost for the computer. What selling price would yield a profit of 50 percent of the computer's cost?

(A) $2,400
(B) $2,464
(C) $2,650
(D) $2,732
(E) $2,800

Algebra Applied Problems

Let $$C$ be the store's cost for the computer. Then the store's profit from selling the computer would be $$(2{,}240 - C)$, which is equal to 40 percent of the store's cost.

$2{,}240 - C = 0.4C$	given
$2{,}240 = 1.4C$	add C to both sides
$C = 1{,}600$	divide both sides by 1.4

Thus, the store's cost for the computer is $1,600. Therefore, to yield a profit of 50 percent of the computer's cost, the selling price would have to be 1.5($1,600) = $2,400.

The correct answer is A.

146. If a certain coin is flipped, the probability that the coin will land heads up is $\frac{1}{2}$. If the coin is flipped 5 times, what is the probability that it will land heads up on the first 3 flips and not on the last 2 flips?

(A) $\frac{3}{5}$
(B) $\frac{1}{2}$
(C) $\frac{1}{5}$
(D) $\frac{1}{8}$
(E) $\frac{1}{32}$

Arithmetic Probability

Because the 5 flips of the coin are independent of each other, the probability of the coin landing heads up on the first 3 flips and tails up (i.e., not heads up) on the last 2 flips is

$P(H) \times P(H) \times P(H) \times P(T) \times P(T)$,

where $P(H)$ and $P(T)$ are the probabilities, respectively, that a single flip of the coin lands heads up and tails up. Since $P(T) = 1 - P(H)$ and $P(H) = \frac{1}{2}$, it follows that $P(T) = \frac{1}{2}$. Therefore, the requested probability is $\frac{1}{2} \times \frac{1}{2} \times \frac{1}{2} \times \frac{1}{2} \times \frac{1}{2} = \frac{1}{32}$.

The correct answer is E.

147. The operation ⊗ is defined for all nonzero numbers a and b by $a \otimes b = \frac{a}{b} - \frac{b}{a}$. If x and y are nonzero numbers, which of the following statements must be true?

I. $x \otimes xy = x(1 \otimes y)$
II. $x \otimes y = -(y \otimes x)$
III. $\frac{1}{x} \otimes \frac{1}{y} = y \otimes x$

(A) I only
(B) II only
(C) III only
(D) I and II
(E) II and III

Algebra Simplifying Algebraic Expressions

I. CAN BE FALSE: Let $x = 2$ and $y = 3$. Then $\frac{1}{y} - y = -\frac{8}{3}$ and $x\left(\frac{1}{y} - y\right) = -\frac{16}{3}$, so $x \otimes xy = x(1 \otimes y)$ can be false.

II. MUST BE TRUE: $x \otimes y = \frac{x}{y} - \frac{y}{x} = -\left(\frac{y}{x} - \frac{x}{y}\right) = -(y \otimes x)$

III. MUST BE TRUE:

$$\frac{1}{x} \otimes \frac{1}{y} = \frac{\frac{1}{x}}{\frac{1}{y}} - \frac{\frac{1}{y}}{\frac{1}{x}} = \frac{y}{x} - \frac{x}{y} = y \otimes x$$

The correct answer is E.

148. If each term in the sum $a_1 + a_2 + \ldots + a_n$ is either 7 or 77 and the sum equals 350, which of the following could be equal to n?

(A) 38
(B) 39
(C) 40
(D) 41
(E) 42

Arithmetic Operations with Integers

Since $a_1 + a_2 + \ldots + a_n = 350 = 7 \times 50$, if each term in the sum were a 7, then n would equal 50. But the only answer options are the consecutive integers from 38 to 42. So, suppose $a_1 = 77 = 7 \times 11$, while each of the other terms is a 7. Then $a_1 + a_2 + \ldots + a_n = 7 \times 50 = 7 \times (11 + 39) = (7 \times 11) + (7 \times 39)$. In that case, in addition to $a_1 = 77$, the sum has 39 other terms, each equal to 7: $a_2, \ldots, a_{40}$. Thus, $n = 1 + 39 = 40$.

The correct answer is C.

149. (1.00001)(0.99999) – (1.00002)(0.99998) =

(A) 0
(B) 10^{-10}
(C) $3(10^{-10})$
(D) 10^{-5}
(E) $3(10^{-5})$

Arithmetic Equations

$(1.00001)(0.99999) - (1.00002)(0.99998) = (1 + 0.00001)(0.99999) - (1 + 0.00002)(0.99998) = (0.99999 + 0.00069999) - (0.99998 + 0.0000199996) = 0.9999999999 - 0.9999999996 = 0.0000000003 = 3(10^{-10})$.

The correct answer is C.

150. A certain rectangular photograph has an area of $6\frac{1}{2}$ square feet. What is the area of the photograph in square inches? (1 foot = 12 inches)

(A) 36
(B) 78
(C) 432
(D) 864
(E) 936

Arithmetic Rational Numbers

Since 1 foot is 12 inches, 1 square foot is $12^2 = 144$ square inches. So, the photograph's area of 6.5 square feet is $6.5 \times 144 = 936$ square inches.

The correct answer is E.

151. The toll for crossing a certain bridge is \$0.75 each crossing. Drivers who frequently use the bridge may instead purchase a sticker each month for \$13.00 and then pay only \$0.30 each crossing during that month. If a particular driver will cross the bridge twice on each of x days next month and will not cross the bridge on any other day, what is the least value of x for which this driver can save money by using the sticker?

(A) 14
(B) 15
(C) 16
(D) 28
(E) 29

Algebra First-Degree Equations

We need to find the least whole-number value of x for which $0.75(2x) > 13 + 0.3(2x)$; that is, the least whole number value for which $(1.5 - 0.6)x = 0.9x > 13$, and thus for which $x > \frac{130}{9} = 14\frac{4}{9}$. This value is 15.

The correct answer is B.

Questions 152 to 207 — Difficulty: Hard

152. Two numbers differ by 2 and sum to S. Which of the following is the greater of the numbers in terms of S?

(A) $\frac{S}{2} - 1$
(B) $\frac{S}{2}$
(C) $\frac{S}{2} + \frac{1}{2}$
(D) $\frac{S}{2} + 1$
(E) $\frac{S}{2} + 2$

Algebra First-Degree Equations

Let x represent the greater of the two numbers that differ by 2. Then, $x - 2$ represents the lesser of the two numbers. The two numbers sum to S, so $x + (x - 2) = S$. It follows that $2x - 2 = S$, or $2x = S + 2$, or $x = \frac{S}{2} + 1$.

The correct answer is D.

153. If m is an integer and $m = 10^{32} - 32$, what is the sum of the digits of m?

(A) 257
(B) 264
(C) 275
(D) 284
(E) 292

Arithmetic Arithmetic Operations

When written in standard base 10 notation, 10^{32} is the digit 1 followed by 32 digits of 0. Now consider the following subtractions and the digit pattern they suggest, a pattern which is easily seen to continue.

$$\begin{aligned} 100 - 32 &= 68 \\ 1{,}000 - 32 &= 968 \\ 10{,}000 - 32 &= 9{,}968 \\ 100{,}000 - 32 &= 99{,}968 \\ 1{,}000{,}000 - 32 &= 999{,}968 \end{aligned}$$

Using this digit pattern, $m = 10^{32} - 32$ in standard base 10 notation consists of $32 - 2 = 30$ occurrences of the digit 9 followed by the digits 6 and 8. Therefore, the sum of the digits of m is $30(9) + 6 + 8 = 270 + 14 = 284$.

The correct answer is D.

154. In a numerical table with 10 rows and 10 columns, each entry is either a 9 or a 10. If the number of 9s in the nth row is $n - 1$ for each n from 1 to 10, what is the average (arithmetic mean) of all the numbers in the table?

(A) 9.45
(B) 9.50
(C) 9.55
(D) 9.65
(E) 9.70

Arithmetic Operations with Integers

There are $(10)(10) = 100$ entries in the table. In rows $1, 2, 3, \ldots, 10$, the number of 9s is $0, 1, 2, \ldots, 9$, respectively, giving a total of $0 + 1 + 2 + \ldots + 9 = 45$ entries with a 9. This leaves a total of $100 - 45 = 55$ entries with a 10. Therefore, the sum of the 100 entries is $45(9) + 55(10) = 405 + 550 = 955$, and the average of the 100 entries is $\frac{955}{100} = 9.55$

The correct answer is C.

155. In 2004, the cost of 1 year-long print subscription to a certain newspaper was \$4 per week. In 2005, the newspaper introduced a new rate plan for 1 year-long print subscription: \$3 per week for the first 40 weeks of 2005 and \$2 per week for the remaining weeks of 2005. How much less did 1 year-long print subscription to this newspaper cost in 2005 than in 2004?

(A) \$64
(B) \$78
(C) \$112
(D) \$144
(E) \$304

Arithmetic Applied Problems

The cost, in dollars, of 1 year-long print subscription in 2004 was $52(4) = 208$ and the cost, in dollars, of 1 year-long print subscription in 2005 was $40(3) + 12(2) = 120 + 24 = 144$. Therefore, the cost in 2005 was less than the cost in 2004 by $208 - 144 = 64$ dollars.

The correct answer is A.

156. A positive integer n is a perfect number provided that the sum of all the positive factors of n, including 1 and n, is equal to $2n$. What is the sum of the reciprocals of all the positive factors of the perfect number 28?

(A) $\frac{1}{4}$
(B) $\frac{56}{27}$
(C) 2
(D) 3
(E) 4

Arithmetic Properties of Integers

The factors of 28 are 1, 2, 4, 7, 14, and 28. Therefore, the sum of the reciprocals of the factors of 28 is $\frac{1}{1} + \frac{1}{2} + \frac{1}{4} + \frac{1}{7} + \frac{1}{14} + \frac{1}{28} =$

$$\frac{28}{28} + \frac{14}{28} + \frac{7}{28} + \frac{4}{28} + \frac{2}{28} + \frac{1}{28} =$$

$$\frac{28 + 14 + 7 + 4 + 2 + 1}{28} = \frac{56}{28} = 2.$$

The correct answer is C.

157. The infinite sequence $a_1, a_2, \ldots, a_n, \ldots$ is such that $a_1 = 2$, $a_2 = -3$, $a_3 = 5$, $a_4 = -1$, and $a_n = a_{n-4}$ for $n > 4$. What is the sum of the first 97 terms of the sequence?

(A) 72
(B) 74
(C) 75
(D) 78
(E) 80

Arithmetic Sequences and Series

Because $a_n = a_{n-4}$ for $n > 4$, it follows that the terms of the sequence repeat in groups of 4 terms:

Values for n	Values for a_n
1, 2, 3, 4	2, −3, 5, −1
5, 6, 7, 8	2, −3, 5, −1
9, 10, 11, 12	2, −3, 5, −1
13, 14, 15, 16	2, −3, 5, −1

Thus, since $97 = 24(4) + 1$, the sum of the first 97 terms can be grouped into 24 groups of 4 terms each, with one remaining term, which allows the sum to be easily found:

$$(a_1 + a_2 + a_3 + a_4) + (a_5 + a_6 + a_7 + a_8) + \dots + (a_{93} + a_{94} + a_{95} + a_{96}) + a_{97}$$

$$= (2 - 3 + 5 - 1) + (2 - 3 + 5 - 1) + \dots + (2 - 3 + 5 - 1) + 2$$

$$= 24(2 - 3 + 5 - 1) + 2 = 24(3) + 2 = 74$$

The correct answer is B.

158. The sequence $a_1, a_2, \dots, a_n, \dots$ is such that $a_n = 2a_{n-1} - x$ for all positive integers $n \geq 2$ and for a certain number x. If $a_5 = 99$ and $a_3 = 27$, what is the value of x?

(A) 3

(B) 9

(C) 18

(D) 36

(E) 45

Algebra Sequences and Series

An expression for a_5 that involves x can be obtained using $a_3 = 27$ and applying the equation $a_n = 2a_{n-1} - x$ twice, once for $n = 4$ and once for $n = 5$.

$a_4 = 2a_3 - x$	using $a_n = 2a_{n-1} - x$ for $n = 4$
$= 2(27) - x$	using $a_3 = 27$
$a_5 = 2a_4 - x$	using $a_n = 2a_{n-1} - x$ for $n = 5$
$= 2[2(27) - x] - x$	using $a_4 = 2(27) - x$
$= 4(27) - 3x$	combine like terms

Therefore, using $a_5 = 99$, we have

$99 = 4(27) - 3x$	given
$3x = 4(27) - 99$	adding $(3x - 99)$ to both sides
$x = 4(9) - 33$	dividing both sides by 3
$x = 3$	arithmetic

The correct answer is A.

159. In a certain medical survey, 45 percent of the people surveyed had the type A antigen in their blood and 3 percent had both the type A antigen and the type B antigen. Which of the following is closest to the percent of those with the type A antigen who also had the type B antigen?

(A) 1.35%

(B) 6.67%

(C) 13.50%

(D) 15.00%

(E) 42.00%

Arithmetic Applied Problems; Percents

Let n be the total number of people surveyed. Then, the proportion of the people who had type A who also had type B is $\frac{(3\%)\cancel{n}}{(45\%)\cancel{n}} = \frac{3}{45} = \frac{1}{15}$, which as a percent is approximately 6.67%. Note that by using $\frac{1}{15} = \frac{1}{3} \times \frac{1}{5}$, which equals $\frac{1}{3}$ of 20%, we can avoid dividing by a 2-digit integer.

The correct answer is B.

160. On a certain transatlantic crossing, 20 percent of a ship's passengers held round-trip tickets and also took their cars aboard the ship. If 60 percent of the passengers with round-trip tickets did not take their cars aboard the ship, what percent of the ship's passengers held round-trip tickets?

(A) $33\frac{1}{3}\%$

(B) 40%

(C) 50%

(D) 60%

(E) $66\frac{2}{3}\%$

Arithmetic Percents

Since the number of passengers on the ship is immaterial, let the number of passengers on the ship be 100 for convenience. Let x be the number of passengers that held round-trip tickets. Then, since 20 percent of the passengers held a round-trip ticket and took their cars aboard the ship, $0.20(100) = 20$ passengers held round-trip tickets and took their cars aboard the ship. The remaining passengers with round-trip tickets did not take their cars aboard, and they represent $0.6x$ (that is, 60 percent of the passengers with round-trip tickets). Thus $0.6x + 20 = x$, from which it follows that $20 = 0.4x$, and so $x = 50$. The percent of passengers with round-trip tickets is, then, $\frac{50}{100} = 50\%$.

The correct answer is C.

161. If x and k are integers and $(12^x)(4^{2x+1}) = (2^k)(3^2)$, what is the value of k?

(A) 5
(B) 7
(C) 10
(D) 12
(E) 14

Arithmetic Exponents

Rewrite the expression on the left so that it is a product of powers of 2 and 3.

$$\begin{aligned}(12^x)(4^{2x+1}) &= [(3 \cdot 2^2)^x][(2^2)^{2x+1}] \\ &= (3^x)[(2^2)^x][2^{2(2x+1)}] \\ &= (3^x)(2^{2x})(2^{4x+2}) \\ &= (3^x)(2^{6x+2})\end{aligned}$$

Then, since $(12^x)(4^{2x+1}) = (2^k)(3^2)$, it follows that $(3^x)(2^{6x+2}) = (2^k)(3^2) = (3^2)(2^k)$, so $x = 2$ and $k = 6x + 2$. Substituting 2 for x gives $k = 6(2) + 2 = 14$.

The correct answer is E.

162. If S is the sum of the reciprocals of the 10 consecutive integers from 21 to 30, then S is between which of the following two fractions?

(A) $\frac{1}{3}$ and $\frac{1}{2}$
(B) $\frac{1}{4}$ and $\frac{1}{3}$
(C) $\frac{1}{5}$ and $\frac{1}{4}$
(D) $\frac{1}{6}$ and $\frac{1}{5}$
(E) $\frac{1}{7}$ and $\frac{1}{6}$

Arithmetic Estimation

The value of $\frac{1}{21} + \frac{1}{22} + \frac{1}{23} + \ldots + \frac{1}{30}$ is LESS than $\frac{1}{20} + \frac{1}{20} + \frac{1}{20} + \ldots + \frac{1}{20}$ (10 numbers added), which equals $10\left(\frac{1}{20}\right) = \frac{1}{2}$, and GREATER than $\frac{1}{30} + \frac{1}{30} + \frac{1}{30} + \ldots + \frac{1}{30}$ (10 numbers added), which equals $10\left(\frac{1}{30}\right) = \frac{1}{3}$. Therefore, the value of $\frac{1}{21} + \frac{1}{22} + \frac{1}{23} + \ldots + \frac{1}{30}$ is between $\frac{1}{3}$ and $\frac{1}{2}$.

The correct answer is A.

163. For every even positive integer m, $f(m)$ represents the product of all even integers from 2 to m, inclusive. For example, $f(12) = 2 \times 4 \times 6 \times 8 \times 10 \times 12$. What is the greatest prime factor of $f(24)$?

(A) 23
(B) 19
(C) 17
(D) 13
(E) 11

Arithmetic Properties of Integers

Rewriting $f(24) = 2 \times 4 \times 6 \times 8 \times 10 \times 12 \times 14 \times \ldots \times 20 \times 22 \times 24$ as $2 \times 4 \times 2(3) \times 8 \times 2(5) \times 12 \times 2(7) \times \ldots \times 20 \times 2(11) \times 24$ shows that all of the prime numbers from 2 through 11 are factors of $f(24)$. The next prime number is 13,

but 13 is not a factor of $f(24)$ because none of the even integers from 2 through 24 has 13 as a factor. Therefore, the largest prime factor of $f(24)$ is 11.

The correct answer is E.

$$3, k, 2, 8, m, 3$$

164. The arithmetic mean of the list of numbers above is 4. If k and m are integers and $k \neq m$ what is the median of the list?

(A) 2
(B) 2.5
(C) 3
(D) 3.5
(E) 4

Arithmetic Statistics

Since the arithmetic mean $= \frac{\text{sum of values}}{\text{number of values}}$, then $\frac{3+k+2+8+m+3}{6} = 4$, and so $\frac{16+k+m}{6} = 4$, $16 + k + m = 24$, $k + m = 8$. Since $k \neq m$, then either $k < 4$ and $m > 4$ or $k > 4$ and $m < 4$. Because k and m are integers, either $k \leq 3$ and $m \geq 5$ or $k \geq 5$ and $m \leq 3$.

Case (i): If $k \leq 2$, then $m \geq 6$ and the six integers in ascending order are k, 2, 3, 3, m, 8 or k, 2, 3, 3, 8, m. The two middle integers are both 3 so the median is $\frac{3+3}{2} = 3$.

Case (ii): If $k = 3$, then $m = 5$ and the six integers in ascending order are 2, k, 3, 3, m, 8. The two middle integers are both 3 so the median is $\frac{3+3}{2} = 3$.

Case (iii): If $k = 5$, then $m = 3$ and the six integers in ascending order are 2, m, 3, 3, k, 8. The two middle integers are both 3 so the median is $\frac{3+3}{2} - 3$.

Case (iv): If $k \geq 6$, then $m \leq 2$ and the six integers in ascending order are m, 2, 3, 3, k, 8 or m, 2, 3, 3, 8, k. The two middle integers are both 3 so the median is $\frac{3+3}{2} = 3$.

The correct answer is C.

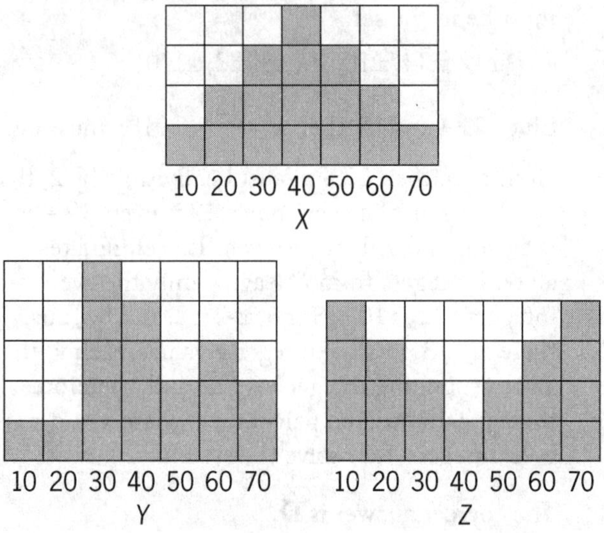

165. If the variables X, Y, and Z take on only the values 10, 20, 30, 40, 50, 60, or 70 with frequencies indicated by the shaded regions above, for which of the frequency distributions is the mean equal to the median?

(A) X only
(B) Y only
(C) Z only
(D) X and Y
(E) X and Z

Arithmetic Statistics

The frequency distributions for both X and Z are symmetric about 40, and thus both X and Z have mean = median = 40. Therefore, any answer choice that does not include both X and Z can be eliminated. This leaves only answer choice E.

The correct answer is E.

$$2x + y = 12$$
$$|y| \leq 12$$

166. For how many ordered pairs (x, y) that are solutions of the system above are x and y both integers?

(A) 7
(B) 10
(C) 12
(D) 13
(E) 14

Algebra Absolute Value

From $|y| \leq 12$, if y must be an integer, then y must be in the set

$S = \{\pm 12, \pm 11, \pm 10, \ldots, \pm 3, \pm 2, \pm 1, 0\}$.

Since $2x + y = 12$, then $x = \frac{12 - y}{2}$. If x must be an integer, then $12 - y$ must be divisible by 2; that is, $12 - y$ must be even. Since 12 is even, $12 - y$ is even if and only if y is even. This eliminates all odd integers from S, leaving only the even integers $\pm 12, \pm 10, \pm 8, \pm 6, \pm 4, \pm 2$, and 0. Thus, there are 13 possible integer y-values, each with a corresponding integer x-value and, therefore, there are 13 ordered pairs (x, y), where x and y are both integers, that solve the system.

The correct answer is D.

167. The United States Mint produces coins in 1-cent, 5-cent, 10-cent, 25-cent, and 50-cent denominations. If a jar contains exactly 100 cents worth of these coins, which of the following could be the total number of coins in the jar?

I. 91
II. 81
III. 76

(A) I only
(B) II only
(C) III only
(D) I and III only
(E) I, II, and III

Arithmetic Operations with Integers

Letting p, n, d, q, and h, respectively, represent the numbers of pennies (1-cent coins), nickels (5-cent coins), dimes (10-cent coins), quarters (25-cent coins), and half-dollars (50-cent coins) with a total worth of 100 cents, it follows that $p + 5n + 10d + 25q + 50h = 100$. Then $p = 100 - (5n + 10d + 25q + 50h) = 5(20 - n - 2d - 5q - 10h)$, so p must be a multiple of 5.

I. If the jar contained 90 pennies and 1 dime, the total number of coins would be $90 + 1 = 91$ and the coins would be worth $90 + 10 = 100$ cents.

II. For the jar to contain 81 coins with a total worth of 100 cents, there could be 80 pennies, but then the one coin remaining would have to amount to 20 cents to make the coins' total worth 100 cents. This is not possible since none of the coins is a 20-cent coin. If there were 75 pennies, then the remaining 6 coins would have to amount to 25 cents. This is not possible because 6 coins of the next smallest denomination would be worth 30 cents. If there were 70 pennies, then the remaining 11 coins would have to amount to 30 cents. This is not possible because 11 coins of the next smallest denomination would be worth 55 cents. Continuing in this manner shows that it is not possible for the jar to contain 81 coins with a total worth of 100 cents.

III. If the jar contained 70 pennies and 6 nickels, the total number of coins would be $70 + 6 = 76$ and the coins would be worth $70 + 30 = 100$ cents.

The correct answer is D.

168. A certain university will select 1 of 7 candidates eligible to fill a position in the mathematics department and 2 of 10 candidates eligible to fill 2 identical positions in the computer science department. If none of the candidates is eligible for a position in both departments, how many different sets of 3 candidates are there to fill the 3 positions?

(A) 42
(B) 70
(C) 140
(D) 165
(E) 315

Arithmetic Elementary Combinatorics

To fill the position in the math department, 1 candidate will be selected from a group of 7 eligible candidates, and so there are 7 sets of 1 candidate each to fill the position in the math department. To fill the positions in the computer science department, any one of the 10 eligible candidates can be chosen for the first position and any of the remaining 9 eligible candidates can be chosen for the second position, making a total of $10 \times 9 = 90$ sets of 2 candidates to fill the computer science positions. But this number includes the set in which Candidate A was chosen to fill the first position and Candidate B

was chosen to fill the second position as well as the set in which Candidate B was chosen for the first position and Candidate A was chosen for the second position. These sets are not different essentially since the positions are identical and in both sets Candidates A and B are chosen to fill the 2 positions. Therefore, there are $\frac{90}{2} = 45$ sets of 2 candidates to fill the computer science positions. Then, using the multiplication principle, there are $7 \times 45 = 315$ different sets of 3 candidates to fill the 3 positions.

The correct answer is E.

169. A survey of employers found that during 1993 employment costs rose 3.5 percent, where employment costs consist of salary costs and fringe-benefit costs. If salary costs rose 3 percent and fringe-benefit costs rose 5.5 percent during 1993, then fringe-benefit costs represented what percent of employment costs at the beginning of 1993?

(A) 16.5%
(B) 20%
(C) 35%
(D) 55%
(E) 65%

Algebra; Arithmetic First-Degree Equations; Percents

Let E represent employment costs, S represent salary costs, and F represent fringe-benefit costs. Then $E = S + F$. An increase of 3 percent in salary costs and a 5.5 percent increase in fringe-benefit costs resulted in a 3.5 percent increase in employment costs. Therefore $1.03S + 1.055F = 1.035E$. But, $E = S + F$, so $1.03S + 1.055F = 1.035(S + F) = 1.035S + 1.035F$.

Combining like terms gives $(1.055 - 1.035)F = (1.035 - 1.03)S$ or

$0.02F = 0.005S$. Then, $S = \frac{0.02}{0.005}F = 4F$. Thus, since $E = S + F$, it follows that $E = 4F + F = 5F$.

Then, F as a percent of E is $\frac{F}{E} = \frac{F}{5F} = \frac{1}{5} = 20\%$.

The correct answer is B.

170. The subsets of the set {w, x, y} are {w}, {x}, {y}, {w, x}, {w, y}, {x, y}, {w, x, y}, and { } (the empty subset). How many subsets of the set {w, x, y, z} contain w?

(A) Four
(B) Five
(C) Seven
(D) Eight
(E) Sixteen

Arithmetic Sets

As shown in the table, the subsets of $\{w, x, y, z\}$ can be organized into two columns, those subsets of $\{w, x, y, z\}$ that do not contain w (left column) and the corresponding subsets of $\{w, x, y, z\}$ that contain w (right column), and each of these collections has the same number of sets. Therefore, there are 8 subsets of $\{w, x, y, z\}$ that contain w.

subsets not containing w	subsets containing w
$\{\ \}$	$\{w\}$
$\{x\}$	$\{w, x\}$
$\{y\}$	$\{w, y\}$
$\{z\}$	$\{w, z\}$
$\{x, y\}$	$\{w, x, y\}$
$\{x, z\}$	$\{w, x, z\}$
$\{y, z\}$	$\{w, y, z\}$
$\{x, y, z\}$	$\{w, x, y, z\}$

The correct answer is D.

171. The number $\sqrt{63 - 36\sqrt{3}}$ can be expressed as $x + y\sqrt{3}$ for some integers x and y. What is the value of xy?

(A) −18
(B) −6
(C) 6
(D) 18
(E) 27

Algebra Operations on Radical Expressions

Squaring both sides of $\sqrt{63 - 36\sqrt{3}} = x + y\sqrt{3}$ gives $63 - 36\sqrt{3} = x^2 + 2xy\sqrt{3} + 3y^2 = (x^2 + 3y^2) + (2xy)\sqrt{3}$, which implies that $-36 = 2xy$, or $xy = -18$. Indeed, if $-36 \neq 2xy$, or equivalently, if $36 + 2xy \neq 0$, then we could write

$\sqrt{3}$ as a quotient of the two integers $63 - x^2 - 3y^2$ and $36 + 2xy$, which is not possible because $\sqrt{3}$ is an irrational number. To be more explicit, $63 - 36\sqrt{3} = x^2 + 2xy\sqrt{3} + 3y^2$ implies $63 - x^2 - 3y^2 = (36 + 2xy)\sqrt{3}$, and if $36 + 2xy \neq 0$, then we could divide both sides of the equation $63 - x^2 - 3y^2 = (36 + 2xy)\sqrt{3}$ by $36 + 2xy$ to get $\frac{63 - x^2 - 3y^2}{36 + 2xy} = \sqrt{3}$.

The correct answer is A.

172. There are 10 books on a shelf, of which 4 are paperbacks and 6 are hardbacks. How many possible selections of 5 books from the shelf contain at least one paperback and at least one hardback?

(A) 75
(B) 120
(C) 210
(D) 246
(E) 252

Arithmetic Elementary Combinatorics

The number of selections of 5 books containing at least one paperback and at least one hardback is equal to $T - N$, where T is the total number of selections of 5 books and N is the number of selections that do not contain both a paperback and a hardback. The value of T is

$$\binom{10}{5} = \frac{10!}{5!(10-5)!} = \frac{(6)(7)(8)(9)(10)}{(1)(2)(3)(4)(5)}$$
$$= (7)(2)(9)(2) = 252.$$

To find the value of N, first note that no selection of 5 books can contain all paperbacks, since there are only 4 paperback books. Thus, the value of N is equal to the number of selections of 5 books that contain all hardbacks, which is equal to 6 since there are 6 ways that a single hardback can be left out when choosing the 5 hardback books. It follows that the number of selections of 5 books containing at least one paperback and at least one hardback is $T - N = 252 - 6 = 246$.

The correct answer is D.

173. If x is to be chosen at random from the set {1, 2, 3, 4} and y is to be chosen at random from the set {5, 6, 7}, what is the probability that xy will be even?

(A) $\frac{1}{6}$
(B) $\frac{1}{3}$
(C) $\frac{1}{2}$
(D) $\frac{2}{3}$
(E) $\frac{5}{6}$

Arithmetic; Algebra Probability; Concepts of Sets

By the principle of multiplication, since there are 4 elements in the first set and 3 elements in the second set, there are $(4)(3) = 12$ possible products of xy, where x is chosen from the first set and y is chosen from the second set. These products will be even EXCEPT when both x and y are odd. Since there are 2 odd numbers in the first set and 2 odd numbers in the second set, there are $(2)(2) = 4$ products of x and y that are odd. This means that the remaining $12 - 4 = 8$ products are even. Thus, the probability that xy is even is $\frac{8}{12} = \frac{2}{3}$.

The correct answer is D.

174. The function f is defined for each positive three-digit integer n by $f(n) = 2^x 3^y 5^z$, where x, y, and z are the hundreds, tens, and units digits of n, respectively. If m and v are three-digit positive integers such that $f(m) = 9f(v)$, then $m - v =$

(A) 8
(B) 9
(C) 18
(D) 20
(E) 80

Algebra Place Value

Let the hundreds, tens, and units digits of m be A, B, and C, respectively; and let the hundreds, tens, and units digits of v be a, b, and c, respectively. From $f(m) = 9f(v)$ it follows that $2^A 3^B 5^C = 9(2^a 3^b 5^c) = 3^2(2^a 3^b 5^c) = 2^a 3^{b+2} 5^c$. Therefore, $A = a$, $B = b + 2$, and $C = c$. Now calculate $m - v$.

$m - v =$	$(100A + 10B + C) - (100a + 10b + c)$	place value property
$=$	$(100a + 10(b + 2) + c) - (100a + 10b + c)$	obtained above
$=$	$10(b + 2) - 10b$	combine like terms
$=$	$10b + 20 - 10b$	distributive property
$=$	20	combine like terms

The correct answer is D.

175. If $10^{50} - 74$ is written as an integer in base 10 notation, what is the sum of the digits in that integer?

(A) 424

(B) 433

(C) 440

(D) 449

(E) 467

Arithmetic Properties of Numbers

$10^2 - 74$	=	$100 - 74$	=	26
$10^3 - 74$	=	$1{,}000 - 74$	=	926
$10^4 - 74$	=	$10{,}000 - 74$	=	9,926
$10^5 - 74$	=	$100{,}000 - 74$	=	99,926
$10^6 - 74$	=	$1{,}000{,}000 - 74$	=	999,926

From the table above it is clear that $10^{50} - 74$ in base 10 notation will be 48 digits of 9 followed by the digits 2 and 6. Therefore, the sum of the digits of $10^{50} - 74$ is equal to $48(9) + 2 + 6 = 440$.

The correct answer is C.

176. A certain company that sells only cars and trucks reported that revenues from car sales in 1997 were down 11 percent from 1996 and revenues from truck sales in 1997 were up 7 percent from 1996. If total revenues from car sales and truck sales in 1997 were up 1 percent from 1996, what is the ratio of revenue from car sales in 1996 to revenue from truck sales in 1996?

(A) 1:2

(B) 4:5

(C) 1:1

(D) 3:2

(E) 5:3

Algebra; Arithmetic First-Degree Equations; Percents

Let C_{96} and C_{97} represent revenues from car sales in 1996 and 1997, respectively, and let T_{96} and T_{97} represent revenues from truck sales in 1996 and 1997, respectively. A decrease of 11 percent in revenue from car sales from 1996 to 1997 can be represented as $(1 - 0.11)C_{96} = C_{97}$, and a 7 percent increase in revenue from truck sales from 1996 to 1997 can be represented as $(1 + 0.07)T_{96} = T_{97}$.

An overall increase of 1 percent in revenue from car and truck sales from 1996 to 1997 can be represented as $C_{97} + T_{97} = (1 + 0.01)(C_{96} + T_{96})$.

Then, by substitution of expressions for C_{97} and T_{97} that were derived above, $(1 - 0.11)C_{96} + (1 + 0.07)T_{96} = (1 + 0.01)(C_{96} + T_{96})$ and so $0.89C_{96} + 1.07T_{96} = 1.01(C_{96} + T_{96})$ or $0.89C_{96} + 1.07T_{96} = 1.01C_{96} + 1.01T_{96}$.

Then, combining like terms gives $(1.07 - 1.01)T_{96} = (1.01 - 0.89)C_{96}$ or $0.06T_{96} = 0.12C_{96}$. Thus $\frac{C_{96}}{T_{96}} = \frac{0.06}{0.12} = \frac{1}{2}$. The ratio of revenue from car sales in 1996 to revenue from truck sales in 1996 is 1:2.

The correct answer is A.

177. Becky rented a power tool from a rental shop. The rent for the tool was \$12 for the first hour and \$3 for each additional hour. If Becky paid a total of \$27, excluding sales tax, to rent the tool, for how many hours did she rent it?

(A) 5

(B) 6

(C) 9

(D) 10

(E) 12

Arithmetic Applied Problems

Becky paid a total of \$27 to rent the power tool. She paid \$12 to rent the tool for the first hour and \$27 – \$12 = \$15 to rent the tool for the additional hours at the rate of \$3 per additional hour. It follows that she rented the tool for $\frac{15}{3} = 5$ additional hours and a total of $1 + 5 = 6$ hours.

The correct answer is B.

178. If $4 < \frac{7-x}{3}$, which of the following must be true?

I. $5 < x$

II. $|x + 3| > 2$

III. $-(x + 5)$ is positive.

(A) II only
(B) III only
(C) I and II only
(D) II and III only
(E) I, II, and III

Algebra Inequalities

Given that $4 < \frac{7-x}{3}$, it follows that $12 < 7 - x$. Then $5 < -x$ or, equivalently, $x < -5$.

I. If $4 < \frac{7-x}{3}$, then $x < -5$. If $5 < x$ were true, then, by combining $5 < x$ and $x < -5$, it would follow that $5 < -5$, which cannot be true. Therefore, it is not the case that, if $4 < \frac{7-x}{3}$, then Statement I must be true. In fact, Statement I is never true.

II. If $4 < \frac{7-x}{3}$, then $x < -5$, and it follows that $x + 3 < -2$. Since $-2 < 0$, then $x + 3 < 0$ and $|x + 3| = -(x + 3)$. If $x + 3 < -2$, then $-(x + 3) > 2$ and by substitution, $|x + 3| > 2$. Therefore, Statement II must be true for every value of x such that $x < -5$. Therefore, Statement II must be true if $4 < \frac{7-x}{3}$.

III. If $4 < \frac{7-x}{3}$, then $x < -5$ and $x + 5 < 0$. But if $x + 5 < 0$, then it follows that $-(x + 5) > 0$ and so $-(x + 5)$ is positive. Therefore Statement III must be true if $4 < \frac{7-x}{3}$.

The correct answer is D.

179. On a certain day, a bakery produced a batch of rolls at a total production cost of \$300. On that day, $\frac{4}{5}$ of the rolls in the batch were sold, each at a price that was 50 percent greater than the average (arithmetic mean) production cost per roll. The remaining rolls in the batch were sold the next day, each at a price that was 20 percent less than the price of the day before. What was the bakery's profit on this batch of rolls?

(A) \$150
(B) \$144
(C) \$132
(D) \$108
(E) \$90

Arithmetic Applied Problems

Let n be the number of rolls in the batch and p be the average production price, in dollars, per roll. Then the total cost of the batch is $np = 300$ dollars, and the total revenue from selling the rolls in the batch is $\left(\frac{4}{5}n\right)(1.5p) + \left(\frac{1}{5}n\right)(0.8)(1.5p) =$

$$\left(\frac{4}{5}n\right)\left(\frac{3}{2}p\right) + \left(\frac{1}{5}n\right)\left(\frac{4}{5}\right)\left(\frac{3}{2}p\right) = \left(\frac{6}{5} + \frac{6}{25}\right)np$$

$= \left(\frac{36}{25}\right)np$. Therefore, the profit from selling the rolls in the batch is $\left(\frac{36}{25}\right)np - np = \left(\frac{11}{25}\right)np =$ $\left(\frac{11}{25}\right)(300)$ dollars $= 132$ dollars.

The correct answer is C.

180. A set of numbers has the property that for any number t in the set, $t + 2$ is in the set. If -1 is in the set, which of the following must also be in the set?

I. -3

II. 1

III. 5

(A) I only
(B) II only
(C) I and II only
(D) II and III only
(E) I, II, and III

Arithmetic Properties of Numbers

It is given that -1 is in the set and, if t is in the set, then $t + 2$ is in the set.

I. Since $\{-1, 1, 3, 5, 7, 9, 11, \ldots\}$ contains -1 and satisfies the property that if t is in the set, then $t + 2$ is in the set, it is not true that -3 must be in the set.

II. Since −1 is in the set, $-1 + 2 = 1$ is in the set. Therefore, it must be true that 1 is in the set.

III. Since −1 is in the set, $-1 + 2 = 1$ is in the set. Since 1 is in the set, $1 + 2 = 3$ is in the set. Since 3 is in the set, $3 + 2 = 5$ is in the set. Therefore, it must be true that 5 is in the set.

The correct answer is D.

181. A couple decides to have 4 children. If they succeed in having 4 children and each child is equally likely to be a boy or a girl, what is the probability that they will have exactly 2 girls and 2 boys?

(A) $\frac{3}{8}$

(B) $\frac{1}{4}$

(C) $\frac{3}{16}$

(D) $\frac{1}{8}$

(E) $\frac{1}{16}$

Arithmetic Probability

Representing the birth order of the 4 children as a sequence of 4 letters, each of which is B for boy and G for girl, there are 2 possibilities (B or G) for the first letter, 2 for the second letter, 2 for the third letter, and 2 for the fourth letter, making a total of $2^4 = 16$ sequences. The table below categorizes some of these 16 sequences.

# of boys	# of girls	Sequences	# of sequences
0	4	GGGG	1
1	3	BGGG, GBGG, GGBG, GGGB	4
3	1	GBBB, BGBB, BBGB, BBBG	4
4	0	BBBB	1

The table accounts for $1 + 4 + 4 + 1 =$ 10 sequences. The other 6 sequences will have 2Bs and 2Gs. Therefore the probability that the couple will have exactly 2 boys and 2 girls is $\frac{6}{16} = \frac{3}{8}$.

For the mathematically inclined, if it is assumed that a couple has a fixed number of children, that the probability of having a girl each time is p, and that the sex of each child is independent of the sex of the other children, then the number of girls, x, born to a couple with n children is a random variable having the binomial probability distribution. The probability of having exactly x girls born to a couple with n children is given by the formula $\binom{n}{x} p^x (1 - p)^{n-x}$. For the problem at hand, it is given that each child is equally likely to be a boy or a girl, and so $p = \frac{1}{2}$. Thus, the probability of having exactly 2 girls born to a couple with 4 children is

$$\binom{4}{2}\left(\frac{1}{2}\right)^2\left(\frac{1}{2}\right)^2 = \frac{4!}{2!2!}\left(\frac{1}{2}\right)^2\left(\frac{1}{2}\right)^2 =$$

$$(6)\left(\frac{1}{4}\right)\left(\frac{1}{4}\right) = \frac{6}{16} = \frac{3}{8}.$$

The correct answer is A.

182. The closing price of Stock X changed on each trading day last month. The percent change in the closing price of Stock X from the first trading day last month to each of the other trading days last month was less than 50 percent. If the closing price on the second trading day last month was \$10.00, which of the following CANNOT be the closing price on the last trading day last month?

(A) \$3.00

(B) \$9.00

(C) \$19.00

(D) \$24.00

(E) \$29.00

Arithmetic Applied Problems; Percents

Let P be the first-day closing price, in dollars, of the stock. It is given that the second-day closing price was $(1 + n\%)P = 10$, so $P = \frac{10}{1 + n\%}$, for some value of n such that $-50 < n < 50$. Therefore, P is between $\frac{10}{1 + 0.50} \approx 6.67$ and $\frac{10}{1 - 0.50} = 20$. Hence, if Q is the closing price, in dollars, of the stock on the last day, then Q is between

$(0.50)(6.67) \approx 3.34$ (50% decrease from the lowest possible first-day closing price) and $(1.50)(20) = 30$ (50% increase from the greatest possible first-day closing price). The only answer choice that gives a number of dollars not between 3.34 and 30 is the first answer choice.

The correct answer is A.

183. How many different positive integers are factors of 441?

(A) 4
(B) 6
(C) 7
(D) 9
(E) 11

Arithmetic Properties of Numbers

Like any integer, 441 has itself and 1 as factors. To find all its other positive factors, we first use prime factorization to write 441 as a product of its prime factors: $441 = 3 \times 3 \times 7 \times 7$. Then we can group those two 3s and two 7s in various ways to find all their products, which will be the other positive factors of 441. That is, $441 = 3 \times (3 \times 7 \times 7) = (3 \times 3) \times (7 \times 7) = (3 \times 7) \times (3 \times 7) = (3 \times 3 \times 7) \times 7$. This shows that 441 has 7 different positive integer factors other than itself and 1. These are 3, 7, $3 \times 3 = 9$, $3 \times 7 = 21$, $7 \times 7 = 49$, $3 \times 3 \times 7 = 63$, and $3 \times 7 \times 7 = 147$. So altogether, 441 has 9 different positive integers as factors: 1, 3, 7, 9, 21, 49, 63, 147, and 441.

The correct answer is D.

184. If n is a positive integer and n^2 is divisible by 72, then the largest positive integer that must divide n is

(A) 6
(B) 12
(C) 24
(D) 36
(E) 48

Arithmetic Properties of Numbers

Since n^2 is divisible by 72, $n^2 = 72k$ for some positive integer k. Since $n^2 = 72k$, then $72k$ must be a perfect square. Since $72k = (2^3)(3^2)k$, then $k = 2m^2$ for some positive integer m in order for $72k$ to be a perfect square. Then, $n^2 = 72k = (2^3)(3^2)(2m^2) = (2^4)(3^2)m^2 = [(2^2)(3)(m)]^2$, and $n = (2^2)(3)(m)$. The positive integers that MUST divide n are 1, 2, 3, 4, 6, and 12. Therefore, the largest positive integer that must divide n is 12.

The correct answer is B.

185. A certain grocery purchased x pounds of produce for p dollars per pound. If y pounds of the produce had to be discarded due to spoilage and the grocery sold the rest for s dollars per pound, which of the following represents the gross profit on the sale of the produce?

(A) $(x - y)s - xp$
(B) $(x - y)p - ys$
(C) $(s - p)y - xp$
(D) $xp - ys$
(E) $(x - y)(s - p)$

Algebra Simplifying Algebraic Expressions; Applied Problems

Since the grocery bought x pounds of produce for p dollars per pound, the total cost of the produce was xp dollars. Since y pounds of the produce was discarded, the grocery sold $x - y$ pounds of produce at the price of s dollars per pound, yielding a total revenue of $(x - y)s$ dollars. Then, the grocery's gross profit on the sale of the produce is its total revenue minus its total cost or $(x - y)s - xp$ dollars.

The correct answer is A.

186. If x, y, and z are positive integers such that x is a factor of y, and x is a multiple of z, which of the following is NOT necessarily an integer?

(A) $\frac{x+z}{z}$
(B) $\frac{y+z}{x}$
(C) $\frac{x+y}{z}$
(D) $\frac{xy}{z}$
(E) $\frac{yz}{x}$

Arithmetic Properties of Numbers

Since the positive integer x is a factor of y, then $y = kx$ for some positive integer k. Since x is a multiple of the positive integer z, then $x = mz$ for some positive integer m.

Substitute these expressions for x and/or y into each answer choice to find the one expression that is NOT necessarily an integer.

A $\frac{x+z}{z} = \frac{mz+z}{z} = \frac{(m+1)z}{z} = m+1$, which MUST be an integer

B $\frac{y+z}{x} = \frac{y}{x} + \frac{z}{x} = \frac{kx}{x} + \frac{z}{mz} = k + \frac{1}{m}$, which NEED NOT be an integer

Because only one of the five expressions need not be an integer, the expressions given in C, D, and E need not be tested. However, for completeness,

C $\frac{x+y}{z} = \frac{mz+kx}{z} = \frac{mz+k(mz)}{z} = \frac{mz(1+k)}{z}$ $= m(1+k)$, which MUST be an integer

D $\frac{xy}{z} = \frac{(mz)y}{z} = my$, which MUST be an integer

E $\frac{yz}{x} = \frac{(kx)(z)}{x} = kz$, which MUST be an integer

The correct answer is B.

187. Running at their respective constant rates, Machine X takes 2 days longer to produce w widgets than Machine Y. At these rates, if the two machines together produce $\frac{5}{4}w$ widgets in 3 days, how many days would it take Machine X alone to produce 2w widgets?

(A) 4
(B) 6
(C) 8
(D) 10
(E) 12

Algebra Applied Problems

If x, where $x > 2$, represents the number of days Machine X takes to produce w widgets, then Machine Y takes $x - 2$ days to produce w widgets. It follows that Machines X and Y can produce $\frac{w}{x}$ and $\frac{w}{x-2}$ widgets, respectively, in 1 day and together they can produce $\frac{w}{x} + \frac{w}{x-2}$ widgets in 1 day. Since it is given that, together, they can produce $\frac{5}{4}w$ widgets in 3 days, it follows that, together, they can produce $\frac{1}{3}\left(\frac{5}{4}w\right) = \frac{5}{12}w$ widgets in 1 day. Thus,

$$\frac{w}{x} + \frac{w}{x-2} = \frac{5}{12}w$$
$$\left(\frac{1}{x} + \frac{1}{x-2}\right)w = \frac{5}{12}w$$
$$\left(\frac{1}{x} + \frac{1}{x-2}\right) = \frac{5}{12}$$
$$12x(x-2)\left(\frac{1}{x} + \frac{1}{x-2}\right) = 12x(x-2)\left(\frac{5}{12}\right)$$
$$12[(x-2)+x] = 5x(x-2)$$
$$12(2x-2) = 5x(x-2)$$
$$24x - 24 = 5x^2 - 10x$$
$$0 = 5x^2 - 34x + 24$$
$$0 = (5x-4)(x-6)$$
$$x = \frac{4}{5} \text{ or } 6$$

Therefore, since $x > 2$, it follows that $x = 6$. Machine X takes 6 days to produce w widgets and $2(6) = 12$ days to produce $2w$ widgets.

The correct answer is E.

188. What is the greatest positive integer n such that 5^n divides $10! - (2)(5!)^2$?

(A) 2
(B) 3
(C) 4
(D) 5
(E) 6

Arithmetic Properties of Numbers; Exponents

The greatest positive integer n such that 5^n divides a given integer is the number of factors of 5 in the prime factorization of the given integer. By repeated identification of common factors, the indicated difference can be factored sufficiently to determine the number of factors of 5 in its prime factorization. In the computations that follow, we have used the equalities $10! = (5!)(6)(7)(8)(9)(10)$ and $5! = (2)(3)(4)(5)$.

$$
\begin{aligned}
&10! - (2)(5!)^2 \\
&= (5! \cdot 6 \cdot 7 \cdot 8 \cdot 9 \cdot 10) - (2 \cdot 5! \cdot 5!) \\
&= (5!)(6 \cdot 7 \cdot 8 \cdot 9 \cdot 10 - 2 \cdot 5!) \\
&= (5!)(6 \cdot 7 \cdot 8 \cdot 9 \cdot 10 - 2 \cdot 2 \cdot 3 \cdot 4 \cdot 5) \\
&= (5!)(2^4)(3 \cdot 7 \cdot 9 \cdot 10 - 3 \cdot 5) \\
&= (5!)(2^4)(3)(7 \cdot 9 \cdot 10 - 5) \\
&= (5!)(2^4)(3)(5)(7 \cdot 9 \cdot 2 - 1) \\
&= (5!)(2^4)(3)(5)(63 \cdot 2 - 1) \\
&= (5!)(2^4)(3)(5)(126 - 1) \\
&= (5!)(2^4)(3)(5)(125)
\end{aligned}
$$

Since there is exactly 1 factor of 5 in $5! = (2)(3)(4)(5)$, no factors of 5 in either 2^4 or 3, exactly 1 factor of 5 in 5, and exactly 3 factors of 5 in $125 = 5^3$, it follows that there are $1 + 1 + 3 = 5$ factors of 5 in $10! - (2)(5!)^2 = (5!)(2^4)(3)(5)(125)$.

The correct answer is D.

189. Yesterday, Candice and Sabrina trained for a bicycle race by riding around an oval track. They both began riding at the same time from the track's starting point. However, Candice rode at a faster pace than Sabrina, completing each lap around the track in 42 seconds, while Sabrina completed each lap around the track in 46 seconds. How many laps around the track had Candice completed the next time that Candice and Sabrina were together at the starting point?

(A) 21
(B) 23
(C) 42
(D) 46
(E) 483

Arithmetic Applied Problems; Properties of Integers

Let C and S be the number of laps around the track, respectively, whenever Candice and Sabrina were together again at the starting point. Since Candice completes each lap in 42 seconds, Candice had been riding for a total of $42C$ seconds, and since Sabrina completes each lap in 46 seconds, Sabrina had been riding for a total of $46S$ seconds. Because they had been riding for the same total amount of time, we have $42C = 46S$, or $21C = 23S$, where C and S are positive integers.

Because 23 is a prime number that divides the product of 21 and C (note that 23 divides $23S$ and $23S = 21C$), it follows that 23 divides 21 (not true) or 23 divides C, and hence 23 divides C. Also, because 3 is a prime number that divides the product of 23 and S (note that 3 divides $21C$ and $21C = 23S$), it follows that 3 divides 23 (not true) or 3 divides S, and hence 3 divides S. Finally, because 7 is a prime number that divides the product of 23 and S (note that 7 divides $21C$ and $21C = 23S$), it follows that 7 divides 23 (not true) or 7 divides S, and hence 7 divides S

It follows that C is a multiple of 23 and S is a multiple of both 3 and 7. The least positive integer values for C and S with this property are $C = 23$ and $S = 3 \times 7 = 21$. Therefore, the next time after beginning that Candice and Sabrina were together at the starting point, Candice had completed 23 laps and Sabrina had completed 21 laps.

The correct answer is B.

190. If $n = 9! - 6^4$, which of the following is the greatest integer k such that 3^k is a factor of n?

(A) 1
(B) 3
(C) 4
(D) 6
(E) 8

Arithmetic Properties of Integers

The following charts isolate and count the occurrences of 2 and of 3 in the factorizations of $9! = (9)(8)(7)(6)(5)(4)(3)(2)$ and $6^4 = (6)(6)(6)(6)$.

9!	=	(9)	(8)	(7)	(6)	(5)	(4)	(3)	(2)
Occurrences of 2		0	3	0	1	0	2	0	1
Occurrences of 3		2	0	0	1	0	0	1	0

6^4	=	(6)	(6)	(6)	(6)
Occurrences of 2		1	1	1	1
Occurrences of 3		1	1	1	1

So, $9! - 6^4 = (2^7 \cdot 3^4 \cdot 5 \cdot 7) - (2^4 \cdot 3^4) = (2^4 \cdot 3^4)(2^3 \cdot 5 \cdot 7 - 1) = (2^4 \cdot 3^4)(279) = (2^4 \cdot 3^4)(3^2 \cdot 31) = 2^4 \cdot 3^6 \cdot 31$, where 31 is prime. Therefore $k = 6$.

Alternatively, express $n = 9! - 6^4$ as $(9)(8)(7)(6)(5)(4)(3)(2)(1) - 6^4 = [(9)(8)](7)(6)(5)(4)[(3)(2)](1) - 6^4$. Then factor (9)(8) as $(36)(2) = (6^2)(2)$ and multiply (3)(2) to get 6. Factoring 6^4 from $n = (6^2)(2)(7)(6)(5)(4)(6)(1) - 6^4$ gives $n = 6^4[(2)(7)(5)(4)(1) - 1] = 6^4(279)$. It follows that 6^4 has 4 factors of 3 and 279 has 2 additional factors of 3 since $279 = (3^2)(31)$, so the greatest integer k such that 3^k is a factor of n is $4 + 2 = 6$.

The correct answer is D.

191. The integer 120 has many factorizations. For example, 120 = (2)(60), 120 = (3)(4)(10), and 120 = (–1)(–3)(4)(10). In how many of the factorizations of 120 are the factors consecutive integers in ascending order?

(A) 2
(B) 3
(C) 4
(D) 5
(E) 6

Arithmetic Properties of Integers

All of the positive factors of 120 listed in ascending order are 1, 2, 3, 4, 5, 6, 8, 10, 12, 15, 20, 24, 30, 40, 60, and 120. The negative factors of 120 listed in ascending order are –120, –60, –40, –30, –24, –20, –15, –12, –10, –8, –6, –5, –4, –3, –2, and –1. Examining these lists for groups of consecutive factors whose product is 120 gives (1)(2)(3)(4)(5), (2)(3)(4)(5), (4)(5)(6), and (–5)(–4)(–3)(–2).

The correct answer is C.

192. Jorge's bank statement showed a balance that was \$0.54 greater than what his records showed. He discovered that he had written a check for \$*x.yz* and had recorded it as \$*x.zy*, where each of *x*, *y*, and *z* represents a digit from 0 though 9. Which of the following could be the value of *z*?

(A) 2
(B) 3
(C) 4
(D) 5
(E) 6

Arithmetic Place Value

Since the amount Jorge recorded for the check (\$*x.zy*) was \$0.54 more than the actual amount of the check (\$*x.yz*), it follows that \$*x.zy* – \$*x.yz* = \$0.54. This is equivalent to $x + \frac{z}{10} + \frac{y}{100} - (x + \frac{y}{10} + \frac{z}{100}) = \frac{54}{100}$. Then $\frac{10z + y}{100} - \frac{10y + z}{100} = \frac{54}{100}$ or, equivalently, $10z + y - (10y + z) = 54$. It follows that $9z - 9y = 54$ or $z - y = 6$. Since y and z are digits, the possible values of y and z, respectively, are 0 and 6, 1 and 7, 2 and 8, and 3 and 9. Of the possible values of z, only 6 is given as one of the answer choices.

The correct answer is E.

193. One side of a parking stall is defined by a straight stripe that consists of *n* painted sections of equal length with an unpainted section $\frac{1}{2}$ as long between each pair of consecutive painted sections. The total length of the stripe from the beginning of the first painted section to the end of the last painted section is 203 inches. If *n* is an integer and the length, in inches, of each unpainted section is an integer greater than 2, what is the value of *n*?

(A) 5
(B) 9
(C) 10
(D) 14
(E) 29

Algebra Applied Problems

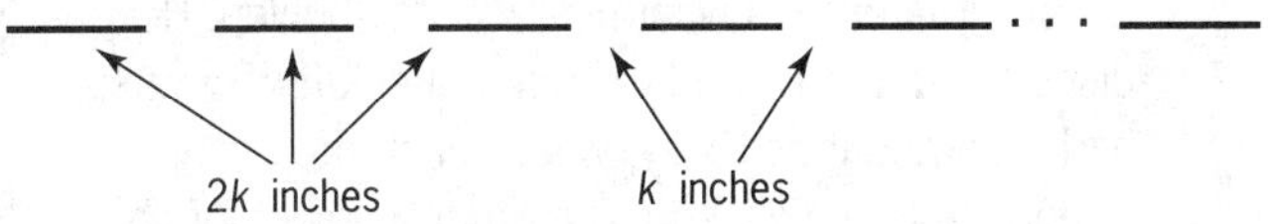

The figure above is a schematic diagram of the parking stall's painted sections, where each painted section has length $2k$ inches and each unpainted section has length k inches. Since there is a total of n painted sections and a total of $(n - 1)$ unpainted sections, it follows that $n(2k) + (n - 1)k = 203$, or $(3n - 1)k = 203$. Also, since n and k are positive integers with $n \geq 2$, and $203 = (7)(29)$ is the only factorization of 203 with integer factors greater than or equal to 2, we have two cases.

Case 1: $3n - 1 = 7$ and $k = 29$. In this case we have $n = \frac{8}{3}$.

Case 2: $3n - 1 = 29$ and $k = 7$. In this case we have $n = 10$.

Because $\frac{8}{3}$ is not an integer, we discard Case 1, and hence $n = 10$.

The correct answer is C.

194. This year, Henry will save a certain amount of his income, and he will spend the rest. Next year, Henry will have no income, but for each dollar that he saves this year, he will have $1 + r$ dollars available to spend. In terms of r, what fraction of his income should Henry save this year so that next year the amount he has available to spend will be equal to half the amount that he spends this year?

(A) $\frac{1}{r} + 2$

(B) $\frac{1}{2r} + 2$

(C) $\frac{1}{3r} + 2$

(D) $\frac{1}{r} + 3$

(E) $\frac{1}{2r} + 3$

Algebra Sets

Let x be the number of dollars Henry should save this year and y be his total income in dollars this year. Then for him to have an amount available to spend next year equal to half the amount he spends this year, $x(1 + r)$ must equal $\frac{y - x}{2}$. Thus, $(2 + 2r)x$ must equal $y - x$, so y must equal $(3 + 2r)x$. Therefore, the fraction of his income he must save this year is $\frac{x}{y} = \frac{x}{(3 + 2r)x} = \frac{1}{2r + 3}$.

The correct answer is E.

Machine	Consecutive Minutes Machine Is Off	Units of Power When On
A	17	15
B	14	18
C	11	12

195. At a certain factory, each of Machines A, B, and C is periodically on for exactly 1 minute and periodically off for a fixed number of consecutive minutes. The table above shows that Machine A is on and uses 15 units of power every 18th minute, Machine B is on and uses 18 units of power every 15th minute, and Machine C is on and uses 12 units of power every 12th minute. The factory has a backup generator that operates only when the total power usage of the 3 machines exceeds 30 units of power. What is the time interval, in minutes, between consecutive times the backup generator begins to operate?

(A) 36
(B) 63
(C) 90
(D) 180
(E) 270

Arithmetic Applied Problems

The given table shows that the backup generator will not operate when only one of the machines is operating, since none of the machines uses more than 30 units of power. The table below shows the power usage when more than one machine is operating at the same time.

Machines	Units of power when on	Backup generator
A & B	15 + 18 = 33	On
B & C	18 + 12 = 30	Off
C & A	12 + 15 = 27	Off
A & B & C	15 + 18 + 12 = 45	On

Thus, the backup generator will be on whenever Machines A and B are both on, this being true regardless of whether Machine C is on. We are given that Machine A is on for 1 minute every 18 minutes and Machine B is on for 1 minute every 15 minutes. Therefore, if Machines A and B are both on for a certain minute, then the following are the minutes when these machines are again on.

Minutes when Machine A is on: 1st, 19th, 37th, 55th, 73rd, $\mathbf{91^{st}}$, 109th, …

Minutes when Machine B is on: 1st, 16th, 31st, 46th, 61st, 76th, $\mathbf{91^{st}}$, 106th, …

Therefore, the next time Machines A and B are both on is the 91st minute, which is 90 minutes after the first minute.

Alternatively, Machine A is on every $18 = (2)(3^2)$ minutes and Machine B is on every $15 = (3)(5)$ minutes, so the machines are both on every $(2)(3^2)(5) = 90$ minutes (least common multiple of 18 and 15).

The correct answer is C.

196. In a certain region, the number of children who have been vaccinated against rubella is twice the number who have been vaccinated against mumps. The number who have been vaccinated against both is twice the number who have been vaccinated against mumps. If 5,000 have been vaccinated against both, how many have been vaccinated against rubella only?

(A) 2,500
(B) 7,500
(C) 10,000
(D) 15,000
(E) 17,500

Algebra Simultaneous Equations; Sets (Venn Diagrams)

Let R, M, and B be the number, respectively, of children who have been vaccinated against rubella, against mumps, and against both. Then the number of children who have been vaccinated against rubella only is $R - B$ and the number of children who have been vaccinated against mumps only is $M - B$, as shown in the Venn diagram below.

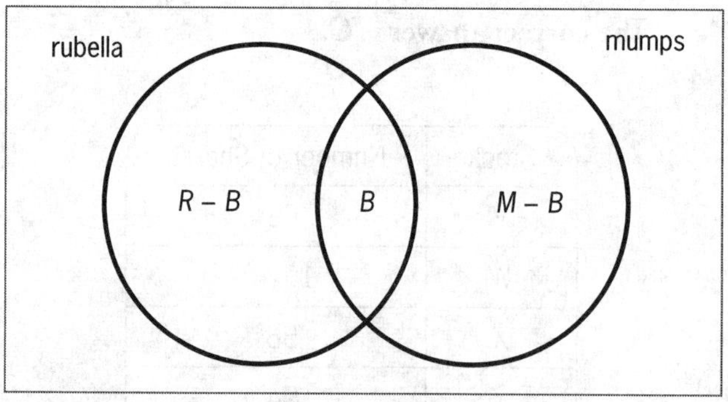

From the given information, we have (i) $R = 2M$, (ii) $B = 2(M - B)$, and (iii) $B = 5{,}000$. Substituting the value of B given in (iii) into (ii) gives $5{,}000 = 2(M - 5{,}000)$, or $M = 7{,}500$. Using this value of M in (i) gives $R = 2(7{,}500) = 15{,}000$. Therefore, the number vaccinated against rubella only is $R - B = 15{,}000 - 5{,}000 = 10{,}000$.

The correct answer is C.

197. Three boxes of supplies have an average (arithmetic mean) weight of 7 kilograms and a median weight of 9 kilograms. What is the maximum possible weight, in kilograms, of the lightest box?

(A) 1
(B) 2
(C) 3
(D) 4
(E) 5

Algebra Statistics

Let x, y, and z be the weights, in kilograms, of the boxes, where $x \le y \le z$. Since the average weight of the boxes is 7 kilograms and the median weight of the boxes is 9 kilograms, we

have $x + y + z = 3(7) = 21$ and $y = 9$. Hence, $x + 9 + z = 21$, or $z = 12 - x$. Since $z = 12 - x$, $z \geq y$, and $y = 9$, it follows that $12 - x \geq 9$, or $x \leq 3$. Therefore, the maximum possible value of x, which is the maximum possible weight of the lightest box in kilograms, is less than or equal to 3. Since $x = 3$ is a possible value of x, which can be seen by considering $x = 3, y = 9$, and $z = 9$, the maximum possible weight of the lightest box is equal to 3 kilograms.

The correct answer is C.

Stock	Number of Shares
V	68
W	112
X	56
Y	94
Z	45

198. The table shows the number of shares of each of the 5 stocks owned by Mr. Sami. If Mr. Sami were to sell 20 shares of Stock X and buy 24 shares of Stock Y, what would be the increase in the range of the numbers of shares of the 5 stocks owned by Mr. Sami?

(A) 4
(B) 6
(C) 9
(D) 15
(E) 20

Arithmetic Statistics

The table below shows the numbers of shares of the 5 stocks before and after the change in the numbers of shares of Stocks X and Y.

Stock	Number of Shares (before)	Number of Shares (after)
V	68	68
W	112	112
X	56	36
Y	94	118
Z	45	45

Before the change in the number of shares of Stocks X and Y, the range was $112 - 45 = 67$. After the change in the number of shares of Stocks X and Y, the range was $118 - 36 = 82$. Therefore, the increase in the range is $82 - 67 = 15$.

The correct answer is D.

199. Last year, sales at Company X were 10% greater in February than in January, 15% less in March than in February, 20% greater in April than in March, 10% less in May than in April, and 5% greater in June than in May. In which month were sales closest to the sales in January?

(A) February
(B) March
(C) April
(D) May
(E) June

Arithmetic Percents; Estimation

Let N be the sales at Company X in January. The table gives numerical expressions for sales in each of the months from January through June. For example, since sales in March were 15% less than sales in February, sales in March can be obtained by multiplying sales in February by 0.85.

Month	Sales
January	N
February	$(1.1)N$
March	$(0.85)(1.1)N$
April	$(1.2)(0.85)(1.1)N$
May	$(0.9)(1.2)(0.85)(1.1)N$
June	$(1.05)(0.9)(1.2)(0.85)(1.1)N$

The month after January with sales closest to sales in January will be the month after January having sales closest to N. To this end, the following two results will be helpful.

(a) $(0.85)(1.1) = 0.935$

(b) $(0.85)(1.2) = 1.02$

From (a) it follows that sales in January were closer to sales in March than to sales in February, since 1 is closer to 0.935 than to 1.1. Hence, the month with sales closest to January is

NOT February. From (b) it follows that sales in January were closer to sales in February than to sales in April, since $(1.2)(0.85)(1.1) = (1.02)(1.1) > 1.1$. Hence, the month with sales closest to January is NOT April. For May, because $(0.9)(1.1) = (1 - 0.1)(1 + 0.1) = 1^2 - (0.1)^2 = 0.99$, it follows from (b) that $(0.9)(1.2)(0.85)(1.1) = (0.99)(1.02) = (0.99)(1 + 0.02)$, which is 0.99 plus a little less than 0.02 (0.99×0.02 is 99% of 0.02). Thus, sales in January were closer to sales in May (between N and $1.02N$) than to sales in March (sales were $0.935N$). Hence, the month with sales closest to January is NOT March. Finally, because sales in June were greater than sales in May, and both were greater than N, sales in January were closer to sales in May than to sales in June. Hence, the month with sales closest to January is NOT June. Therefore, the month with sales closest to January is May.

Alternatively, multiply the indicated products and determine which is closest to N.

Month	Sales
January	N
February	$1.1N$
March	$0.935N$
April	$1.122N$
May	$1.0098N$
June	$1.06029N$

The correct answer is D.

200. If s and t are integers greater than 1 and each is a factor of the integer n, which of the following must be a factor of n^{st}?

I. s^t

II. $(st)^2$

III. $s + t$

(A) None
(B) I only
(C) II only
(D) III only
(E) I and II

Algebra Factoring; Simplifying Algebraic Expressions

Since each of s and t is a factor of n, it follows that there are positive integers a and b such that $n = as$ and $n = bt$.

I. MUST BE A FACTOR: nst divided by st is an integer, since $\frac{n^{st}}{s^t} = \frac{(as)^{st}}{s^t} = \frac{a^{st}s^{st}}{s^t} = a^{st}s^{st-t} = a^{st}s^{t(s-1)}$ and each of a^{st} and $st(s-1)$ is an integer. Note that $st(s-1)$ is an integer because s is greater than 1, and hence the exponent $t(s-1)$ is not negative.

II. MUST BE A FACTOR: Since $s \geq 2$ and $t \geq 2$, we have $st \geq 4$, or $st - 4 \geq 0$. Hence, n^{st-4} is an integer because the exponent $st - 4$ is not negative. Therefore, because $n^{st} = n^4 n^{st-4}$, it follows that n^4 is a factor of n^{st}. Also, because $n^4 = (n)(n)(n)(n) = (as)(as)(bt)(bt) = (ab)^2(st)^2$, it follows that $(st)^2$ is a factor of n^4. Finally, because $(st)^2$ is a factor of n^4 and n^4 is a factor of n^{st}, it follows that $(st)^2$ is a factor of n^{st}.

III. CAN FAIL TO BE A FACTOR. Let $s = 2$, $t = 3$, and $n = 6$. Then s and t are integers greater than 1 and each is a factor of n. However, $s + t = 5$ is not a factor of $n^{st} = 6^6$.

The correct answer is E.

201. How many 4-digit positive integers are there in which all 4 digits are even?

(A) 625
(B) 600
(C) 500
(D) 400
(E) 256

Arithmetic Elementary Combinatorics

There are 4 possibilities for the left-most digit (2, 4, 6, and 8) and 5 possibilities for each of the 3 remaining digits (0, 2, 4, 6, and 8). Therefore, the number of 4-digit positive integers in which all 4 digits are even is $4 \times 5 \times 5 \times 5 = 500$.

The correct answer is C.

202. If $0 < r < 1 < s < 2$, which of the following must be less than 1?

I. $\frac{r}{s}$

II. rs

III. $s - r$

(A) I only
(B) II only
(C) III only
(D) I and II
(E) I and III

Arithmetic Inequalities

I. MUST BE LESS THAN 1: We have $0 < r < s$ from the given information. Dividing throughout by the positive number s gives $0 < \frac{r}{s} < 1$.

II. CAN FAIL TO BE LESS THAN 1: If $r = 0.9$ and $s = 1.9$, then $0 < r < 1 < s < 2$ and $rs = 1.71$ is not less than 1.

III. CAN FAIL TO BE LESS THAN 1: If $r = 0.1$ and $s = 1.9$, then $0 < r < 1 < s < 2$ and $s - r = 1.8$ is not less than 1.

The correct answer is A.

203. Last month, 15 homes were sold in Town X. The average (arithmetic mean) sale price of the homes was \$150,000 and the median sale price was \$130,000. Which of the following statements must be true?

I. At least one of the homes was sold for more than \$165,000.

II. At least one of the homes was sold for more than \$130,000 and less than \$150,000.

III. At least one of the homes was sold for less than \$130,000.

(A) I only
(B) II only
(C) III only
(D) I and II
(E) I and III

Arithmetic Statistics

I. MUST BE TRUE: Since the average sale price of the 15 homes was \$150,000, the total of the 15 sale prices was 15(\$150,000) = \$2,250,000. Also, since the median sale price of the 15 homes was \$130,000, 7 of the homes each had a sale price less than or equal to \$130,000, 7 of the homes each had a sale price greater than or equal to \$130,000, and the remaining home had a sale price equal to \$130,000.

$$\underbrace{\leq \$130{,}000 \text{ each}}_{7 \text{ homes}} \quad \underbrace{= \$130{,}000}_{1 \text{ home}} \quad \underbrace{\geq \$130{,}000 \text{ each}}_{7 \text{ homes}}$$

If none of the homes was sold for more than \$165,000, then the total of the 15 sale prices would be less than or equal to 7(\$130,000) + \$130,000 + 7(\$165,000) = \$2,195,000, which is less than \$2,250,000, contradicting what we know is the total of the 15 sale prices. Therefore, it is not possible for none of the homes to be sold for more than \$165,000, and thus it must be true that at least one of the homes was sold for more than \$165,000.

II. CAN BE FALSE: If 13 of the sale prices were each \$130,000 and 2 of the sale prices were each \$280,000, then the median of the sale prices would be \$130,000 and the average of the sale prices would be $\frac{13(\$130{,}000) + 2(\$280{,}000)}{15} = \$150{,}000$.

However, in this example none of the homes was sold for more than \$130,000 and less than \$150,000.

III. CAN BE FALSE: If 13 of the sale prices were each \$130,000 and the 2 remaining sale prices were \$140,000 and \$420,000, then the median of the sale prices would be \$130,000 and the average of the sale prices would be $\frac{13(\$130{,}000) + \$140{,}000 + \$420{,}000}{15} =$ \$150,000.

However, in this example none of the homes was sold for less than \$130,000.

The correct answer is A.

204. Pumps A, B, and C operate at their respective constant rates. Pumps A and B, operating simultaneously, can fill a certain tank in $\frac{6}{5}$ hours; Pumps A and C, operating simultaneously, can fill the tank in $\frac{3}{2}$ hours; and Pumps B and C, operating simultaneously, can fill the tank in 2 hours. How many hours does it take Pumps A, B, and C, operating simultaneously, to fill the tank?

(A) $\frac{1}{3}$
(B) $\frac{1}{2}$
(C) $\frac{2}{3}$
(D) $\frac{5}{6}$
(E) 1

Algebra Work Problem

Let t_A, t_B, and t_C be the number of hours, respectively, for Pumps A, B, and C operating alone to fill the tank, and let t be the number of hours for Pumps A, B, and C operating simultaneously to fill the tank.

Since Pumps A and B, operating simultaneously, can fill the tank in $\frac{6}{5}$ hours, it follows that $\frac{1}{t_A}+\frac{1}{t_B}=\frac{1}{\frac{6}{5}}=\frac{5}{6}$, and similarly for the other two pairs of pumps we are given information about.

$\frac{1}{t_A}+\frac{1}{t_B}=\frac{5}{6}$

$\frac{1}{t_A}+\frac{1}{t_C}=\frac{2}{3}$

$\frac{1}{t_B}+\frac{1}{t_C}=\frac{1}{2}$

Adding these 3 equations gives $2\left(\frac{1}{t_A}+\frac{1}{t_B}+\frac{1}{t_C}\right)=\frac{5}{6}+\frac{2}{3}+\frac{1}{2}=2$, or $\frac{1}{t_A}+\frac{1}{t_B}+\frac{1}{t_C}=1$. Since $\frac{1}{t_A}+\frac{1}{t_B}+\frac{1}{t_C}=\frac{1}{t}$, it follows that $\frac{1}{t}=1$, or $t=1$.

The correct answer is E.

205. If n is a positive integer, then $(-2^n)^{-2}+(2^{-n})^2=$

(A) 0
(B) 2^{-2n}
(C) 2^{2n}
(D) 2^{-2n+1}
(E) 2^{2n+1}

Algebra Simplifying Algebraic Expressions

$(-2^n)^{-2}+(2^{-n})^2$	given
$=\frac{1}{(-2^n)^2}+\left(\frac{1}{2^n}\right)^2$	use $a^{-b}=\frac{1}{a^b}$
$=\frac{1}{(-1)^2(2^n)^2}+\left(\frac{1}{2^n}\right)^2$	$-2^n=(-1)(2^n)$ and use $(ab)^c=a^cb^c$
$=\frac{1}{(2^n)^2}+\frac{1}{(2^n)^2}$	$(-1)^2=1$ and use $\left(\frac{a}{b}\right)^c=\frac{a^c}{b^c}$
$=\frac{2}{(2^n)^2}$	adding fractions with a common denominator
$=\frac{2}{2^{2n}}$	use $(a^b)^c=a^{bc}$
$=2^{1-2n}$	$2=2^1$ and use $\frac{a^b}{a^c}=a^{b-c}$
$=2^{-2n+1}$	$1-2n=-2n+1$

The correct answer is D.

206. Which of the following is equal to $\left(\frac{2\sqrt[3]{3}}{\sqrt{2}}\right)^3$?

(A) $\frac{3\sqrt{2}}{2}$
(B) $3\sqrt{2}$
(C) $6\sqrt{2}$
(D) 12
(E) $12\sqrt{2}$

Arithmetic Operations on Radical Expressions

$$\left(\frac{2\sqrt[3]{3}}{\sqrt{2}}\right)^3 = \frac{\left(2\sqrt[3]{3}\right)^3}{\left(\sqrt{2}\right)^3} \qquad \text{use } \left(\frac{a}{b}\right)^c = \frac{a^c}{b^c}$$

$$= \frac{(2)^3\left(\sqrt[3]{3}\right)^3}{(\sqrt{2})(\sqrt{2})(\sqrt{2})} \qquad \text{use } (ab)^c = a^c b^c$$

$$= \frac{(8)(3)}{2\sqrt{2}} \qquad (\sqrt{2})(\sqrt{2}) = 2 \text{ and } \left(\sqrt[3]{3}\right)^3 = 3$$

$$= \frac{12}{\sqrt{2}} \qquad \text{reduce}$$

$$= \frac{12}{\sqrt{2}} \times \frac{\sqrt{2}}{\sqrt{2}} \qquad \text{multiply by 1}$$

$$= \frac{12\sqrt{2}}{2} \qquad (\sqrt{2})(\sqrt{2}) = 2$$

$$= 6\sqrt{2} \qquad \text{reduce}$$

The correct answer is C.

207. Dara ran on a treadmill that had a readout indicating the time remaining in her exercise session. When the readout indicated 24 min 18 sec, she had completed 10% of her exercise session. The readout indicated which of the following when she had completed 40% of her exercise session?

(A) 10 min 48 sec
(B) 14 min 52 sec
(C) 14 min 58 sec
(D) 16 min 6 sec
(E) 16 min 12 sec

Arithmetic Rate Problem

Since 24 min 18 sec (or 1,458 sec) represents 90% of the total time for the exercise session, it follows that the total time for the exercise session was $\frac{1{,}458}{0.9}$ sec = 1,620 sec. Thus, when she had completed 40% of the exercise session, the readout would have indicated 60% of the total time, which is 0.6(1,620 sec) = 972 sec = 16 min 12 sec.

The correct answer is E.

5.0 GMAT™ Official Guide Quantitative Review Question Index

5.0 GMAT™ Official Guide Quantitative Review Question Index

The Quantitative Review Question Index is organized by the section, difficulty level, and then by mathematical concept. The question number, page number, and answer explanation page number are listed so that questions within the book can be quickly located.

Quantitative Reasoning — Chapter 4 – Page 74

Difficulty	Concept	Question #	Question ID #	Page	Answer Explanation Page
Easy	Absolute Value	32	300212	82	120
Easy	Applied Problems	11	300199	79	113
Easy	Applied Problems	12	300189	79	113
Easy	Applied Problems	13	300332	79	113
Easy	Applied Problems	14	300333	80	114
Easy	Applied Problems	18	300188	80	115
Easy	Applied Problems	19	300334	80	115
Easy	Applied Problems	47	300193	84	123
Easy	Applied Problems	48	300216	84	124
Easy	Applied Problems	61	300100	86	127
Easy	Applied Problems	71	300207	88	131
Easy	Applied Problems; First-Degree Equations	77	300291	89	133
Easy	Applied Problems; Operations with Fractions	46	300147	84	123
Easy	Applied Problems; Percents	56	300191	85	126
Easy	Applied Problems; Proportions	9	300173	79	112
Easy	Applied Problems; Substitution	16	300104	80	114
Easy	Average	78	300292	89	133
Easy	Equations	43	300342	84	122
Easy	Estimation	54	300105	85	125
Easy	Estimation	79	300293	89	133
Easy	Exponents	41	300341	83	122
Easy	Exponents	44	300343	84	122
Easy	Factoring	3	300198	78	110

(Continued)

Difficulty	Concept	Question #	Question ID #	Page	Answer Explanation Page
Easy	Factors, Multiples, and Divisibility	4	300208	78	111
Easy	First-Degree Equations	27	300250	81	118
Easy	First-Degree Equations	39	300247	83	121
easy	First-Degree Equations	40	300340	83	122
Easy	First-Degree Equations	49	300213	85	124
Easy	First-Degree Equations	80	300294	89	134
Easy	First-Degree Equations; Substitution	36	300134	83	120
Easy	Formulas	53	300120	85	125
Easy	Formulas	66	300260	87	129
Easy	Fractions	23	300146	81	117
Easy	Inequalities	7	300242	79	111
Easy	Inequalities	34	300145	82	120
Easy	Interpretation of Graphs	63	300129	87	128
Easy	Interpretation of Tables	37	300338	83	121
Easy	Operations on Integers	5	300220	78	111
Easy	Operations on Integers	65	300228	87	129
Easy	Operations on Integers	68	300214	87	130
Easy	Operations on Rational Numbers	21	300218	81	116
Easy	Operations with Fractions	59	300112	86	127
Easy	Operations with Fractions	60	300136	86	127
Easy	Operations with Fractions	64	300226	87	128
Easy	Operations with Integers	33	300337	82	120
Easy	Operations with Integers	58	300102	86	126
Easy	Operations with Integers	62	300168	86	128
Easy	Operations with Integers; Measurement Conversion	73	300155	88	132
Easy	Order	8	300331	79	112
Easy	Order	15	300209	80	114
Easy	Percents	10	300258	79	112
Easy	Percents	20	300335	80	115
Easy	Percents	24	300336	81	117
Easy	Percents	29	300170	82	119
Easy	Percents	35	300285	82	120

Difficulty	Concept	Question #	Question ID #	Page	Answer Explanation Page
Easy	Percents	50	300116	85	124
Easy	Percents	57	300101	86	126
Easy	Percents	70	300232	88	131
Easy	Place Value	30	300175	82	119
Easy	Place Value	74	300117	88	132
Easy	Properties of Integers	25	300182	81	117
Easy	Properties of Integers	82	300296	89	134
Easy	Properties of Numbers	6	300330	78	111
Easy	Properties of Numbers	28	300178	81	118
Easy	Properties of Numbers	55	300174	85	126
Easy	Properties of Numbers	72	300119	88	131
Easy	Rate	1	300203	78	110
Easy	Rate Problem	17	300239	80	115
Easy	Rate Problem	42	300181	84	122
Easy	Ratio and Proportion	51	300252	85	125
Easy	Second-Degree Equations	2	300107	78	110
Easy	Second-Degree Equations	22	300131	81	116
Easy	Second-Degree Equations	52	300130	85	125
Easy	Sequences	67	300172	87	130
Easy	Series and Sequences	26	300186	81	118
Easy	Series and Sequences	45	300185	84	123
Easy	Series and Sequences	75	300289	89	132
Easy	Series and Sequences; Simplifying Algebraic Expressions	76	300290	89	133
Easy	Simplifying Algebraic Expressions	81	300295	89	134
Easy	Simultaneous Equations	31	300202	82	119
Easy	Simultaneous Equations	38	300339	83	121
Easy	Statistics	69	300103	88	131
Medium	Absolute Value	113	300118	94	144
Medium	Applied Problems	84	300160	90	135
Medium	Applied Problems	87	300161	90	136
Medium	Applied Problems	102	300283	93	141
Medium	Applied Problems	109	300187	94	143

(Continued)

Difficulty	Concept	Question #	Question ID #	Page	Answer Explanation Page
Medium	Applied Problems	112	300204	94	144
Medium	Applied Problems	122	300284	95	148
Medium	Applied Problems	124	300221	96	148
Medium	Applied Problems	145	300306	98	155
Medium	Applied Problems; Formulas	95	300272	92	139
Medium	Applied Problems; Percents	130	300245	96	150
Medium	Arithmetic Operations	141	300302	98	154
Medium	Decimals	110	300171	94	143
Medium	Equations; Inequalities	93	300269	91	138
Medium	Equations	149	300345	99	156
Medium	Estimation	131	300286	96	151
Medium	Exponents; Simplifying Algebraic Expressions	139	300300	97	153
Medium	Factoring	99	300277	92	140
Medium	First-Degree Equations	83	300159	90	134
Medium	First-Degree Equations	94	300271	92	139
Medium	First-Degree Equations	96	300273	92	139
Medium	First-Degree Equations	151	300347	99	157
Medium	Formulas	98	300276	92	140
Medium	Formulas; Percents	105	300140	93	142
Medium	Functions	142	300303	98	154
Medium	Functions; Absolute Value	92	300267	91	137
Medium	Inequalities	106	300176	93	142
Medium	Inequalities	108	300244	93	143
Medium	Inequalities	117	300241	95	146
Medium	Inequalities	126	300114	96	149
Medium	Inequalities; Absolute Value	120	300268	95	147
Medium	Measurement Conversion	101	300282	93	141
Medium	Measurement Conversion	138	300299	97	153
Medium	Measurement Conversion; Rate Problem	136	300297	97	152
Medium	Operations with Integers	89	300165	91	137
Medium	Operations with Integers	148	300344	99	156
Medium	Order	86	300163	90	135

Difficulty	Concept	Question #	Question ID #	Page	Answer Explanation Page
Medium	Percents	127	300229	96	149
Medium	Percents	132	300154	97	151
Medium	Percents; Estimation	114	300210	94	145
Medium	Percents; Estimation	125	300222	96	149
Medium	Place Value	115	300287	94	145
Medium	Place Value	134	300223	97	152
Medium	Probability	146	300307	98	155
Medium	Probability; Sets (Venn Diagrams)	140	300301	98	153
Medium	Properties of Integers	90	300166	91	137
Medium	Properties of Integers	133	300261	97	151
Medium	Properties of Integers	137	300298	97	152
Medium	Properties of Numbers	107	300133	93	143
Medium	Properties of Numbers	118	300111	95	146
Medium	Properties of Numbers	119	300192	95	147
Medium	Properties of Numbers	128	300179	96	150
Medium	Ratio and Proportion	123	300280	95	148
Medium	Rate Problem; Measurement Conversion	144	300305	98	155
Medium	Rational Numbers	150	300346	99	156
Medium	Ratios	85	300162	90	135
Medium	Second-Degree Equations	100	300279	92	141
Medium	Second-Degree Equations	104	300127	93	142
Medium	Series and Sequences	135	300141	97	152
Medium	Series and Sequences	143	300304	98	154
Medium	Sets (Venn Diagrams)	88	300164	90	136
Medium	Simplifying Algebraic Expressions	147	300308	99	156
Medium	Simultaneous Equations	97	300275	92	139
Medium	Simultaneous Equations	103	300126	93	142
Medium	Simultaneous Equations	116	300255	94	145
Medium	Simultaneous Equations	129	300196	96	150
Medium	Statistics	91	300266	91	137
Medium	Statistics	111	300262	94	144
Medium	Statistics	121	300115	95	147

(*Continued*)

Difficulty	Concept	Question #	Question ID #	Page	Answer Explanation Page
Hard	Absolute Value	166	300201	101	161
Hard	Applied Problems	155	300139	100	158
Hard	Applied Problems	177	300135	103	165
Hard	Applied Problems	179	300137	103	166
Hard	Applied Problems	187	300263	104	169
Hard	Applied Problems	193	300157	105	171
Hard	Applied Problems	195	300156	105	172
Hard	Applied Problems; Percents	159	300113	100	159
Hard	Applied Problems; Percents	182	300183	103	167
Hard	Applied Problems; Properties of Integers	189	300143	104	170
Hard	Arithmetic Operations	153	300167	99	157
Hard	Elementary Combinatorics	168	300197	101	162
Hard	Elementary Combinatorics	172	300180	102	164
Hard	Elementary Combinatorics	201	300314	106	175
Hard	Estimation	162	300106	100	160
Hard	Exponents	161	300205	100	160
Hard	Factoring; Simplifying Algebraic Expressions	200	300313	106	175
Hard	First-Degree Equations	152	300158	99	157
Hard	First-Degree Equations; Percents	169	300233	102	163
Hard	First-Degree Equations; Percents	176	300281	102	165
Hard	Inequalities	178	300243	103	166
Hard	Inequalities	202	300315	106	176
Hard	Operations on Radical Expressions	171	300153	102	163
Hard	Operations on Radical Expressions	206	300319	107	177
Hard	Operations with Integers	154	300190	99	158
Hard	Operations with Integers	167	300234	101	162
Hard	Percents	160	300219	100	159
Hard	Percents; Estimation	199	300312	106	174
Hard	Place Value	174	300211	102	164
Hard	Place Value	192	300138	105	171
Hard	Probability	181	300215	103	167

Difficulty	Concept	Question #	Question ID #	Page	Answer Explanation Page
Hard	Probability; Concepts of Sets	173	300206	102	164
Hard	Properties of Integers	156	300264	100	158
Hard	Properties of Integers	163	300274	101	160
Hard	Properties of Integers	190	300148	104	170
Hard	Properties of Integers	191	300144	105	171
Hard	Properties of Numbers	175	300237	102	165
Hard	Properties of Numbers	180	300230	103	166
Hard	Properties of Numbers	183	300348	104	168
Hard	Properties of Numbers	184	300253	104	168
Hard	Properties of Numbers	186	300152	104	168
Hard	Properties of Numbers; Exponents	188	300142	104	169
Hard	Rate Problem	207	300320	107	178
Hard	Sequences and Series	157	300108	100	158
Hard	Sequences and Series	158	300288	100	159
Hard	Sets	170	300195	102	163
Hard	Sets	194	300349	105	172
Hard	Simplifying Algebraic Expressions	205	300318	107	177
Hard	Simplifying Algebraic Expressions; Applied Problems	185	300151	104	168
Hard	Simultaneous Equations; Sets (Venn Diagrams)	196	300309	106	173
Hard	Statistics	164	300257	101	161
Hard	Statistics	165	300217	101	161
Hard	Statistics	197	300310	106	173
Hard	Statistics	198	300311	106	174
Hard	Statistics	203	300316	107	176
Hard	Work Problem	204	300317	107	177

Appendix A Answer Sheet

Quantitative Reasoning Answer Sheet

1.	36.	71.	106.	141.
2.	37.	72.	107.	142.
3.	38.	73.	108.	143.
4.	39.	74.	109.	144.
5.	40.	75.	110.	145.
6.	41.	76.	111.	146.
7.	42.	77.	112.	147.
8.	43.	78.	113.	148.
9.	44.	79.	114.	149.
10.	45.	80.	115.	150.
11.	46.	81.	116.	151.
12.	47.	82.	117.	152.
13.	48.	83.	118.	153.
14.	49.	84.	119.	154.
15.	50.	85.	120.	155.
16.	51.	86.	121.	156.
17.	52.	87.	122.	157.
18.	53.	88.	123.	158.
19.	54.	89.	124.	159.
20.	55.	90.	125.	160.
21.	56.	91.	126.	161.
22.	57.	92.	127.	162.
23.	58.	93.	128.	163.
24.	59.	94.	129.	164.
25.	60.	95.	130.	165.
26.	61.	96.	131.	166.
27.	62.	97.	132.	167.
28.	63.	98.	133.	168.
29.	64.	99.	134.	169.
30.	65.	100.	135.	170.
31.	66.	101.	136.	171.
32.	67.	102.	137.	172.
33.	68.	103.	138.	173.
34.	69.	104.	139.	174.
35.	70.	105.	140.	175.

176.
177.
178.
179.
180.
181.
182.
183.
184.
185.
186.
187.
188.
189.
190.
191.
192.
193.
194.
195.
196.
197.
198.
199.
200.
201.
202.
203.
204.
205.
206.
207.

Notes

Notes

Notes

Notes

Notes

GPSR Compliance
The European Union's (EU) General Product Safety Regulation (GPSR) is a set of rules that requires consumer products to be safe and our obligations to ensure this.

If you have any concerns about our products, you can contact us on

ProductSafety@springernature.com

In case Publisher is established outside the EU, the EU authorized representative is:

Springer Nature Customer Service Center GmbH
Europaplatz 3
69115 Heidelberg, Germany

www.ingramcontent.com/pod-product-compliance
Ingram Content Group UK Ltd.
Pitfield, Milton Keynes, MK11 3LW, UK
UKHW052128231225
466357UK00015B/254
* 9 7 8 1 4 3 0 2 6 6 5 5 6 *

Application Name:

Screen Name:

Notes:

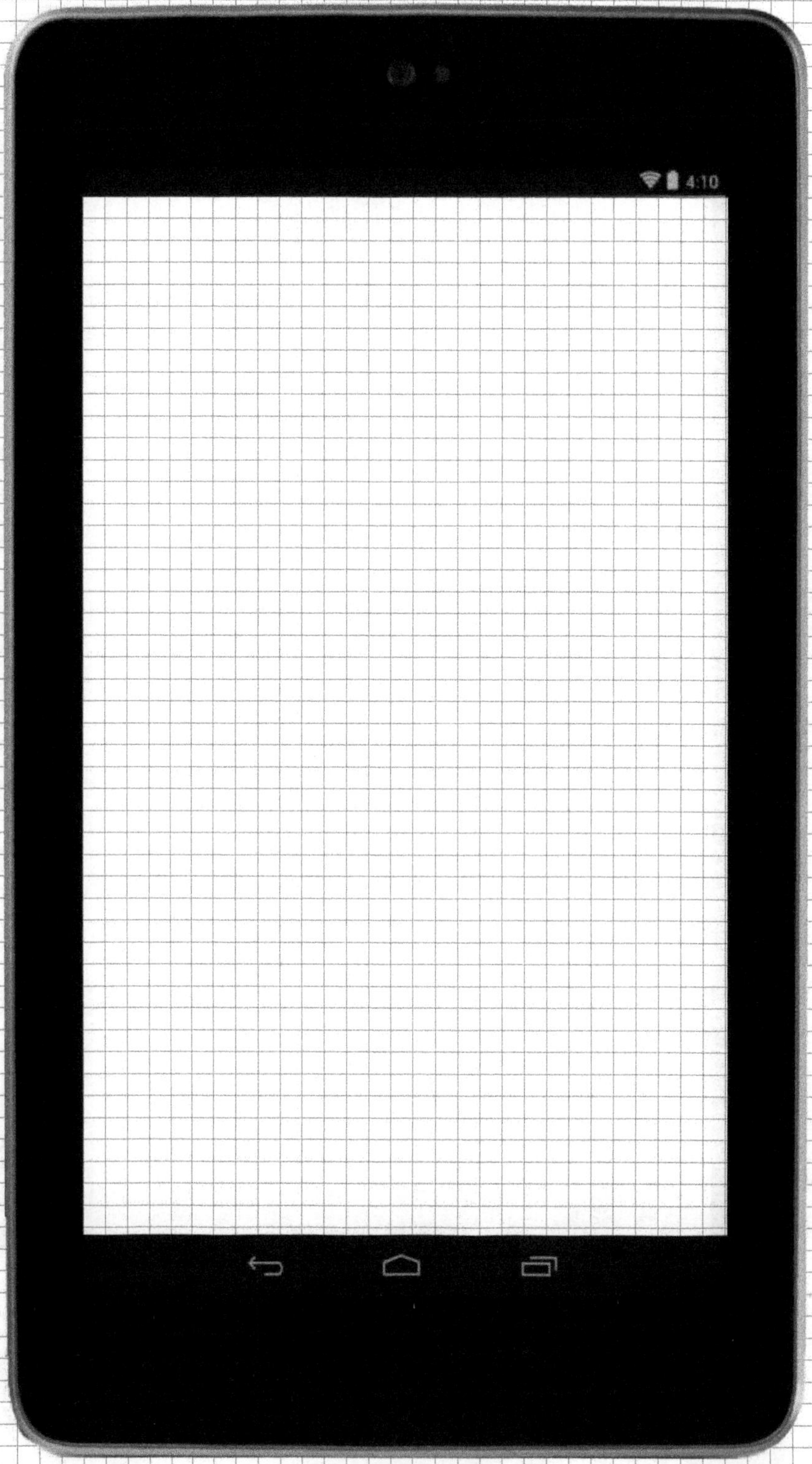

Application Name:

Screen Name:

Notes:

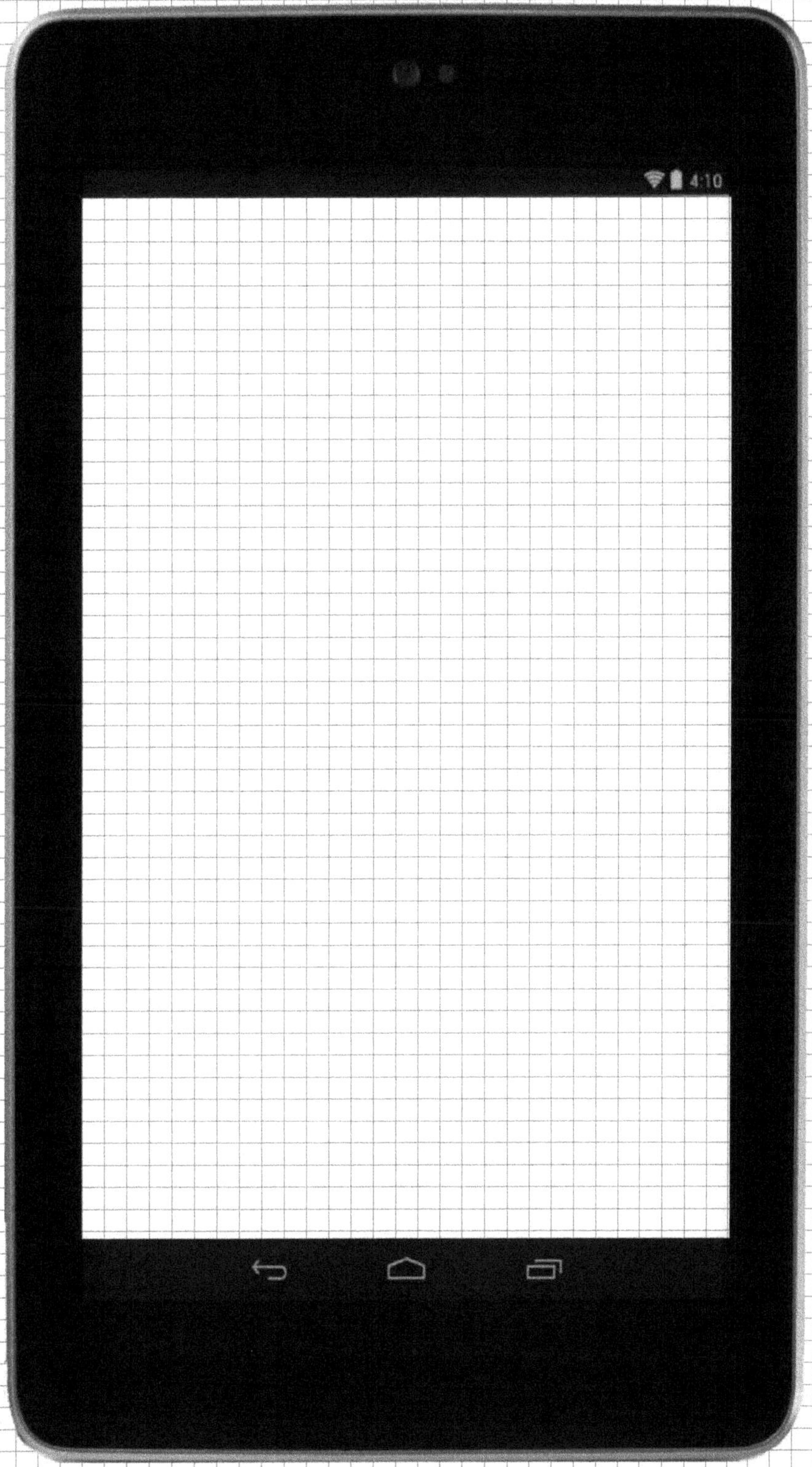

Application Name:

Screen Name:

Notes:

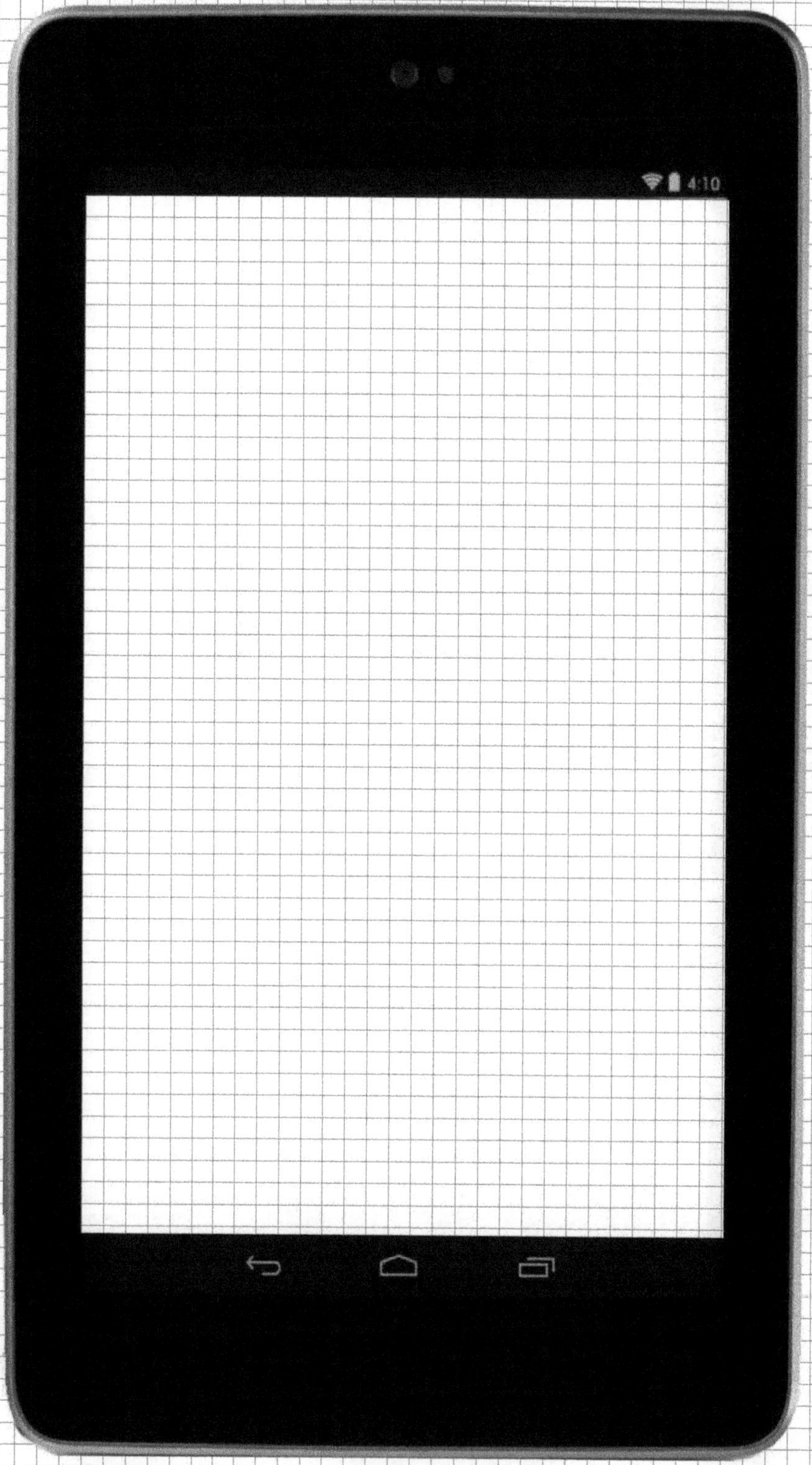

Application Name:

Screen Name:

Notes:

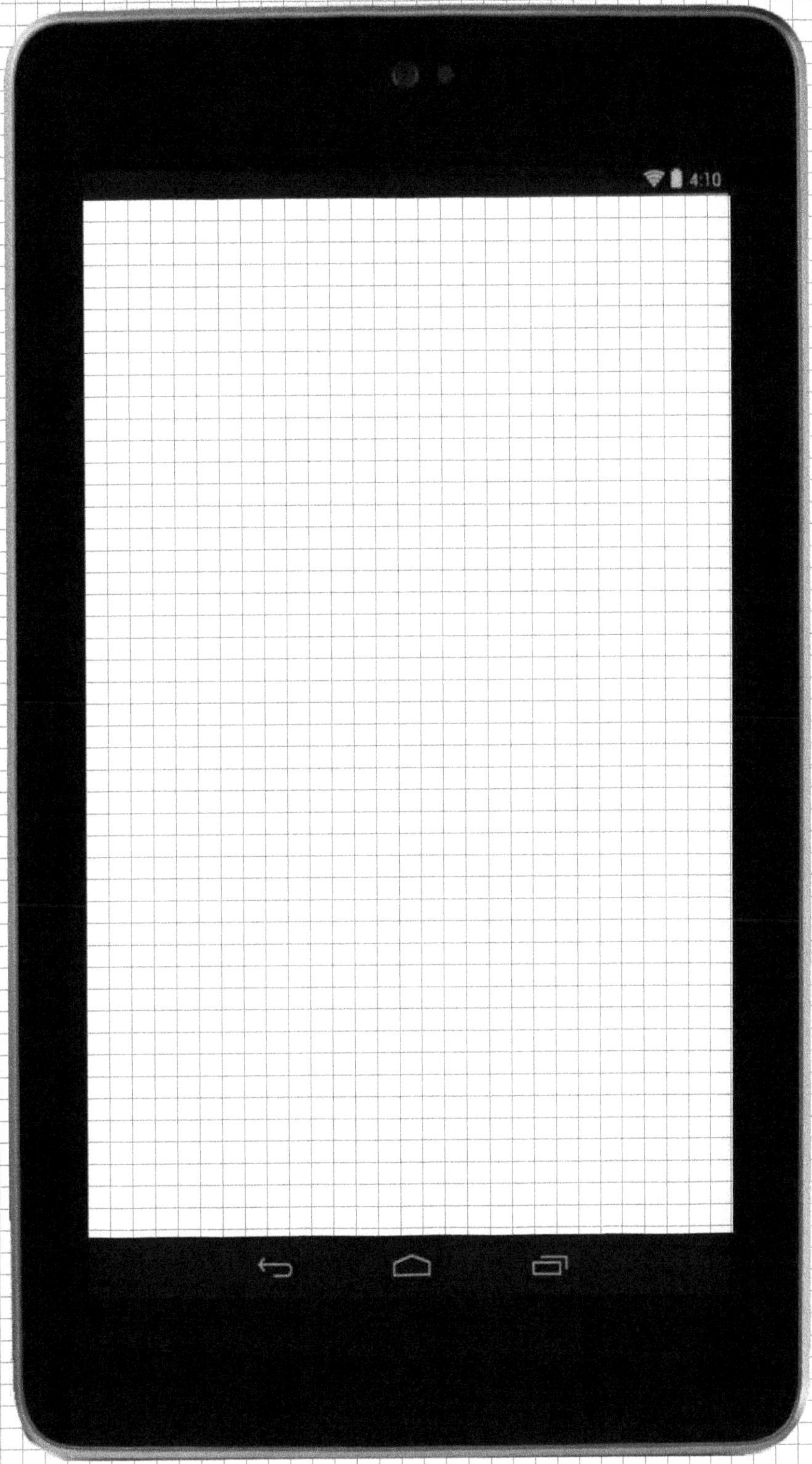

Application Name:

Screen Name:

Notes:

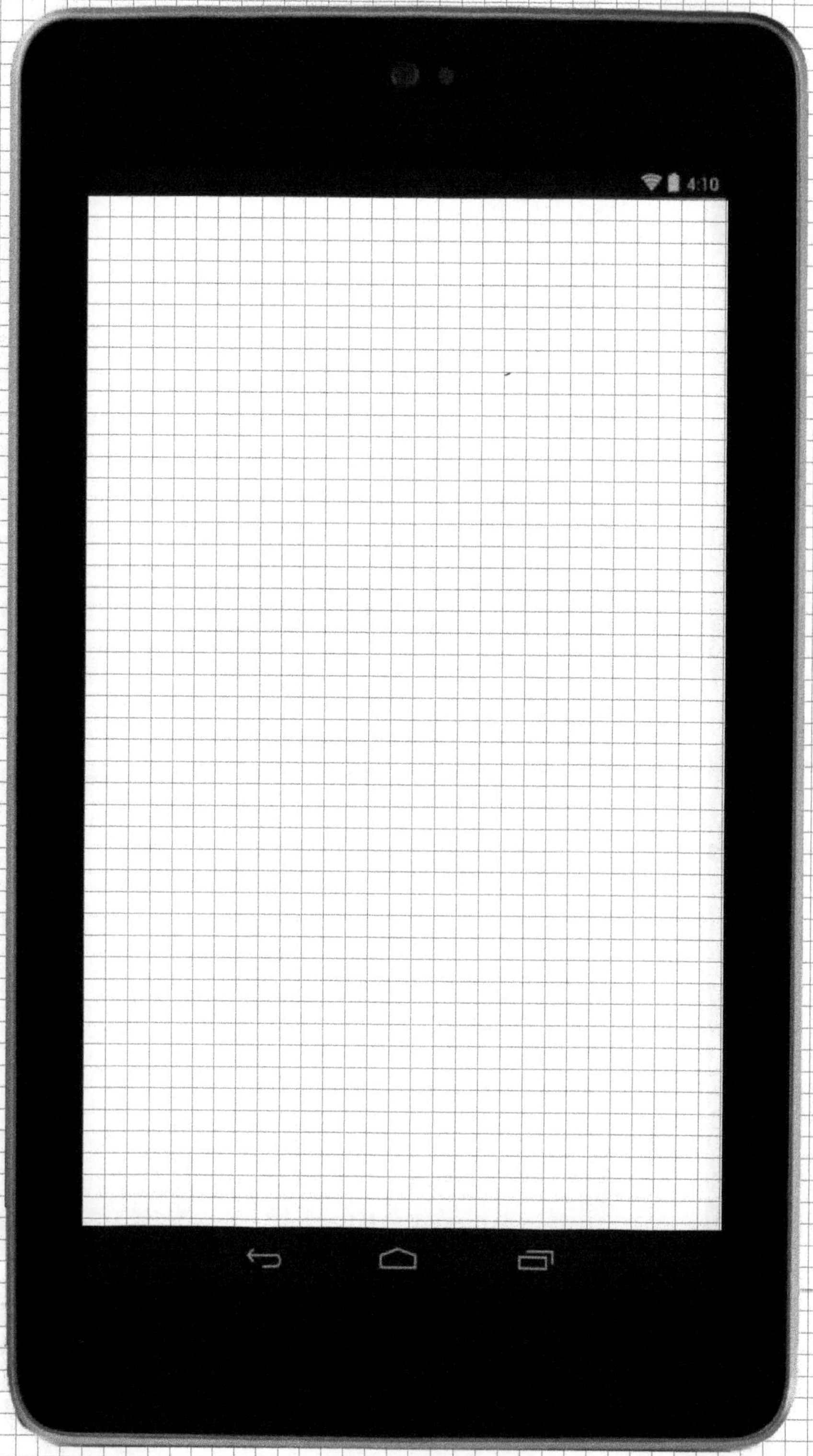

Application Name:

Screen Name:

Notes:

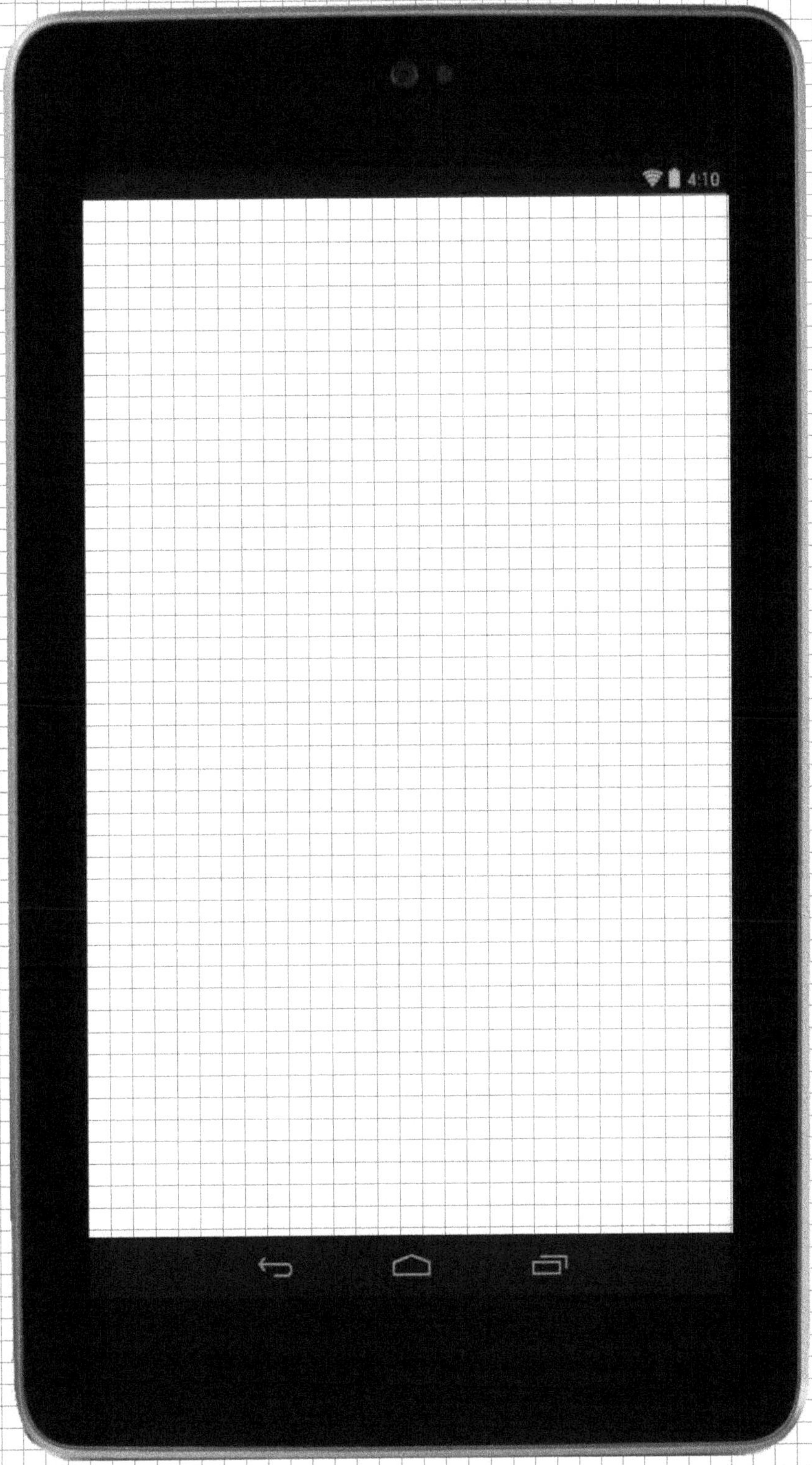

Application Name:

Screen Name:

Notes:

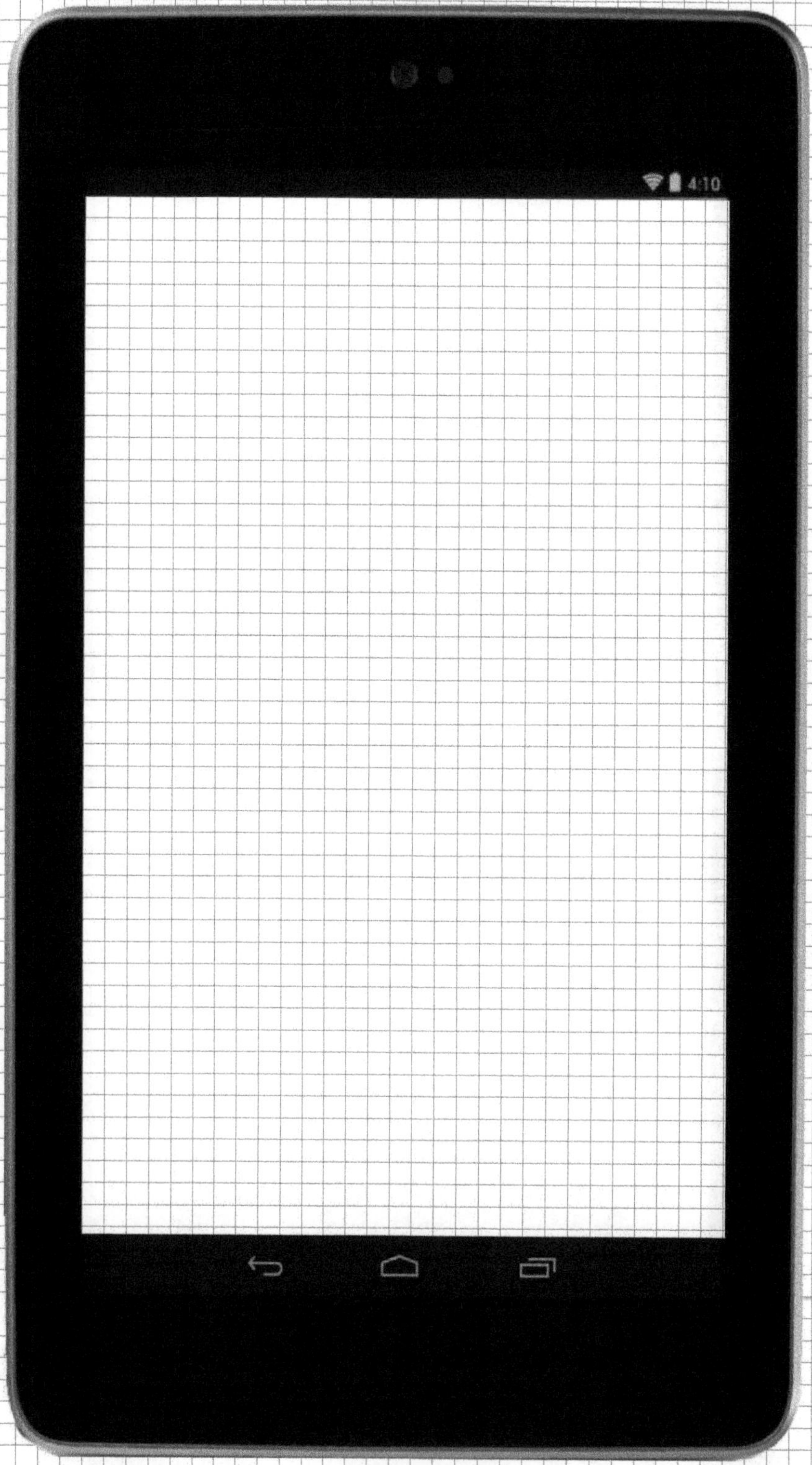

Application Name:

Screen Name:

Notes:

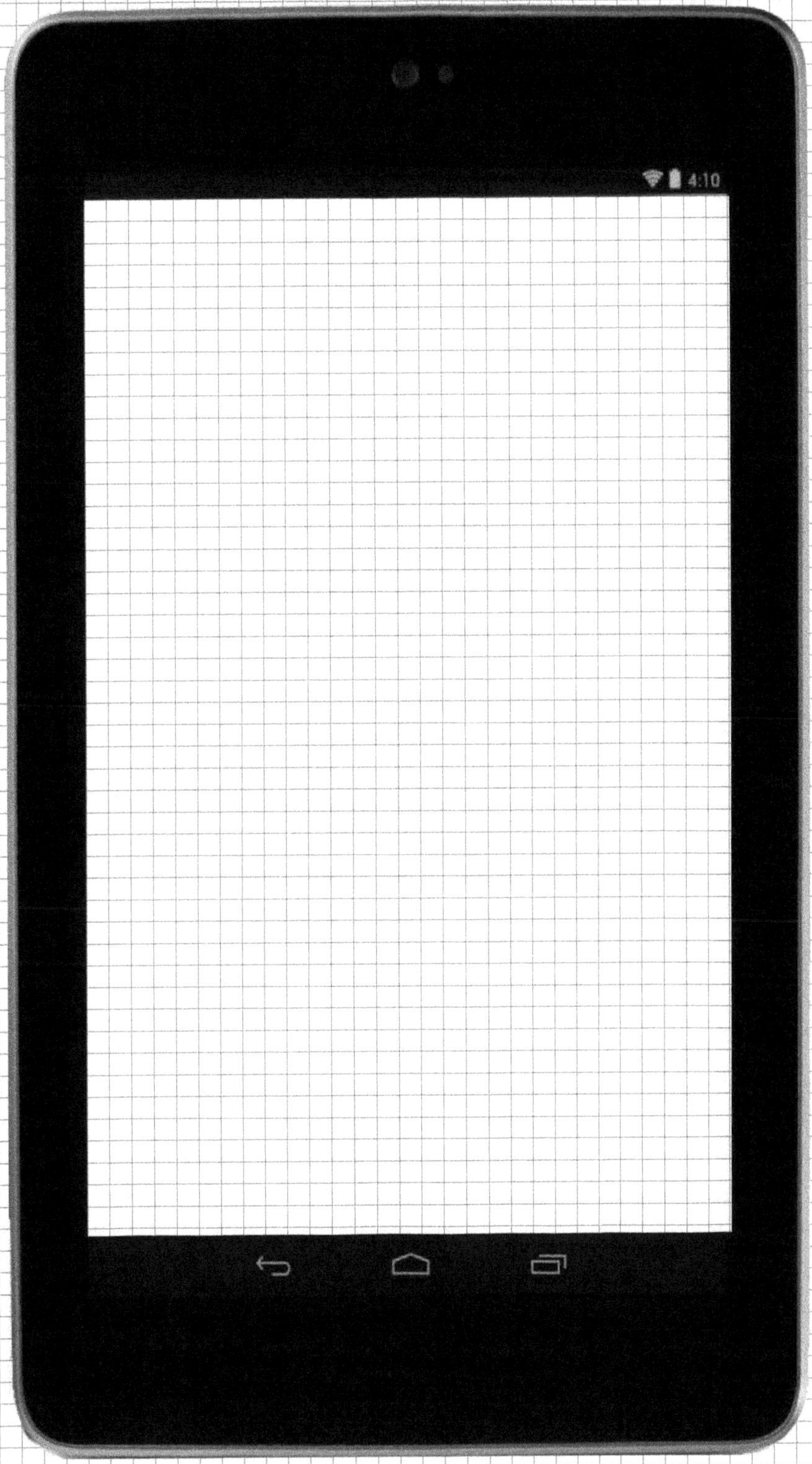

Application Name:

Screen Name:

Notes:

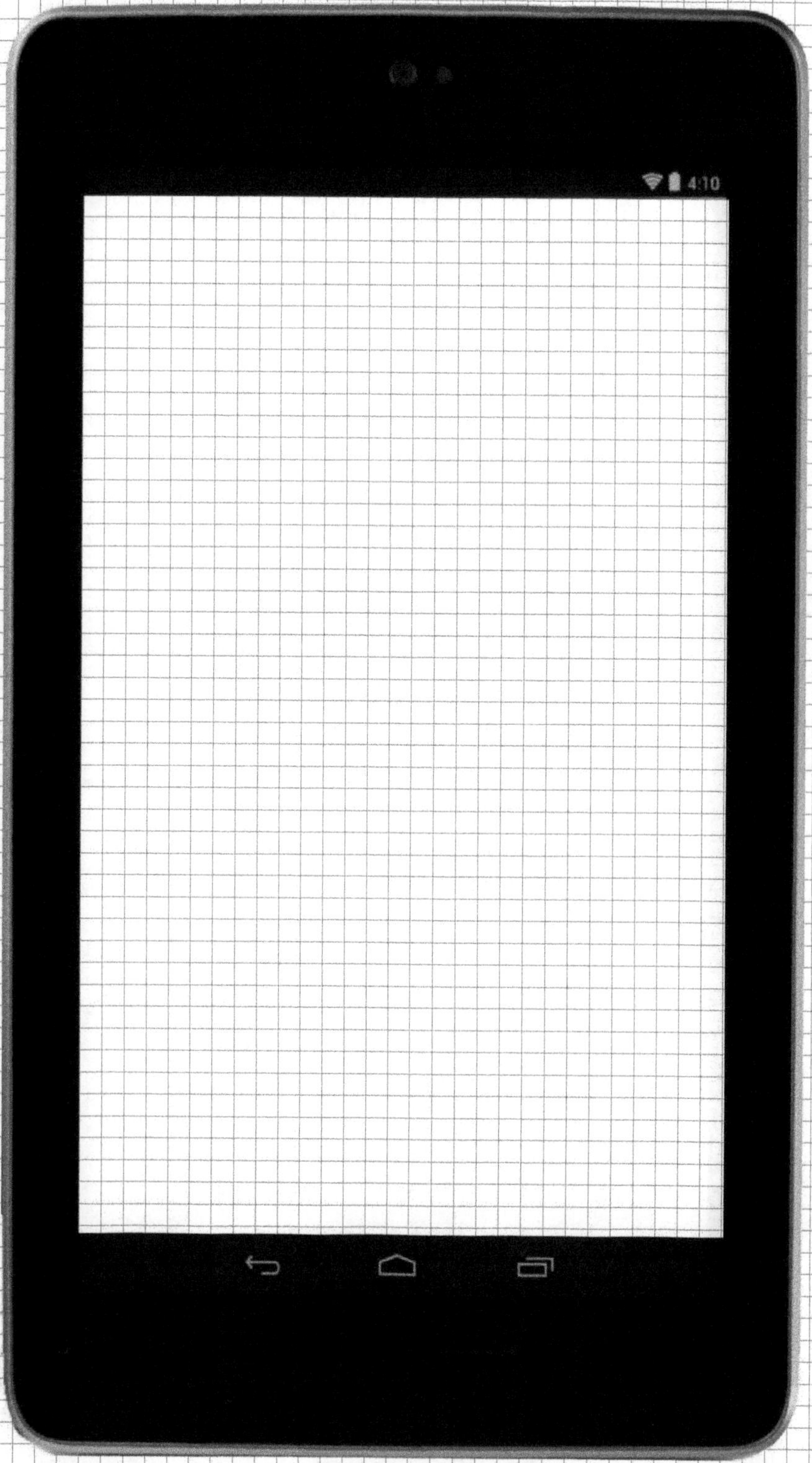

Application Name:

Screen Name:

Notes:

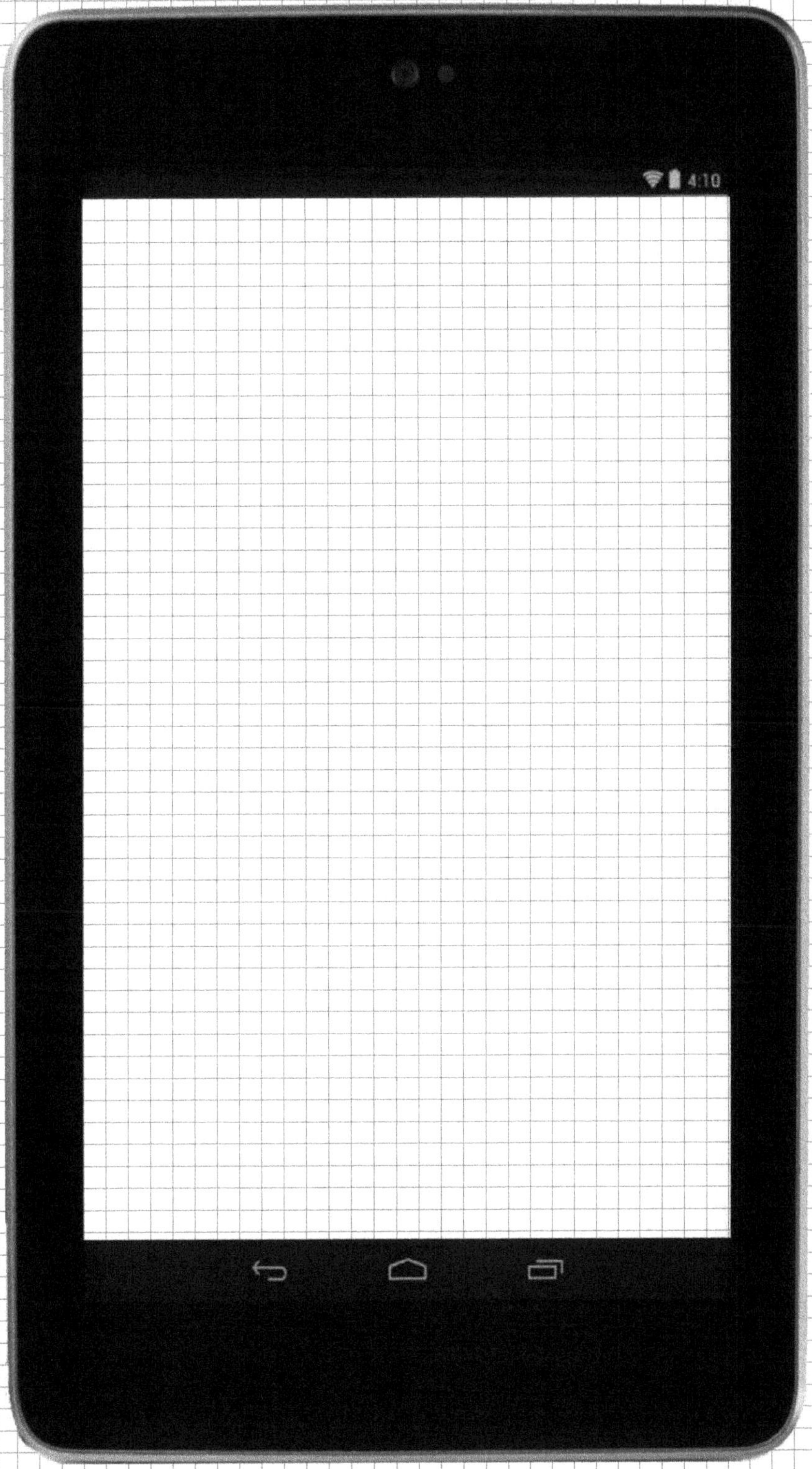

Application Name:

Screen Name:

Notes:

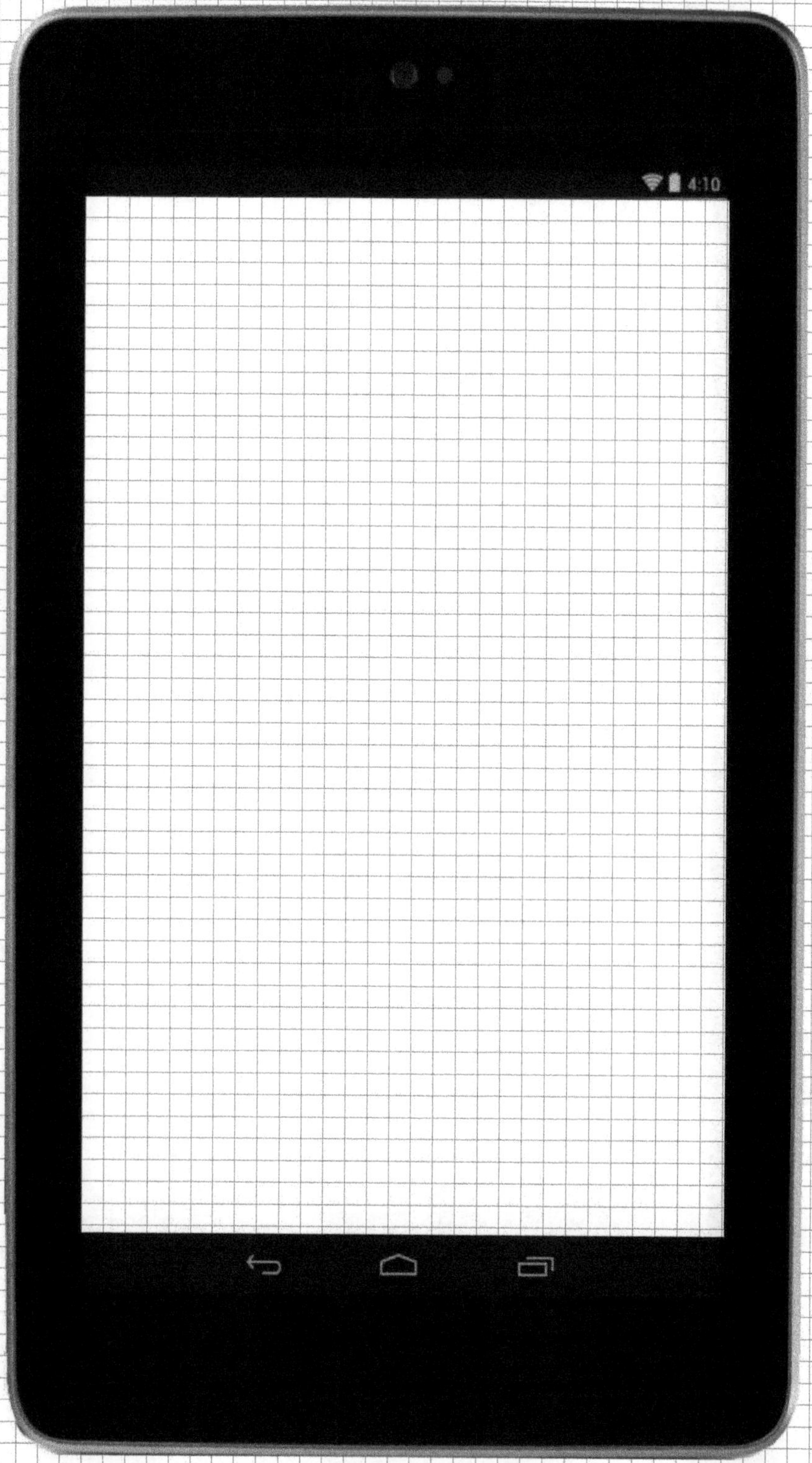

Application Name:

Screen Name:

Notes:

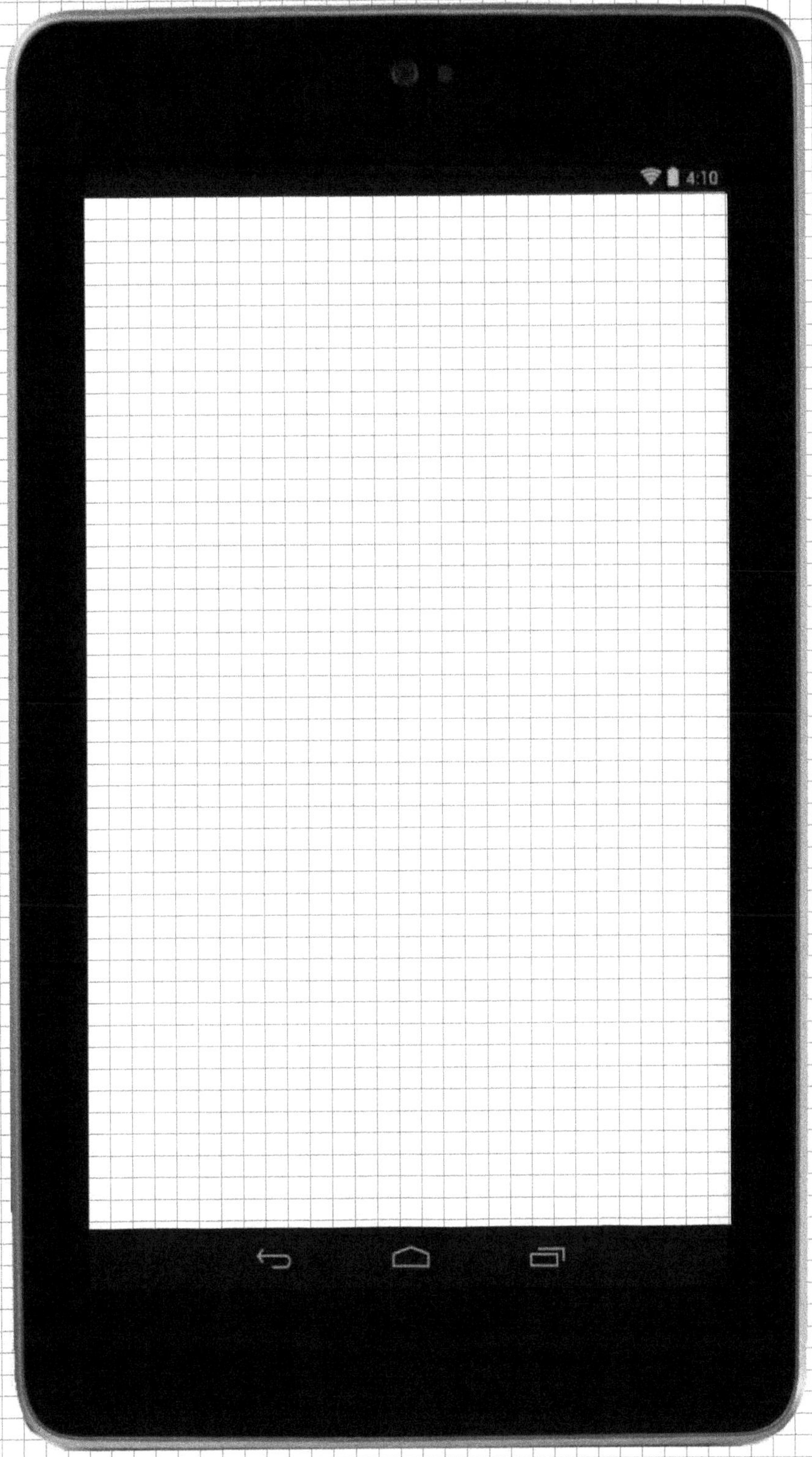

Application Name:

Screen Name:

Notes:

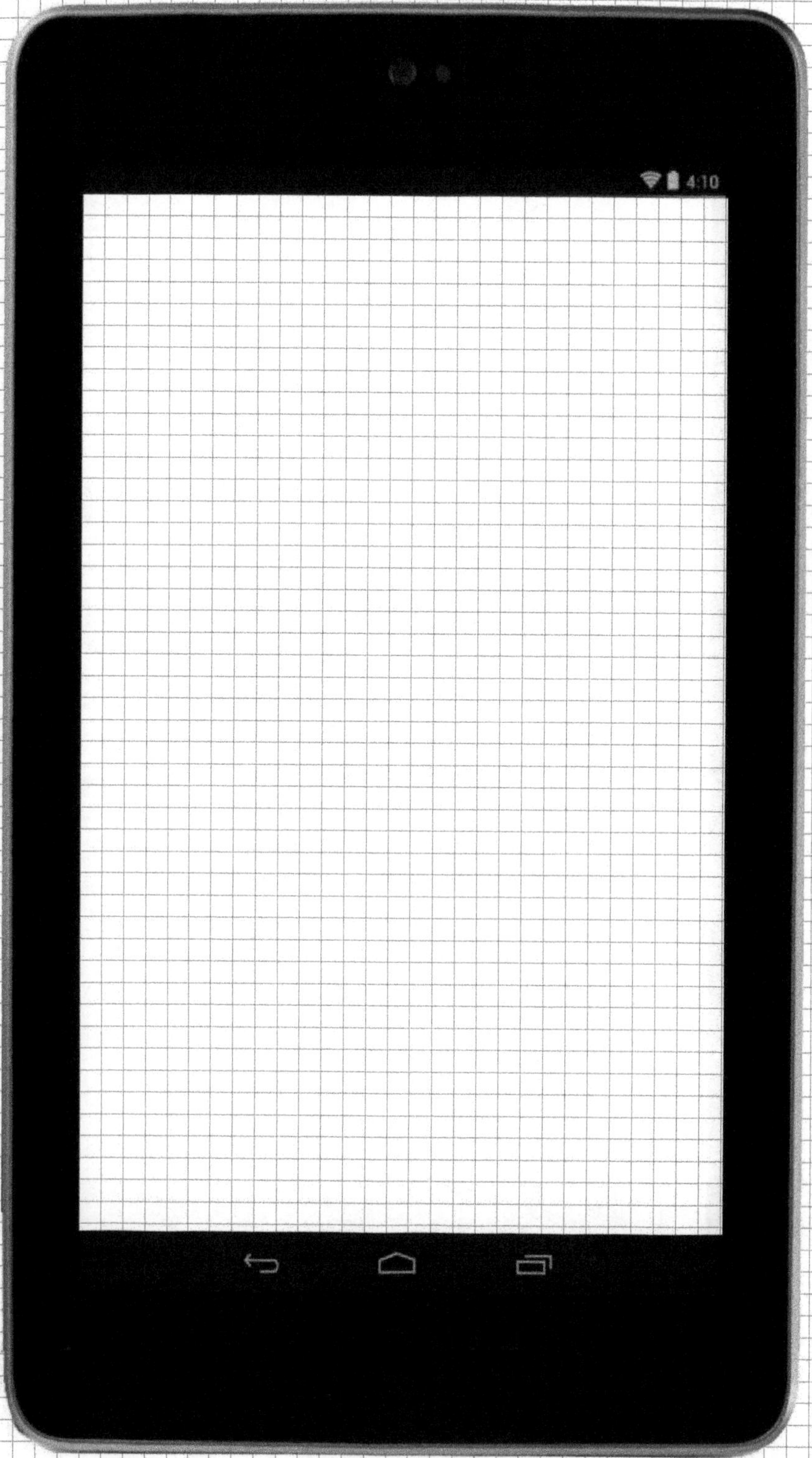

Application Name:

Screen Name:

Notes:

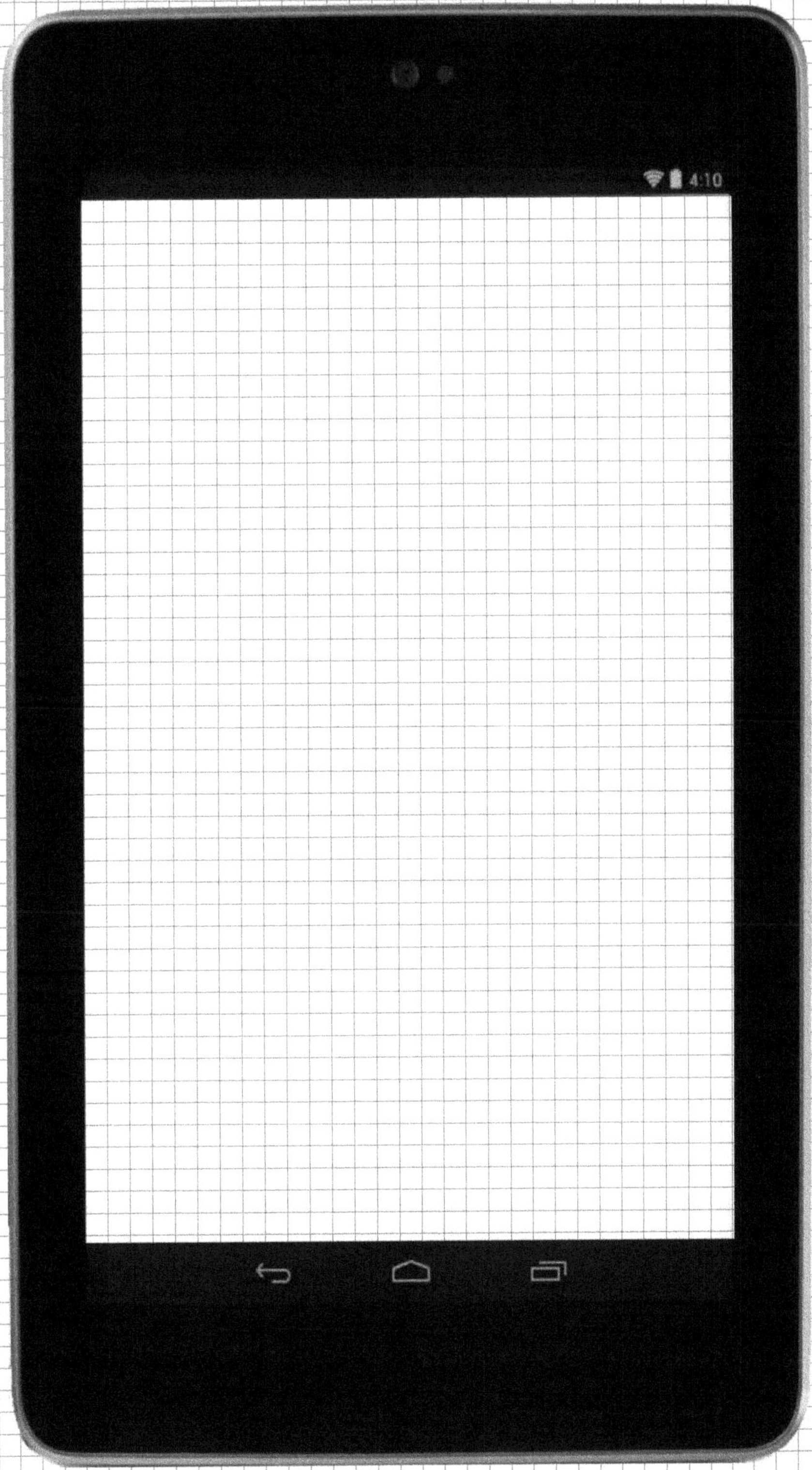

Application Name:

Screen Name:

Notes:

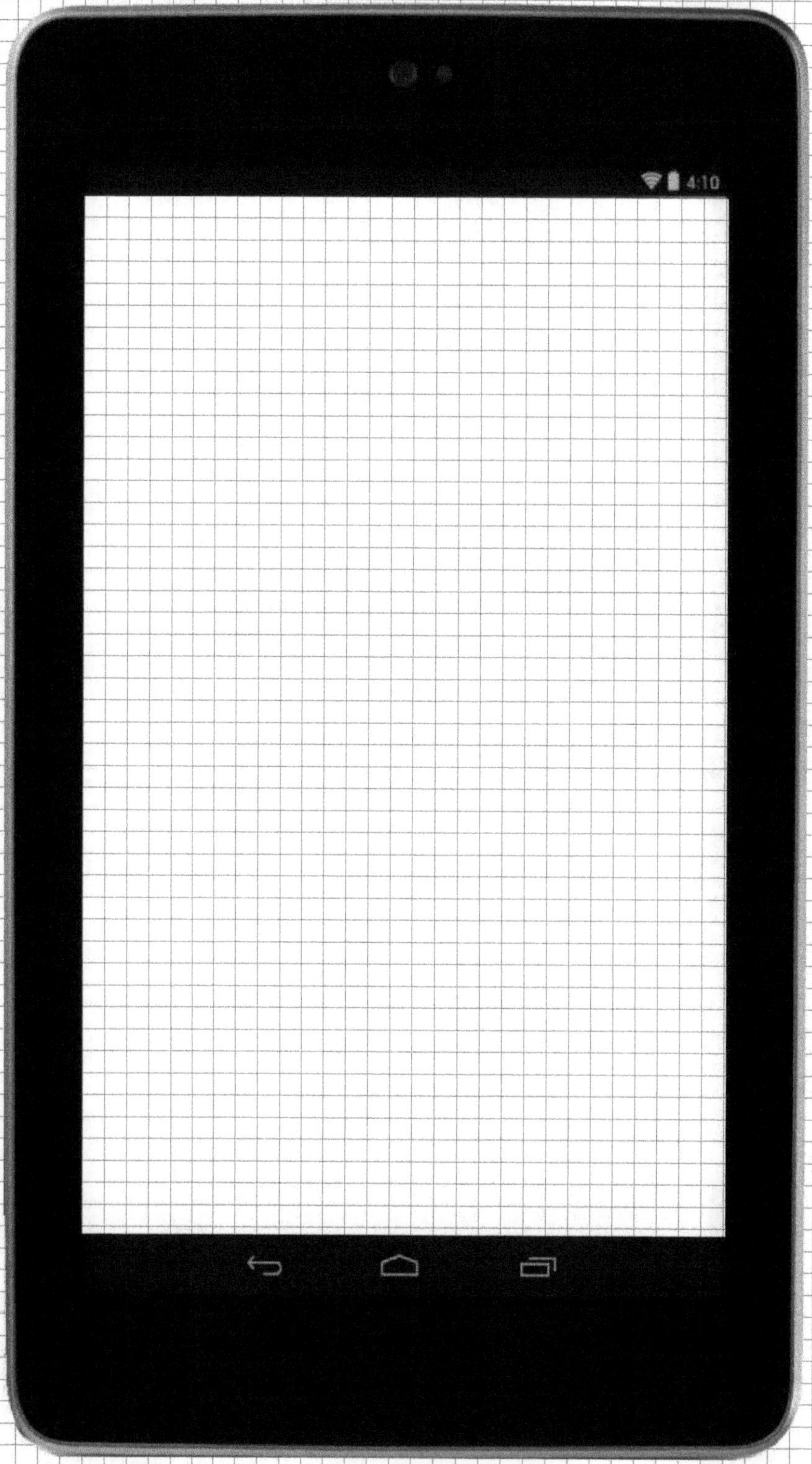

Application Name:

Screen Name:

Notes:

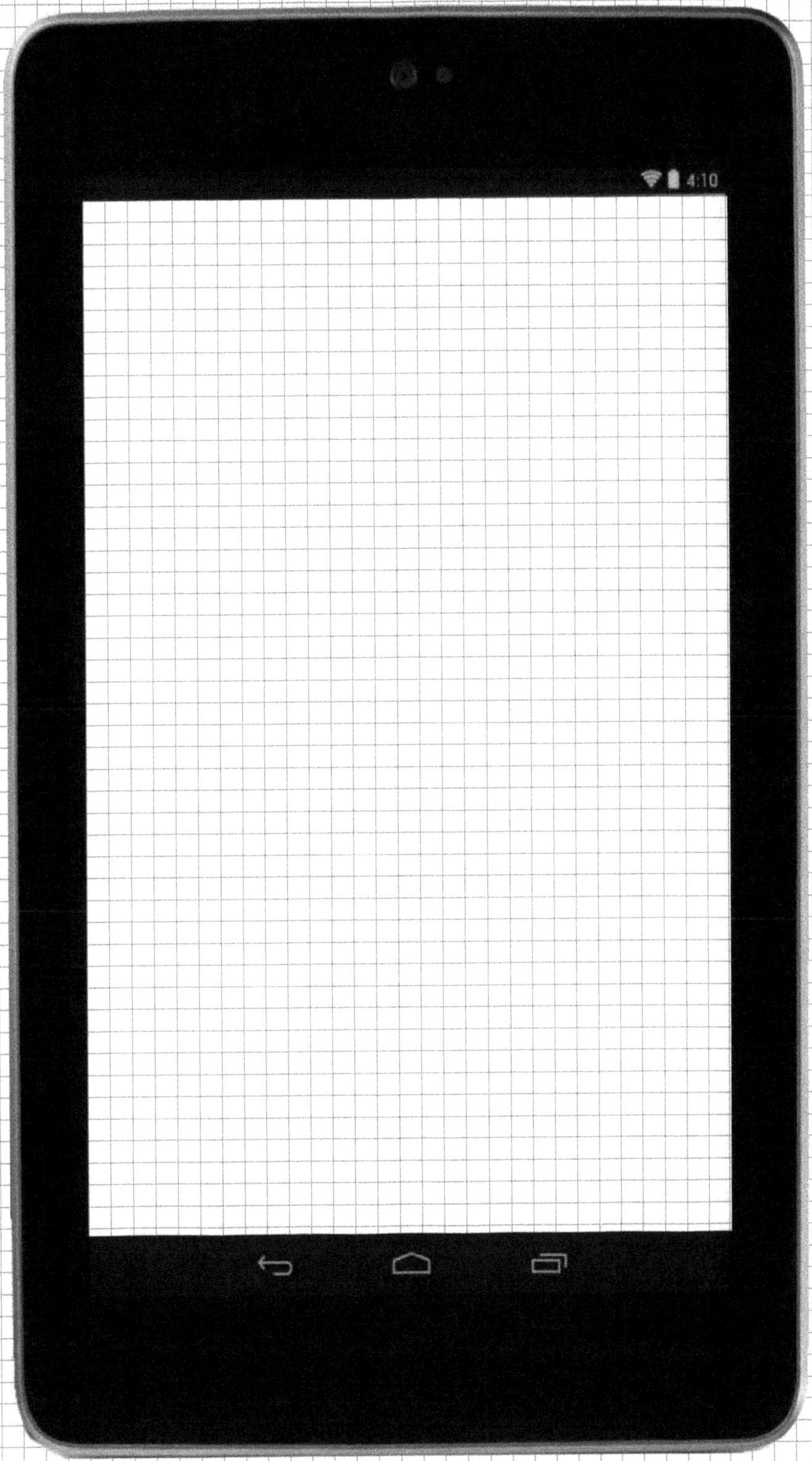

Application Name:

Screen Name:

Notes:

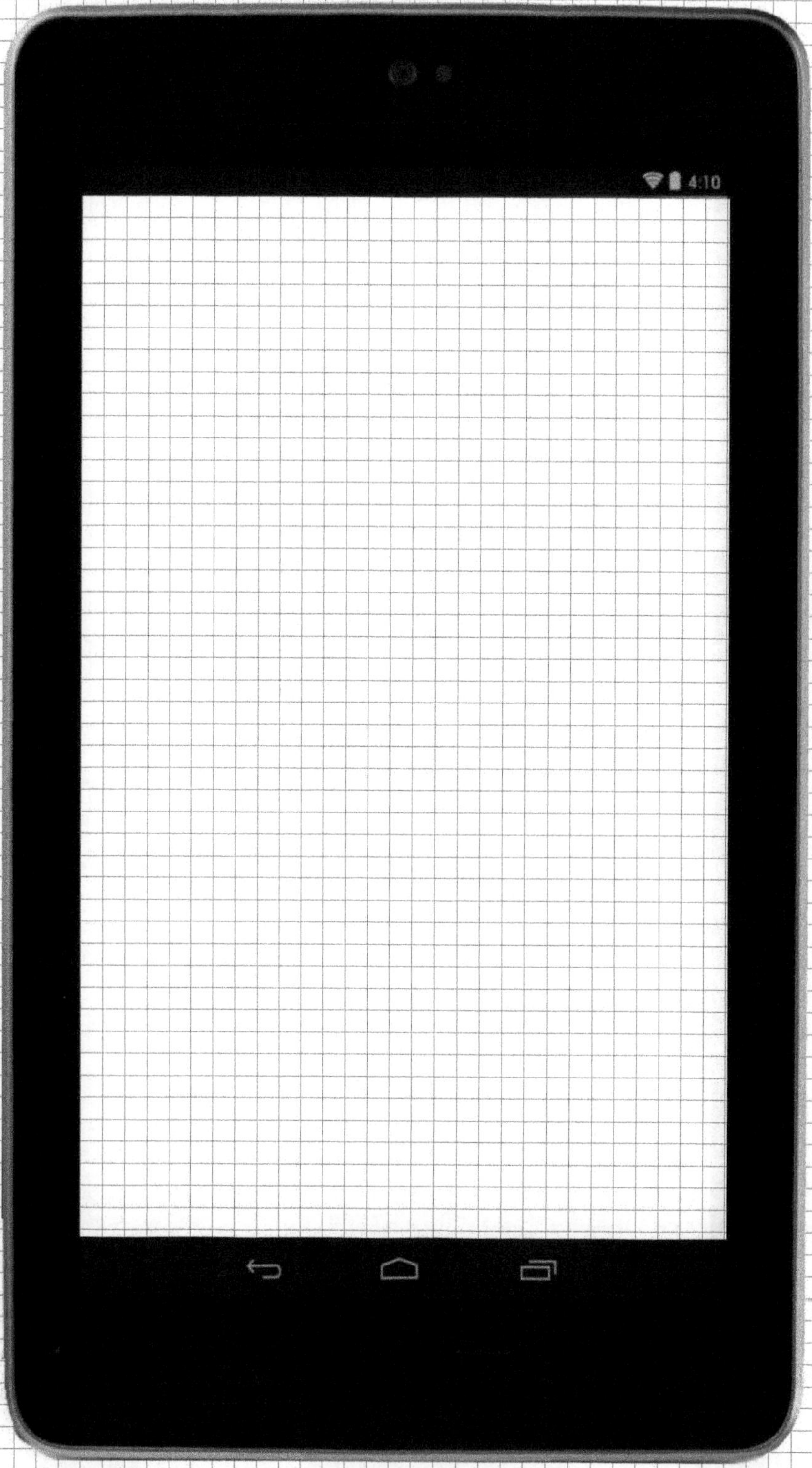

Application Name:

Screen Name:

Notes:

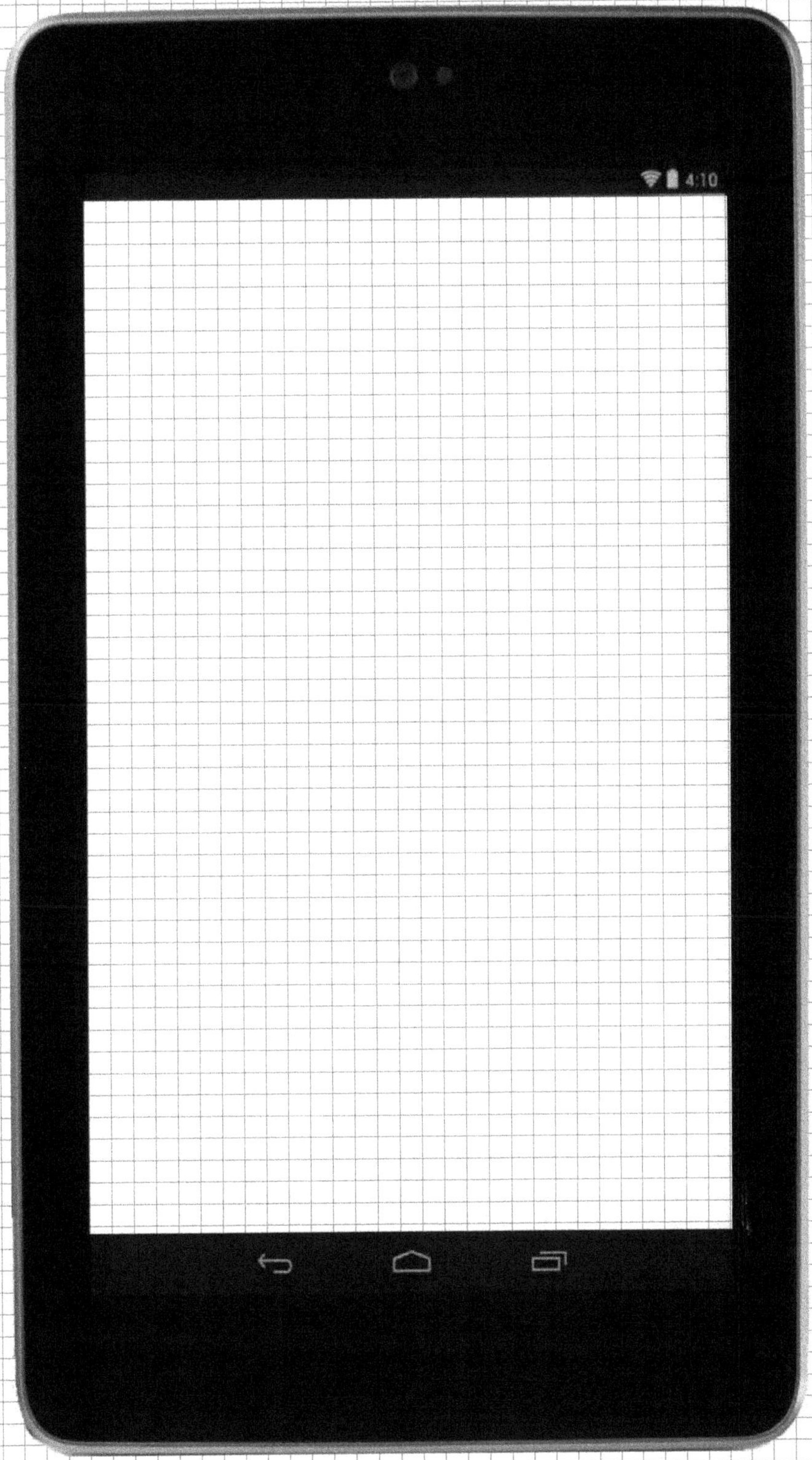

Application Name:

Screen Name:

Notes:

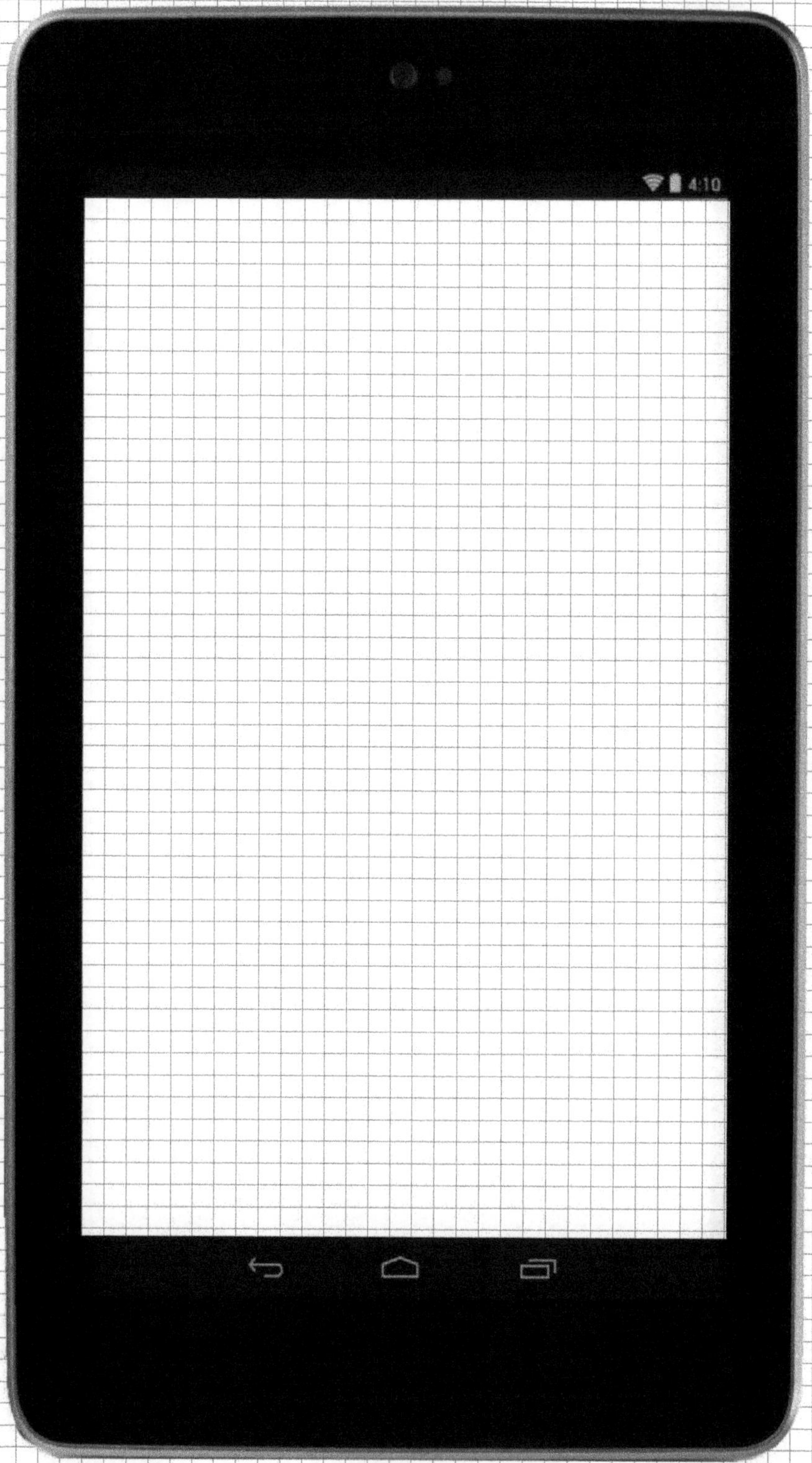

Application Name:

Screen Name:

Notes:

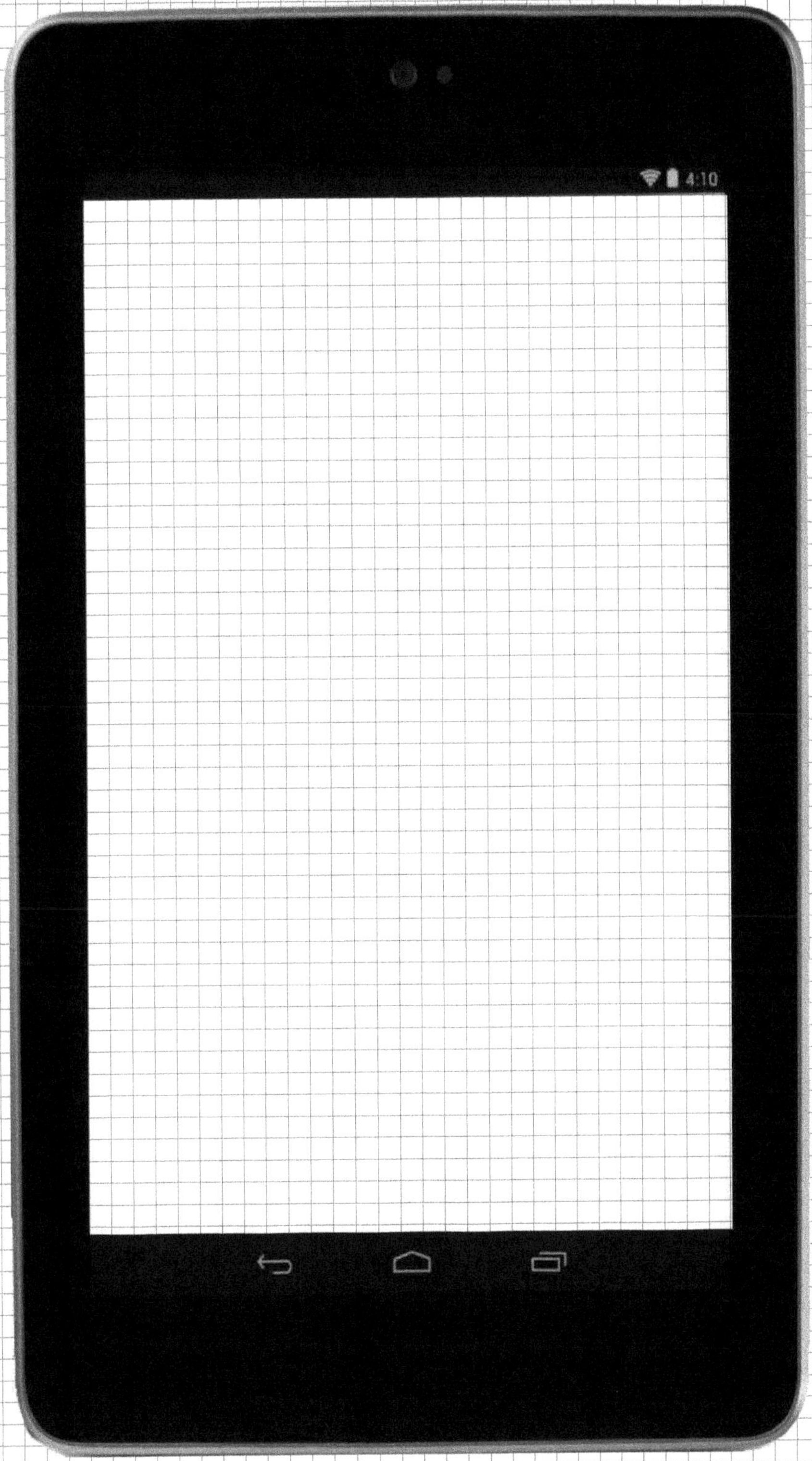

Application Name:

Screen Name:

Notes:

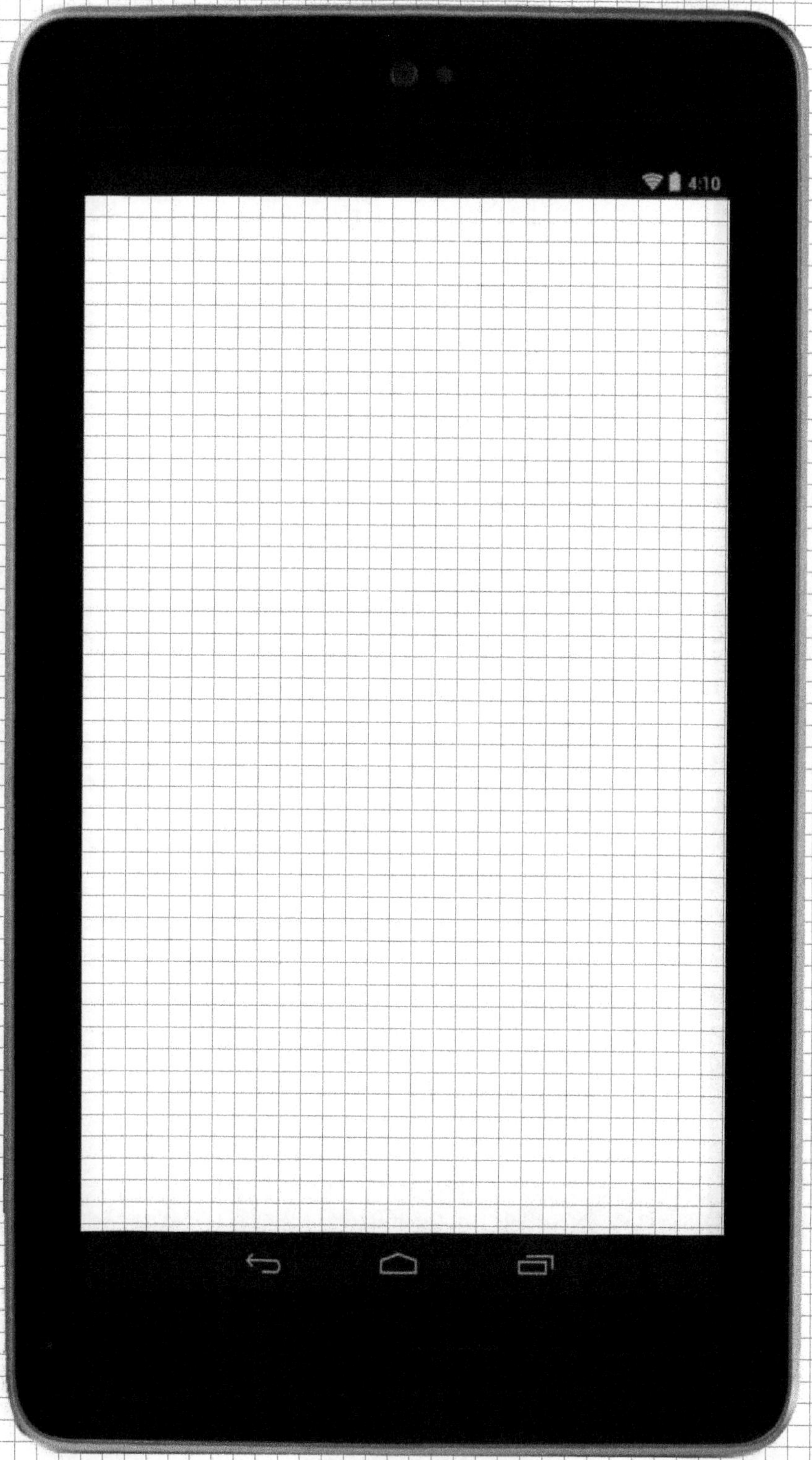

Application Name:

Screen Name:

Notes:

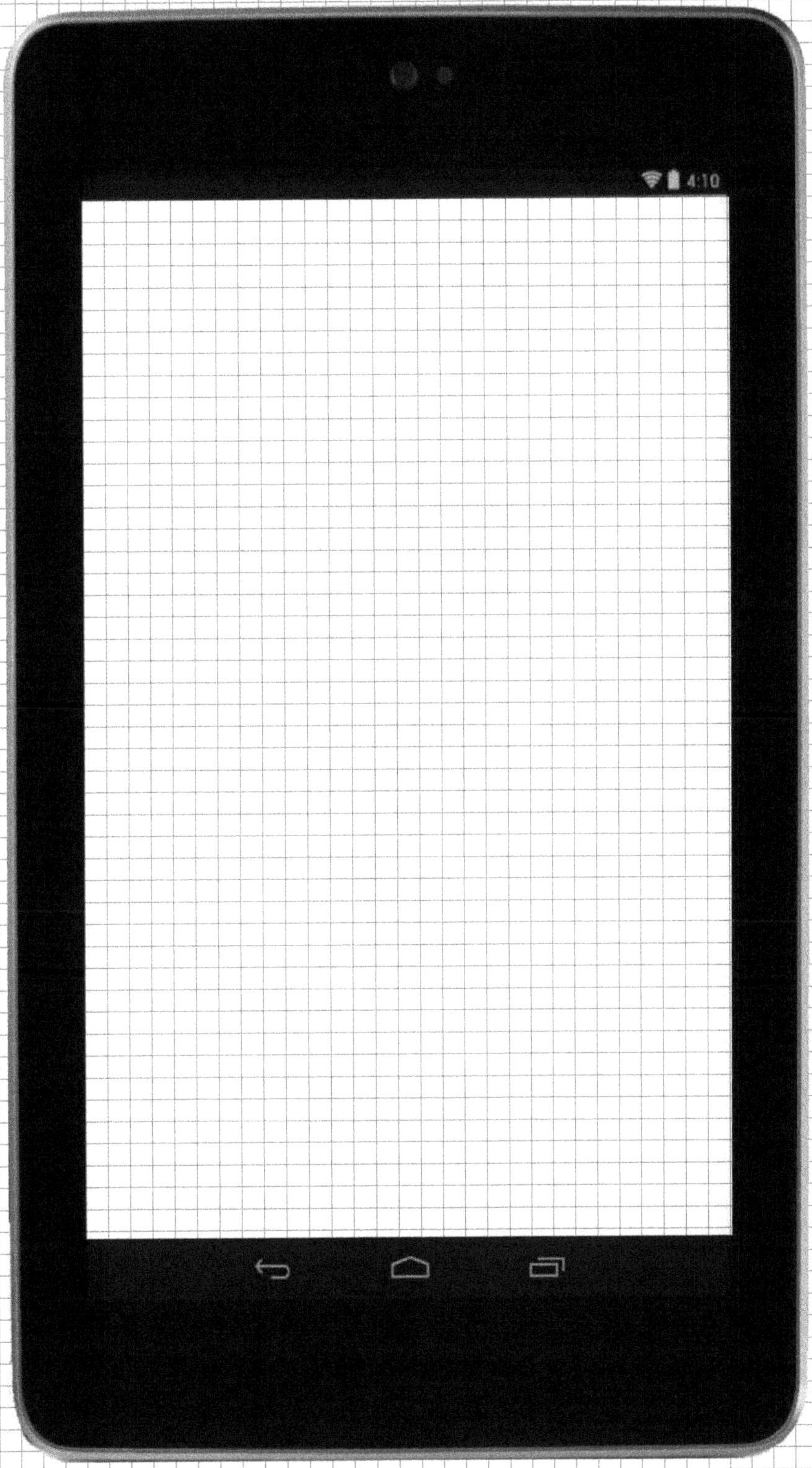

Application Name:

Screen Name:

Notes:

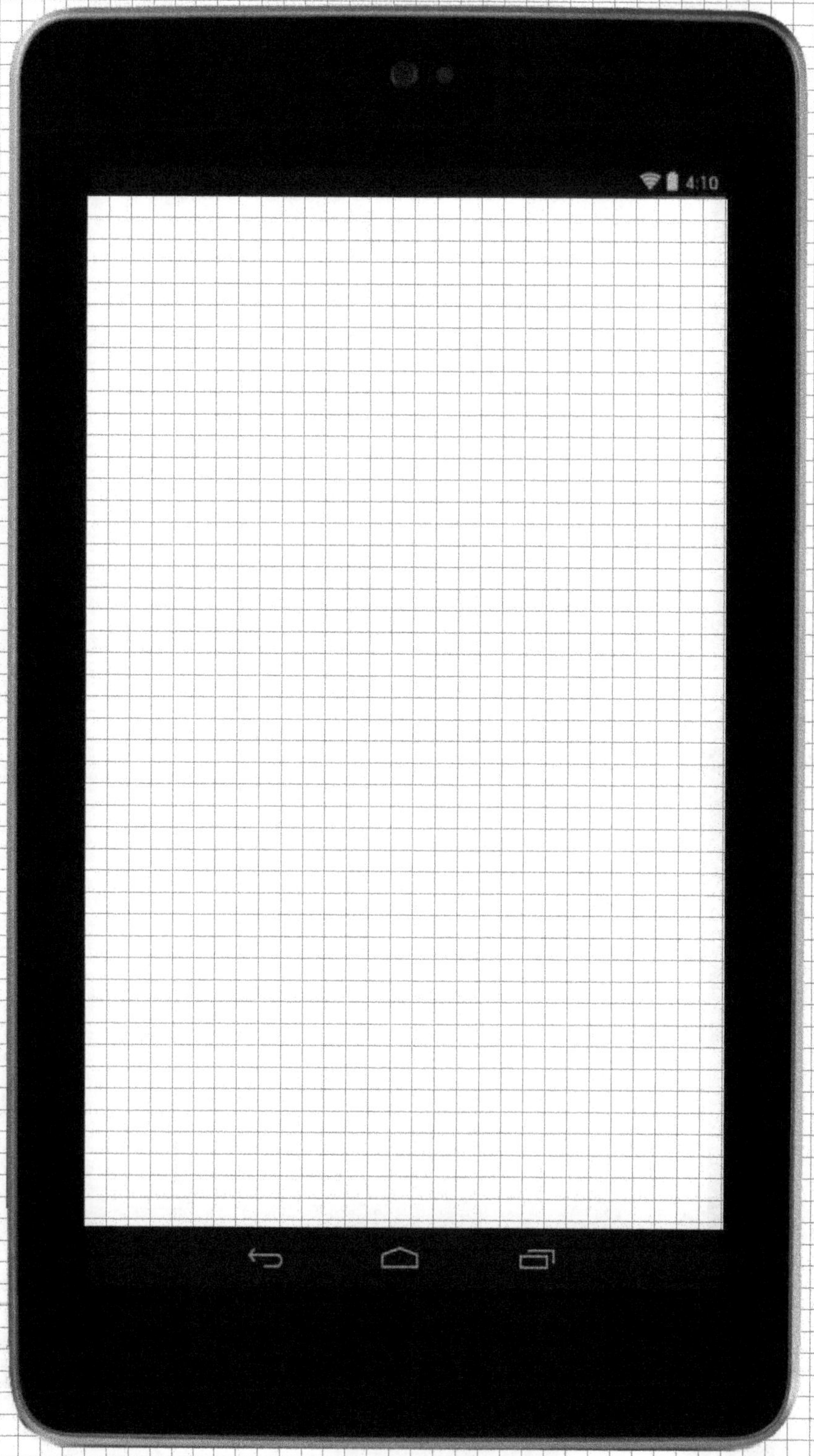

Application Name:

Screen Name:

Notes:

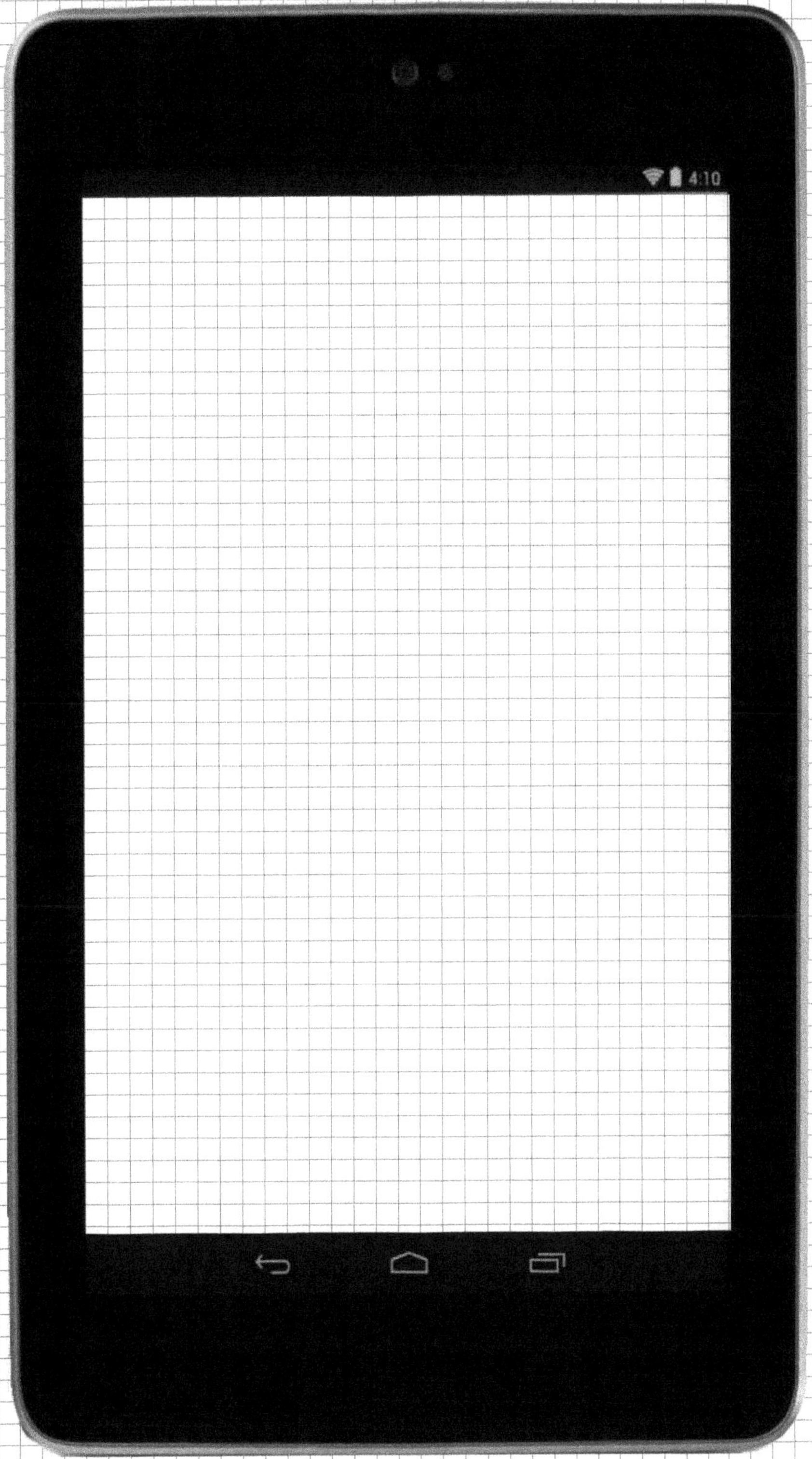

Application Name:

Screen Name:

Notes:

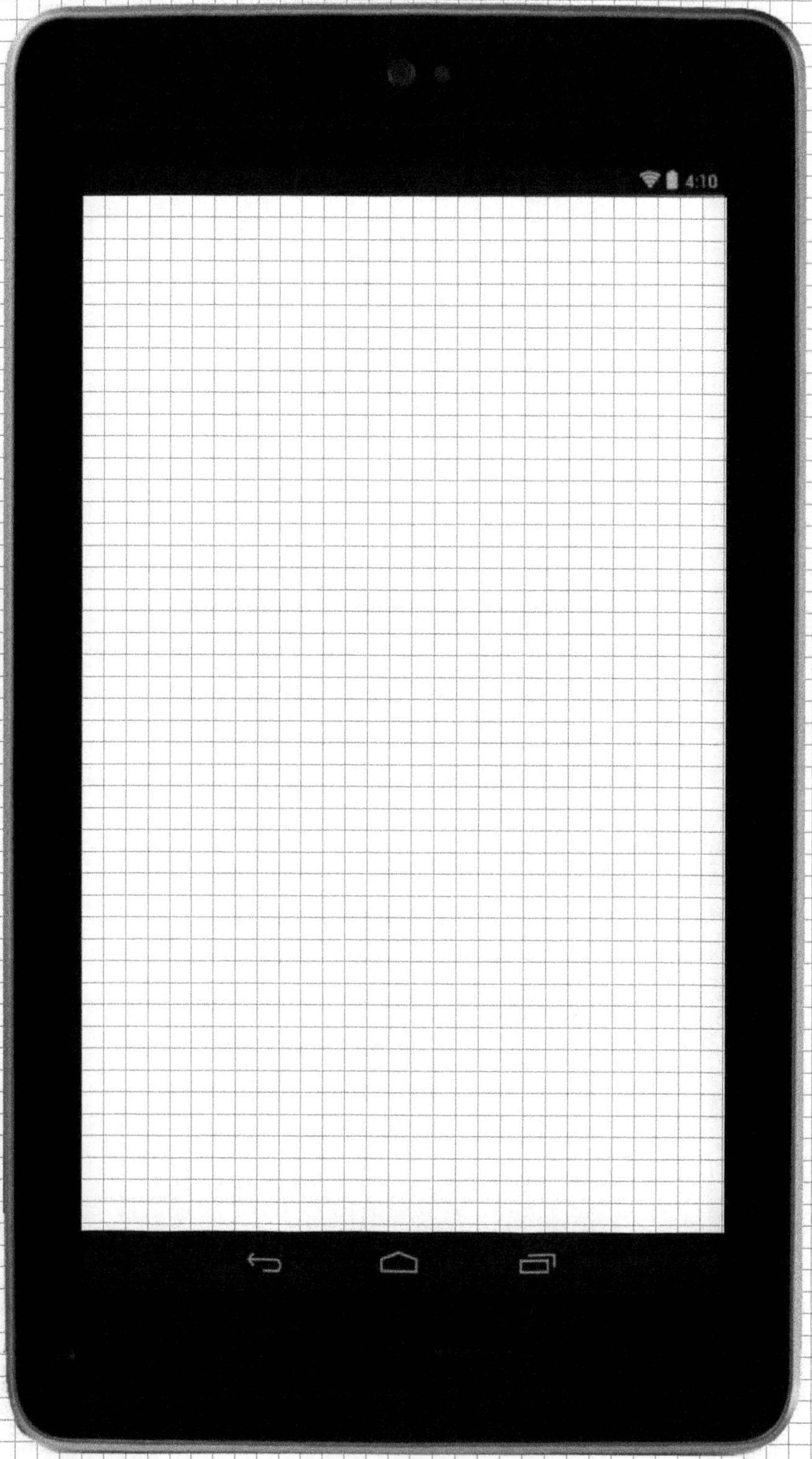

Application Name:

Screen Name:

Notes:

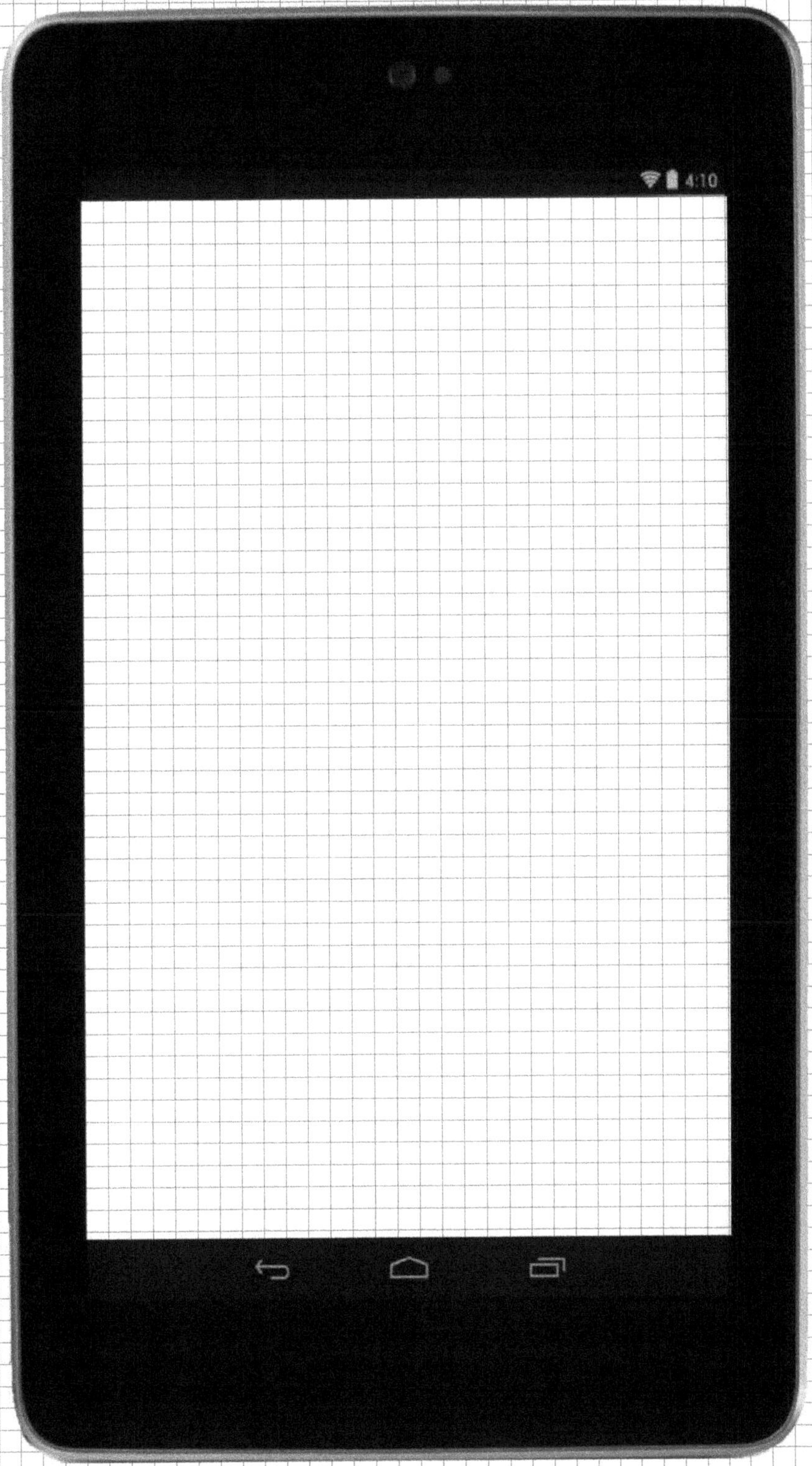

Application Name:

Screen Name:

Notes:

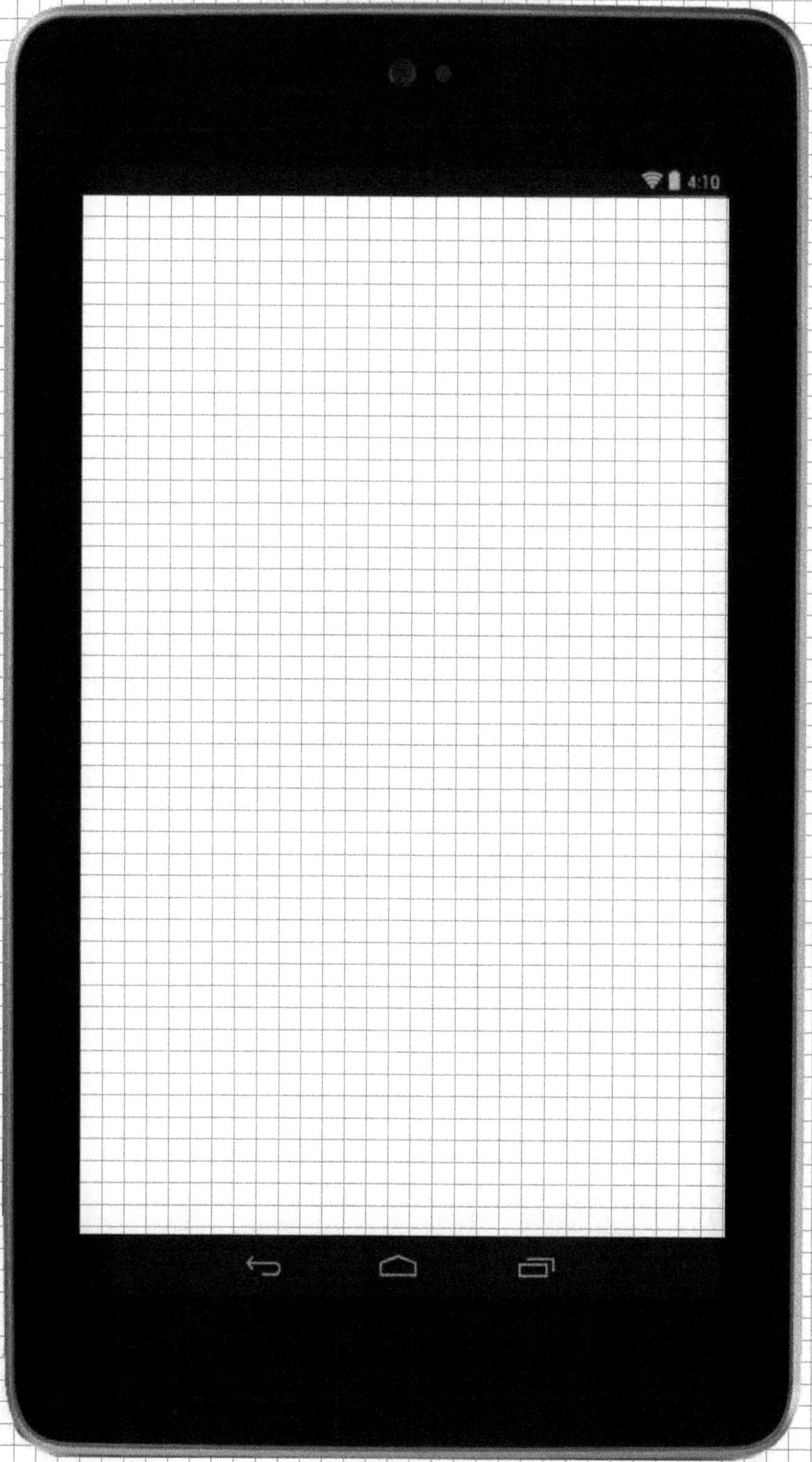

Application Name:

Screen Name:

Notes:

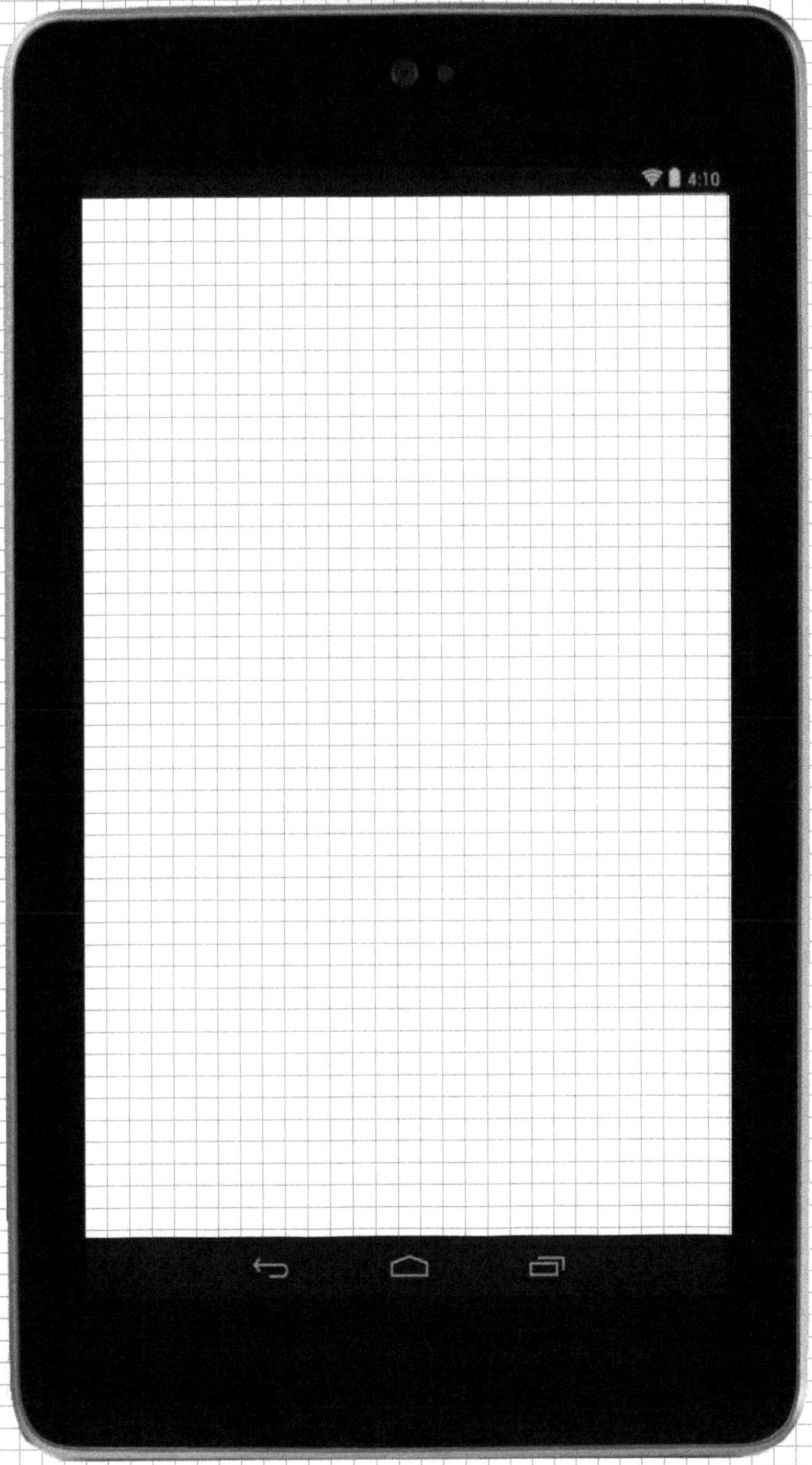

Application Name:

Screen Name:

Notes:

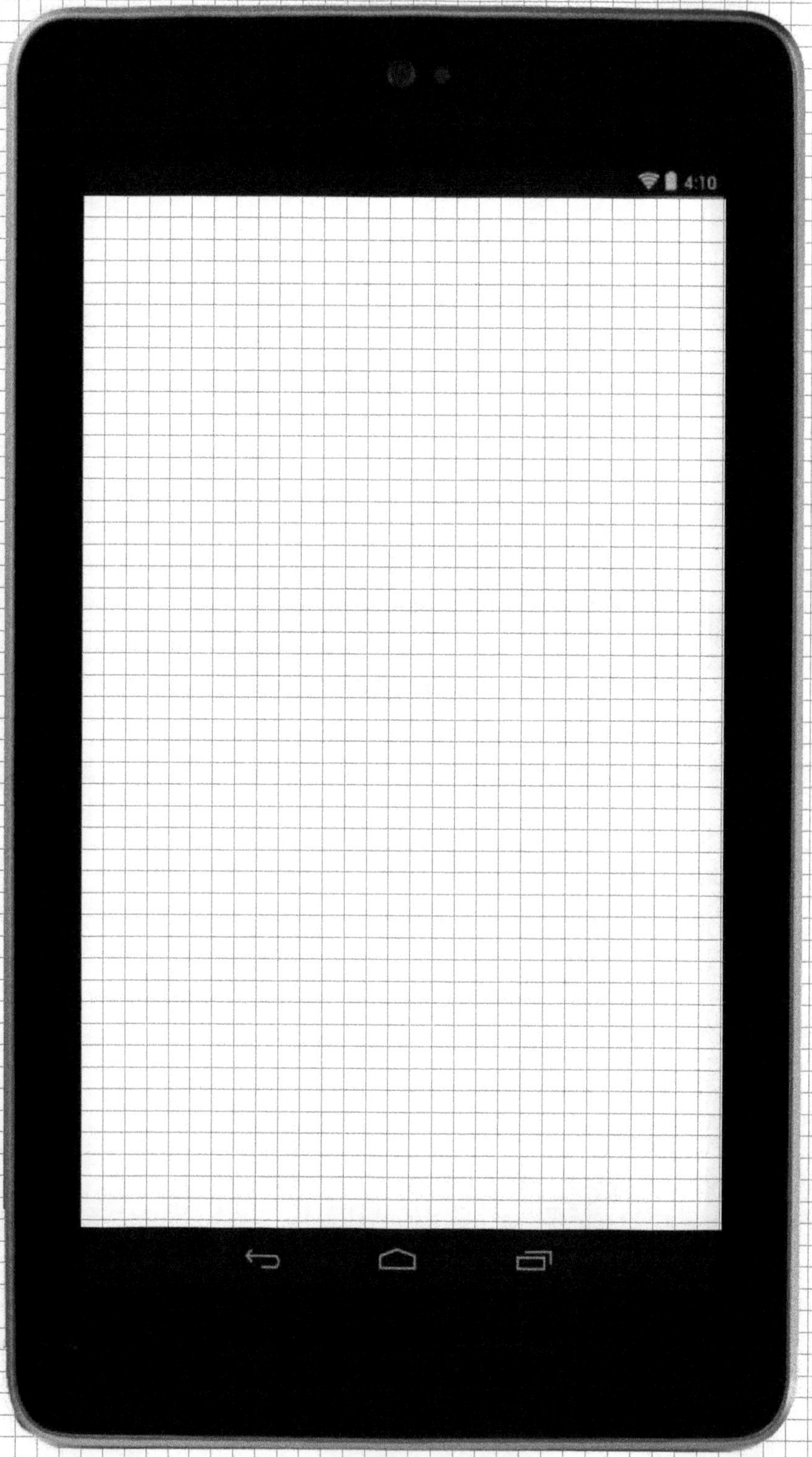

Application Name:

Screen Name:

Notes:

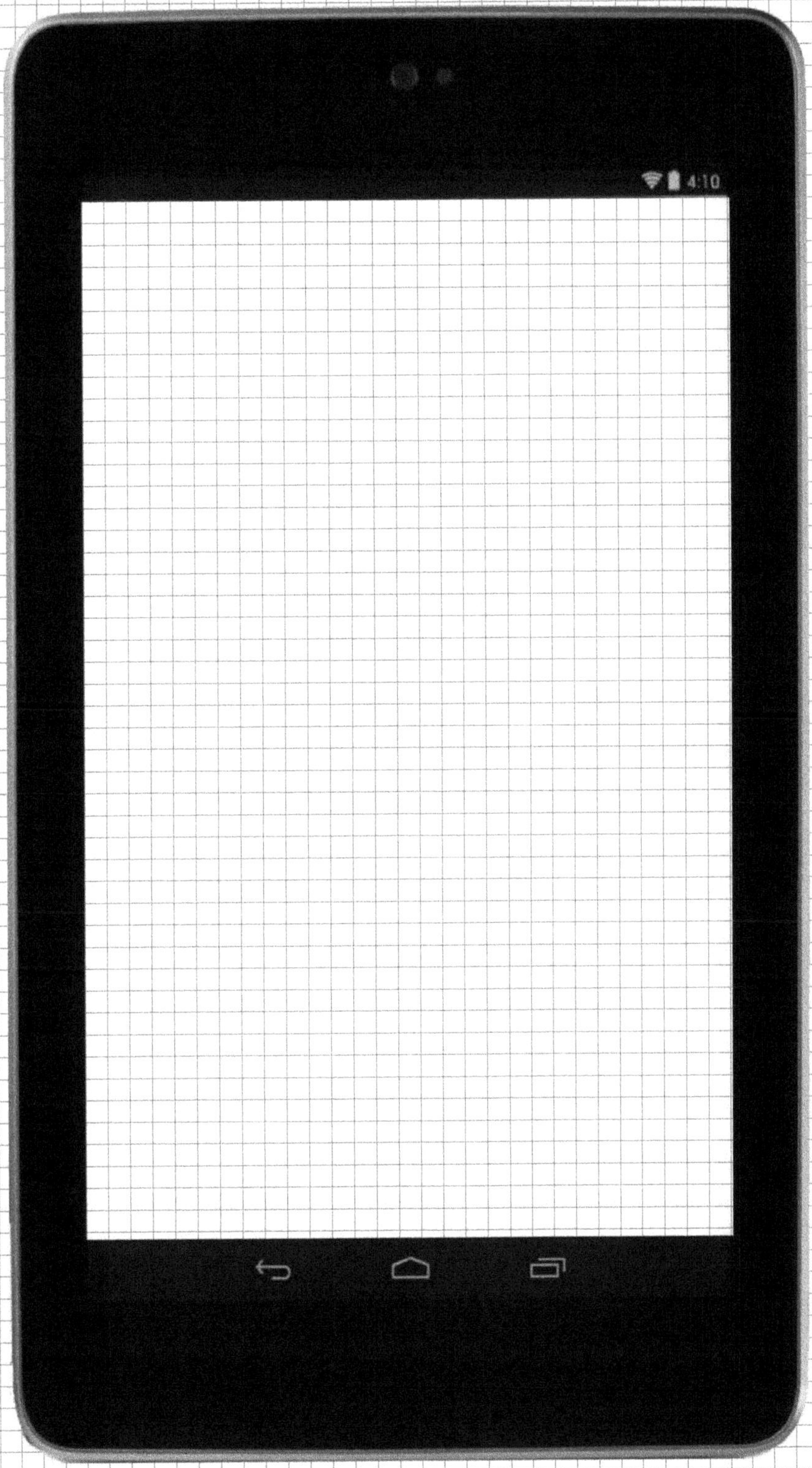

Application Name:

Screen Name:

Notes:

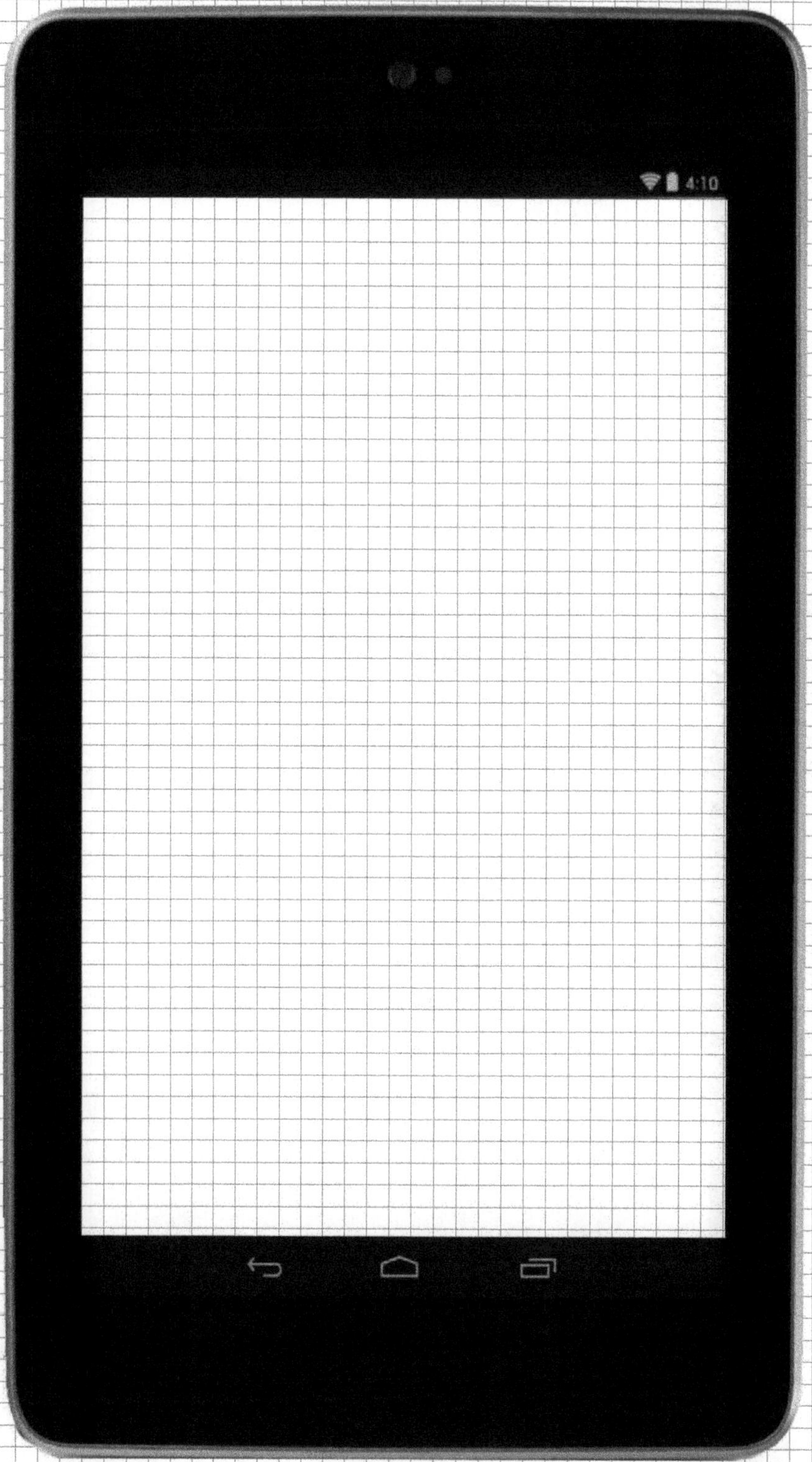

Application Name:

Screen Name:

Notes:

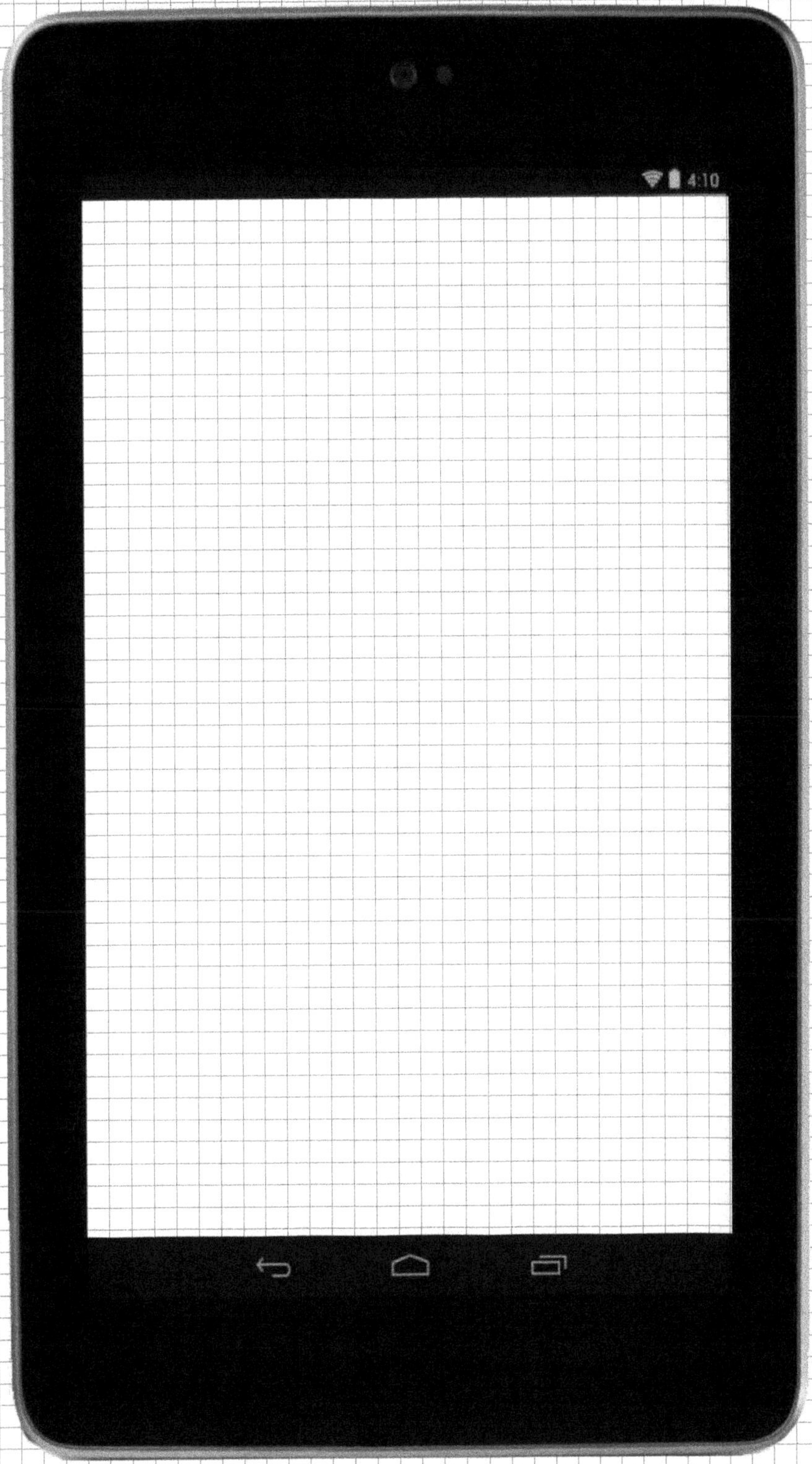

Application Name:

Screen Name:

Notes:

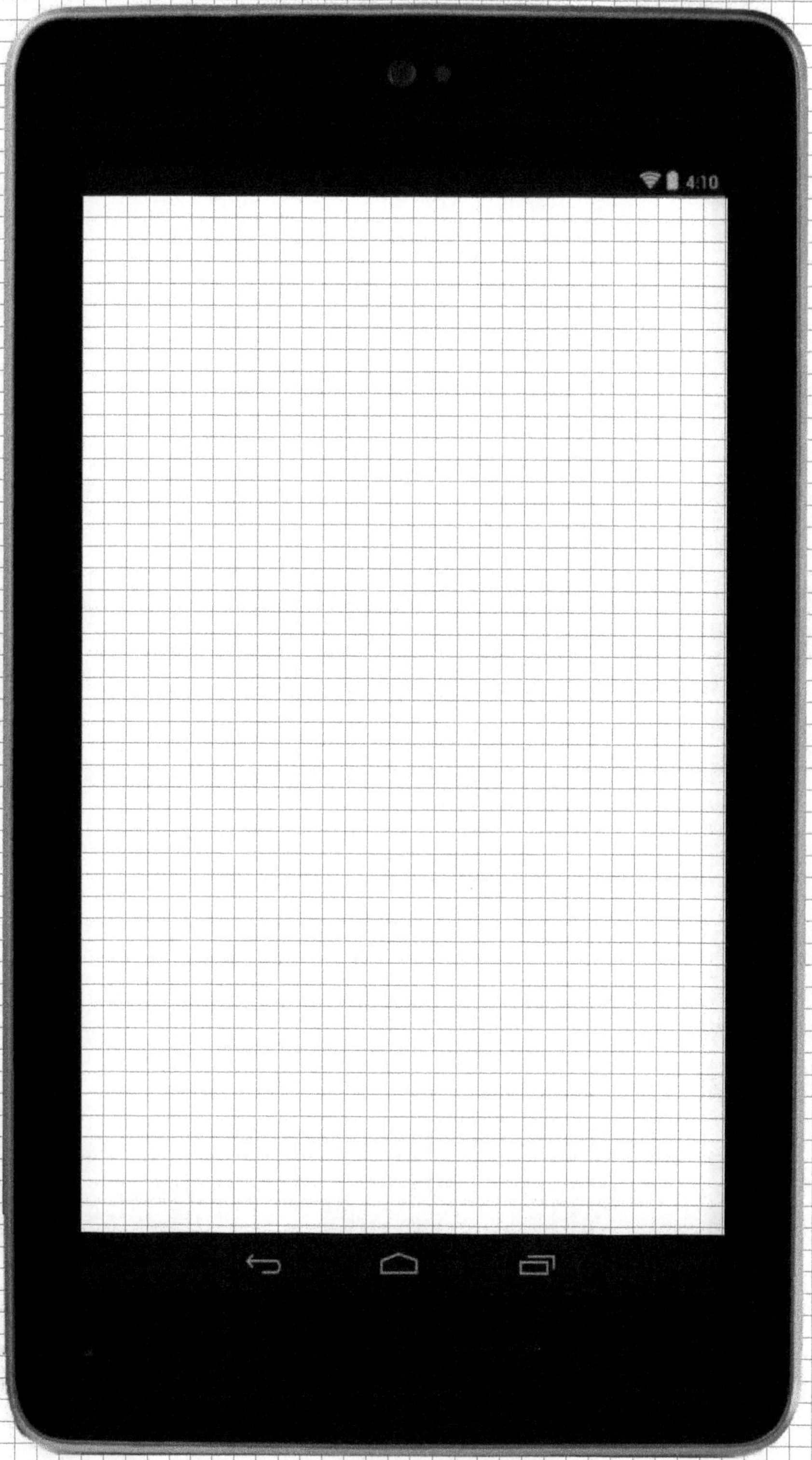

Application Name:

Screen Name:

Notes:

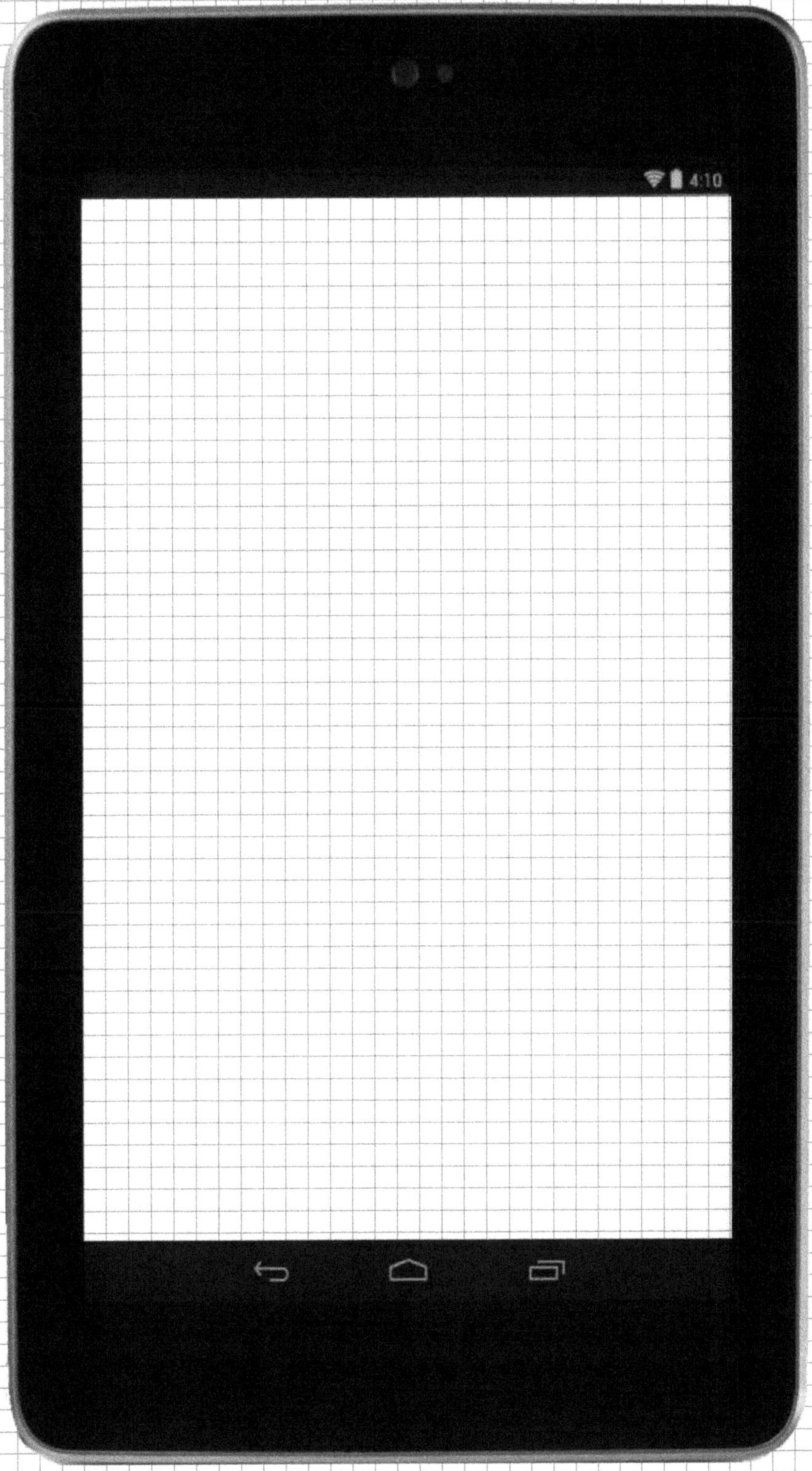

Application Name:

Screen Name:

Notes:

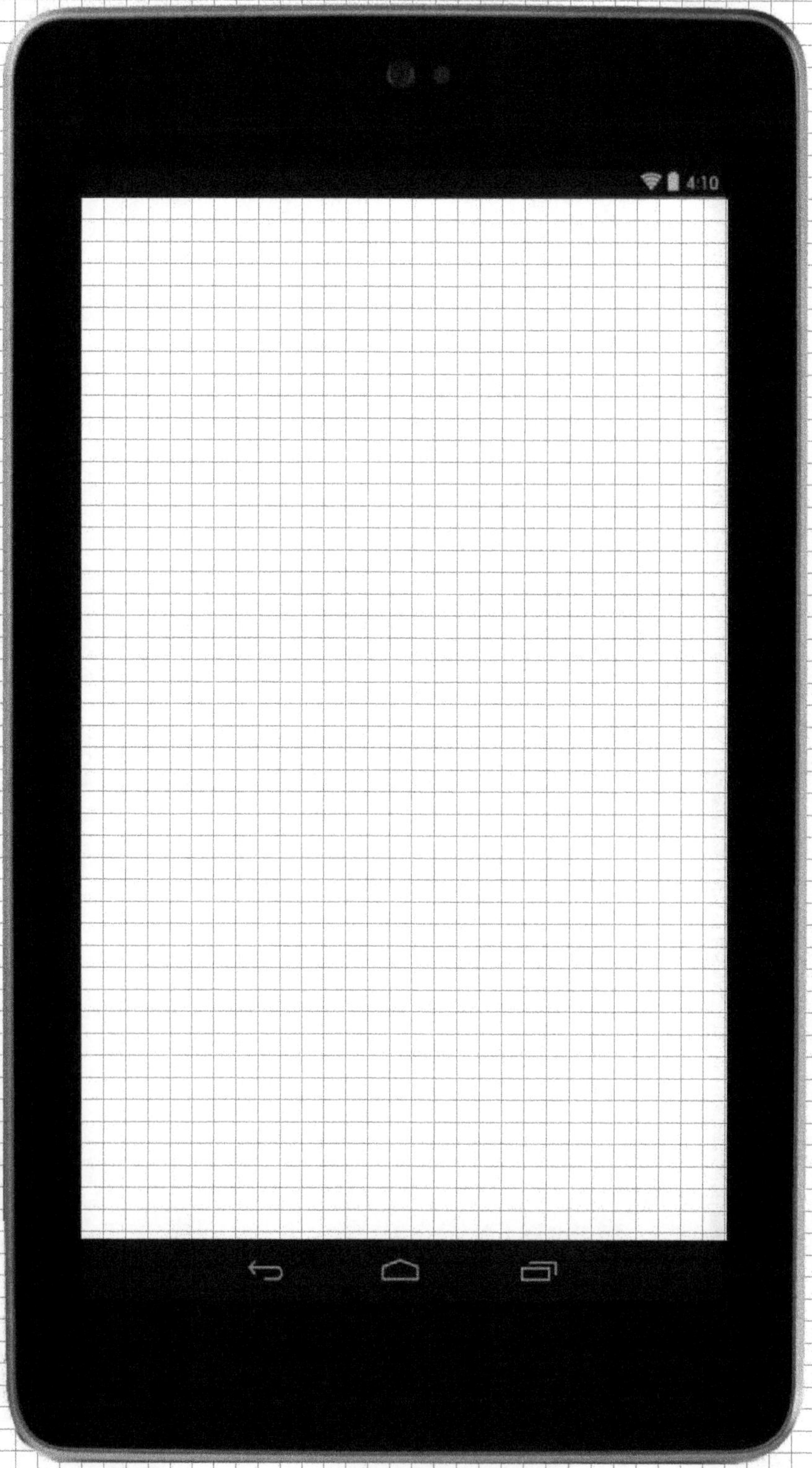

Application Name:

Screen Name:

Notes:

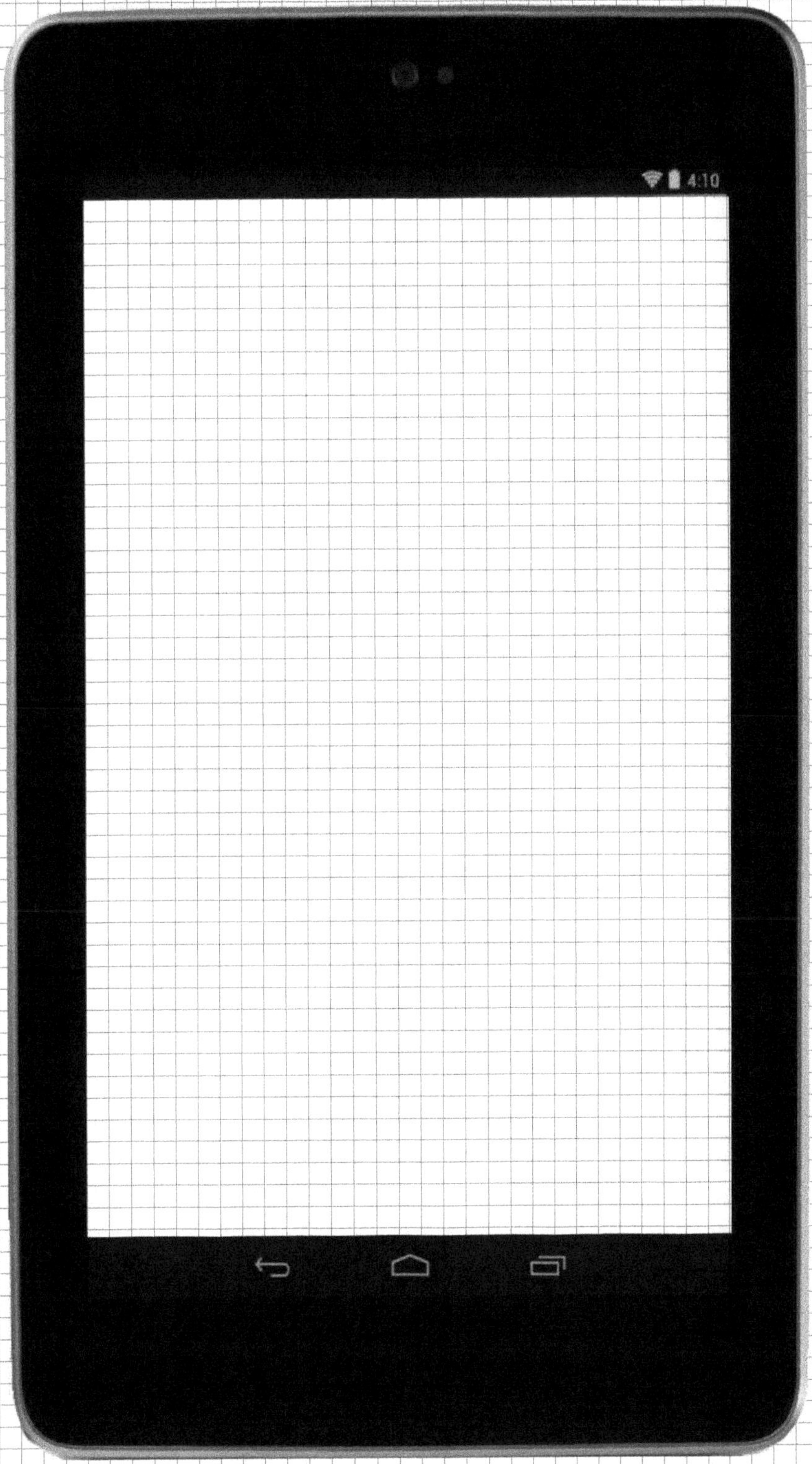

Application Name:

Screen Name:

Notes:

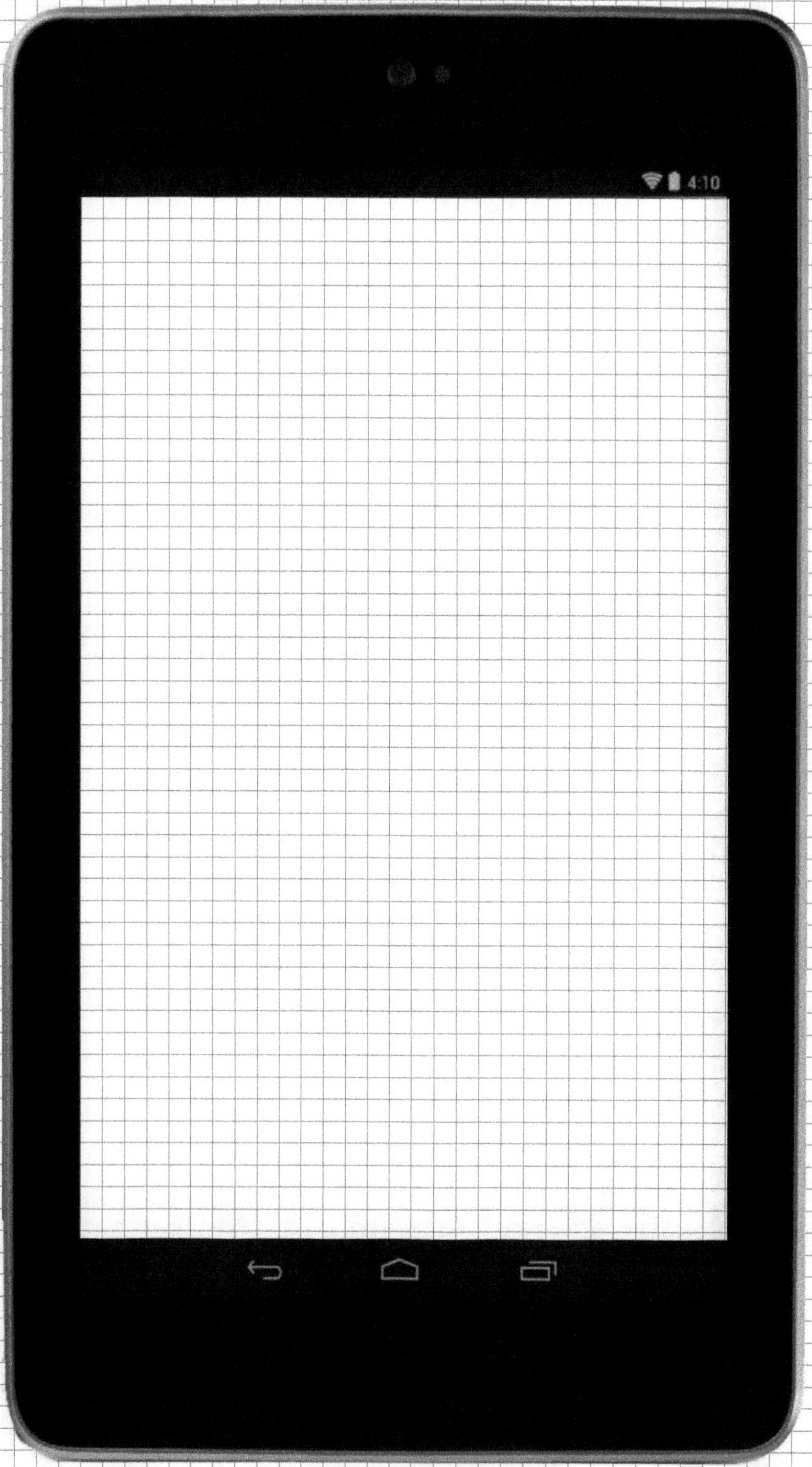

Application Name:

Screen Name:

Notes:

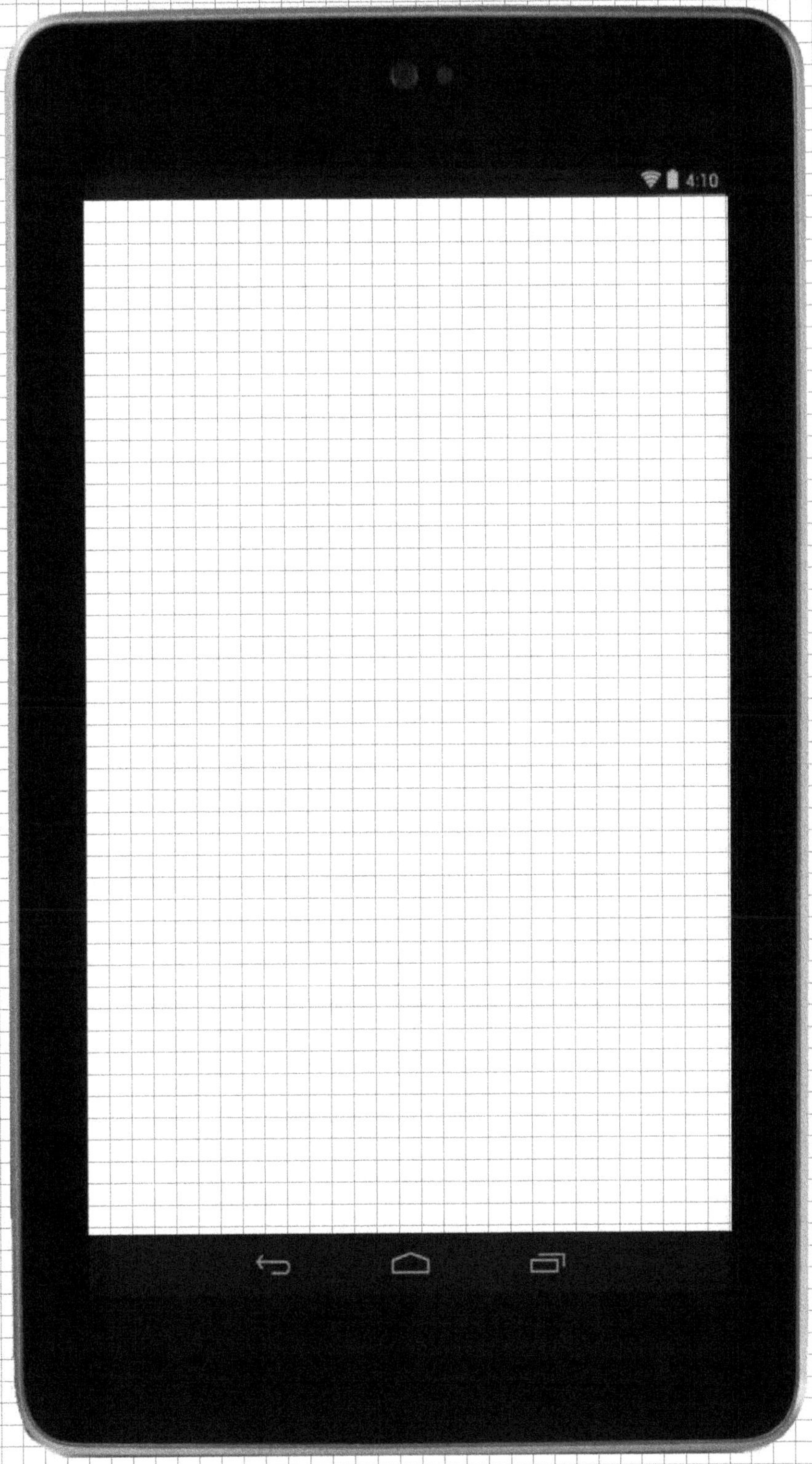

Application Name:

Screen Name:

Notes:

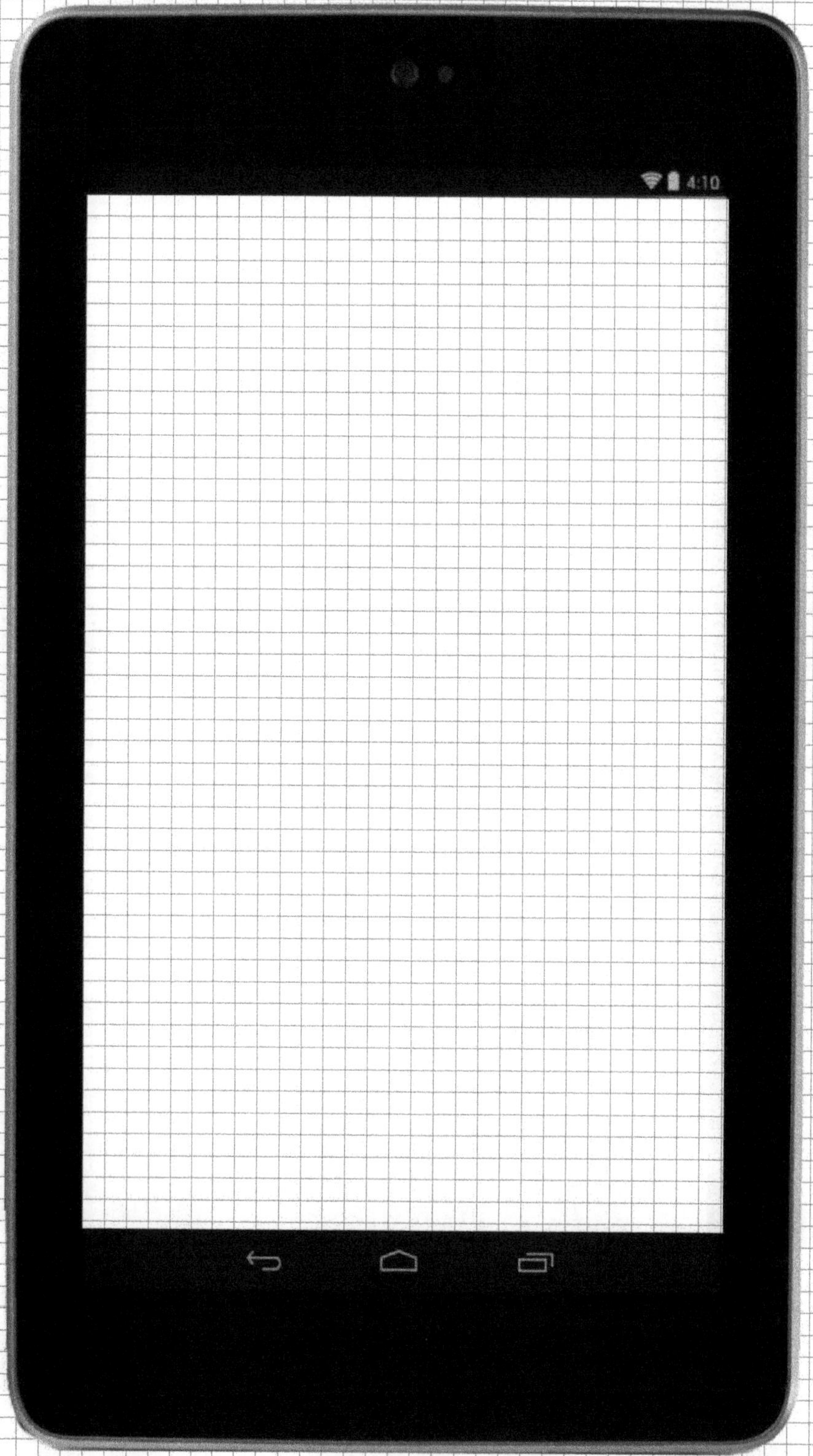

Application Name:

Screen Name:

Notes:

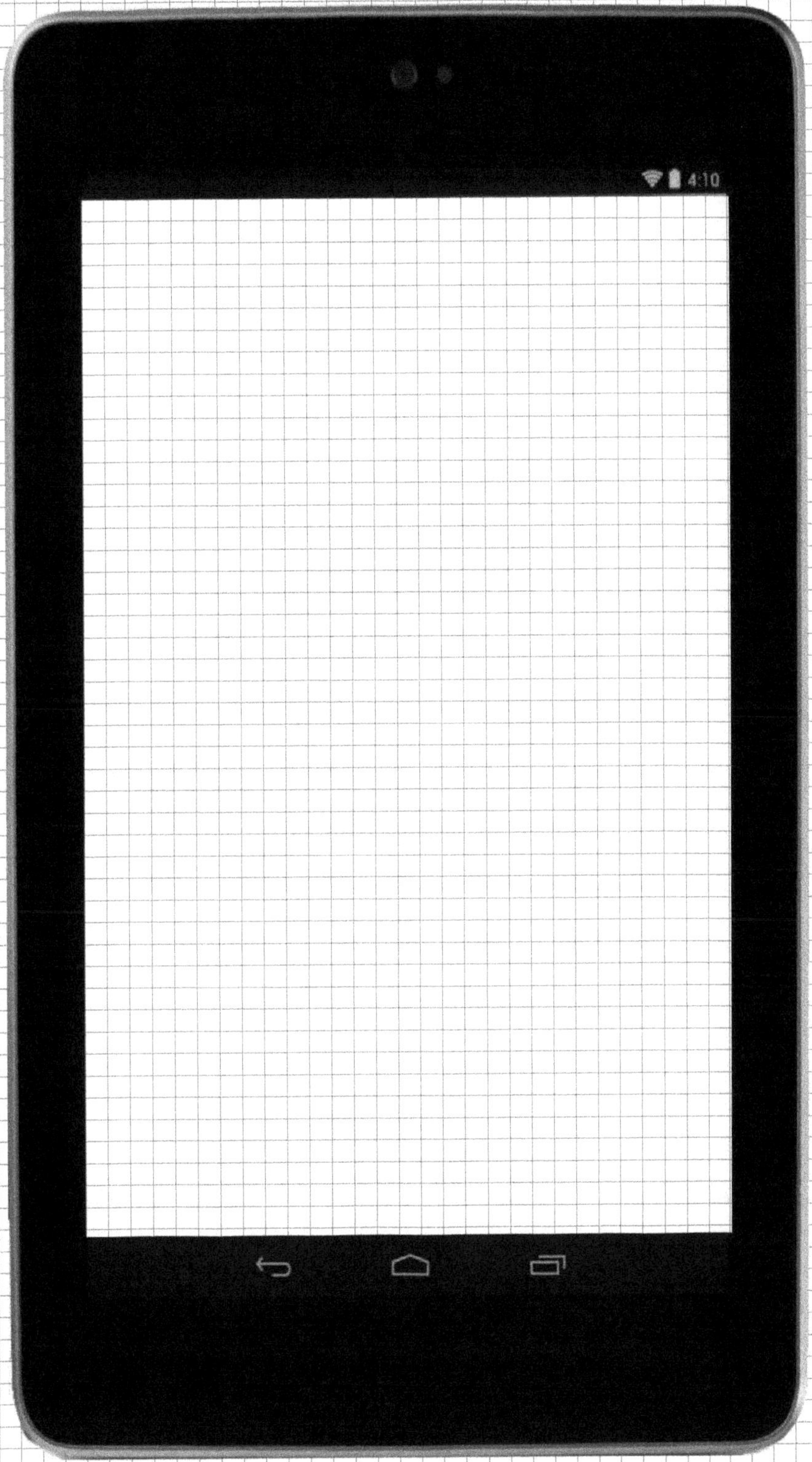

Application Name:

Screen Name:

Notes:

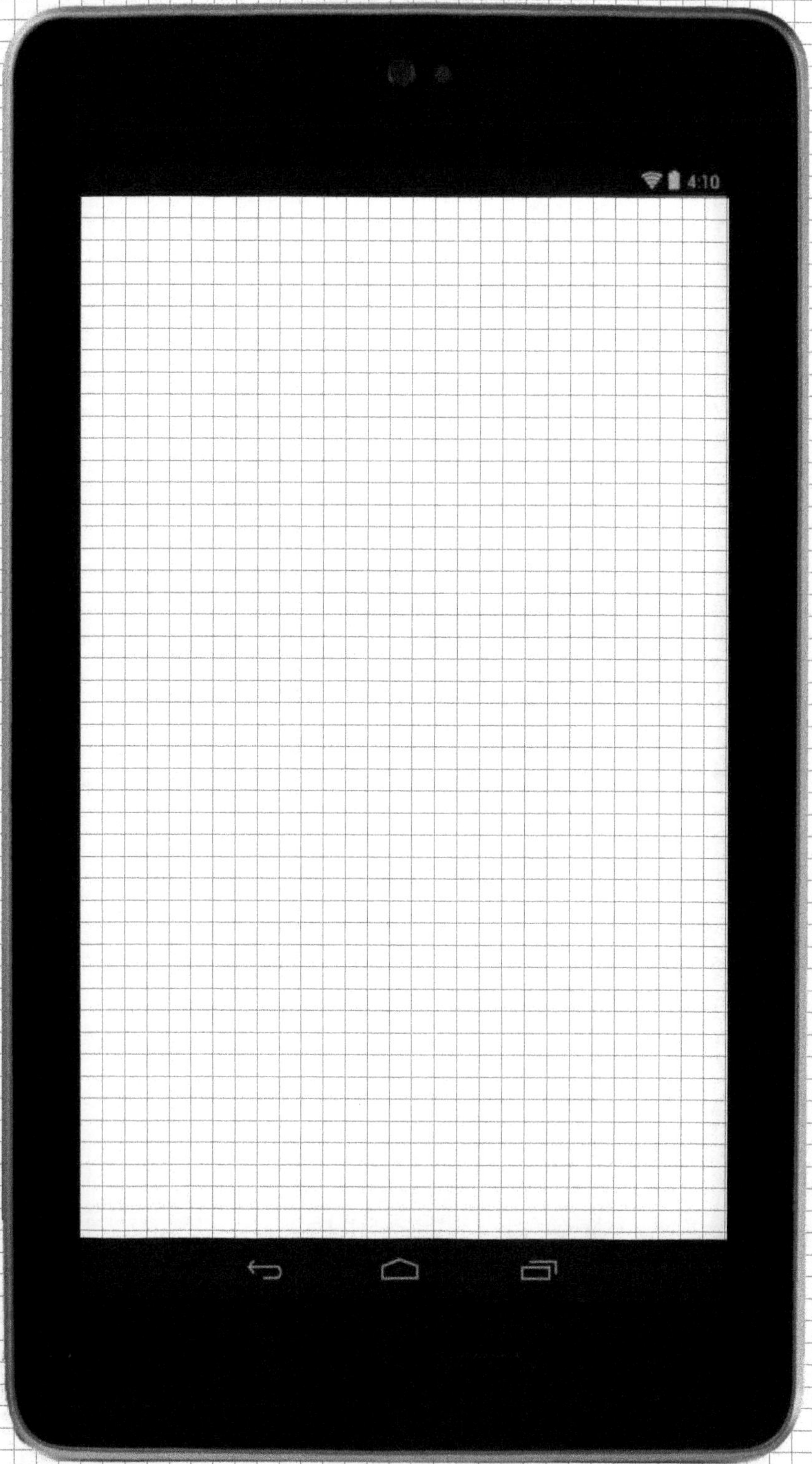

Application Name:

Screen Name:

Notes:

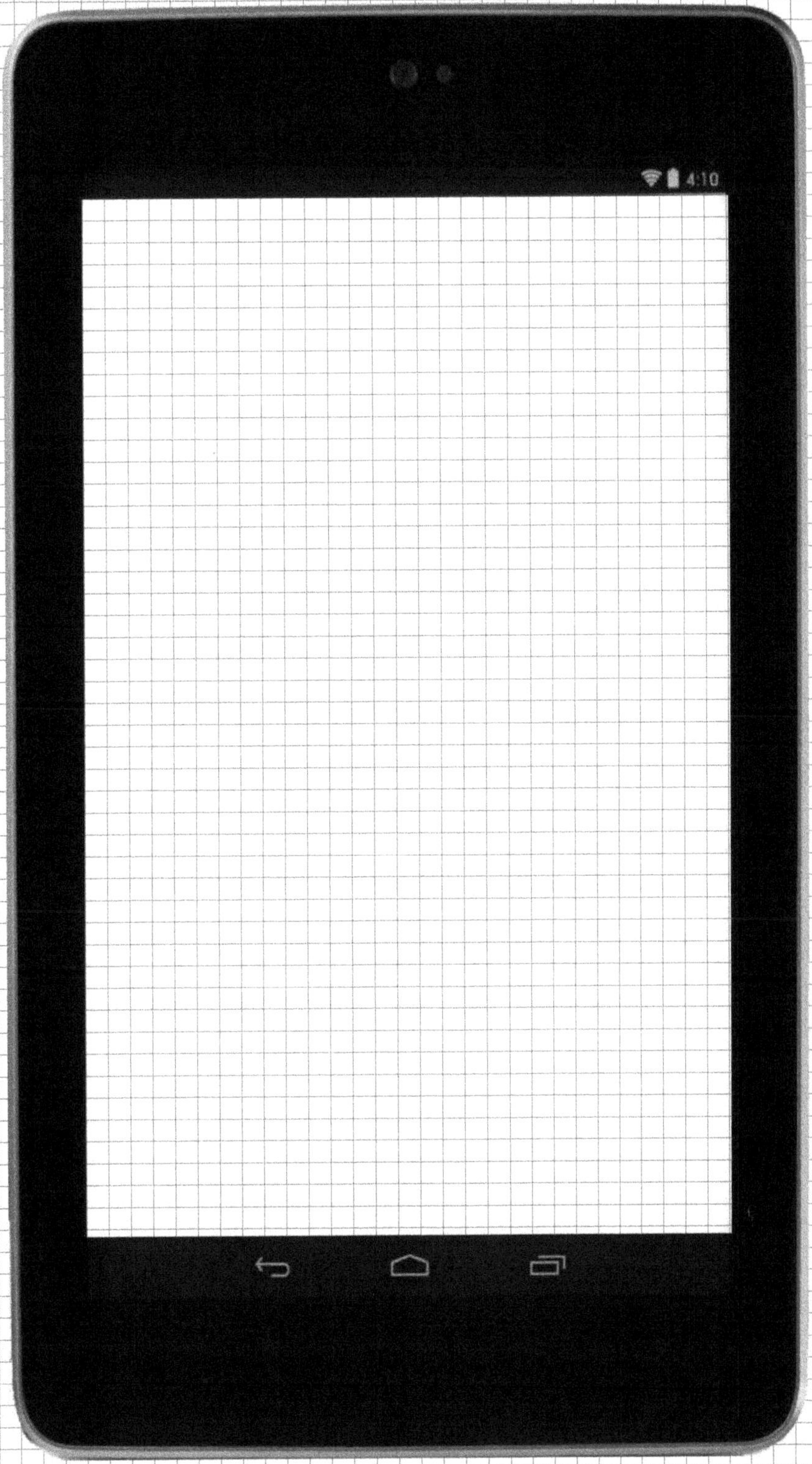

Application Name:

Screen Name:

Notes:

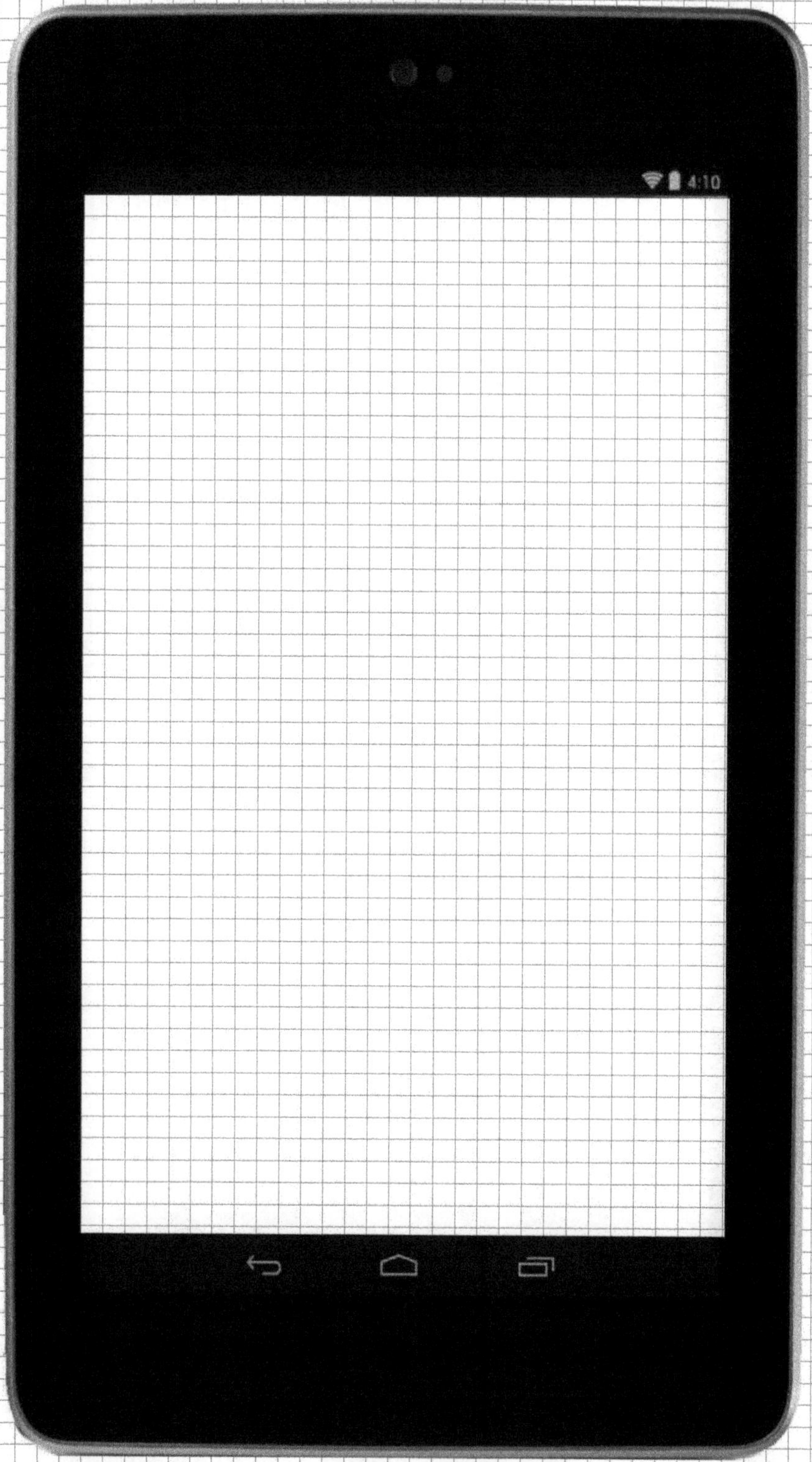

Application Name:

Screen Name:

Notes:

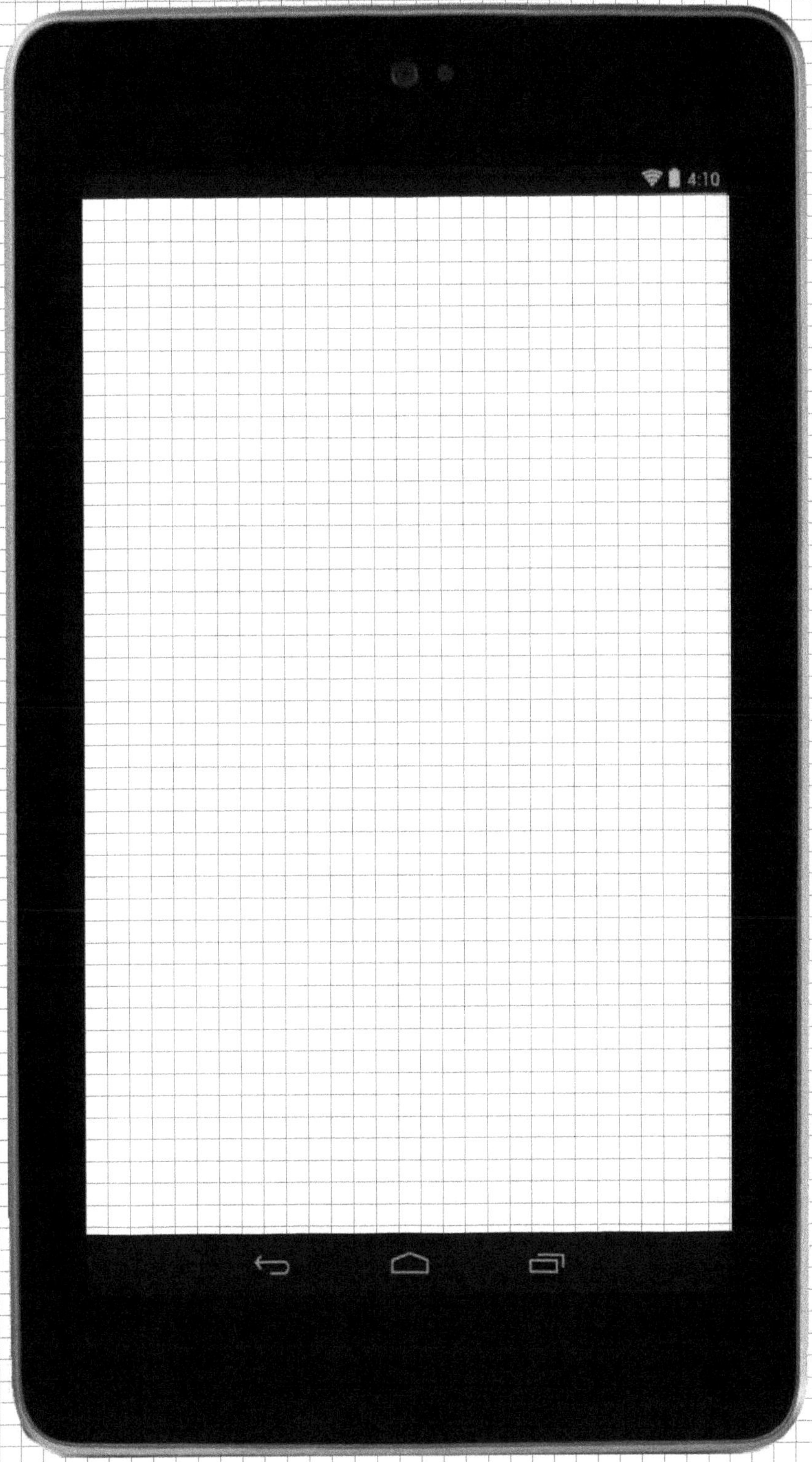

Application Name:

Screen Name:

Notes:

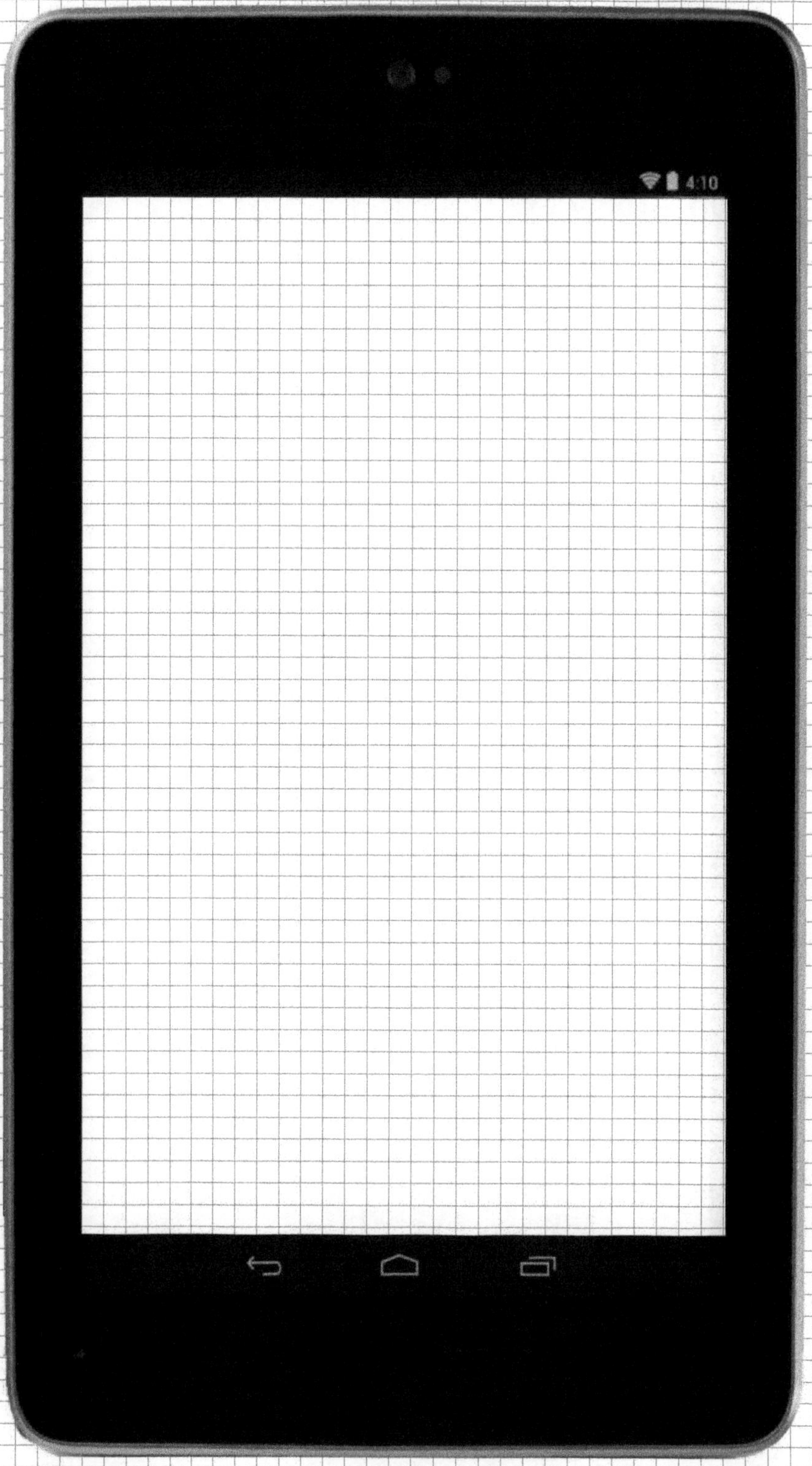

Application Name:

Screen Name:

Notes:

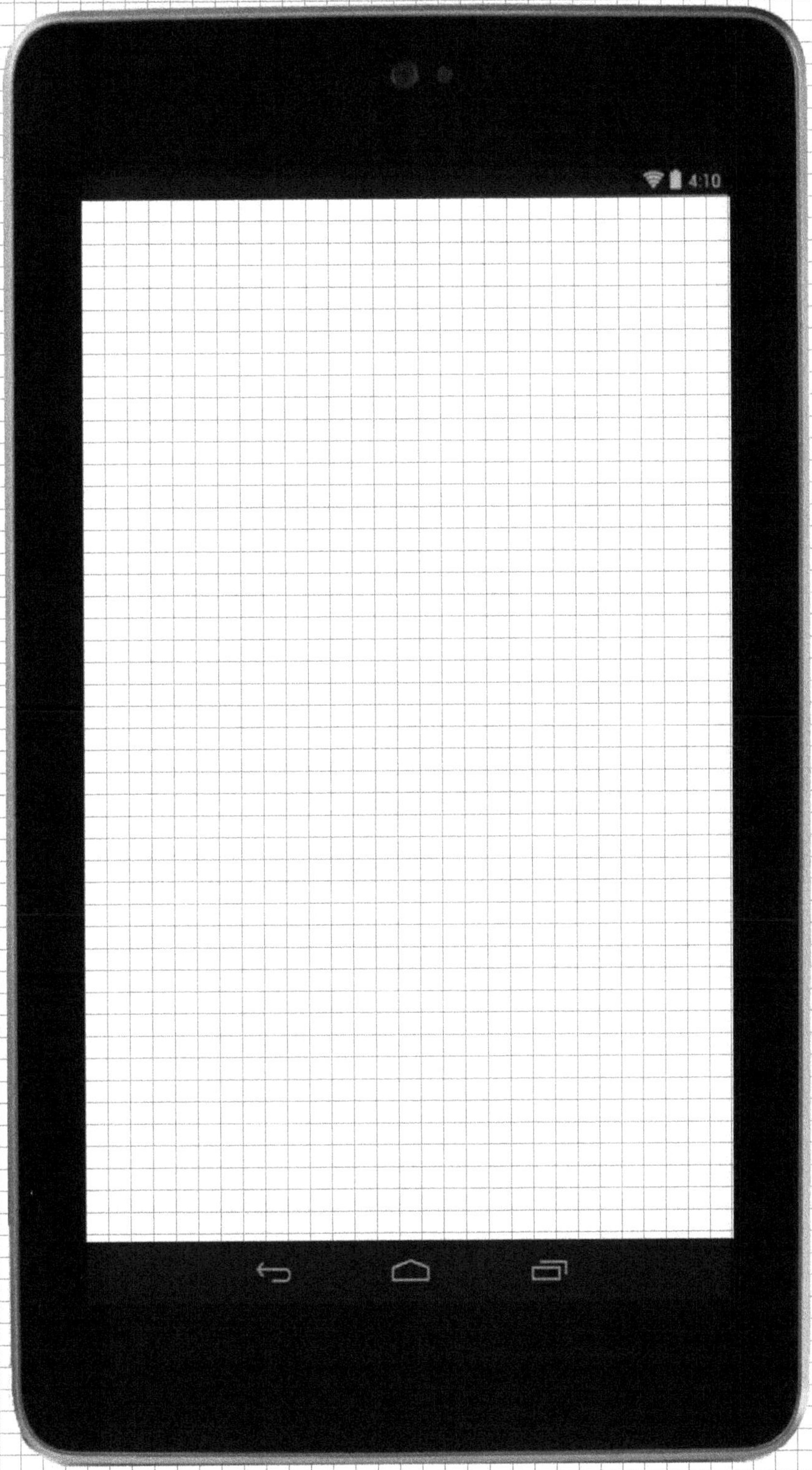

Application Name:

Screen Name:

Notes:

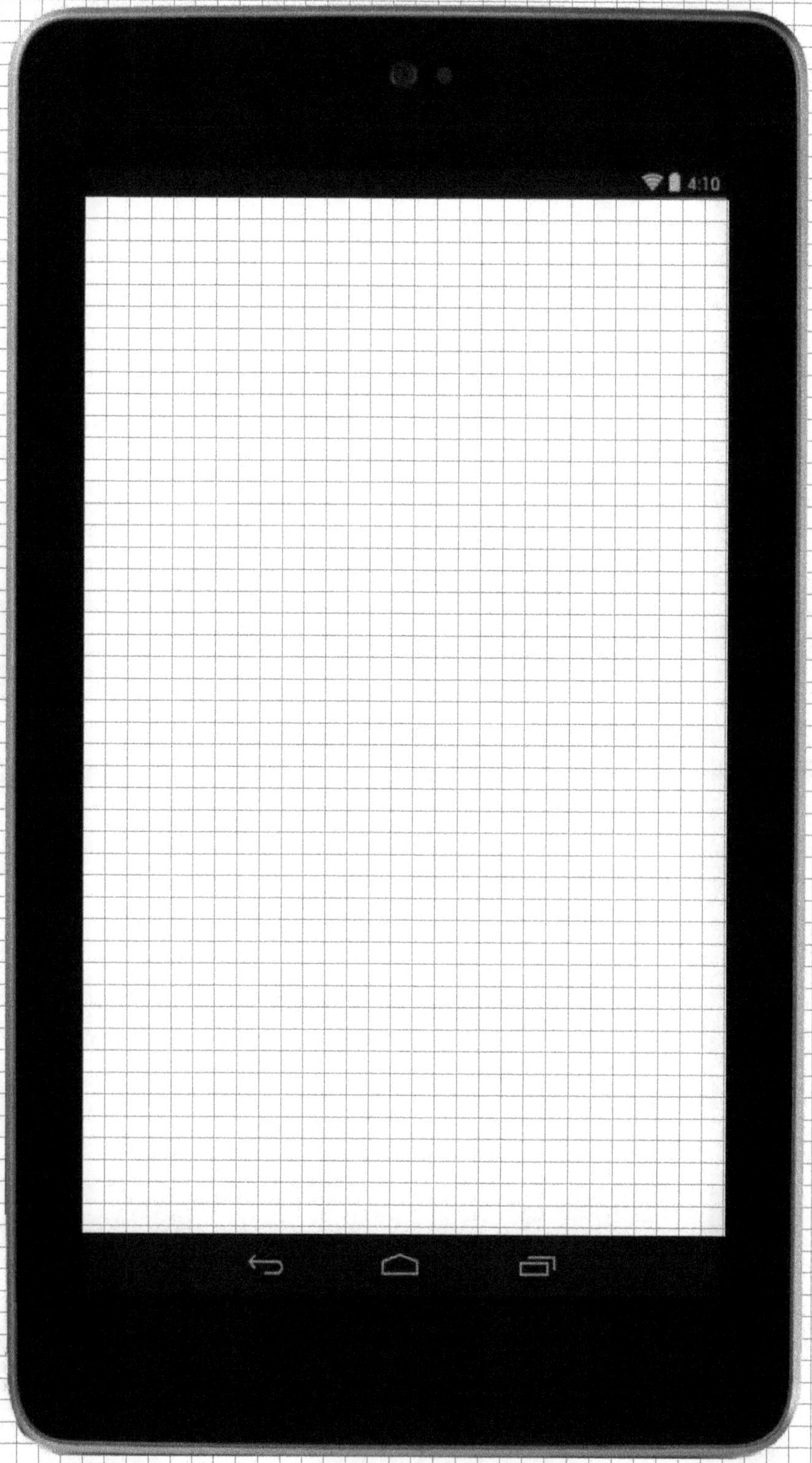

Application Name:

Screen Name:

Notes:

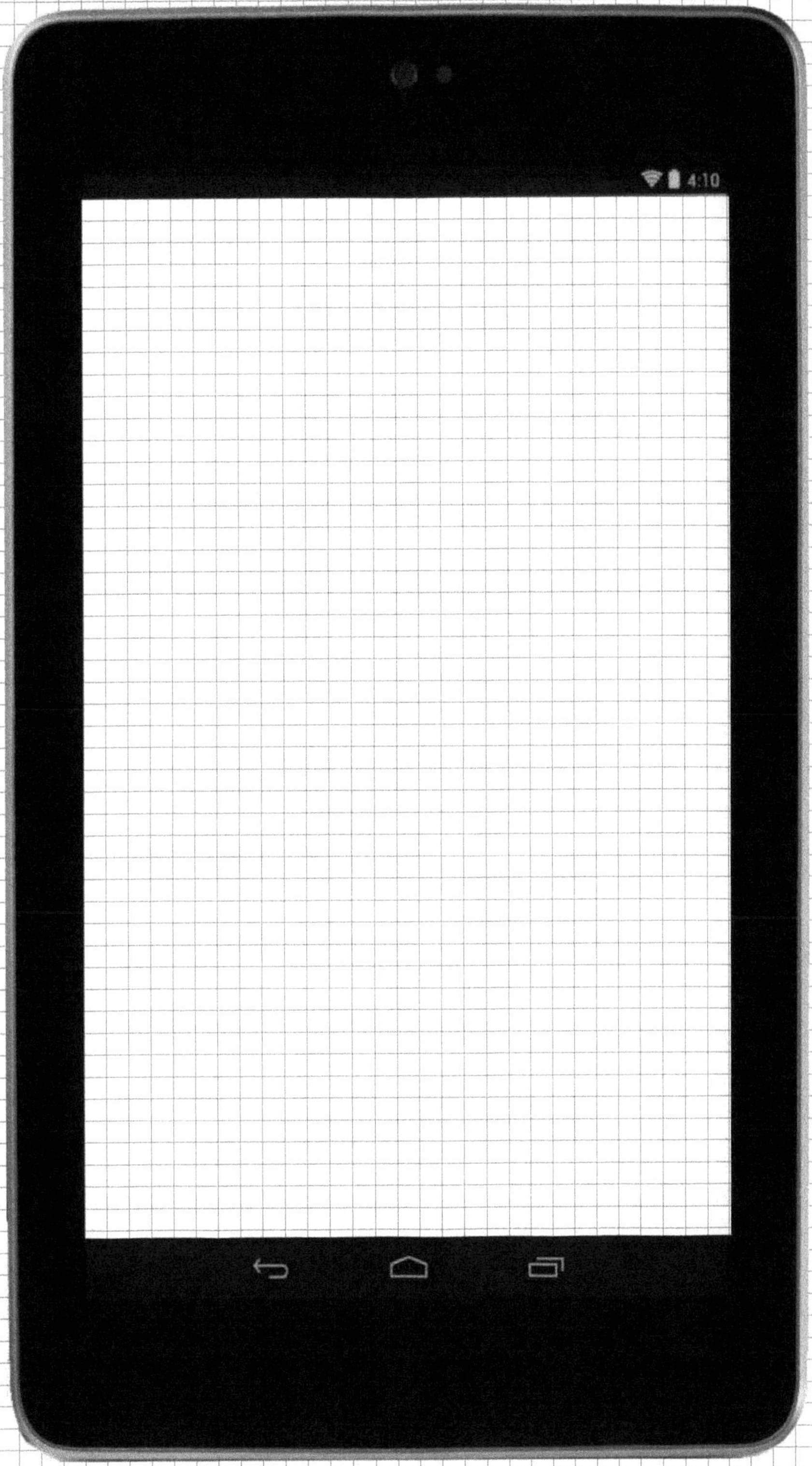

Application Name:

Screen Name:

Notes:

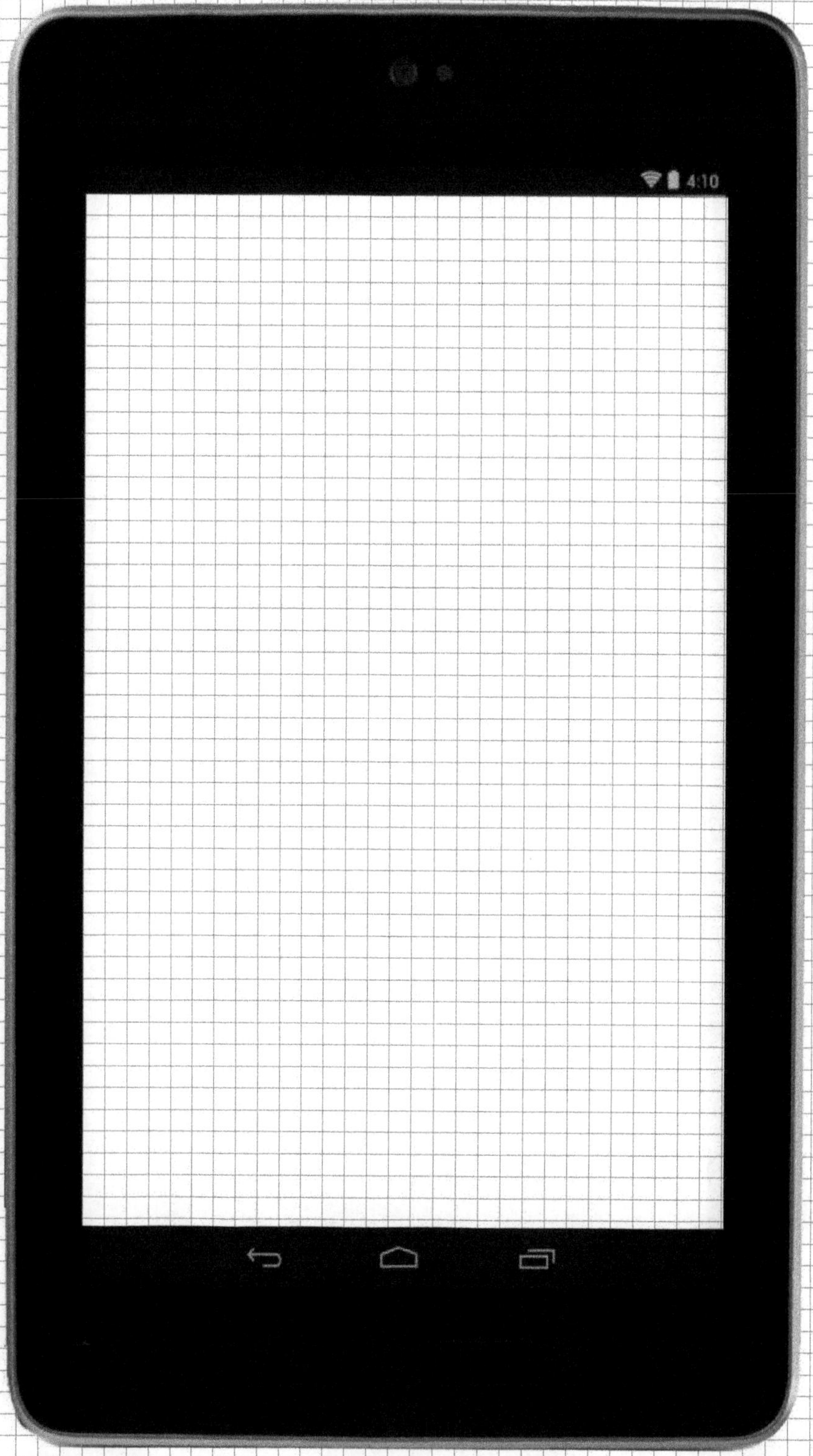

Application Name:

Screen Name:

Notes:

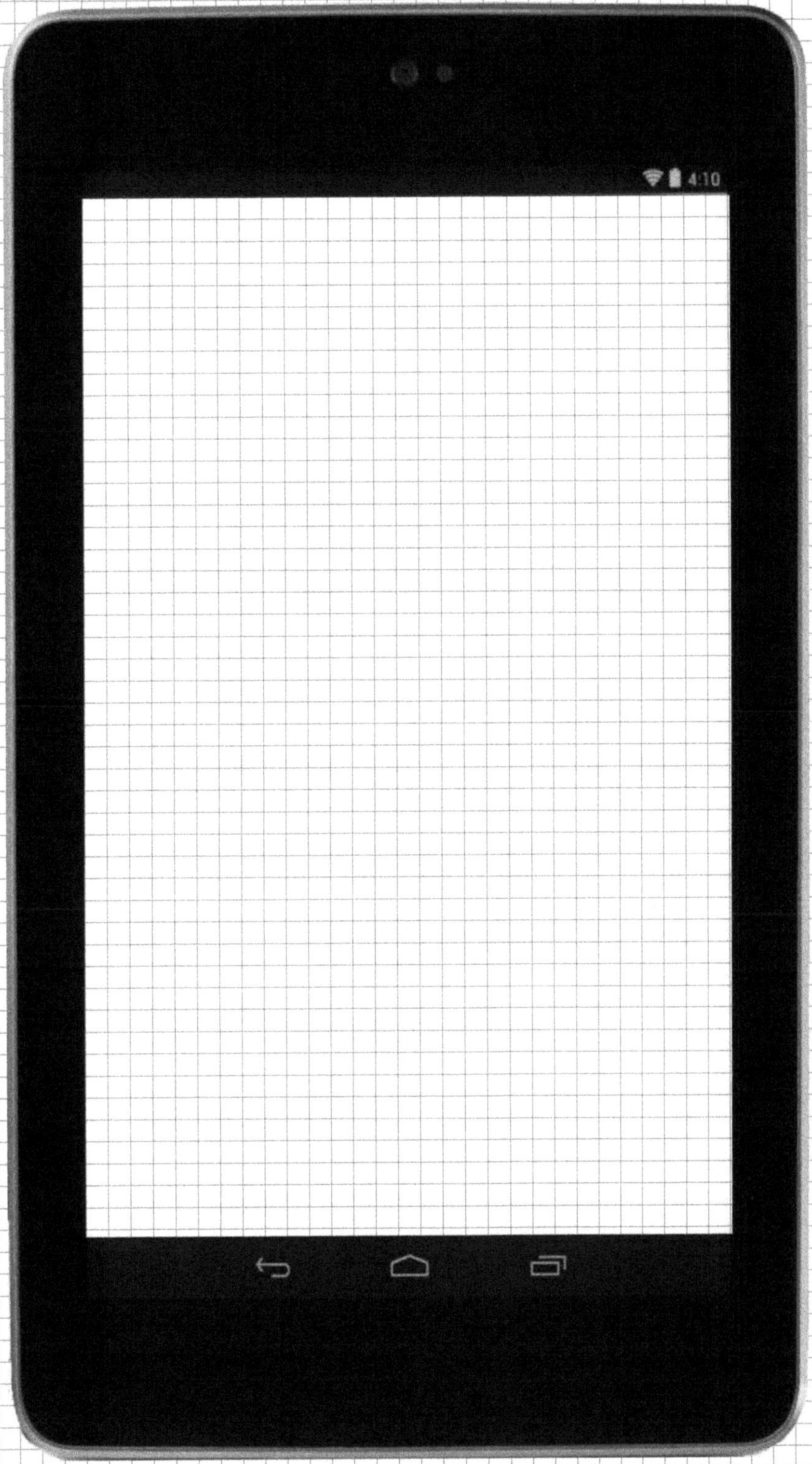

Application Name:

Screen Name:

Notes:

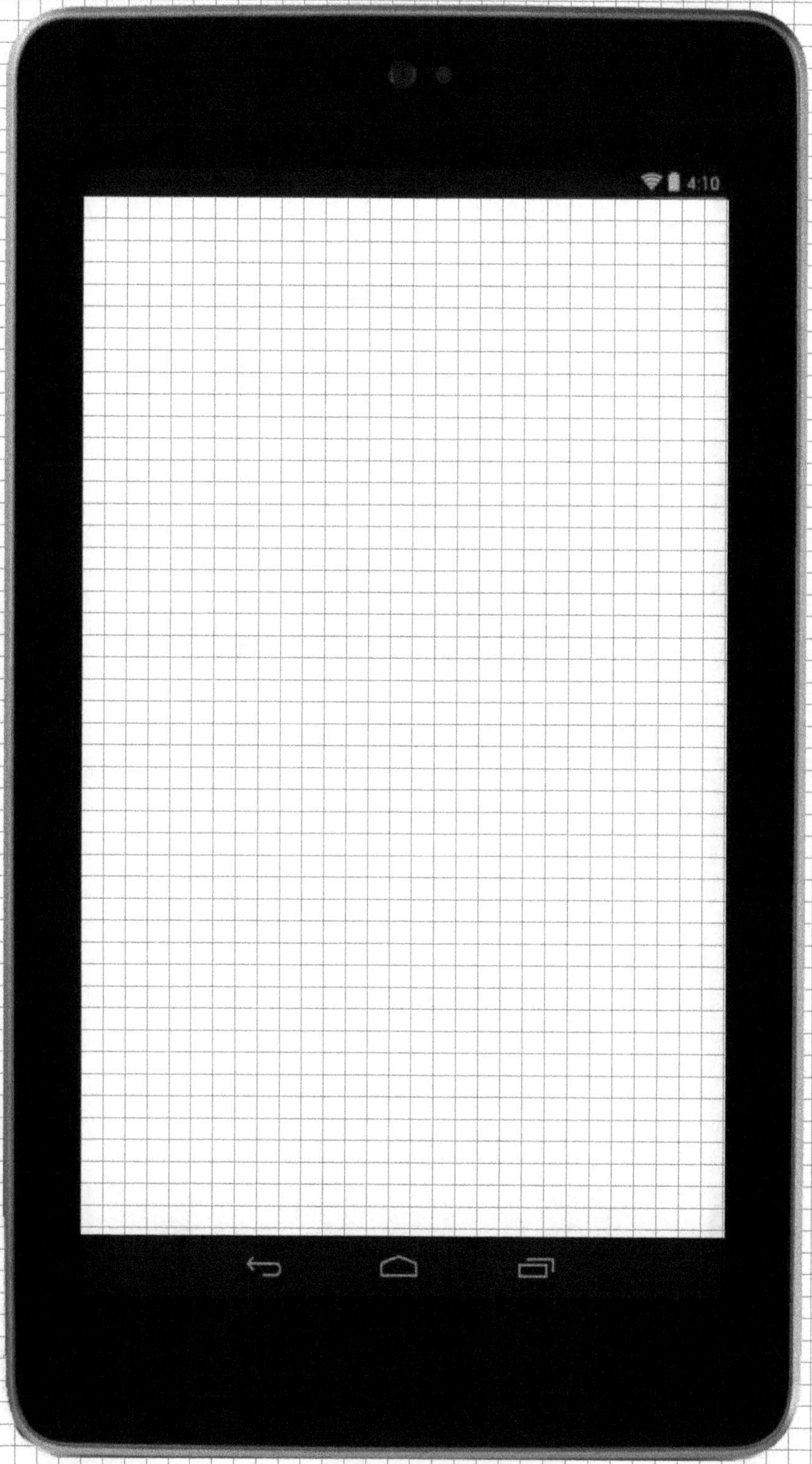

Application Name:

Screen Name:

Notes:

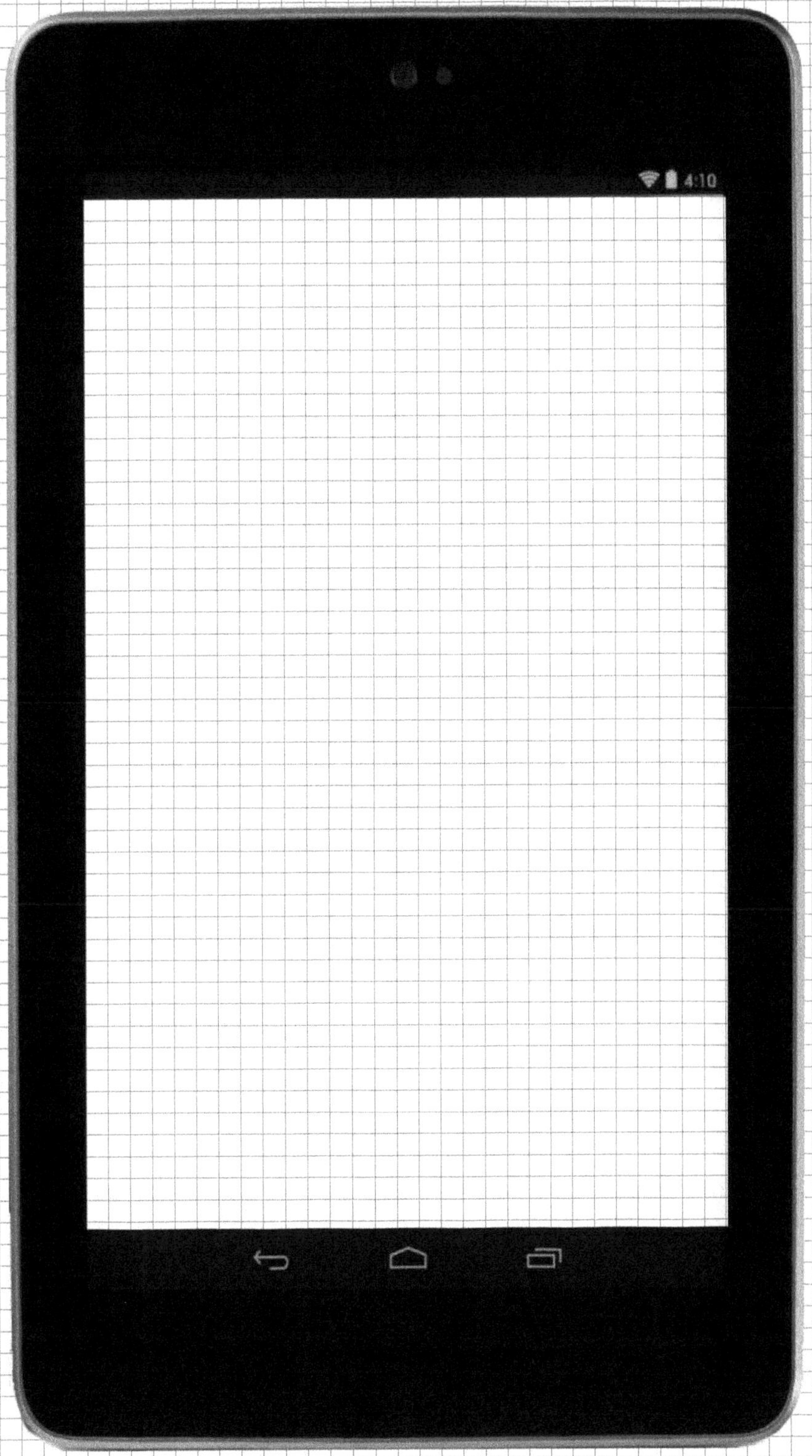

Application Name:

Screen Name:

Notes:

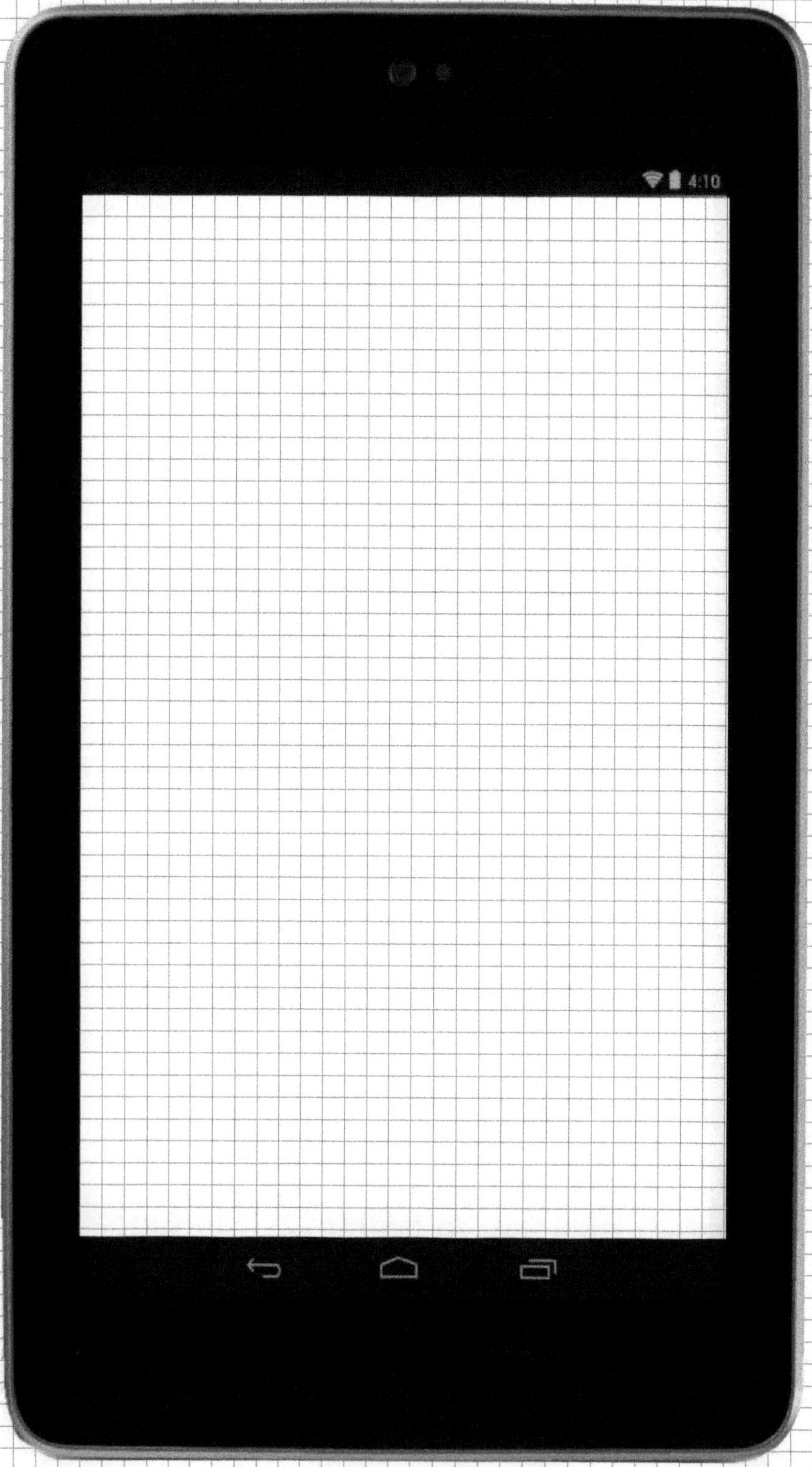

Application Name:

Screen Name:

Notes:

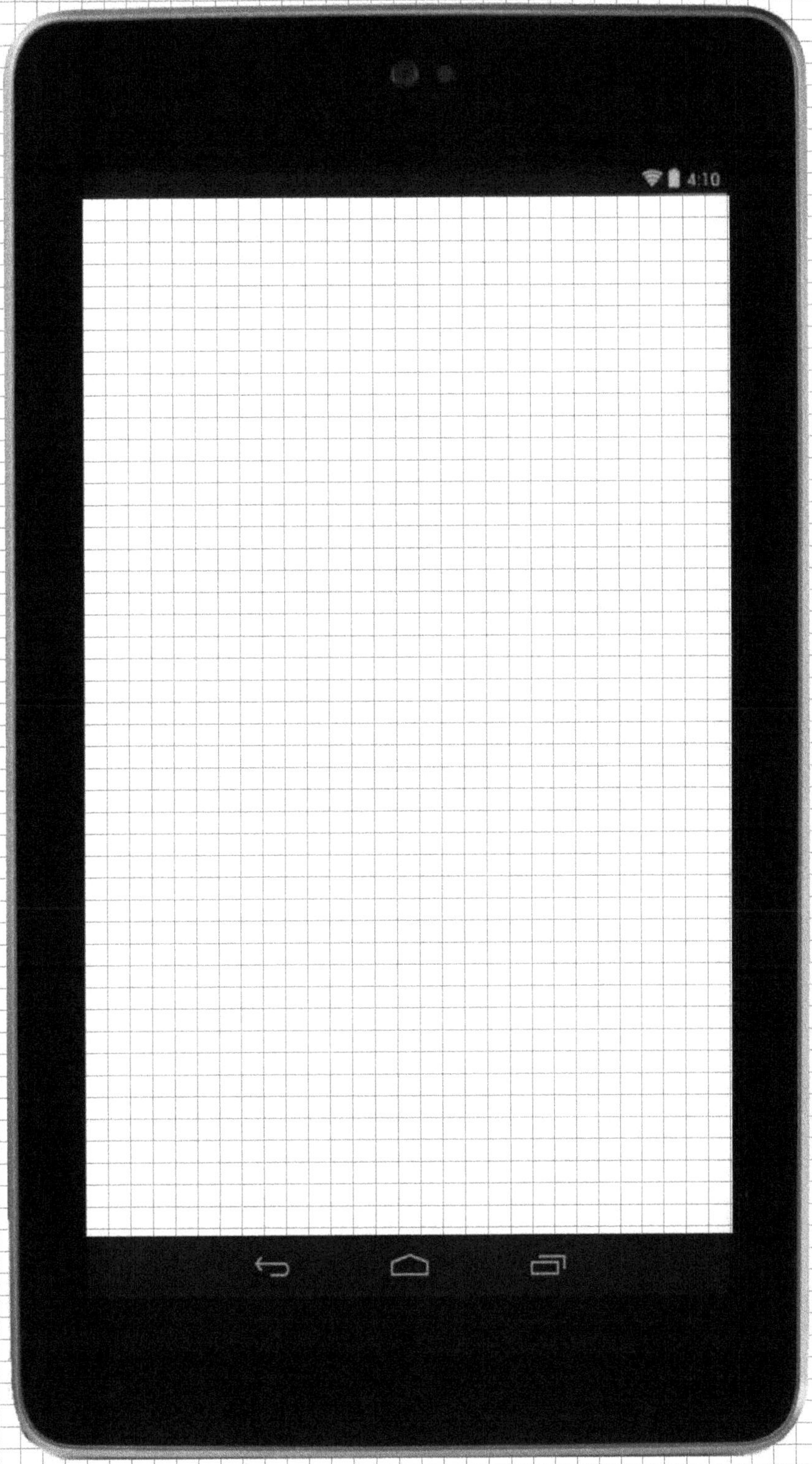

Application Name:

Screen Name:

Notes:

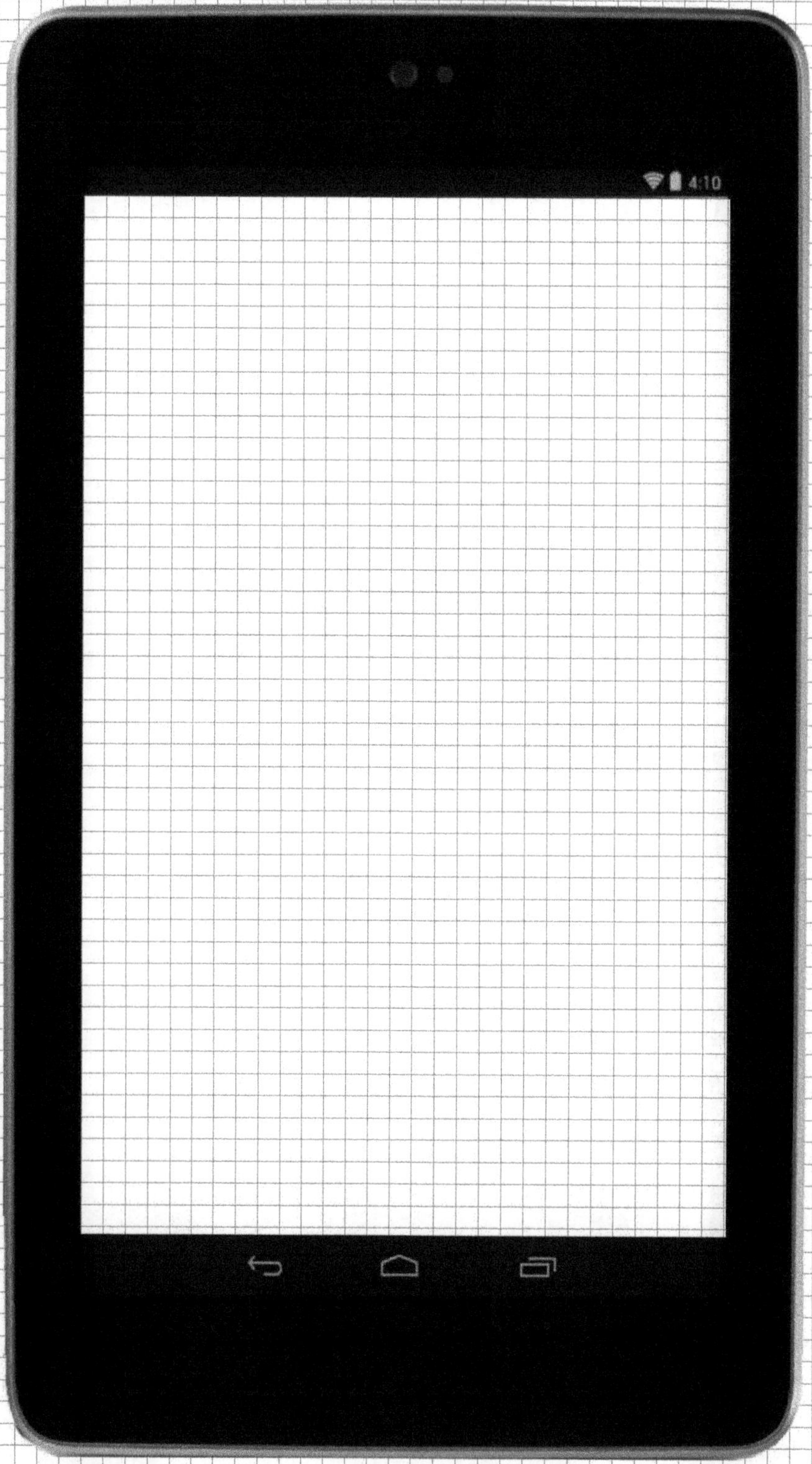

Application Name:

Screen Name:

Notes:

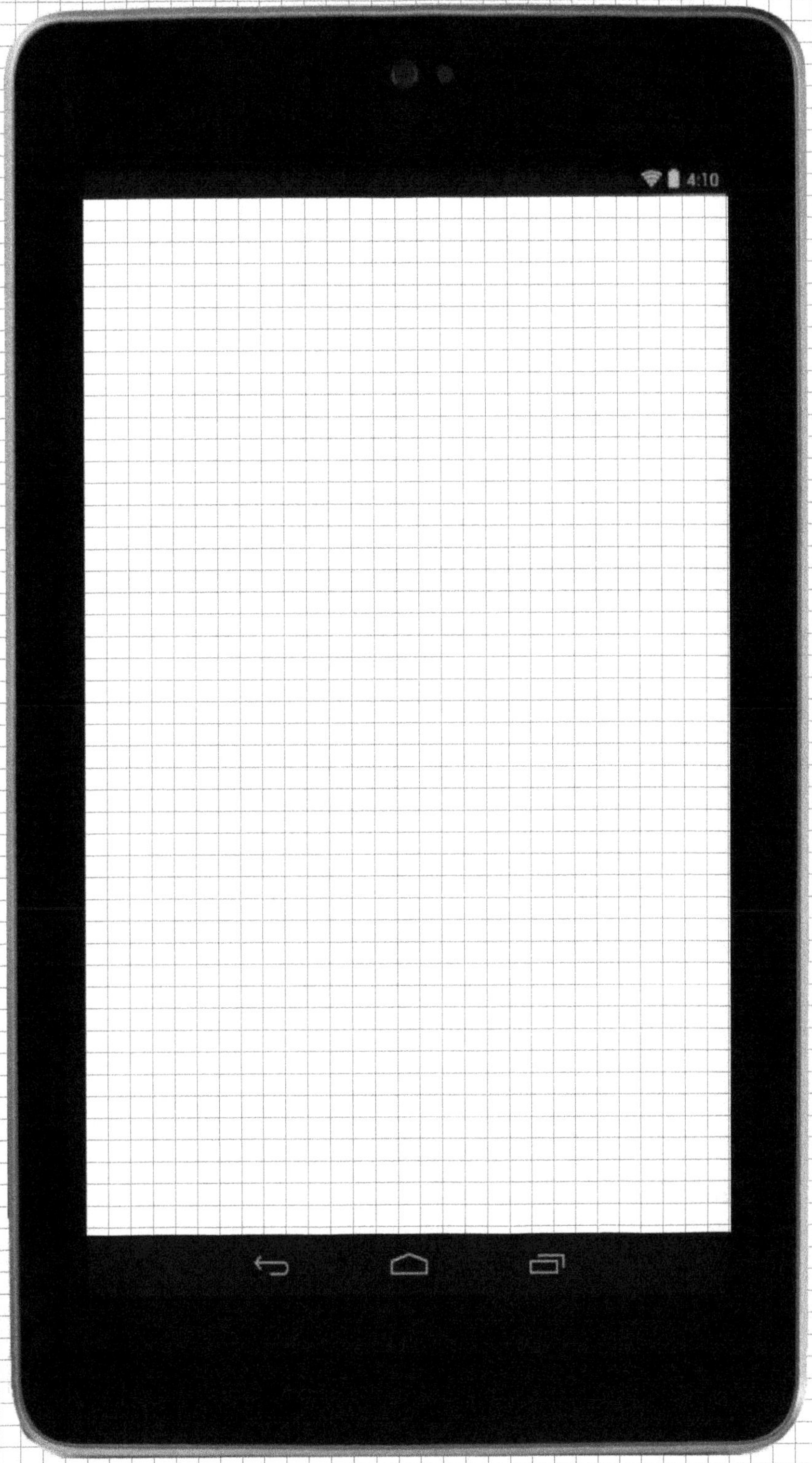

Application Name:

Screen Name:

Notes:

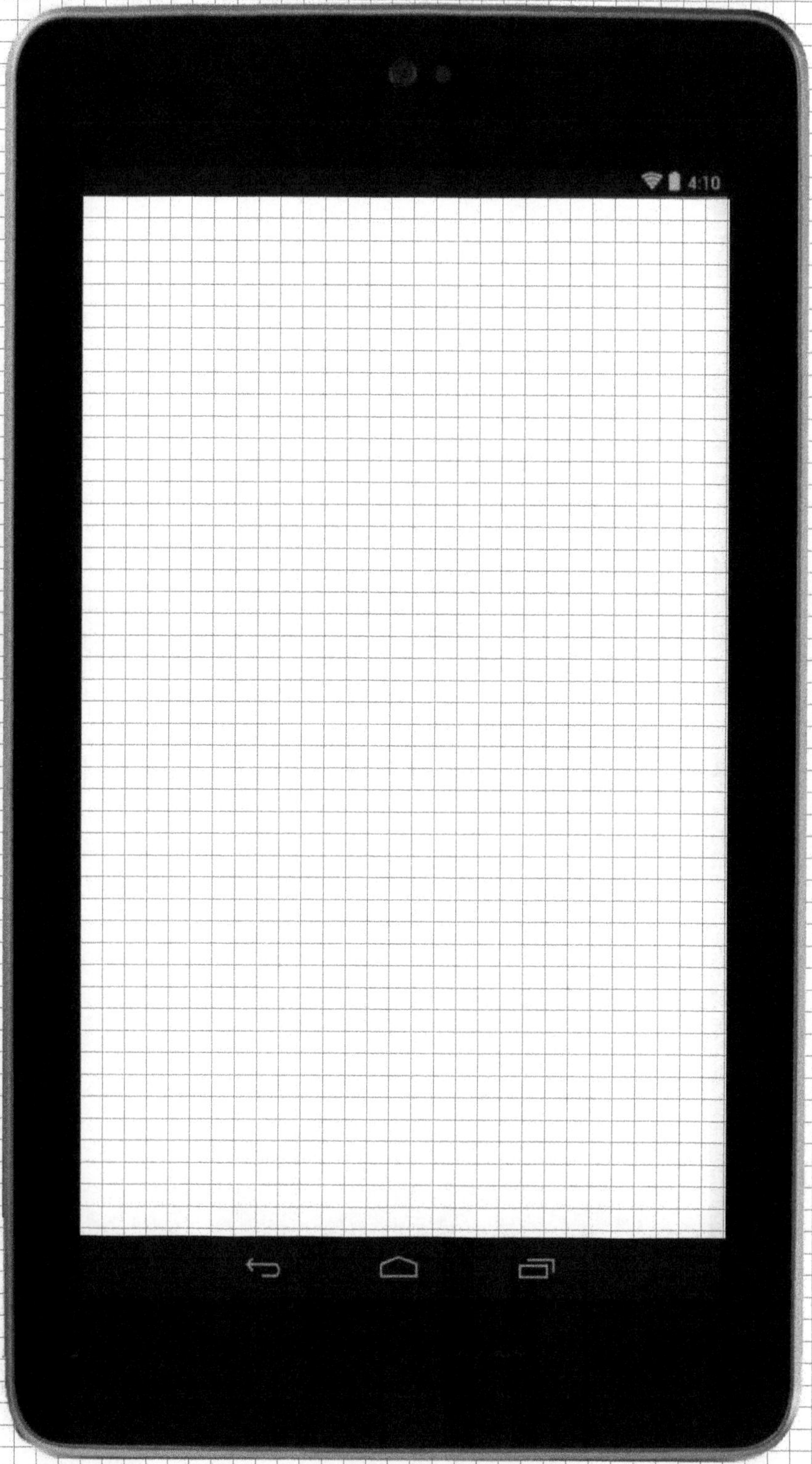

Application Name:

Screen Name:

Notes:

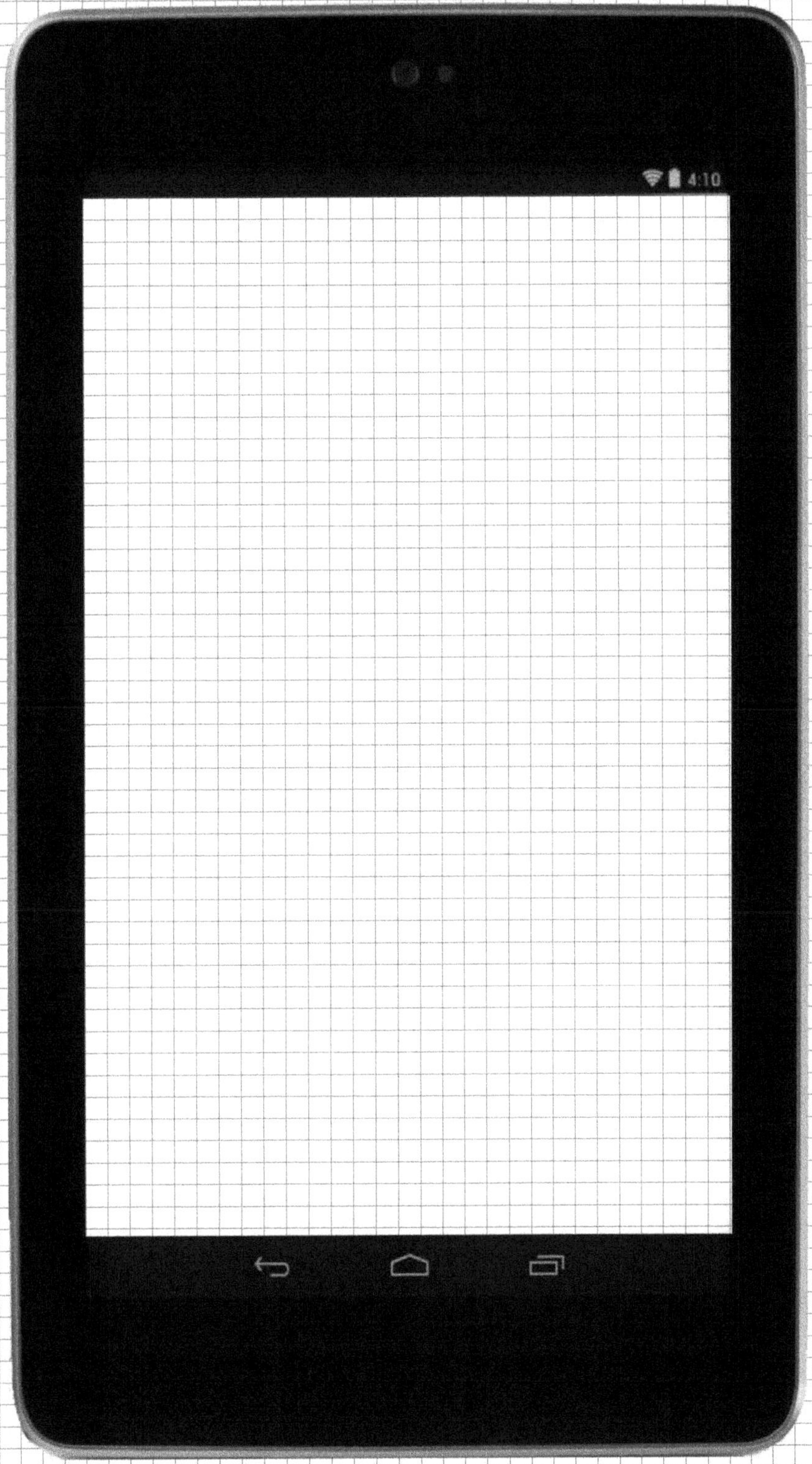

Application Name:

Screen Name:

Notes:

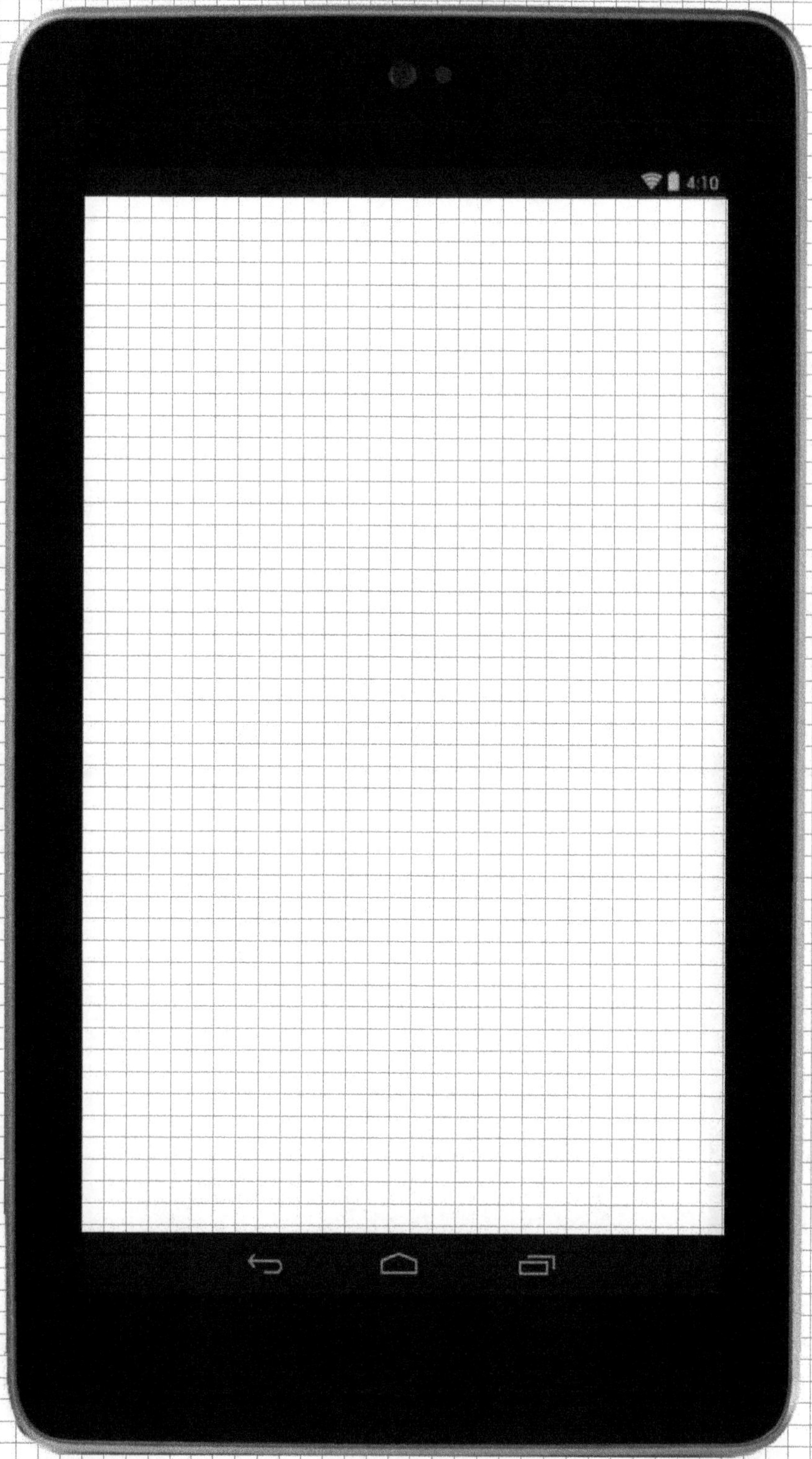

Application Name:

Screen Name:

Notes:

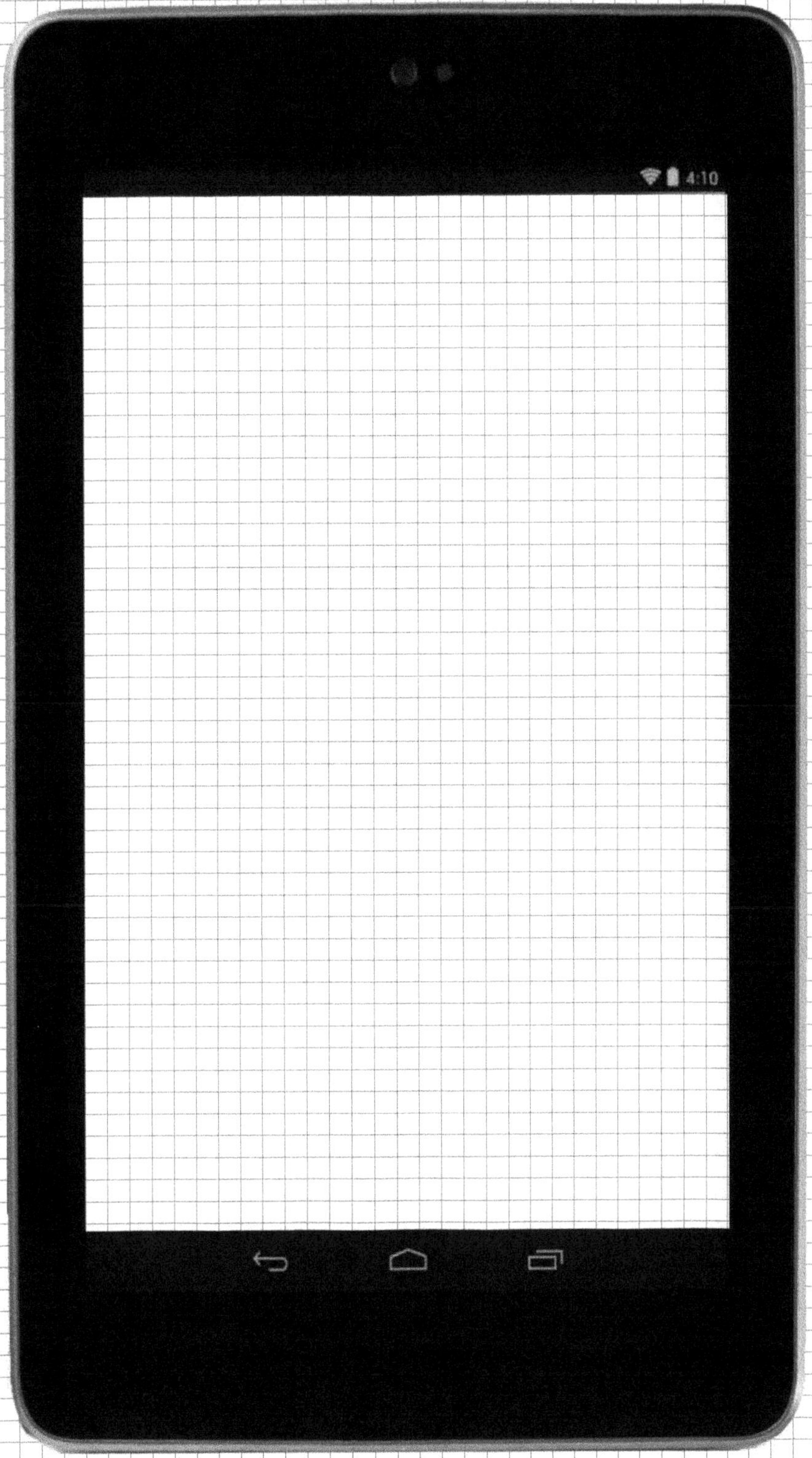

Application Name:

Screen Name:

Notes:

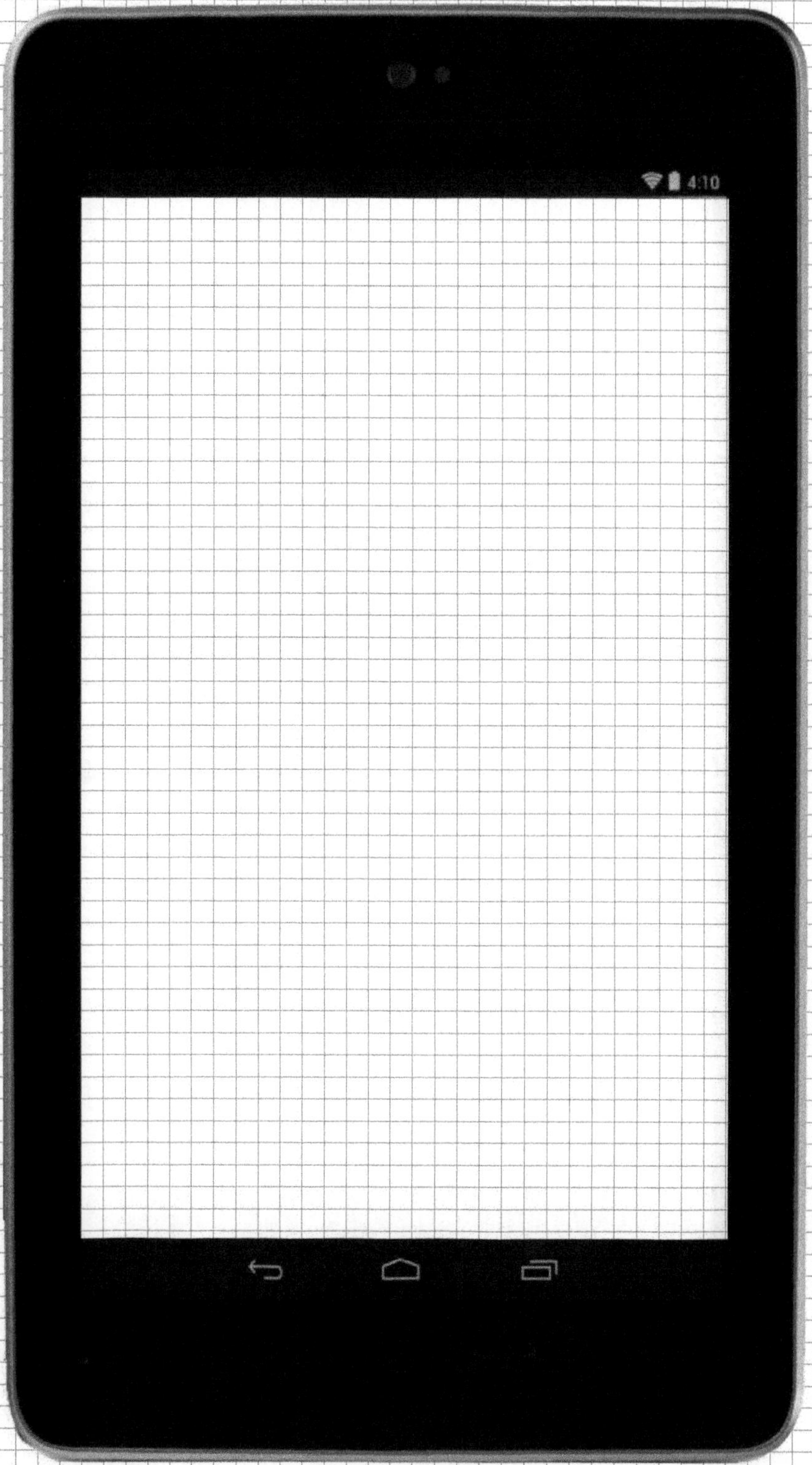

Application Name:

Screen Name:

Notes:

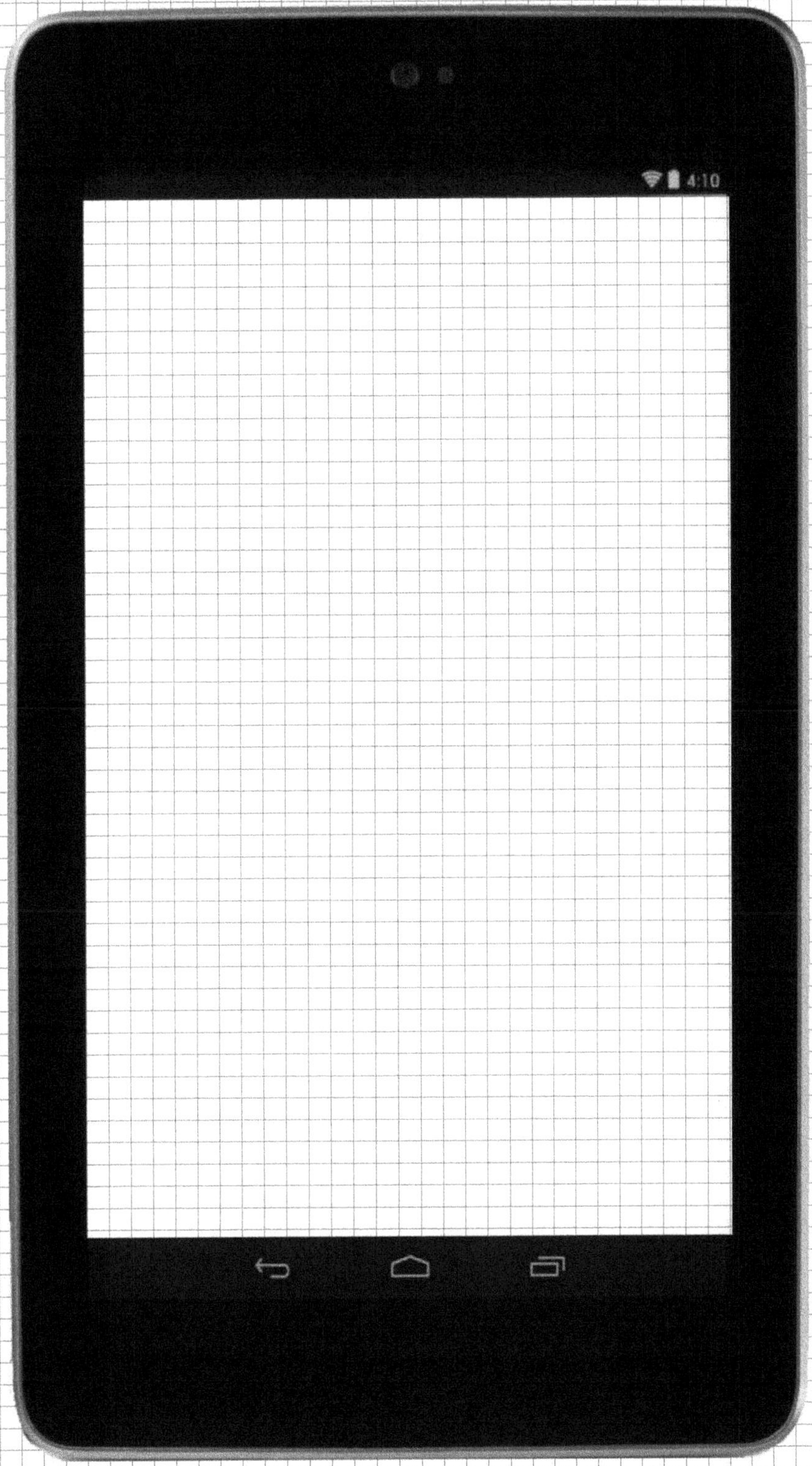

Application Name:

Screen Name:

Notes:

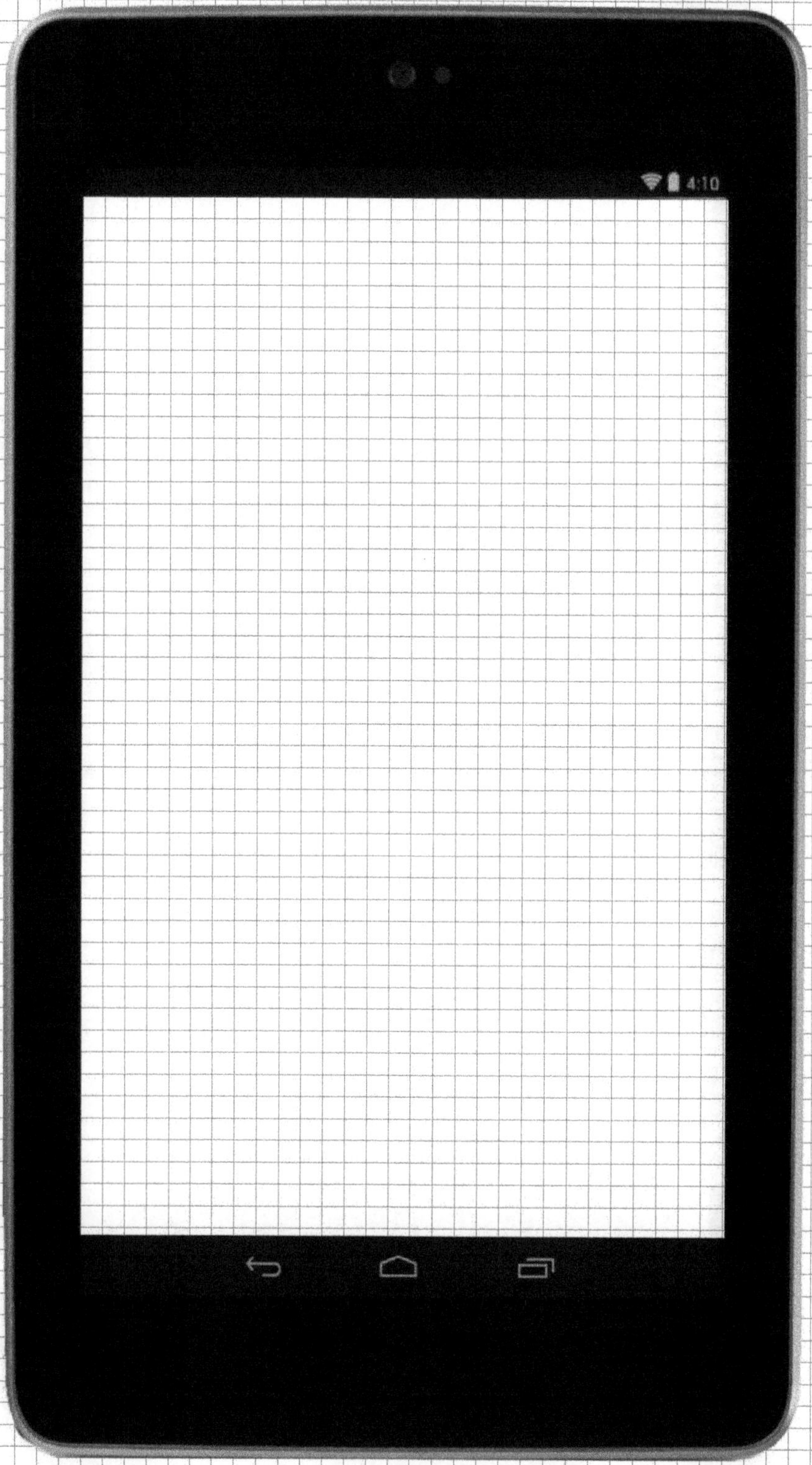

Application Name:

Screen Name:

Notes:

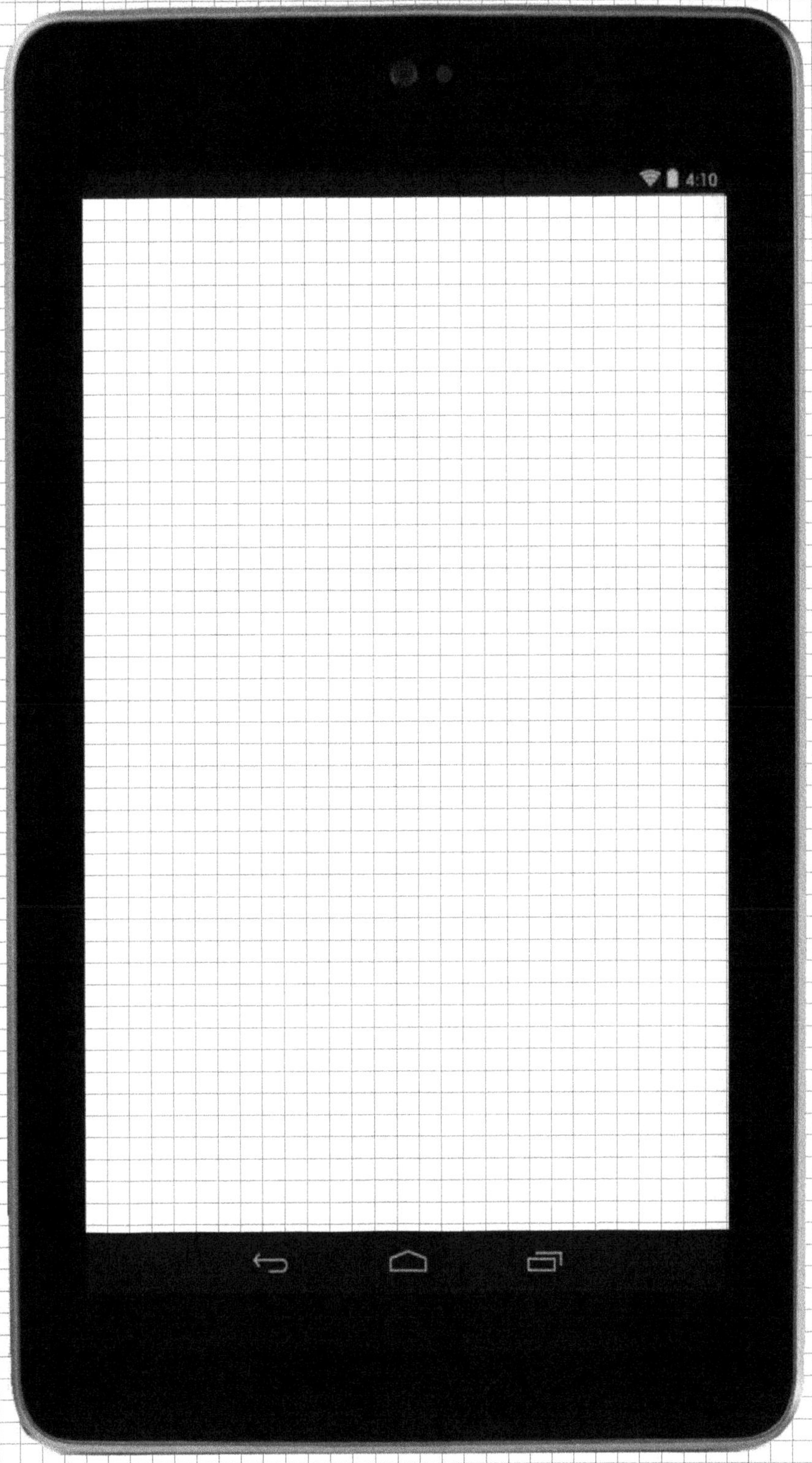

Application Name:

Screen Name:

Notes:

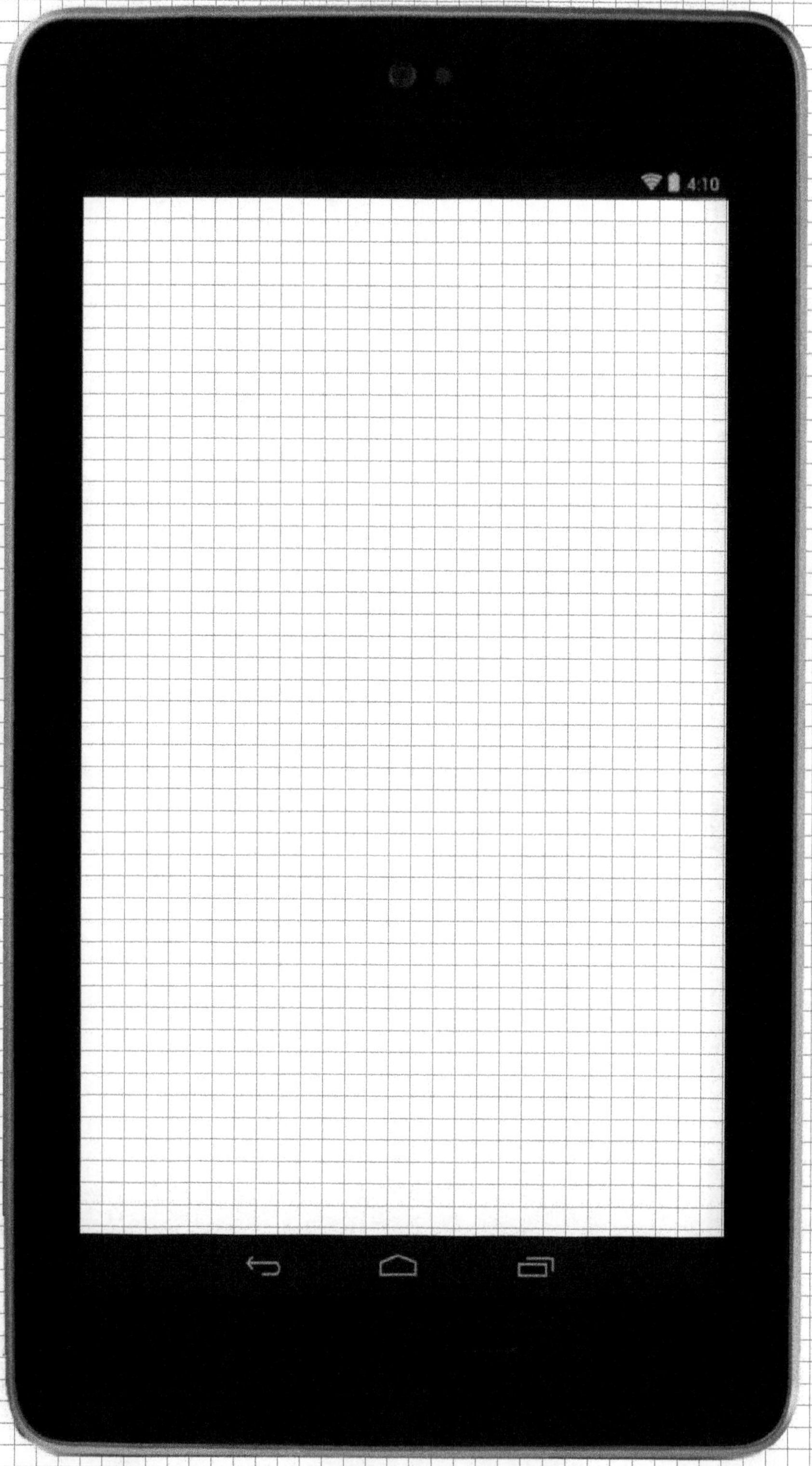

Application Name:

Screen Name:

Notes:

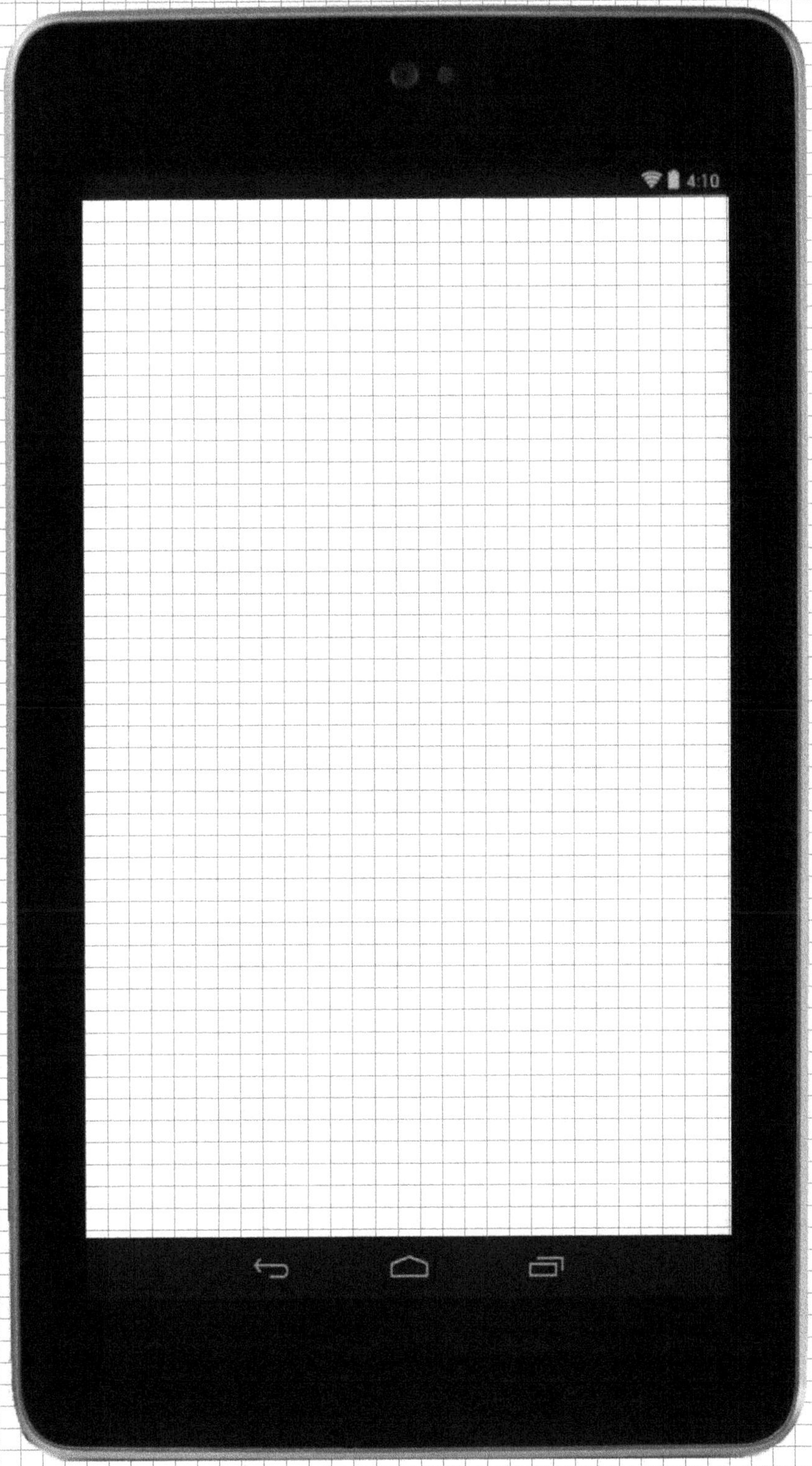

Application Name:

Screen Name:

Notes:

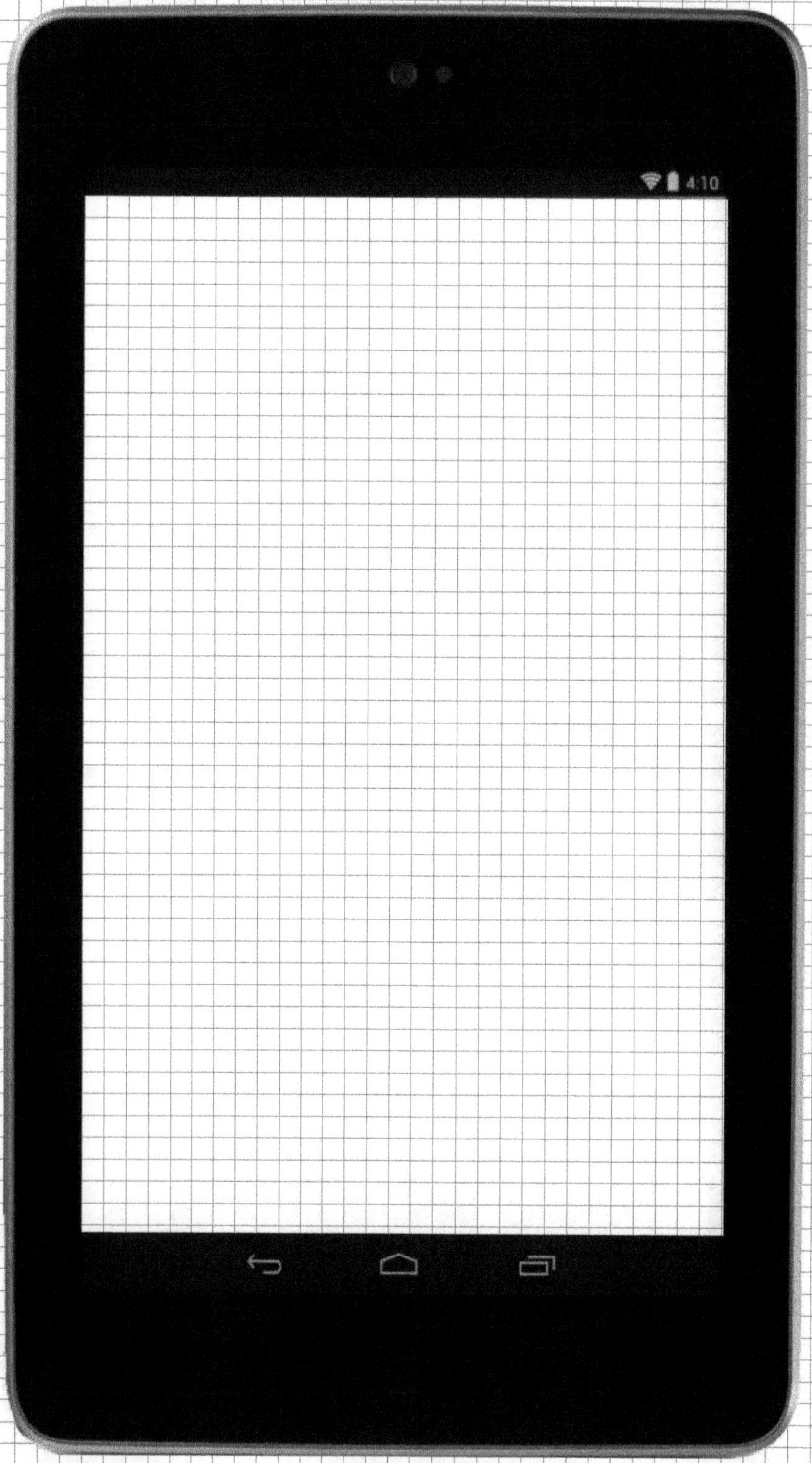

Application Name:

Screen Name:

Notes:

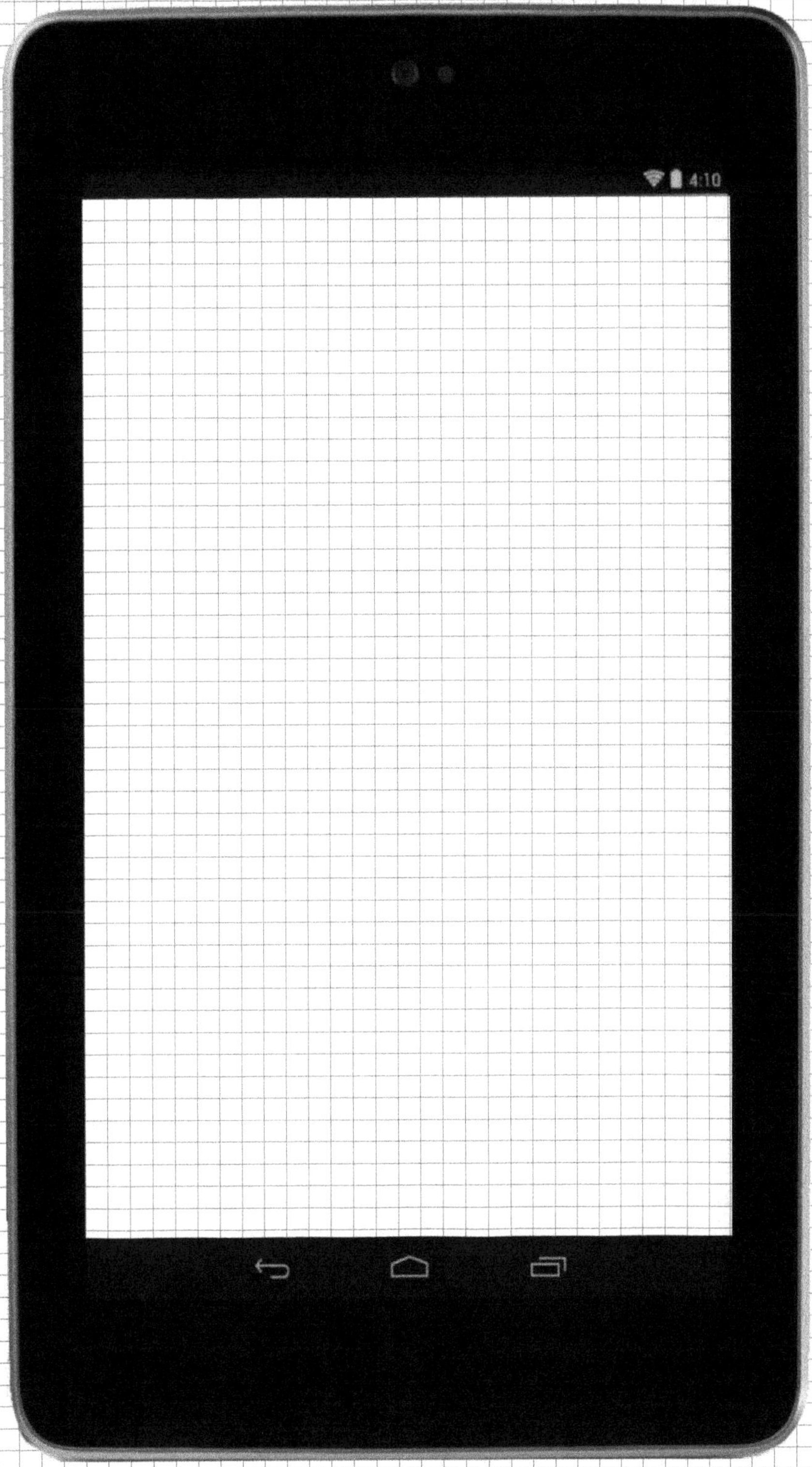

Application Name:

Screen Name:

Notes:

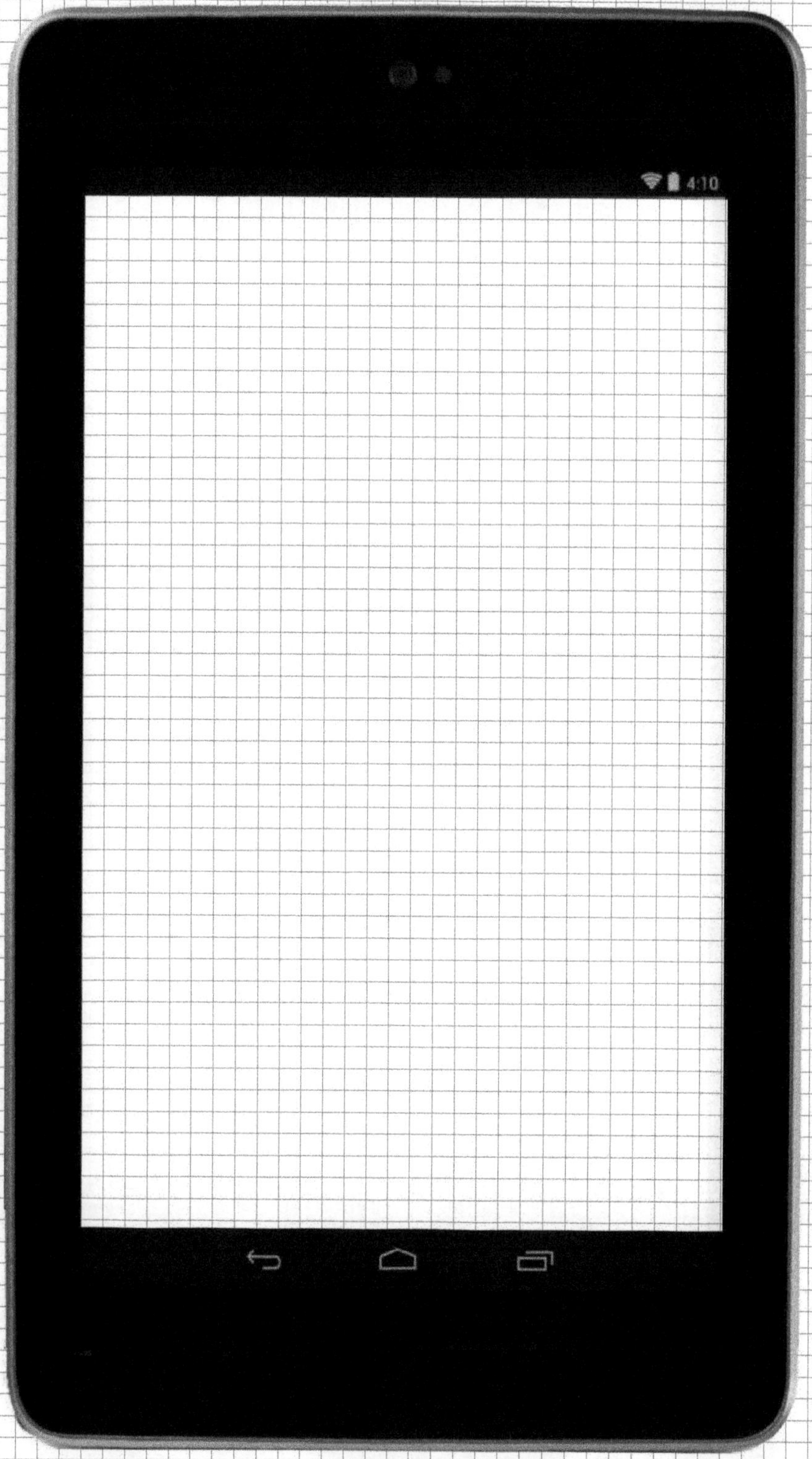

Application Name:

Screen Name:

Notes:

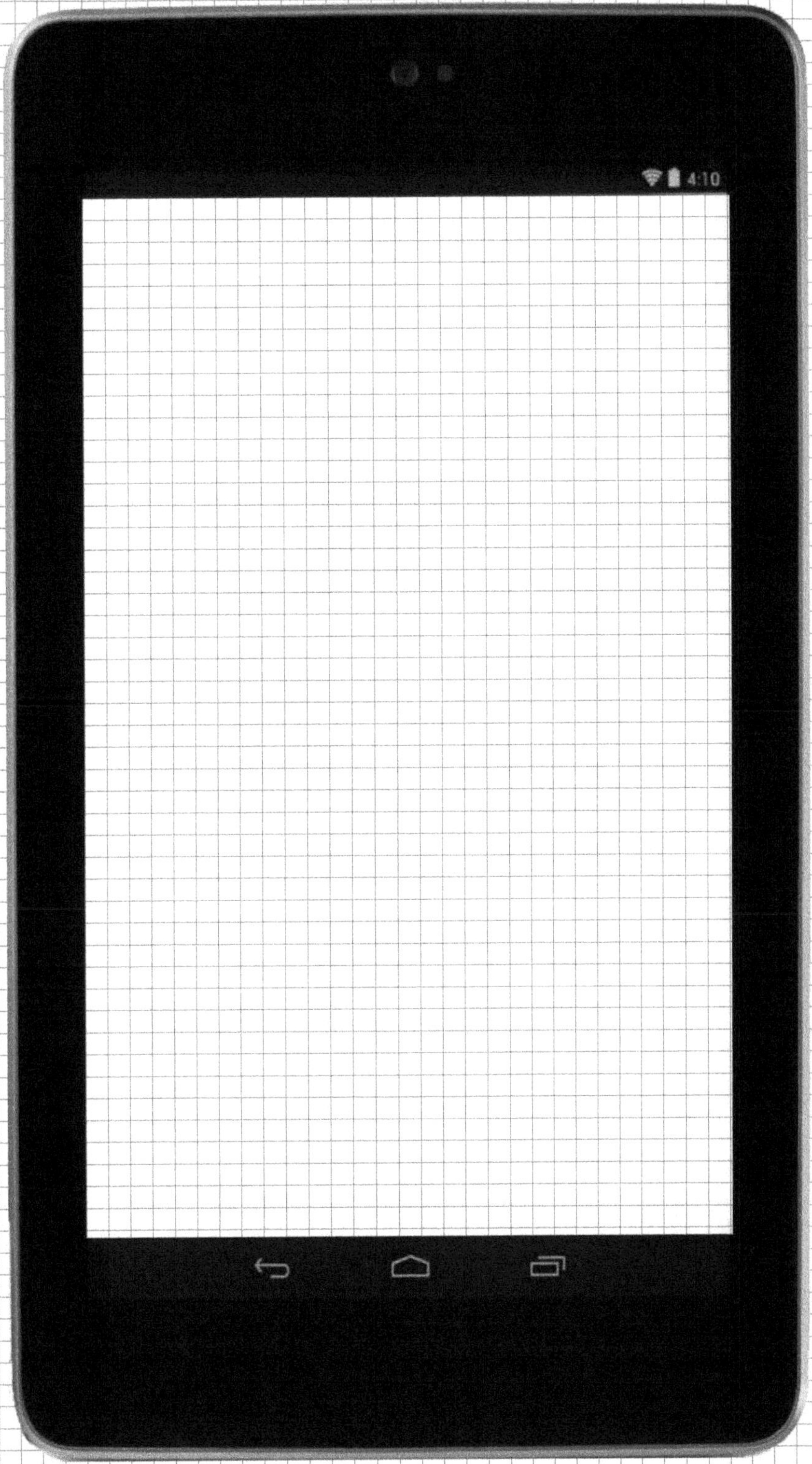

Application Name:

Screen Name:

Notes:

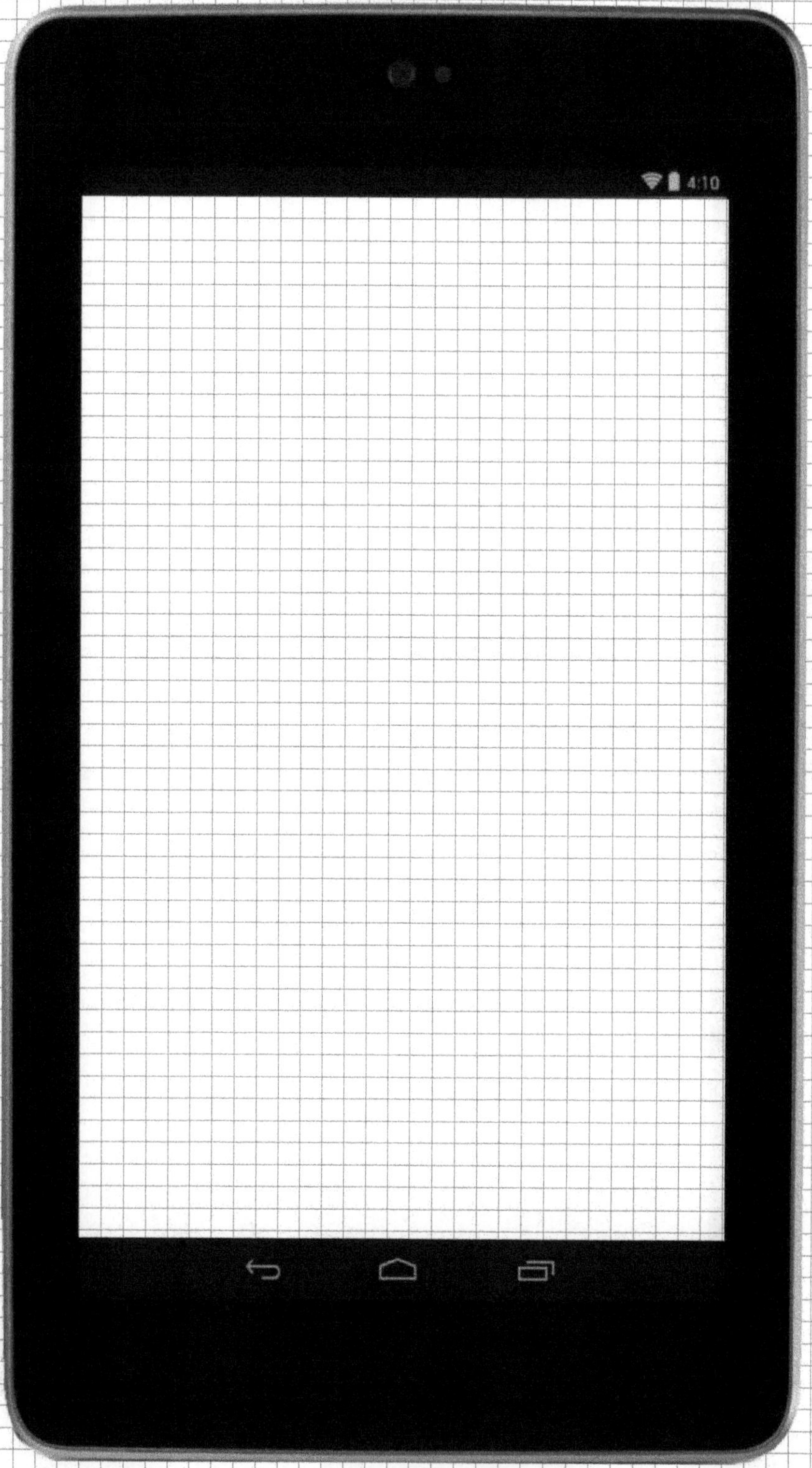

Application Name:

Screen Name:

Notes:

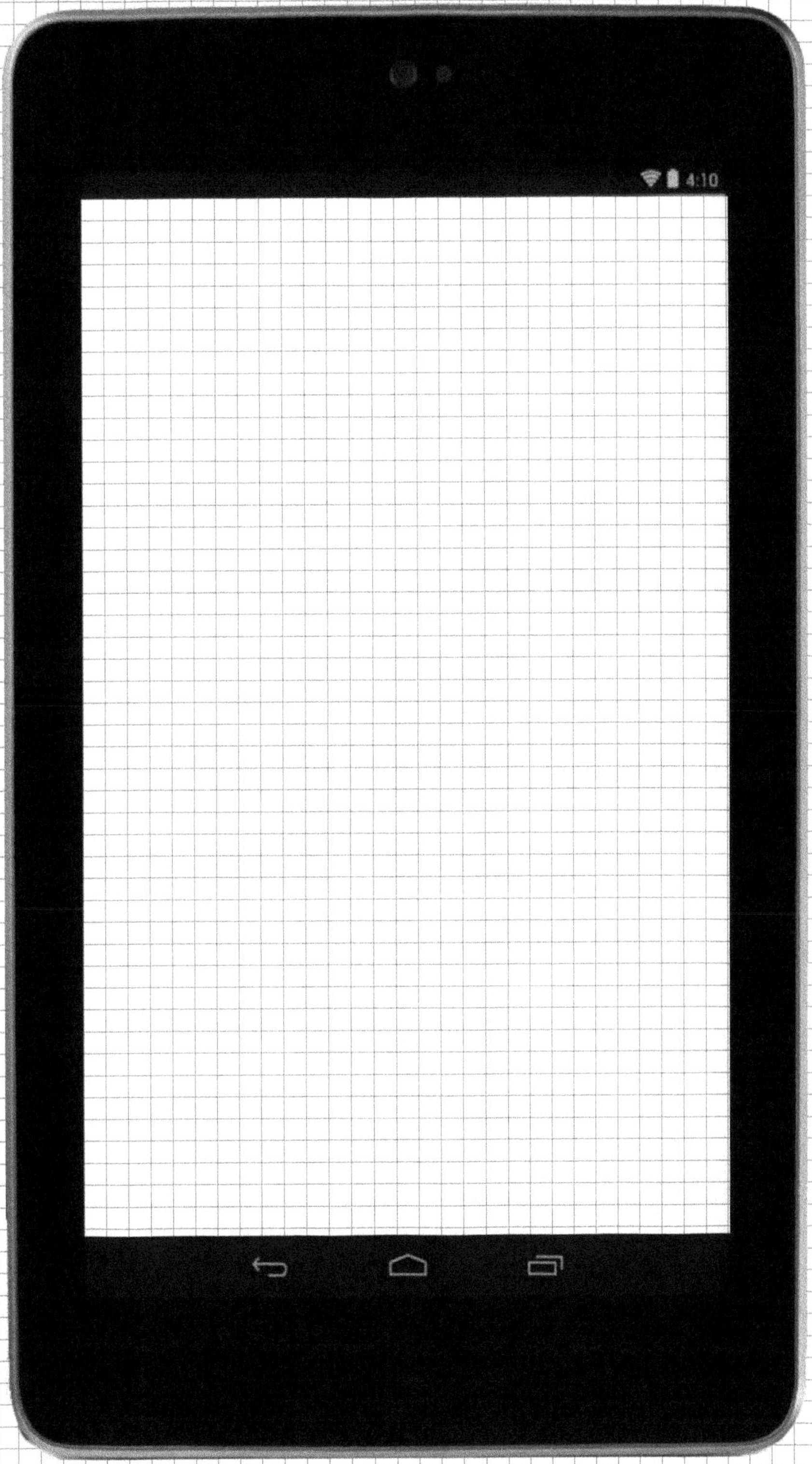

Application Name:

Screen Name:

Notes:

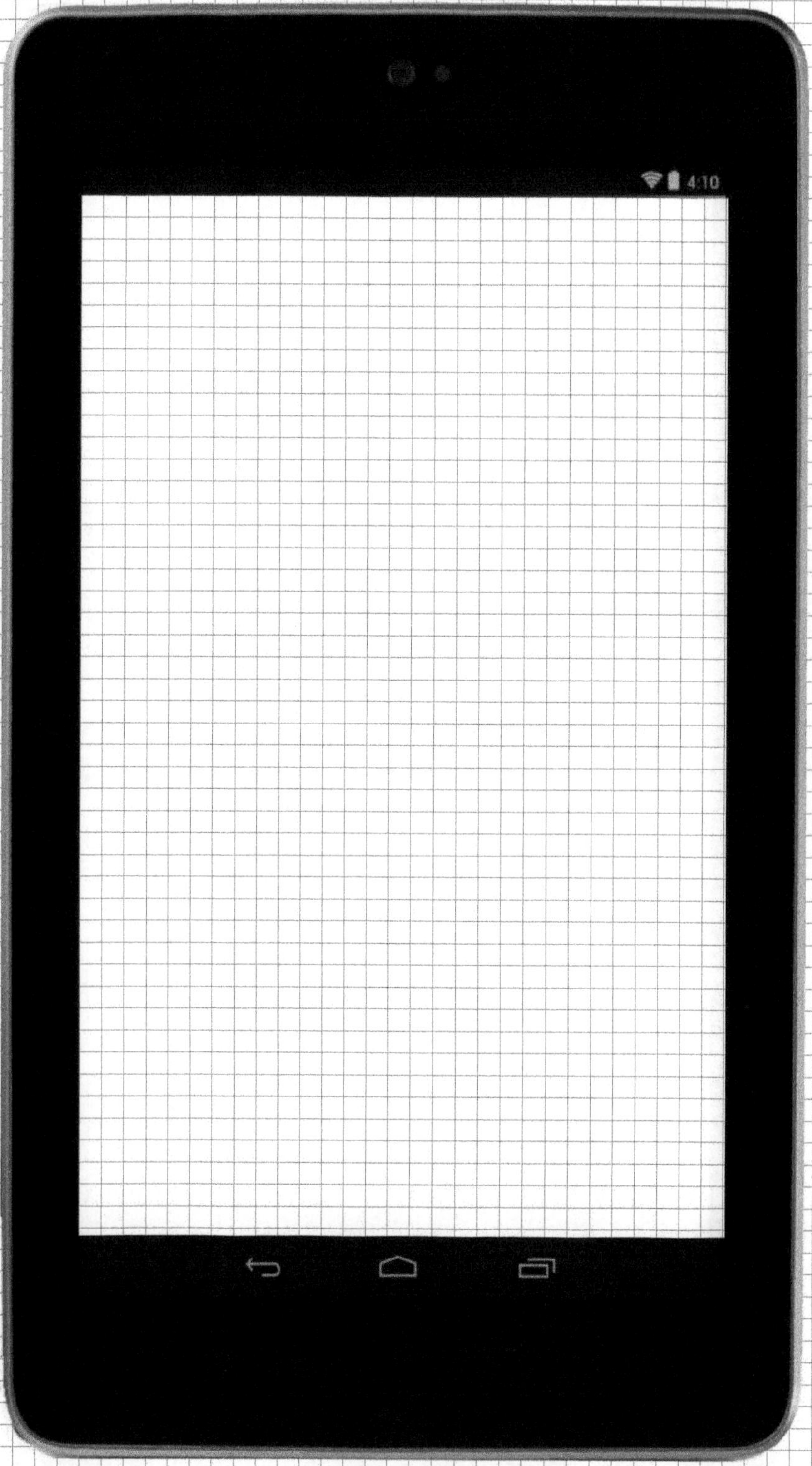

Application Name:

Screen Name:

Notes:

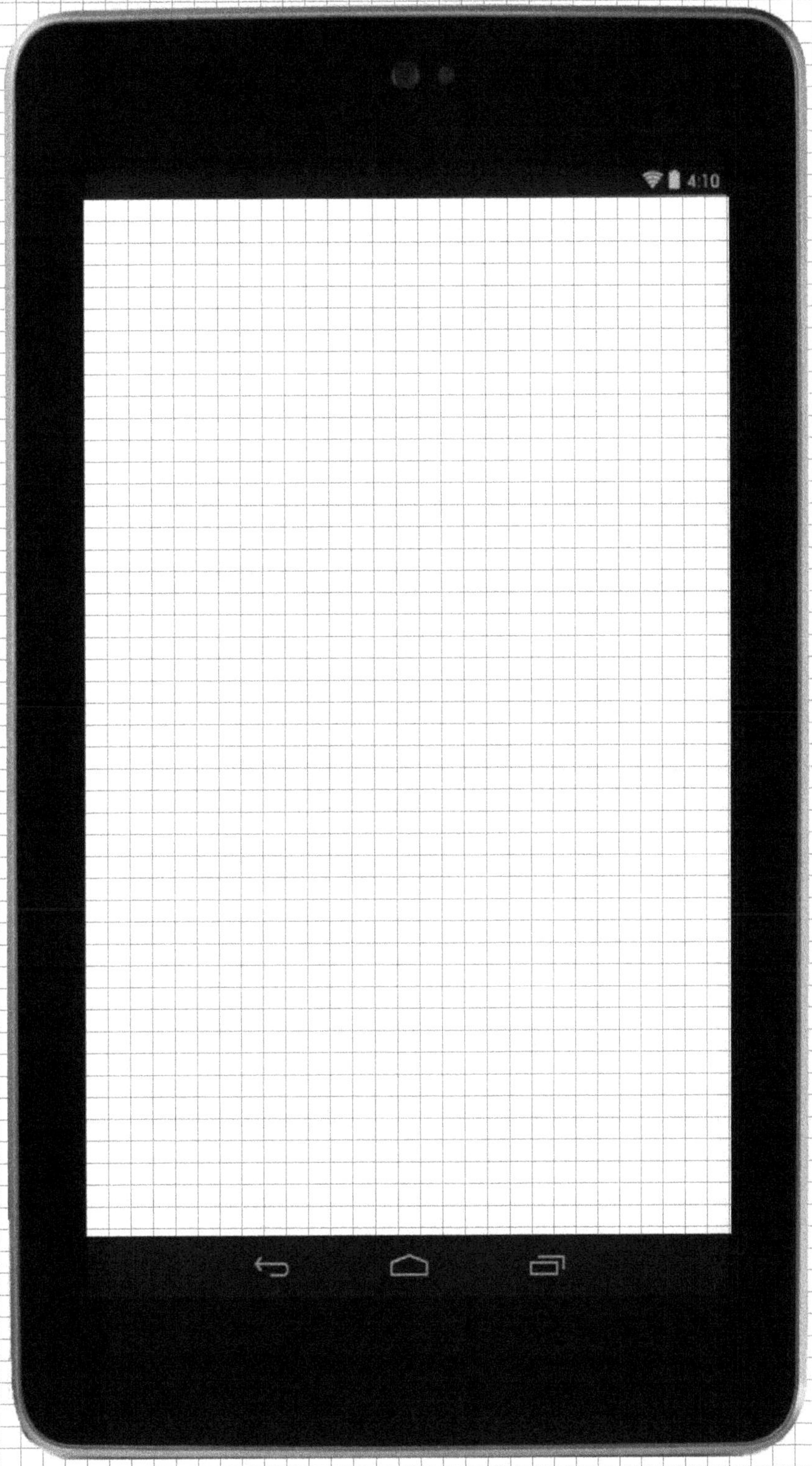

Application Name:

Screen Name:

Notes:

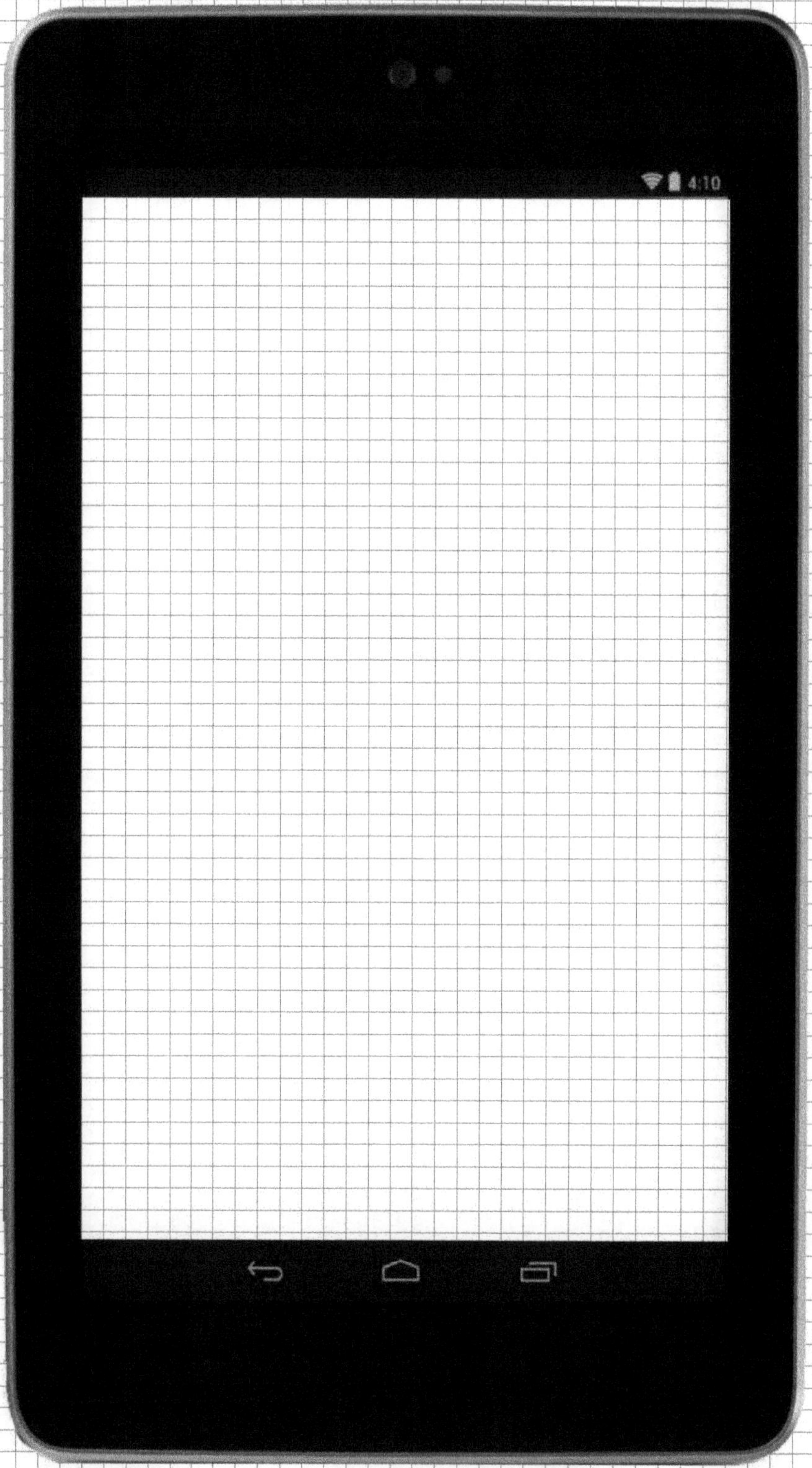

Application Name:

Screen Name:

Notes:

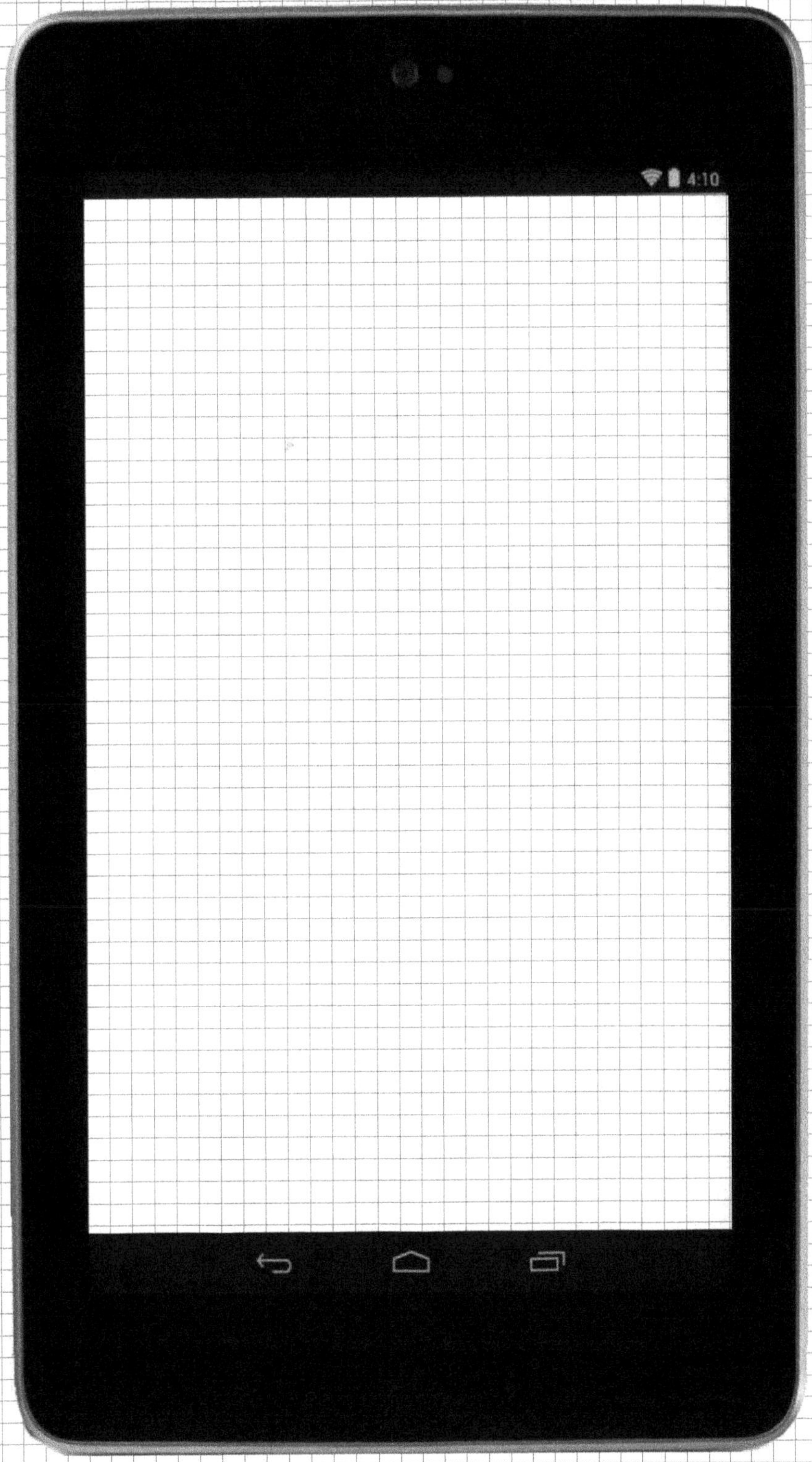

Application Name:

Screen Name:

Notes:

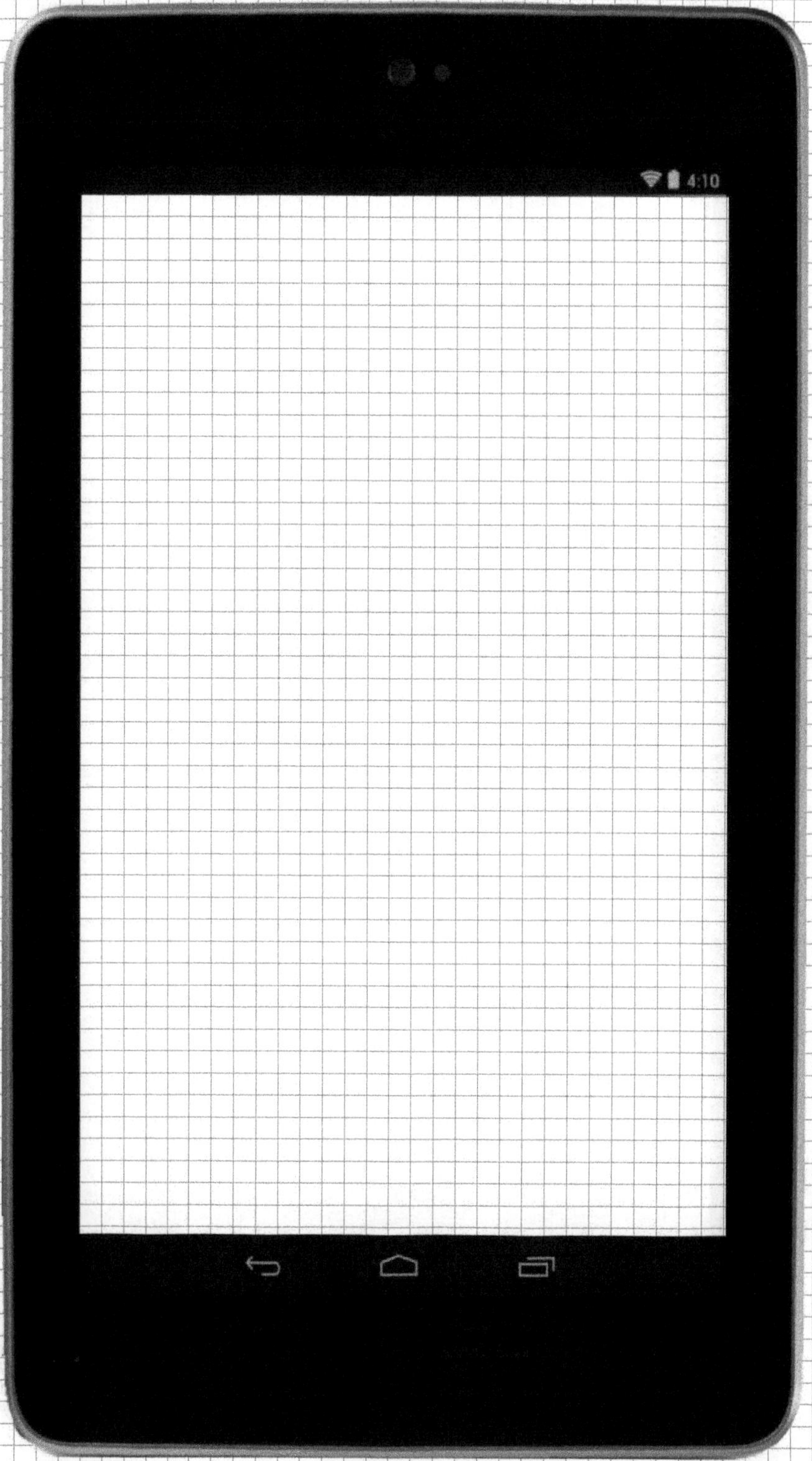

Application Name:

Screen Name:

Notes:

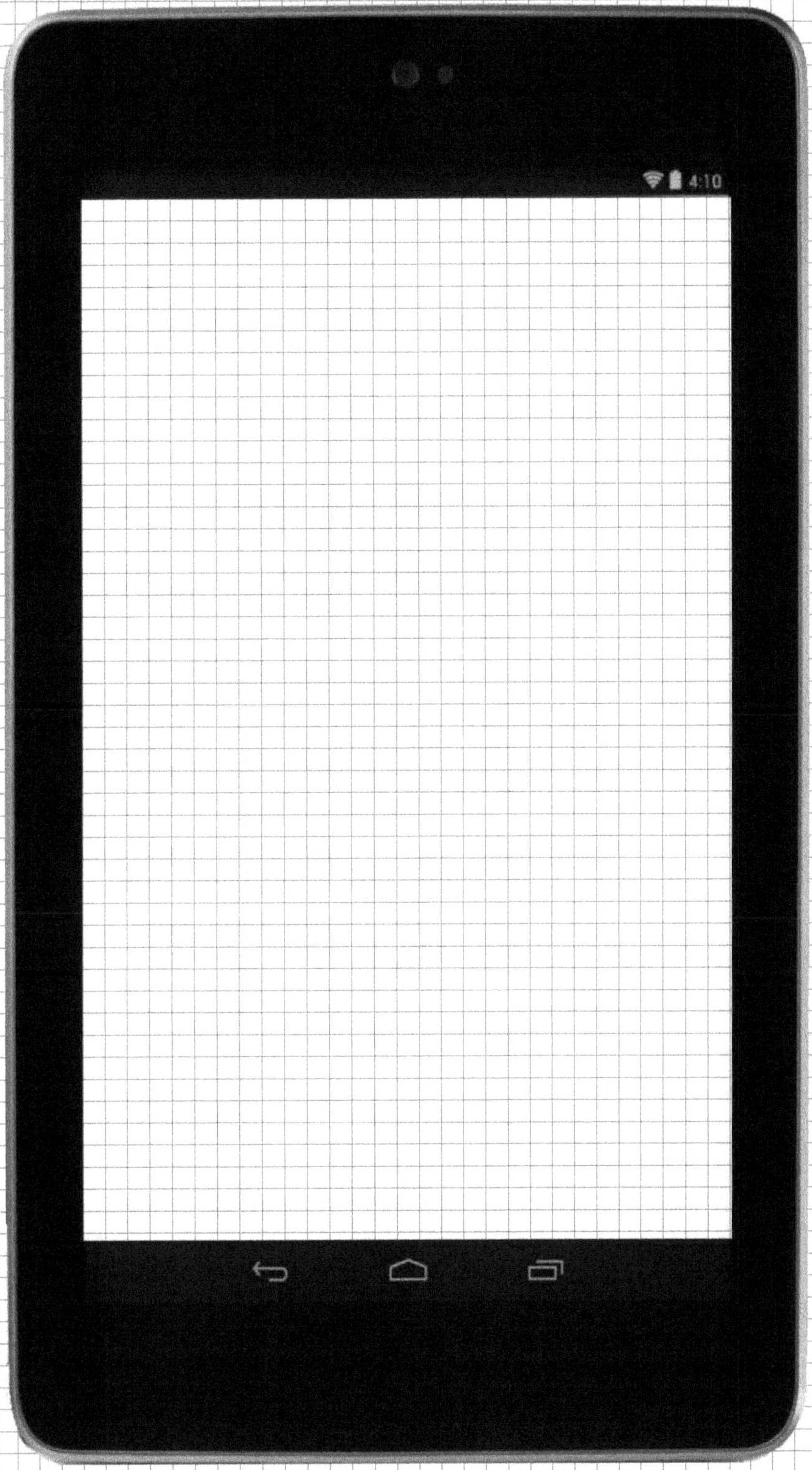

Application Name:

Screen Name:

Notes:

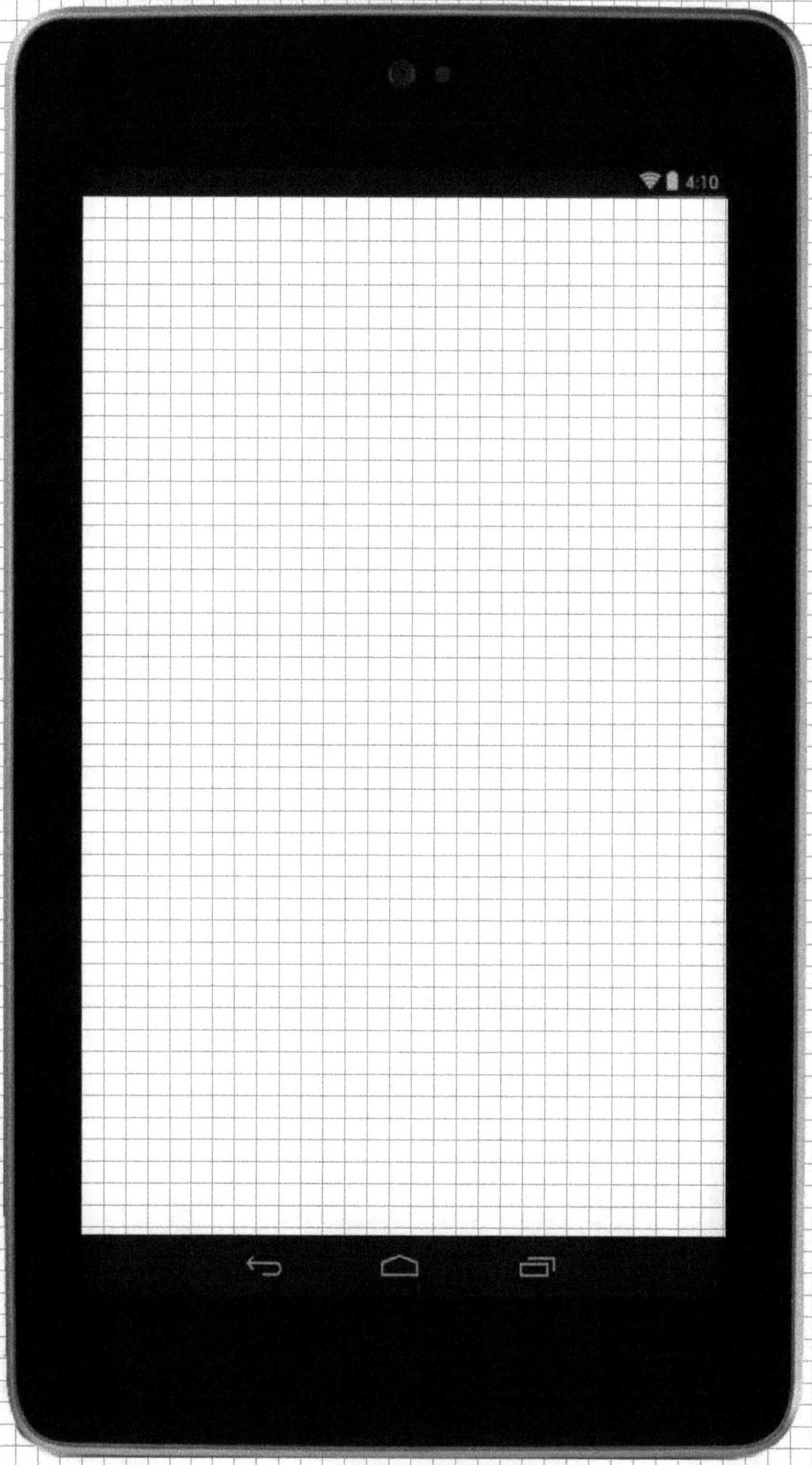

Application Name:

Screen Name:

Notes:

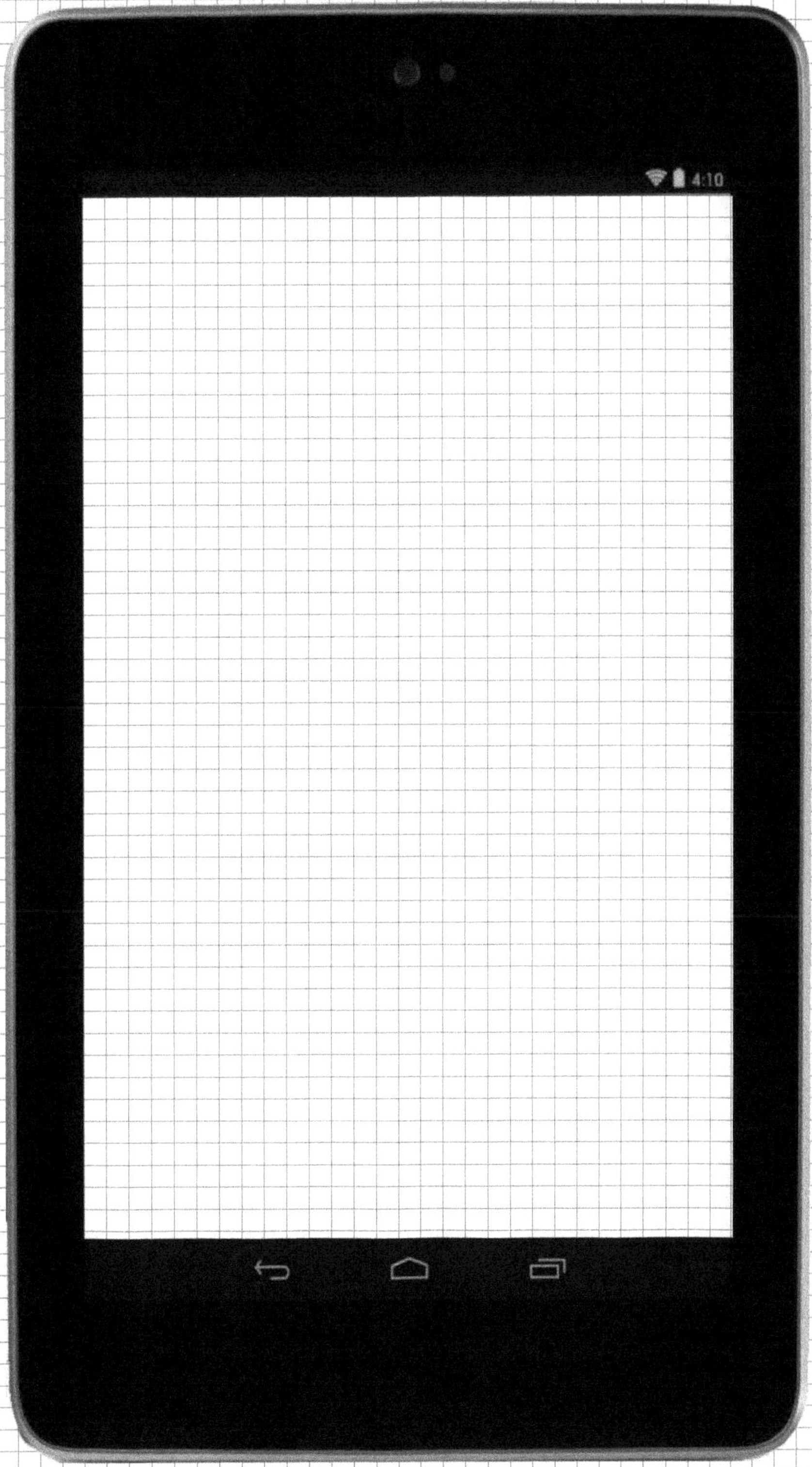

Application Name:

Screen Name:

Notes:

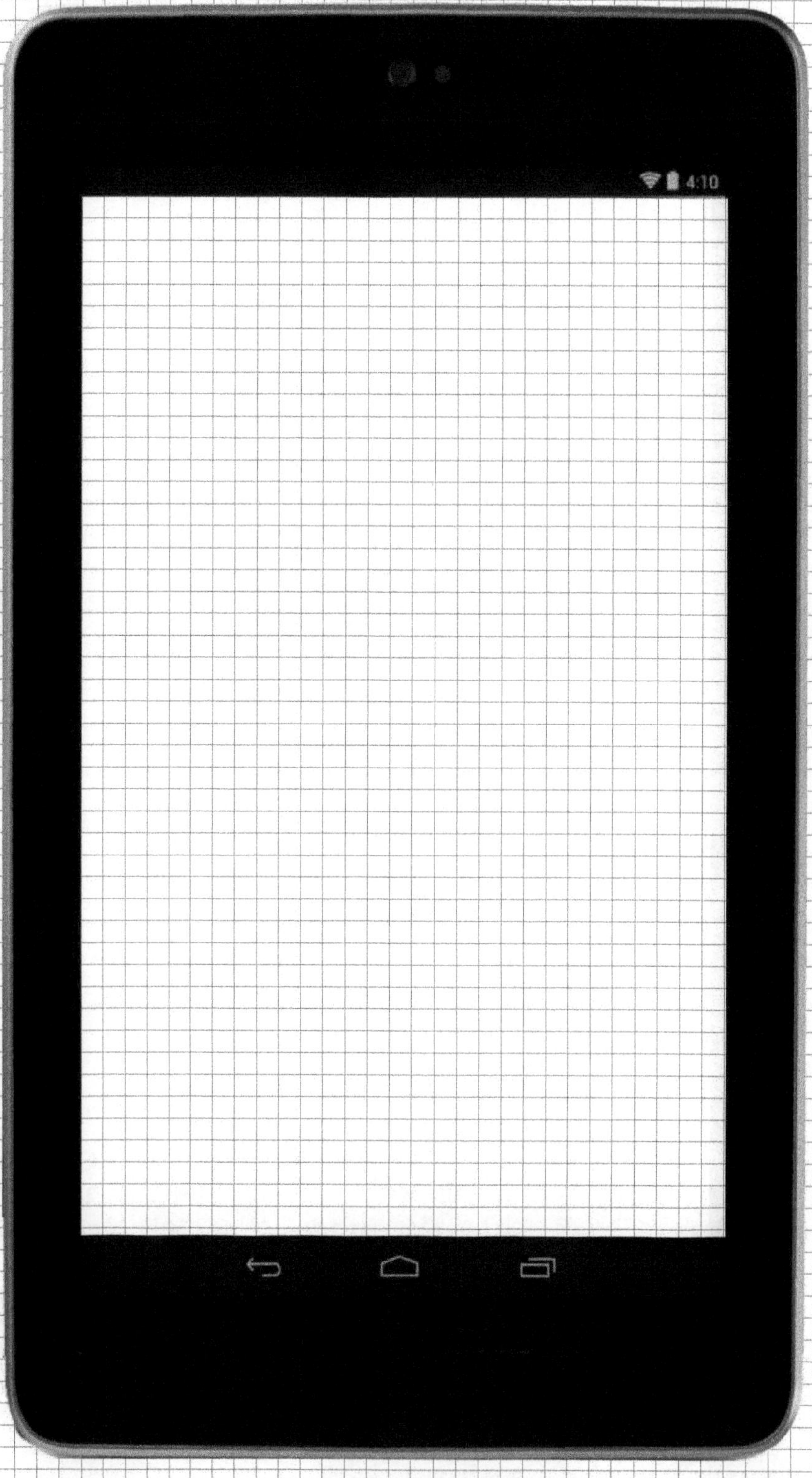

Application Name:

Screen Name:

Notes:

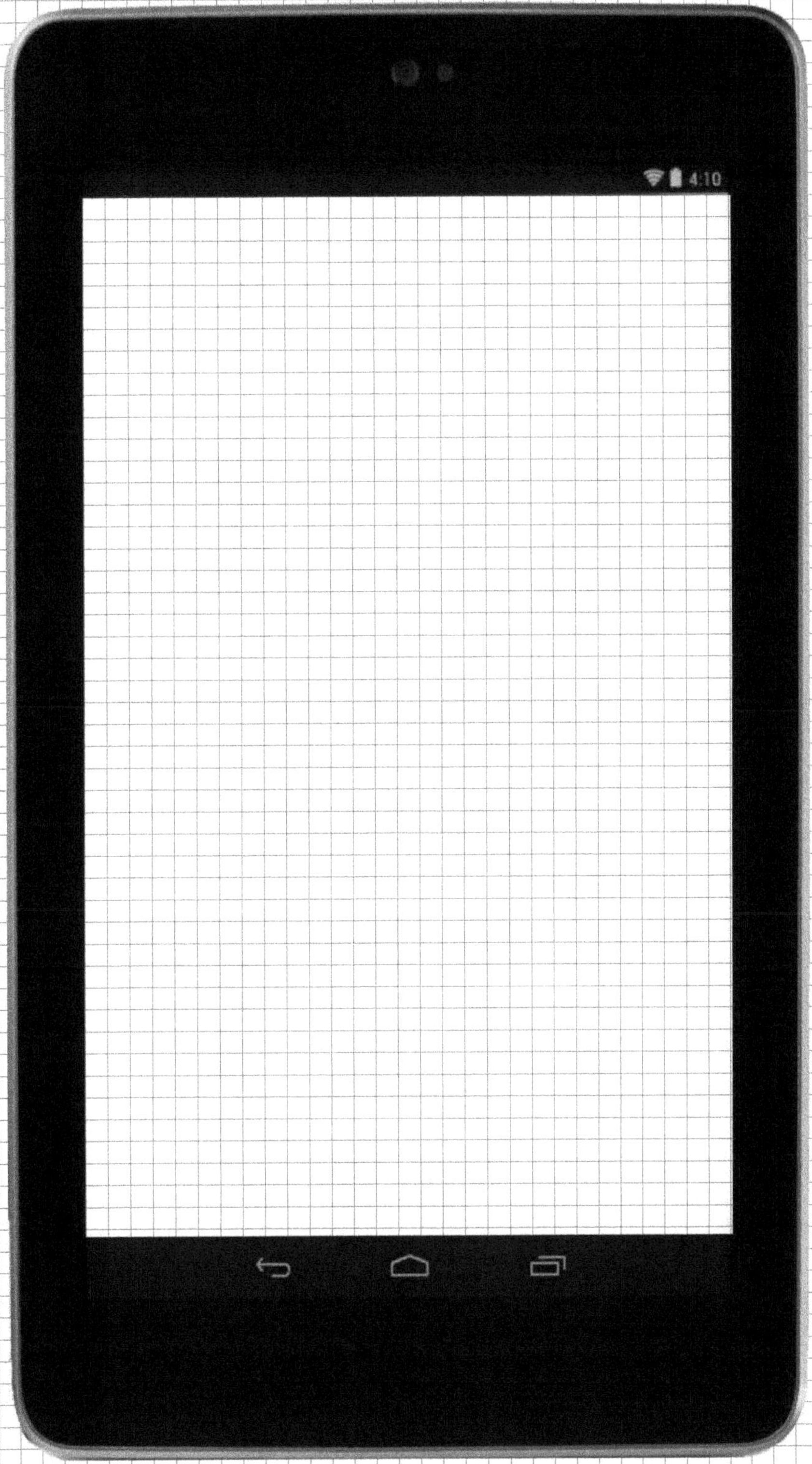

Application Name:

Screen Name:

Notes:

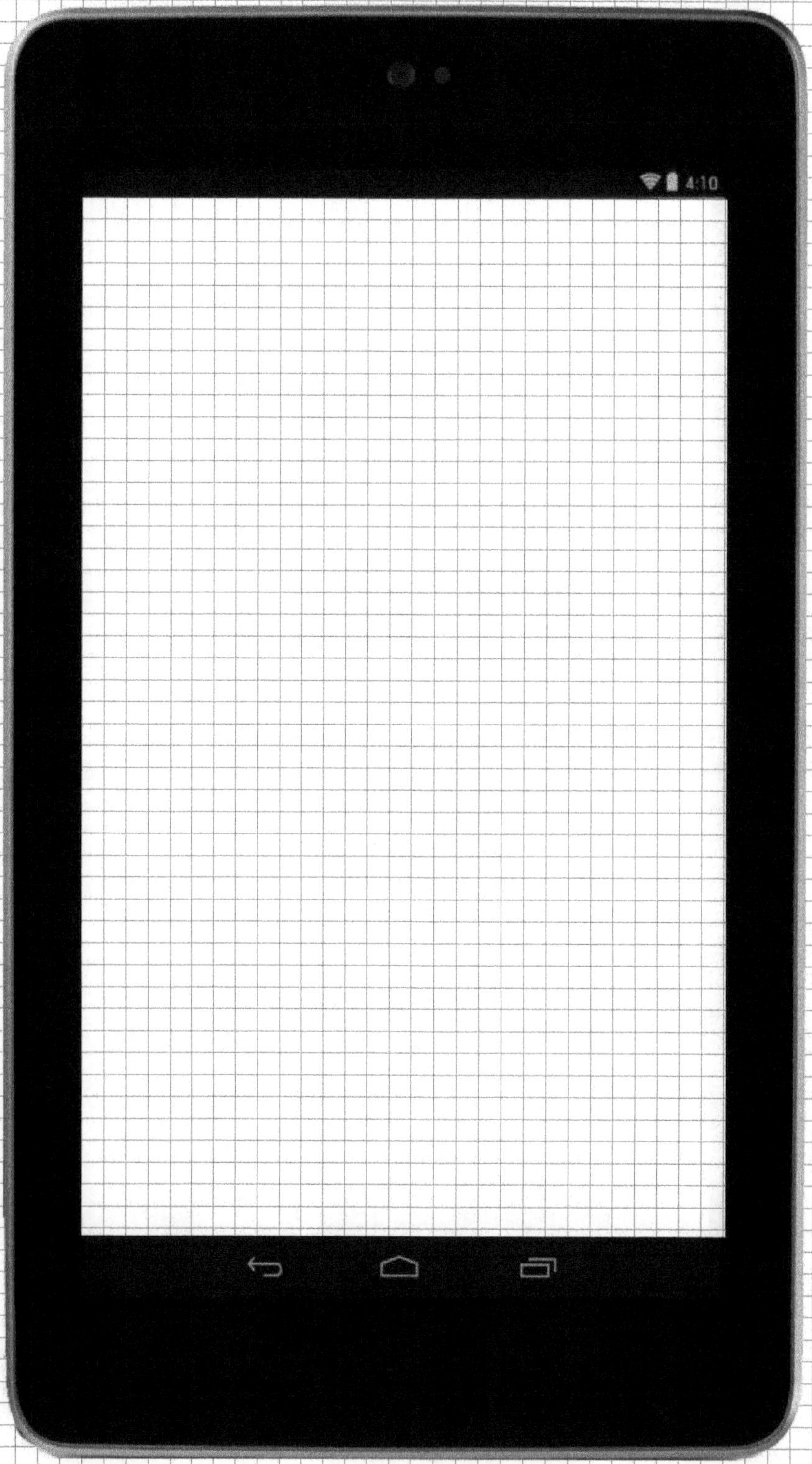

Application Name:

Screen Name:

Notes:

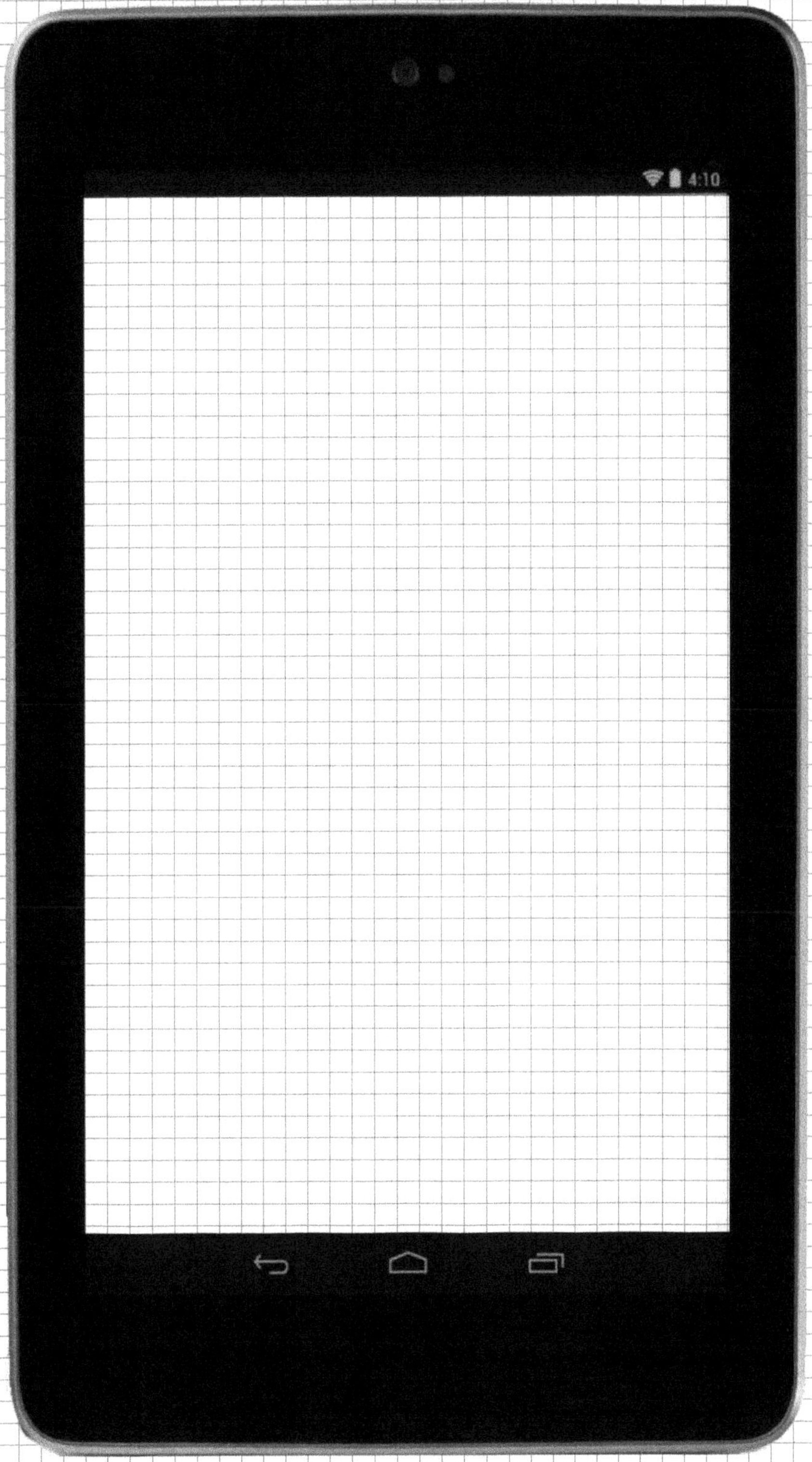

Application Name:

Screen Name:

Notes:

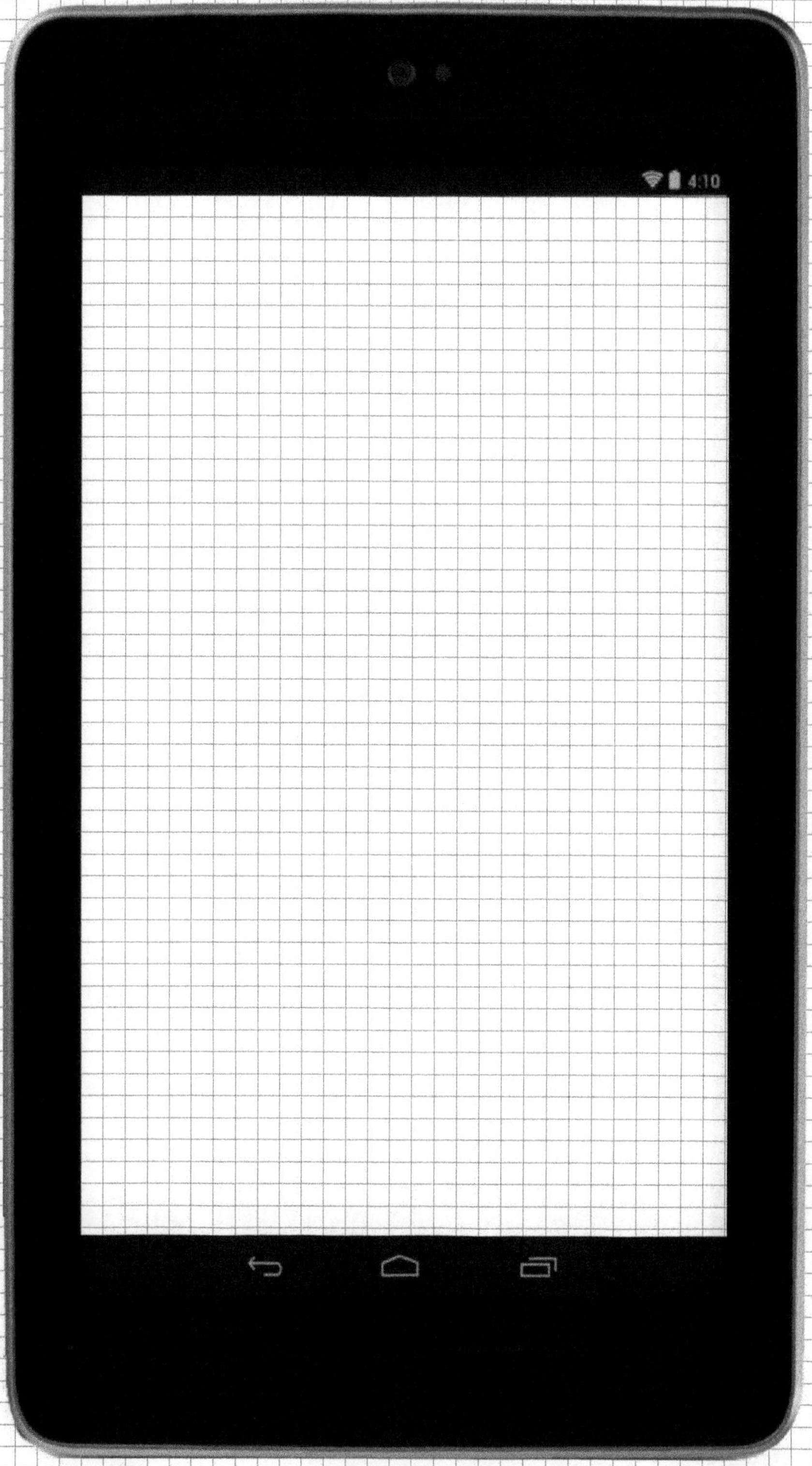

Application Name:

Screen Name:

Notes:

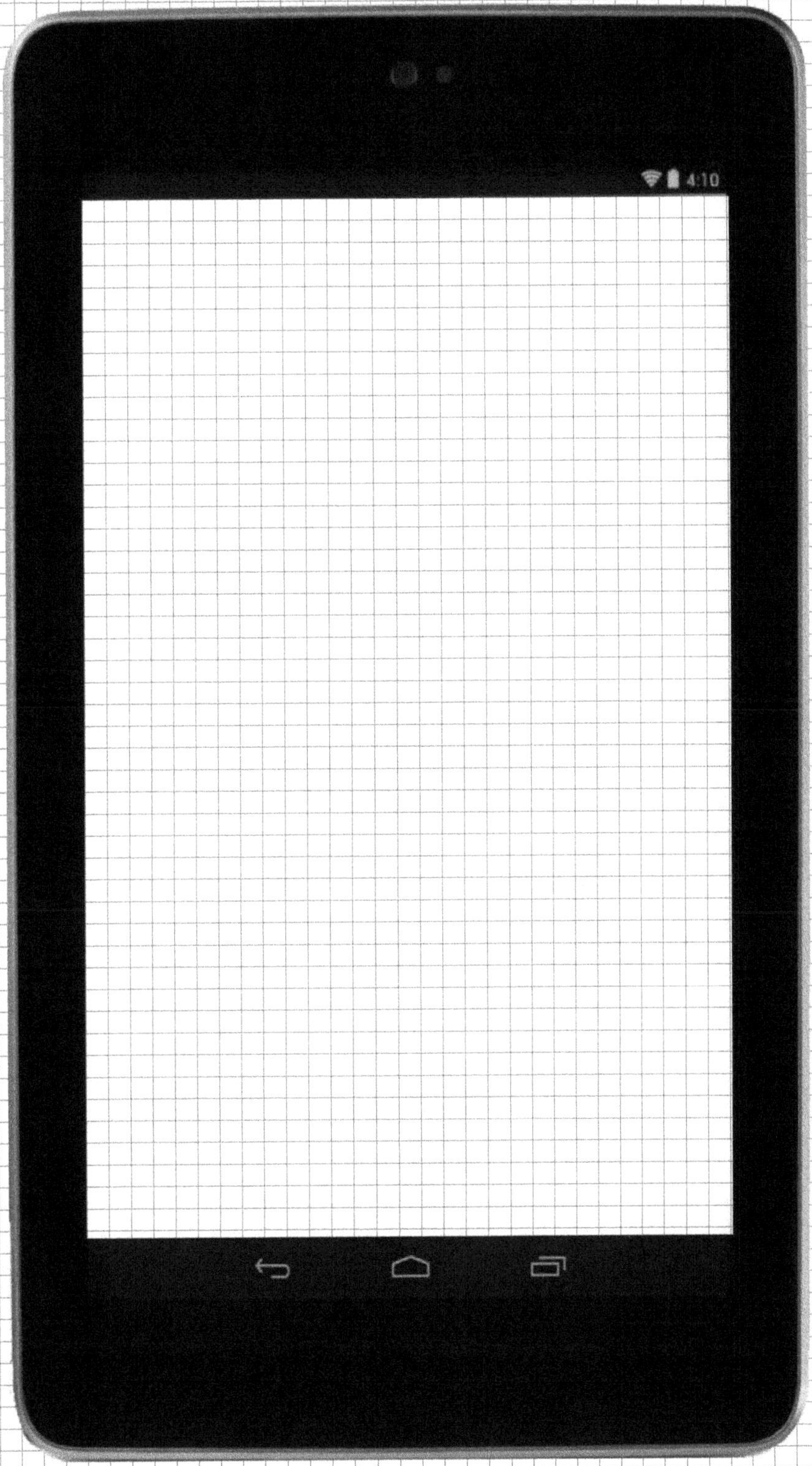

Application Name:

Screen Name:

Notes:

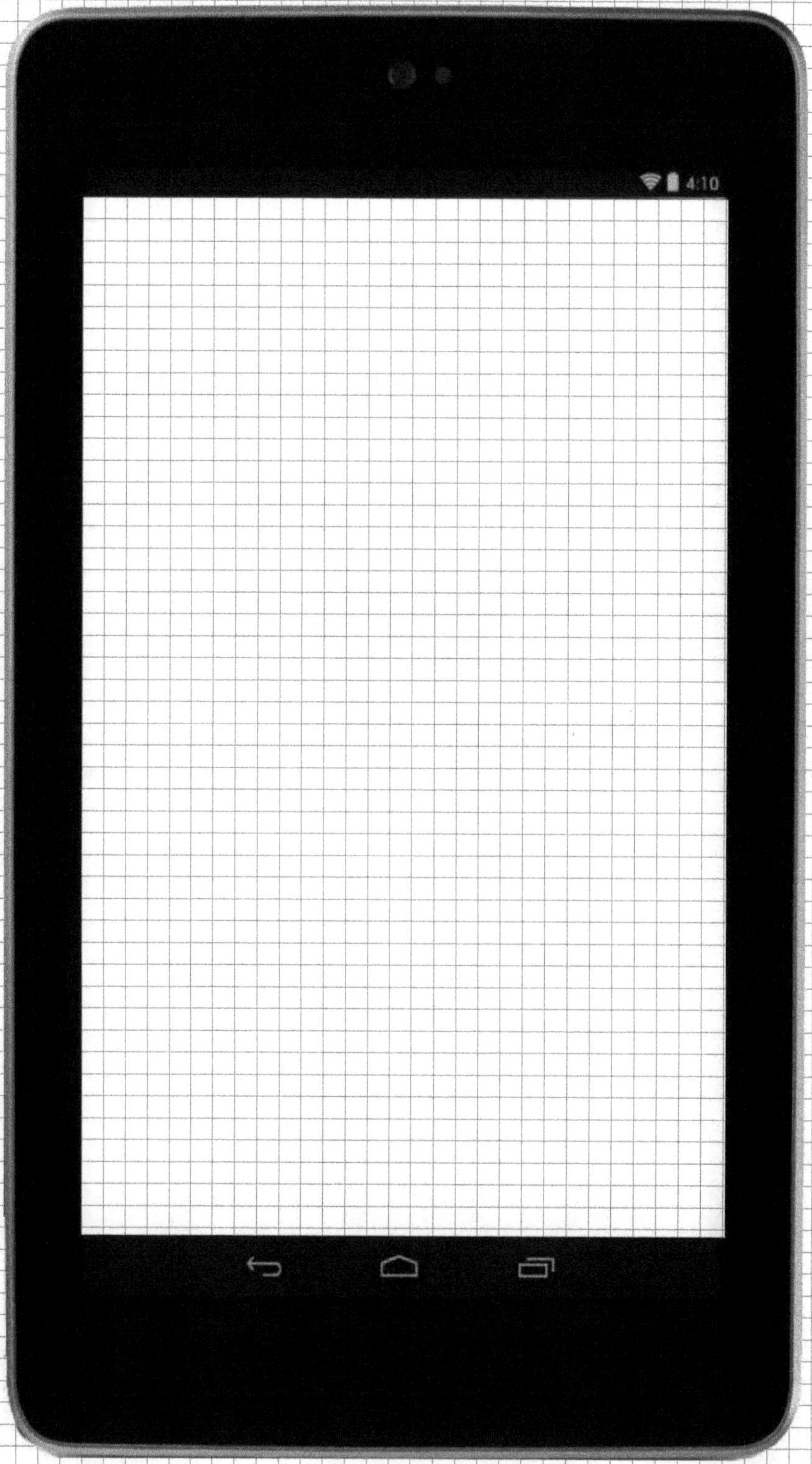

Application Name:

Screen Name:

Notes:

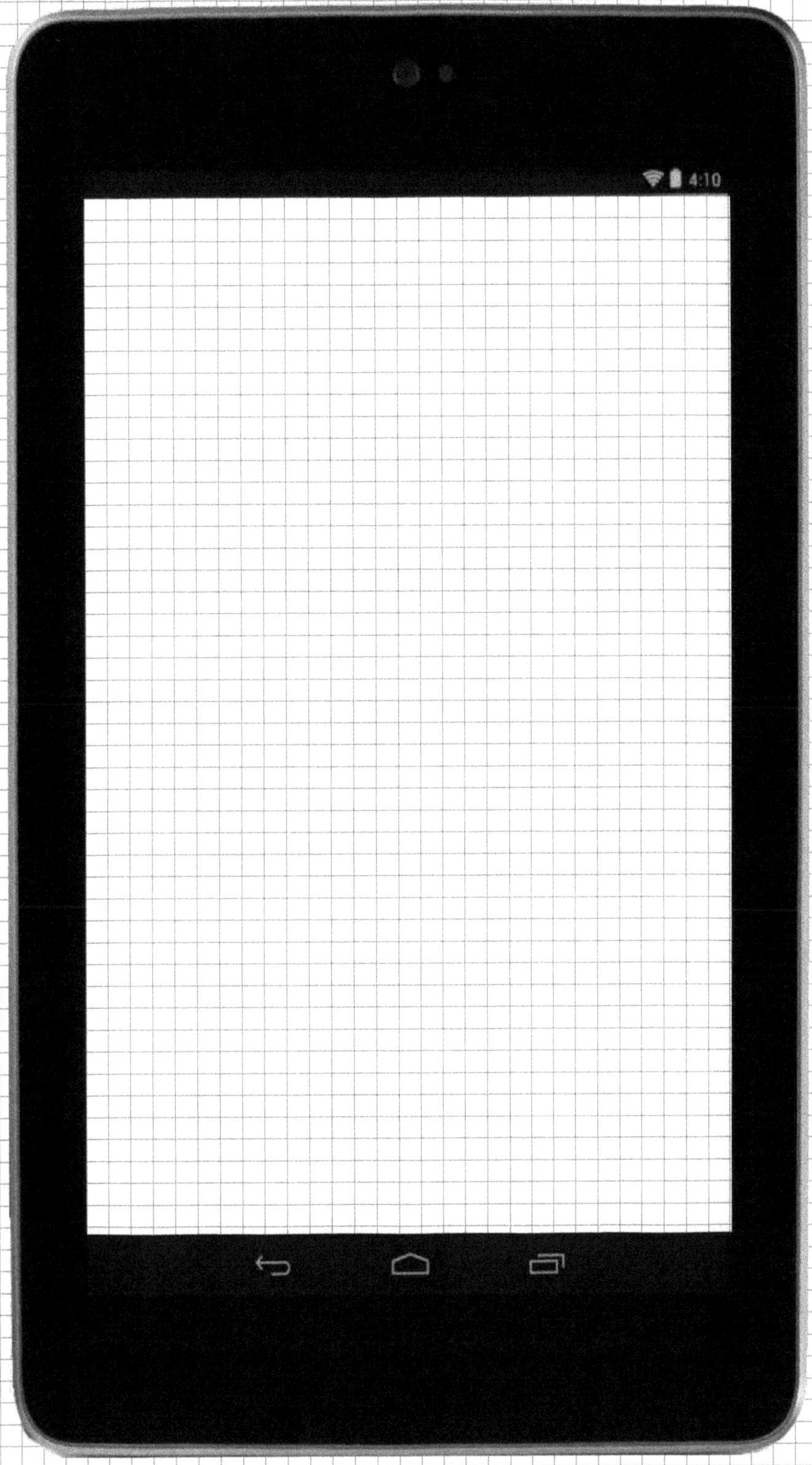

Application Name:

Screen Name:

Notes:

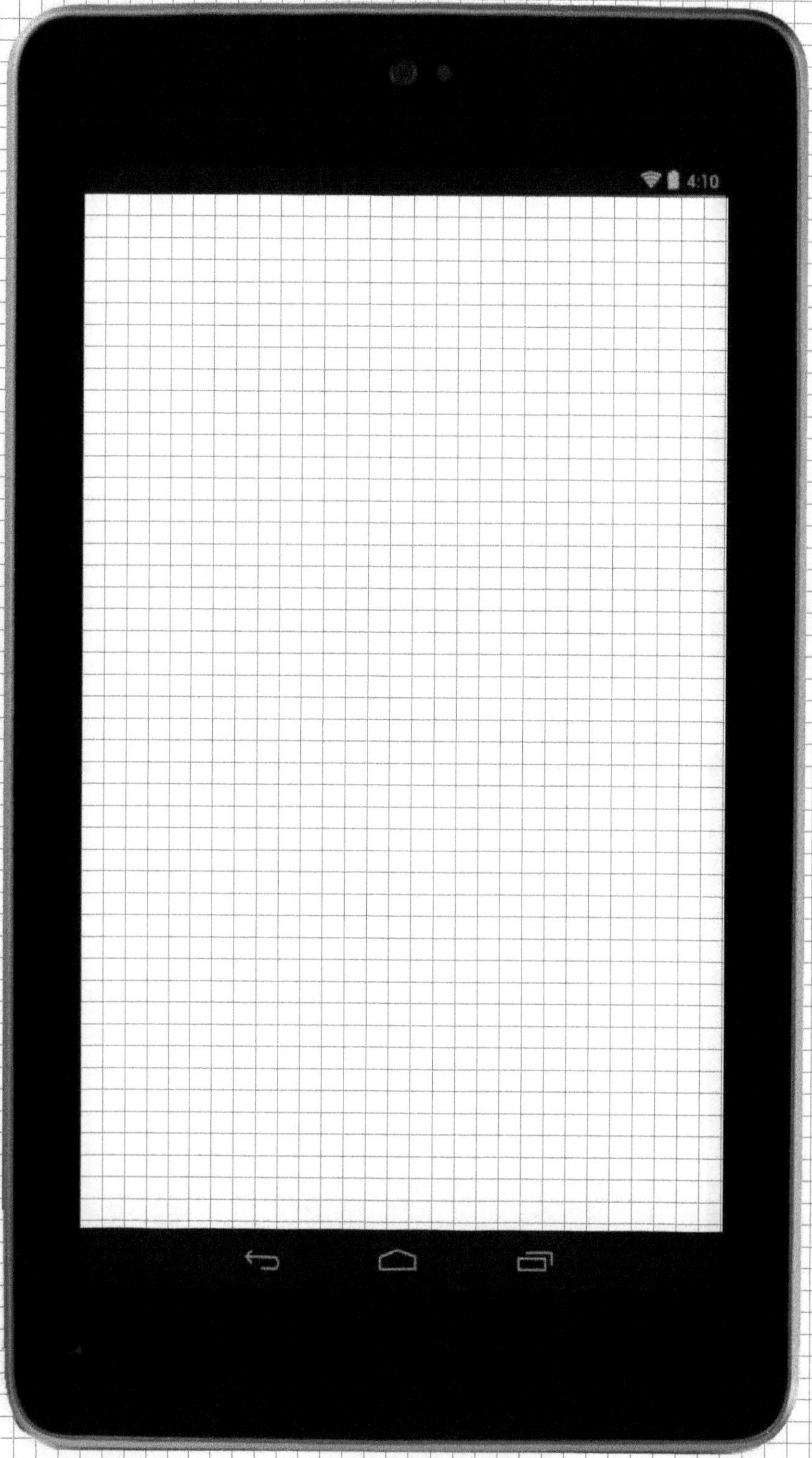

Application Name:

Screen Name:

Notes:

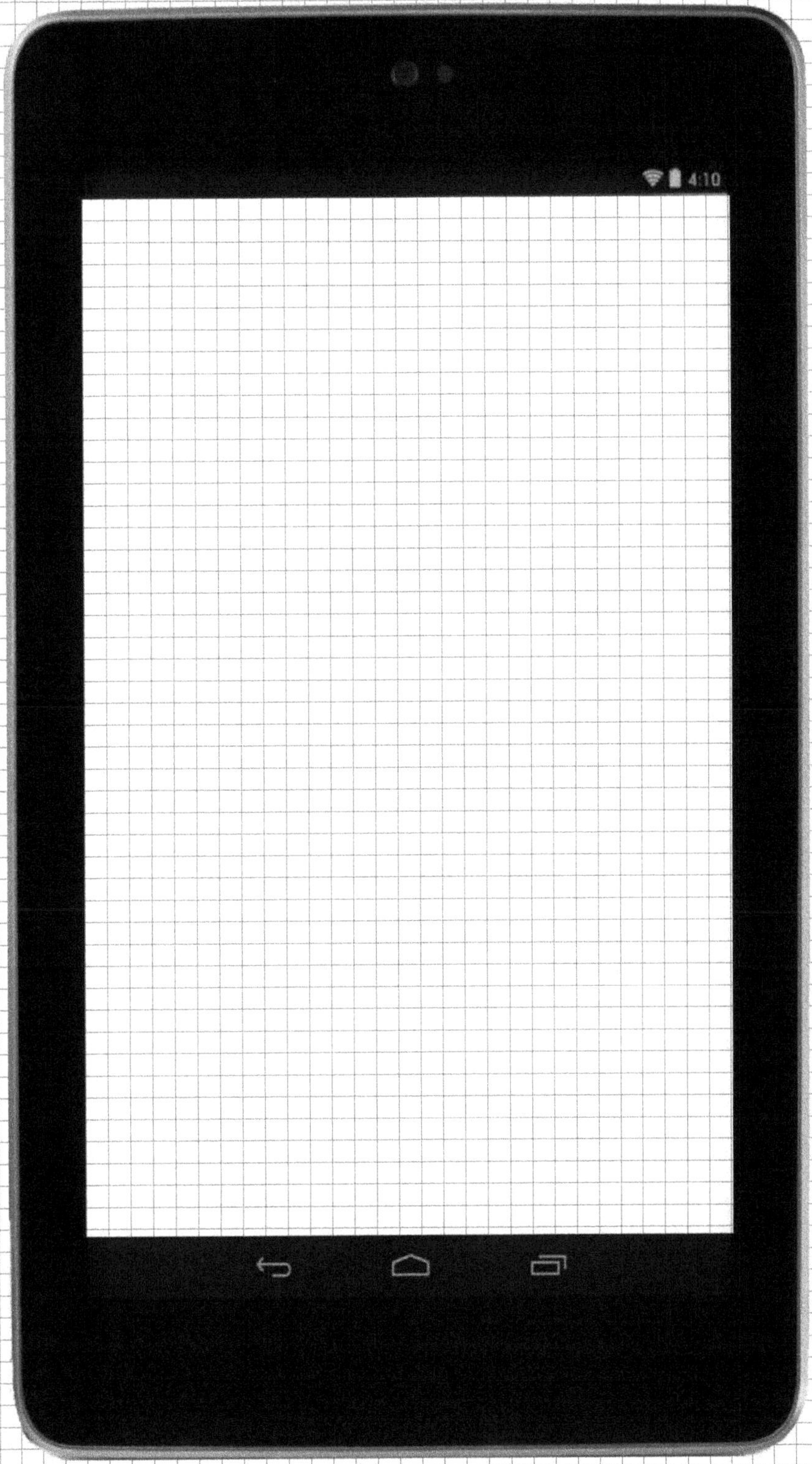

Application Name:

Screen Name:

Notes:

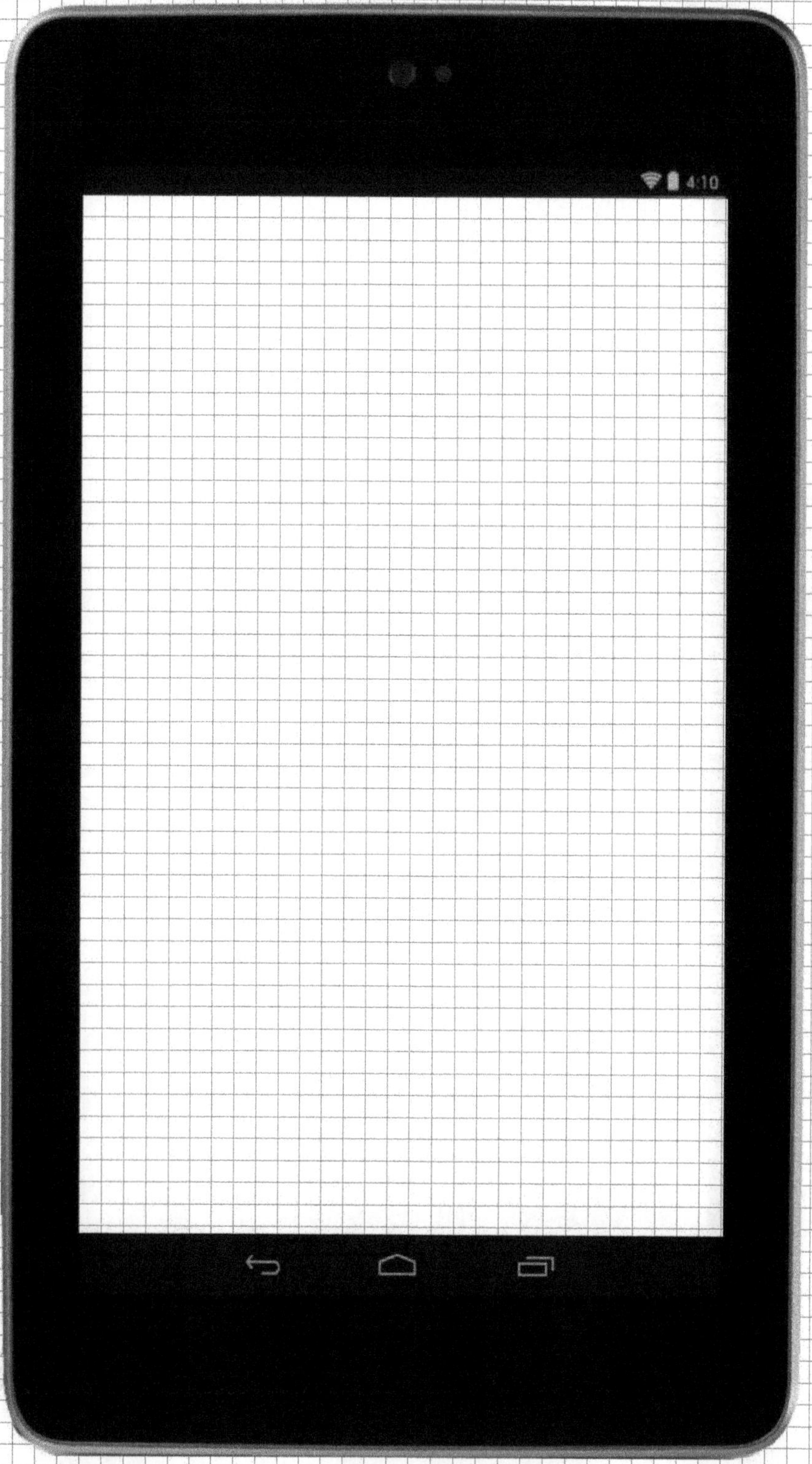

Application Name:

Screen Name:

Notes:

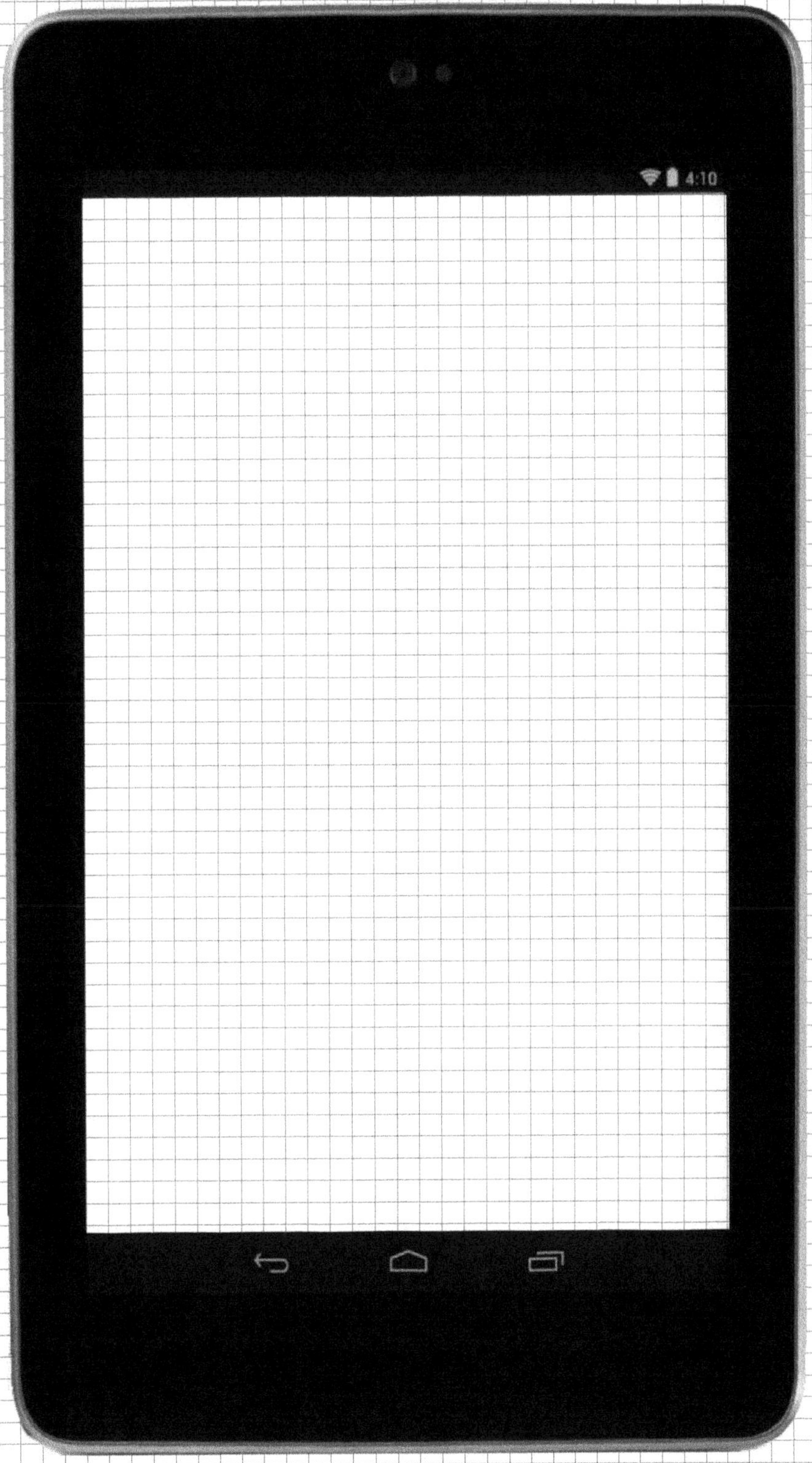

Application Name:

Screen Name:

Notes:

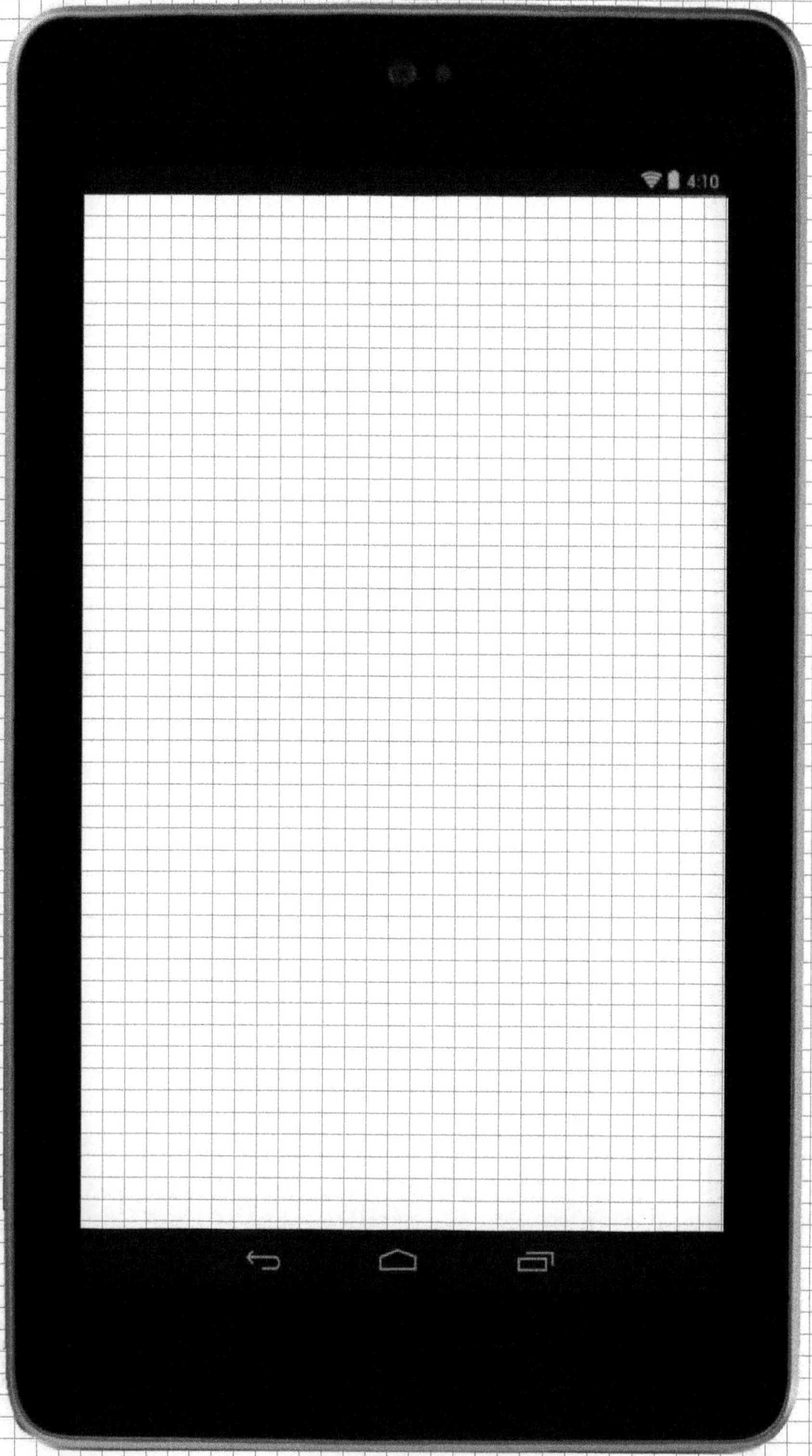

Application Name:

Screen Name:

Notes:

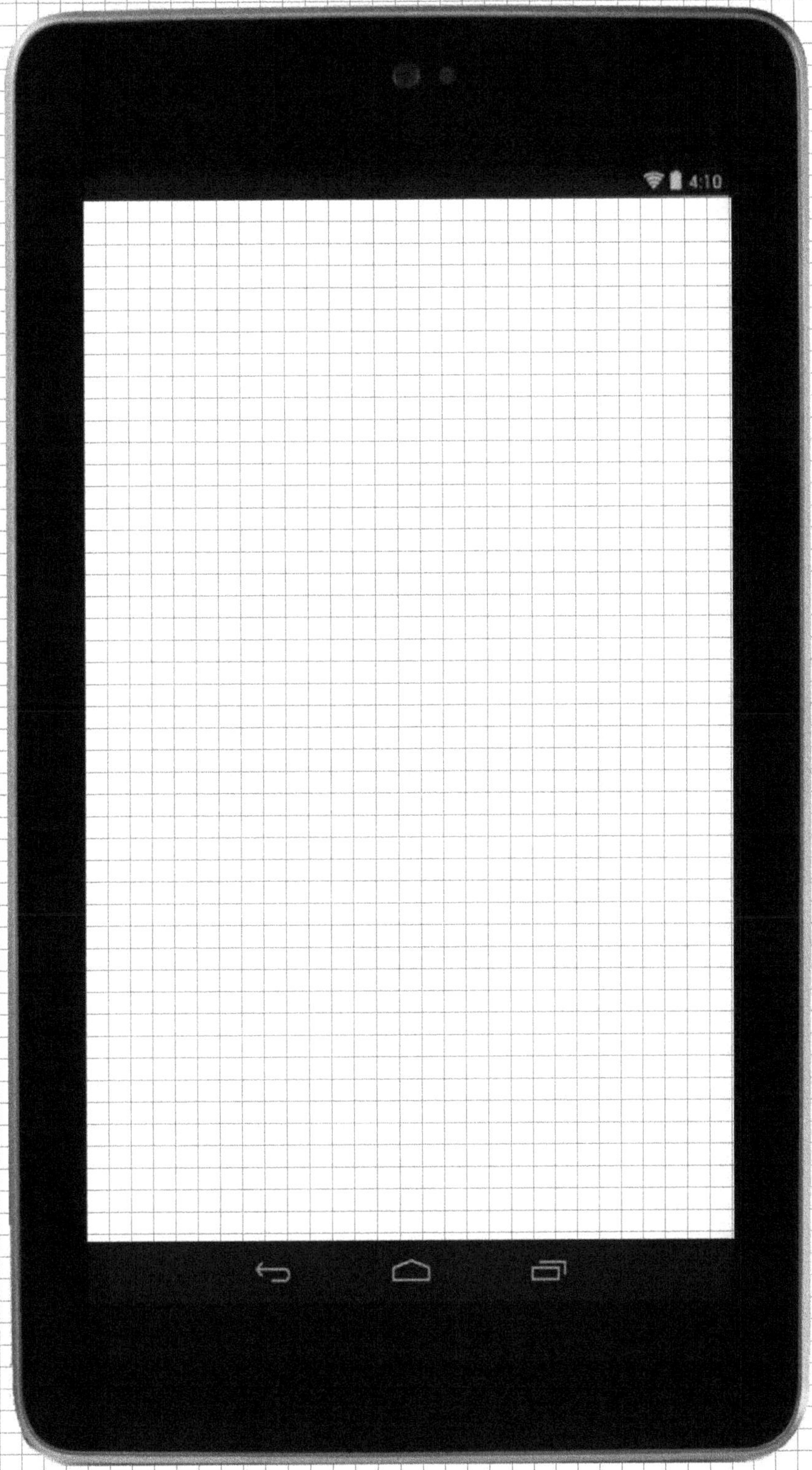

Application Name:

Screen Name:

Notes:

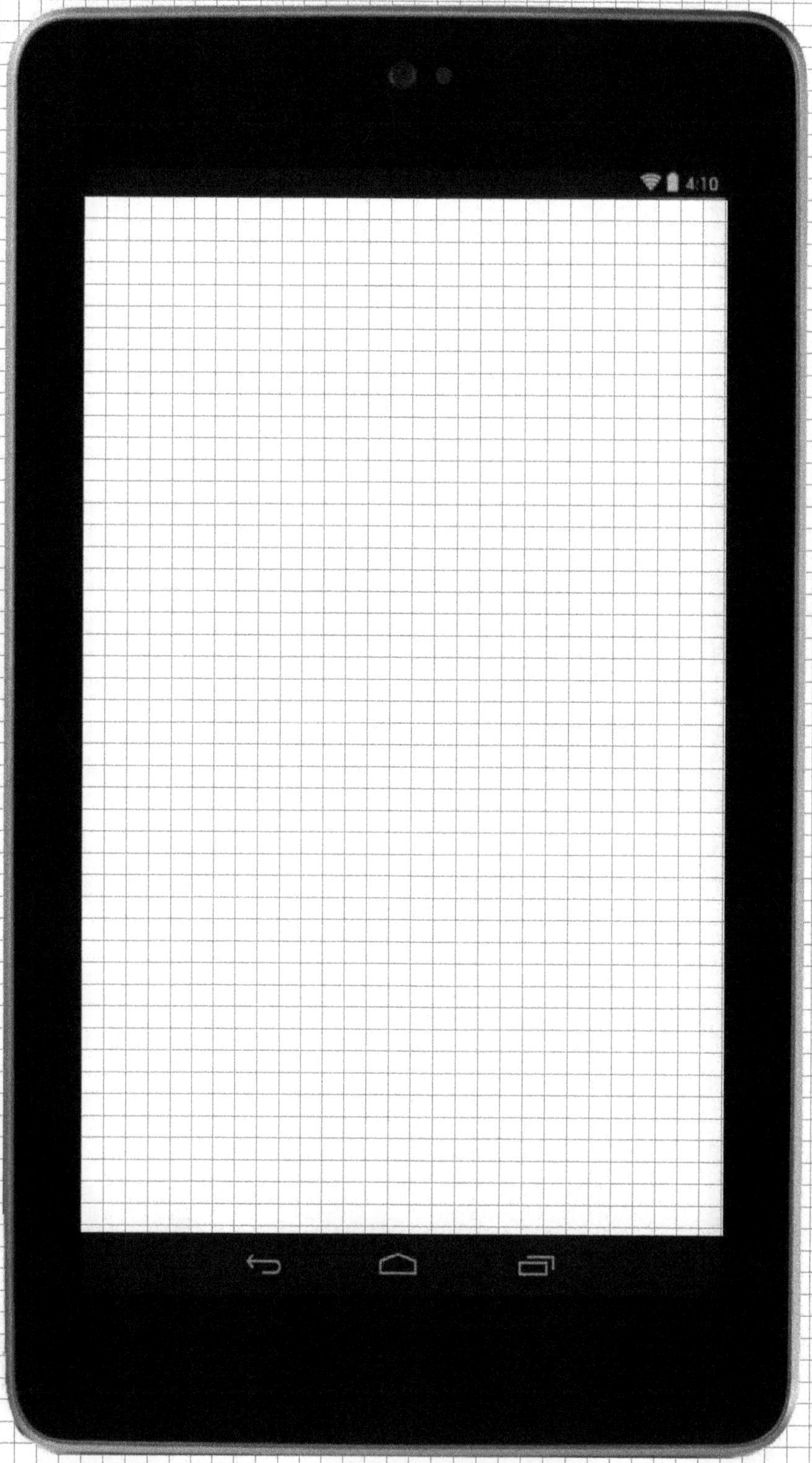

Application Name:

Screen Name:

Notes:

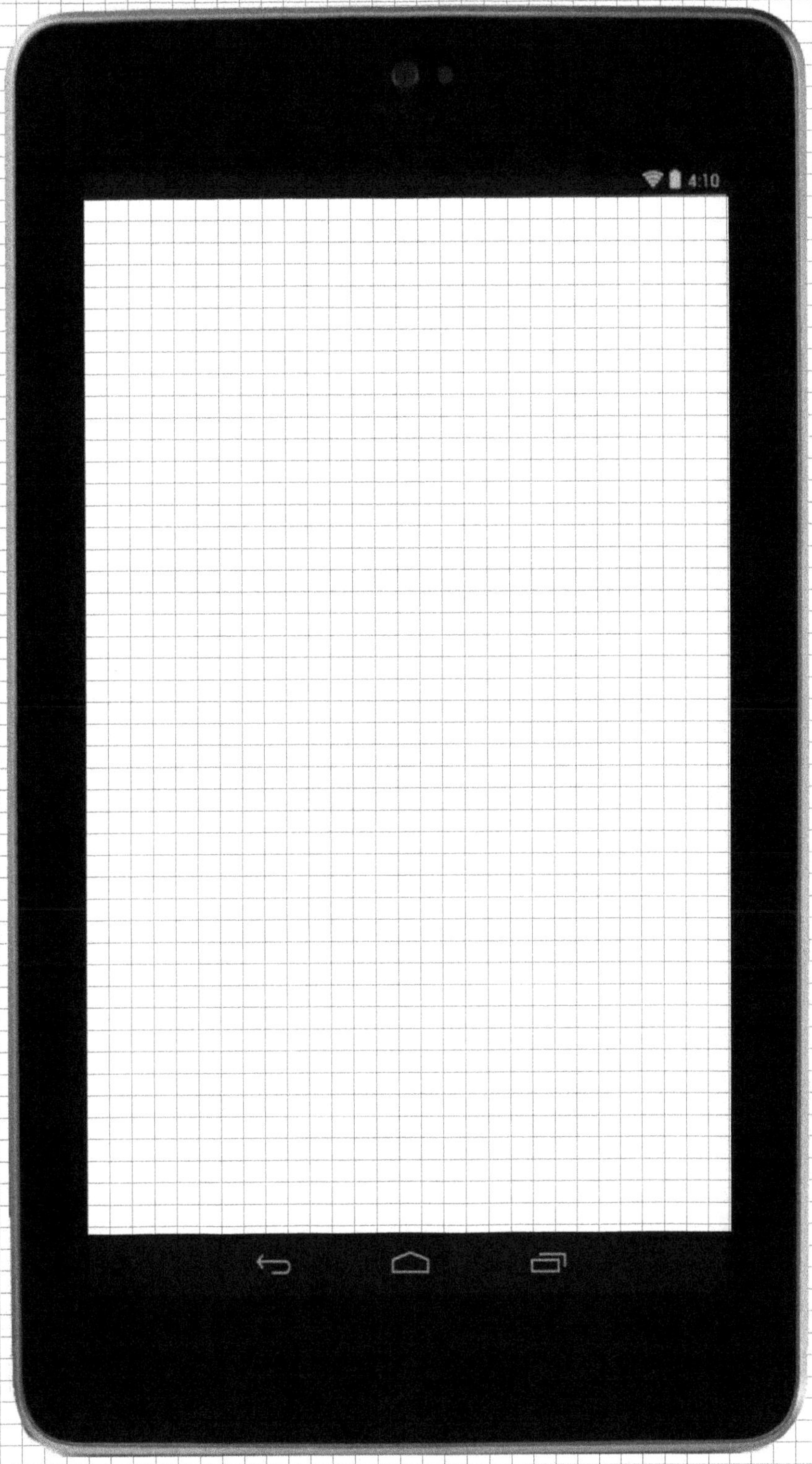

Application Name:

Screen Name:

Notes:

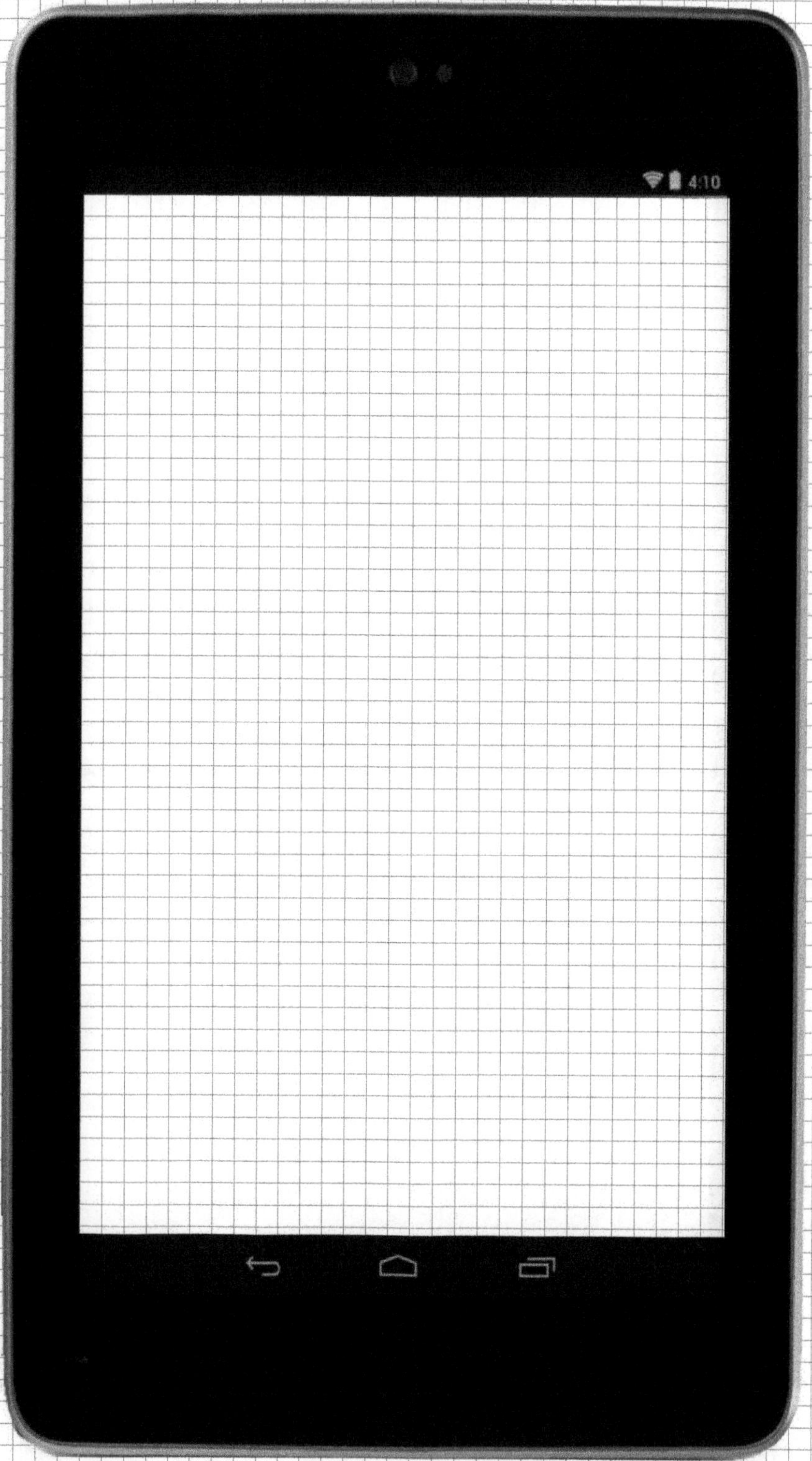

Application Name:

Screen Name:

Notes:

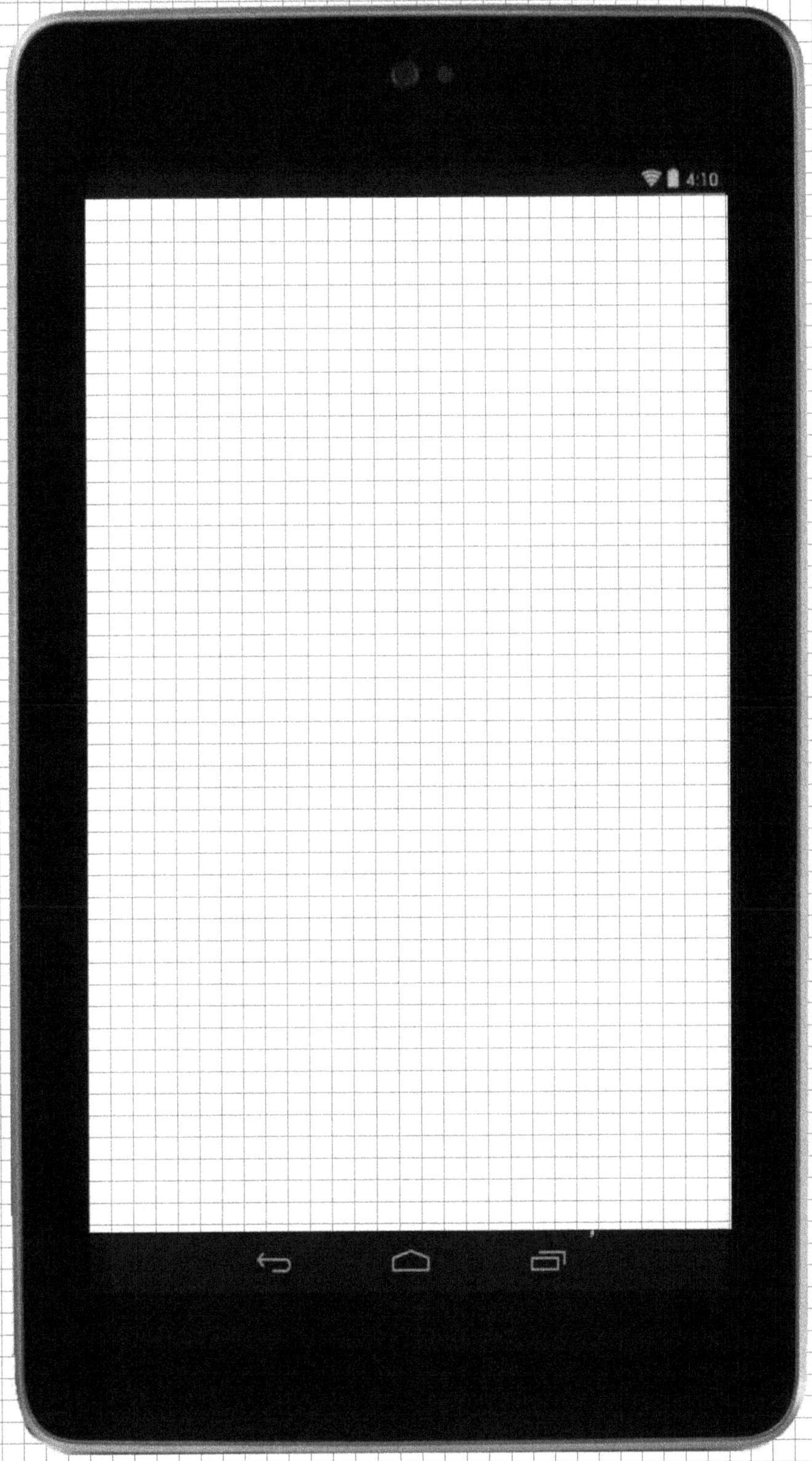

Application Name:

Screen Name:

Notes:

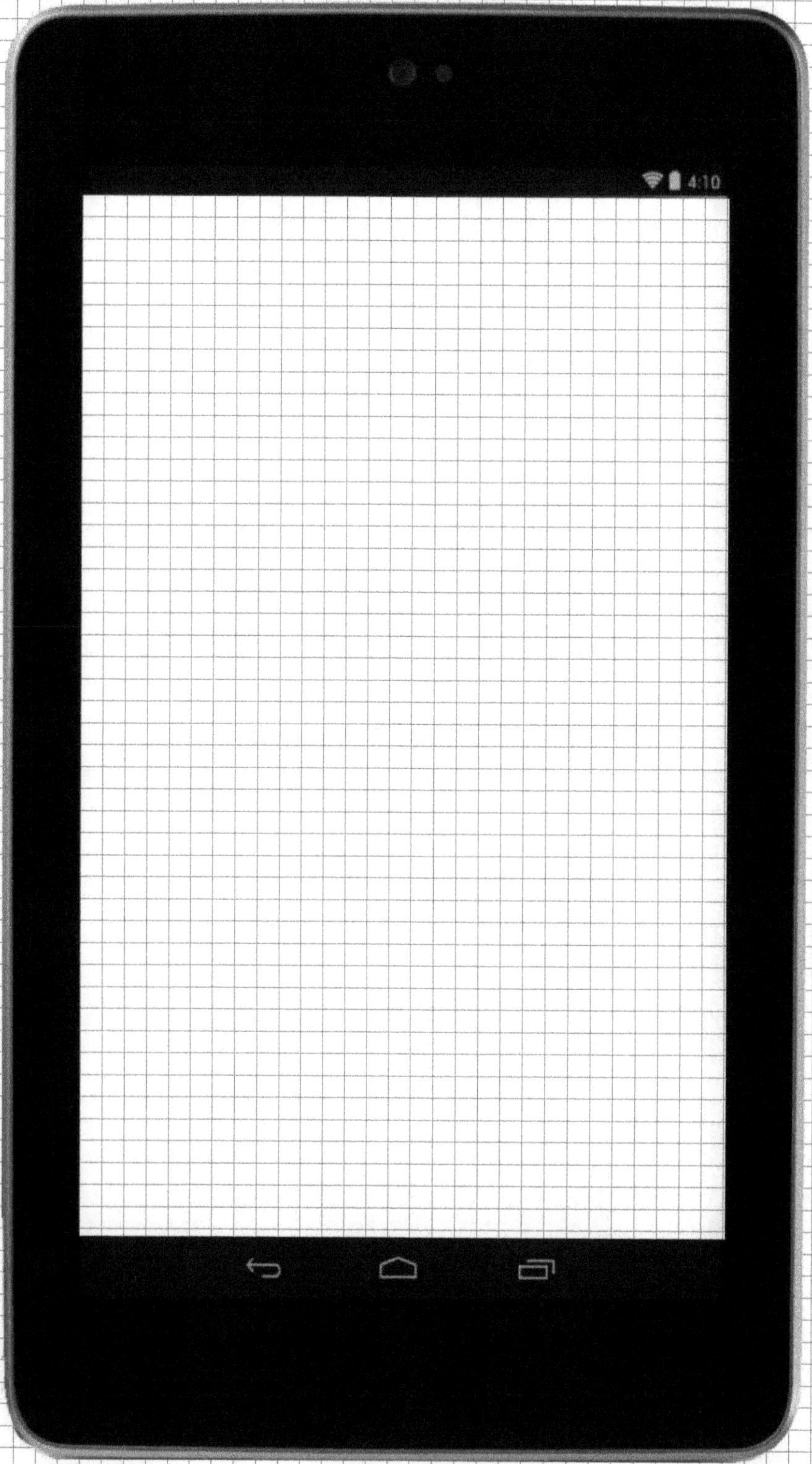

Application Name:

Screen Name:

Notes:

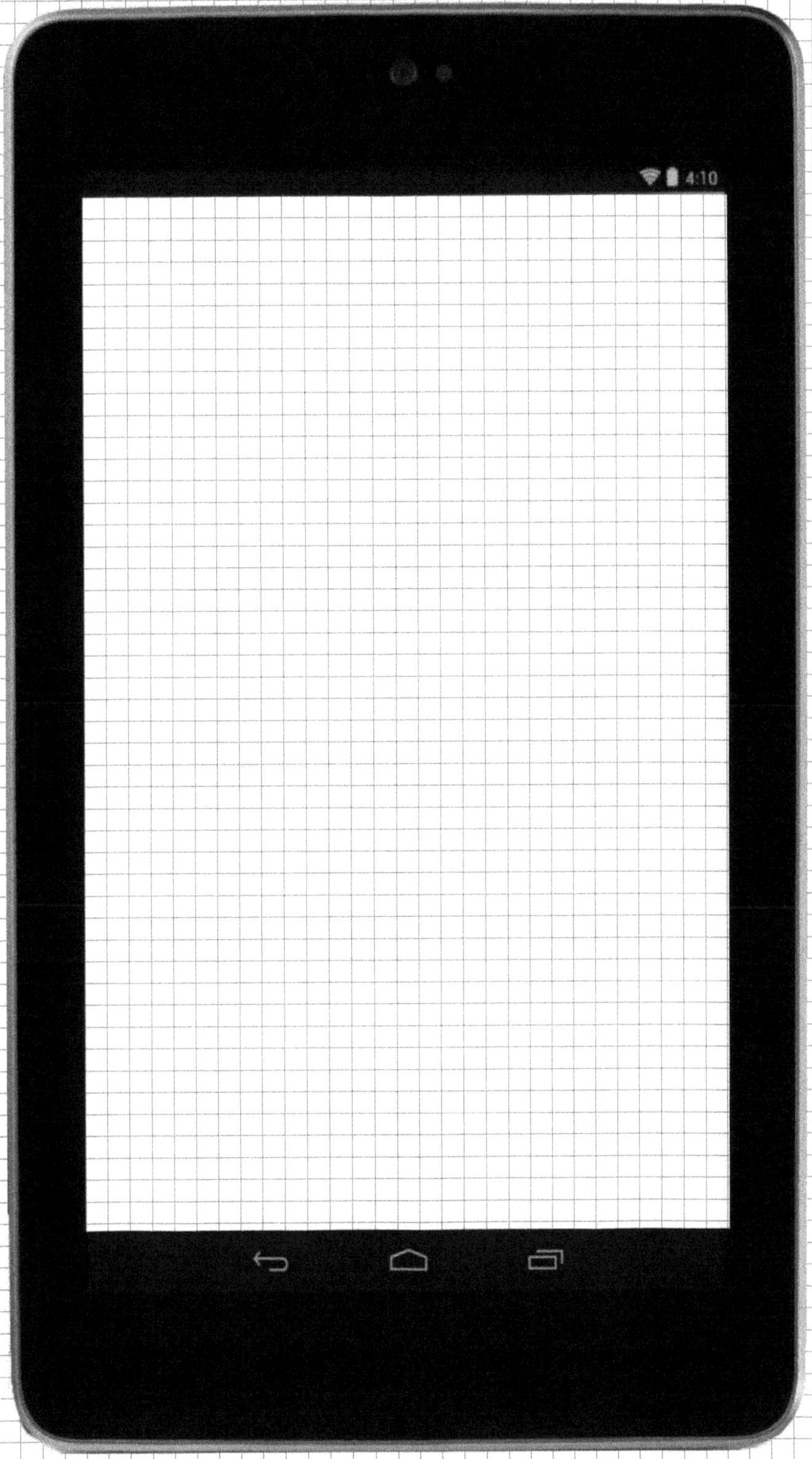

Application Name:

Screen Name:

Notes:

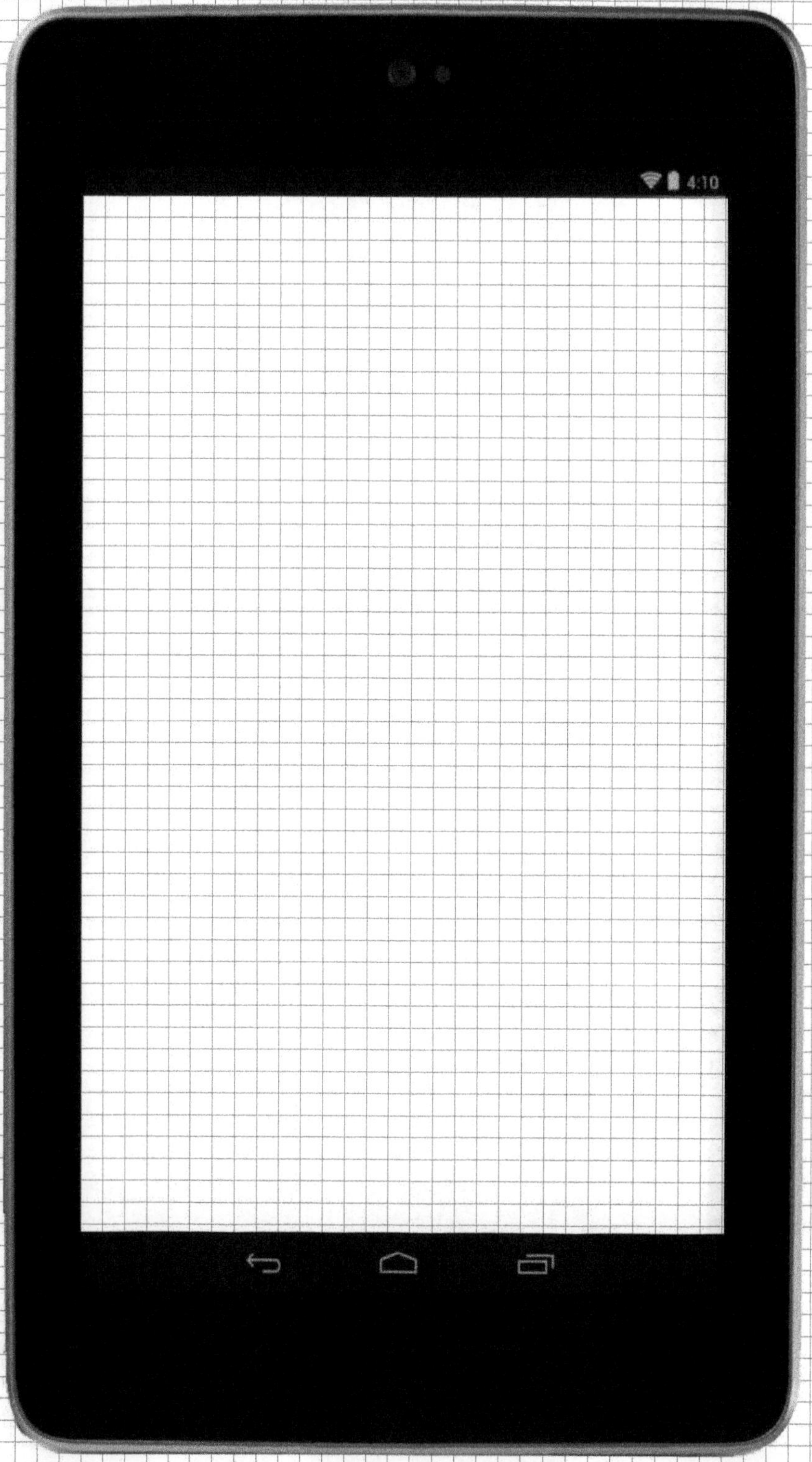

Application Name:

Screen Name:

Notes:

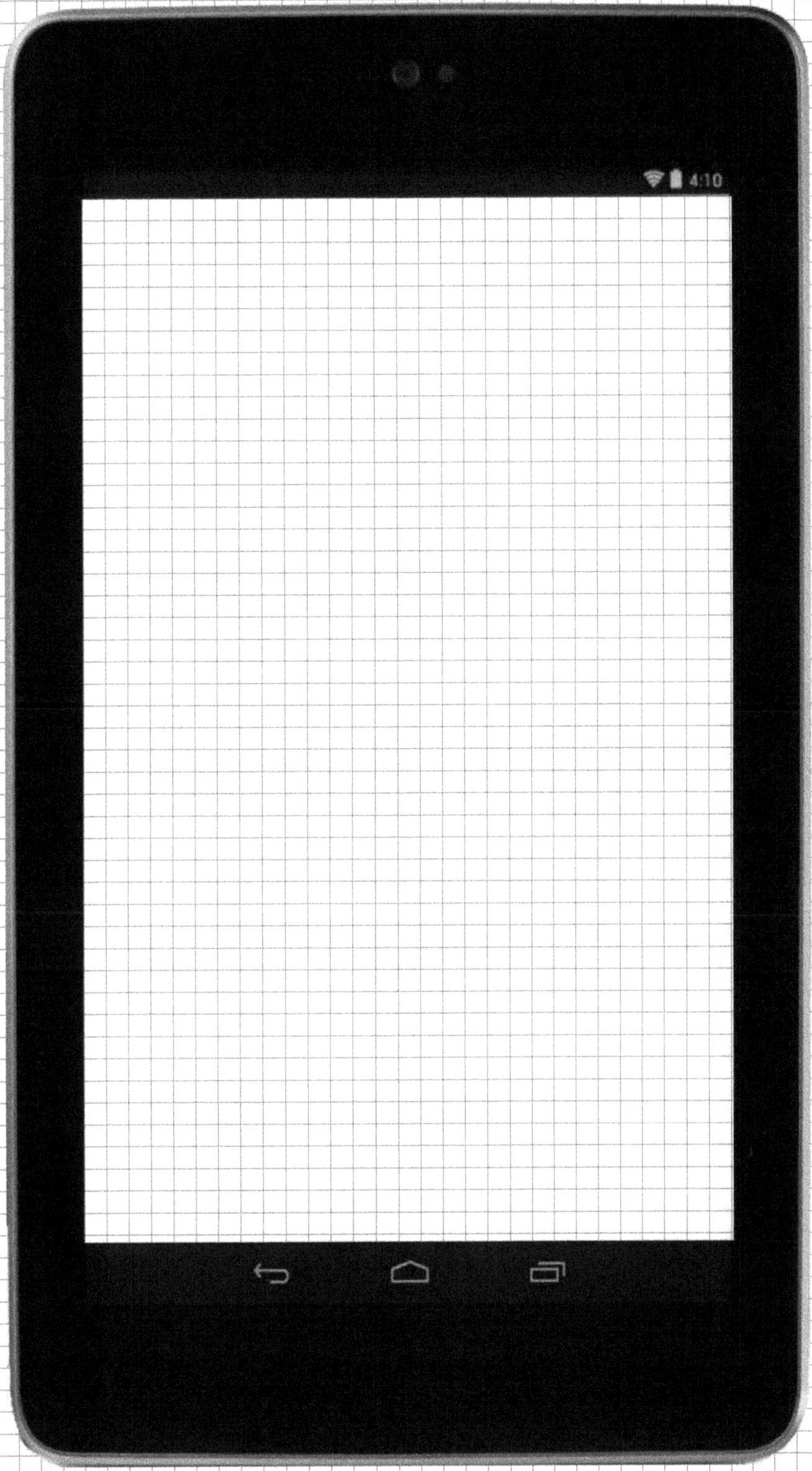

Application Name:

Screen Name:

Notes:

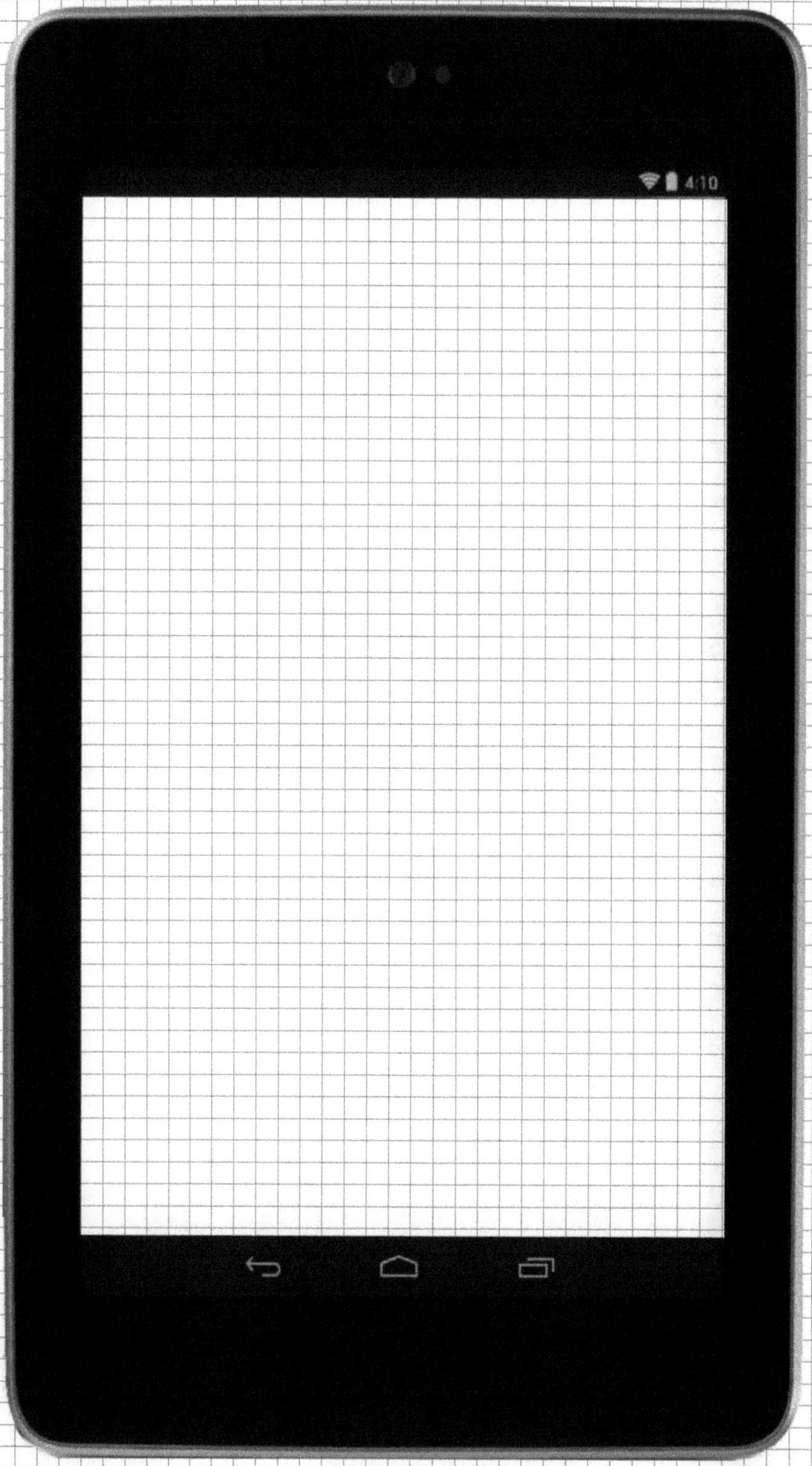

Application Name:

Screen Name:

Notes:

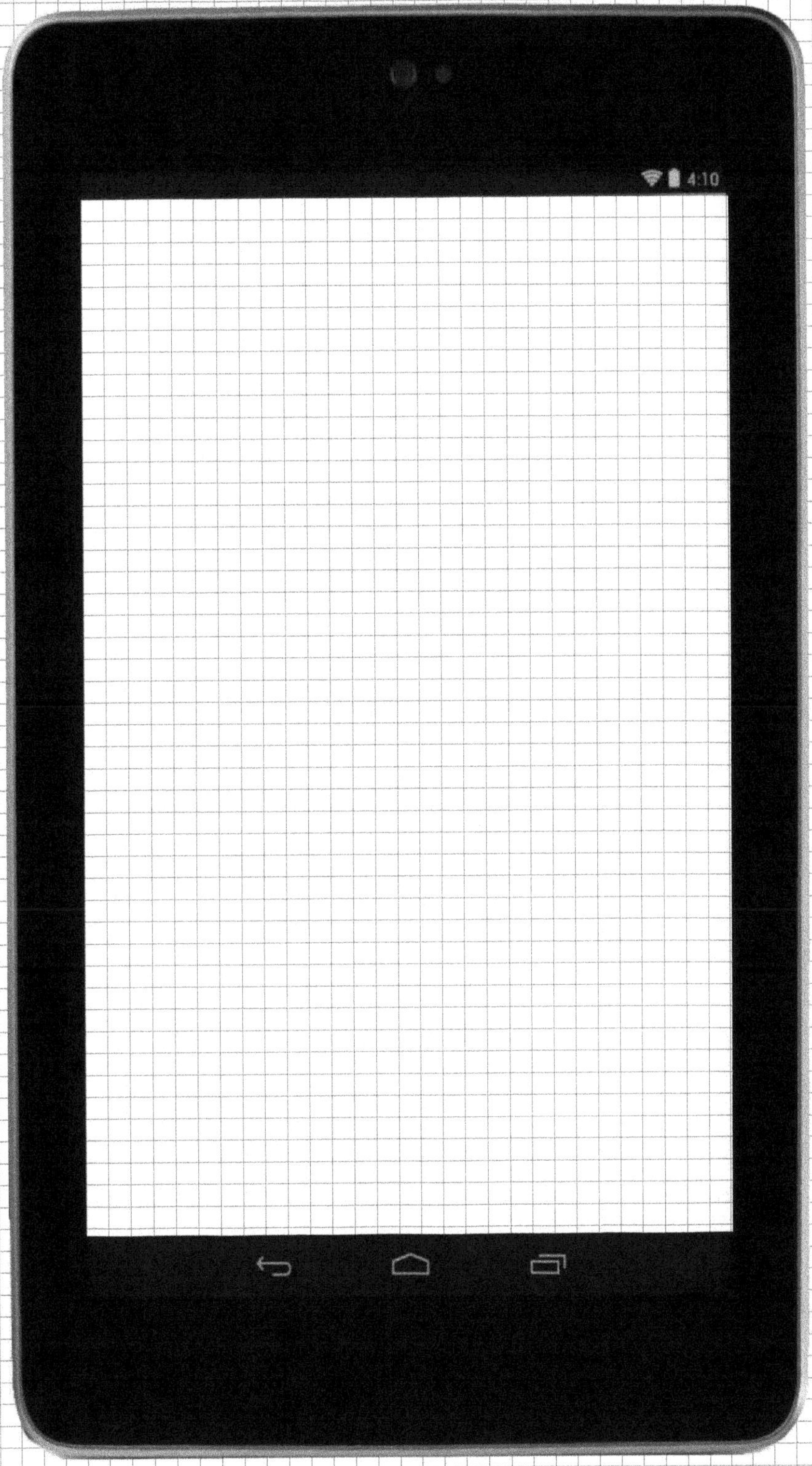

Application Name:

Screen Name:

Notes:

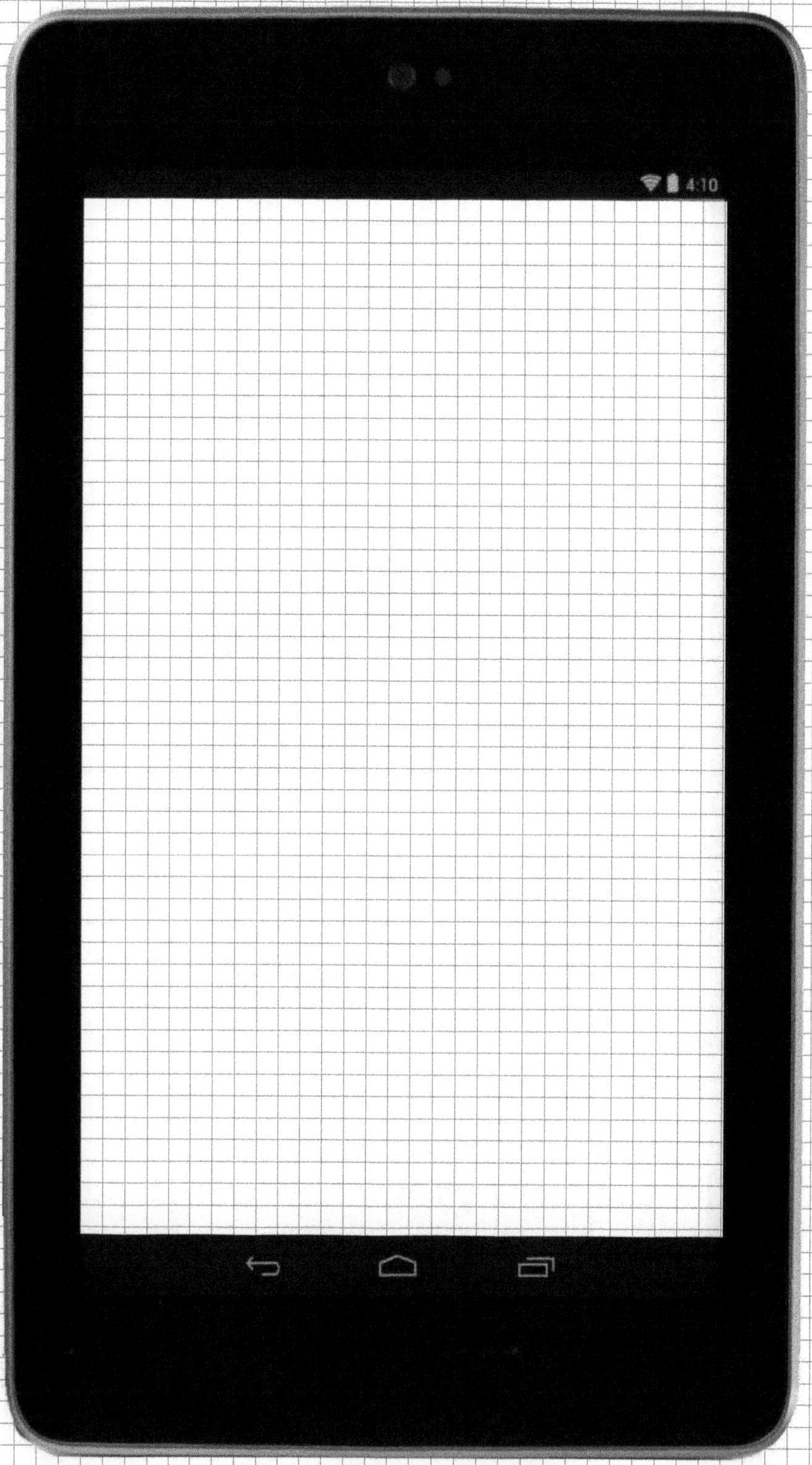

Application Name:

Screen Name:

Notes:

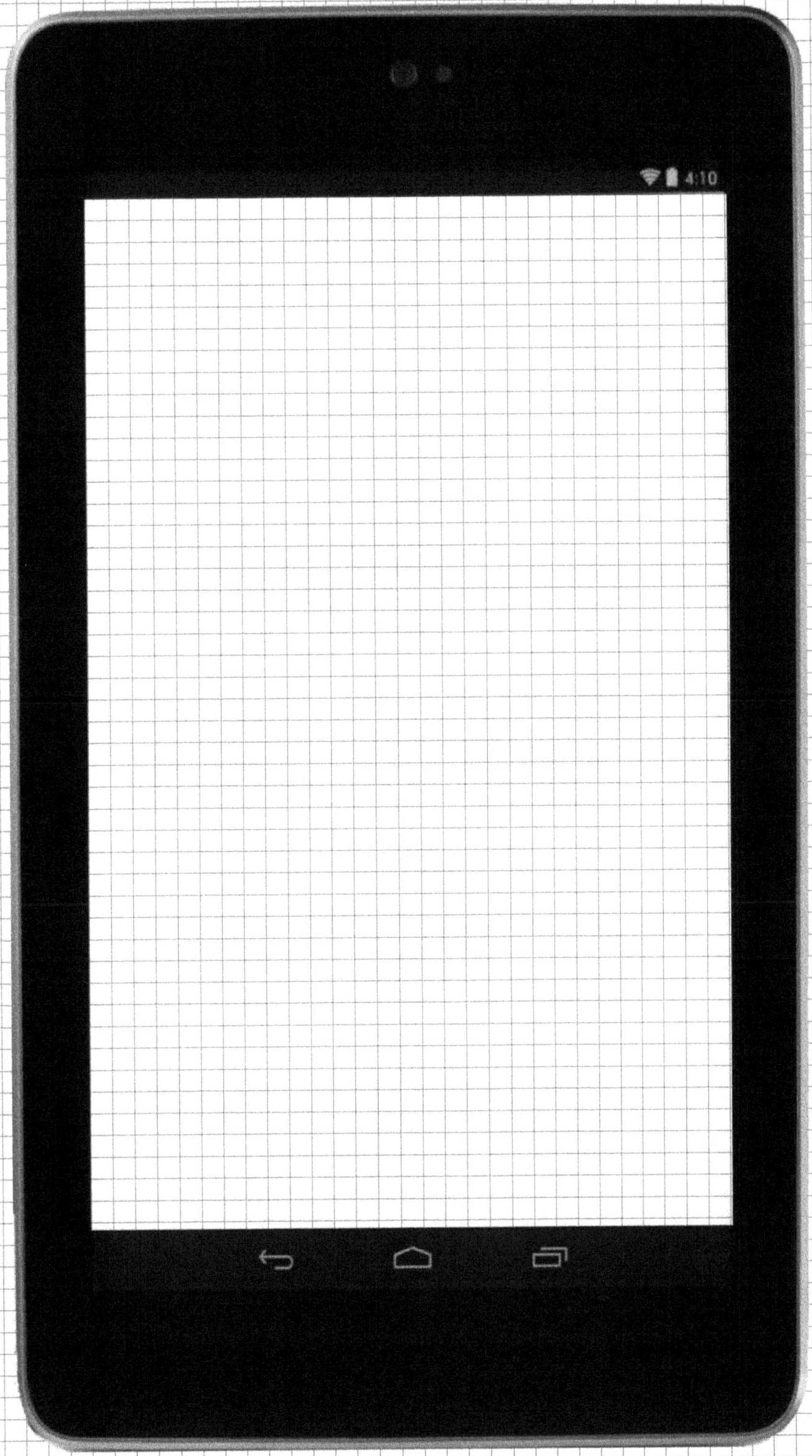

Application Name:

Screen Name:

Notes:

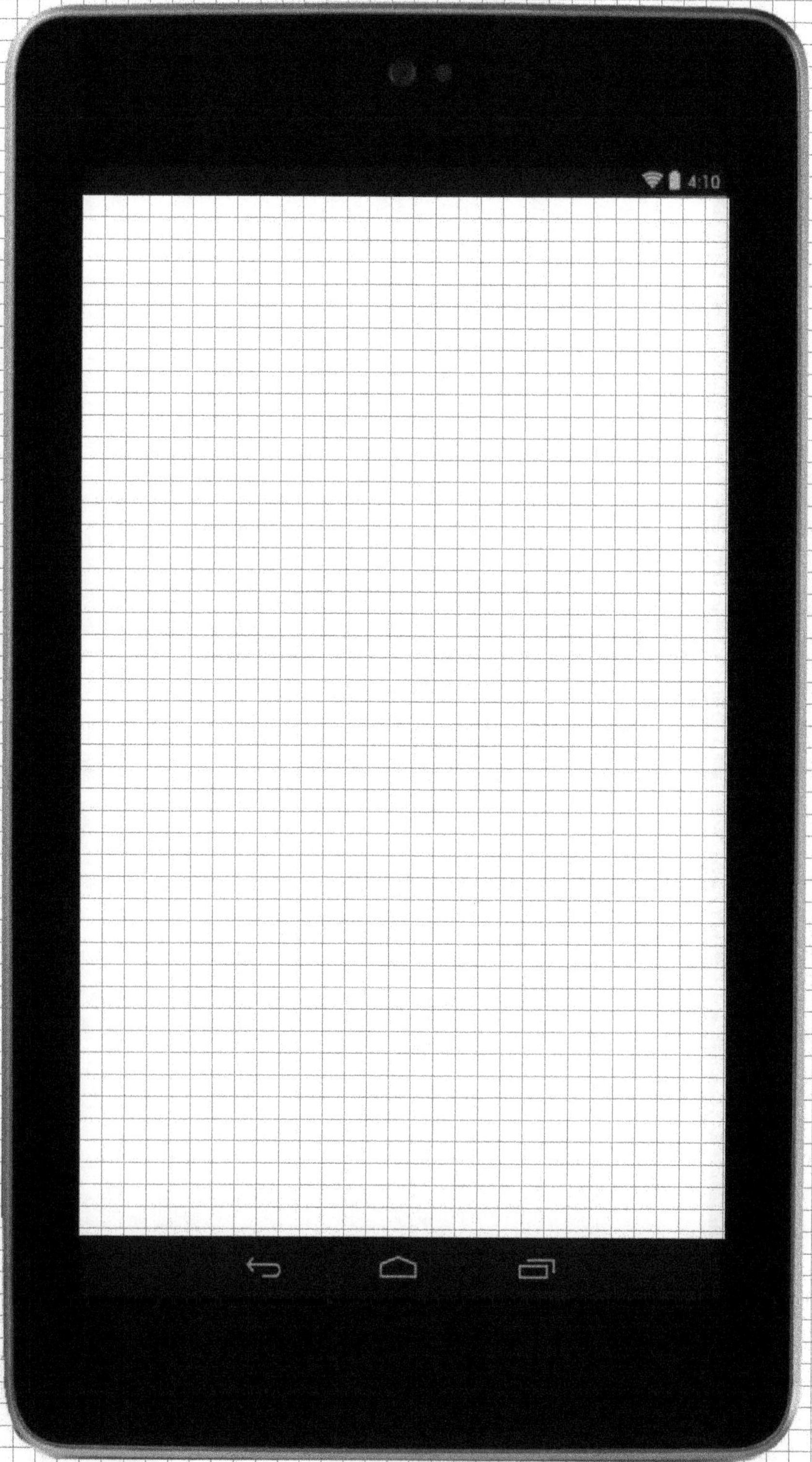

Application Name:

Screen Name:

Notes:

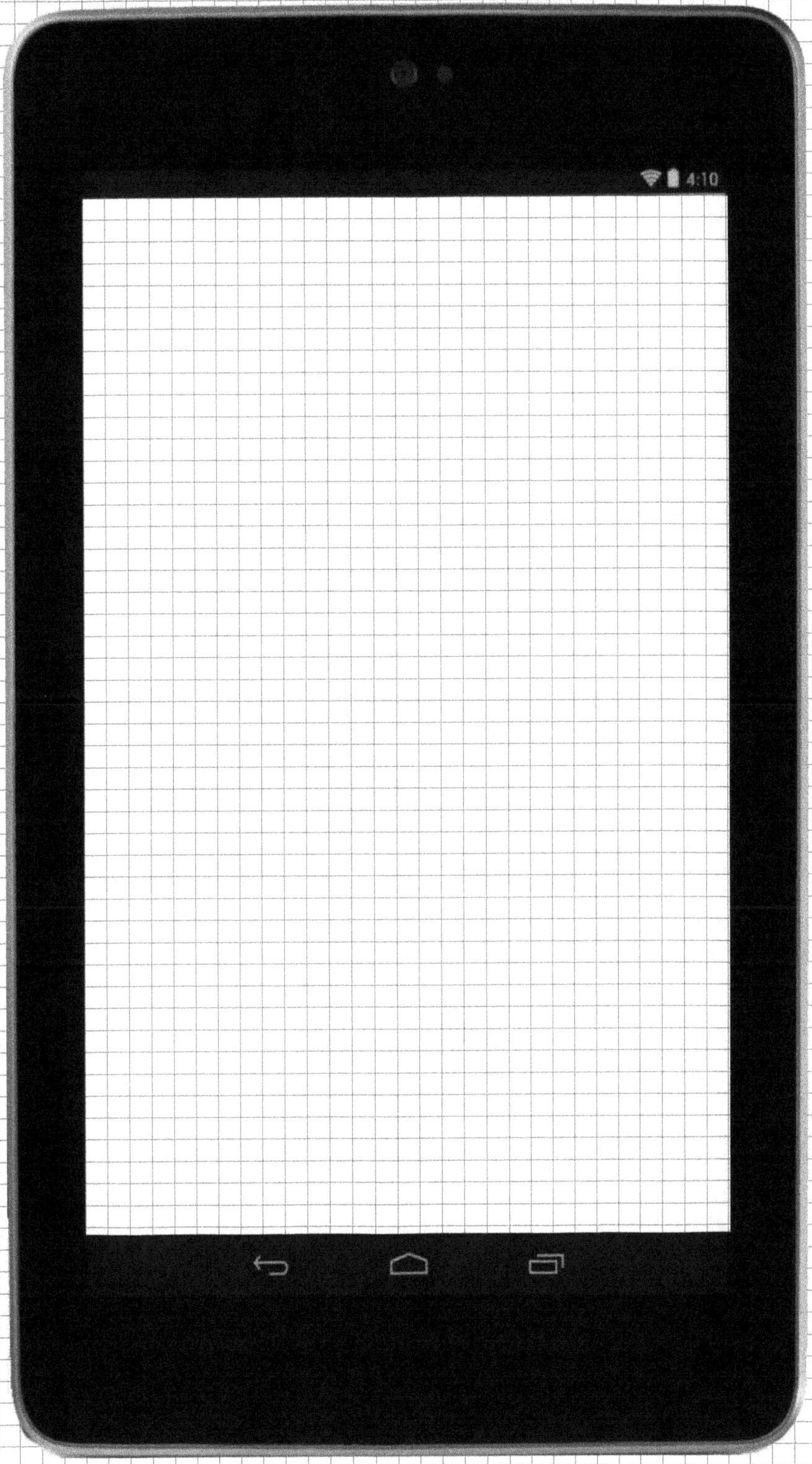

Application Name:

Screen Name:

Notes:

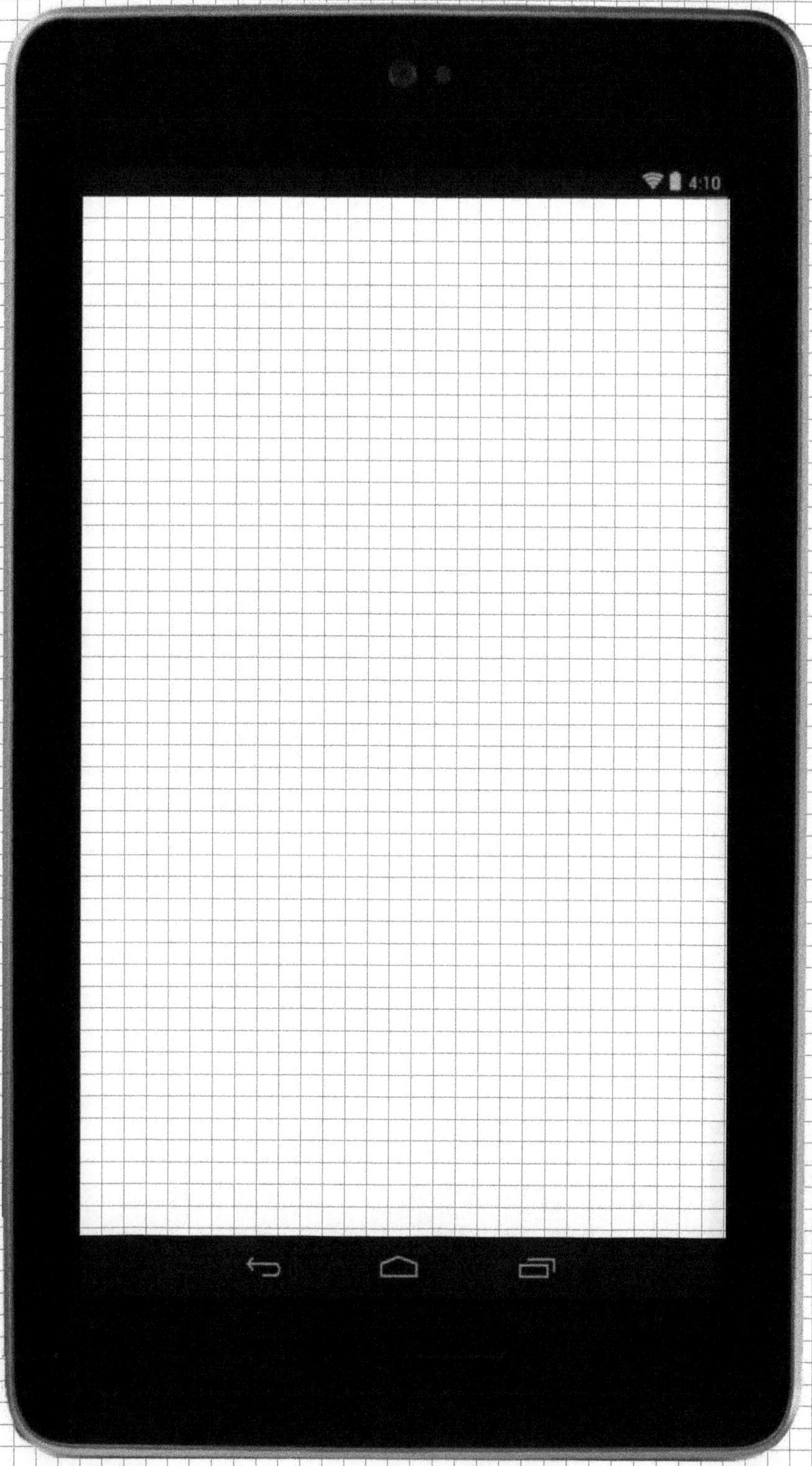

Application Name:

Screen Name:

Notes:

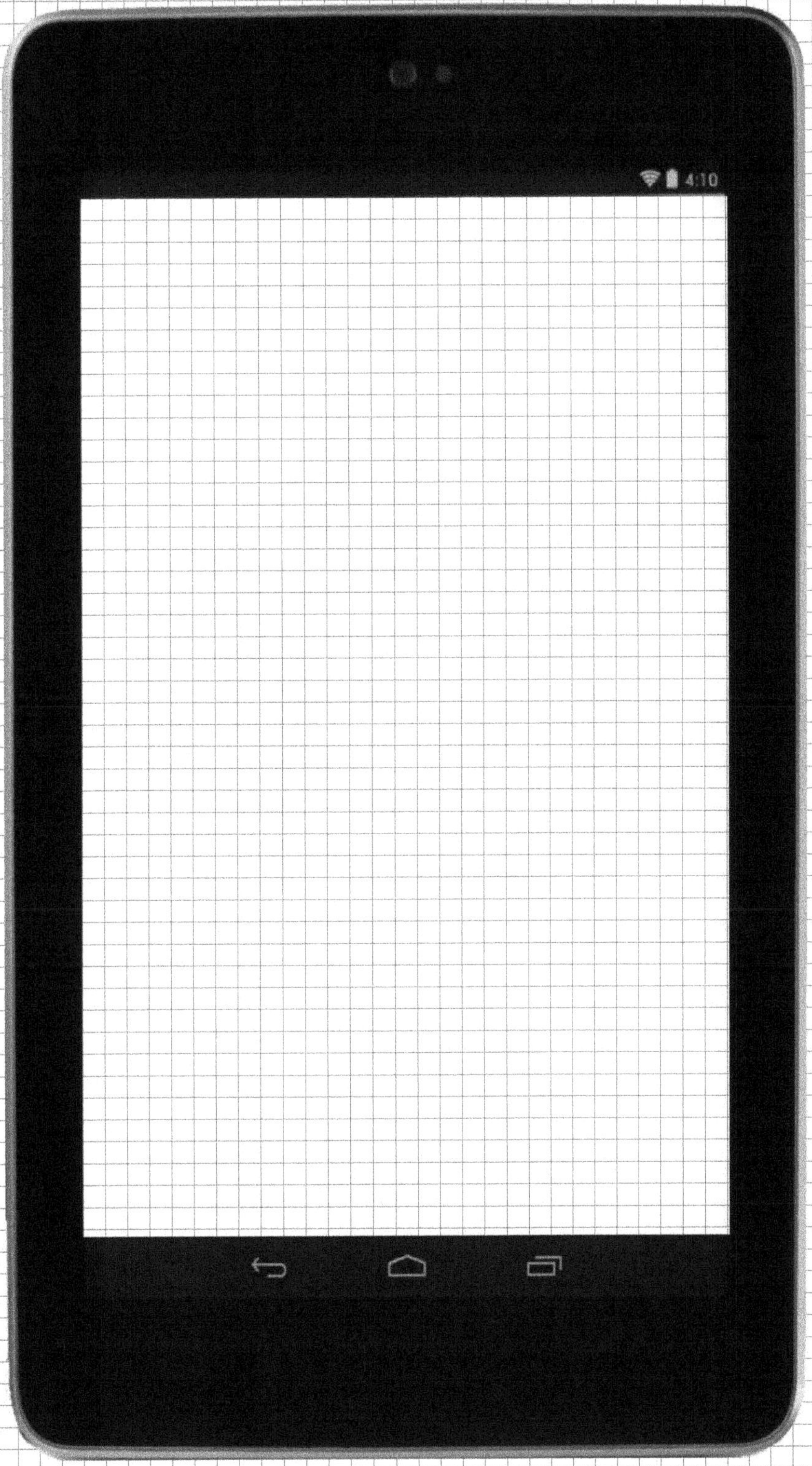

Application Name:

Screen Name:

Notes:

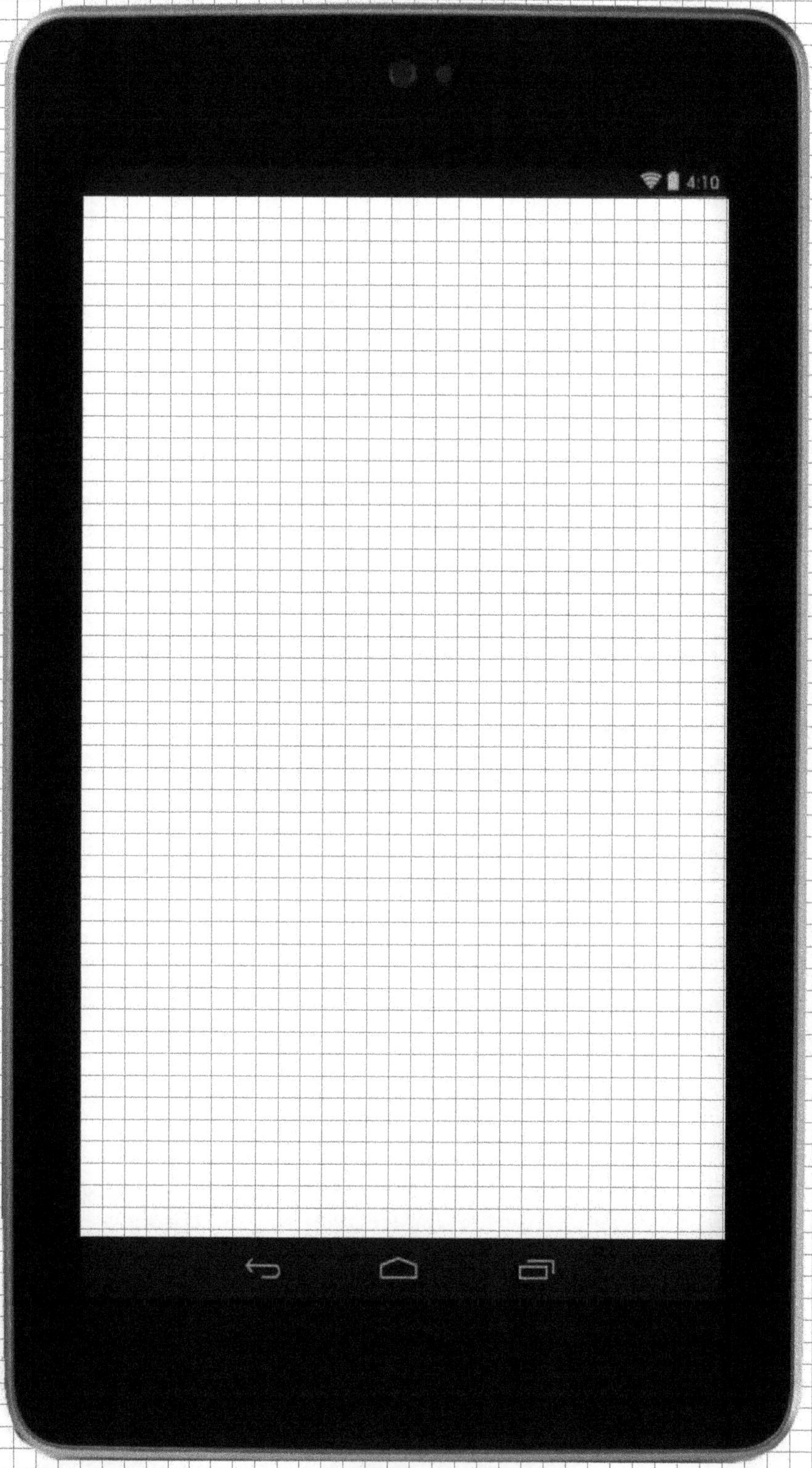

Application Name:

Screen Name:

Notes:

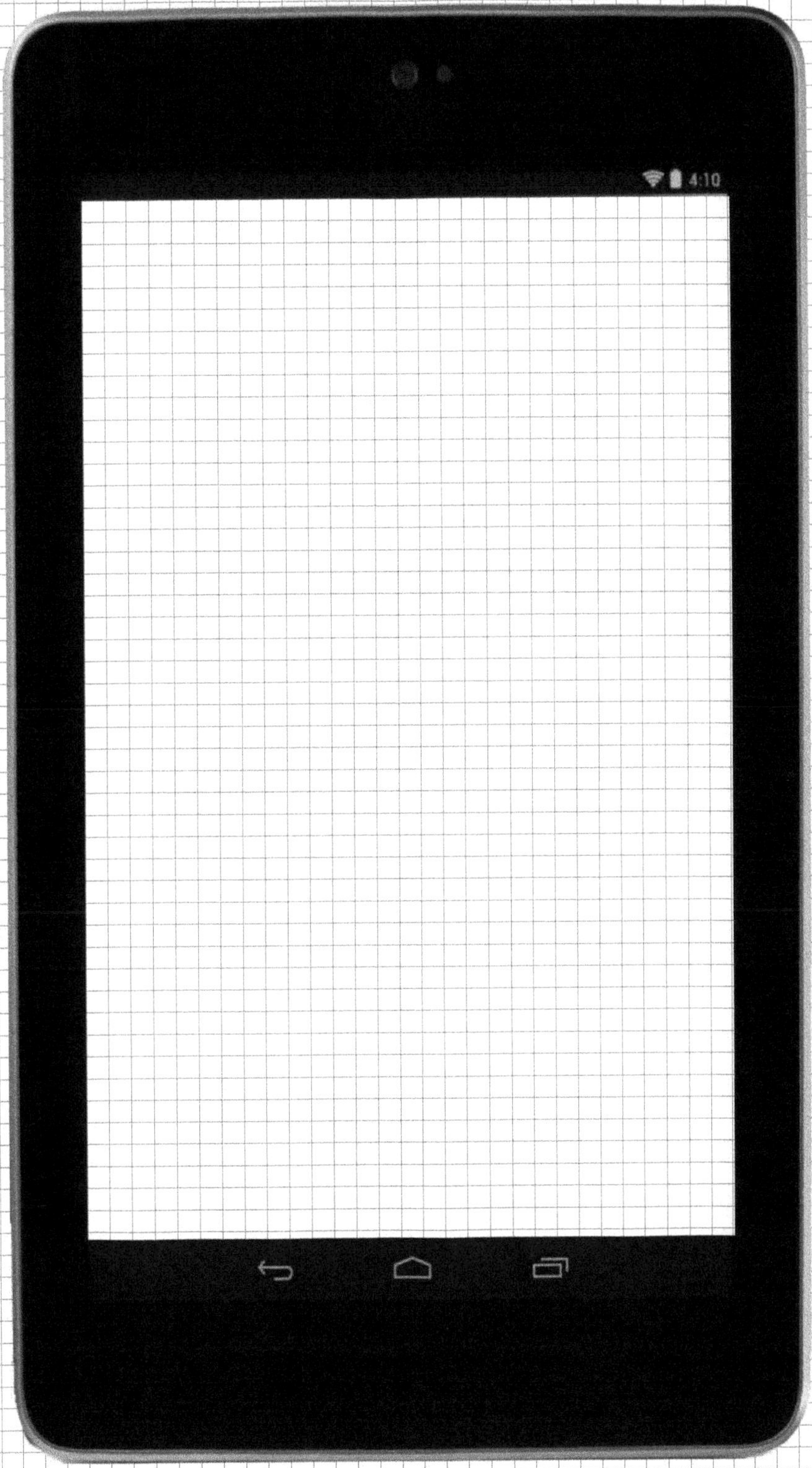

Application Name:

Screen Name:

Notes:

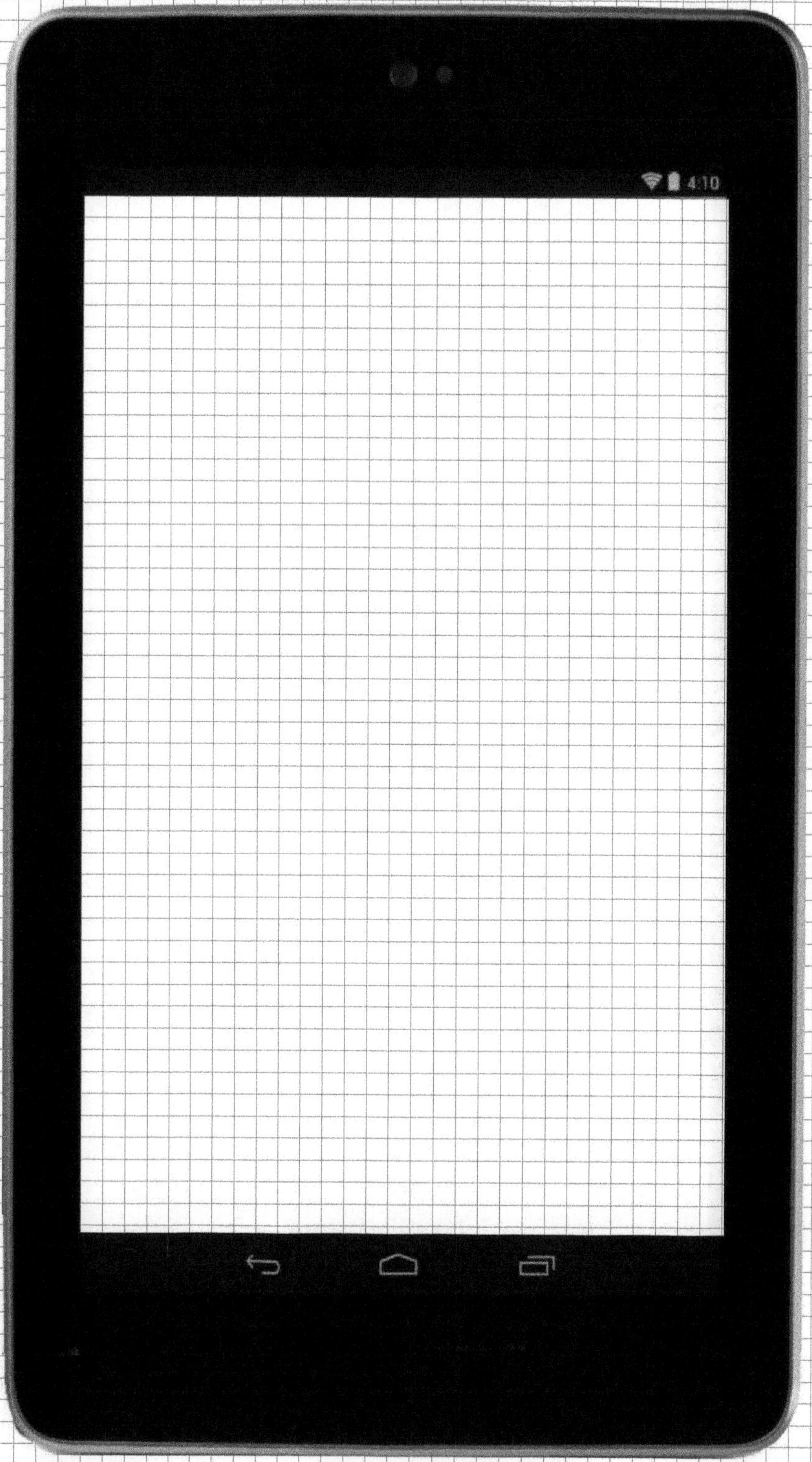

Application Name:

Screen Name:

Notes:

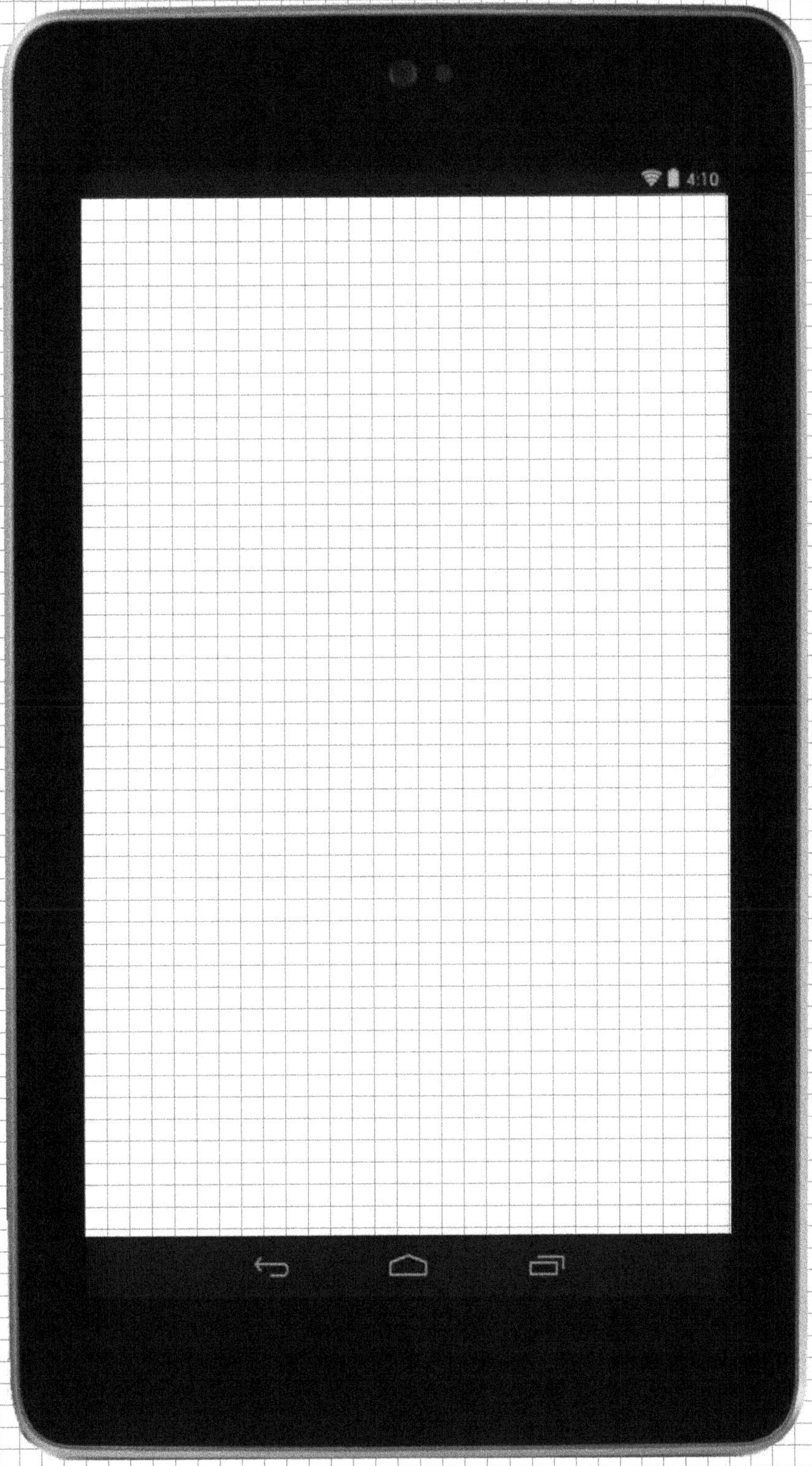

Application Name:

Screen Name:

Notes:

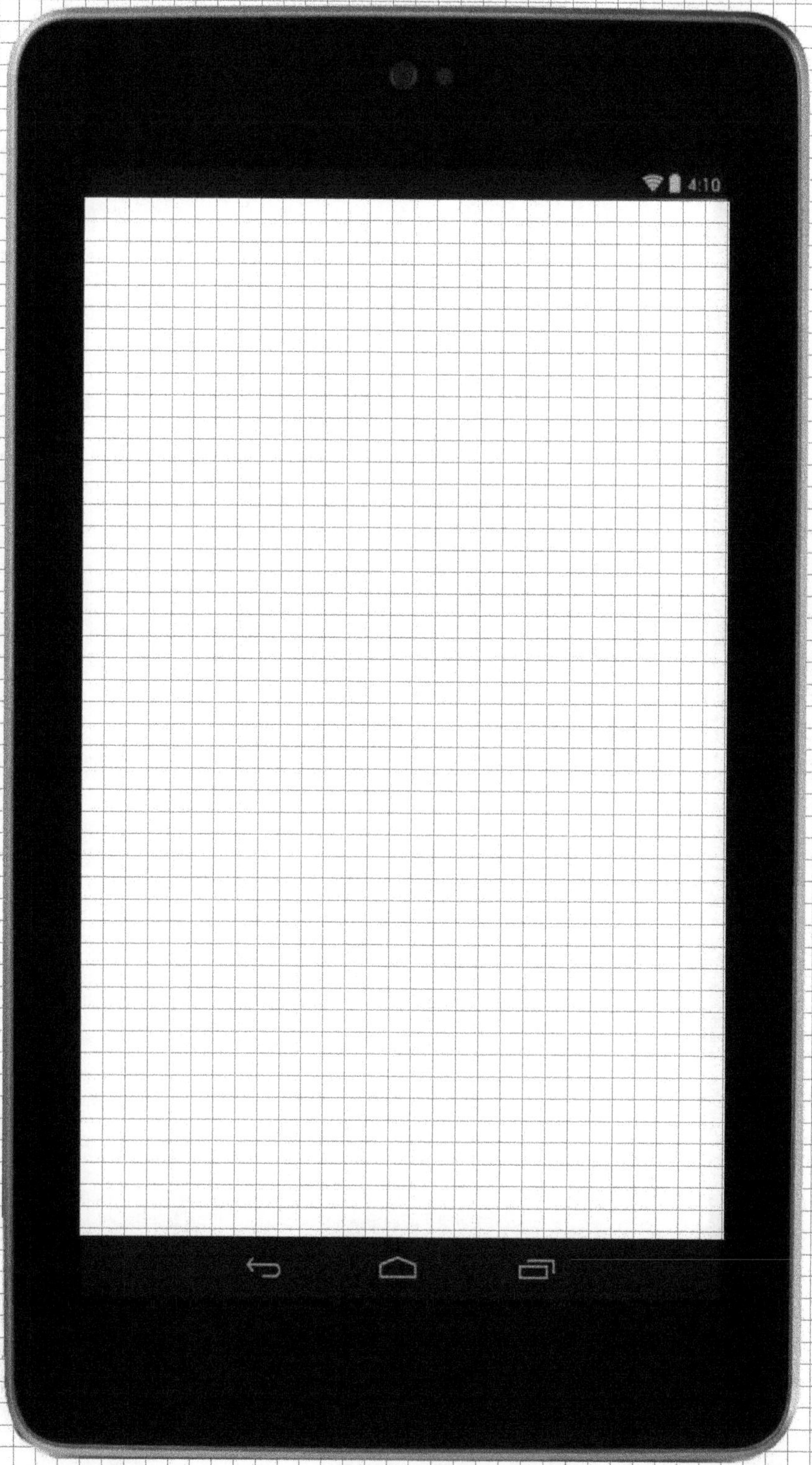

Application Name:

Screen Name:

Notes:

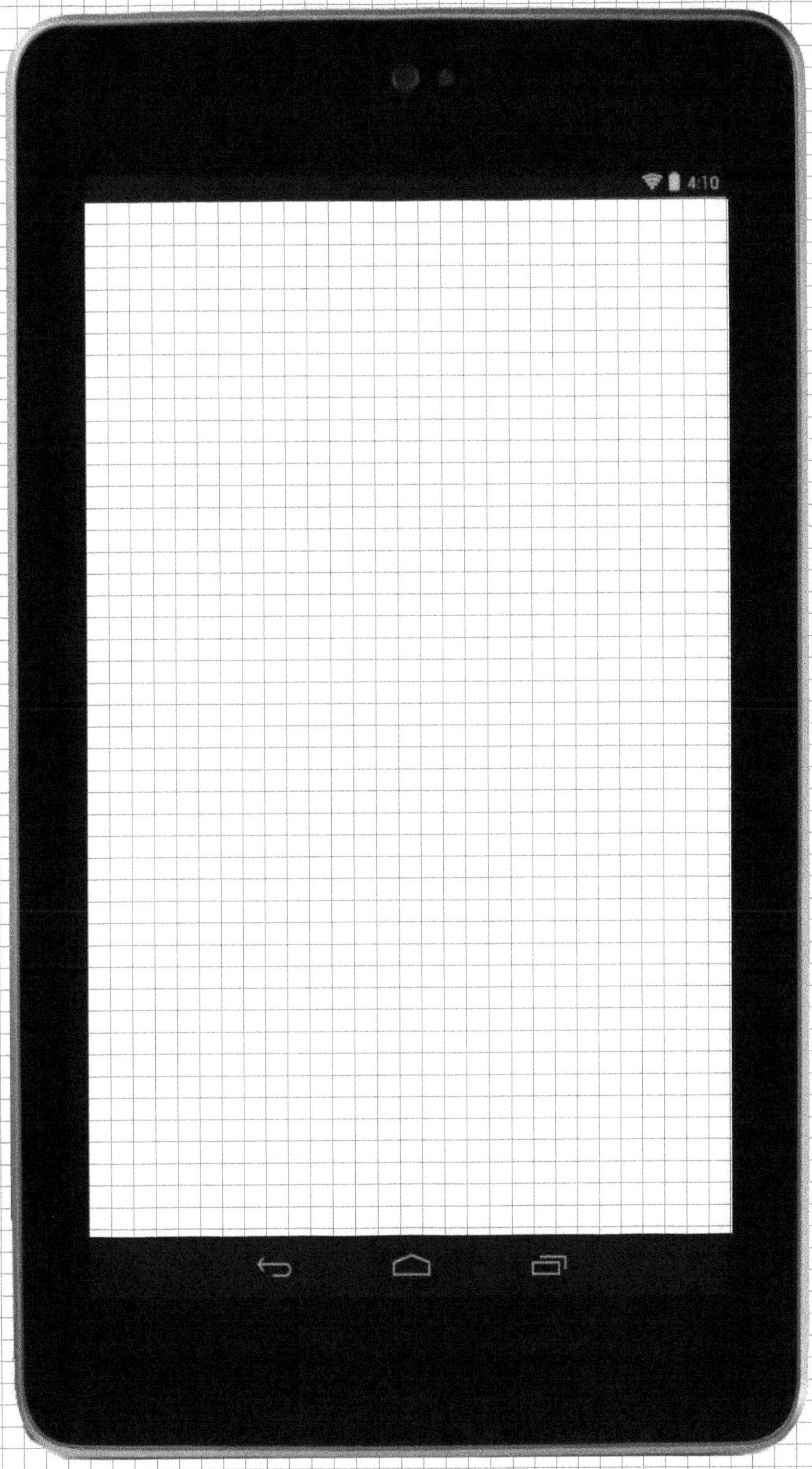

Application Name:

Screen Name:

Notes:

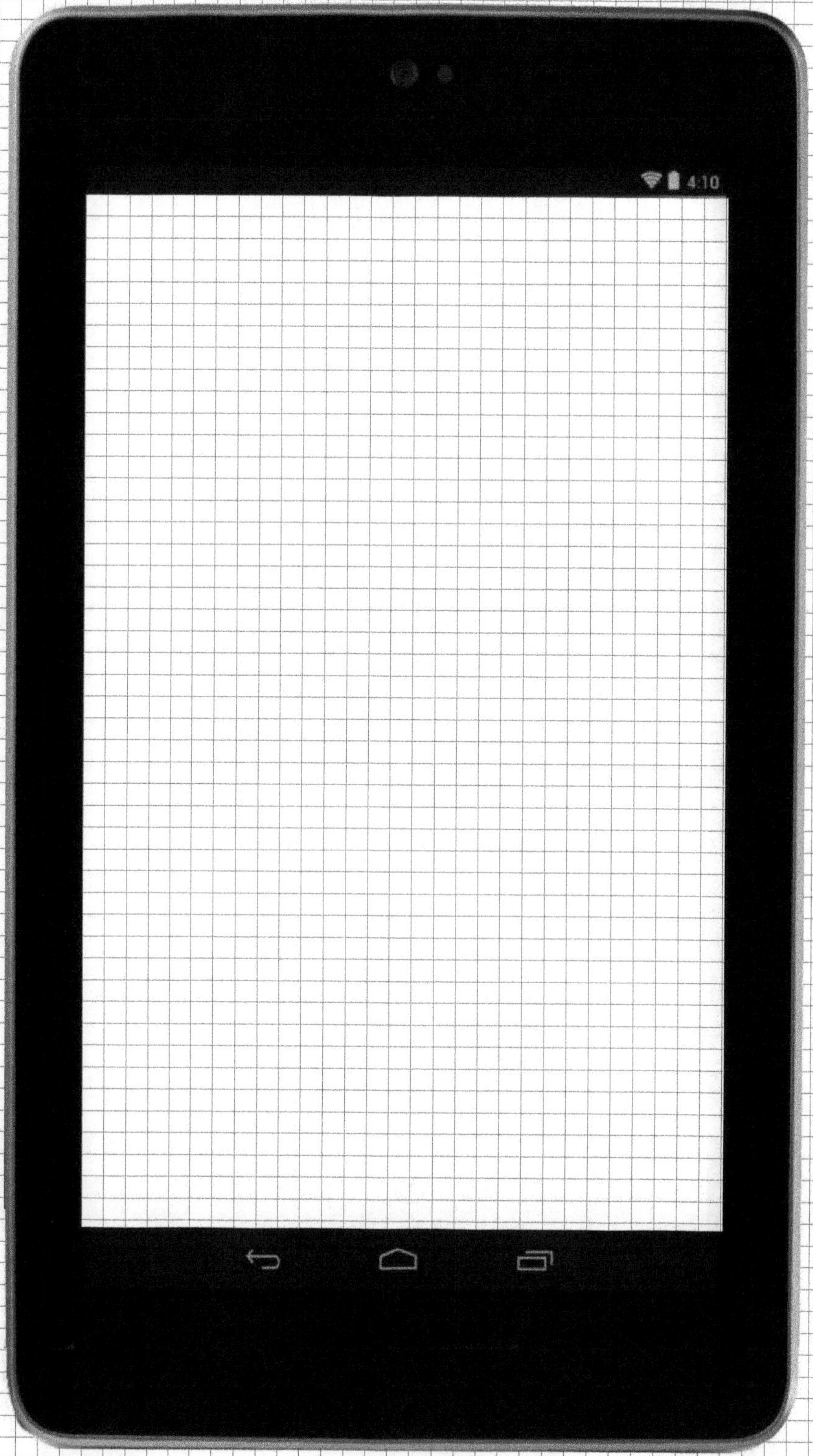

Application Name:

Screen Name:

Notes:

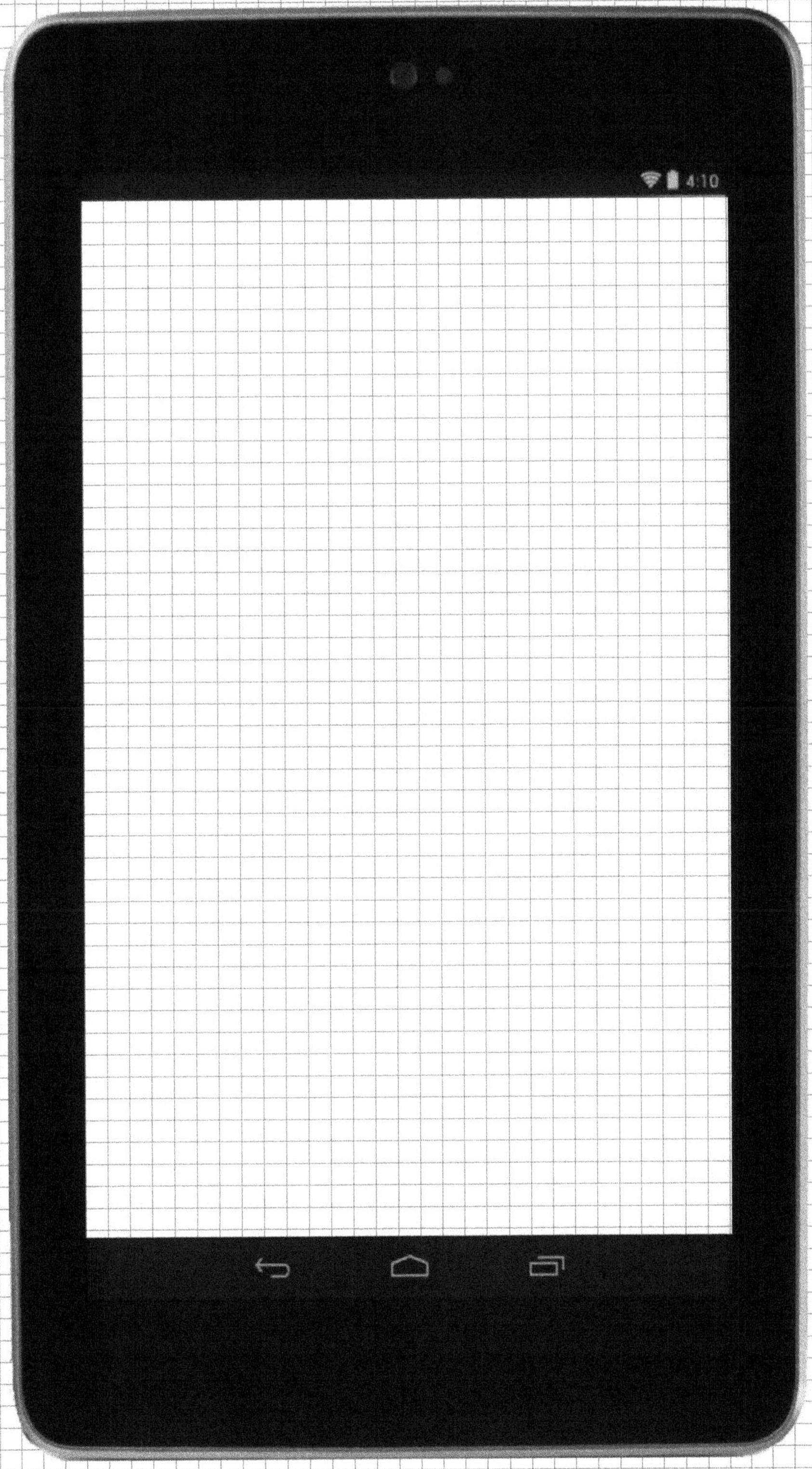

Application Name:

Screen Name:

Notes:

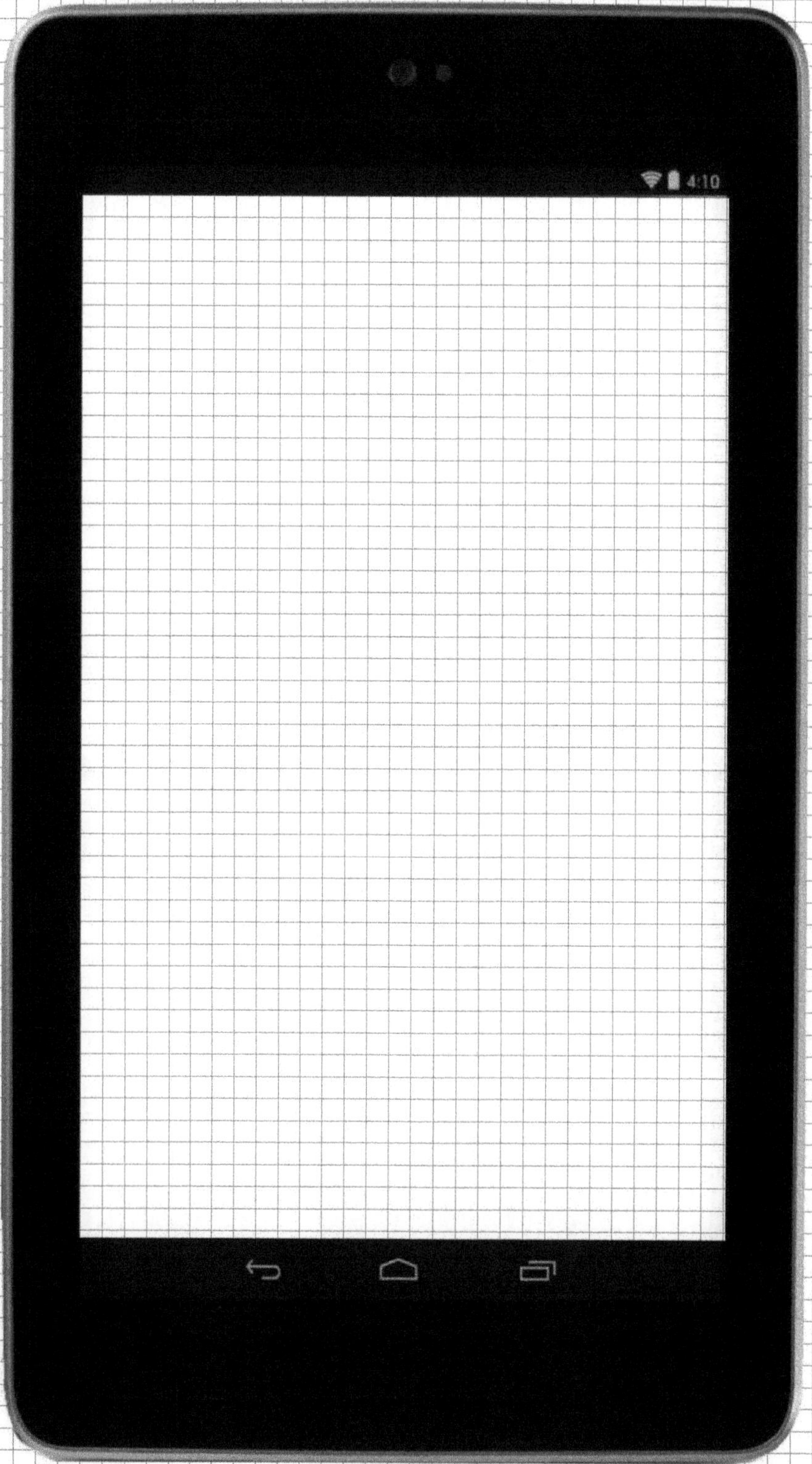

Application Name:

Screen Name:

Notes:

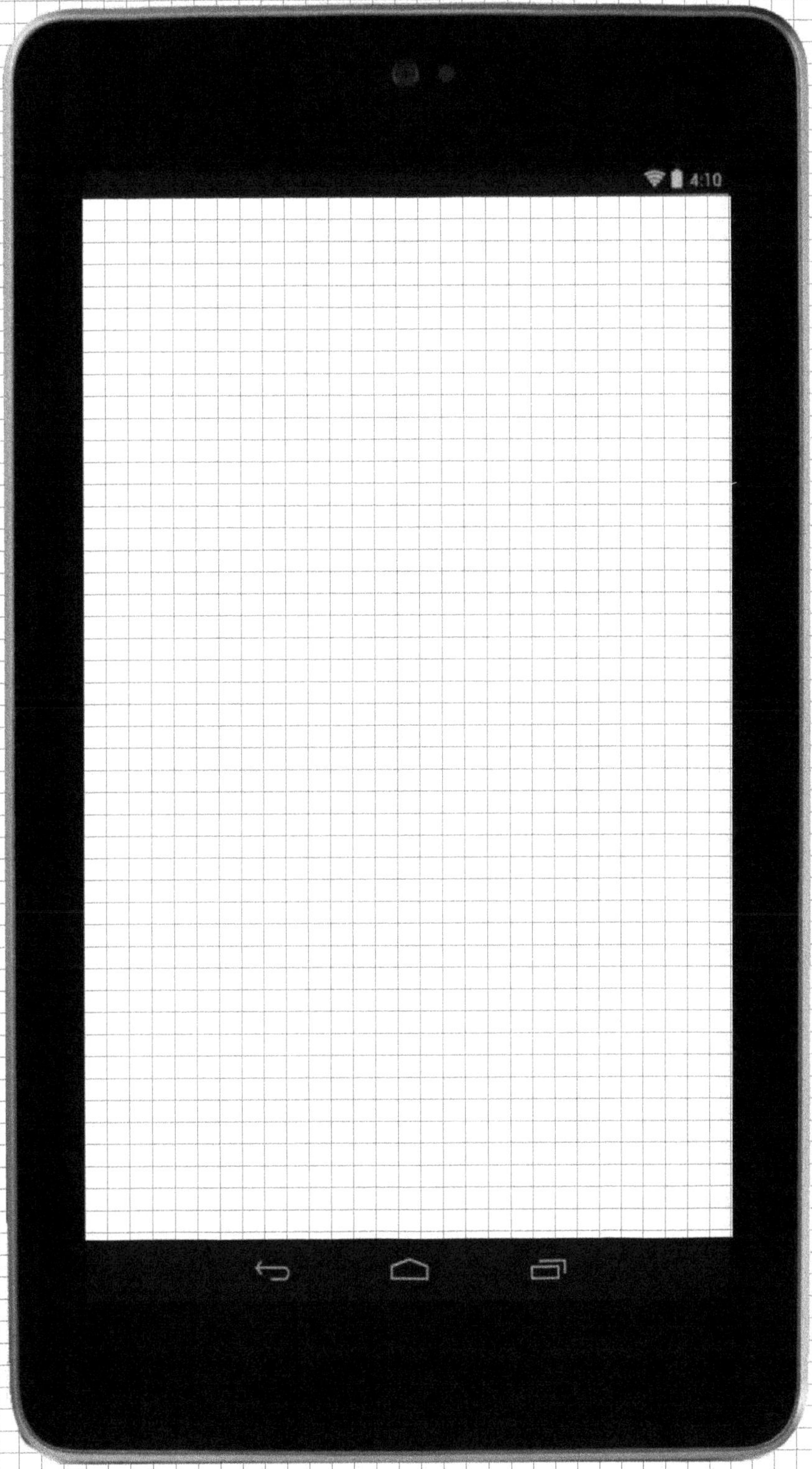

Application Name:

Screen Name:

Notes:

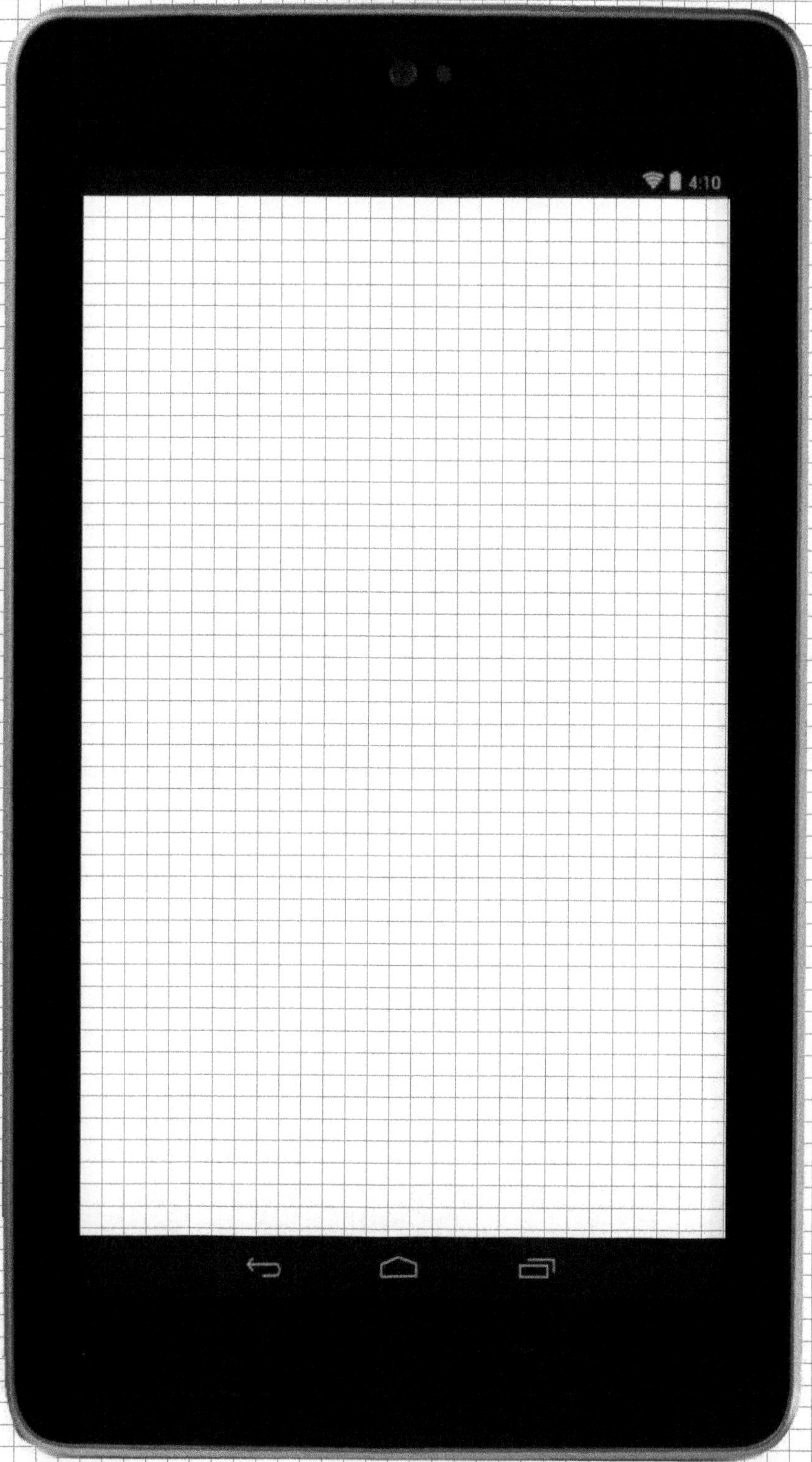

Application Name:

Screen Name:

Notes:

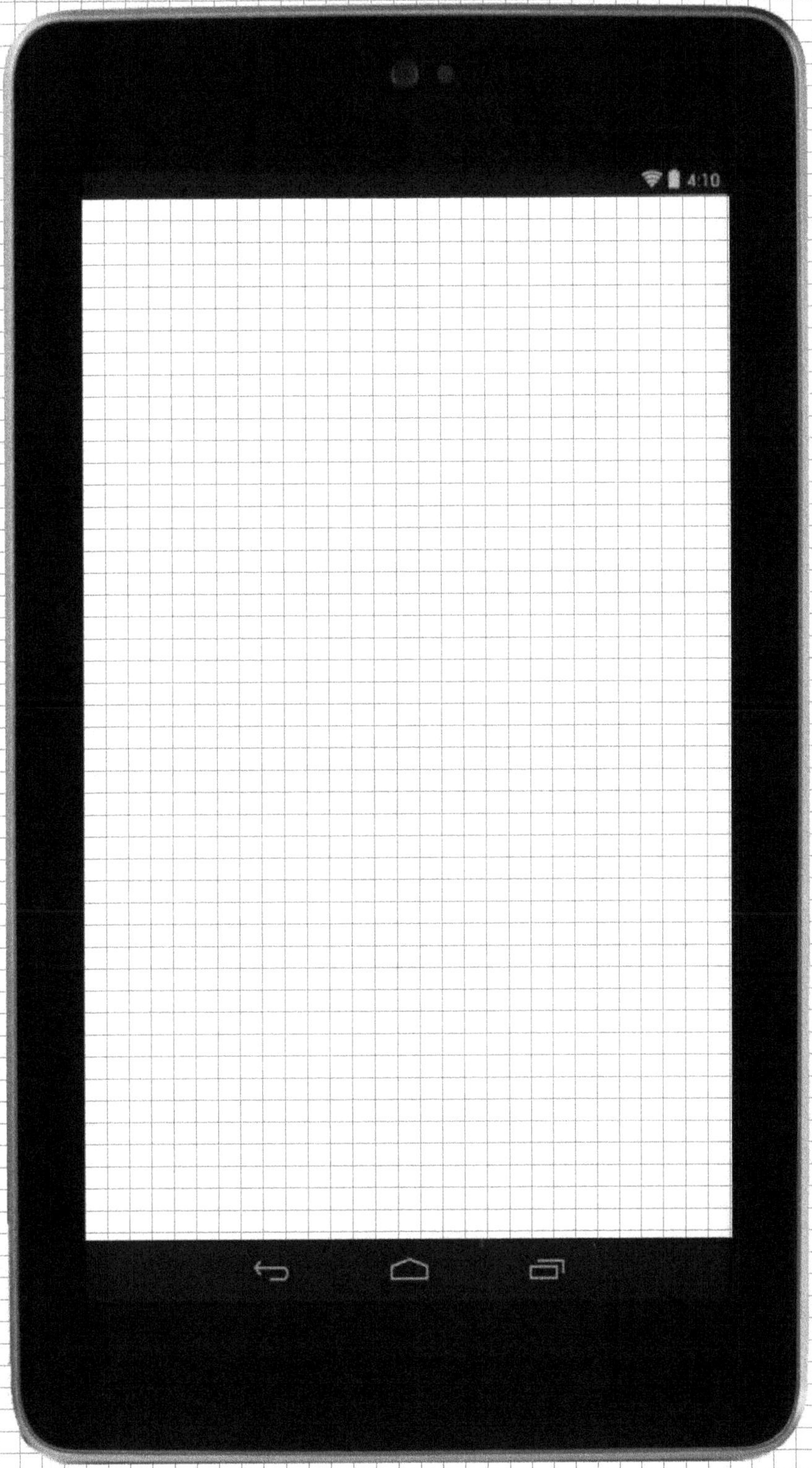

Application Name:

Screen Name:

Notes:

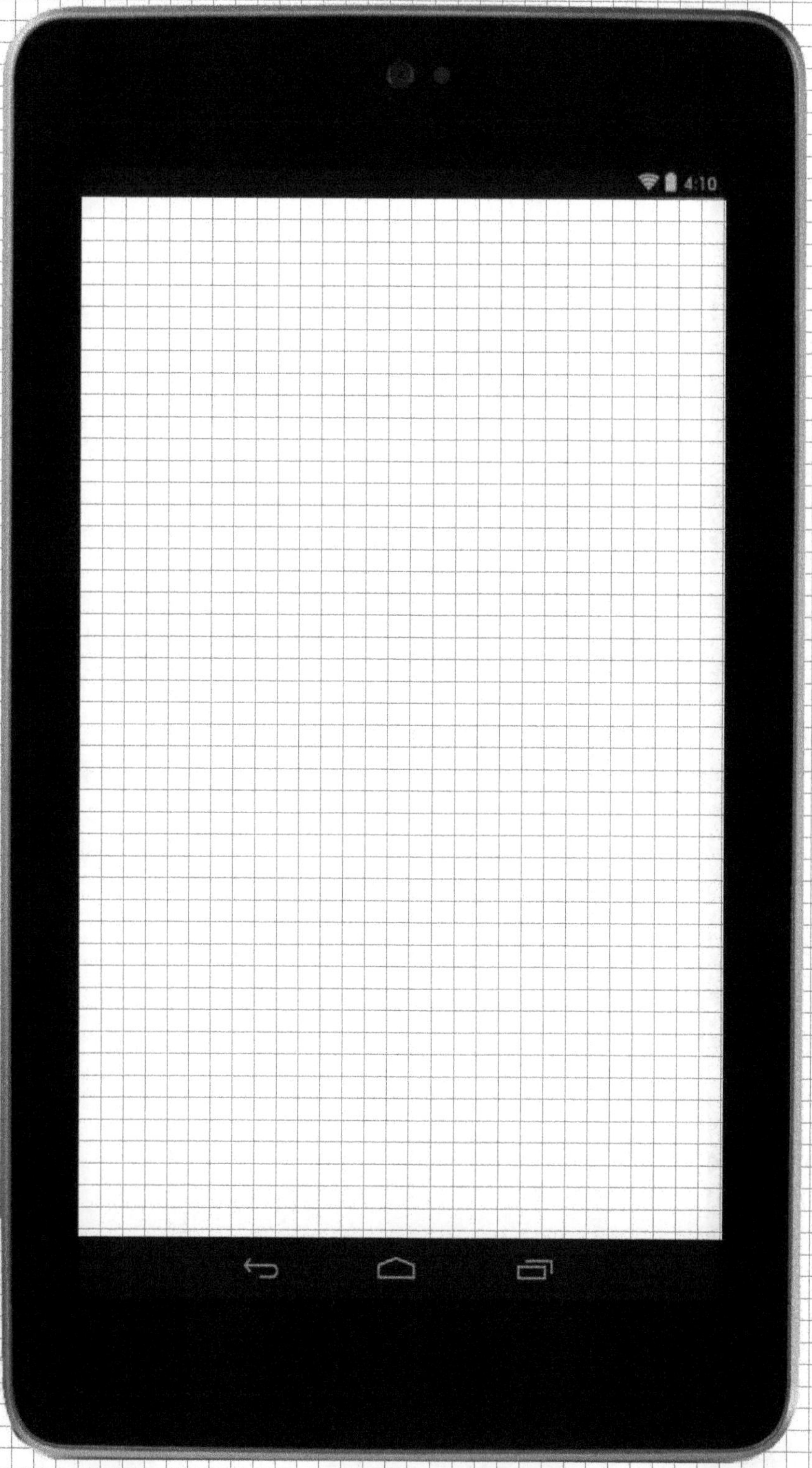

Application Name:

Screen Name:

Notes:

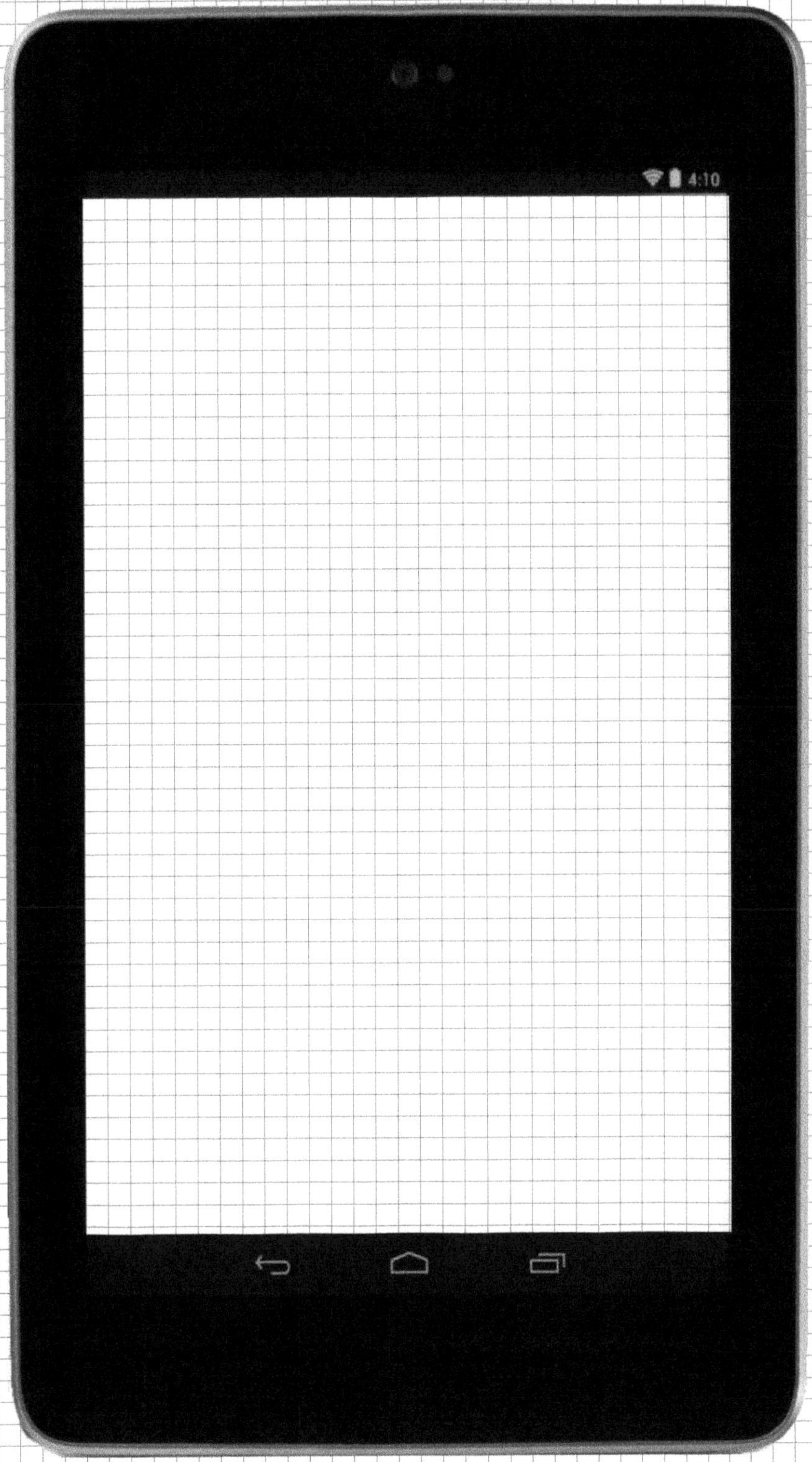

Application Name:

Screen Name:

Notes:

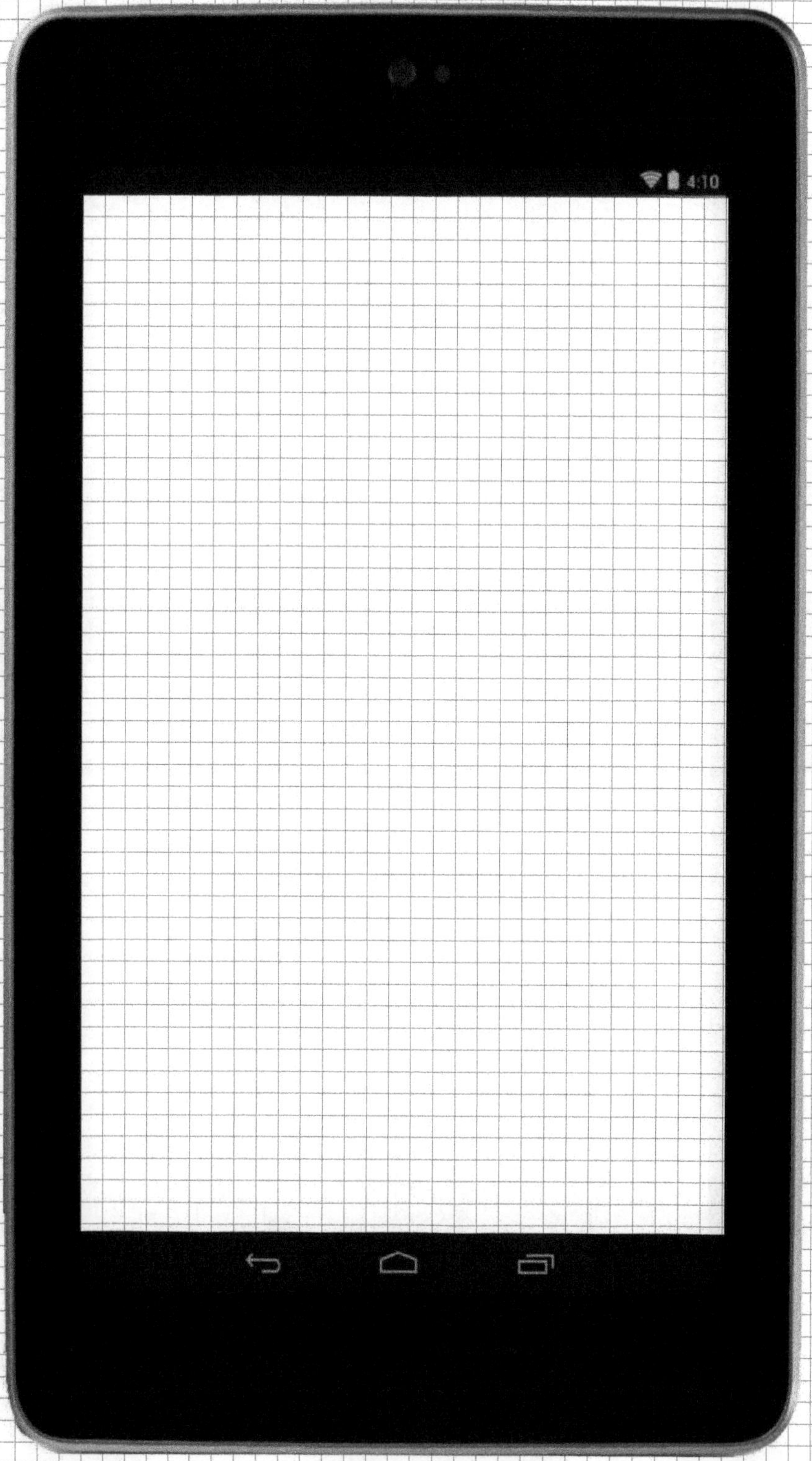

Application Name:

Screen Name:

Notes:

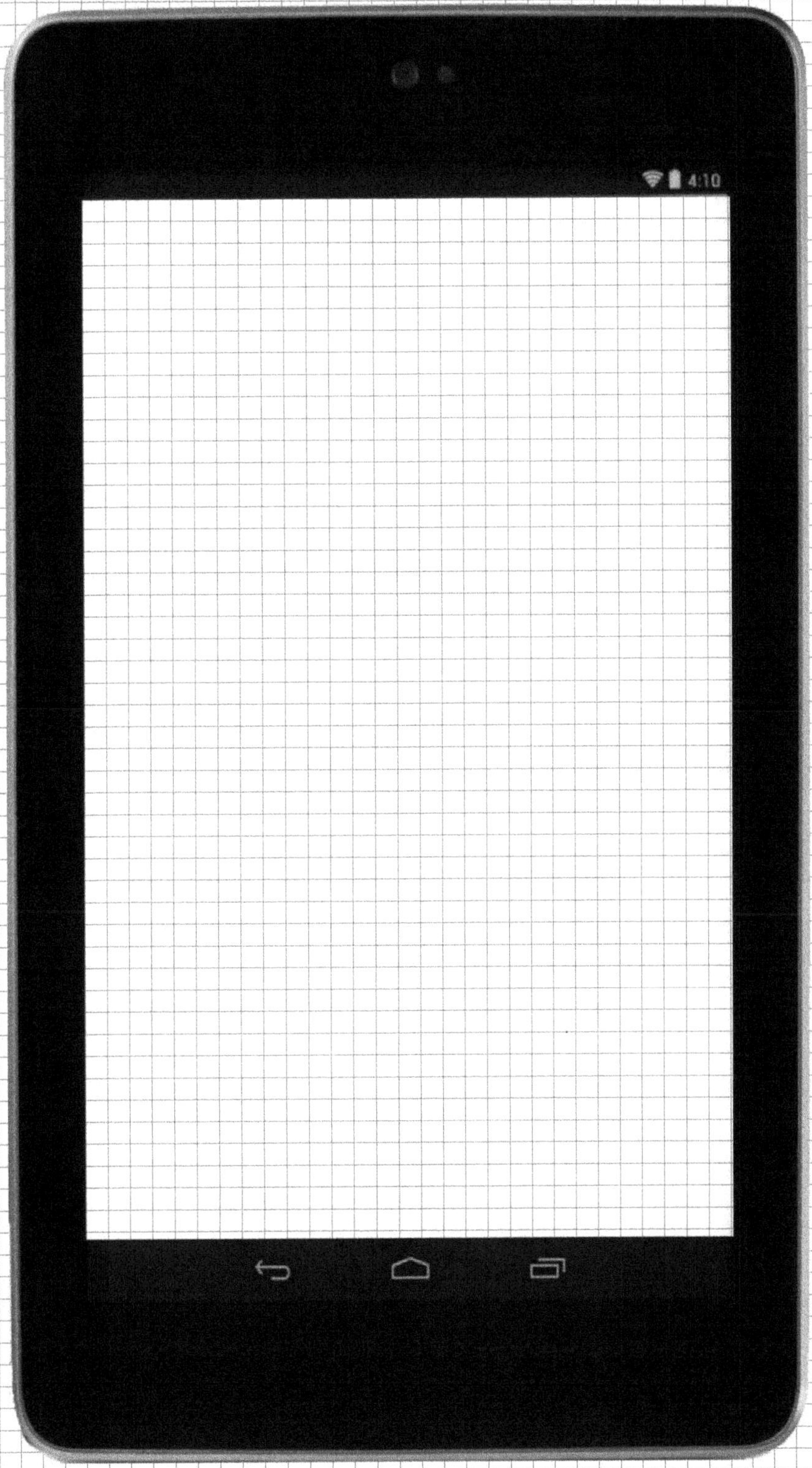

Application Name:

Screen Name:

Notes:

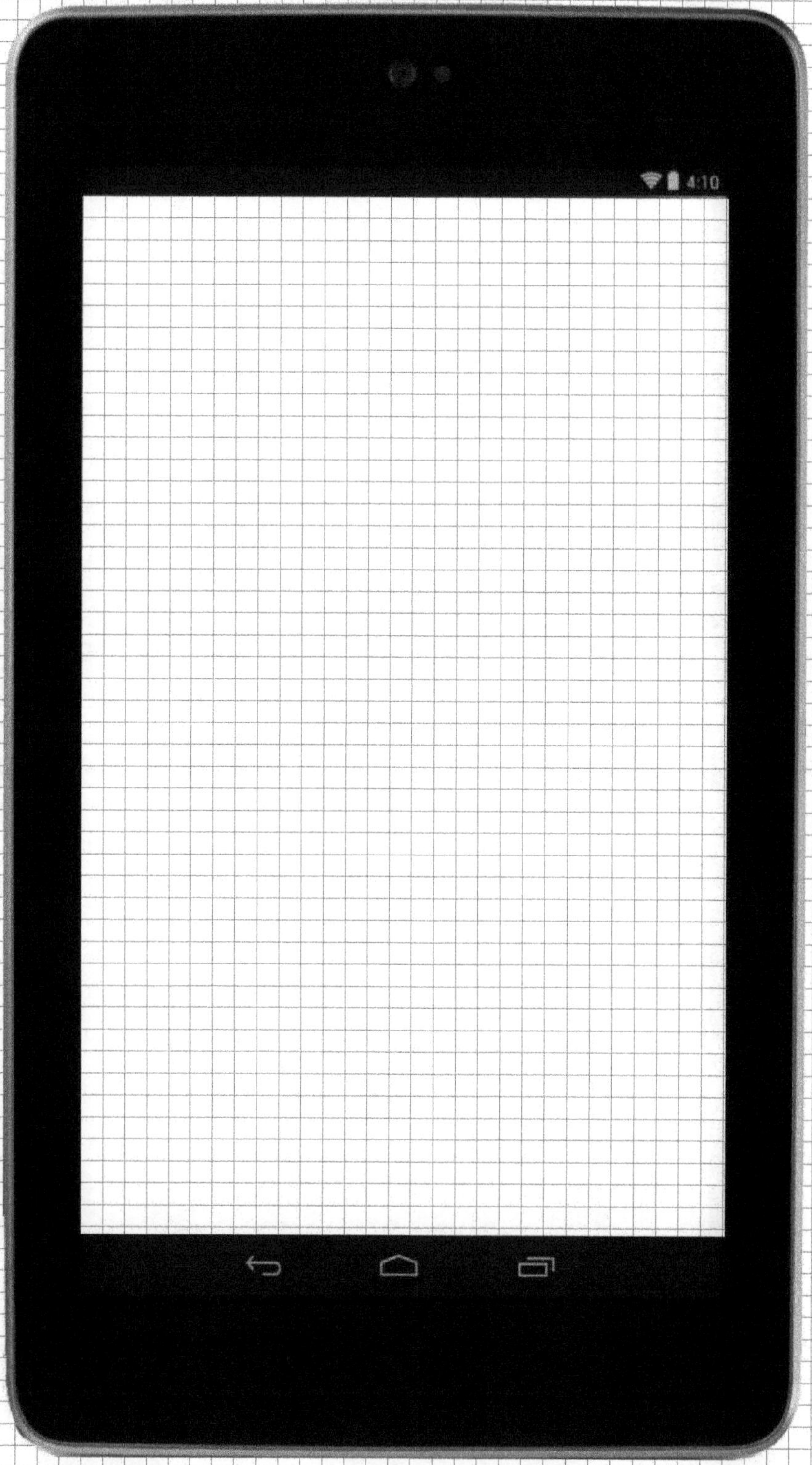

Application Name:

Screen Name:

Notes:

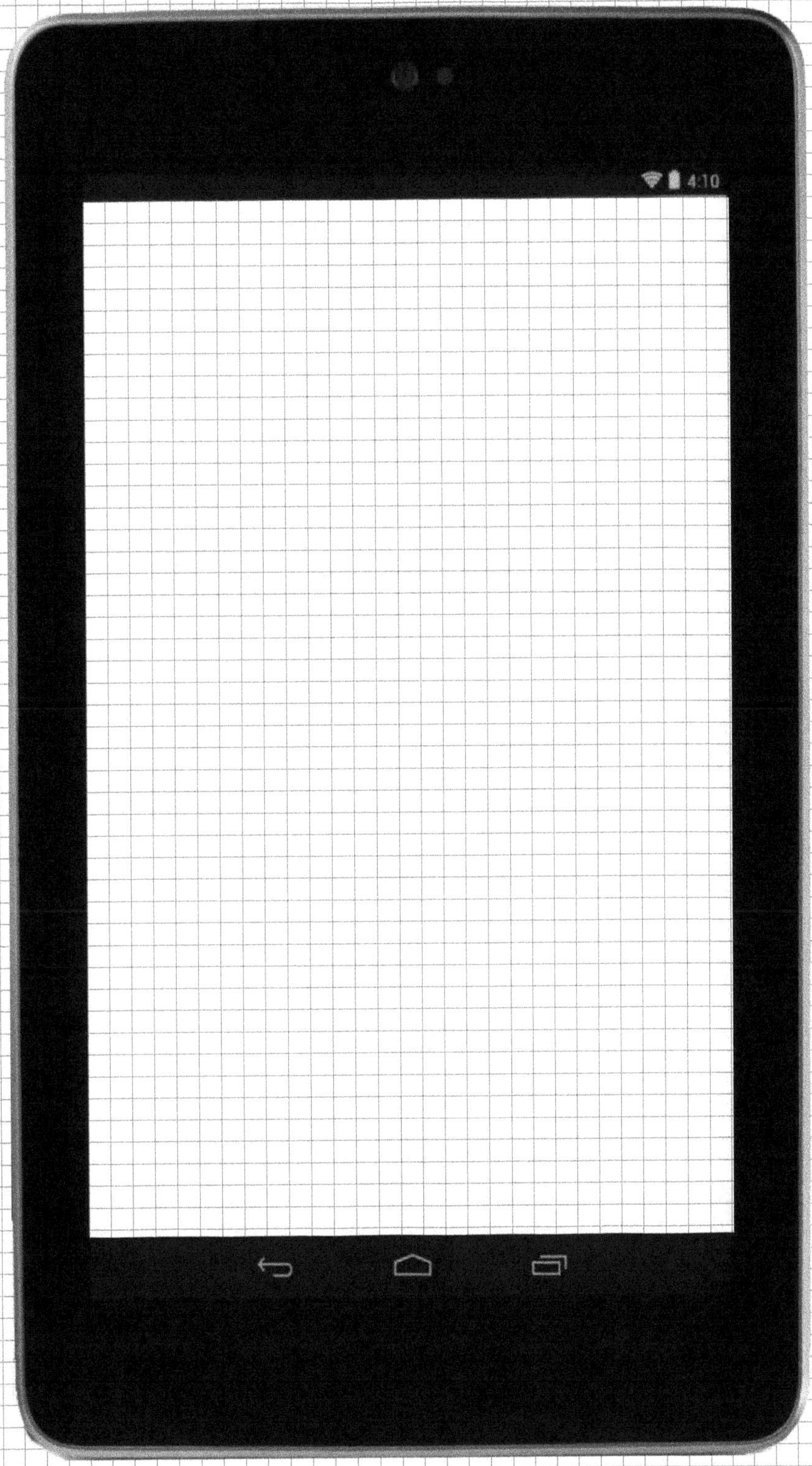

Application Name:

Screen Name:

Notes:

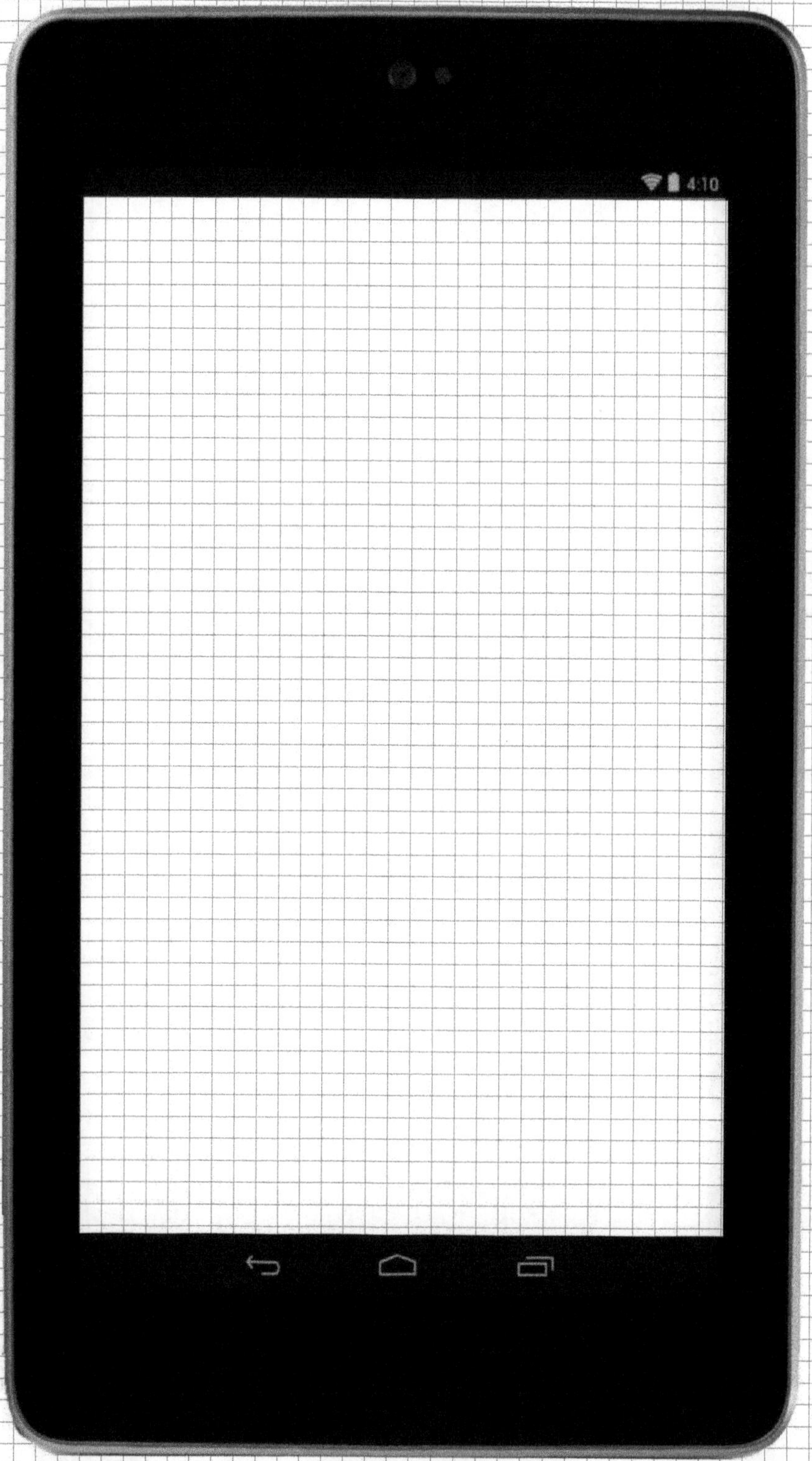

Application Name:

Screen Name:

Notes:

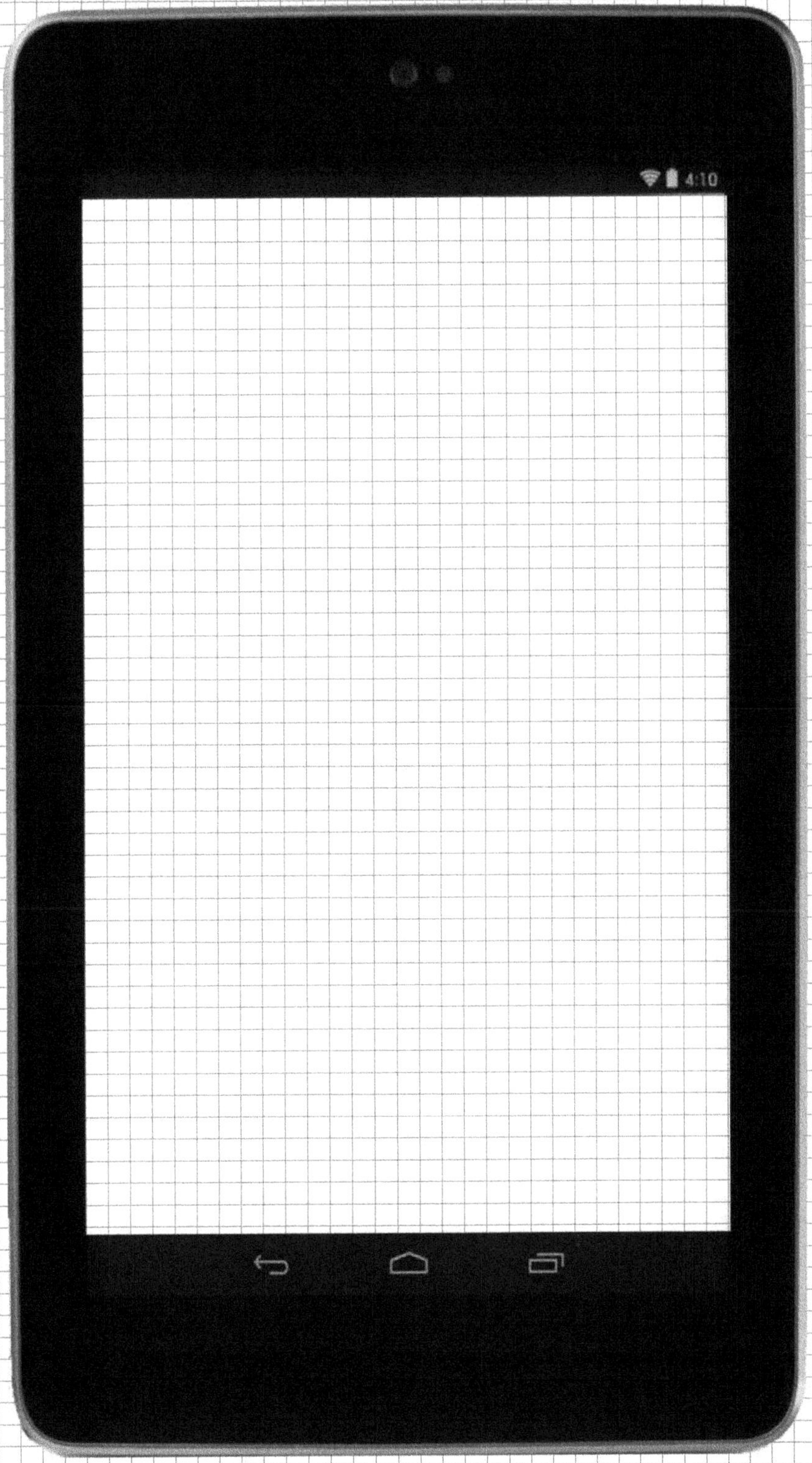

Application Name:

Screen Name:

Notes:

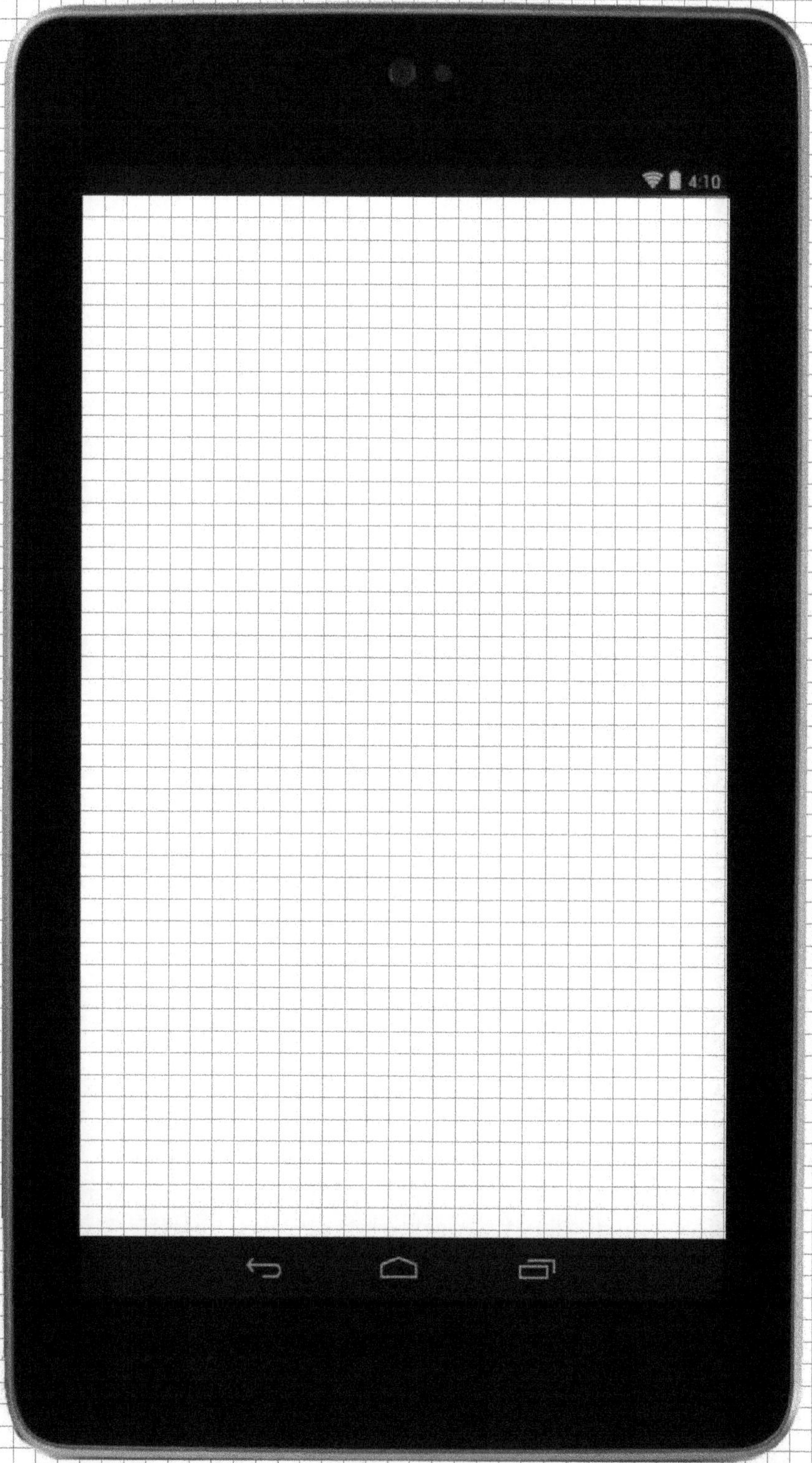

Application Name:

Screen Name:

Notes:

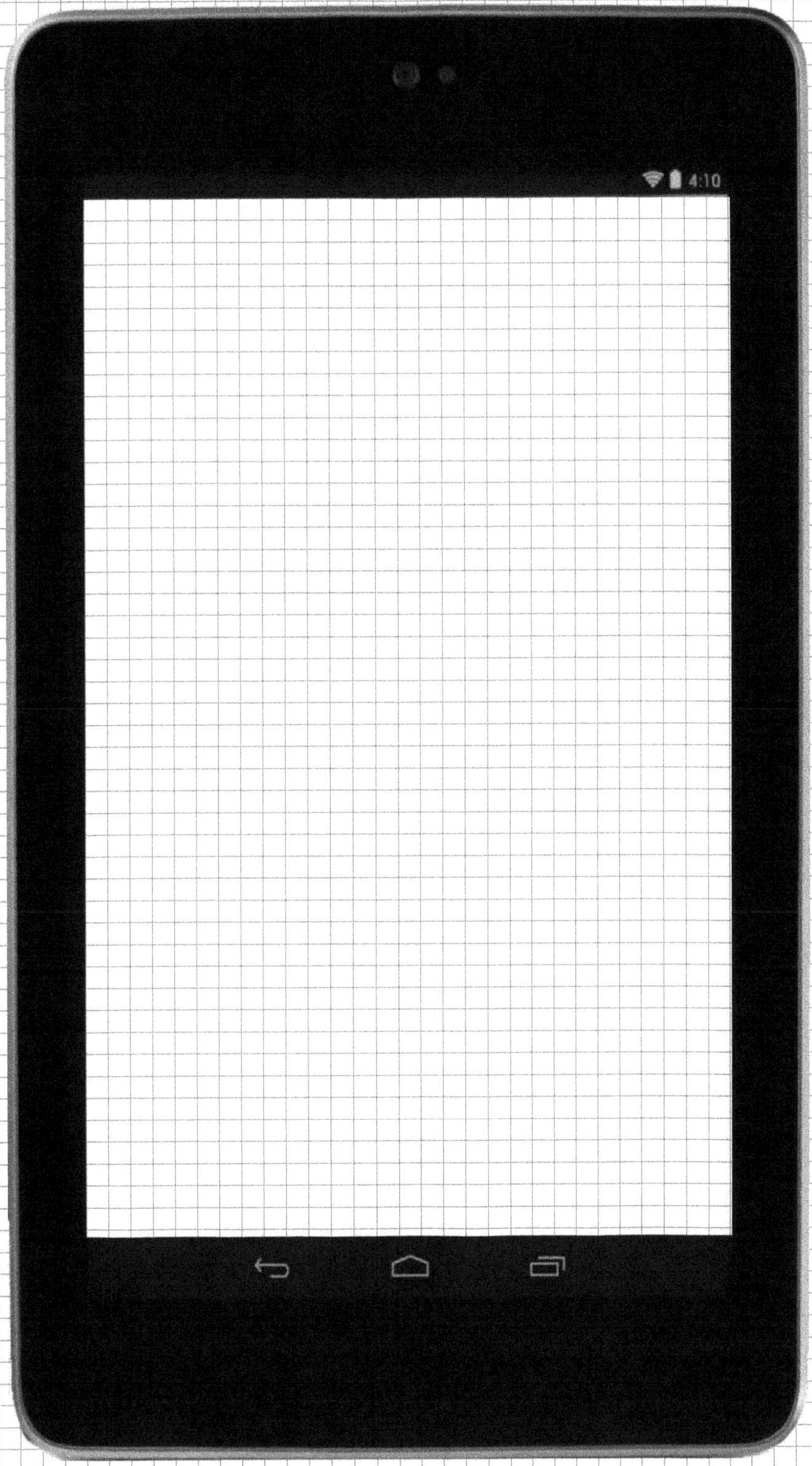

Application Name:

Screen Name:

Notes:

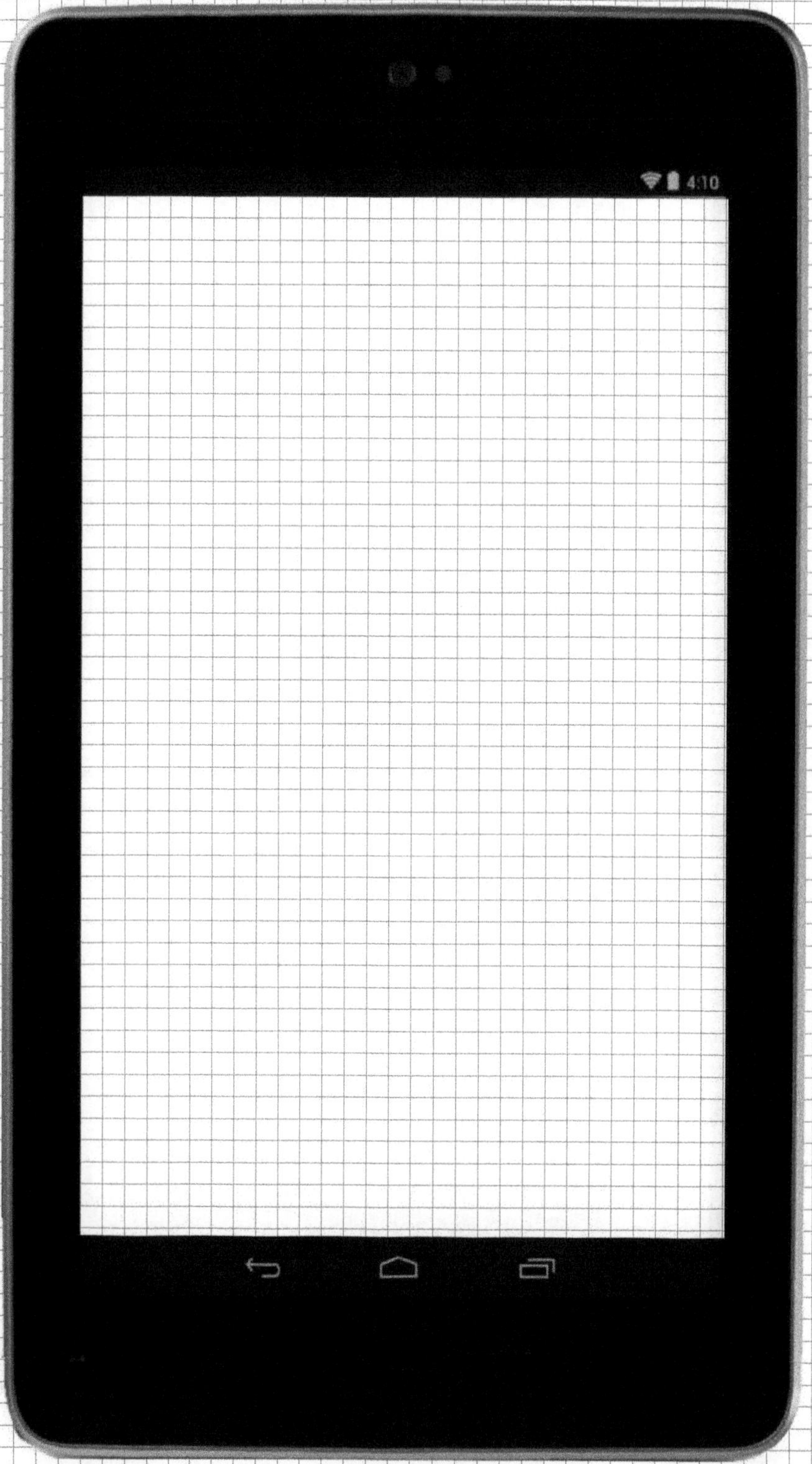

Application Name:

Screen Name:

Notes:

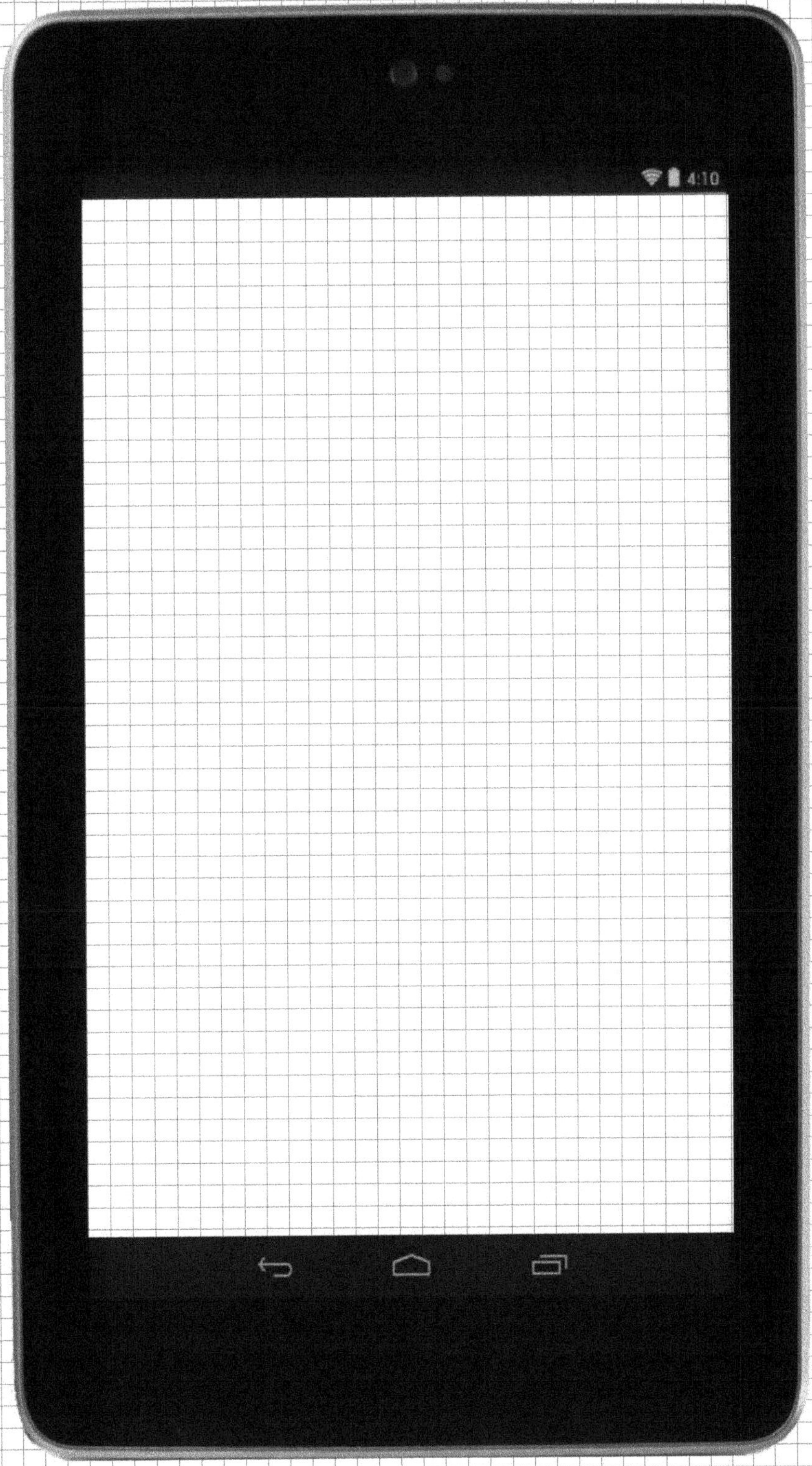

Application Name:

Screen Name:

Notes:

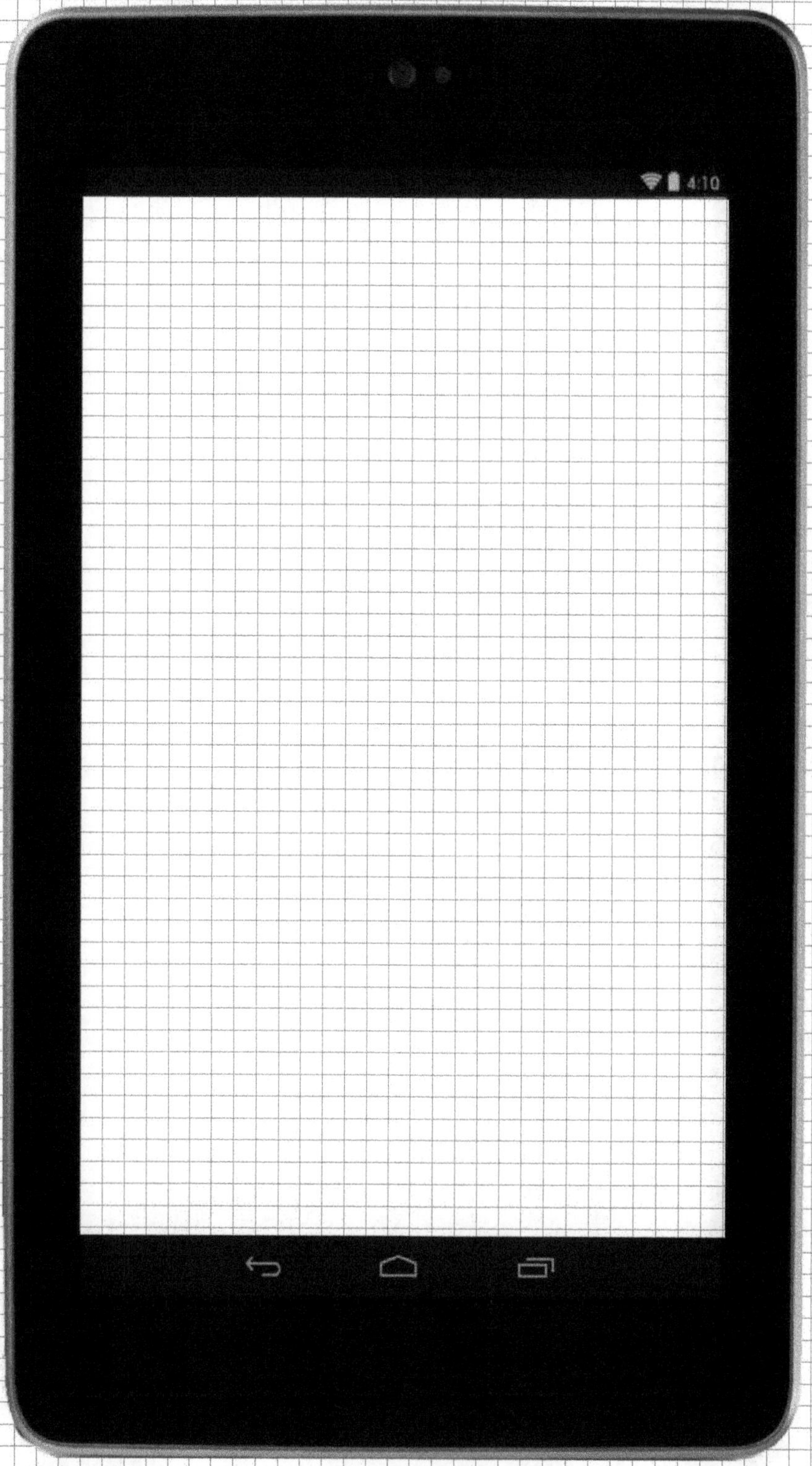

Application Name:

Screen Name:

Notes:

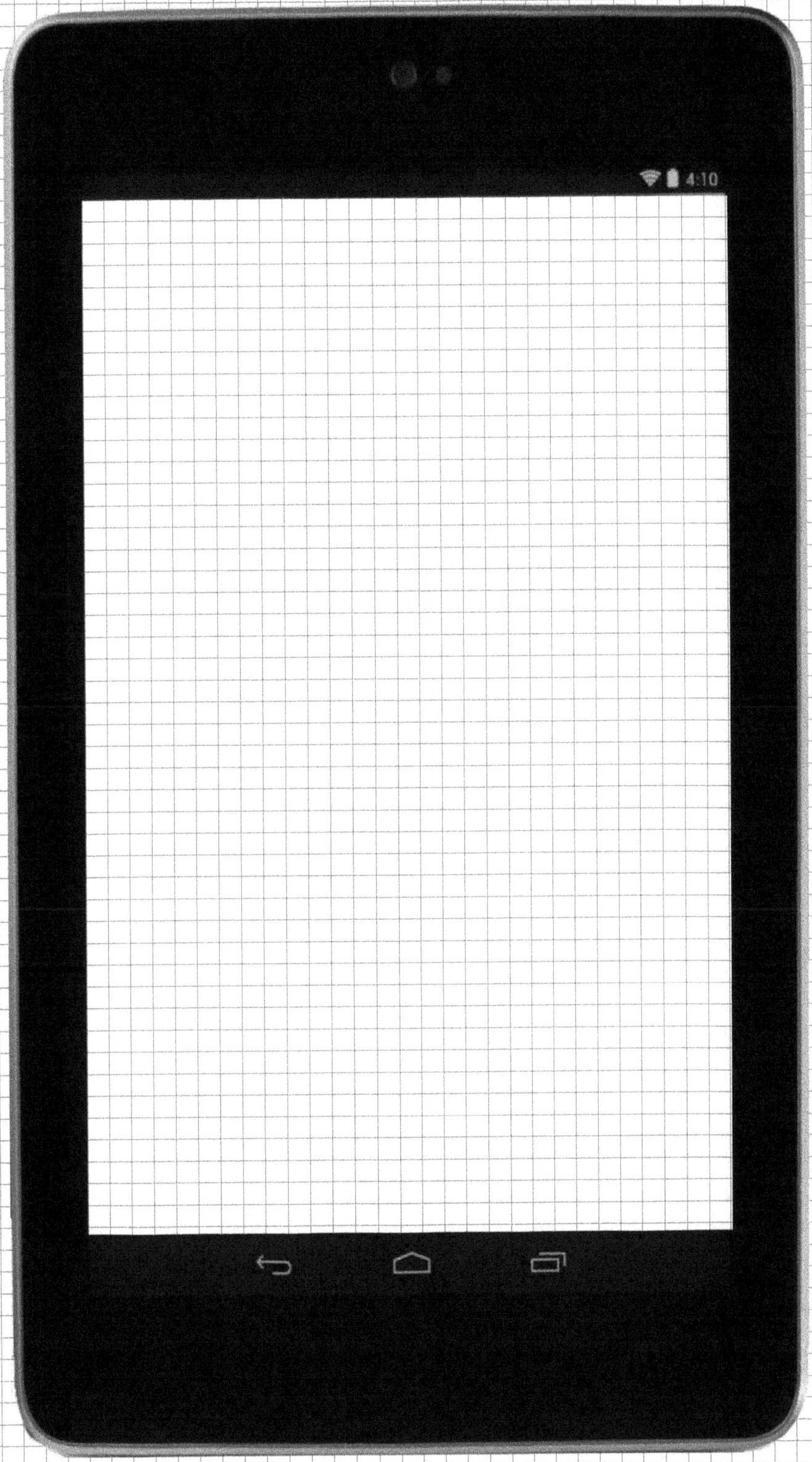

Application Name:

Screen Name:

Notes:

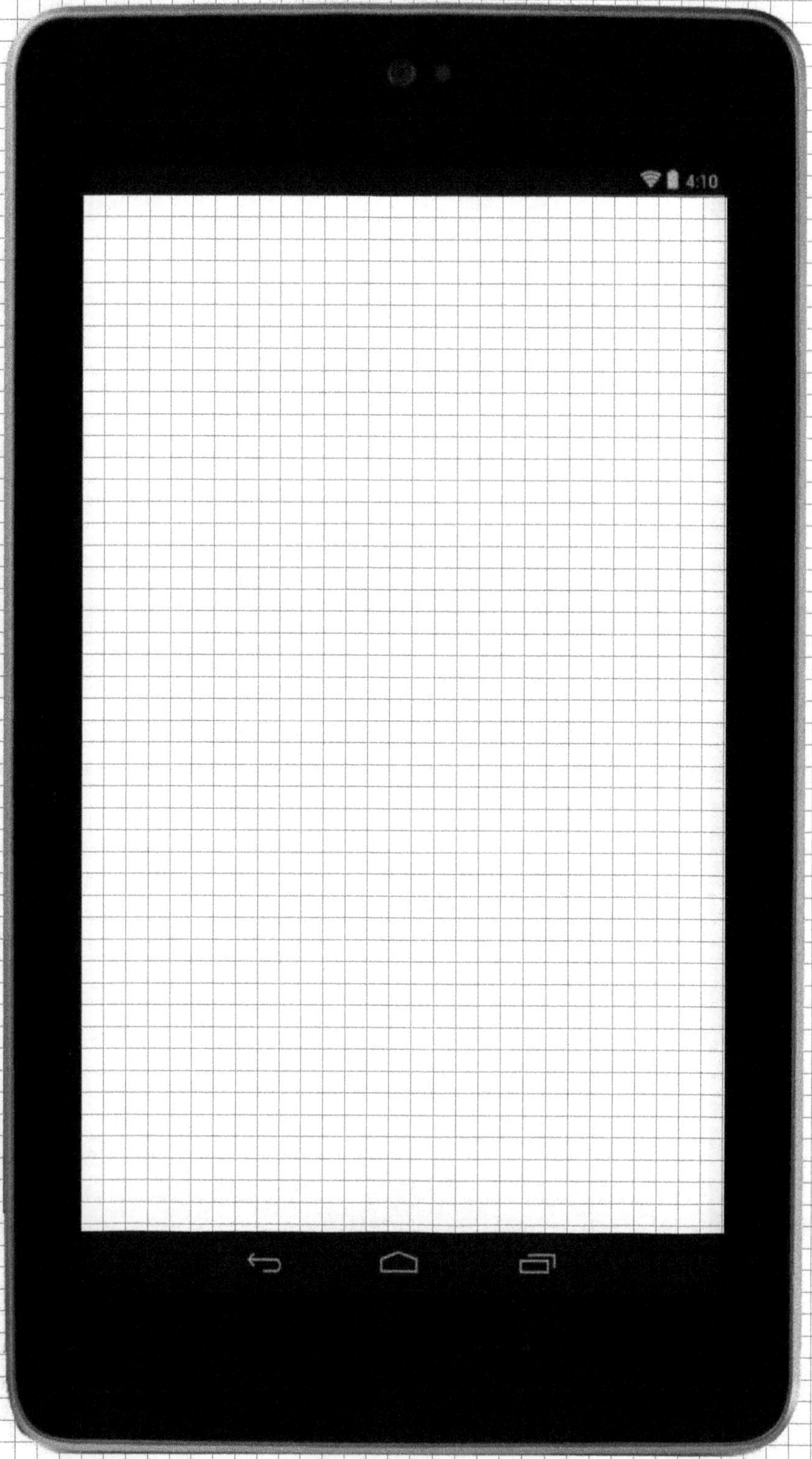

Application Name:

Screen Name:

Notes:

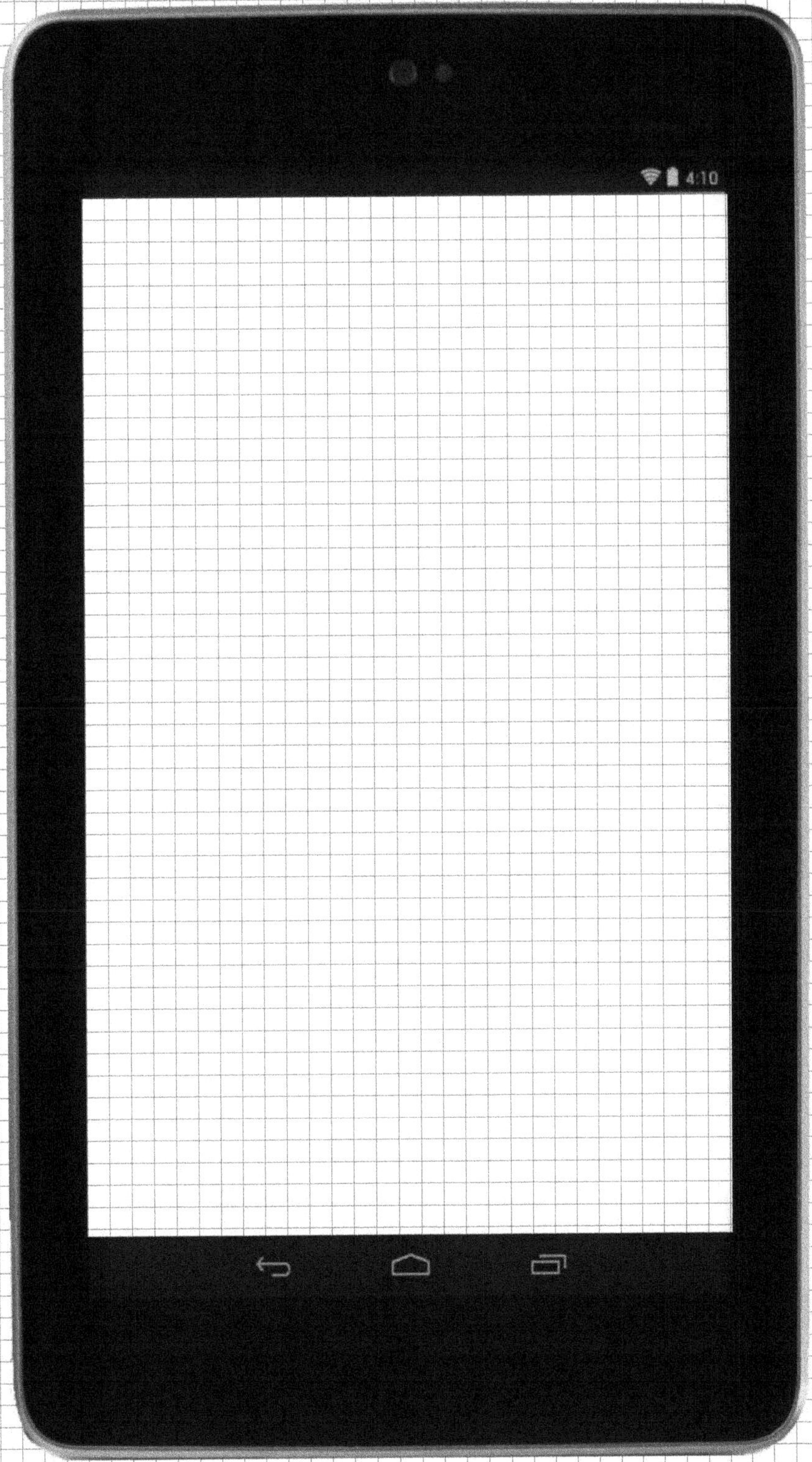

Application Name:

Screen Name:

Notes:

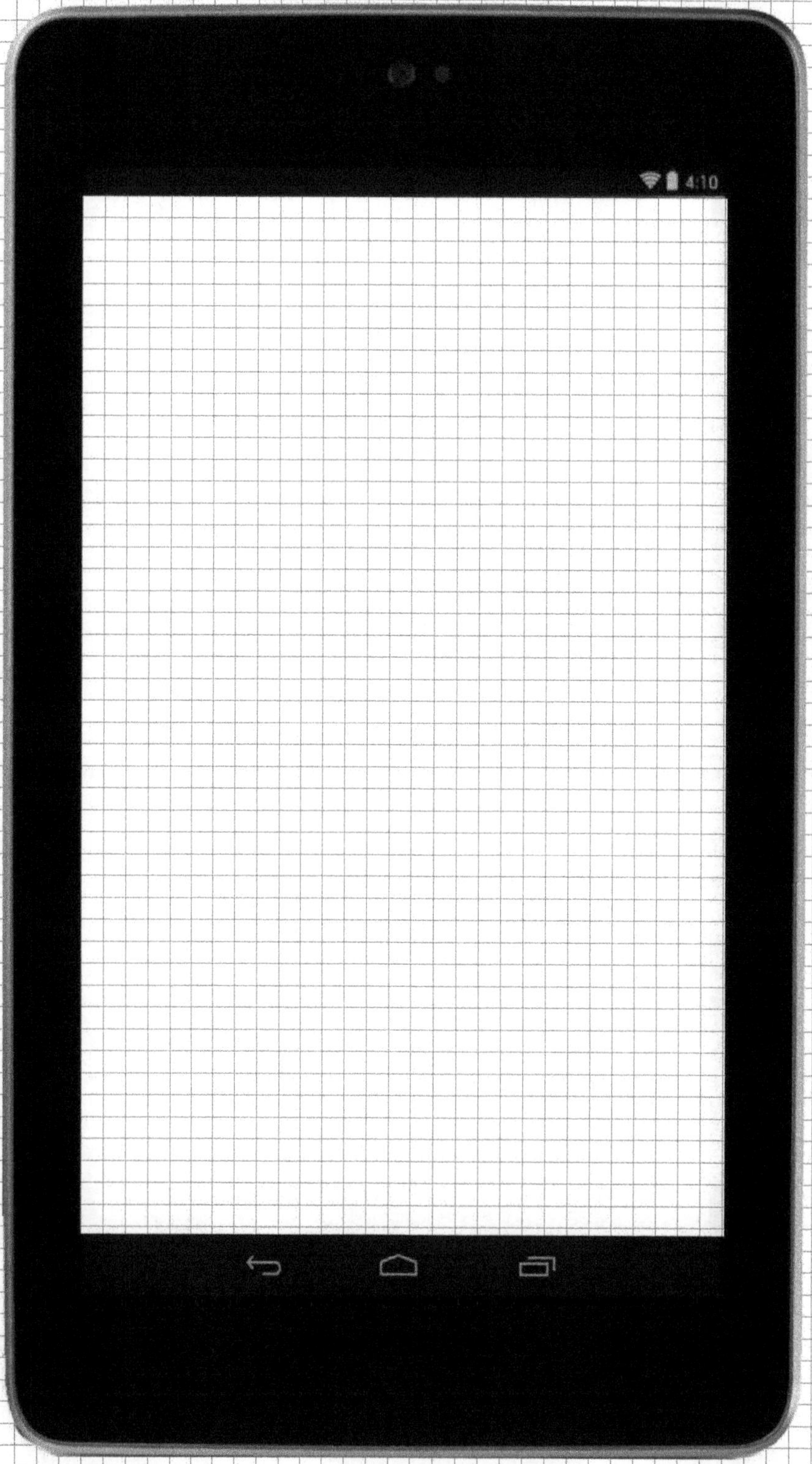

Application Name:

Screen Name:

Notes:

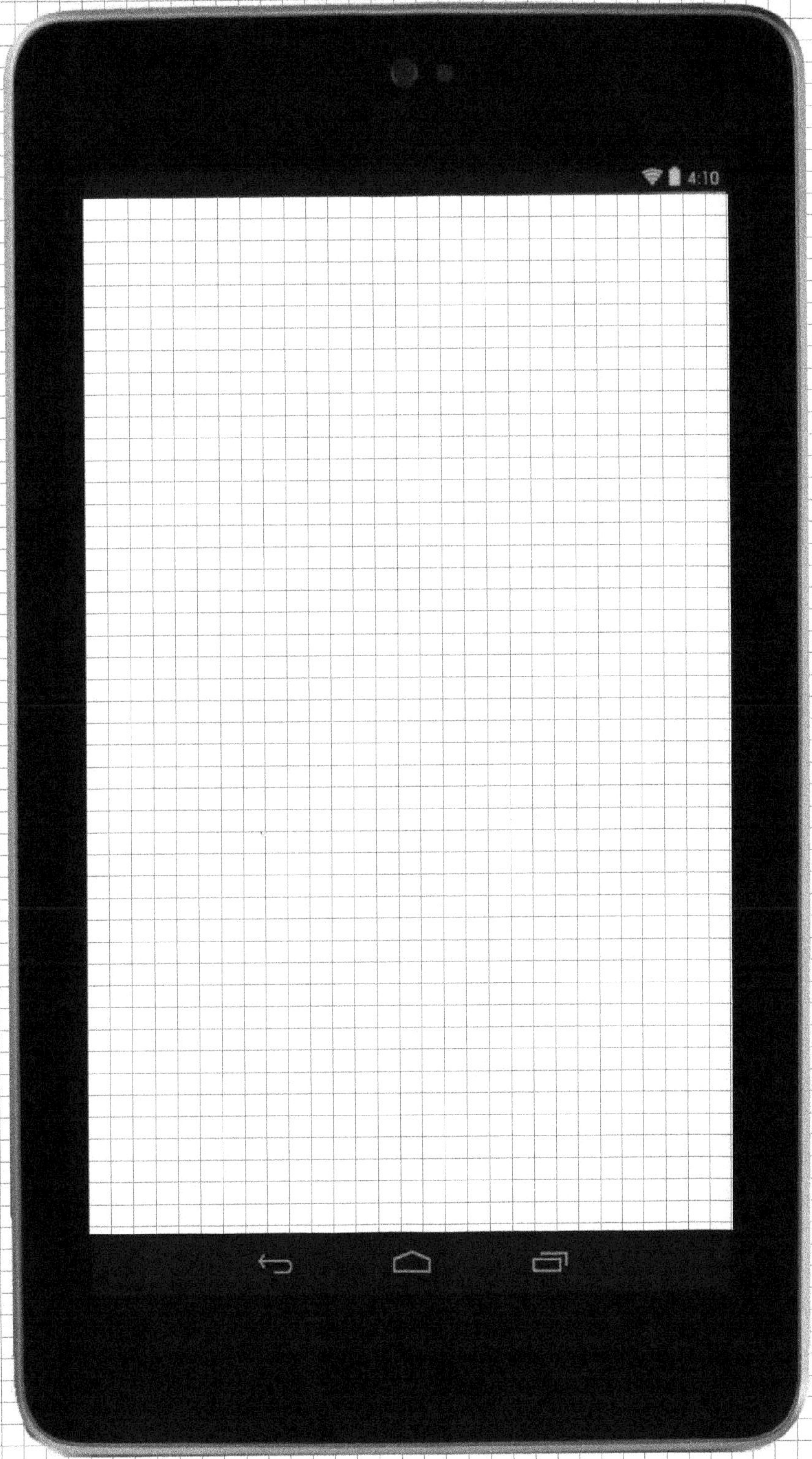

Application Name:

Screen Name:

Notes:

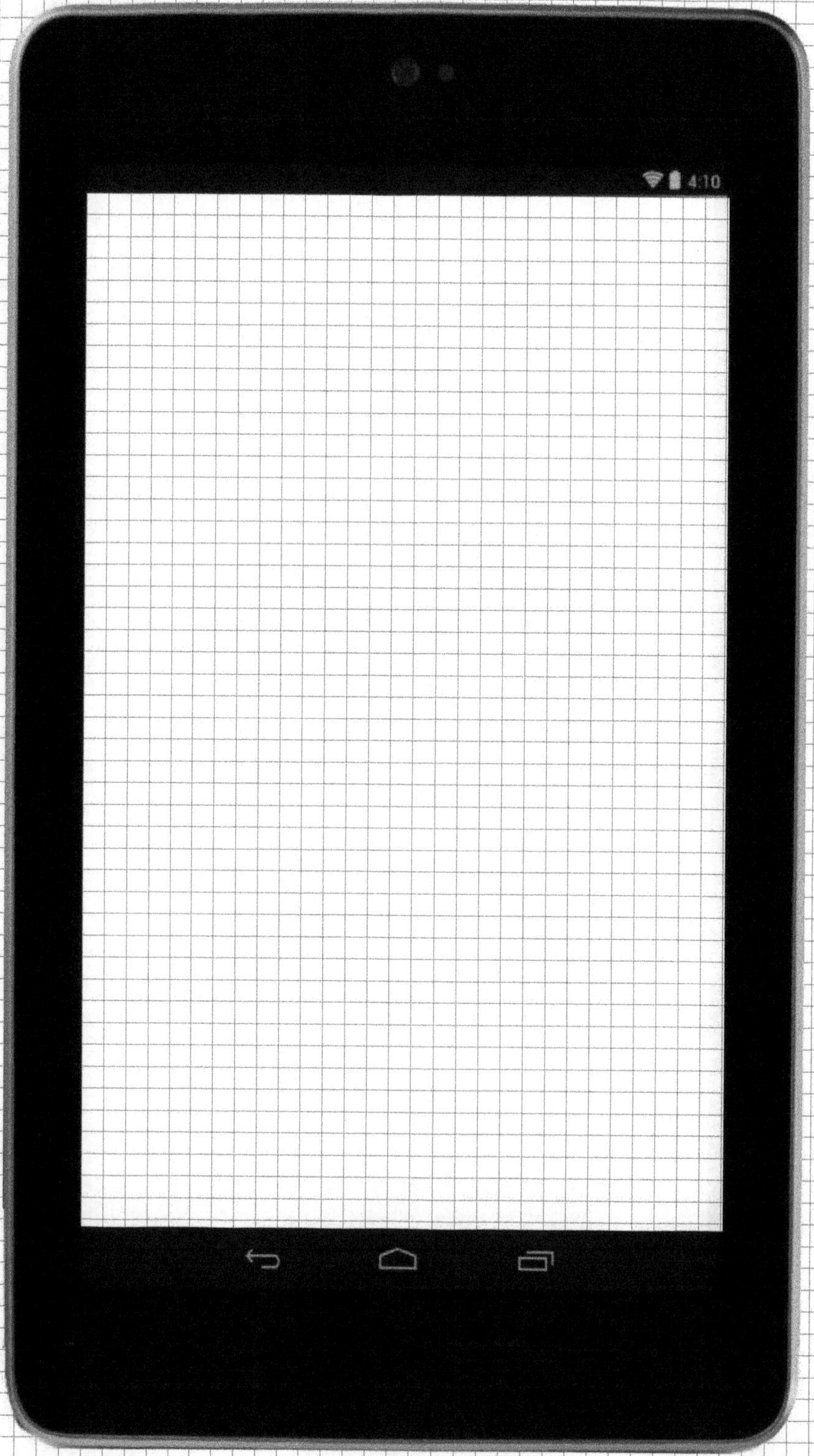

Application Name:

Screen Name:

Notes:

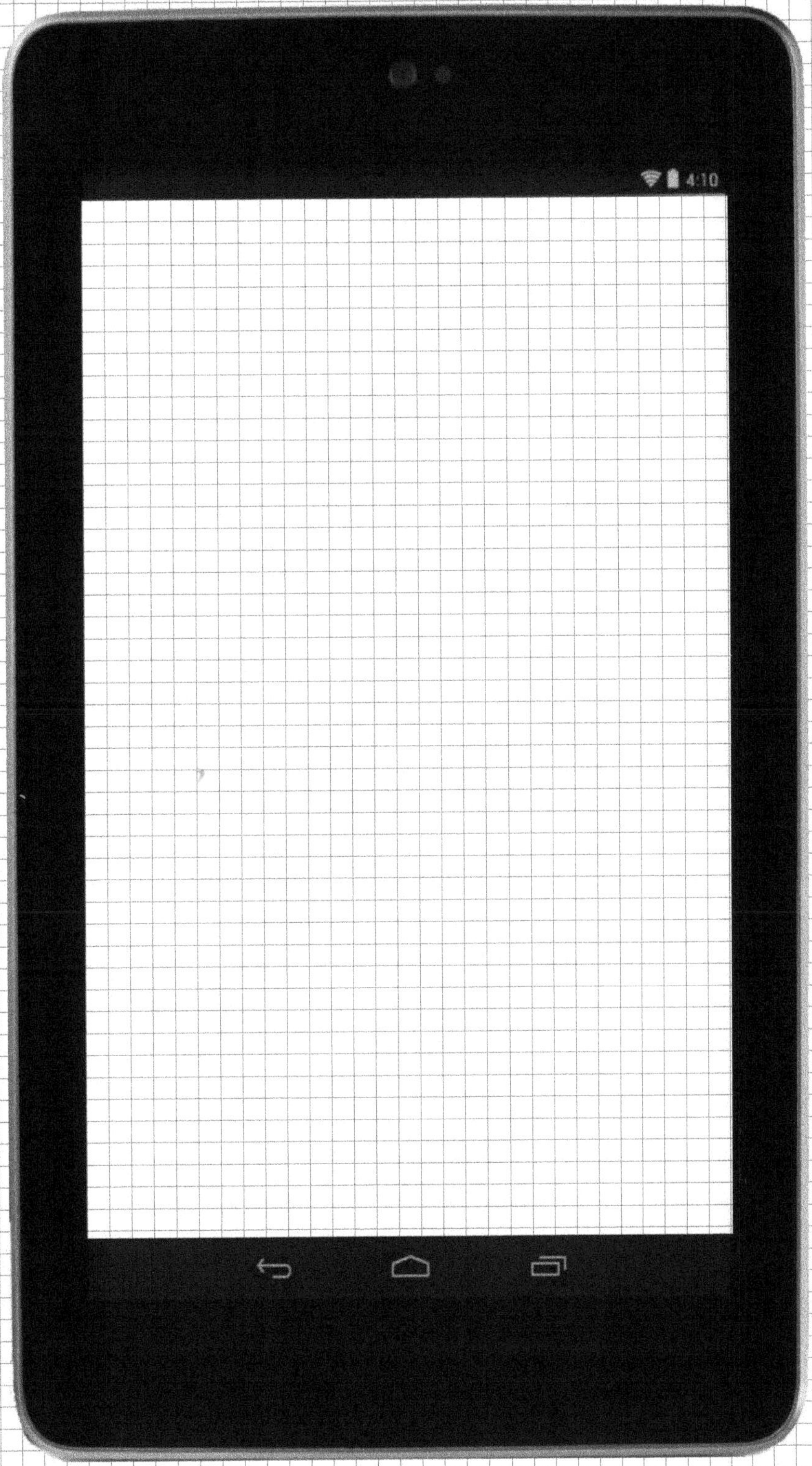

Application Name:

Screen Name:

Notes:

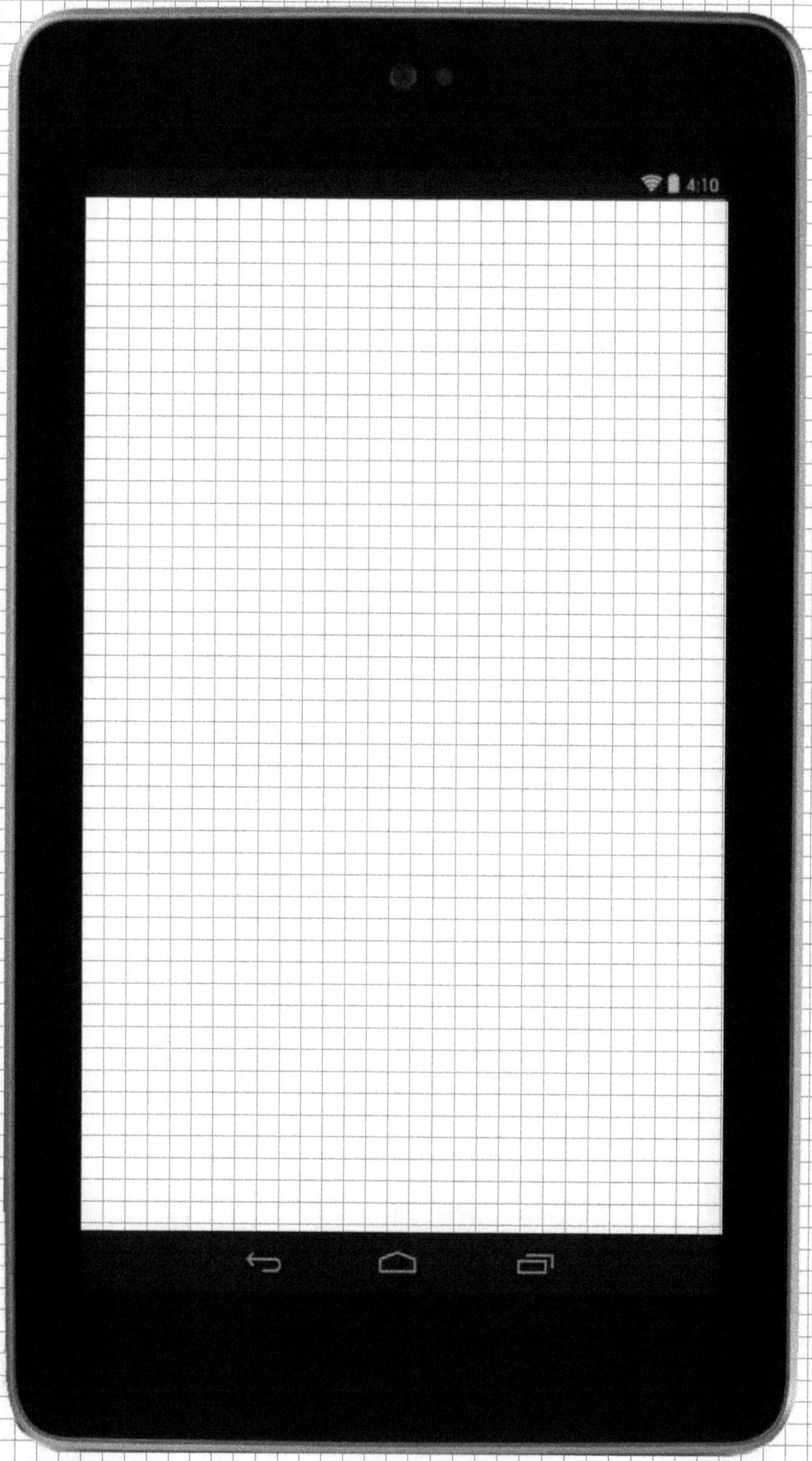

Application Name:

Screen Name:

Notes:

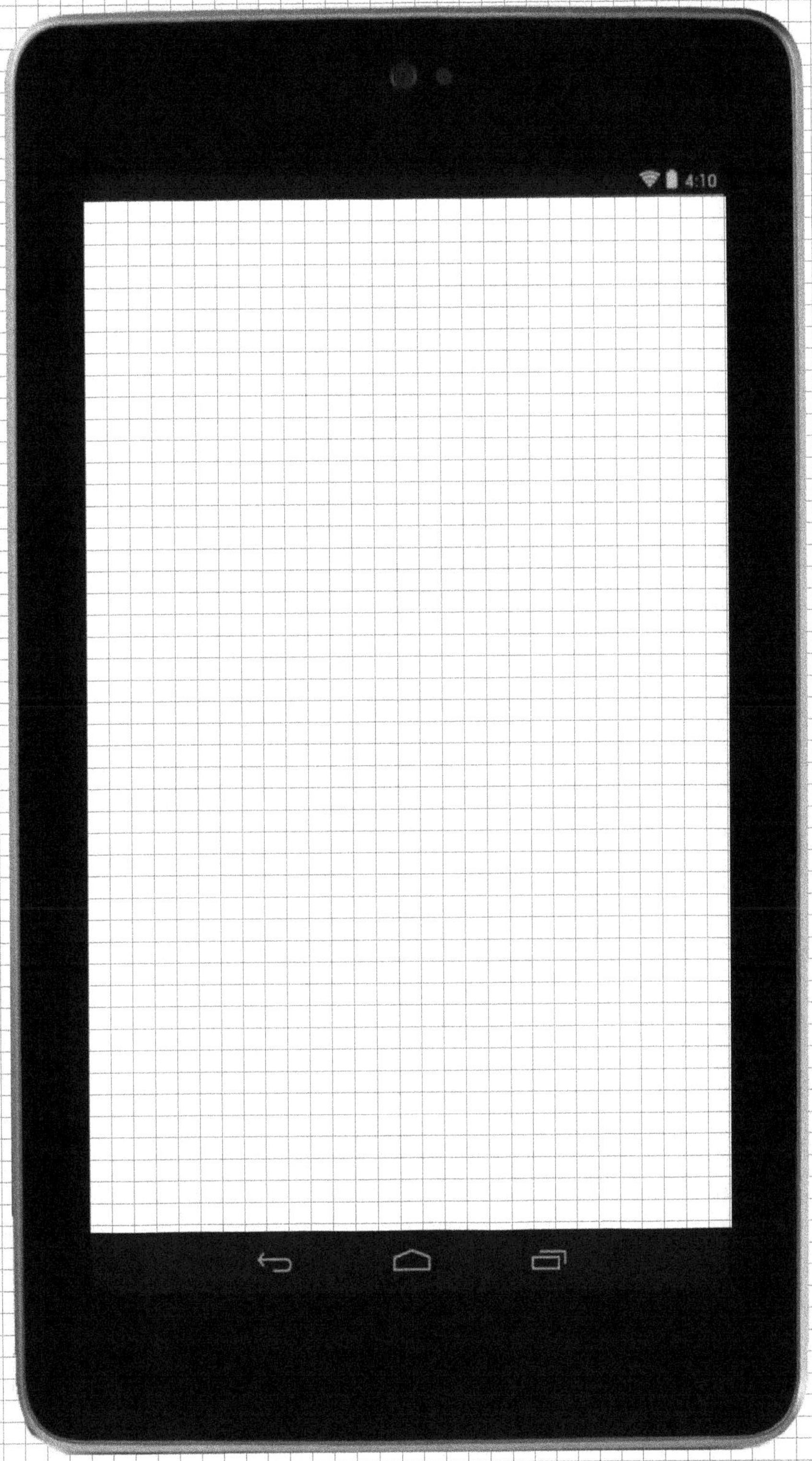

Application Name:

Screen Name:

Notes:

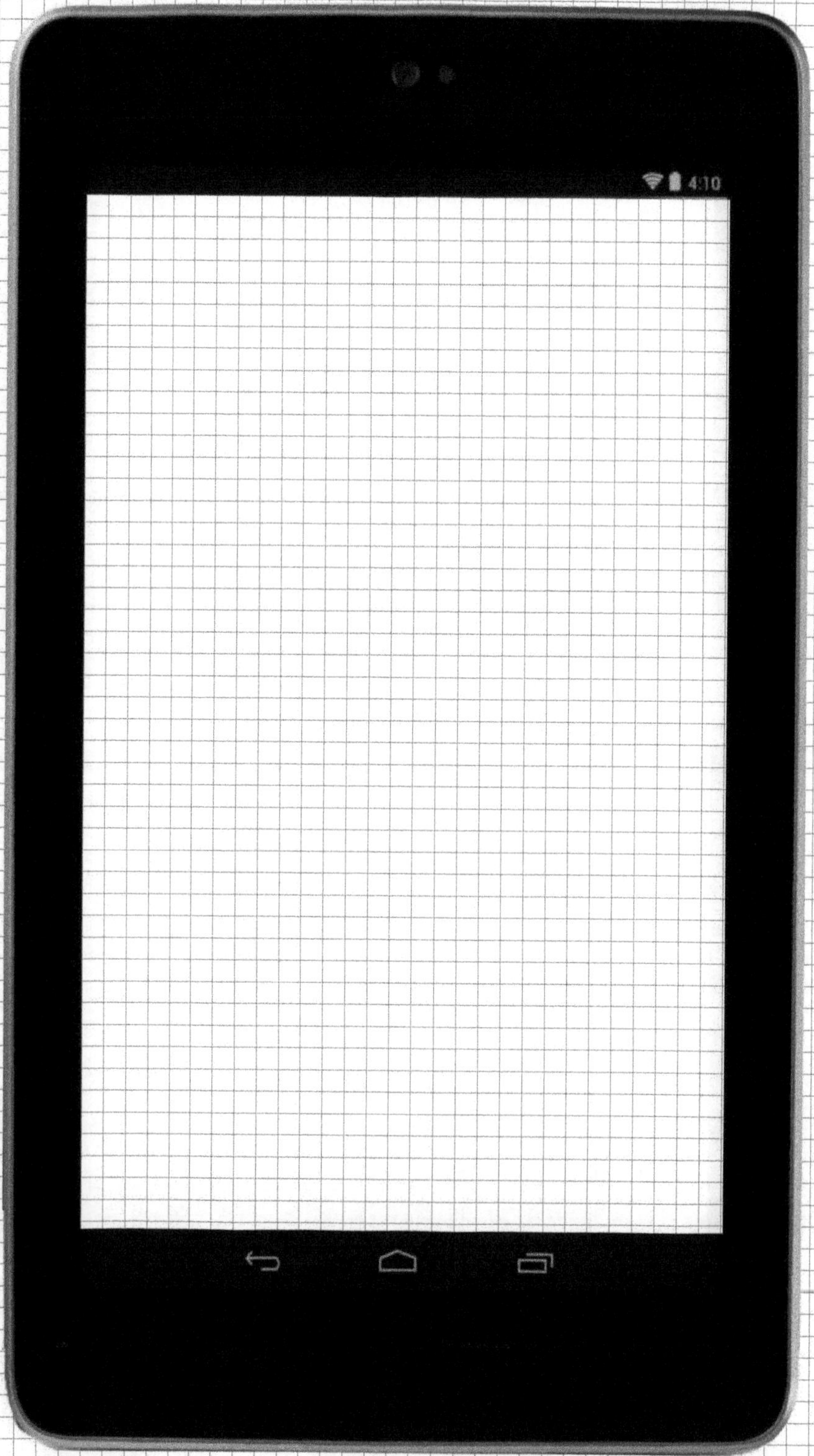

Application Name:

Screen Name:

Notes:

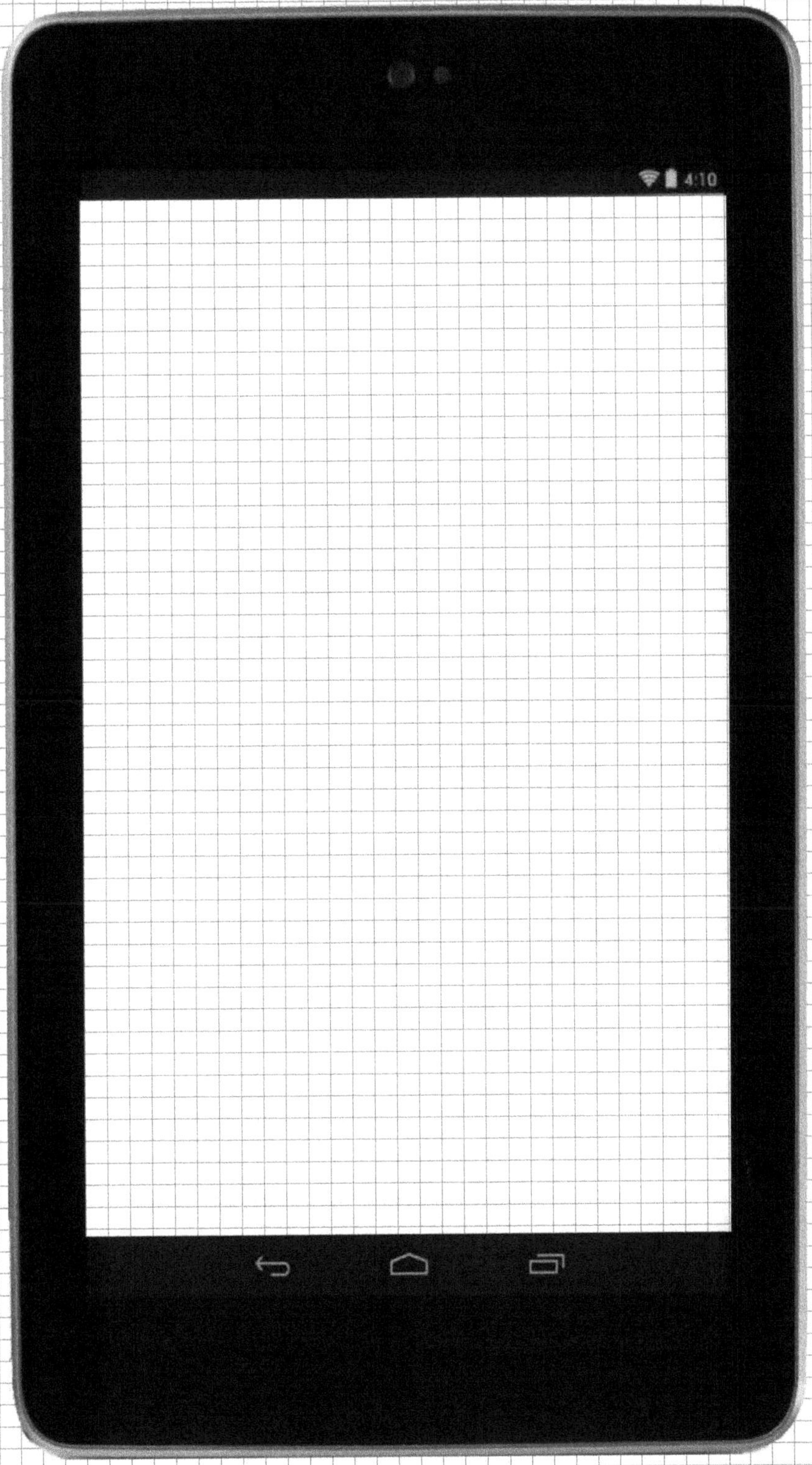

Application Name:

Screen Name:

Notes:

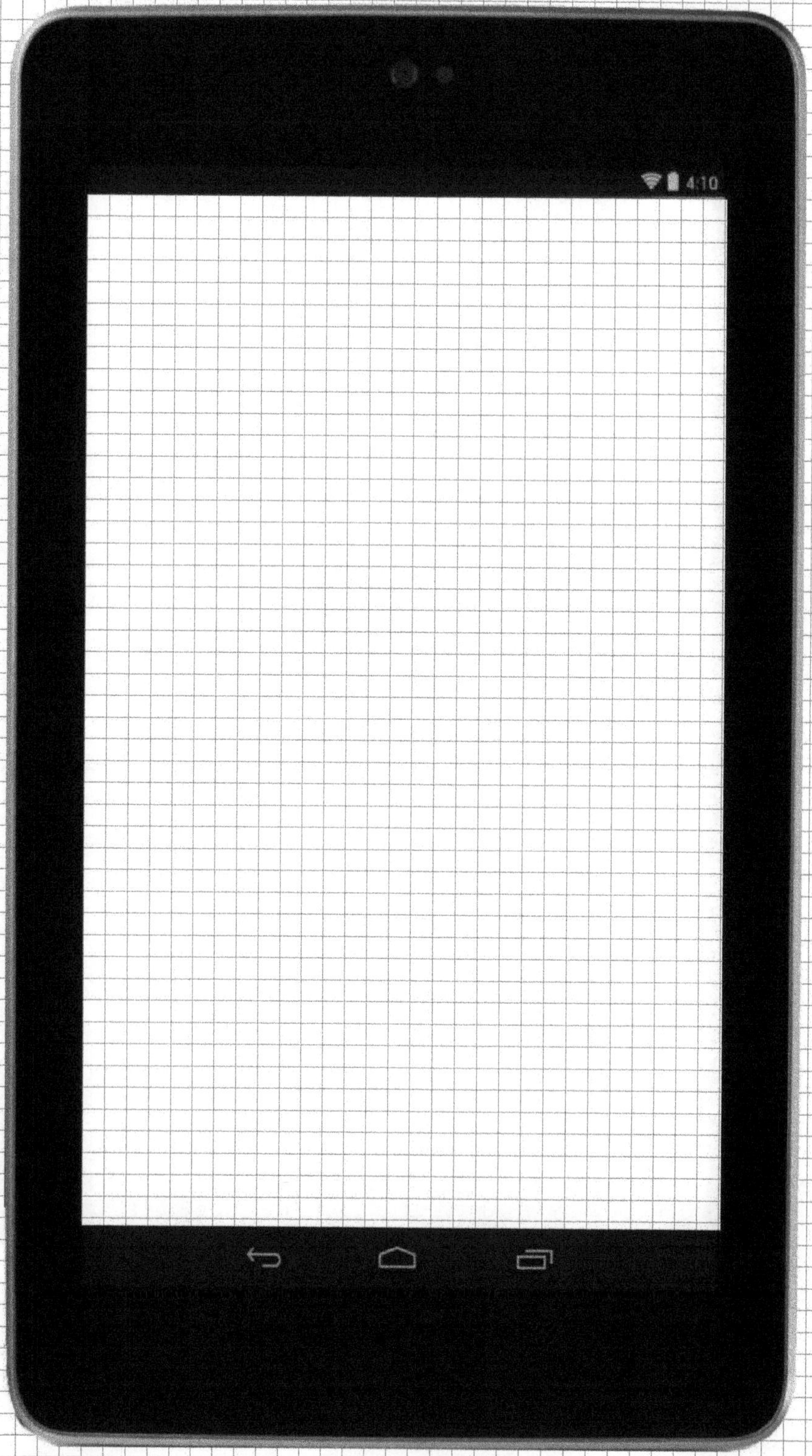

Application Name:

Screen Name:

Notes:

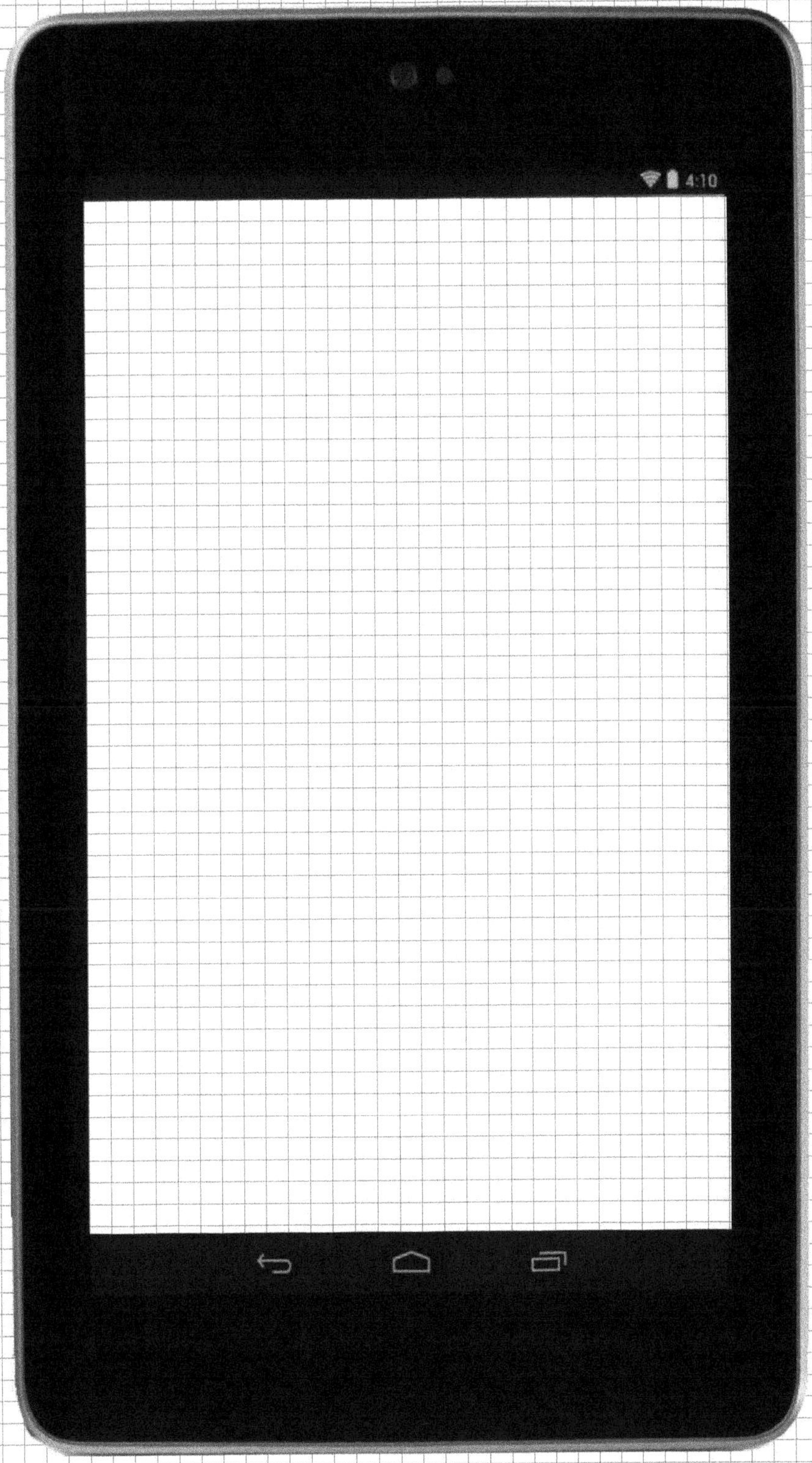

Application Name:

Screen Name:

Notes:

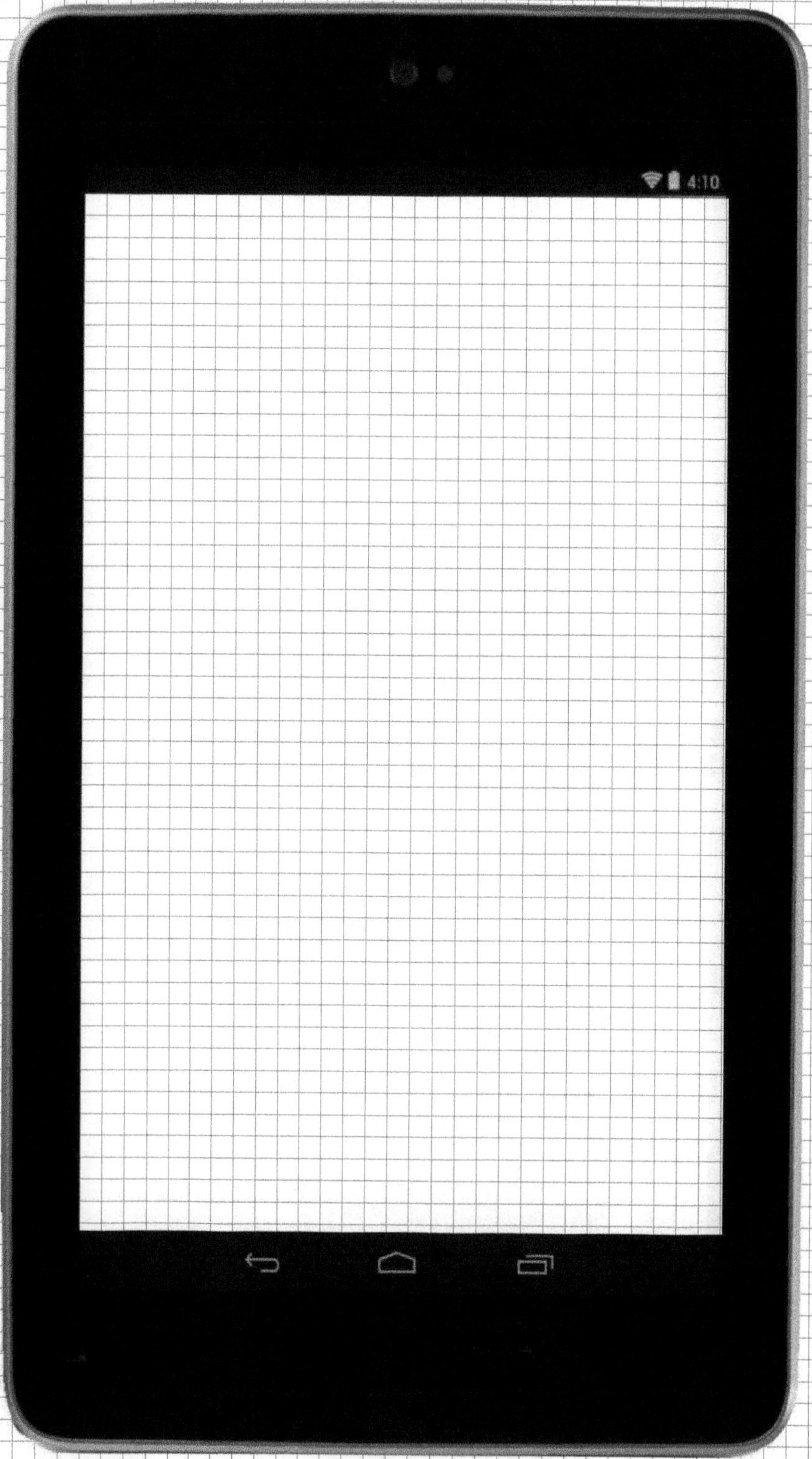

Application Name:

Screen Name:

Notes:

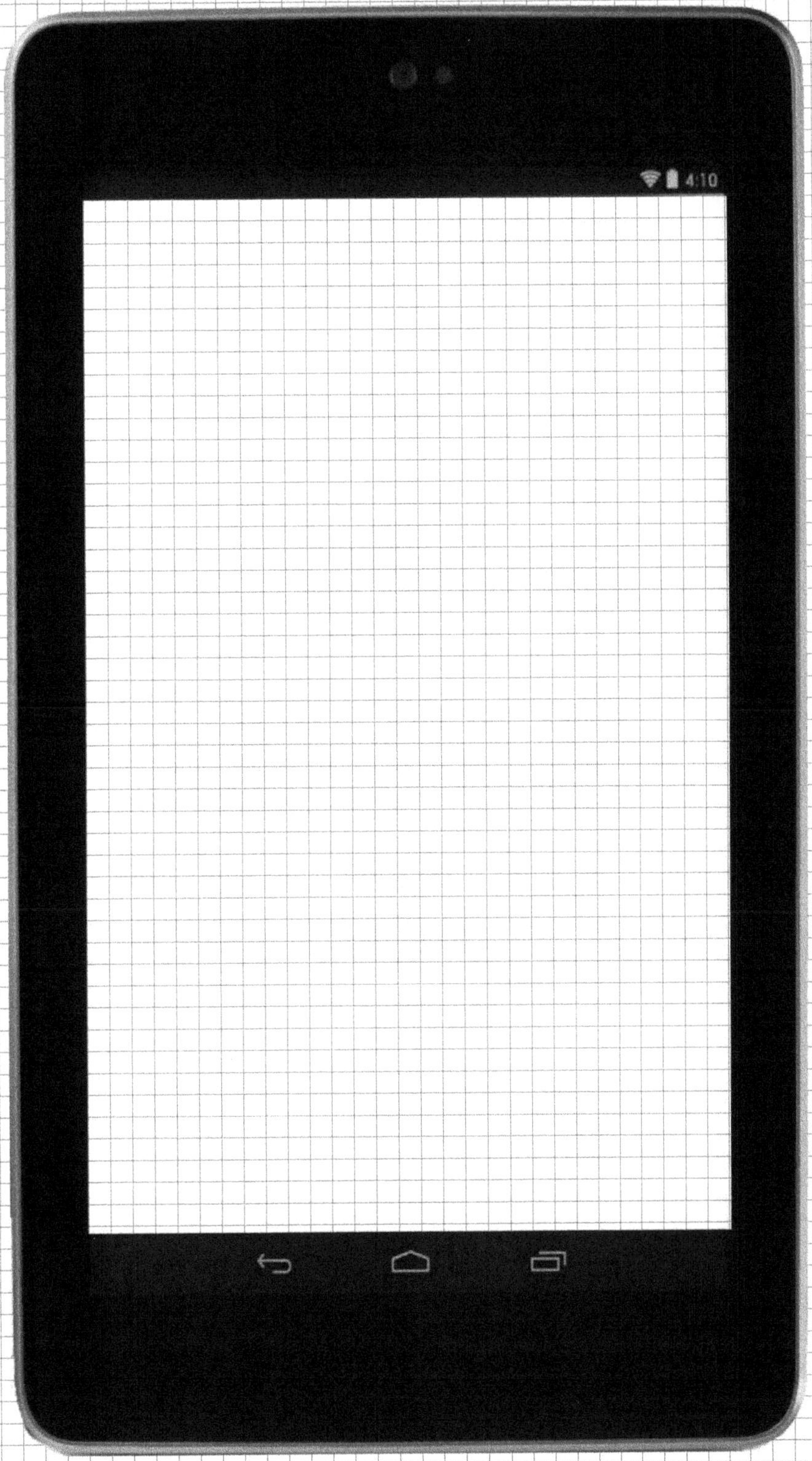

Application Name:

Screen Name:

Notes:

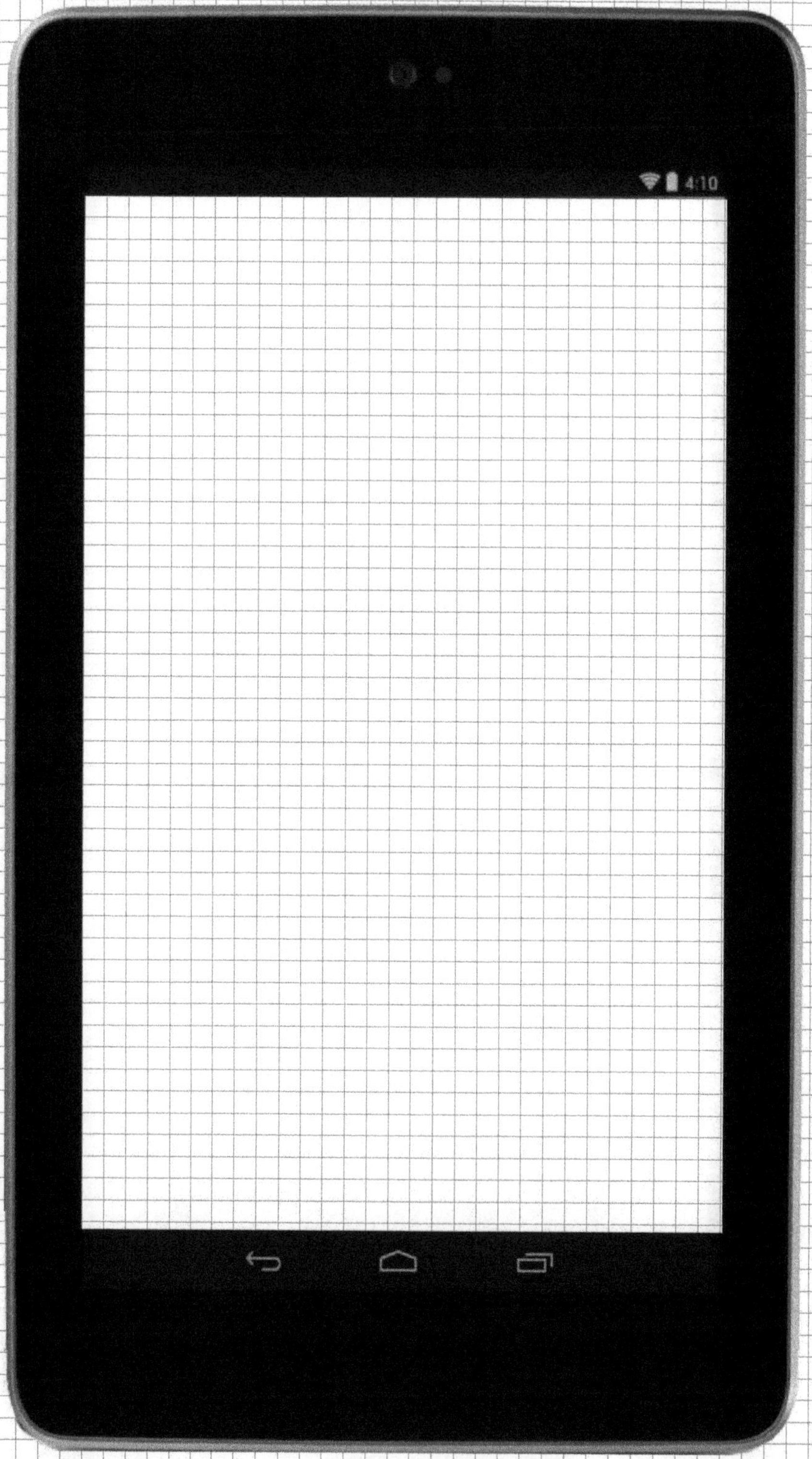

Application Name:

Screen Name:

Notes:

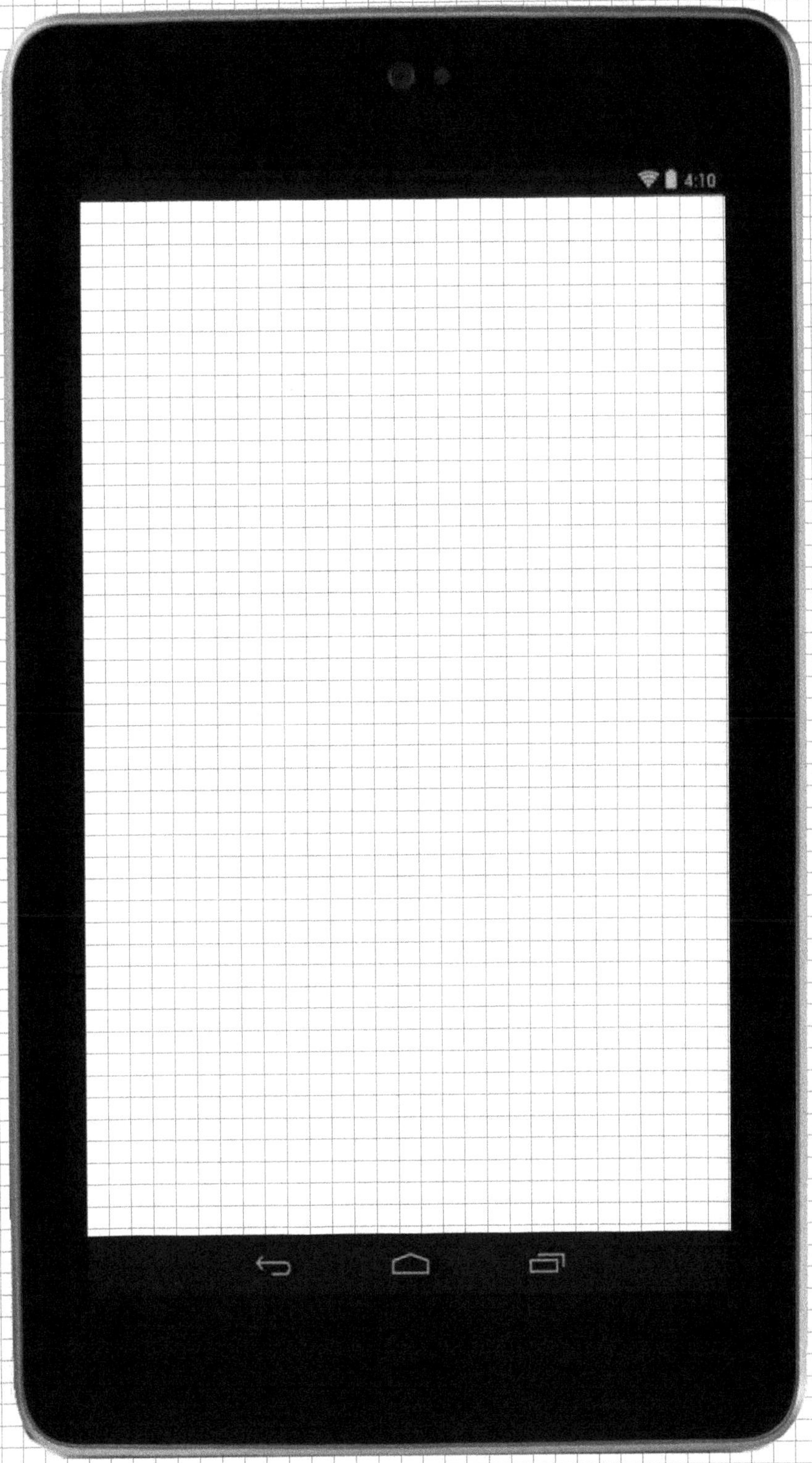

Application Name:

Screen Name:

Notes:

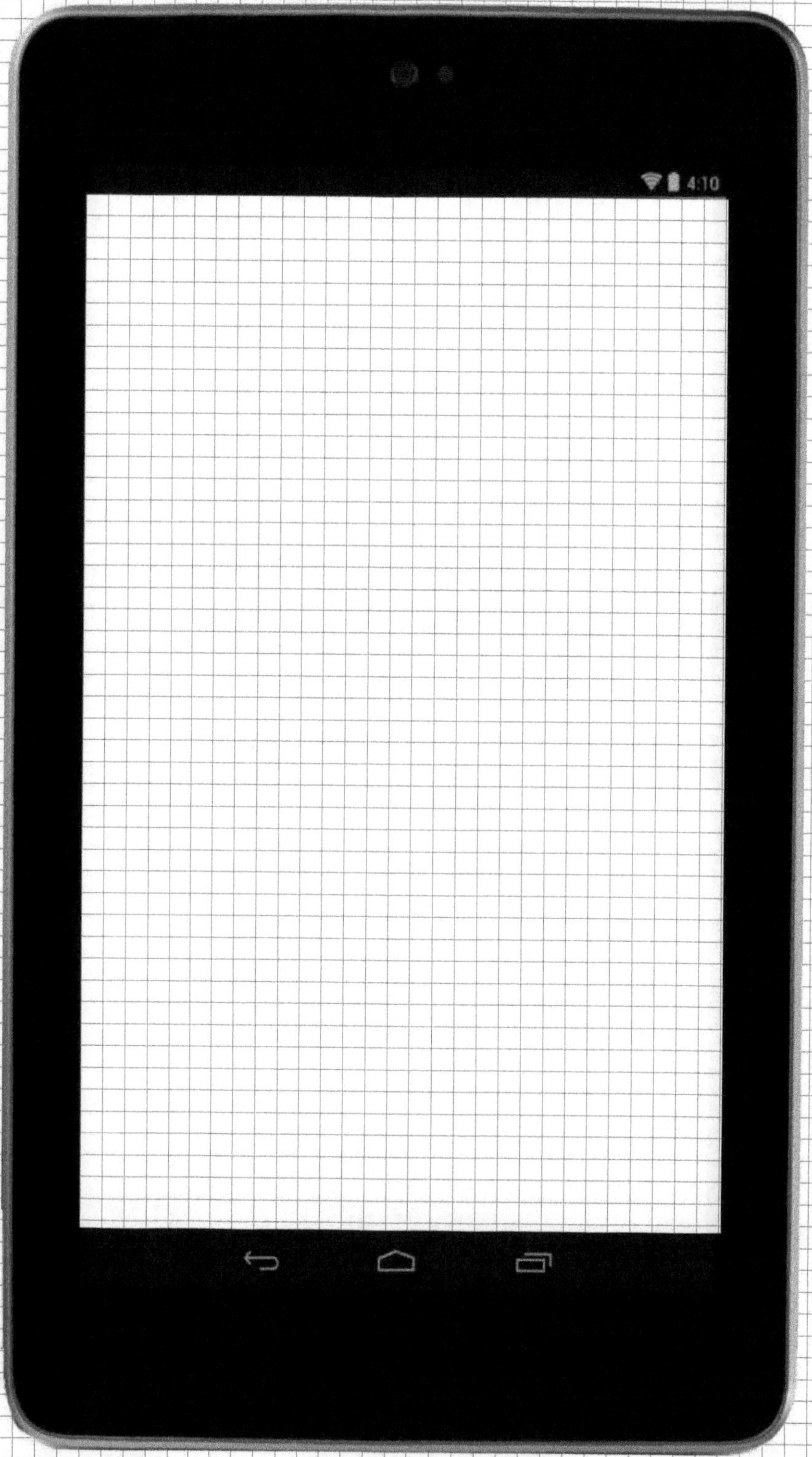

Application Name:

Screen Name:

Notes:

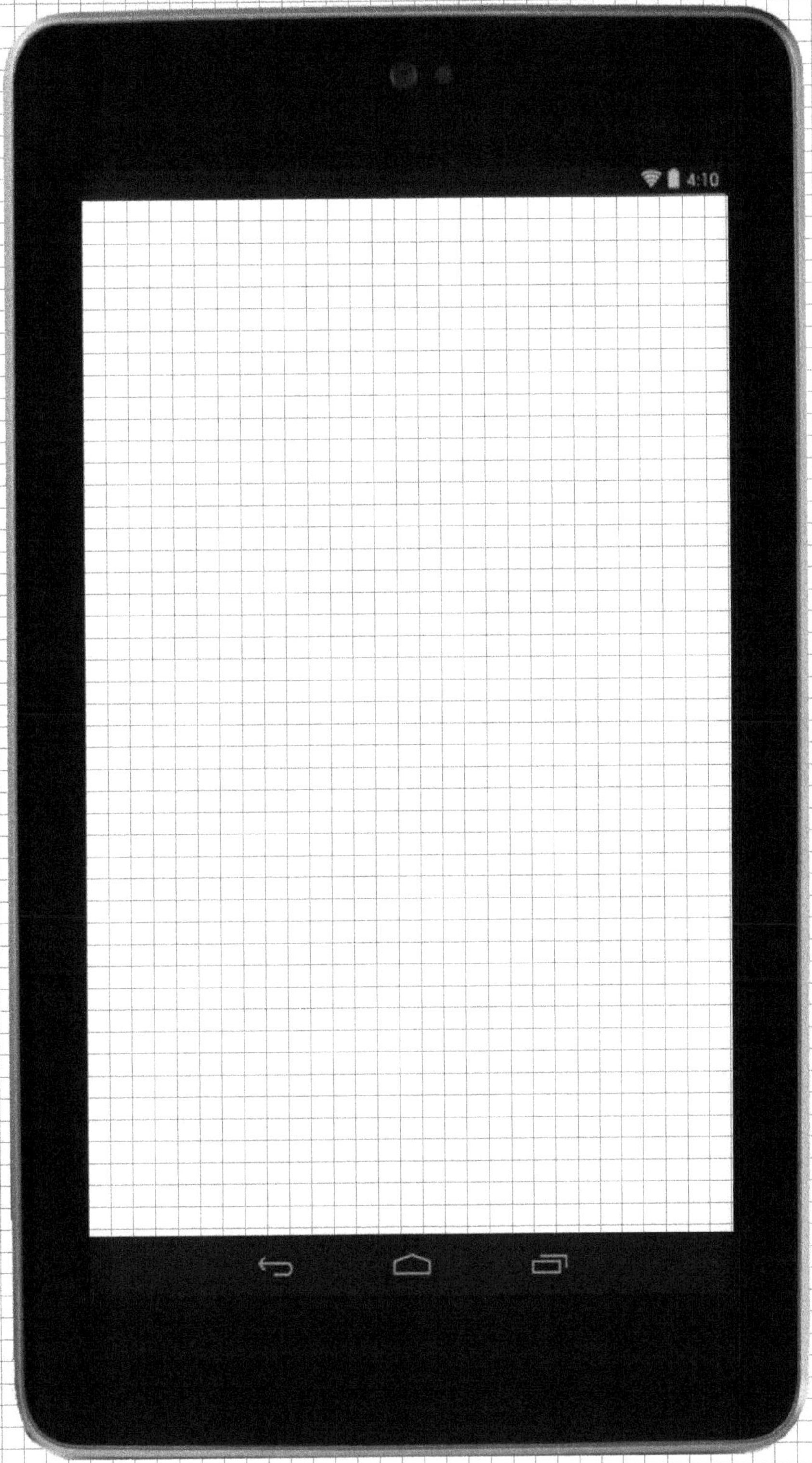

About the Author

Dean Kaplan is founder and owner of Kapsoft, a technology consulting firm specializing in software applications for engineering applications. Kapsoft provides a full spectrum of product design and development services including manufacturing automation, cellular and location services, material handling, automatic identification, network analysis and protocols, telecommunications, telecom billing, healthcare, and bond trading. Dean recently designed and executed a new synthetic instrument product serving as a replacement for five or more legacy RF test instruments.

Dean anticipated a need for simple effective smartphone design tools and created Application Sketch Books for the iPhone and the iPad to fill that void. Kapsoft is currently deeply involved in new exciting accessory development for the various smartphone platforms including the creation of stencils. More information about other related Kapsoft smartphone products may be obtained at `mobilestencil.com`.

Dean Kaplan was born in Philadelphia and to this day still resides in nearby Haverford, Pennsylvania. Dean has a Bachelor of Science in Electrical Engineering Technology obtained from Temple University in 1982. Dean writes a contemporary technology blog at `DeanOnSoftware.com`. For info about Kapsoft, please see `Kapsoft.com`. You can also follow Dean on Twitter at `@Kapsoft`.

Kapsoft

Purchase a Companion Android Stencil at Mobilestencil.com

Introduction

The *Nexus 7 Application Sketch Book* is the brainchild of Dean Kaplan who understood the need of tablet application designers for a place to sketch and keep sketches of their design ideas. He has taken this idea and transferred it to the Nexus tablet. With the knowledge that people often write their ideas on a whiteboard, only to lose them or other important details later, we created a sketchbook appropriate for the Nexus 7.

The idea, of course, is really simple. Give the user 150 pages of grid space to draw or layout their plans, sketches or whatever, for their Android applications. Users have found a number of unexpected uses for the book.

The book features:

- A grid background on each page.
- A lay flat binding so that you can have a hand on your Nexus 7 and one on a pencil.
- 150 pages to write, draw, compose or doodle on.
- An organized place for your user interface designs.

To use the lay flat binding, simply open the book to the page you wish and in the gutter crease both pages with your hand.

We hope that you will find the book useful for whatever purpose you choose.

Nexus 7 Application Sketch Book

ISBN-13 (pbk): 978-1-4302-6655-6

President and Publisher: Paul Manning

Lead Editor: Jeffrey Pepper
Editorial Board: Steve Anglin, Mark Beckner, Ewan Buckingham, Gary Cornell, Louise Corrigan, Jonathan Gennick, Jonathan Hassell, Robert Hutchinson, Michelle Lowman, James Markham, Matthew Moodie, Jeff Olson, Jeffrey Pepper, Douglas Pundick, Ben Renow-Clarke, Dominic Shakeshaft, Gwenan Spearing, Matt Wade
Coordinating Editor: Jill Balzano
Compositor: SPi Global
Indexer: SPi Global
Cover Designer: Anna Ishchenko

Distributed to the book trade worldwide by Springer Science+Business Media New York, 233 Spring Street, 6th Floor, New York, NY 10013. Phone 1-800-SPRINGER, fax (201) 348-4505, e-mail **orders-ny@springer-sbm.com**, or visit **www.springeronline.com**. Apress Media, LLC is a California LLC and the sole member (owner) is Springer Science + Business Media Finance Inc (SSBM Finance Inc). SSBM Finance Inc is a Delaware corporation.

For information on translations, please e-mail **rights@apress.com**, or visit **www.apress.com**.

Apress and friends of ED books may be purchased in bulk for academic, corporate, or promotional use. eBook versions and licenses are also available for most titles. For more information, reference our Special Bulk Sales–eBook Licensing web page at **www.apress.com/bulk-sales**.

Any source code or other supplementary materials referenced by the author in this text is available to readers at www.apress.com. For detailed information about how to locate your book's source code, go to **www.apress.com/source-code/**.

Nexus 7 Application Sketch Book

For the Google Nexus 7 Tablet

Dean Kaplan

Apress®